INDIAN PLAN OF ATTACK

Pontiac wasted no time in getting to the point of this council.

"My brothers, everywhere the tomahawk is raised and ready to fall as soon as ours falls here. Therefore, let us strike! There is no longer any time to lose, and when the English shall be defeated, we will stop up the way so that no more of them shall ever return again upon our lands. *We must destroy them now!*"

A wild, raucous shrieking burst from the throats of his listeners and everywhere in the assemblage the chiefs leaped to their feet brandishing tomahawks, and they slashed and struck the air with them at an imaginary English foe.

It was a declaration of war.

The Conquerors

Dedication

*With warmth and great esteem,
this book is dedicated to
a truly good friend,*

RICHARD REINAUER

Without any exaggeration, I look upon the Northern Indians to be the most formidable of any uncivilized body of people in the world. Hunting and war are their sole occupation, and the one qualifies them for the other; they have few wants, and those are easily supplied; their properties of little value, consequently, expeditions against them, however successful, cannot distress them, and they have courage sufficient for their manner of fighting, the nature and situation of their countries require not more.

—SIR WILLIAM JOHNSON
Diary of the Siege of Detroit, ix–x

The chronicles of the American borders are filled with the deeds of men who, having lost all by the merciless tomahawk, have lived for vengeance alone; and such men will never cease to exist so long as a hostile tribe remains within striking distance of an American settlement.

—FRANCIS PARKMAN
The Conspiracy of Pontiac, II, 117

I mean to destroy the English and leave not one upon our lands.

—PONTIAC
The Conspiracy of Pontiac, I, 251

AUTHOR'S NOTE

THE CONQUERORS is fact, not fiction. It is living history; the narrative of the day by day, often minute by minute, experiences of the people and events of the time period it covers. Every incident described herein actually occurred; every date is historically accurate; every character, regardless of how major or how minor, actually lived the role in which he is portrayed.

For the reader who seeks the entertainment of a good story, written history all too often becomes burdensomely pedantic and tedious; on the other hand, the historical novel, while often dramatic and interesting, can rarely—if indeed ever—be relied upon for historical accuracy. It has long been my belief that this gap could and should be bridged; that there is no reason why these two literary forms could not be wedded in a new and perhaps better form which combines the inherent vitality, depth of characterization, drama and entertainment of the historical novel with the unswerving reliability of the truly historical work.

It is this marriage, this blending of the two forms, that I have attempted in *The Conquerors*, as was similarly done in its two predecessors in the author's projected series entitled *The Winning of America*. In this present book, as was the case in those previous two—*The Frontiersmen* and *Wilderness Empire*—many of the techniques normally associated with the novel form have been utilized in order to help provide continuity and maintain a high degree of reader interest, but in no case has this been at the intentional expense of historical accuracy.

Within the text there are occasional numbered notes keyed to an Amplification Notes section at the back of the book. These are notes which provide material that is primarily tangential to the subject under discussion but nevertheless of added interest and value in providing the reader with a greater understanding of the events portrayed and a stronger sense of orientation where geographic locales are concerned. They are numbered consecutively from beginning to end of the book, but they need never intrude; the reader may choose for himself whether he wishes to read them as he reaches them, but it is not essential that he do so. Also at the rear of the book there is a bibliography of the principal sources of reference for this volume, as well as a complete index of characters, places and events.

As in *Wilderness Empire*, as much as possible I have adhered to use of Indian names for Indian individuals rather than the often clumsy or derogatory translations or nicknames given to them by the English or French. I feel there is a much greater dignity and a certain charm and musical ring to the actual Indian names. Hokolesqua of the Shawnees, for example, was called Cornstalk by the English, while Chief Unemakemi of the Miami tribe was called Damoiselle by the French and Old Britain by the English. In those few cases where the reader might be more familiar with the English or French name than with the Indian name, correlation is always shown between them. Admittedly, many of the Indian names appear almost unpronounceable at first glance, but such is not really the case. To aid the reader in this respect, at the back of the book is an alphabetical listing by tribe of all the Indian characters who appear herein and, where called for, these names are also spelled phonetically for correct pronunciation. Included as well are other names the same Indian was known by, his rank or status in the tribe and, in some cases, family relationships.

The Conquerors takes up the thread of narrative where it left off in the preceding volume, *Wilderness Empire*. However, chronologically speaking, the first volume of this series, *The Frontiersmen*, comes after the time period of *The Conquerors*. The individual volumes of this series, even though there is some overlapping of characters between them, are not dependent upon one another; yet, they strongly complement each other and all of them contribute to the principal theme of the series, which is a presentation of precisely how the white man took North America from the Indians.

Step by step *The Winning of America* series will move across the continent, showing clearly and in the most fundamentally human terms, how the land was won—through encroachment, warfare, trickery, grant, treachery, alliance, deceit, fraud, theft, and treaty. It is a story which began at the first white contact with the Indians of this continent, and which continued through the centuries until subjugation or extinction of the tribes was total.

As in the past volumes—and those to come in the future—it is neither the intention nor the desire of the author to champion either the cause of the Indians or that of the whites; there were heroes and rascals on both sides, humanity and atrocity on both sides, rights and wrongs on both sides. The facts are presented chronologically, just as they occurred, and with the greatest possible degree of accuracy. There has been no author intrusion, no editorializing, no moralizing. It has not been necessary. The facts speak amply for themselves, and whatever conclusions are drawn must be drawn by the reader himself.

ALLAN W. ECKERT

Englewood, Florida
May, 1970

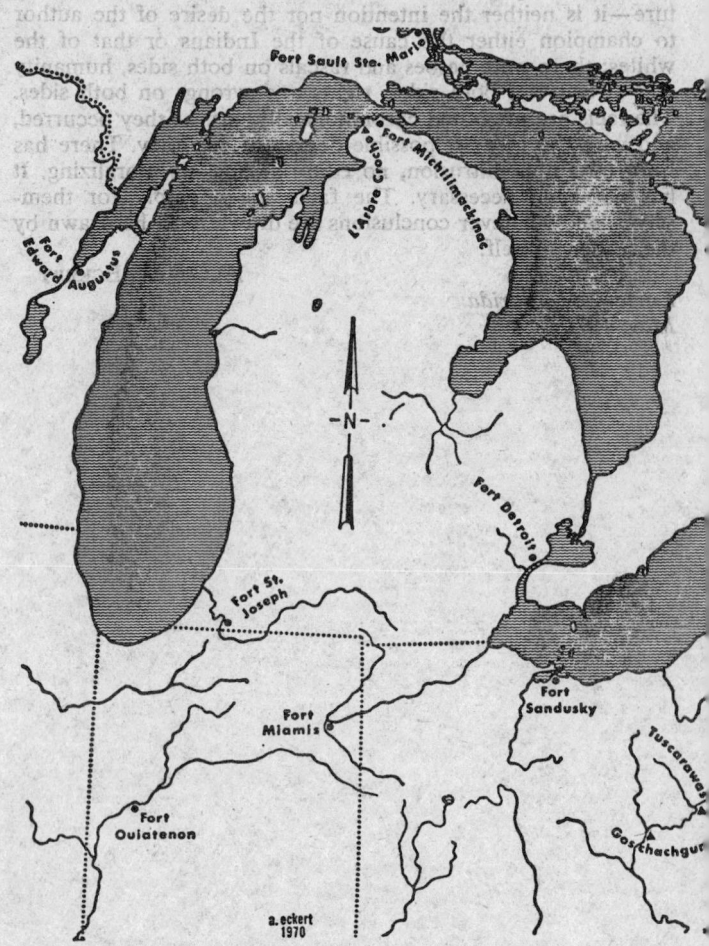

Fort Sault Ste. Marie

Fort Michilimackinac

L'Arbre Croche

Fort Edward Augustus

Fort Detroit

Fort St. Joseph

Fort Sandusky

Fort Miamis

Tuscarawas

Fort Ouiatenon

Goschachgunk

a. eckert
1970

–N–

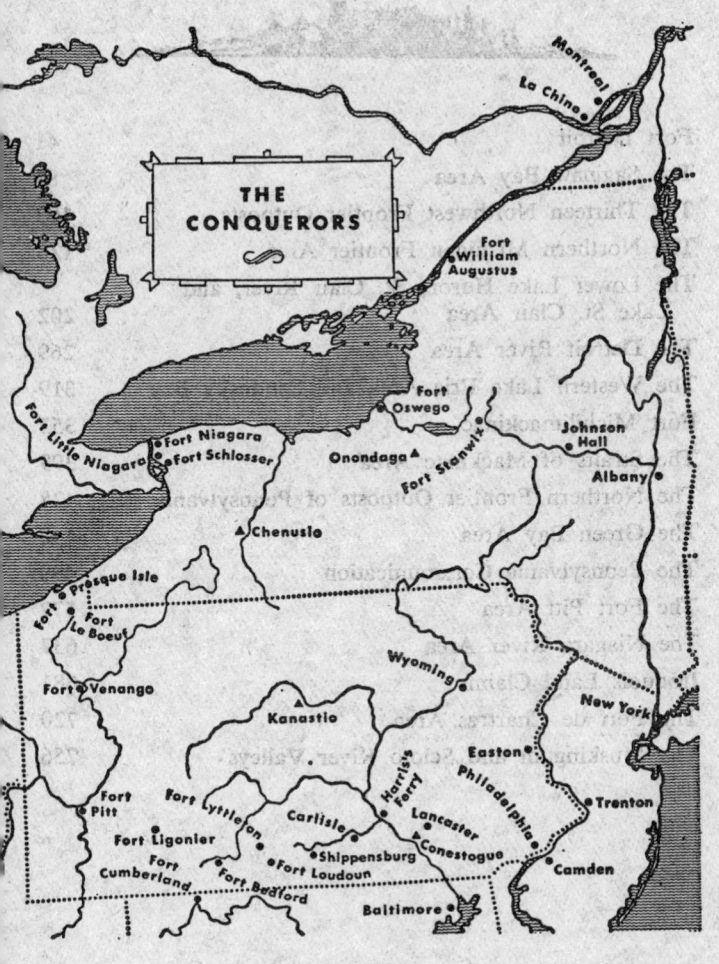

THE CONQUERORS

ILLUSTRATIONS

PROLOGUE

THE fur-wrapped figure sitting on the high ledge jutting from the cliff was as motionless as the rock formation behind him and the barren shelf upon which he sat. He had been in this position as the first gray of dawn had begun thrusting back the night and he had not moved as gradually the stars were extinguished and the sliver of moon paled in the brightening sky.

He had not turned to watch as the sun lifted free from the slightly rippled waters of vast Lake Huron, which stretched to the horizon behind and to the left of him, nor did he indicate any appreciation of the warmth of its rays, which dispelled the cold grip of night that had held him so long. Even when several hours more passed and the waters of the lake below had changed from black to gray and then to greenish and now to startling blue as the sun rose ever higher in a cloudless sky, he did not move, although great beads of perspiration glistened on his forehead.

He had taken this position late in the afternoon, two days and three nights ago. In the woods below he had divested himself of all clothing and with nothing but the beaver-skin robe and his medicine pouch he had climbed to this lofty perch. He sat cross-legged, with his hands in his lap and the robe pulled around him. He had remained motionless until now.

It was difficult at first, as it always was. First had come the discomfort of his stationary position, followed by the chill of the breeze blowing off the lake. Then had come the thirst and the hunger in great engulfing waves, but he remained motionless and they passed. Several times during the first night and the day which followed, he dozed; but even during these brief sleeps his rigidly disciplined muscles held him in place and he did not sway, nor did his head nod. Another night and another day and another night had passed and yet he waited for the vision that he knew would come, just as such visions had come to him numerous times over these many years—just as they had come to him three times in the past on this very rocky ledge.

He was an Indian, lean and muscular and tall, though hunched as he was beneath the fur robe, he seemed drawn down in size, dwarfed by the great rocky outcroppings. His unbraided hair was thick and black, falling unadorned to his shoulders. His features were angular, expressionless, reflecting the gray cragginess of the face of this cliff.

His tribe was Chippewa[1] and he had been born forty years before on this very island, as had his father and his grandfather and perhaps even fathers before them. Their bones remained here, as perhaps would his own someday, for this was a sacred island. It was the home of the Great Spirit, and as this deity was the Great Turtle, so the island was named after Him in the Chippewa language—Michilimackinac.[2]

Although well known and respected in his own village, this Indian sitting silently on the ledge was not markedly outstanding in the tribe. He was a minor village chief, a relatively ordinary individual, the head of his own large family but not from a line of tribal chiefs nor inclined to such leadership. He was satisfied with his lot.

His name was Wawatam.

The life he led was an essentially simple one. Below him on the level ground about a half-mile away, his family was at this moment engaged in caring for the newly sprouting crops—the corn, turnips and squash that were the vegetable mainstays of the village, along with the peas and watermelons which came from seeds gotten in trade from the French, although the melons never seemed to amount to much. The family would be finished by the time Wawatam returned and then he would lead them, as he always did, to the great rapids to the north, which the Frenchmen called the Sault Sainte Marie, and here they would spend the summer catching and drying, for trade and their own winter use, great numbers of the large whitefish which traveled in incredible abundance through the frothy, thundering strait from spring to fall.

When they finished there, they would return here and remain for a few weeks to do their trading and harvest their crops, after which he would lead them to the winter hunting grounds far to the south and inland from the eastern shore of Lake Michigan. In the following spring or early summer they would return here to trade their winter catch of furs and plant their crops and begin the whole cycle anew.

But first Wawatam must have his guiding vision, for which purpose he had come to this place. Perhaps this vision would show him that the fishing at the Sault this year would be better than ever before in his memory, or that the following winter's hunt would be as incredibly successful as that winter hunt of eighty-eight years ago that his father had told him about—when, during that single winter, a small band of Chippewas hunting on Manitoulin Island had slain twenty-four hundred moose in their snares![3] Perhaps the vision would tell him that his three daughters would bear him many fine grandchildren or that his two sons would become great hunters and fishermen, excelled by none, and that they would become heads of their own large families. After all, one already had taken a wife and with her his son had sired a daughter who was now eight summers old.

Although he had speculated on these things before arriving up here on the ledge, Wawatam really had no idea what the vision would be; only that whatever it was, it would be important and that he should—*he must!*—be guided by it in the future.

Since the dawn his unwavering gaze had been southwestward across the water toward the vaguely discernible shoreline marking the northeastern lip of the Straits of Mackinac. But now, with the sun approaching its meridian, the gaze in those dark eyes suddenly became amazingly vacant and the occasional automatic blinking ceased.

For a long while he stayed this way and then very fluidly, without conscious volition, he stood and the robe slid from him and lay unheeded in a pile at his heels. His arms came up and forward as if beseeching; and though his expression changed not at all, his entire naked body was wracked by a great convulsive trembling. Abruptly he fell backward stiffly, rapping his head smartly on the shelf. His hands slapped to his chest and the strong fingers dug into the flesh until his nails had gouged furrows from which the blood began welling. One hand had caught in the rawhide thong of the medicine bag hung from his neck and as his arms suddenly jerked spastically away, the thong snapped and the pouch described an arc through the air and disappeared, plummeting down into the trees and brush below.

As quickly as the spasm had come, it left. The trembling died away and he lay on his back, his body shiny with perspiration, his breath coming in great sucking gasps. A return of awareness to his surroundings was slower in coming and it was fully five minutes before he came to a sitting position and then stood. There was expression on his face now as he looked down at himself and then touched the lump on the back of his head and looked at his fingers tinged with blood seeping from that wound. There was expression, but of an indescribable nature, as he was swept with a sense of awe and gratification mingled with puzzlement and perhaps even a touch of fear. At length he reached down and picked up the beaver-skin robe and wadded it under his arm. Then he turned and began the treacherous descent, his mind going over what had come to him in his vision, marveling and wondering at it.

What a vision! Never before one so clear, so strong, yet so bewildering. He had seen a man. It was not the Great Turtle or a lesser deity, but simply a man. He was a young man, certainly no more than a score of summers in age; a man with extremely handsome features and dark hair; a man of medium height and medium build; a man whose appearance was now so sharply engraved in Wawatam's mind that even should twoscore summers pass, he would recognize him in an instant if he ever saw him; a man who was dressed in the clothing of an Englishman! With the vision had come a command:

This man will appear to you in a day to come. You will watch for him. You will rejoice in his arrival. You will clasp him to your heart and you will adopt him as your son, your brother, and your friend. This you will do.

How could this be? Wawatam's brow wrinkled as he continued down the cliff face. This was a land where only Frenchmen were tolerated by the Indians; where no Englishman dared set foot lest he be slain, if not by the Indians then by the French themselves, since the two were fighting a great war just now. The Frenchmen were here in numbers—soldiers at nearby Fort Michilimackinac on the south shore of this Strait, a smaller number of them garrisoning the little fort to the north at the Sault, and a great many more to the south in and around the fort at Detroit. Along with the soldiers there were many French traders who had established themselves in this land at the favor of the Indians.

Yes, the French and the English were at war, and many were the warriors from this region who had joined with their French brothers to fight the English. Often these warriors had returned with scalps and plunder taken from the Englishmen and over the lodge fires at night they told of how in all of the battles, whether fighting against Indians or French or both, the English had been severely defeated. How then would it be possible for an Englishman to come here?

Wawatam did not know the answer, but he knew that the Englishman would come. Never before had any vision been so strong, nor the will of the Great Turtle so manifest. Had not this Great Spirit ripped away Wawatam's medicine bag with such force that His fingers had scored Wawatam's breast? Had He not violently tapped the back of Wawatam's head with His finger to gain his attention? And had He not commanded him to accept this Englishman—*adopt him!*—not just as brother or friend or son, but as all three? Such a multiple adoption of one person was unheard of, and obviously it must be the most powerful bond of all—for Wawatam would have to care for this man as if he were his son, and love him as if he were his brother, and honor him as if he were his friend.

Yes, it was a powerful vision. The Englishman would certainly come and when he came, Wawatam would be so bidden, for he would recognize the man at once.

CHAPTER I

GEORGE CROGHAN was disgusted.

For weeks now he and his men, along with the garrison here at Pittsburgh, had been walking a tightrope that was being stretched ever tighter each day. If relief did not come very soon, all the talks he had concluded with the Indians here would be for nothing. That tightrope would break, Pittsburgh would be lost, his own plans would be wrecked and every man here would be lucky to get away with his scalp still attached.

With sour expression he poured a healthy dollop of rum into a pewter mug and drank it down with no more reaction than if it had been water. He squinted across the room toward the desk and then shook his head and snorted. Not much use in writing Johnson or Bouquet again; he'd told his situation here in the last four or five letters and still no supplies or reinforcements had been sent up. What did it take to convince them?

He wished he were back in Philadelphia again and sighed longingly as he thought of what a good time he'd been having there before General Stanwix gave him orders to come back here. Ever since then he'd been bucking odds and he didn't like it. True, all modesty aside, nobody else could handle the Shawnees and Delawares like George Croghan could—no, not even Johnson, and no one knew it better than Sir William himself—but what was the use of being able to sway the tribes with words if there weren't trade goods to hold them and strength to cow them?

Ever since Sir William Johnson had named him an assistant Indian supervisor under Sir William himself some three and a half years ago, Croghan's influence had grown among the tribes of western Pennsylvania and the Ohio country. They had known him well as a trader before and respected him for his fair treatment of them, but now they revered him even above Johnson. Croghan had become, in fact, to these western tribes, what Johnson himself was to the Six Nations[4]—the most influential and trusted Englishman. But there was a difference. Where at least five of these Iroquois nations were, at Johnson's behest, maintaining something of a neutrality in this war between the French and English, the western Indians had long been the strong allies of the French. Over these past weeks Croghan had held council after council with them, gradually drawing them into a treaty of sorts, but one that would swiftly evaporate if abundant men and supplies did not arrive at Pittsburgh soon.

George Croghan was a methodical Irishman with a keen if relatively uneducated mind, and now he concisely reviewed in his own mind's eye the events that had transpired since he left Philadelphia. Though he was not privy to the war plans of William Pitt in London and the new military commander in chief of North America, Sir Jeffrey Amherst, he nevertheless had a reasonably good grasp of the overall situation. A massive, three-pronged attack was shaping up right now against the French, with three wings of Amherst's army—the largest under the general himself—closing in to converge on Quebec and Montreal from the east, the south, and the west. Even Johnson was part of the plan. Along with a party of nearly a thousand of his more faithful Iroquois, he was at this moment en route with Colonel John Prideaux's force to attack Fort Niagara. Naturally, every available man was needed for these campaigns and so this meant that the border outposts, such as they were, suffered severe shortages of men, arms, ammunition and supplies.

More precariously balanced, of course, was this fort at Pittsburgh. Built on the point of land where the Monongahela River from the south and the Allegheny from the north converged to form the westward-flowing Ohio River, the fort had been called Fort Duquesne by the French until last November when the dying English commander, General John Forbes, took it. The retreating French had blown up the place before hightailing it for the three little posts north of here—Fort Venango, Fort Le Boeuf and Fort Presque Isle. They had, however, left behind quite a large number of cabins and barracks of a sort which were essentially undamaged and which formed something of a village. This was the area Forbes had enclosed with a stockade and named Pittsburgh. When Forbes left, Colonel Hugh Mercer had stayed behind to erect a temporary bastion. It was being called Fort Mercer, but the colonel was no engineer and the place was, by and large, a pretty sad example of a defensive works. While it might succeed in holding off an attack from Indians armed with muskets or bows, it wouldn't have a ghost of a chance against even the lightest of artillery. In fact, so untenable was it that Mercer had been given standing orders to destroy it at once and retreat if attack threatened.

Nevertheless, the value of the post—or at least of the highly strategic location—was realized and steps were taken to preserve it if possible by negotiations with the Indians until a strong military force could be sent. The great danger at the moment had been that the Indians would take it upon themselves to attack while the French were occupied elsewhere and, by sheer force of numbers, overrun it. That was where Croghan came in. With his knack for handling the Delawares and Shawnees, as well as that loose little confederation called Mingoes,[5] he might be able to keep them temporarily appeased. This plan was spelled out to the Pittsburgh commander in a letter from Lieutenant Colonel Henry Bouquet written on May 8, in which Bouquet had told Mercer:

Mr. Croghan, with your direction and assistance, will, I hope, be able to support our interests with the Indians till we can raise troops and enforce your arguments by the weight of an army.

The only thing wrong was that Colonel Bouquet hadn't even given a hint about when such support might be expected here and matters at Pittsburgh were degenerating daily.

Laden with goods for both the garrison at Pittsburgh and the Indians with whom he was to treat, Croghan left Philadelphia accompanied by two of his assistants, William Trent and Thomas McKee, both of whom were skilled frontiersmen and Indian traders in their own right. He also brought along as interpreter, though he scarcely needed him in that office, his good friend and companion of many years, Andrew Montour, a French-Seneca half-breed with his loyalty to Croghan and the English already many times proved.

Croghan and his supply train had almost reached the town of Lancaster on the Susquehanna River when an express from Fort Ligonier thundered up, paused briefly, then sped on. The word he left behind was not encouraging; just recently in the Fort Ligonier area, large marauding bands of

French and Indians had killed some thirty people, including a party of eleven sick and wounded people en route eastward from Fort Ligonier, all of whom were scalped before they could reach Fort Bedford.

Croghan had pressed morosely on and reached Fort Bedford all night, only to discover there that on May 21 the same enemy had routed a rather well-protected supply train which was being escorted by a detachment of one hundred and ten soldiers. That attack had occurred within three miles of Fort Ligonier.

Since it was obviously too hazardous to go on unless very well escorted, this meant a considerable delay at Fort Bedford until some troops could be brought up. While they waited, Croghan sent Montour out toward Pittsburgh with orders to gather together all the Indians he could, to meet Croghan's convoy en route, and also to employ others to carry the word that he would be holding important peace councils with the Indians soon at Pittsburgh, to which they were invited. This was an indirect way of letting the Indians know that the convoy carried goods destined for themselves and it would be senseless for them to undergo the hazards of attacking the train when they were going to be given these same goods anyway.

At last, on June 8, escorted by three hundred men under Colonel Adam Stephen, Croghan's party had left Fort Bedford. Shortly after passing Fort Ligonier they were joined by Montour and a party of thirty Indians. Montour assured Croghan that word about the forthcoming parlays at Pittsburgh had been sent out. The journey continued without further incident until finally, a month ago today—on June 18—they had reached Pittsburgh and its ramshackle defensive works, Fort Mercer.

The situation was very bad. Hugh Mercer's garrison of four hundred and fifty soldiers was crammed into barracks built to house a maximum of two hundred and the men were weakened by illness and extremely short rations. Food had become so scarce that the men had been contemplating eating the dogs and horses of the place. So relieved were the soldiers at the appearance of Croghan's supply train that many of the men merely stood in place and wept. Others rushed forward, though not so much to greet Croghan and his men as to throw themselves upon the beef herd that had been brought along. In a short time they had butchered forty head of them. These animals were spitted and barely seared over hastily built fires and then devoured virtually raw. Even the intestines were eaten.

That was the beginning of an extremely busy and hectic time for George Croghan. Shortly after Colonel Stephen's force left to return east, one hundred and sixty-four Indians arrived at Pittsburgh, but they were primarily warriors unaccompanied by the important chiefs of their nations.

"Our chiefs could not be certain you were coming," their spokesman told Croghan, "as they have been so often deceived this past spring and winter by being told you were on the road here. This time they sent us to discover the truth."

Croghan had nodded understandingly. "You are not now deceived," he told them. "Your chiefs know that Croghan has not deceived them in the past, nor will he do so now. Send messengers back to them, to bring them here at once. It is time for there to be peace between us."

Accepting clothing, food and other gifts, the Indians set off, assuring Croghan that their most powerful chiefs would soon be on hand here for the peace councils. Croghan sent out some spies toward Venango and set about immediately erecting a huge shedlike council house several hundred yards upstream on the Allegheny for the forthcoming meetings, then reviewed in his mind the points on which he meant to concentrate.

His orders in this respect had been specific: as much as possible, alienate the Indians from the French; send spying parties out to evaluate the situation up around Venango, from whence the majority of the Indian marauding parties seemed to be originating; send regular reports of progress and intelligence to Lieutenant Colonel Bouquet and General Stanwix and, if possible, to Sir William, even though Johnson was himself on the march against Niagara; take strong steps to regulate the Indian trade.

No white men knew better than George Croghan and Sir William Johnson that the principal fear the Indians had of the English was one of encroachment. These Indians not only had to be reassured that such encroachment into their country would not occur, they must also be assured of a stabilized, fair and substantial trade to provide them the supplies they sorely needed. In the final analysis, the only possible way to hold their goodwill and encourage them toward allegiance to the English would be by providing them with the supplies upon which they had become so dependent. This matter of establishing the trade was, therefore, Croghan's principal objective.[6] As Johnson himself put it to the Board of Trade in his letter of May 17:

An equitable, an open, and a well-regulated trade with the Indians is, and ever will be, the most natural and the most efficacious means to improve and extend his Majesty's Indian interest.

The Indians came back to Pittsburgh in force. The chiefs of nine tribes, along with five hundred of their warriors, assembled in the huge council shed to hear what Croghan had to say. Among them were even the Hurons of the Ohio country, who called themselves Wyandots, and who claimed to represent eight other far western tribes. Yet, even while these talks were in progress, attacks by marauding Indian bands went on, especially eastward in the vicinities of Fort Bedford and Fort Ligonier. The latter post, in fact, was attacked in force but withstood the onslaught.

Nevertheless, Croghan gradually won these assembled Indians over, holding daily councils which began July 4 and did not conclude until a week ago, on July 11. For eight solid days Croghan spoke, hoping to convince the chiefs to go to Philadelphia to establish the formal peace treaty or, if not that, then at least to wait until General John Stanwix arrived to represent the English government.

The chiefs were not inclined toward either idea, even though leaning toward peace. The largest single tribal contingent present was that of the Delawares.[7] The last time Croghan had had dealings with them, their principal chief had been old Tollema. Now, however, even though he was present, Tollema had stepped down in favor of a squat, powerful chief named Shingas—The Beaver[8]—who insisted on a solemn and official treaty immediately. It meant that Croghan would have to exceed his authority considerably, but that was something he had often done in the past, so it didn't bother him to do so again here.

Although many of these Indians presently on hand—including both Tollema and Shingas—had attended the big nineteen-day council held with the English at Easton, Pennsylvania last October, which had resulted in the Easton Treaty, Croghan nevertheless went over the points covered there, reaffirming them.

"Brothers," he said, "at that time a boundary was established, which was what you requested of the English. They were not to permit any settlement beyond the Allegheny

Mountains, and this agreement remains firm. It has been declared against the law for anyone to attempt to encroach into your territory to settle there. Further, as soon as the French have been driven away—*as I promise you, they will be!*—our own army will leave this place and it will no longer be a military post, but only a post of trade with you. Brothers, this will be a trade far more of benefit to you than you could ever hope to receive from the French."

The Indians were openly impressed and the peace agreed to at Easton was reaccepted here. These chiefs, however, pointed out that they spoke only for their own tribesmen actually under their command at the moment. They refused to be held accountable for the hostile acts being committed even at this moment by other Indians or by some of their own uncontrollable young men who had left the tribe, heated with passion for English blood, and who had now banded together under the name Mingo. Such Indians, Chief Shingas declared, Croghan would have to deal with separately.

It was about what Croghan expected. Though the counciling had to be considered a success, he was not particularly buoyed by it. Mainly this was in view of the fact that conditions at Pittsburgh were degenerating while these very peace talks progressed. Not only had it been necessary to give these Indians an enormous amount of goods, but they were being fed from the supplies Croghan had brought, and the appetites of four hundred and fifty troops and another five hundred hungry Indians depleted the food stores with incredible speed. By the time the councils ended, the food situation was once again perilous.

Of this the Indians were well aware and it did little to encourage their allegiance, such as it was. They were openly skeptical of Croghan's assurance that another huge supply train was en route here. As a matter of fact, even though he himself had been assured of it, Croghan was hardly any less skeptical. Already the promised convoy was long overdue and no further word of it had come. If it did not make an appearance very soon, all the counciling and agreements would have been in vain and he didn't like to speculate beyond that point. And on top of all this had come some very bad news. Two days after the talks ended, but while the Indians were still encamped in force near Pittsburgh, Montour returned with some of his spies and reported directly to Croghan and Mercer.

"French an' Injens 're massin' at Venango," he reported dourly. "They're aimin' t' hit us here. Cap'n Ligneris is gettin' artillery ready to bring with 'im, an' he's got seven hunnerd men, plus 'bout a thousand Injens. There'll be hell t'pay when he gits here. He's got all his Injens liquored up an' they're all steamed up t'take English scalps. They were still there at Venango when I left 'em, but I reckon they're on the march here by now. Couple of Beaver's men was with us an' now they're out there tellin' him all about it. We ain't got a prayer of holdin' this place."

There was an immediate coolness apparent in the attitude of the nearby Indians and it bore the promise of rapidly becoming open hostility. Croghan cursed the ill fortune of it all and silently damned the relief force which was supposed to have arrived weeks ago.

Montour was right, of course: Pittsburgh and its pitiful Fort Mercer were as good as gone if the reinforcements didn't arrive. Last November Forbes had driven Captain Ligneris and his garrison from Fort Duquesne and the French officer undoubtedly bore a grudge about it. If he could crush Pittsburgh in return, he'd certainly do so with a vengeance. The allegiance so laboriously gained from the Indians here these past days was rapidly crumbling and already many parties of them were slipping away to join the supposedly approaching French force.

But then, four days ago—on July 14—a miraculous reprieve had come. More of Croghan's spies returned and this time with the news that two days before, only hours before Ligneris was to begin his march against Pittsburgh, he had received emergency orders from Captain François Pouchot, commander at Fort Niagara, to come to his aid. A siege had been placed against that fort by Colonel John Prideaux, who was supported by a thousand Iroquois under Sir William Johnson.[9] Immediately Ligneris and his army, along with most of his Indians, had headed for Niagara.

In his quarters now, Croghan poured another few fingers of rum into his cup, quaffed it and shook his head. It had been a last-minute reprieve, yes, but things right here were still damned bad. Starvation was a viable threat and continued reports of his spies indicated an alarming increase of Indian attacks all along the Forbes road, from Lancaster right to here.

Abruptly there was a firing of guns and a great shouting outside and Croghan's heart sank. Certain that the Indians had launched an attack against them, he snatched up his rifle and raced out. He almost wept at what he saw.

14

It was the King's 62nd Regiment—over five hundred of the Royal Americans—with a supply train of considerable proportions and bringing word that orders had come from William Pitt himself for the construction of an impregnable fortress here at the forks of the Ohio River—construction that would undoubtedly begin later this summer, now that Pittsburgh was no longer menaced by attack . . . at least from the French.

[March 16, 1760—Sunday]

While never particularly fond of military men, the high-ranking officers in particular, George Croghan couldn't help feeling a little sorry for Major General John Stanwix. The officer was a bit stuffy, perhaps, and it was common knowledge that he deemed a military order as being next in importance to the Ten Commandments, but he was neither proud nor arrogant, as were so many of his fellow officers. He seemed to be, more than anything else, a sadly resolute man.

For over seven months he had been here at Pittsburgh and now he was leaving; not only leaving the fort he had built here, but determined to leave America as well and return to his beloved England for musty retirement. He reminded Croghan of nothing so much as an old faithful stud horse being retired at last and wistfully looking back across the fence at his career of conquests.

Croghan could not help but admit that Stanwix was leaving behind here at Pittsburgh the finest English-built fortification in America. It was, in effect, a memorial to the aging general. To one who had been here as short a time ago as last July, when the installation was a shabby, poorly armed and highly vulnerable frontier post, the transformation to what it had become under Stanwix was little short of incredible.

So *much* had happened since last July, Croghan reflected, both here and elsewhere. The fortunes of the English, which had been at such a nadir in their conflict with the French and Indians, had taken a sudden and marvelous upswing beginning with the capture of Fort Niagara by Sir William Johnson. Up until then it had been one shattering defeat after another. Even the triumph of General Forbes having taken Fort Duquesne on this spot had rung somewhat hollow, since the French had abandoned and destroyed the place before Forbes even got here.

But then had come Niagara. Prideaux has launched his siege and then promptly had his head blown off by his own cannon, whereupon Sir William, as second-in-command, had stepped in, maintained the siege, smashed the arriving French reinforcements—including those under Ligneris—and forced the capitulation of the fort. The French who escaped, realizing that communication with Montreal was severed, fled westward in panic to hole up at Detroit, their largest bastion in the upper Great Lakes country, leaving behind them the smoldering remains of the three forts they abandoned in Presque Isle, Le Boeuf, and Venango.[10]

Almost immediately, to keep control of Lake Erie, the English built a shipyard on a small island in the Niagara River about five miles upstream from the falls and here the keels for two ships were laid. The island was quickly named Navy Island and soon both of the ships were completed and launched. They were the eighty-ton armored sloop which had been named the *Michigan*, and the slightly smaller schooner named the *Huron*. These two ships gave the English uncontested dominance of Lake Erie.[11]

And far down the St. Lawrence River, after an extended siege, General James Wolfe took Quebec in a battle that cost both him and the French commanding general, Louis Montcalm, their lives. Montreal still held out, but this year's campaign was almost certain to take it. Everywhere, it seemed, things augured well for the English.

With the pressure from the French at Venango gone following Niagara's capitulation, Pittsburgh breathed a little easier and relations with the Indians thereabout improved considerably, although their menace hadn't ended immediately. All through the summer Croghan had continued holding talks with various bands of Indians as they defected from the faltering French; yet there were still numerous incidents occurring of individuals being scalped and horses stolen in the vicinities of Pittsburgh and Fort Ligonier and Fort Bedford. Little by little, however, the hostilities dwindled and the last serious engagement with them was on August 5 when they attacked a large supply train en route to Fort Ligonier.

It was on August 29 that General Stanwix had arrived with a detachment of men at Pittsburgh, increasing the size of the garrison there to thirteen hundred men. On September 1 he had his chief engineer, Captain Harry Gordon, already hard at work on the new fort which William Pitt had ordered he should build here. And for the first time, where Indian incidents were concerned, there was tranquility.

Croghan had corresponded with John Stanwix often and even met him on several occasions, but he had never gotten

16

to know the man well. Now he did, and he sympathized with him. Stanwix was tall and unpretentious. His hair was entirely gray and he was almost seventy years old. For fifty-four years he had been in the English army and his career had been honorable always, and quite often distinguished.

General John Stanwix, however, was a disappointed man. He had expected that when a new commander in chief of American forces was named, it would be himself. Certainly he had the seniority and felt deserving of it. But when the bumbling commander, General James Abercromby, had been recalled, it was not Stanwix who had been named to the top post but, instead, General Jeffrey Amherst, a man who wasn't even born until Stanwix already had eleven years of military service behind him. Understandably, especially since he considered Amherst an officer inferior in ability to himself, Stanwix was affronted at being passed over and the fact that he had himself been promoted to major general last June had been insufficient balm.

Because he was ordered to do so, he came to Pittsburgh to build the new fort, but he had made it clear that this was to be his final act in uniform, as he could not bear to serve beneath the new commander. Now he was leaving. The fort was not yet quite finished, but was complete enough that it no longer required his supervision.

Croghan looked around him and marveled anew at the change in this place. The Indian trade had grown prodigiously and a constant flow of fine hides and furs came in, for which Croghan made certain the Indians received fair payment. For the first time Pittsburgh was no longer just a scattering of shanty buildings and log cabins, but rather an actual town with intersecting streets, a blacksmith and a number of different shops, an abundance of pubs and even more trading houses. The place was thriving.

And then there was the fort. The old rickety installation known as Fort Mercer had been torn down at once by Captain Gordon's men and the new defensive works was situated within a pentagon of thick earthworks and protected from the Monongahela all the way across the triangular point to the Allegheny by a deep ditch. The ditch was in turn protected by the bastions of the fort proper, on which there were presently mounted eighteen pieces of artillery, with room for more. More than enough barracks had been raised and the storerooms were crammed with enough provisions—food, powder, lead, clothing, medical supplies, and spirits—to last a thousand men for seven months.

Tomorrow morning, Major General John Stanwix would be returning to the East and then to England, leaving behind him here a town which was the gateway to a vast untapped empire; and leaving behind as well a formidable bastion that he had named Fort Pitt.

At the age of thirty-two, Henry Gladwin[12] was a ruggedly handsome officer. Though not quite six feet tall, he gave the impression of being a big man. His shoulders were exceptionally broad and his features could only be described as craggy. More often than not his sand-colored hair was hidden behind the powdered wig which he, like all others of His Majesty's officers, was required to wear, but this same sandiness was reflected in his eyebrows. His jawline and nose were angular, yet not unattractive, and his forehead was broad and high. But it was his eyes and mouth which commanded attention. His lips were full and just slightly turned upward at the corners, imparting at one and the same time an impression of good-natured determination. His eyes were a pale icy blue with direct, penetrating gaze, yet somehow without the coldness so often evident in eyes of this hue.

A quietly competent man, Gladwin had been in His Majesty's service for very nearly a decade now, and had his manner been a shade more aggressive or had he been willing, as were so many of his fellow officers, to depend on family connections in England to help him in advancement, he might now be a colonel, or at least a lieutenant colonel.[13] As it was, his permanent rank was still that of captain, even though last summer he had been appointed temporary major and this was the rank by which he was most often addressed.

For some months now, ever since the major campaign of last year had ended in the late autumn, he had been billeted with the rest of his regiment—the 48th Regiment of Foot—in New York City. He expected, as did his fellow officers, that the upcoming campaign would be the decisive one of this war and that orders would soon be given directing his regiment to move to the front somewhere. All military attention was directed now at Montreal, at which the massive three-pronged drive would be made, and it was impossible to conceive of that campaign failing. Every officer in the service wanted to be in on it, for in all likelihood here would be the final great opportunity of this war to gain promotion. Henry Gladwin was no exception.

It was therefore a crushing disappointment today when a special courier came to him directly from General Amherst with the long-anticipated orders. They were not orders sending him to Quebec to be in on Brigadier General James Murray's thrust up the St. Lawrence at Montreal, nor did they call for him to join Brigadier Haviland for the push north on Lake Champlain with the same objective. Even the chance to be with the biggest drive of all—the commander in chief's in which Amherst would move to Oswego and then down Lake Ontario and the St. Lawrence to unite with the other two thrusts, even this was apparently being denied him.

He read the orders through a second time now and shook his head resignedly. Amherst was directing him to lead his detachment out of New York directly to Fort Pitt, where he was to report to the commander of the Southern Military District, Brigadier General Robert Monckton. There he and his men were to join with four hundred men of the Royal American Regiment, whom Monckton had been ordered to send up to garrison Fort Niagara, and secure the communication between Niagara and Fort Pitt by rebuilding those three posts the French had abandoned and destroyed—Presque Isle, Le Boeuf and Venango. Gladwin was to leave one hundred and fifty of his men to work on the Presque Isle entrenchment and he was then to move eastward on Lake Erie, charting the coastline all the way to the Niagara River, and then move directly to Fort Niagara to relieve the garrison there. It was hardly an ideal assignment. On the face of it, he was being buried in frontier outposts at precisely the time when the decisive battles of the war were expected to be fought, and it was a huge disappointment.

In characteristic tranquil manner, however, Henry Gladwin began making preparations immediately for his departure. He thought of Fort Pitt with mixed emotions, remembering the tragedy of his last journey to the forts of the Ohio. It had been in 1755, when Colonel Dunbar had been commanding the 48th, and they had marched with General Edward Braddock in an attempt to take Fort Duquesne from the French. In memory he could clearly relive again that frightful battle of July 9, feel again the searing pain of the rifle ball that had torn through his upper arm, recall only too vividly the death of General Braddock and the frightful defeat and retreat of that awful day.

Now, on the ashes of Fort Duquesne, had sprung up the new Fort Pitt, reputed to be the finest English fort in the land; and in his customary manner of optimism, Gladwin decided that it would be interesting to see what had been done there and perhaps, as was always a possibility regardless of the remoteness of a post, he might unknowingly be on hand in an area where unforeseen difficulties would break out which would test his mettle.

[September 8, 1760—Monday]

Even though he was considered to be a brilliant administrator, Lieutenant General Sir Jeffrey Amherst found the writing of reports and orders to be among the most distasteful of chores. As his rank and responsibility had increased, so too had the number of such documents he was required to prepare. When taken into consideration with the amount of correspondence he had to write, journal notes to record, campaign plans to draw up and the like, it often seemed to him that he was gradually being buried by a slow-moving avalanche of paperwork. Yet, there was no way he could devise to circumvent this necessary evil. As it always had been, and apparently always would be, voluminous paperwork was the cross every commander had to bear.

Sitting comfortably now in the privacy of his temporary chambers in Montreal, the forty-three-year-old commander of the British forces in America leaned back in his desk chair, stretched prodigiously and ran a stubby hand through the short, stringy red hair covering his crown. His expensive and elegant powdered wig had been removed and was now perched on the oval-shaped pedestal resting on a dressing table on the other side of the room near his bed. Without it, without the pompous dignity it imparted, the fundamental ugliness of this man was intensified.

He had thin reddish eyebrows which jutted on a high double arc over small, intense gray eyes. The center of his face was dominated by a huge hooked nose which gave him a decidedly vulturine appearance. His mouth was almost always pursed into an incongruous babylike pouting expression, especially when he was steeped in thought, as now. Nor were his features enhanced any by the large fleshy mole at the left corner of the thick, moist lips.

The merest trace of a smile thinned his lips at this moment as he reflected on the events of this year's campaign, which had culminated in today's stunning triumph. A feeling of exultation rose in him when he realized that because of the events of this day, his name would forevermore play an important part in history. It was late at night now and he was weary, but he savored again in his thoughts the knowledge that on this day he had accepted from the French governor of Canada, Pierre Vaudreuil, not only the surrender of Montreal, but the surrender of the entire French domain in Canada; a domain twelve times the size of England! This fact alone must be recorded in the annals as one of the most triumphant moments in the whole history of the British Empire. An entire continent had suddenly been opened and Sir Jeffrey Amherst was at the helm. His smile broadened.

He straightened in his chair, adjusted the small lamp so that its glow fell onto the blank pages before him and not in his eyes, and then he dipped the tip of his goose quill pen into the inkpot. Throughout this campaign he had sent report after report across the Atlantic to William Pitt in London. Earlier in the day he had sent off a relatively brief announcement of this day's grand accomplishment, but now it was time for a summing-up; it was time to detail for the prime minister what had been done to effect this triumph, what was being done at this moment, and what was planned for the future, if it met with His Majesty's gracious approval.

There was, of course, the completion of Fort Pitt, which was a superb fortress from whence, Amherst declared, no enemy could dislodge His Majesty's troops. It was now commanded by Brigadier General Robert Monckton, under whose directions had been carried out Amherst's orders for the rebuilding of Fort Presque Isle, Fort Le Boeuf and Fort Venango, along with the strengthening of Fort Niagara, which was in itself a sturdy bastion.

Lieutenant Colonel Henry Bouquet, second-in-command of the Southern Department under Monckton, was presently commanding Fort Presque Isle and continuing with the work of improving and adding to its defenses, as this was a vital median post in the communication between Fort Niagara and Fort Pitt and a most important outpost for future moves of His Majesty's interests into the western Great Lakes region.

With these western posts well under control, Amherst had begun his own massive advance down Lake Ontario from his assembly point at Oswego in August with over ten thousand men, plus some seven hundred Indians under Sir William Johnson. Most of these Indians were Senecas, whom Amherst hated as he hated all Indians. Despite the arguments of the Indian supervisor to the contrary, he considered Indians generally to be far more a liability than an asset. Not unexpectedly, Amherst went on in his report, these Indian allies, so-called, had almost all deserted him en masse because he had refused to give them free hand with the loot and prisoners when Fort Lévis was taken at the head of the St. Lawrence River rapids later the same month. This fort, incidentally, he had renamed Fort William Augustus and he had left a garrison there under the command of acting Major Henry Gladwin, which rank Amherst hoped His Majesty would see fit to confirm, since Gladwin was an extremely capable and reliable officer.

Amherst continued, that about this same time, on his orders, General Haviland began his thrust to the north on Lake Champlain from Crown Point with thirty-four hundred regulars, provincials and some Indians; and Brigadier Murray ascended the St. Lawrence from Quebec with his force of nearly four thousand. Amherst himself, with time running short for effecting the planned rendezvous of these three army wings at Montreal, elected to run the hazardous La Chine Rapids of the St. Lawrence in boats, rather than to make the laborious and time-consuming portage around them. In doing so, unfortunately, forty-six boats transporting troops were upset on the rocks and another eighteen were badly damaged, resulting in a total of eighty-four men drowned; but Amherst was glad to report that the rendezvous was kept and that Montreal was quickly surrounded by his combined forces of seventeen thousand men. Since the French inside the city had only twenty-two hundred regulars and two hundred militia, they wisely decided to capitulate rather than fight it out. As a result, today he had accepted the surrender of the King of France's domain here and Canada now belonged to England.

To make this triumph complete, he reported, he was at this time preparing to send a strong detachment westward with copies of Governor Vaudreuil's capitulation and orders for the French garrisons in the numerous western Great Lakes outposts, of which Detroit was the hub, to give them up and vacate the country.

Amherst declared that he expected no difficulty from the French there. As for their Indian allies, many of whom were still openly hostile to the English, in his opinion they were merely a disorganized lot of barbarians and of little concern. However, in an effort to prevent possible bloodshed, he would also send along with the detachment an experienced Indian agent to treat with them and warn them against becoming an annoyance to His Majesty's interests.

While on the subject of these Indians, Amherst reported that numerous conferences had been held with them during this year thus far and a substantial number of peace treaties had been enacted. There was little doubt in Amherst's mind that when the remainder discovered that they were now dealing with a commander in chief who was not as lenient as his predecessors had been with them, they would quickly fall in line and assume a proper subservience. To further this end, he was at this very moment initiating a program to withhold from them the great amount of presents they had grown accustomed to receiving through His Majesty's bounty. No longer, he declared, would they be provided with abundant supplies of gunpowder, lead, rum, clothing, blankets, food, tomahawks and tools. Complete subjugation was in order and one did not subjugate by providing weapons and supplies to those being subjugated. The English were the conquerors of all Canada and Amherst meant to see that they acted the part; kowtowing to Indian demands was one thing which would end now. Amherst was sure His Royal Majesty would approve of these measures taken and planned.

Whether or not the Indians would approve was of very little concern to General Amherst.

[*September 9, 1760—Tuesday*]

Even though it was still relatively early in the morning and he had not finished his reports until dawn was beginning to streak the eastern sky, Sir Jeffrey Amherst seemed remarkably alert. He was again sitting in the chair in which he had spent most of the night, and now he regarded with a speculative eye the rangy, green-clad man standing at ease before him. He knew of no one better qualified than this officer to undertake the mission he had in mind now.

For his own part, Major Robert Rogers[14] felt a stirring of excitement within him. He had no idea why the commanding general had summoned him, but evidently it was something of considerable importance. Though the major appeared relaxed, his attention was closely riveted to Amherst and what the general was saying. He paid no attention whatever to Lieutenant James Dalyell of the 60th Regiment, recently appointed Amherst's aide-de-camp, who now stood quietly against the wall near the door. Amherst, too, ignored the younger officer.

"Major Rogers," the general said, "according to the terms of the capitulation signed yesterday,[15] all of Canada and the French frontier posts on the lakes are now the possession of our own sovereign. It is to our interest to move without delay to each post and assume occupancy thereof. It is essential that word of the capitulation be carried to the commanders of these forts at once, together with official orders from the Marquis de Vaudreuil for these garrisons to remove themselves in peace. Since the French commanders of these posts must still be under the impression that the war continues, the mission to take possession must be regarded as a most hazardous one."

A faint smile grew on the lips of Robert Rogers as he now guessed what was coming, but he said nothing and General Amherst continued:

"Throughout our campaigns you have shown ingenuity and zeal in performing duties of a hazardous nature, which is why I have selected you for this mission. As soon as possible you are to embark with two companies of your Rangers and proceed directly to Fort Niagara, and from there to Fort Presque Isle. At that point, leaving your detachment to await your return, you will proceed quickly to Fort Pitt, carrying with you a packet of dispatches and instructions to be delivered to General Monckton there. These papers will inform that officer what has transpired here and what steps he is to take at that point. In essence, he is to appoint an officer and detachment from his own force to return with you from Pitt to Presque Isle, and from there directly to the principal French establishment on the lakes, Detroit. As soon as you have informed the commander of that post—a Captain named Belêtre, I believe—of the capitulation, and accepted from him the surrender of Detroit, the officer appointed by General Monckton will assume command there. Since you will be carrying with you a letter to Belêtre in the hand of the Marquis de Vaudreuil, advising the captain of what has transpired and ordering him to lay down his arms and surrender Detroit and all its dependencies, it is to be hoped that you will have no difficulty effecting this object."

Amherst paused and then handed a large oilskin-wrapped package to Rogers, who accepted it with scarcely a glance and without comment. The general remained standing and regarded the Ranger for a long moment. Rogers waited quite patiently, holding the packet of orders for Monckton carelessly under one arm. Abruptly Amherst nodded and took another packet, considerably smaller than the first, from his desktop and handed this, too, to Rogers.

"These are your own orders in detail. What I have not covered orally here today will be found written within. At Fort Niagara you have authority to take whatever boats, supplies, cattle or equipment will be necessary to sustain you and your men, as well as the garrisons which will be left behind under the officer appointed by General Monckton.

"The season is already well advanced," he continued, "and you may not be able to occupy all the dependent posts of Detroit this year. You will, however, occupy as many of them as possible in accordance with these written instructions, especially Forts Michilimackinac, Miamis and Ouiatenon.[16] Now, how soon can you be in shape to leave?"

Rogers was ready with his reply. "At least four days, sir. The whaleboats are pretty well banged up from descending the rapids and they'll need a certain amount of repair. Gathering up necessaries, loading and the like, all that'll take time, too. But we should be ready on Saturday, if that meets the general's approval?"

Amherst nodded, pleased. It was sooner than he expected. Rogers was a good man and he was glad he had picked him for this mission.

"Excellent, Major," he said. "That will give me time to prepare some additional dispatches for you to carry along. Keep your line of communication open and send reports of your progress at intervals to General Monckton, who in turn will keep me informed. We both have much to do. You are dismissed."

The commanding general was already occupied with other matters when Lieutenant Dalyell quietly closed the door behind Major Rogers.

At almost the same moment in his own quarters a short distance away, Governor the Marquis Pierre de Vaudreuil was also giving some important instructions. He addressed himself to a pair of poorly dressed Canadians, speaking in a voice so low they had to lean closer to hear him. They accepted thin dispatch pouches from him. These two men would also soon be heading for the western French outposts, but with a difference: they would be traveling the old fur-trading route—up the Ottawa River and its tributary, the Mattawa River, to Lake Nipissing, then down the French River to Lake Huron. Here they would separate, one going southward to Detroit, the other northward to the Straits of Mackinac. They would be leaving Montreal by canoe first thing in the morning tomorrow and they should reach Fort Michilimackinac and Detroit and others of the outposts enough in advance of the English that the reception those conquerors received might be considerably different than anticipated.

For the moment Canada was lost for the French, but perhaps this secret measure might aid in making that loss only temporary instead of permanent.

[October 19, 1760—Sunday]

Ever since the word had reached Fort Pitt of the surrender of Canada, the atmosphere in the garrison and throughout the whole of Pittsburgh was one of bubbling excitement. Traders had suddenly flocked to the town in droves, clamoring for permits from General Monckton to set up Indian trading posts, not only here but also at the rebuilt posts of Presque Isle, Le Boeuf and Venango.

Some of the traders, particularly those who had traded with Indians of the Ohio country before the war—men such as Hugh Crawford and John Hart, Mike Teaffe and William Trent, Robert Callender and Alexander Lowry—were even asking permission to go deep into the Northwest Territory to reestablish the posts they had once operated in competition with the French traders. Now, with the French gone, the Shawnees in the valley of the Scioto, the Delawares along the Muskingum, the Hurons at Sandusky Bay and the Miamis on the headwaters of the Wabash, Miami and Maumee, all these would be desperate for supplies. Fortunes were there to be made and these men were determined to be among those who made them.

For the moment, no such permits were being given, although Robert Monckton had given every assurance that they soon would be. As a result, Pittsburgh virtually bulged at the seams with trade goods and traders poised for the opening of the trade.

Nor was trading fever the only excitement prevailing. The military, too, were considerably keyed up, wondering what would take place now; wondering who would get commands at the remote outposts and, particularly, who would get command of the hub of all these posts—Detroit.

Then, three days ago on a drizzly Thursday morning, a new ripple of excitement swept over the fort at the arrival of Major Robert Rogers directly from Amherst at Montreal, carrying with him numerous orders and dispatches, along with an abundance of news. It did not take long for the word to spread: Rogers was en route to demand the surrender of Detroit, and Monckton would now soon be naming an officer to lead a detachment and accompany Rogers there, to take command of that post when the surrender was effected. The big question in everyone's mind was who would it be?

Captain Donald Campbell of the 60th Regiment—the Royal Americans[17]—was both pleased and honored when he was ordered to report to the general this morning and was told by Monckton that the responsibility for taking over command of Detroit would be his. Gray-haired already, although he was only thirty, Campbell was relatively short, quite fat and decidedly nearsighted. He was a Scotsman with a pleasing personality and a well developed administrative ability. Until now, his military career had been relatively uneventful. The few times he had participated in campaigns, he had performed his duties well enough, though certainly no one—himself least of all—considered him as being of heroic stature or an exceptional leader of men.

Captain Campbell was grateful at being chosen for the command, but was honest enough with himself to realize that probably the deciding factor in his favor was his command of the French language, which he could speak with enviable fluency. Since the entire white civilian population at Detroit was French, such bilingual ability on the commander's part was virtually imperative. He determined to prove to himself as well as to his fellow officers, however, that he had what it took in other respects, also, to be commander of an important post.

Now in his quarters preparing for his departure on the morrow, Campbell paused and leaned against the wall as he read, for the fourth time today, the special instructions he had been given by General Monckton:

GENERAL MONCKTON, INSTRUCTIONS TO CAPTAIN CAMPBELL

You are, with your detachment, to proceed with all possible dispatch to Presque Isle and to put yourself under the command of Major Rogers, to proceed with him to assist in putting in execution the instructions he has received from General Amherst—as the detachment of Royal Americans under your command are to remain and keep possession of the posts now possessed by the French at Detroit, Michilimackinac, and their dependencies, as far as it may be found practicable. I herewith enclose you a copy of the capitulation for your guidance in this command and by which I refer you. I have, in my instructions to Major Rogers, fully set forth the steps necessary to be taken for lading in provisions for your detachment and desired him to consult with you in regard to the posts you may be able to garrison, supply with provisions and keep up a communication with for the winter.

As by the Major's instructions from General Amherst and in consequence of the capitulation, all the inhabitants [French] are to be disarmed and their arms brought off. I have (as the subsistence of the inhabitants greatly depends on their arms) recommended to him, to leave with you some few, that you may deliver them out to such of the inhabitants as may, by their attachment to the British Government, merit such indulgence.

By the capitulation, the inhabitants become his Majesty's servants, by which they enjoy great privileges. They must therefore be made (if necessary) to assist, as in others of his Majesty's colonies, in transporting provisions and other services for the British good with their boats and canoes, for which they will be paid.

You will, during your command, endeavor to procure the release of as many prisoners as you can that may be with the Indians of that post. You will maintain the strictest discipline in your troops and suffer no insults to be committed on the inhabitants, as by the capitulation of the 8th September, they are become his Majesty's subjects. Major Rogers will leave such boats as you may want, and a detachment of his Rangers if it should be necessary, upon your consulting together. You will take care, upon Major Rogers' return, not to keep more men with you than you can well maintain. I have ordered some blankets and palliasses[18] for your detachment.

Everything is so fully set forth in the capitulation that I have only to add that you will, as opportunity offers or necessity requires, transmit to General Amherst accounts of your proceedings and any material occurrences: make all necessary observations and explore the country as much as the season will admit of: you will likewise try to reconcile the minds of the Indian inhabitants of those posts to the British interests, by acquainting them that a free trade will be opened to all nations, they showing and manifesting by their behavior and conduct, a due and proper attachment to the British Government now possessed of all Canada.

When any boats are sent for provisions, either to Niagara or Presque Isle, a proper person should be sent to receive and give receipt for the same. You will make known these orders to Colonel Bouquet, that he may be informed of the steps taken to supply you with provisions and stores.

Given under my hand at Fort Pitt the 19th day of October 1760.

Robt. Monckton

Donald Campbell refolded the document, put it back into the packet and continued his packing. He had also been told by General Monckton that in an effort to avert any possible misunderstanding with the Indians of the Detroit area, Sir William Johnson's chief Indian Department deputy here, George Croghan, would be accompanying the detachment, along with several of his men and a small party of Iroquois Indians. Having himself had little experience in dealing with the Indians, Campbell was glad of it. Croghan had considerable influence among the natives and Campbell hoped to learn a great deal from him during their time together.

Abruptly he grinned and slapped his thigh. For the first time in years he felt like a boy preparing to embark on a great adventure. He was extremely anxious to get going.

[*November 30, 1760—Sunday*]

In the council house of the Seneca village on the banks of the Genesee River a couple of days' journey from Fort Niagara, the tribal council was drawing to a close.[19] It was a huge council house, fully one hundred and twenty feet long and a third that in width, yet so many warriors were gathered in the dimness within that hardly another individual could have been accommodated.

For many days the deliberations had been going on here and, not long before that, similar deliberations had been held far to the east at Onondaga, seat of the Iroquois Confederacy.[20] There the Six Nations which made up the Iroquois—Cayuga, Mohawk, Onondaga, Oneida, Tuscarora, Seneca—had assembled to discuss their situation now that the war had ended between the white men. The speeches were long, sometimes angry, often plaintive.

For the first time in the history of the League, which was now over two hundred years old, the name Iroquois no longer struck terror into the hearts of the other tribes. This, they determined, was the work of the English and the French, but most especially the English. For too long these white people had used the Iroquois for their own purposes. Too often the Iroquois had shed blood in fighting white men's battles until now the population of the Six Nations was but a mere fraction of what it had once been. No longer did the Cherokees and Creeks and other tribes far to the south tremble at the mention of the Iroquois. No longer did the Delawares and Shawnees, the Miamis, the Kaskaskias, the Peorias fear them. No longer did the Hurons and Ottawas, the Chippewas and Potawatomies hide themselves if a little bird brought word that the Iroquois were coming. No! Now the Iroquois had grown weak and would grow weaker yet, so long as the white men were tolerated here.

The Senecas dominated in this speechmaking. They, more than any others of the League, had sympathized with the French. When at last it had become obvious that the French must lose this war, the Senecas had had no choice other than to join the English against them, if they wished to preserve themselves. And so they had joined with Sir William Johnson—their adopted Mohawk brother whom they knew as Warraghiyagey—and fought first in the great battle at Niagara; a battle which, without them, the English would surely have lost, as even Warraghiyagey admitted. Following that, they had aided in the taking of Fort Lévis on the great river to the sea, the St. Lawrence. What then had happened? Had they been given their rightful plunder? No! Had they been allowed to take a share of the prisoners? No! Had they been allowed to indulge in a massacre of the defeated, as had always been their right? No! They had been ordered under pain of death to desist, and so they had gone away from General Amherst, but his insult to them was not forgotten, nor would it go unavenged.

Further, had it not been promised by the English that at the end of the war they would vacate all those forts that had been built on the Iroquois land? Had they not solemnly declared that they would either destroy them or else abandon them and turn them over to the Iroquois? Had any been vacated? No! Had any been destroyed? No! Had any been turned over to the Six Nations? No! Instead, they were rebuilding forts the French themselves had destroyed, and they were building many new forts. More and more English people were coming in and the Iroquois land was being devoured at an even more alarming rate.

But now the Iroquois alone were too weak to drive out the conquerors who had beaten the French. To do this, they must have help. Was it not possible that the Six Nations and the tribes of the west and the upper lakes could bury the hatchet that had so long been bloody between them? Could they not all join hands and rise as one to wipe out the white conquerors?

Now these same conquerors were preparing to move into the lands upon which the Indians had permitted the French to build small forts and trading posts. The English were claiming it to be their land by right of conquest. But this land had never belonged to the French at all, so how could the English claim it as a prize from the French? Yet they were already moving themselves into Canada and into the Ohio country and into the country of the upper lakes, saying that it was theirs and that the Indians were only to be tolerated there. Would this not give those tribes whose land this had always been, good reason to forget past differences between the tribes and join the Iroquois in a drive to destroy these English?

On and on went the harangues and in the end it was decided to let the Senecas, who were the westernmost tribe of the Six Nations, send emissaries to the tribes of the far west to learn their feelings in the matter. With this the Onondaga council had concluded.

But now, in the Seneca council just coming to an end, the wrinkled, leathery-skinned Chief Kaendae spoke. His voice no longer carried in it the thunder of youth and strength, but it reached every ear and it raised in every breast the lust for war. He appointed two strong young chiefs—Kyashuta and Teantoriance[21]—to carry to the Indians of the Ohio country, Illinois country and upper lakes country, especially those in the area of Detroit, red war belts. These belts, often called red hatchets, were invitations to the recipient tribes to rise up with the Iroquois and strike down all Englishmen.

No sanction had been given at the Onondaga council for the actual circulation of war belts in the Iroquois name, but no one of this Seneca council voiced objection. Kyashuta and Teantoriance accepted the belts and set off at once on their long journey. The council ended and Chief Kaendae retired to his own cabin, where two Frenchmen from Detroit dressed as Indians, heard from him what had transpired at the council and congratulated him. They promised to help convince the tribes around Detroit to agree to an uprising. With great sincerity the two declared that the King of France would soon send a great army to join them and support the Indians in this purpose. In the meanwhile, they whispered, every Frenchman left in Canada would support the Indians in every way possible . . . though unobtrusively, of course.

Captain Donald Campbell was extremely pleased with how well things had gone in the transference of Detroit from the French to the English. True, the French commandant, Captain François de Belêtre,[22] was not at all happy about it, but Campbell hardly expected him to be. For a brief while it had even appeared that he might resist but, under the circumstances, he really had no choice but to give the place up. The most surprising thing, to George Croghan as well as to Campbell, was the easy acceptance of the French inhabitants of Detroit to the changeover, even though it meant they had to swear an oath of allegiance to the King of England in order to stay.

Supplies were scarce here, to be sure, and Campbell determined to urge the speedy arrival of traders to provide not only what he and his men would need here at Detroit, but equally the French residents and Indians who were in the area in great numbers. With their own supply system from the French severed, they were just as dependent on English goods as he.

Now, having had possession of Detroit for three days, it was time to get a report off to Lieutenant Colonel Bouquet at Presque Isle. As he moved to his desk and prepared his writing materials, he thought of the events of their arrival here.

The entire English military force here totaled two hundred and seventy-five men. Of these, two hundred were the Ranger detachment under Major Rogers, clad in their trademark garb of forest green buckskins and Scottish tams of the same hue. The remaining men, Campbell's own detachment, wore the colors of the Royal American Regiment—blue trousers and scarlet coats.

The force left Presque Isle on November 4—the cattle herd having been sent ahead on land the day before under a small detachment commanded by Lieutenant Robert Brewer and Croghan's man, Andrew Montour—and arrived at the mouth of the Detroit River on November 28, prepared for trouble. Croghan, Rogers and Campbell had held several minor conferences with the Indians encountered en route and, though the red men had not been outwardly hostile, still they had warned the English that the French garrison at Detroit would not give up their fort without a fight.

The reports proved to be unfounded. The next day, when six miles up the river, they were met by a French officer carrying a flag of truce. He had reported to Major Rogers and

Captain Campbell that the commandant had heard of their approach and of the news they brought that Governor Vaudreuil had capitulated. He wished to see a copy of the capitulation and also the letter that Vaudreuil had written to him to give up the fort, which letter Major Rogers had in his pocket.

Campbell returned with him to the fort while Rogers and the detachments moved a little closer to Detroit to camp for the night. The troops were still edgy, but there had been no problem at all. Captain Campbell recalled now how impressed he had been—and still was—at the worthiness of these Detroit fortifications. They were every bit as good as Fort Pitt's, if not better, with the outer pickets enclosing an area of considerable size, having a perimeter of some thirty-six hundred feet. In addition to the fortifications themselves inside, there were seventy or eighty well-built frame houses and business places fronting on a regular system of streets. By comparison, Campbell thought, Pittsburgh seemed rather primitive.

Captain François de Belêtre was cordial enough and read the documents Campbell brought with seeming interest. He then agreed, without further discussion of the matter, to surrender the fort—Fort Pontchartrain, as he called it—at noon the next day. And just that simply, the change had been made. A number of the French inhabitants of Detroit and fully seven hundred Indians—mostly Potawatomies, Hurons and Ottawas, though with a scattering of Chippewas and Miamis as well—were on hand to watch soberly as the French colors were lowered for the last time and the British flag hoisted. At this there was a great cheer from the English and then, with Campbell interpreting to French, Major Rogers administered the oath of allegiance to the whole assemblage of French inhabitants at once, having them repeat it after him, phrase by phrase:

"Say 'I' and then repeat your name!" Rogers shouted.

The crowd did so and when the babble had died away, he added. "And now repeat after me: '. . . swear that I shall be faithful . . . and that I shall behave myself honestly . . . towards his sacred Majesty . . . George the Second[23] . . . by the grace of God . . . King of Great Britain, France and Ireland . . .'"

At this Campbell noted a look of consternation on the faces of many of the French inhabitants, some of whom now resolutely clamped their mouths shut, while others merely made wordless mouthings. Short of administering the oath individually, however, there was nothing to be done. Besides,

Rogers commented in an undertone to Campbell, the requirement was now being met; the oath of allegiance was being administered. With Campbell's help, Rogers continued:

"'. . . defender of the faith . . . and that I will defend him and his . . . in this country . . . with all my power . . . against his or their enemies . . . and further I swear . . . to make known and reveal . . . to His Majesty . . . his general . . . or their assistants in place present . . . as much as depends on me . . . all traitors or all conspirators . . . that could be formed . . . against his sacred person . . . his country . . . or his government.'"

There were notably fewer who finished repeating the oath than who began it, but Robert Rogers overlooked it. Immediately following the oath the name of the fort was officially changed from Fort Pontchartrain to Fort Detroit, but practically everyone continued to refer to the place simply as Detroit, as they had been accustomed to doing, including even the French residents and soldiers.

Since then, everything had moved along smoothly. Rogers was preparing temporary garrisoning detachments to Forts Miamis and Ouiatenon,[24] while he intended going himself to take over Fort Michilimackinac, despite the dire prediction by all the inhabitants here that it was too late, the weather becoming too bad and he could get himself killed. Rogers remained unconvinced. George Croghan had already held several conferences with the Indians, reported them to be quite tranquil and remarkably amenable to the change in government. They had even, in fact, effected the release of fifteen of their prisoners to Croghan and promised to deliver up many more. The Indian agent told Campbell that as soon as his business was done here, he would escort what liberated prisoners remained here back to Fort Pitt.

Belêtre was at this moment at one of the nearby Indian villages, giving a farewell message to them. His request to be allowed to do so had been granted without question. It was a request he had made early this morning when he and his soldiers were ordered to make ready to be transported to Fort Pitt under an escort of some of Rogers's Rangers. There they would be taken to Philadelphia or New York as prisoners and exchanged, although this was obviously in opposition to Article 39 of the capitulation, which stated:

None of the French at those colonies or posts, neither the married nor unmarried soldiers, should be transported to the

American Colonies or Old England, and they shall not be troubled for having carried arms . . .

Nevertheless, under the order of Major Rogers, they were made ready to leave as soon as the new Detroit commander finished his report to Lieutenant Colonel Bouquet, which the Rangers would deliver at Presque Isle as they passed. With them, too, would be going the fifteen prisoners of the Indians already liberated by Croghan.

On the whole, then, Captain Campbell was quite proud of what they had accomplished here in this short time. Now, with a smooth, sure hand, he bent to the task of writing the required letter report to Henry Bouquet:

Detroit December 2d 1760

Sir:

Major Rogers and his detachment came safe to this place the 29th of November.[25] *We had only the misfortune to lose a man of my company who fell overboard by some accident, and some batteaux drove ashore and some boxes of cartridges damaged. There is no dependence on the lake at this season of the year. It is at least one hundred leagues from this* [post] *to Presque Isle, but people here say it is still a better navigation than the north coast.*

Two days after we left you we were joined by some of the principal people of the Tawa [Ottawa] *Nation, who came to make peace with you at Presque Isle, who returned with us; and then by the Wyandots,*[26] *whom we were obliged to humor and give them provisions, as we did not know what reception we were to have at this place. They were highly pleased with what we told them, but all this added to the consumption of our provisions. You know how little we could spare, but we could not help it and some of it was anyway not fit to be made use of.*

Mr. Belêtre would give no credit to the report of our coming as friends, but when I brought him the Marquis Vaudreuil's letters, he did everything with a good grace. I am certain when you see him you will not be so much prejudiced against him; besides, he is now your prisoner.

Your prospect of sending the cattle by land has turned [out] *very well; they have been of the greatest use to us.*[27]

Mr. Navarre[28] *thinks the inhabitants can supply our detachment with flour until next spring, or very near that time, but how we shall be supplied with meat will be the difficulty. We are still in hopes of five boats from Niagara, but there is no dependence on the lake; they expect it to be frozen every hour. I believe we could get some people to go from this [post, though] I do not know how far it would answer, [as] their horses must be worn out before they got there and could not return with a load. I shall be better judge of what we want when Captain Cochrane returns. You could get Indians to undertake it from Pittsburgh. We found the King's stores here almost empty; some barrels of powder and not much of anything else. I have not got a return [i.e., inventory] of it as yet, but Major Rogers took all that on himself. He is to give me over everything that belongs to the fort tomorrow.*

Major Rogers is preparing to send to the posts to bring off the people. He cannot possibly send any of us as the season is too far advanced and [there is] a want of provisions. Everybody here says he will find great difficulty to go himself to Michilimackinac. Even with a small detachment, they doubt even it is possible to be done.

We are to have a treat [council] with Indians the day after tomorrow; I shall have a good deal of difficulty to manage them for the first time, as they are so much accustomed to come to the French commandant for everything they want.

The Inhabitants seem very happy at the change of government, but they are in great want of everything. It has been a very flourishing place here before the war; plenty of everything. The fort is much better than we expected. It is one of the best stockades I have seen, but the commandant's house and what belongs to the King is in very bad repair. We got our people quartered in the fort for the first time this night: I shall be able to write more fully about everything in a few days. I shall be glad to hear from you however soon it is possible.

I am, with the greatest respect,

> *Your most obedient humble servant,*
> *Donald Campbell*

To Lt. Col. Bouquet
Commd. at Presque Isle

Campbell sealed the letter and strode out to give it to an officer of the Ranger detachment ready to head eastward. With that taken care of, the Rangers could leave here as soon as Captain Belêtre returned from giving his farewell address to the Indians, taking along with them the French garrison and liberated prisoners.

Captain François de Belêtre was thankful that neither Major Rogers nor Captain Campbell had insisted that George Croghan accompany him to this Potawatomi village for his farewell address to the Indians. The ensign and their privates of the Royal Americans who had escorted him here and who now stood nearby waiting to take him back did not understand the Algonquian tongue, so there was little danger that what he meant to say would get back to Campbell or Rogers before he left Detroit.

He stood now before the assembled Indians in this village a short distance southwest of the fort and looked out over their faces. He was pleased to see some of the most important chiefs on hand: Teata of the Hurons, Washee of the Potawatomies, Wasson and Perwash of the Chippewas, and Oulamy, Pontiac and Mehemah of the Ottawas. Even the aged and dying Messeaghage, eldest chief of the Ottawas, was on hand. There were about eighty Indians here before him, all of them waiting patiently for his final words to them.

Belêtre was in no hurry. The longer he kept them waiting, the greater would be the impact of the few words he had to say. He smiled humorlessly as he thought of how well he had masked the hatred burning in him for the English and how he loathed giving up Detroit to them. He thought he had feigned surprise rather well at the news they brought of the capitulation. They, of course, had no way of knowing that a messenger from Governor Vaudreuil had arrived here some time ago with all that news and with instructions for the Detroit commander. What the captain was doing now, in fact, was a part of those instructions. With the seed he would plant in the minds of his Indian listeners now, perhaps one day these English would realize the depth of his own and Vaudreuil's hatred. The thought gave him pleasure. Abruptly he raised his arms, then lowered them again at the resultant silence and began his address:

"My children, the time has come for me to bid you farewell. I do so now and carry away with me a great love for you in my heart. But I have more to say to you than just that.

"My children, the English today overthrow your father. As long as they have the upper hand, you will not have what you stand in need of, *but this will not last!*

"My children, keep your ear tuned to the wind, for soon it will carry a whisper to you that the time has come to reverse what you see happening here now. Listen well, my children, for the French voice which will come and tell you that we are returning, for then, as always, we will need your support.

"My children, farewell . . . *for now!*"

He turned swiftly then and stepped over to the waiting guards. He smiled pleasantly at the ensign and said, "I'm ready to return. I have given my farewell."

The ensign nodded and the five of them moved off at once for the fort. Wordlessly, without expression, the assembled Indians watched them go.

[*December 31, 1760—Wednesday*]

It could hardly have been possible for Captain Donald Campbell to have been more pleased with a command than he was with this duty at Detroit. He could not quite recall now just what conditions he had expected to find here before his arrival, but certainly he had not pictured what he found.

In comparison to this place, the English forts in which he had previously served could only be described as austere. Almost without exception they had been as roughly crude as the frontier cabins which so often surrounded them. They bore little similarity to what he found here at Detroit and his opinion of the French had increased appreciably.

His own house within the walls of the fort, although admittedly in need of considerable repair work, was reasonably representative of the majority of the French domiciles inside the walls. Many of the numerous French homes which lined the Detroit River on either side, above and below the fort for eight or ten miles, were also quite similar, at least in exterior appearance, to the quarters Campbell had inherited with his command.

The house fronted on the Rue Saint Louis, which many of the Royal Americans were already calling Saint Louis Street. It was constructed on a well-laid stone foundation measuring thirty-two feet in width and forty-three in depth. The roof was neatly shingled and the walls were sided with board and painted white. A small front yard was surrounded by a low white picket fence.

It was a two-story dwelling, with most of the downstairs devoted to a formal dining room and a large, beautifully furnished living room that had obviously been designed with the entertainment of guests in mind. Both of these rooms had large stone fireplaces. In addition to the well-apportioned bedrooms upstairs, there was already a nicely furnished office

38

with fireplace. Each of the upper rooms had its own window dormer projecting from the steeply sloped roof. The interior woodwork had been well finished and in some places, such as the balustrade, was intricately carved with figures. All of the interior walls of the house had been plastered.

Such quarters as this Campbell had never before had in his service career, and he was impressed. True, the roof needed some reshingling, the outer walls stood in need of repainting, the woodwork was badly marred in some places and each of the plastered walls had some pretty bad cracks, but on the whole it was a charming place.

One of the first self-appointed tasks the new commander performed was a thorough inspection of the fort. There was, within these walls, four streets running parallel with the Detroit River, which practically lapped against the south wall as it hissed past. Farthest street to the north was the Rue Saint Joseph, followed by the Rue Saint Jacques, the Rue Sainte Anne, and the Rue Saint Louis, which was closest to the river wall. An unnamed street, somewhat narrower, bisected all four streets, running from the south wall's water gate to the north wall, which had no gate at all. All around the inside perimeter of the walls ran a spacious lane called the Chemin du Ronde—or Patrol Road—with no building coming closer than fifteen feet to any wall. Main gates were in the center of both east and west walls.

In most respects Campbell was pleased with what he found, although he did note what he considered to be a few fundamental flaws in the defenses. The palisades were in generally good shape, with a rampart scaffolding around the whole. Each of the three sturdy bastions had mounted within it a trio of three-pounder cannon and three brass coehorn mortars. One of the prime deficiencies of the fort, however, as Campbell saw it, was the fact that it was not on level ground. From the river wall on the south to the north wall there was a rise of some thirty feet. This permitted the interior of the fort to be exposed to the view of anyone in a boat in the middle of the river, or to anyone on the half-mile distant opposite shore. Too, the lower portion of the fort's interior was rather marshy ground.

Another factor he considered a deficiency was the lack of a wharf running out into the river from the water gate. The French had nothing larger than batteaux where vessels were concerned, but next spring supplies would undoubtedly be arriving here aboard the ships *Michigan* and *Huron* from the Niagara River and they would be forced to anchor in this deep, swift water here while batteaux shuttled materials back and forth. Also, there were altogether too many buildings inside the walls to suit him. The houses and business places, though neatly placed, were built close together, sometimes even touching, and this could be a hazard if fire broke out. Nearly all the residences and numerous shops fronted on those principal east-west streets. The barracks for the garrison, he was glad to see, were in reasonably good shape.

The French civilian population here, both inside and outside the fort, numbered about eight hundred. Almost all the homes that were not inside the fort fronted on the river. Generally, those properties had anywhere from four hundred to eight hundred feet of river frontage, but all were upwards of two or three miles in depth. Campbell had been told that the backs of these properties were rarely farmed, that most of the residents contented themselves with their own little family garden plot. Fronting on the river also, at the southeast corner of the fort, was the garrison's own garden plot, an area about one hundred and twenty feet square.

Inspection completed, Captain Donald Campbell decided that Detroit was undoubtedly the finest station he had ever been assigned to and, as he soon learned, not the least of its appeal was the French people themselves. They were a genuine, convivial lot with whom he soon found himself engaged in all sorts of social affairs. Rare indeed was the evening when there were not numerous get-togethers going on in which there was dancing, card playing, parlor games and stimulating conversation. The inhabitants always dressed in their finest raiment on Sundays and special religious days— of which there were a great many—when they all came to attend services inside the fort at Sainte Anne's Church, located at the east end of the Rue Saint Jacques. Lately, in fact, it had become something of a pattern for Captain Campbell to entertain on Sunday evenings at his own house. Often a dinner of venison purchased from the Indians would be served to the twenty or more inhabitants in attendance, and the festivities seldom broke up before midnight.

Campbell smiled to himself as he thought of these evenings and the people who came. He found the men extremely interesting to converse with and was thankful for his own fluency in the French tongue, as few of them spoke English. As for the women, a fair proportion of them were unmarried and some of these were extremely attractive. Not infrequently the officer found himself vaguely wishing he were not so fat nor his hair so prematurely gray, both of which combined to

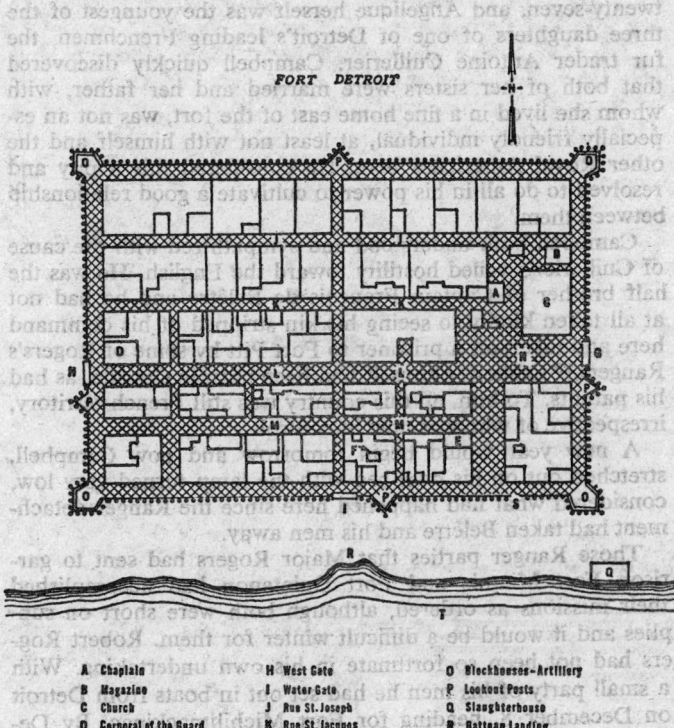

FORT DETROIT

A Chaplain
B Magazine
C Church
D Corporal of the Guard
E Commanding Officer
F Guardhouse
G East Gate
H West Gate
I Water Gate
J Rue St. Joseph
K Rue St. Jacques
L Rue Ste. Anne
M Rue St. Louis
N Parade Ground
O Blockhouses—Artillery
P Lookout Posts
Q Slaughterhouse
R Batteau Landing
S Secret Entry Port
T Detroit River

make him look more like a man in his fifties than one of thirty. He found himself wishing this even more whenever he saw twenty-five-year-old Angelique Cuillerier dit Beaubien, who was beyond any doubt one of the most strikingly beautiful women he had ever laid eyes upon.

She had an older brother named Alexis, who was about twenty-seven, and Angelique herself was the youngest of the three daughters of one of Detroit's leading Frenchmen, the fur trader Antoine Cuillerier. Campbell quickly discovered that both of her sisters were married and her father, with whom she lived in a fine home east of the fort, was not an especially friendly individual, at least not with himself and the other Royal Americans here. He considered this a pity and resolved to do all in his power to cultivate a good relationship between them.

Campbell both understood and sympathized with the cause of Cuillerier's veiled hostility toward the English. He was the half brother of Captain François de Belêtre and he had not at all taken kindly to seeing his kin stripped of his command here and taken off a prisoner to Fort Pitt by some of Rogers's Rangers.[29] Cuillerier himself had been born in Canada, as had his parents. To him, all this country was still French territory, irrespective of who was now in control.

A new year would begin tomorrow and now Campbell, stretched out on his own bed with the lamp turned very low, considered what had happened here since the Ranger detachment had taken Belêtre and his men away.

Those Ranger parties that Major Rogers had sent to garrison Fort Miamis and Fort Ouiatenon had accomplished their missions as ordered, although both were short on supplies and it would be a difficult winter for them. Robert Rogers had not been so fortunate in his own undertaking. With a small party of his men he had set out in boats from Detroit on December 8, heading for Fort Michilimackinac. By December 16 he had gone many miles north along the shoreline of Lake Huron, only to find further progress blocked by ice floes. The French inhabitants of Detroit had warned him that he would not make it to his destination, nor did he. The party was forced to turn back and very nearly perished from exposure before reaching Detroit again on December 21.

Two days later Campbell had said a final farewell to Rogers as he and the Ranger detachment headed for Fort Pitt. This time he had not returned and Campbell could only assume they had made it back safely. With Rogers gone for good, Campbell found himself in sole command of Detroit, and there was more to the job than socializing with the inhabitants.

There were two problems here already that concerned him a great deal. One of these was the dangerous lack of supplies and the fact that with winter now solidly set in, there was little likelihood of any further supplies reaching Detroit before the ice broke up next spring. The Frenchmen, for the most part, were quite agreeable to furnishing the garrison with what they had to spare—some flour, peas and corn—but the war had left them almost destitute and they themselves were in great need of supplies. Campbell hoped that the coming of spring would also bring English traders to establish themselves here and at the dependent posts. Nothing could more quickly restabilize the economy in the area.

The second problem had to do with the Indians. George Croghan had established remarkably good relations with them while he was here. Numerous councils had been held with them and Campbell, who attended most of them, quickly saw why this Indian agent always seemed to get along so well with them.

In the beginning of the talks there had been a disturbing coldness on the part of many of these Indians, but with each meeting this had diminished. Croghan always listened to them with great care and he stubbornly refused to take offense at their often imperious demeanor. He never failed to take the time to explain in detail to them why certain things were as they were, or why certain things would be changing. He never flatly gave them orders or laid down ultimatums, however minor, or acted in any way superior to them. For all this, they respected him deeply.

Croghan had met with the Hurons, Ottawas, Chippewas, Potawatomies, Mississaugis, and even with a scattered few of the Delawares, Shawnees and Miamis. The Indians asked for traders to be permitted to come among them and supply their needs for tools, ammunition, weapons, clothing and other such goods at prices lower than the French traders had demanded, which the English had often said they could and would do if the Indians gave them the chance. Croghan nodded and promised them that this would happen in the spring; that the French inhabitants here were now British subjects and that both they and the Indians would be permitted a free and open trade. General Amherst, he added, had given his word on this.

They asked for a gunsmith to repair their faulty weapons

for them at the fort, and for a doctor to care for them and their families when they were ill. He promised them that the fort's surgeon, Dr. George Christian Anthon, would help them all he could and that a gunsmith, though not available at the fort now, would undoubtedly be sent here later on and that he would repair such weapons as he could.

In addition to the fifteen liberated prisoners that he had already sent east with the Rangers, Croghan during these meetings effected the release of yet another forty-two prisoners, most of them having been taken during the past war. All of these forty-two were prisoners released by the Indians because they had wanted to go back with Croghan. There were others, however, who much preferred to stay with the tribes that had adopted them, and these the Indians would not surrender, nor was Croghan so unwise as to demand that they do so. The forty-two he took back personally with him to Fort Pitt when he left Detroit on December 11.

So skilled had he been in the discussions with the Ottawas, that Croghan had even managed to calm the ruffled waters between them and the Iroquois party who had accompanied him here. He wound up the meetings with the incredible accomplishment of getting the Ottawas to invite the Iroquois back to another conference in the spring to settle the differences that had risen between them at the Fort Niagara battle, at which time their cross-purposes and sharp words for one another had very nearly resulted in a resumption of bloody warfare between them.

But with Croghan gone away now, the Indian problem here was threatening to grow rather than diminish. Suspected, though not yet clearly understood by them, was the gradually firming policies of General Amherst to completely alter English treatment of the Indians, now that they no longer had the French to support them. It had always irked Amherst that presents were given to the tribes at each meeting. His long-range planning called for a stop to be put to that practice, just as he planned to cease listening to any complaints or demands they might have, to cease providing them with gunpowder and lead, to cease treating them as if they were human beings and instead to consider them as little more than annoying and not particularly dangerous creatures who had best tread lightly around the English if they did not wish to suffer the consequences.

It was just as well that they did not yet understand what was shaping up, or the manner in which Amherst considered them. Campbell understood it to a degree, mainly through conversations with Croghan. The Indian agent had no idea where things would go from here, but he fervently hoped that Amherst would mellow his outlook. In the meanwhile, he recommended that Campbell, as much as it was possible for him to do so, provide the tribes with what they so badly needed.

Campbell had been doing so, continuing to provide them with powder and goods out of his own meager supplies, but the time had to come when he could no longer do this, and that would be the time when the full understanding of what was happening to them would dawn on the Indians.

That was what worried Campbell now.

[*June 18, 1761—Thursday*]

Kyashuta and Teantoriance, the two Seneca chiefs, had arrived at Sandusky eight days ago, along with a number of Delaware and Shawnee chiefs they had been joined by in their travels. All of them were astounded to find that close at hand to this Huron village under Chief Orontony was a sizable storage shed only recently erected by English traders. In it a great supply of goods was stored and a large number of packhorses were penned beside it.

Here and there in their travels throughout the Ohio and Illinois country the pair of Senecas had encountered evidence of English traders afoot in this Indian territory. They learned from several sources that ever since earliest spring, English traders had begun flocking to Detroit and Presque Isle, but somehow they had not expected to find them already ensconced at Sandusky.

Ever since he had more or less separated himself from the Hurons in the Detroit area, Orontony had been referring to himself and his people as Wyandots, rather than Hurons. Though he lived apart from them, he feared his brother Hurons in the Detroit area, just as he feared the Ottawas and other tribes gathered there. Rarely had he ever agreed with their policies or gone their way in matters. He and his Wyandot Hurons were not strong and he knew it only too well. Even the fact that recently another Huron faction from Detroit, led by a big, square-jawed chief named Odinghquanooron, had come to take up residency here at Sandusky Bay, too, did little to ease his fears. He neither liked nor trusted the man and he was glad that chief was absent when these Senecas had come here to council.

When Chiefs Kyashuta and Teantoriance remarked about

their surprise at finding English traders here, Orontony only shrugged. But, since the Senecas apparently expected some sort of explanation, he had muttered words to the effect that it was obvious that he and his people had to have supplies and, without the French to provide them any longer, they were forced to trade with the English. He did not mention the fact that for many years he had preferred English traders to the French. It was why he had broken with his fellow Hurons at Detroit. It was also the reason why Pontiac, war chief of the Ottawas, had once burned his villages here.[30]

The two Senecas nodded, dismissing the matter for now, and requested an immediate council. Orontony agreed. The Senecas also suggested that it might be wise for two Frenchmen from the Detroit area, who were in the village this day, to sit in on the council. Again Orontony agreed. Finally, Kyashuta said that even though the Frenchmen could attend, any Englishmen on hand here must be excluded from the council. Reluctantly, Orontony nodded and runners were sent to announce the formation of the council.

Thus far in their journey, Kyashuta and Teantoriance had met with signal success. They had carried the Iroquois war belts and red war hatchet from village to village all winter and spring. They had been among the Mingoes, the Delawares and Shawnees of the eastern, central and southern Ohio country; they had carried the belts to the scattered tribes in the Illinois country—the Kaskaskias, Peorias, Cahokias, and other tribes making up the Illinois confederacy—and had even been encouraged there in their mission by the French in and around Fort de Chartres on the Mississippi,[31] they had carried their message to the Weas and Muncees, the Piankeshaws and Kickapoos and Miamis of the upper Wabash and Miami River valleys, and now they had come to the Hurons—the *Wyandot* Hurons—at Sandusky Bay. Their message was clearly stated by Kyashuta:

"Brothers, since the English have taken possession of Detroit, they have encouraged you to fan to brightness again the fire that burns within your breasts against your and our ancient enemies to the south, the Cherokee. They have encouraged you to lead war parties against them, in order that discord may remain strong among Indian peoples and that you may weaken yourselves in these endeavors.

"Brothers, hear us: we have no love in our hearts for the Cherokee, but there is an enemy much greater to be contended with first. We now desire and request that your young men be not permitted to go to war against the Cherokees, but instead that they remain home for some time."

Kyashuta now held high, for all to see, the war belt. It was an impressive, woven affair of beads and shell bits worked into an intricate design of red and black. It was six inches wide and fully seven feet in length. Twice the Seneca chief turned a complete circle with it and listened with satisfaction to the awed murmur that it elicited from the Indians assembled here. He then faced them again and continued, addressing them with the same flattering terms he and Teantoriance had used with other tribes who had called councils to hear them.

"Brothers, as you are the leading nation here, you have only to say the word and the others will follow your example. We do now invite you, by this belt, to cut off the English at the Detroit fort, which, if you will agree, will give us the greatest joy and pleasure and go far to restore friendship between ourselves and you."

No word was spoken by anyone seated here, but the air was suddenly charged with excitement and wonder. Many of the Hurons leaned forward so as not to miss a word as Kyashuta continued:

"Western brothers, if you will agree to this, with cheerfulness we will return home to our nation and endeavor to do the same with the English forts of Niagara and Pitt. The English treat us and you with much disrespect; their behavior towards us gives us, as it must give you, the greatest reason to believe they intend to cut us off entirely. They have possessed themselves of our country and now, as you have seen, they are possessing themselves of yours. It is now in our power to dispossess them and recover it, if we will only embrace the opportunity before they have the time to assemble themselves strongly together and fortify themselves against us more than they have already done."

His voice rose stridently now and he shook his war belt high above his head until it writhed in his grasp like an angry snake.

"Brothers," he shouted, "there is no time to be lost! Let us strike immediately! Your neighbors to the east and south and west are prepared for our movement, ready to join. Our warriors—the Iroquois—are already prepared and impatiently wait till they hear from you. Attack can be made as early as fifteen or twenty days from now. Our fleetest messengers are poised to run in all directions with the word, so that on the appointed day all may strike as one, wherever they are. Brothers, what is your answer?"

Kyashuta turned and went back to where Teantoriance was seated and sat down himself. For a long while there was no sound. At length Orontony stood and addressed himself in a loud but emotionless voice to the Senecas:

"Iroquois brothers, we are honored that you have come to us and asked us to join our might to yours. You consider us the leading nation here, but we are only a small part of that nation, the heart of which is beside the great river of Detroit. We can give you no reply without knowing their favor, and at the same time the favor of those tribes who are our brothers here, the Ottawas and Potawatomies and Chippewas and the children of the Chippewas, the Mississaugi. We ask that you go with us to that place to repeat what you have told us now and to there receive your answer, which we hope will be pleasing to you."

This did not sit very well with Kyashuta. Frowning, he asked that Orontony send word to those tribes to come here, far away from the Detroit fort, for a grand council. Orontony agreed to this and sent off the runners, but when they returned it was with word that the Detroit area tribes refused to come. However, if this embassy from the Iroquois League was willing to come to the Huron village of Chief Teata, across the river from Detroit, they would hold a council to hear what was said and give their reply.

The Shawnees and Delawares flatly refused to go to Teata's village, but Kyashuta and Teantoriance had little choice but to agree to go. The journey had been made and now they were in this great, sprawling Huron village, waiting for the various tribes to assemble for the promised grand council. No one in the village saw the small flotilla of five batteaux which passed downstream in the darkness, hugging the river's western shore.

Three hours ago the commander of Detroit had learned from some Frenchmen in his employ of the council that had been held at Sandusky Bay. Alarmed at the tidings, Captain Donald Campbell had placed his garrison on full alert. He also accepted gratefully the offered services of James Hambach, one of the most influential of the English traders who had come to Detroit this past spring. Much of the material stored in the structure at Sandusky Bay was Hambach's and he meant to protect his interests if he possibly could. The five batteaux sliding silently downriver with the current at this very moment contained the trader and a large number of men he had rounded up to help. They were en route to Sandusky.

Captain Campbell, for his part, was busily writing at this moment. Already he had completed letters to General Amherst and the Fort Niagara commander, Major Walter. Now he started a third, this one to the new commander of all the western forts, Lieutenant Colonel Henry Bouquet, who now had his headquarters at Fort Pitt:

Detroit, 18 June 1761
Sir

I wrote you lately very fully of all my proceedings at this place. Since that time I have been a little alarmed by the reports of the discontent and bad designs of the Indian Nations, which, as they carried some appearance of truth, put me upon my guard, and made me at pains to find out the true cause of their discontent. It was first told me that it proceeded from the Northern Indians, but I now find it comes from the Six Nations, and for your information, I give you the intelligence I had from my Indian interpreter and several other people of character whom I can depend upon.

The Six Nations have sent deputies and large belts of wampum to all the Indians, from the Bay of Gaspé to the Illinois, inviting them to take up the hatchet against the English. Two of their deputies (Seneca chiefs) came here two days ago to propose it to the nations here, and to invite them to a grand council at the Little Lake, with the Delawares and Shawnees, whose chiefs are already there . . . as I have so good information of everything that passes, I hope to be able to prevent the Indians here from taking any concern.

The scheme laid is that the Indians in general shall at one time cut off all the communications and stop the roads at Niagara, Fort Pitt, and here, and at the same time seize upon all the goods and horses of the traders at Sandusky. In order to prevent their taking advantage of the powder and Indian goods at Sandusky, I have sent Mr. Hambach this night with about fifty of the trader's servants, armed, and five batteaux, to bring all the traders and goods here, which will certainly be a great disappointment to their project.

I have sent this express by Presque Isle that you may have the intelligence as soon as possible, the truth of which is not to be doubted, as it came in confidence from the Senecas themselves who, with the rest of the Six Nations, are to assemble at the head of French Creek, about twenty-five leagues from Presque Isle. I have written to the General and

Major Walters, but in case of any accident, I should be glad you would give information of it to the General and to the officers at the different posts. How far the Indians will be able to put their whole plan into execution, I do not know, but it is certain that they have very bad designs and will do mischief. So far as I can learn, they propose to begin in fifteen days after this.

I expect Ensign Gorrell with the Batteaux from Niagara every day. If he was here with the provisions, I should not be uneasy about my post, as the inhabitants seem well disposed to support me.

I am, with the greatest respect, Sir, your most obedient humble servant,

Donald Campbell

P.S. The Delawares and Shawnees are certainly greatly concerned in the plot.

[July 7, 1761—Tuesday]

Donald Campbell laid his pen down and rubbed both eyes with the heels of his hands and then for a long while he simply sat with his elbows propped on the desk and his hands couching his head. He felt as if he hadn't slept well in a week or more and the truth of the matter was that what sleep he had been able to get was irregularly spaced and brief at best.

Now that the councils were over and the Indian emissaries gone back to where they had come from, he felt drained of all energy. How good it would be to drop into bed tonight, knowing he could really relax now. He wished vaguely that George Croghan had been here to witness how he had comported himself at the councils and how it seemed evident now that he had very likely averted a possible attack by the Indians, if not a full-scale uprising.

Ever since the Senecas had come to the Huron village here from Sandusky, he had been extremely on edge and only now was he able to sort out in reasonably chronological order what had transpired. A grand council had been called for July 3 in which all the Indians and a few of the Detroit Frenchmen had listened to what the visiting Senecas had to say. A few of the French and even two of the Indians in attendance were men that Campbell had deliberately planted to listen to what went on and to report to him of it. They had done their jobs well.

Somewhere over six hundred Indians had come to the council as once again, this time with Teantoriance doing the speaking, the Seneca plan was bared and cooperation of the western Great Lakes tribes requested. The Detroit Indians had promised to reply on the morrow and then had councilled among themselves most of the night. In essence, the councils boiled down to the fact that while these Indians hereabout harbored no great love for the English, yet they had to admit that they were extremely dependent upon English supplies to sustain themselves.

Rumors were spreading, fanned by the Senecas, that the great general in the East was withholding supplies for the Indians, especially lead and gunpowder, knives and tomahawks. The Detroit area tribes considered this at length, unsure of the truth of such allegation, unwilling to be too hastily committed to some plot which might result in their own ruination in the end. True, those items in question were not in the abundance the Indians here at Detroit had been accustomed to receiving from the French, but it was also true that Captain Campbell had obviously given them all he could spare of just such items and certainly things would improve as more and more English traders came. The Indians here would be sore pressed indeed for supplies should they make any effort to attack the English. Who would sustain them while they did so? The French? They were full of promises that the French King would reclaim his rights here, and word had even spread that an army of French soldiers was gathering at Fort de Chartres to come against Detroit, but for now at least this was something that could not be counted upon. Further, and even more importantly, the Ottawas in particular were in no hurry to bury the hatchet that had been raised between themselves and the Senecas ever since Johnson took Niagara. Words had been said there, and deeds done, which still rankled and the Ottawas were not so keen about letting bygones be bygones.

It had come as a great surprise to Campbell, on the morning of July 4, when he and several of his officers, along with a number of the more influential Frenchmen of the city, were invited to attend the day's council to hear the answer of the Detroit area tribes. This answer would be given by the Hurons since the council was being held in their village.

It was Chief Teata who spoke for the tribes of this area, his voice firm and dignified as he directed his remarks not to Chiefs Kyashuta and Teantoriance, but to the English commander. Step by step, to the amazement and chagrin of the Senecas, Teata told Campbell what the Seneca plan was and what they had asked of the tribes of this area. Then he handed over the large war belt to the Detroit commander, who was very nearly as surprised as the Senecas. As soon as Teata had seated himself, it was Teantoriance who arose and, his face suffused with ill-concealed anger, addressed Campbell.

"Being that our mission here is thus far revealed to you," he said accusingly, "I will admit to it and declare to you in the presence of all assembled here that we, the Iroquois, as well as many other nations, hold great grievance against you. Of all the many promises made to us when you needed us as allies against the French, not one has been kept. When we helped you defeat the French at Niagara and again at Fort Lévis, the rights due us as a warrior nation were denied us. The lands you borrowed from us are suddenly no longer ours but yours and we see the whole of our country being eaten away. We are cheated in trade and our voice among you carries no weight and we are insulted and cheated further. It is said that your great general has told his men that there is nothing to fear from the Indians now, for they no longer have the French to support them. Hear these words, Englishman: it was not the French who supported *us*, but rather *we* who supported *them;* and had we stayed with them instead of foolishly believing the English promises, it would be your army now who would be sailing across the great sea to the east, instead of that of the French. You have taken the belt that we brought, but this is of no concern to us, for that belt is but a copy of the original which lies in our nation. It was presented to the Hurons, who have broken a great trust in giving it to you. Nevertheless, it is still upon their heads to reply to us, that we may take this reply, whatever it will be, back to our nation. I have said. I will say no more."

Teantoriance, his expression ugly, resumed his seat beside Kyashuta. There was a general murmuring of voices until Campbell himself strode forward with his interpreter, the Frenchman named Pierre LaButte, beside him. With increased anger, the two Seneca chiefs recognized the interpreter as one of the Frenchmen who had attended the first council at Sandusky. LaButte paid little attention to them, concerning himself with accurately interpreting, at the end of each phrase, what Campbell was saying. The Detroit commander was directing his words to Teata in particular and the other Detroit area chiefs in general.

"My friends, my brothers, I return you my heart and sincere thanks for the important discovery you have made of the bad designs of the Six Nations against the English. That you have so wisely rejected their proposals of war and the means you have used to put a stop to their activities yield me the greatest satisfaction. I shall immediately acquaint his Excellency, General Amherst, of your good behavior and friendship to the English and shall take particular care that you be constantly treated as our friends and allies, which I hope you will always continue to be."

He paused for a moment to let LaButte finish with his interpreting and then directed that a black and white wampum belt being held by one of his men be handed to Teantoriance. When this was done he directed his next remarks to the two Seneca chiefs:

"I am very much surprised at this extraordinary behavior of the Six Nations, who have always before this been considered our greatest friends. Now you are not only threatening to become our enemies, but you are inviting other nations to take up the hatchet against us. Your designs are discovered now, and steps will be taken everywhere to circumvent them. By this belt of wampum just given to you, I advise you with all my heart and in the most friendly manner to return home and, in the most persuasive way possible, recommend it to your chiefs and those of other nations in concert with you, to quit their bad intentions and live in peace; for if they proceed in their designs against the English, it will terminate in their utter ruin and destruction."

With those words the council was terminated for the day and the promise given by Teata to the Senecas that they would be given an official reply on the morrow to the request they had made of the western Great Lakes nations.

The day before yesterday then—on July 5—the council had convened a final time early in the morning and once again Campbell and his attendants were on hand. Campbell looked haggard from lack of sleep because, despite the friendly assurances of the Detroit Indians, he had kept the ramparts manned all night and had himself moved constantly from guard post to guard post. He had no intention of being deceived and letting this fort be taken by surprise.

As the murmuring of the crowd had ceased, Teata had again risen to address the two Senecas. On behalf of his own Hurons as well as the Ottawas, Potawatomies and Chippewas, he delivered to them four narrow strings of wampum and one large belt of it. Then he spoke:

"Brothers of the east, we return you thanks for the agreeable proposals of friendship you have offered up and the assurances that you, for your part, will forget the grievances that have been between us. We do now dig a hole and place into it the bloody hatchet and cover it over, that it may never be lifted again between us.

"But, brothers of the east," he continued, his manner somewhat more stern now, "hear well what we say at this time: we by no means approve of your proposal to go to war against the English. We further desire that you will desist from your design, as it is contrary to our inclinations that there should be any disturbances. We now think ourselves happy, being in peace and quiet. If you go on to engage in joining with other nations against the English, we shall be forced to look upon you as disturbers of our own peace and we will therefore be obliged to interpose, to put a stop to what you are doing and to restore peace and quiet again to the land. This is our answer. We have no more to say to you."

Then it was Chief Teantoriance who stood again to reply. His face was devoid of expression as he did so and Campbell wondered fleetingly what the Seneca was thinking.

"Western brothers," Teantoriance said, his voice steady and far-carrying, "notwithstanding the fact that the Six Nations have great reason to be angry with the English, I am now convinced peace is best. Your nations and the English here have opened my eyes to what are the best interests of my people. I will bury all bad thoughts and return home now to acquaint the chiefs of the Seneca and the chiefs of the other five nations in our League, as well as any others who may have agreed with us on our plans, of the desires and intentions of your nations here at Detroit. I will, as you have recommended I do, urge them in the most positive manner to lay aside all thoughts of war and live in peace."

He hesitated and the only sound was the low voice of Pierre LaButte translating to Captain Campbell. When he had finished, the Seneca chief addressed the fort commander directly:

"English chief, I will leave at once and move swiftly to my people. If I have the good fortune to arrive there before any hostilities have been committed, I will do all in my power to stop any bad intentions on their part. Further, I will recommend it to my chiefs and the chiefs of the entire Six Nations that they go and assemble at the place of Warraghiyagey—he who is called Johnson by you—to hold a council with him and accommodate in peaceful manner all matters of grievance between us and you. When such council is finished, I will return here to acquaint you and the nations around Detroit with what has been done at the council. This I will do. I am finished."

And that pretty well wrapped it up. By nightfall the Senecas had been gone for hours and the other tribes had moved off to their own villages. Campbell was not sure whether or not he could believe what the Senecas had promised, or for that matter even what the Huron chief, Teata, had said on behalf of the nations here. Once more Campbell had kept the ramparts manned all night and the garrison remained under arms through yesterday. Late in the evening yesterday he had begun a letter report of the councils to Bouquet at Fort Pitt, but he had fallen asleep before completing it. Now, still tired and thankful that the crisis had apparently been weathered, he straightened at the desk and began finishing the letter.

Though he had not let on to anyone, Donald Campbell felt very proud of how he had handled matters and once again he wished fleetingly that Croghan had been here to witness it.

[August 4, 1761—Tuesday]

At twenty-two, Alexander Henry was an extremely handsome man, fastidious in his habits, careful in his apparel, gentle in his speech. He was possessed of a rather winning personality and his smile had melted more than one female's heart, though he was still unattached. Reasonably well educated, he was a gifted conversationalist. He also had great plans for making his fortune—plans which were now, after the passage of a year, finally coming to fruition.

Alexander Henry wanted to be in the Indian trade.

Ever since he had moved as part of Amherst's army last year down Lake Ontario in the advance on Montreal, his dream had grown stronger. Because he was only of medium build and height and his smooth good looks made him appear even younger than he was, those who knew of his plans were amused. Indian traders, they contended, had to be experienced frontiersmen, tough and big and unafraid. Henry did not argue with them, realizing the futility of it, but there was no diminishing his resolve. Once, early in the campaign, he had seen a young man who was much like himself in appearance, though perhaps even younger than he himself was now; yet that individual had already gained fame on the Pennsylvania and Virginia frontiers as both frontiersman and Indian trader. His name was David Duncan, and ever since Henry had had that brief encounter with him, he felt that there was no good reason why he could not engage in the business with

55

every bit as much success as Duncan had.[32] Certainly he had a couple of important attributes in his favor: Alexander Henry was tenacious when he set his mind on something and, though he really did not consider himself as such, he was quite a courageous young man.

In coming down the St. Lawrence rapids with Amherst's force after the taking of Fort Lévis, young Henry, traveling with three boats loaded with merchandise, was among the casualties of that treacherous descent. Forty-six troop-carrying boats had been smashed and their men dumped into the cold waters. Eighty-four men had drowned and another eighteen craft had been severely damaged. Alex Henry's only three boats were lost and he saved his own life by grimly hanging to the bottom of the out-of-control craft he had been riding in, clinging tenaciously for several hours before finally being rescued by one of Amherst's aides.

Montreal had been taken soon after that and Henry's half-formulated plans called for setting up his trading headquarters here, where Colonel Thomas Gage—with the temporary rank of brigadier general—was left in command as governor-general of Canada while Amherst returned to New York. Henry himself hastened back to Albany for new supplies, but on his return north, due to the lateness of the season, he was forced to spend the winter at Fort William Augustus, which had so recently been Fort Lévis. During the winter he disposed of his trade goods at a handsome profit to the garrison stationed there under Captain Henry Gladwin. With the advent of spring, Henry had gone down the St. Lawrence to Montreal again in the hope that by now he would be able to procure more trade goods there. In this he was disappointed. Such goods were just not yet available, and so it meant another trip back to Albany.

Before leaving, however, he stayed as a guest in the house of a French resident named Jacques LeDeuke[33] who had, as a younger man, been engaged in the Indian trade at Michilimackinac. For hours he expounded to Henry on the opportunities there and Henry was impressed with his knowledge of the people and their language as well as the fur trade.

"Michilimackinac," LeDeuke declared expansively, "is richer in fur trade potential than any other place in North America, perhaps in the world! Here, Monsieur Henry, is where the fortunes will be made in times to come. As for the Indians there," he shrugged casually, "they are a peaceable race of red men. A European may travel from one side of the continent to the other without experiencing insult."

He paused and eyed Henry with a speculative look and then nodded. "Perhaps you would like confirmation of this. You shall have it! I know of a man living nearby here who has guided many parties to the area and who knows that country as well or better than I. His name is Etienne Campion and he is a good man. Since you are interested, it would be well for you to meet him."

Campion was sent for and arrived at LeDeuke's house an hour later. The conversation of the three men lasted into the light of dawn and it was during this period that the nebulous plans of Alexander Henry finally jelled. He asked Campion to come into his employ as first assistant. While Campion prepared boats here, Henry would go again to Albany for more goods and then he would return here, at which time Campion could lead him to the best location at the Straits of Mackinac. The terms were good and Campion, eager to begin again in the business in which he was engaged before the war, agreed at once.

Armed with a list of items which both LeDeuke and Campion agreed would be most desired by the Indians of the upper Great Lakes, Henry headed for Albany again. Within a few weeks he was returning with kegs and parcels, bundles and bales and barrels of trade goods. Among the goods were many of the coarse blankets called strouds, which were always so desired by the Indians. Some of these were black and others were green or royal blue, but by far the greatest percentage were a gaudy scarlet. There were needles and thread, ropes, awls, finger rings of plain metal or with polished stone insets, combs made from cow horn, and razors, scissors and looking-glasses to go with them in little belt pouches. There were ankle bells and stockings, flowered serge material and bolts of calico. There were colored ribbons and shirts and linen sheets, jews harps and tobacco and pipes and snuffboxes. There was brass wire in wooden spools and there were glass beads, black and white wampum, utensils made of pewter, and gilded cups. There were brass and tin pots and pans, iron kettles, silver gorgets, various trinkets, steel traps and fish spears. Most importantly, there were clasp knives and tomahawks, skinning knives and axes, lead and bullet molds, flints and gunpowder and a considerable supply of rum. All of these goods and more Alexander Henry meant to exchange for the prime pelts of beaver and otter, mink and raccoon and fox, marten and ermine, wolf and bear and wolverine; furs which, when transported back to Albany or New York, would net him a small fortune.

During Henry's absence, Campion had hired men to build the boats for this long journey and the job had been completed in exemplary manner. Each of the four canoes was thirty feet in length and four and a half feet in beam. All were constructed of quarter-inch birchbark fitted and sewn over a resilient cedar ribbing and framework, then sealed with pitch and spruce gum until watertight.

Not until Henry returned to Montreal did he learn that patterns for Indian trade were still not established, as no definitive treaty had yet been drawn between the English and the tribes of the upper Great Lakes. His heart fell as he saw all his well-laid plans and a considerable investment seemingly dashed. Then he learned that another English trader, Henry Bostwick, also with designs on the Michilimackinac fur trade, had been given a special passport by Governor-General Gage to go there shortly after Alexander Henry had left Montreal for Albany.

Immediately Henry went to see Gage and applied for permission to go to Michilimackinac for the trade, pointing out that he had all in readiness. Gage was astounded. Henry was hardly more than a boy. Didn't he realize the dangers of such an undertaking?

"No," Gage said regretfully, "I couldn't give you permission to do such a thing. The hazards are just too great as yet. Perhaps in a year or so, when matters have settled down and we have established proper treaties and garrisoned all the western forts, perhaps then it will be a different matter. But as it is now, the property and lives of His Majesty's subjects in such remote country would be extremely insecure."

Henry argued the matter strongly and, when every other argument failed, he played his trump.

"Sir," he said, "could it possibly be that you are engaging in favoritism? I happen to know that you have already given permission to one Englishman to engage in the trade there—Mr. Henry Bostwick, by name."

Gage was taken aback, not realizing until now that young Henry had known about that. He shook his head in an agitated manner. "No, I just can't do it. Henry Bostwick is a man with years of experience in the Indian trade, which was why I let him go, though it was against my better judgment even where he was concerned."

"Sir," Henry countered, "it is neither proper nor just for you to have given permission to Mr. Bostwick and refuse it to me. I have my men, my boats, my goods all ready. My chief assistant, Monsieur Campion, has lived and traded among the Indians in the Michilimackinac area all of his life. With his assistance I should have no difficulty. Certainly the Indians there, now being deprived of French goods, will welcome trade with us. I ask you, sir, to reconsider."

Gage did not, at least at first he didn't; but as the arguments by Henry went on and on he at last slapped his hands to his sides and gave up. He went to his desk and wrote out a permit for Alexander Henry to engage in the Indian trade.

"It is against my better judgment," he said, handing the paper to Henry, "but good luck to you, young man. I hope you'll prove my fears in vain."

Henry grinned and accepted the paper, then shook hands with Gage.

"I plan to do just that, sir," he said.

For several days following, Henry was extremely busy with final preparations. Because of the very shallow rapids just above Montreal, loaded canoes could not fight the upstream current. The boats therefore, by established custom, were wagon-carted nine miles upstream to a tiny settlement called La Chine.[34] This had always been the departure point for expeditions to north and west. Yesterday Henry had seen the large empty cargo canoes off and then supervised the loading of the trade goods onto wagons to follow them. Now, under the experienced direction of Etienne Campion, the goods had been stowed carefully into the canoes, the crews were ready and the great adventure was about to begin.

Each of the four boats carried sixty large, well-wrapped bundles of merchandise, well distributed in the bottom of the craft and tied securely. Each of these bundles weighed in the vicinity of a hundred pounds and each of the boats, in addition, carried a thousand pounds of provisions. For each boat there were eight men and every man had his own bag. The gross weight of each of the loaded and manned canoes, therefore, was somewhere in the neighborhood of four tons. The end men—the paddlers in bow and stern—had the greatest responsibility and were the more skilled. Their wage for the journey was three hundred livres.[35] The middle rowers received one hundred fifty livres each for the trip.

In a last, long moment, Alexander Henry stood on the bank looking downstream toward Montreal. For the first time he let himself consider the possibility that Thomas Gage's apprehension had been well founded, and he admitted to himself that there was more than a faint possibility that he would never return to a world of Englishmen.

At length he smiled wryly, tossed an offhand salute to his assistant and took his place in the lead canoe.

"Let's go, Etienne," he said. "It's a long trip."

[September 1, 1761—Tuesday]

Henry Gladwin was a dreadfully sick man. This malarial attack had hit him a severe blow almost when they were in sight of arriving here at Detroit and now, with the first night at the fort not even at hand yet, here he was in bed alternating between attacks of fever and chills.

Of one thing he was thankful: the malady had not struck him shortly after he and his three hundred man detachment had left Fort Niagara. The trip had been rigorous enough for a man feeling well; had he been as sick as this, he felt he would have died before arriving here.

There were so many things he had to do, according to his orders from General Amherst, and they were things he very much wanted to do. The garrisoning of the remaining ungarrisoned forts, formerly French, was high on the list and Gladwin had looked forward eagerly to it, never having seen this upper Great Lakes country. Now it appeared he would have to relegate the duty to one of his junior officers and he gritted his teeth in exasperation as much as from a sudden chill.

Along with his orders for this expedition had come a special notice for him personally from Amherst:

To Henry Gladwin, Esqre., Captain in His Majesty's 80th Regiment of Light Armed Foot:

Whereas I have thought it requisite for the better carrying on of his Majesty's service that a Major should be appointed to his Majesty's 80th, or Regiment of Light Armed Foot, I do by the virtue of the power and authority to me given and granted by his Majesty, hereby constitute and appoint you to be Major to the said regiment, during this campaign only; after which you are to return to the rank of Captain unless provided for otherwise; ...

The promotion, such as it was, had not moved Gladwin very much. It was his third appointment to the rank of temporary major and now he was beginning to think that the permanent rank would elude him forever. Nevertheless, that spark of hope was there that the powers that were, in His Majesty's service, would this time give him the permanent rating he felt he had long deserved.

At Fort Niagara he had joined the party under Sir William Johnson, also en route to Detroit to hold massive Indian congresses there with all the western tribes. The Indian supervisor was hoping that somehow, in spite of the growing restrictions Amherst was placing on the Indian Department, he might mollify the tribes and keep them from learning the full truth about the general's feeling toward them.

Johnson had confessed to Gladwin that if the Indians ever did find out, there would be no way possible to prevent an uprising. Nor would it be easy to keep them in the dark. So sharply had Amherst cut down the expenditures budget of Johnson's department that he and his deputies had been forced to cut back severely in their own staffs. Already a fair percentage of the goods and ammunition they continued to give as presents to the Indians, in the traditional manner, was coming out of their own pockets and there was little likelihood of reimbursement. Croghan—who had also been en route at that time to Detroit from Fort Pitt to arrange things for Johnson's arrival—was so disgusted with the Indian service of late that he was talking of resigning.

The news of the war belt circulated by the two Seneca chiefs among the western tribes had caused great concern in Johnson. His first move had been to ascertain whether or not the pair had really represented the Iroquois League in their offering of the war belt. He soon found that though the Iroquois were disgruntled, Kyashuta and Teantoriance had far exceeded their authority and what they said did not represent the consensus of the Six Nations. Before leaving his home on the Mohawk River, Johnson had sent runners to the Genesee to ask the Chenusio Senecas to meet him for a council at Niagara to settle differences. The belts he sent them were pointedly ignored. True, a few Seneca warriors did show up under a minor chief with a belt of their own, proclaiming the tribe's innocence in any anti-English agitation, but Johnson nearly laughed in his scorn and refused the belt. He told them in a very stern manner to tell Chiefs Kyashuta and Teantoriance that either they or their representatives had better be on hand for the grand council at Detroit; if not, it might well be to their own peril. The warriors, visibly impressed, left at once.

On his arrival here at Detroit about noon today, Henry Gladwin had been informed by Captain Campbell that George Croghan had arrived here two weeks ago, after stopping to confer with the Indians at Sandusky Bay. Ever since he got here he had been uncommonly busy meeting with the

61

Indians and preparing them for the forthcoming grand council. He had advised them to send runners far and wide to all tribes and villages that they might be adequately represented here. Gladwin nodded weakly and thanked Campbell for the information, but at the moment he just felt too awful to care about what anyone was doing.

For almost five hours now he had been first roasting and then freezing in these chambers. His hope that the malady would diminish quickly now that he had stopped traveling was fading. If anything, it was getting worse. Twice already he had felt himself approach the fine edge of delirium. Now, in answer to his summons, Captain Henry Balfour, his second-in-command of the detachment brought from the east, reported to him, his face reflecting concern for Gladwin, whom he admired.

"Henry," Gladwin said laboriously, "it looks as if I'm going to be stuck here for a while. The season's growing late and there's a lot to do. Can you take over for me on the trip north?"

"Yes sir, Major," Balfour replied. "When would you like us to leave?"

"Hold off a little while yet," Gladwin said. "Maybe I can shake this thing. Give the men a chance to rest up from the trip here. But if I'm not up and around in another seven or eight days, you'll have to take over."

A spasm of shivering shook Gladwin and he tugged the blankets more tightly around him, blankets that only a short while before Balfour had appeared he had thrown off because he had been so hot. The alternating cycles of fever and chill were coming more swiftly now. When the trembling passed, he continued with his instructions:

"I've written out orders on who is to be placed in command at each of the posts. Take a detachment of a hundred and twenty men with you. We won't concern ourselves with the Sault Sainte Marie right now. Leave a garrison of twenty-eight men at Michilimackinac and seventeen at La Baye. Fifteen at St. Joseph ought to suffice there. I'll take care of sending out relief for Ouiatenon and Miamis from here. Lieutenant Meyer already has his orders about building the new fort at Sandusky Bay and will be leaving here with a detachment tomorrow."

Again there was a long interval when Gladwin did not speak and at last Balfour cleared his throat and said, "Anything else, sir?"

Major Henry Gladwin grunted. "Yes. Have Captain Campbell send me Doctor Anthon. He's going to be busy with me for some time, I'm afraid."

[September 13, 1761—Sunday]

Never in its sixty-year history to this point had Detroit been so bubbling with people, activities and excitement as were evidenced since the arrival ten days ago of Sir William Johnson.[36] From a distance of three hundred miles or more in all directions had come Indians of numerous tribes to hear the great Warraghiyagey in this council he had called. For most, it was their first really official business with a European power since the English conquerors had ousted the French government from Canada.

The French civilian population, too, was all astir and hardly had Johnson settled himself in his quarters in Captain Campbell's house than he was besieged with visits from the two priests and a great number of the more prominent French inhabitants. He greeted all with friendship and managed to keep from committing himself about anything, while at the same time providing them with punch and cakes and listening carefully to all they had to say.

The first real order of business for him, however, was a series of long, closed-door conferences with his chief deputy, George Croghan. Step by step Croghan went over what he had done on his journey here from Fort Pitt and since arriving at Detroit. The deputy's expression clouded a bit as he told of his arrival at Sandusky Bay. In accordance with orders from Amherst, he had set about selecting a site for the erection of a fort as a way station on the communication between Detroit and Fort Pitt. But the Wyandots there had become extremely angry that the English would presume to build a fort there without first getting tribal permission. In fact, Croghan warned, they might even try to prevent its erection.

Johnson shook his head in agitation. It was just as he had feared. He had cautioned Amherst against making such a move without first paving the way by providing gifts and compliments for the Indians involved there. Not to have done so was a considerable insult and now who could tell what they would do? Certainly it would not help in the forthcoming conferences. Sighing, Johnson motioned to Croghan to continue with his report and they went on to discuss the Indians, the French, the trade, the overall English situation here.

On the whole, knowing what he knew about things to come, the situation was much better than he had any right to expect, especially insofar as the Indians were concerned.

Thus far, Croghan said, they had been disappointed in the wares brought to Detroit by the English traders, since these were wares geared more to please the French inhabitants than the Indians, but it was a problem rapidly disappearing as more merchandise from the East was arriving regularly. Satisfied with his deputy's report, Johnson ordered Croghan to make it known that the first session of the grand council would open on the plain outside the fort on the morning of September 9. In the meanwhile, he continued to meet with numerous chiefs for private discussions.

Captain Campbell, anxious to give Sir William a good impression, invited twenty of the most beautiful young women of Detroit to attend a ball at his house. A few Frenchmen were invited, as were some officers. Still severely wracked with fevers and chills and experiencing only occasional times of lucidity of thought, Major Gladwin was unfortunately unable to attend. Early that morning during one such lucid period, he had called Captain Henry Balfour to his bedside and gave him orders to leave at once on the mission to garrison the upper French posts. Balfour and his detachment, in a fleet of batteaux, were gone before noon.

The ball was a huge success, though William Johnson did not see a great deal of it. He had eyes for only one woman in attendance—the stunning, raven-haired beauty, Angelique Cuillerier. As if by magnetism his gaze had gone to her at once and there it had stayed. This fact alone was rather remarkable, since Johnson was widely known as quite a lover, who had possessed dozens, scores, perhaps hundreds of women, and it took more than mere prettiness to so captivate him.[37]

Noting the attraction at once, Captain Campbell led Sir William across the room to her. Angelique smiled as they approached, delicately fingering the exquisite little gold cross she wore on a filigreed golden neckchain, apparently as much impressed by this large frontier baronet as he was by her.

"Mademoiselle," Campbell said properly, speaking in French, "may I present to you his Excellency, Sir William Johnson. Sir," he turned to Johnson and reverted to English, "may I present Mademoiselle Angelique Cuillerier dit Beaubien who, in addition to possessing obviously great beauty and grace, is a fine scholar and undoubtedly the best interpreter of Indian languages in all of Detroit."

Neither Angelique nor Sir William were aware of Captain Campbell's immediate tactful withdrawal. Johnson kissed her hand and bowed deeply and Angelique colored becomingly. In a moment they were laughing delightedly when it became clear to both that she understood English no better than he understood French. A common ground for discourse was quickly discovered and soon both were conversing mirthfully in the Iroquois tongue—Johnson with his Mohawk accent and Angelique with the Huron dialect.

All throughout the evening, though conversation swirled around them and there was much gaiety and music and dancing, they hardly had words or eyes for anyone but each other. About midnight, while the affair was still in full swing, they left and walked together through the quiet streets of Detroit. Here and there in the deeper shadows they paused and their forms merged in the darkness for long periods and there were soft whisperings. The ball was still in progress when they returned to the fort commander's house at about 3 A.M. and once again they talked and drank and danced almost exclusively with one another. When at last, two hours later, the party was over, they parted one another's company only with the greatest of reluctance and with promises to meet again very soon. The Detroit visit for Sir William Johnson, at least on a personal level, had already been a smashing success.

The distraction provided by Angelique Cuillerier did not prevent Johnson from attending to business, however, and on the morning of September 9 he appeared dressed in his finest and stood for a long quiet time letting his gaze rove across the incredible assemblage of Indians here. There was no way of accurately saying how many people were in attendance, but representatives of no less than a quarter-hundred tribes were on hand,[38] along with almost the entire populations of Ottawas, Hurons, Chippewas and Potawatomies.

Johnson's eyes widened slightly as he saw Angelique seated with the Hurons beside their council fire, and he suspected that the Frenchman beside her must be her father, Antoine Cuillerier. Several hundred other French people were also there, as were a great many officers and men of Campbell's garrison. It was the largest group of people ever to assemble at Detroit and a silence fell among them as they awaited Sir William's opening speech.

All such Indian congresses follow a basic pattern and this one was to be no exception. As always, he who calls the congress is first speaker and he may speak to whatever length he desires without interruption, followed, if he wishes it, by speeches from his deputies or assistants. Such councils often took many days to complete, for only in the rarest of circumstances would answers to the speeches be given on the same day. Wampum belts, stressing each point to be brought out in the answering speeches, had to be made and great numbers of nimble-fingered squaws worked through the night on the strings or belts of wampum. These belts would not only emphasize specific points to be made, they would accurately record what the reply of the tribe was. This was the centuries-old method of record keeping for the Indians and from such a piece of wampum with numerous figures and symbols woven into it, they could in later years relate virtually everything that occurred at a council, and with incredible accuracy.

Throughout the vast assemblage there were individuals, some Indian, some French or English, standing among the seated listeners. Theirs was the job, at each pause made by the speaker, to interpret accurately what he had said into the tongue of the tribe for whom he was interpreting. Such councils, therefore, often became necessarily tedious, but there was no other way in which they could be properly and fairly conducted.

"Brothers of the Lakes and of the West and of the Ohio Country," Johnson began, "I bring to you greetings and the hand of friendship as the tongue and the mind and the heart of King George the Third. He has empowered me to say to you that he is pleased with you and with your peaceful acceptance of the English here, where once you only knew the French. I have come here in the name of the King to brighten the chain of friendship which exists between us and to encourage you to hold fast to it."

Sir William stopped and gave the interpreters time to catch up with him. When their loud voices had died away, he continued: "My brothers, I, who am known to many of you as Warraghiyagey and one who speaks only the truth to you, I come here to assure you that King George is forever attentive to the welfare of all his subjects. He has given me leave to assure you that for his part, whatever differences there may have been between us, whatever blood may have been shed, whatever angry words may have been spoken, all are now buried beneath friendship and forgotten by him, and he assures you of his royal clemency and forgiveness if you will enter into peace with the English from this time forward, so long as the grass shall grow and the rivers flow and the wind blow."

It was remarkable how the words flowed from Johnson and how attentive was the entire assemblage to his every word, gesture, expression or inflection. Few white men, if any, had ever been able to grip an Indian audience so thoroughly. On he went, stressing point by point the friendship being offered by the English and the advantages to all the tribes of accepting it.

"Brothers," he continued, "you worry that your lands will be eaten up, as some bad birds have come among you from among the Senecas and other tribes and told you that their lands have been eaten up by the English. I am here to tell you that this is not true, nor need you accept the word of an Englishman. When I finish speaking, you will hear from the chiefs of the Mohawk and Oneida and others of the Six Nations tribes who have accompanied me here and they will assure you that these things the bad birds have sung in your ears have been untrue and related only to stir in you a distrust which is not justified. The King has given me leave to tell you that your land shall not be eaten up; that you will be denied no other land than that to which the English already have lawful claim, or that which you yourselves have already given permission for us to use in the building of posts so that traders with goods needed by you may come among you. Even now, with permission of the Hurons in this assembly, such a post is being erected at Sandusky Bay; but this, as with all others, hopefully is with your permission and forbearance and with your knowledge that it is to your own best interests."

As the interpreters relayed this into the various tongues, there was a sudden angry murmur. *Damn!* Johnson thought, *I warned Amherst about it!* Suddenly finding himself on the defensive, he quickly maneuvered the speech into another channel and his tone became somewhat accusatory and, in a way, sad.

"Brothers, the King is distressed to learn that many of you here assembled still have in your possession horses that have been stolen from the English and prisoners among you who were taken from among the English. I hope you will see it in your hearts to give up these evidences of bad faith between us and blow all the clouds away from our eyes, that they need no longer fill with tears at such acts."

On and on he spoke, skillfully using the highly metaphorical expressions so important in speaking with Indians in formal council, talking of trade and relations and friendship, but skirting with great care any mention of two of the foremost points the Indians wished to hear about; the high cost of goods they bought from English traders, and the scarcity—in fact, almost the total absence—of ammunition or weapons for them.

When he had finished, in midafternoon, Johnson stepped aside and let Croghan take a turn at addressing them, and Croghan was followed by deputies of the Oneida and Mohawk tribes, speaking officially for the Iroquois League. The Mohawk spokesman told them forcefully of the advantages his tribe had gained in its many years of attachment to the English.

"Pay no attention, western brothers," he told them, "to rumors passed by others, even others of the Iroquois, such as the Chenusio Senecas, that you are endangered by the English and that they intend to devour Indian land. We, the Mohawks, live closest to the English and should they do such a thing, it is we who shall know it first and it is we who would rise up and gather to us all other tribes to strike them down if such came to be. But, brothers, such will not come to be, for they are our friends and yours."

Day by day the congress went on, first one tribe and then another answering Johnson, paying respects to him and the English King. The reply by the aged chief of the Hurons—Anaisa—was reasonably representative, as he professed pleasure in the knowledge that the conduct of his tribe had been commended by the King and by General Amherst and by Warraghiyagey. He pledged that henceforth, so long as he lived to lead them, the Hurons would be forever faithful to the English.

"It is true," he then added, "that in our villages there are yet some horses taken from the English, and for this we beg forgiveness, as this is the work of some of our idle young men who are hard to restrain. These animals will be returned to you, just as all the English prisoners who were among us have already been returned to your man Croghan. We beg further that you will keep your promise of an extensive trade to come among us, because thus far goods are so high-priced that we receive too little from our hides and furs to support our families, and our hunting is made very difficult because we have so little ammunition, or none at all."

As always, each chief gave belts of wampum as he spoke, for each point covered. There had been concern that the Ottawas in attendance would cause trouble, for among them especially of late there had been rising discontent at the manner in which they were being denied goods by the English. It was said that the war chief, Pontiac, was behind much of the unrest, but when it came time for the Ottawas to speak, it was not Pontiac but rather an aged civil chief, Macatepilesis, who came to his feet and made the official Ottawa address, directing his remarks to Johnson.

"Brother Warraghiyagey," he said, "we were called to the fort at the forks of the Spay-lay-wi-theepi—that stream which you call the Ohio River—at the time of the war between you and the French, after you had taken from them their Fort Duquesne there. We immediately attended your summons, where we found the man Croghan, who spoke to us by order of the general, that we might acquaint the nations of his intentions to live at peace with them, and to require them to do the same and act as friends and allies to the English; since which time we have begun to look upon you as friends and not in the light in which you have been represented to us by the French.

"Brother Warraghiyagey, I speak on the part of all our confederacy here present,[39] who are charmed with the speech which you made to them yesterday, and determined to act for the future agreeably thereon, and to make all nations of Indians acquainted therewith, even to the setting sun, and with the great work which you have now executed, whereby you have established tranquility throughout the land and made the roads and the waters of our lakes smooth and passable, which were before rough and dangerous.

"Brother Warraghiyagey, you have wisely recommended to us to pay no regard for the future to any evil reports which may spread, and you desire to know the people who sent the bad bird lately amongst us to stir us up against our brethren. It is certain such bad birds have been amongst us, but we should look upon ourselves as a very unhappy people if we paid any attention to such disturbers of the peace whom we shall always despise for attempting to put such evil thoughts into our ears, who are all determined as one man to hold fast by the covenant chain forever."

It was an involved declaration, but Johnson had no difficulty following it and nodding approvingly as a wampum belt was presented at each major point. Now the old Ottawa turned and gave a belt of black and white wampum to the Mohawk spokesman.

"Our eastern brothers," he said, "may now be assured that what evil was raised between us at Niagara is now forever buried and there is nothing between us henceforth but goodwill."

Despite this seeming resolution of troubles, for which Johnson publicly expressed the greatest admiration, the Indian supervisor spent almost every night in closed conferences with individual tribal chiefs, subtly doing all in his power not to promote peace between the tribes of east and west but rather to create greater antagonism between them. With dreadful certainty he knew that the last thing the English needed at this time was the formation of an amalgam of all the Indian tribes.

Without seeming to do so, Sir William even subtly promoted something of an argument between the Senecas represented here again by Kyashuta—and the Ottawas. Kyashuta, he had been privately informed, had admitted to several other chiefs that the Senecas had been both inspired and encouraged in the proposed uprising plot by Frenchmen from Detroit. He let word of this slip to the Ottawas and there were some harsh words between the tribes. It was a little enough rift, but Johnson hoped in time to come he could cause it to widen until it would no longer ever be bridgeable. It was in such undercover intrigue as this, however, that the greatest impact of the Detroit congress lay.

For those who knew Sir William Johnson well and had attended some of the multitude of councils he had held with Indians in the past, this one was a disappointment. There was really little of the flair and fire he had always shown in his years of dealing with them, and his remarks had been, almost without exception, placating but without much substance.

The reason for this was simply that already in what little he had done here, Johnson had trodden the thin line of disobedience to Lieutenant General Sir Jeffrey Amherst's direct orders. Now, hoping for the best, Johnson concluded the congress by openly and flatly disobeying Amherst's orders, knowing it had to be done if the most indescribable of consequences were not to be suffered.

As the congress ended, Johnson ordered half a hundred or more oxen butchered and roasted for a feast and he distributed an immense assortment of goods which the assembled Indians were sorely in need of—goods valued at nearly £6,000 sterling, but for which he intended billing the Crown for only a portion. To all the Indians he gave the impression that this largess was merely a sample of what they could expect from now on from the English. And even as he made the distribution he knew that it might well be the last gifts they would ever receive. All he could hope was that it would keep them content until the English were established in this wilderness of the upper Great Lakes country beyond the point of dislodgment.

The disobedience perpetrated by Johnson here was something he did not like to do. He did not mind cutting corners or pulling certain strings to make things come out as he wanted them to, but rarely had he ever deliberately disobeyed the direct order of his superior. Now he closed his eyes briefly and thought again of the express from Amherst that had reached him while he was en route to Detroit. He had been utterly appalled at the contents. The general had written:

. . . and I find there will be no end to giving, if not put a stop to in time . . . You must give up the practice of purchasing the good behavior of the Indians by presents . . . I think it much better to avoid all presents in the future, since that will oblige them to supply themselves by barter and of course keep them more constantly employed, by means of which they will have less time to concert, or carry into execution, any schemes prejudicial to his Majesty's interests; and keeping them short of ammunition is no less to be recommended. Nothing could be so impolitic as to furnish them with the means of accomplishing the evil which is so much dreaded . . . Tell them if they commit hostilities, they must not only expect the severest retaliation, but an entire destruction of all their nations, for I am firmly resolved whenever they give me occasion, to extirpate them root and branch . . .

Johnson absolutely shuddered to think what would have happened had this message fallen into the wrong hands. Amherst in the past had clearly shown his inability to understand the Indian mind, and this put the exclamation point to it.

Presents! What a term to use, and what a misconception it had made in the general's mind; a misconception he refused utterly to allow Johnson or any other person to correct. The so-called "presents" given to the Indians at the Indian congresses were not so much gifts as they were a form of tribute or, more accurately, rent. It was rent for the privilege the Indians were extending to the English to enter and use their country in peace, to set up trading posts and the like. It was a form of rent which the French had understood perfectly and paid gladly and without question. For Amherst to blandly order the complete cutting off of such "presents" was utter nonsense, and it was damned dangerous as well. It was why Johnson on this occasion had so blatantly disobeyed orders.

By giving to the Indians who had congregated here at Detroit the presents that he had just given them, Sir William Johnson had acted with great prudence. Soon the tribes would learn the truth of Amherst's new policies in regard to them and, when they did, a great seething anger would rise in them. He hoped that for the moment his disobedience had caused a deferment of that anger, but he couldn't be sure of it. If it had, there might be time for the English to strengthen their hold on this wild country; but he doubted it. Of only one thing in this regard was Sir William absolutely certain: trouble—big trouble—was on the way.

CHAPTER II

THOUGH very weary, and glad that the long journey to Michilimackinac was over, young Alexander Henry was still almost numbed by the excitement of that trip. His temporary store quarters here at the Straits of Mackinac were certainly not ideal, but this was something he intended to improve as soon as possible. Just the very fact that he was able to be here was enough for the moment. There had been several times along the way, during encounters with dangerous waters—and with Indians even more dangerous—when he wondered whether he would even arrive at his destination.

Time after time as they had passed dangerous falls and rapids, often making long, arduous portages, Henry marveled that the early French explorers could have carved this route to the West to begin with. Strange to believe that Lake Erie had been the last of the Great Lakes to be discovered and that this hazardous river journey he had just made was for scores of years the established western fur trade route.

At La Chine the river had become so broad that it was more like a lake and had, in fact, been given the name of Lac St. Louis. At its upper end the watercourse split, with the St. Lawrence continuing upstream to the southwest, and the Ottawa River[40] to the northwest. It was the Ottawa River that they had ascended. There had been high waterfalls and dangerous rapids requiring many portages and the hand-carrying of the boats and four tons of merchandise over treacherously rocky ground.

Finally, when Montreal was almost three hundred miles behind them, they had reached the mouth of the Mattawa River entering from the west. Here they left the Ottawa and followed the no less dangerous and rapidly narrowing course of the Mattawa until the final upstream portage took them into the waters of the vast Lake Nipissing. They followed the eastern and then southern shore to its outlet, the French River, which left the western end of the lake. Then they were able to travel more swiftly, moving with the current downstream into the great eastern bay at Lake Huron, which they had reached on August 31.[41]

Soon again they encountered Indians, as they already had on several occasions to this point. They were friendly and greatly concerned for Henry's safety, assuring him that the tribes immediately to the west would certainly kill him when they discovered him to be an Englishman. With an odd sort of logic, they reasoned that since he was going to be killed, they had the right to their share of the plunder now, and so they demanded a keg of the young trader's rum. Deciding that it would be the wiser course to comply than to defy, Henry gave them a keg and the party pushed on.

For the first time Henry was beginning to become afraid and he now began to have serious doubts about having begun this trip in the first place. At this point, with his own provisions of food badly depleted, there could be no turning back. And so, at Campion's insistence that he do so for his own protection, Henry packed away his English garb and dressed himself as a French paddler, donning a shirt hanging loose, a broad sash about his middle, a cheap blanket-coat and a large flop-topped red cap of worsted material. Then, having smeared his face with grease and dirt, he took the place of one of his middle paddlers and whenever Indians approached, he paddled with the rest. It was a wise move. A number of Indian parties passed without recognizing him as an Englishman.

They had continued in this manner until they reached the island of the Great Turtle—Michilimackinac. Up until now, all the Indians encountered had been Algonkins, Nipissings or Mississaugis. On Michilimackinac, however, there was a sizable village of Chippewas containing a population of about three hundred fifty men, women and children. These were the Indians Henry had been warned about and he was very much afraid, but once again the disguise worked well and he remained unrecognized as an Englishman.

They quickly left the island and paddled from there directly to the south shore of the Straits of Mackinac where there stood about thirty French homes and a church within the stockaded enclosure called Fort Michilimackinac. The fort itself included an area of about two acres and the pickets were made of cedar logs. So close was it to the water's edge that when the wind was high, waves broke against the wall.

The only artillery at the fort was in the bastions—two small brass cannon captured from the English in some bygone encounter. Campion, who had taken charge of the expedition when Henry donned the disguise, now went into the village and found quarters for Henry to use, and all the equipment and supplies were quickly taken there. Henry decided that he would retain his disguise a while longer, but some of his men became drunk and the secret was out.

Almost immediately a great number of the French inhabitants, of which there were about one hundred, had come to visit him. They had heard of the capitulation of Montreal and Canada by Governor Vaudreuil and so they greeted him warmly enough, but almost unfailingly warned him of his peril at the hands of the Chippewas or Ottawas as soon as they discovered there was an Englishman here. Another Englishman, they told him—and Henry knew they must have meant Henry Bostwick—had managed to reach here some time ago, but he had become afraid and had quickly left for Detroit, resolving to stay there until a garrison of English soldiers should be sent up to hold this fort. They advised Henry to do the same. There were not, they warned, any French soldiers here to protect Henry and his goods, should he be threatened. Shortly after Montreal was surrendered, they added, a courier had come here from Governor Vaudreuil with a message for the commandant, Captain Louis de Beaujeu. Almost immediately after reading it, Beaujeu had abandoned the fort and took his entire garrison overland through Wisconsin country to the Mississippi River and then downstream to Fort de Chartres, from whence he had promised to continue to harass the English who were coming. He had placed in charge of the French civilians remaining here a half-breed Canadian officer, Lieutenant Charles Michel de Langlade, who was a life-time resident of this area. Langlade was very well-known and respected by both French and Indians and had, in fact, on several occasions in the past, led Ottawas, Chippewas and Hurons against the English.

Yet, despite the warnings, Henry had stayed, and he even resumed the wearing of his English clothing. He felt he had too much at risk now, having invested all he possessed in this endeavor, to leave it behind and seek the protection of Detroit.

At first he had seemed safe enough and even began carrying on a lively trade with the inhabitants. By this morning, in fact, he had almost convinced himself that his own fears and the warnings of the French here had been overblown. And then, not long after noon, word had been brought to him that the Chippewas from Michilimackinac Island had learned of his presence here and a sizable band of warriors, about sixty of them, were on their way for an encounter with him, their boats already visible in the distance.

Immediately Henry had sent Etienne Campion with a message to Pierre Farli, who had acted as interpreter for Captain Beaujeu when the garrison was here. Farli's wife was a Chippewa and he knew these Indians well. Would Farli come to Henry's store to advise him and interpret for him? The voices of the oncoming Indians could be heard across the water before Farli and Campion arrived, along with several other French residents, and Henry felt a lift of his spirits when he saw the men. He shook hands with them, inviting them in, and then asked Farli with a steadiness which surprised himself:

"Are they coming to take me? You know them very well. What do you think they're going to do?"

Farli, a small, aquiline man of about thirty, shook his head. "It is, monsieur, hard to say what comes now. Perhaps there is nothing to fear, but that I cannot say for sure. It is the custom of these Indians, when a stranger arrives, that he be waited upon and welcomed by the chiefs of the nation. On their part, usually they give him a small present and they expect, in return, a larger one. But whether or not this is the sole purpose of their visit now, who is to say?" He shrugged, then added, "I would not care to say that the matter looks good for you at this time. Since you are an Englishman and these Indians have made no treaty with the English, I think you may be in grave danger. I have heard them say on many occasions that they will not permit an Englishman to remain in their part of the country. If you wish to flee, there is perhaps a chance you might be able to reach Detroit."

Henry shook his head. "No. I'm not going to run from them. I have come here to stay and I would have to face them sooner or later, so it may as well be now." There was a marked quaver in his voice this time, but Farli appeared not to notice.

Within half an hour the Chippewas, led by their principal chief, whom Farli pointed out to Henry as being named Minivavana,[42] had beached their canoes and were approaching Henry's store. The trader paled when he saw that each man carried a tomahawk in one hand and a scalping knife in the other. Some had their heads almost entirely shaven, but the majority had long hair which either fell free to below shoulder length or was braided into a single queue. Except for only a few who had blankets tossed casually over their shoulders, they were all bare-chested and had been painted frighteningly with whorls and lines of charcoal mixed with grease and thick white clay. All had one or more eagle feathers in their hair and several had feathers or bones thrust through their noses. By the time they reached the door, Henry was seated in a large chair across the big storeroom and against the far wall. His trouser legs shook faintly from the trembling of his legs, but his expression was remarkably composed.

Wordlessly, Minivavana entered and his men followed in single file. When all were inside, the chief gave a motion and the warriors immediately seated themselves on the floor, their bodies blocking passage to the doorway. Minivavana remained standing and he gazed for a disturbingly long time at Alexander Henry.

The chief was an impressive Indian to say the least. Standing slightly over six feet tall, he was half a head taller than most of his warriors. He appeared to be about fifty years old and his face was deeply lined; a face which appeared to reflect an indescribable mixture of good and evil. When he spoke, however, it was neither to Henry nor Farli, but rather to Etienne Campion.

"How long has it been," he asked, "since you left Montreal with this Englishman?"

"One moon and almost half another," Campion replied.

"The English," Minivavana said then, nodding, "as it would seem, are brave and not afraid of death, since they come, as this one has done, fearlessly and alone among their enemies."

Still he did not speak to Henry and as the young trader watched, the chief turned and motioned to his men. At once all of them reached to their belts and loosened small doeskin pouches. Into these they dipped finger and thumb and extracted *kinnikinnick*, the Indian tobacco,[48] and tamped it into the pipe end of their tomahawks. The chief did the same, and smoldering sticks of punk were passed from man to man until all the pipes were lighted. Now came a long quiet period of smoking and this interval was extremely unnerving to Alexander Henry. Not until every pipe was finished did Chief Minivavana turn his attention back to the Europeans in the room. His gaze finally settled on Henry, who returned it unflinchingly. Minivavana's hand went to his belt and he extracted a number of small strings of wampum that had been looped over it.

"Englishman!" he said abruptly, and Henry sat straighter. "Englishman, it is to you that I speak now and I demand your attention!"

The demand was unnecessary. Henry could hardly have been giving him more attention. His own gaze never left the Indian's eyes as Farli, at his side, interpreted in a voice so low that it could hardly be heard across the room.

"Englishman," Minivavana continued, "you know that the French King is our father. He promised to be such, and we in turn promised to be his children. This promise we have kept.

"Englishman, it is you who have made war with him, our father. You are his enemy. Since you are such, how could you then have the boldness to venture among us, who are his children? You must know that his enemies are our enemies.

"Englishman, we here have been told that our father, the French King, has grown old and infirm. It is said that so long has he made war upon you that he has become over-weary and that now he has fallen asleep. It is said that you have taken advantage of his weariness and have entered into his forts and trading posts in this country of Canada, which is our country, and have taken possession of them while he sleeps, and that he knows not what you have done. But, Englishman, unplug your ears; his nap is almost at an end and I think I hear him stirring and inquiring for his children, the Indians. When he does awake, what then is to become of you? I will tell you: he will destroy you utterly!"

Minivavana frowned and for an instant he fingered the haft of a scalping knife at his waistline. Then he continued, "Englishman, you say you are the conquerors and that you have conquered our father, the French King. We think your words are like those of the Indian boy who, on finding the great bear asleep in his hole in the winter, enters the hole fearfully and whispers, 'I have him; I have conquered him!' Is it perhaps this way that you have conquered?

"Englishman, although as you say you have conquered the French, hear me well: you have not yet conquered us! We are not your slaves. These lakes, these woods, these mountains, all these are ours. They were left to us by our ancestors. They are our inheritance and we will part with them to none. Your nation supposes that we, like your own people, cannot live without bread and pork and beef. But you ought

78

to know that He, the Master of Life, has provided food for us in these wild lakes and in the woods of these mountains."

For each of these points he was making, Minivavana was giving a string of wampum. These were accepted by Farli, as Henry's interpreter. Minivavana continued without pause:

"Englishman, our father, the French King, used our young men to make war on your nation. In this pursuit many of our young men were killed. It is our custom to take a life for a life until such time as the spirits of the dead are satisfied. But the spirits of the dead may be satisfied in two ways. The first, as I have said, is by the spilling of the blood of the nation which spilled theirs; the other is by covering the bodies of the dead and thus smoothing out and calming the resentment of their relations.[44] This is done by making presents.

"Englishman, your King has never sent us any present, nor has he entered into any treaty with us, and therefore he and we are still at war. Until he does these things, we must consider that we have no other father nor no other friend among the white men than the French King."

Alexander Henry's mouth was dry and his heart was beating erratically as Farli's whispered words kept pace with Minivavana expertly. The young trader was now certain, as he had only suspected before, that these Indians intended killing him. Yet, somehow he managed to keep the fear out of his expression and his eyes levelly on those of Chief Minivavana.

"Englishman," the chief continued, and suddenly his tone had softened somewhat, "for you now we have taken into consideration that you have ventured your life among us in the expectation that we should not molest you. You do not come armed and with an intention to make war upon us. We see with our eyes and have heard with our ears and understand with our hearts that you have come in peace, to trade with us, and to supply us with the necessaries of which we are very much in want. We shall therefore regard you as a brother. Englishman, you may sleep peacefully without fear of the Chippewa. As a token of our friendship, we give you now this pipe to smoke."

A warrior suddenly rose and, before Farli had even finished interpreting this last, carried to Henry a lighted pipe. He accepted it and, after another whispered comment by Farli, puffed on it three times and handed it back to the warrior. The man then handed it to Minivavana, who did the same. After that, the pipe was puffed in turn by every Indian in the room.

At the conclusion of this ceremony, by which time the young trader had regained his composure considerably, Minivavana advanced to Henry and shook his hand. Again the action was emulated in turn by the individual warriors. One of these, a man nearly as old as the chief, gripped Henry's hand far more firmly than did the rest and he held it considerably longer than had any other before him. His eyes seemed to be glowing from within and there was a broad smile on his face as he finally relinquished his hold on Henry's hand and resumed his seat.

Farli shrugged slightly and looked somewhat bewildered at the questioning glance Henry gave him. "I don't know why he did that," he told the young trader as the Indian went on. "It's very strange. His name is Wawatam and I know him, but I do not understand his warmth for you."

Minivavana had taken a seat on the floor at the forefront of his warriors after the handshaking ceremony. Now he allowed a slight smile to crease his features and nodded at Henry.

"My young men," he said, "and their chief, would like to be allowed to taste your English milk. It has been long since we have tasted any and we wish to know whether or not it is any different than the French milk."

Farli, grinning now, leaned close to Henry and told him that by this the chief meant rum, and Henry had better promise to give them some when they parted. Henry nodded and instructed Farli to tell the chief that he would do so. Immediately at Farli's declaration, a murmur of anticipation came from every throat.

Now it was Henry's turn to speak and he stood before his chair, directing all his remarks to Chief Minivavana.

"You have said I was bold in coming here, but I did so only because of the many good reports I had been given of you, which have this moment been justified. Your late father, the King of France, has surrendered his posts in Canada to the King of England and it is he that you should now regard as your father. He will be as good to you—or even better!—than your other father has been. You see me now, come among you to provide you with those things you find necessary. Your good treatment of me will be an encouragement to others and soon you will have in abundance all of what you need. I thank you for your friendship and as you have given me yours, so do I give you mine."

After each phrase of his speech had been interpreted by Farli for them, the Chippewas muttered "Eh!" which Farli told him signified that they approved of his words. When the speech was completed, Henry set about distributing to them a substantial gift of knives, tomahawks, trinkets, combs, vermilion and mirrors. These, too, were received with much guttural approval.

Without further ado, then, the Indians filed out behind their chief. The warrior Wawatam was last to leave, his gaze boring into Henry, and even after the room had been cleared of all Indians but himself, still Wawatam remained for a while and only reluctantly, it seemed, at last turned and left, running to overtake the others and be assured of his share of the rum.

Henry now turned and flopped into his chair with a great expulsion of breath. The crisis had been weathered and he grinned rather weakly at Campion. The assistant smiled back, but not very convincingly.

"You are safe now, I think, where these Chippewa are concerned," he said. "But there are Ottawa here, too, who will come. It has been told to me that they are very angry at your being here and that they intend to kill you. The Chippewas will not stop them if they decide to do so."

Alexander Henry's grin faded.

[*September 17, 1761—Thursday*]

George Croghan and Sir William Johnson watched the expanse of water between themselves and the shoreline crowded with waving Indians broaden abruptly as the Detroit River current caught them and swept their boat downstream. Both men waved to the Indians a final time and then, after Croghan had shouted an admonition for the other boats to remain close, they took a seat together in the large batteau. In moments the Huron village, as well as Detroit, was lost in the distance behind.

The pair congratulated each other on the success of the congress which, considering the orders of Amherst under which they had been forced to labor, had come off quite well. Following the grand council, both Johnson and Croghan had continued to meet with individual chiefs in private council, encouraging the western tribes to refuse the Iroquois offer to join in an alliance with them. Instead, the idea was somehow raised among them that they make their own confederacy of tribes similar to that of the Iroquois, but not bound to them. The idea was found appealing and now some of the western chiefs were taking steps in that direction, delighted with the idea of their own confederacy separate from the Iroquois.

At the same time, although still seeming to be trying to draw the Indians together in friendship, both Johnson and Croghan used every wile they could devise to broaden the healing rift between the tribes of the east and those of the west.

"Nothing," Johnson had told Croghan in private prior to the secret councils, "could be more dangerous for our own interests now than a coalition of the eastern and western tribes. What we have to do now—and damned carefully!—is to create misunderstanding between the Six Nations and the western tribes."

They had done just that and in this fact alone Johnson considered the whole mission successful. He was equally pleased with the success he had met with in his relations with Angelique Cuillerier. The Detroit beauty had fallen in love with him in this short time and they had spent as much time as possible together. Three nights ago Johnson had given a great dinner for the most influential Frenchmen at Detroit, and Angelique was among those in attendance. The night before last he had given a ball to reciprocate for the one given in his honor shortly after his arrival, and once again he had had eyes for no one but Angelique. For several hours they had disappeared from among the dancers and when they returned Angelique clung most possessively to him.

Johnson was no stranger to affairs of the heart, but his normal preference was for them to be momentary things and in no way binding. Now he abruptly seemed to be teetering close to the edge of matrimony. It was Angelique who asked him to marry her and it had taken skillful maneuvering for him to keep from giving her a definite answer without hurting her feelings and spoiling things. As it was, he had managed to put her off and they returned to the dance and waltzed across the floor in each other's arms until seven o'clock in the morning.

Though he might have arranged it differently had he been so inclined, Johnson fixed his own schedule so that it allowed no time for them to meet in private after that and they had ultimately parted with the big question unanswered. The last full day had been spent in conference with the officers at the fort, at which time Johnson had established the Indian trade regulations to be followed by the English traders.

It would be the responsibility of Captain Donald Campbell and his officers here at Detroit as well as at the dependency forts to see to it that the regulations were not broken. Trade was to be based on the value of a beaver skin, which was worth one buck—a buck being a buckskin, the hide of one large prime male deer. Three martens were worth one beaver, or one buck, as were six raccoon pelts. A whole list of prices were set on various commodities: a large blanket—stroud—could be purchased for three bucks, and a small striped blanket for two bucks. An ordinary man's shirt was given a valuation of one buck, and a ruffled shirt would be sold for two bucks. On and on the list went and it was vital that all traders be familiar with it and stick to it.

"The officers," Johnson told Campbell, "are to keep up a good understanding with all the Indians living near their posts. In order to do this, they will have to keep in frequent communication with the commanders of the other posts, so that all may act uniformly. Each commander should hire interpreters for his fort, regulate the English trade—since no trading will be permitted yet to the north or west of Detroit except at forts commanded by officers—and the Indians are to be permitted to have their guns repaired at Crown expense at the forts. No one is to be allowed to engage in trade except those who have received a license from Mr. Croghan or myself."

With their business concluded, Johnson and Croghan had this morning shoved off from Detroit, crossed the river and put ashore briefly for a talk with the Huron chief, Anaisa, at the old man's request.

"I do not live much longer, Warraghiyagey," he told Johnson, "and soon the younger chiefs—Teata and Takee, for example—will see to my people. But it is my dying wish that my people be allowed the right to be advanced goods by the English traders on credit, which is what was done by the French. We need hoes for the cultivation of our corn, and we need someone to repair our guns and our tomahawks. We suffer from need. We are drained from the last war, having neglected our planting and our hunting in order to fight. Many of our better hunters were killed in that fighting. We have used up all of our goods and have none to replace them, nor skins with which to buy new goods and ammunition. Without credit being given to us, how then will we survive?"

Once again Johnson skirted the question of ammunition. "I will see to it personally, Anaisa," he assured the chief, "that two hundred hoes are sent to you, and a gunsmith, who will repair free for you any weapon that is sick. As for English goods being advanced to you on credit, this is a matter which you must bring up yourselves with the traders, for it is up to them. I can regulate your trade and theirs, but I cannot compel them to sell their goods on credit; however, I am sure you will find them agreeable to doing so."

Soon after that he had bidden the chief good-by and now they were afloat and on their way to Sandusky Bay. There they would inspect the new fort being built by a detachment under Lieutenant Elias Meyer and also they would try to calm the Wyandot Hurons there who were still not pleased about it and who had originally been led to believe the construction was to be no more than a trading post. There, too, Croghan and Johnson planned to part company; Croghan to return to Fort Pitt on horseback, through the Delaware and Shawnee territory of the Ohio country, and Johnson to continue by boat back to Fort Niagara, Fort Oswego, and down the Mohawk River to his home, Johnson Hall.

It had been an extremely busy time and both men were glad it was coming to an end.

[September 26, 1761—Saturday]

The fright that Alexander Henry had undergone with the appearance of the Chippewas after his arrival here at Fort Michilimackinac was as nothing compared to what he felt now. As Etienne Campion had grimly predicted, the Ottawas had come and they were anything but in a friendly mood.

Immediately after the departure of Chief Minivavana and his Chippewas twelve days ago, Henry had hired a number of French inhabitants to work in the Indian trade for him. He planned to send various parties out toward Lake Superior's western end to trade with the Dakotah or Sioux, toward Green Bay across Lake Michigan to trade with the Winnebago, Sac, Fox and Menominee, and toward the Sault Sainte Marie and northward to trade with the Chippewa and Mississaugi. He had outfitted these parties with a considerable portion of his goods and was on the point of sending them out when, yesterday afternoon, two hundred painted Ottawas arrived from the village known as L'Arbre Croche,[45] about twenty miles to the west of Fort Michilimackinac.

Two other English traders—James Stanley Goddard and Ezekiel Solomon—who had come here about a week ago with goods from Montreal, rushed to Henry with the news that the Indians had come and were staying in a number of French houses. Both men were as frightened as Henry himself had been at the approach of the Chippewas. He reassured them as best he could and, in truth, despite the warning given earlier by Campion, he was not greatly worried. After all, nothing serious had resulted from the visit of the Chippewas.

His shell of confidence was harshly cracked this morning. The Ottawas had assembled themselves shortly after dawn before the home of Charles Langlade and had sent orders for the three traders to appear before them. Fearful of angering them, Henry, Goddard, and Solomon went there at once. The interpreter, Pierre Farli, immediately detached himself from the crowd of Frenchmen standing nearby and took a position next to Henry to interpret for him. In a low voice he told Henry that the chief in charge of this party was Mackinac, who was principal chief of the Ottawa tribe.

Chief Mackinac wasted no time with formalities. He strode to a point only ten feet from the three traders and regarded them for a moment with a look that was anything but friendly.

"Englishmen," he said, his voice extremely deep and distinctive, "we, the Ottawa, were some time ago informed of your arrival in this country. We were told that you have brought with you the goods that we are much in need of. Upon hearing this news we were greatly pleased, for we believed that with what you could provide us, our wives and children would be able to pass another winter without fear of death, which has ridden our shoulders of late because our need is so great. But what was our surprise," his voice became suddenly hard, "when a few days ago we were again informed that the goods we had expected were intended for us, were on the eve of departure for distant countries, some of which are inhabited by our enemies!

"Englishmen, with these stories being told, our wives and children come to us crying and begged that we come here to this place to learn with our own ears their truth or falsehood. We therefore have come, almost naked as you see, and very much in want. On our arrival here yesterday we inquired into the matter and we found to our displeasure that the stories are true. Before us we see your canoes readied to depart and your men engaged for trading with the Indians on the Mississippi and beyond, and into other distant regions.

"Englishmen," he continued flatly, "knowing then the circumstances, we counciled together throughout this night past, considering what now we should do. You have been sent for, that you may hear our will in the matter. Englishmen, our will is this: that you shall give to each of our men, young and old, merchandise and ammunition to the amount of fifty beaver skins on credit, and for which I have no doubt of their repaying you in the summer, on their return from winter hunting."

Henry's mouth fell open as Farli quietly interpreted. Fifty beaver skins worth of credit to each man! That was a total of ten thousand beaver skins' worth of goods, which was not only all of what Henry had here, but all of Goddard's and Solomon's goods besides. To further add to their consternation, Farli added that these Ottawa were unfortunately accustomed to treating credit lightly and though they might pay it back, they also might not, especially if winter hunting was bad. Henry shook his head and told Farli to tell the chief that he must reduce his demands a great deal.

Chief Mackinac's expression became sour when he heard Farli's words. He grunted once, savagely, and then broke out in a short harsh statement. Farli sighed and turned to the three traders.

"He won't hear of it, won't even discuss it anymore with you. He says that they have nothing further to say to you and that they will give you until noon tomorrow to think about it. If by that time you do not agree to give them the goods they have demanded, they will not ask again but will come and take this property which they already regard as their own because it was brought into this country before any conclusion of peace between themselves and the English."

Chief Mackinac had now turned his back and so, without further conversation, the traders went back to Henry's store. For the past hour or so they had been discussing what to do, unwilling to let their goods go on credit, yet not sure whether or not the Indians would really follow through with their plans of taking them. Now it was growing dark and all three men started abruptly as there was a light knocking on the door. Henry opened it a crack, saw Farli and let him in. The interpreter did not look happy.

"The Ottawas have decided," he told them, "to come during the darkness tonight and kill all of you. I advise you to give in at once to their demands as your only means of safety."

For the first time since they had become acquainted, Henry suddenly had the suspicion that Farli was not telling the truth. He had heard it said here that Farli was himself interested in the Indian trade, was envious of what Henry had and would like to see all these English traders out of it. Might this not be a way for him to prey on their fears and make them voluntarily give up the toehold they had gained in the trade?

"Tell them," Henry said tightly, without even discussing the matter with the other two, "that we are not rabbits who run at the growl of the wolf. If they come here this night, they will find us more than ready."

Farli looked surprised, then frowned. He nodded and left without farewell. Solomon looked at Henry and shook his head. "You could have asked us first," he said, a trifle bitterly. Then he shrugged and smiled. "But I guess we'd of answered the same way. Hell, I guess you can only die once."

They both laughed and Goddard, who had been standing quietly, finally joined them in it. "You should have been in the army," he told Henry.

By the time full darkness had come, the store was crowded with thirty men, all of them armed and ready. Etienne Campion had rounded them up, assuring Henry that they were going to be as dependent as anyone on the English trade now, so they might as well commit themselves to it. Of the Frenchmen Henry had hired in Montreal to further his enterprises, only a few had declined to be on hand for this possible showdown.

But no matter how any of them looked at it, the odds of nearly seven to one were not encouraging.

[September 30, 1761—Wednesday]

In his service career, Lieutenant William Leslye[46] had been given many assignments he did not care for, but never before had he been given command of so isolated a post. From first sight of it he had not liked Fort Michilimackinac, and in the two days since his arrival he had grown to like it even less. Now, with Captain Henry Balfour on the point of moving out, a depression bred of equal measures of fear and a lack of self-confidence settled shroudlike over his shoulders.

Though his personal quarters were probably better than any in the fort, they were crude and distasteful and he wished for perhaps the hundredth time since leaving Detroit on September 9 that Major Gladwin had not named him to take command here. He paused in the writing he was doing, glanced out of the window and shook his head. Balfour's detachment was already gathering its things preparatory to leaving and who could tell what would happen as soon as they were gone? Obviously, from what they had learned already from the traders here—young Alexander Henry in particular—the place was a powder keg with a fuse already lighted.

Leslye sighed and rubbed his eyes. He was still weary from

the long journey up here from Detroit. He had not at all enjoyed the trip in the string of batteaux under command of Captain Balfour of Gage's Light Infantry. The detachment of a hundred and twenty men of the 60th Regiment had rowed the remainder of the way up the Detroit River into Lake St. Clair,[47] crossed it and then rowed up the fast, treacherous current of the stream which connected with Lake Huron. From that point on, in weather that was generally foul, they had hugged the western shore of the lake, not even leaving it when they came to the thirteen-mile wide mouth of Saginaw Bay.

They could have saved themselves perhaps forty or fifty miles of rowing had they cut directly across the bay when they reached the long peninsula which Balfour's map showed to be called Sand Point. From here they could just barely make out a pair of islands six or seven miles away in the mouth of the bay, but if a storm were to come up they would almost surely wreck and it was just about as far from Sand Point to the islands as it was from the islands to Point Lookout on the other side.[48] They had camped overnight on Sand Point and discussed whether or not they ought to try the crossing, but the decision went against it and in the morning they had once again begun following the shoreline.

It had taken nineteen days for them to reach Fort Michilimackinac and the only pleasure Leslye took in their arrival on September 28 was that it marked the end of the laborious travel. He did not envy Balfour's detachment having to go on from here to even more remote posts.

Though in command now, Leslye was still under orders of Balfour until the captain would leave, and together he and Balfour had conferred at once with the French residents and the three English traders who, to Balfour's surprise, had already set themselves up here. They had expected that there might be some opposition from the French garrison and were further surprised when they were met by Lieutenant Charles Michel de Langlade, who represented the only soldiery there. Langlade respectfully turned the fort over to Balfour and Leslye and informed them that only a month after the fall of Montreal a messenger from Governor Vaudreuil had arrived with orders for the commandant, Captain Louis de Beaujeu, to abandon Fort Michilimackinac and lead his garrison down to Fort de Chartres on the Mississippi to avoid falling into the hands of the English. Beaujeu, Langlade told them, had done just that, leaving him in charge since this was his home and he had no intention of leaving it. The messenger, he

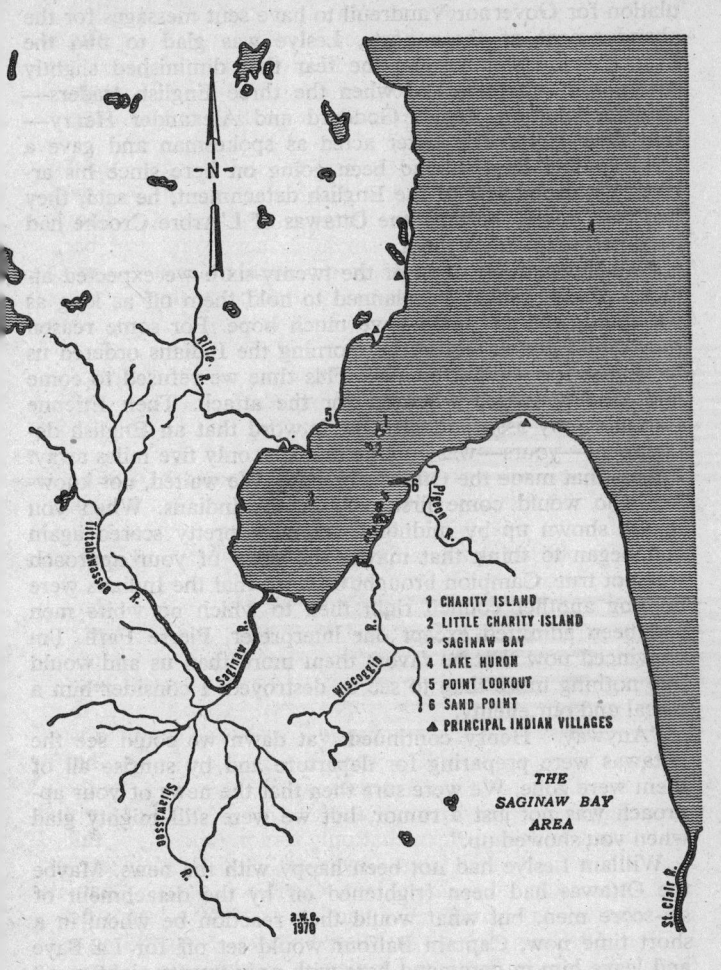

THE
SAGINAW BAY
AREA

1 CHARITY ISLAND
2 LITTLE CHARITY ISLAND
3 SAGINAW BAY
4 LAKE HURON
5 POINT LOOKOUT
6 SAND POINT
▲ PRINCIPAL INDIAN VILLAGES

a.w.e.
1970

added, had gone on to Fort La Baye at the Bay des Puants,[49] and to Fort La Pointe at Madeline Island in Lake Superior. He was fairly certain that both these installations had also been abandoned by the French.

Although it had been a violation of the terms of the capitulation for Governor Vaudreuil to have sent messages for the abandonment of these posts, Leslye was glad to find the French soldiers gone. But the fear that diminished slightly within him was restoked when the three English traders—Ezekiel Solomon, James Goddard and Alexander Henry—told their story. The latter acted as spokesman and gave a brief résumé of what had been going on here since his arrival. On the arrival of the English detachment, he said, they had been saved, because the Ottawas of L'Arbre Croche had been poised to attack them.

"All through the night of the twenty-sixth we expected attack," Henry said. "We planned to hold them off as long as we could, but we didn't have much hope. For some reason they didn't attack and in the morning the Indians ordered us to appear for another council. This time we refused to come and all day long we waited for the attack. Then Etienne Campion, my assistant, brought in word that an English detachment—yours—was coming and was only five miles away. I guess that made the Ottawas hesitate. We waited, not knowing who would come first, you or the Indians. When you hadn't shown up by midnight, we were pretty scared again and began to think that maybe the story of your approach was not true. Campion brought us word that the Indians were holding another council right then to which no white men had been admitted except our interpreter, Pierre Farli. I'm convinced now that he favors them more than us and would like nothing more than to see us destroyed. I consider him a rascal and our enemy.

"Anyway," Henry continued, "at dawn we could see the Ottawas were preparing for departure and by sunrise all of them were gone. We were sure then that the news of your approach was not just a rumor, but we were still mighty glad when you showed up."

William Leslye had not been happy with the news. Maybe the Ottawas had been frightened off by the detachment of six-score men, but what would their reaction be when, in a short time now, Captain Balfour would set off for La Baye and leave him in command here with only twenty-eight men? He shuddered slightly and looked out the window at the fortifications. They were none too strong. The stockade of posts was formed in a square on the south side of the Straits of Mackinac, with the north wall only a few feet from the water. Inside the stockade were a few houses and storerooms, a guard house, and a powder magazine, a church and the priest's house, along with a few other buildings. There were also five long barracks for the garrison and traders.

It was considerably smaller than Detroit and nowhere near as crowded. The French population, both inside the walls and scattered around the stockade on the outside, was about thirty-five families. With unpleasant visions of what they might do if they should decide to join the Ottawas and rise up against the garrison, Leslye had set about writing his first order to the inhabitants. It was what he had been working on at his desk and he returned to it now and quickly finished it. By the time he carried it out to the main point of the interior of the fort, Balfour had his men all assembled and ready for the march. With the order in his left hand, Leslye strode over to him and saluted.

"Ready to leave now, sir?"

Balfour nodded. "We'll cut directly across the Straits here and follow the north shore of Lake Michigan westward, and then down to the post on Stinking Bay. We're not going to worry about putting a post at La Pointe yet. Season's too advanced. We don't plan to linger at Stinking Bay—Green Bay, if you prefer—as long as we did here, either. We'll go right on to Fort St. Joseph, leave a garrison and head back for Detroit."

Balfour motioned to an ensign, who nodded and began moving the remaining eighty-nine men out of the fort toward the beached batteaux. The captain turned his attention to Leslye again.

"Assemble the inhabitants and render the oath," he said, "as Major Rogers did at Detroit. Take whatever steps are necessary to maintain yourself and your garrison here safely. Avoid, if possible, any detrimental incidents between your men and the Indians. The traders are getting ready to send their men out now. Give them whatever assistance it is in your power to give them, but be sure they are doing no trade in either rum or ammunition."

The two officers shook hands then and wished each other good luck. Balfour instructed Leslye to keep communications open as much as possible to Detroit, from whence Fort Michilimackinac would get supplies as they became available. Then, after tossing a hasty salute in reponse to Leslye's, he spun on his heel and followed the detachment.

Fort Michilimackinac seemed suddenly a lonely place. Leslye looked at his own men who were now separating from the cluster they had drawn themselves into as Balfour's detachment marched out. Here and there a few groups of Frenchmen stood watching them idly. Charles Langlade was one of them and Leslye walked directly to him and handed him the written order. It said:

Monsieur Langlade is ordered to notify all the inhabitants residing at Michilimackinac, whether they live there or are only spending the winter there, that they are to bring to me, without delay, all the arms they have in their possession, whether they be rifles, muskets, carbines, pistols, or swords of any nature; and all those discovered with arms from now on will be punished rigorously.
Made at Michilimackinac, 30th Sept., 1761
William Leslye, Commandant

Langlade read the order and, though his eyes narrowed and his lips tightened, he made no comment. He stared at Leslye for a long moment and then nodded almost imperceptibly and left. Leslye watched until he disappeared into one of the French houses and then the officer returned to his own quarters.

The operation of Fort Michilimackinac as an English post was now begun, and once again Lieutenant William Leslye wished he was back in Detroit.

[October 1, 1761—Thursday]

Pontiac, war chief of the Ottawa Nation, found himself in a peculiar position. The occasions in his life when he didn't know exactly what would be best for him to do had been few, but this was one of them. It all boiled down to a matter of deciding whom he disliked most and upon whom he wished to inflict the most harm—his ancestral enemies far to the south of Detroit, the Cherokees; his more recent enemies to the east, the Iroquois League, who no longer had the ferocious strength they once wielded; or the white invaders, the conquerors, the men who had thrust his French friends from this land and who were here in Detroit now, the English.

He had no love for any of them but, if nothing else, Pontiac was a practical man. He had the capacity for projecting ideas into the future and determining, through logic, what the end result might be. His bravery, his skill in battle, his dominance, his ability to think—all these had resulted in his assumption of the role of war chief of the Ottawas, second most powerful position in the tribe to that of the principal chief himself, Mackinac, at L'Arbre Croche.[50] There were always young men who clamored for war and old men who spoke for peace, but it was he, Pontiac, who had the most influence in weighing the advantages or disadvantages of either and setting the course in such matters for his people here at Detroit, and this would normally be the course followed by the entire tribe.

He sat now beside the fire in his own longhouse at the Ottawa village across the river from Detroit and just slightly upstream from the Huron village. He was oblivious of two of his wives who worked quietly nearby, and aloof from the warriors and subchiefs who padded down the long central aisle of the quonset-shaped longhouse, going to and from their own quarters in this 180-foot-long apartmented structure. Pontiac merely looked into the fire and thought his thoughts, divorced from all that was occurring around him.

At forty-one years of age, Pontiac was not a very pleasant-appearing individual. Only slightly taller than medium height, he was well built and still appeared to be in the prime of his physical condition. Normally he wore paint of some kind on his face and body, but at the moment this had been scrubbed away and the firelight reflected now in little glinting highlights from the bear oil that had been rubbed all over his skin by one of his wives.

He was naked, as was usual when in his own quarters. In fact, quite frequently in summer he wore nothing at all, regardless of whether he was inside his dwelling or out. As the days cooled, however, he would take to wearing first a breechcloth and then leggings and finally a motley assortment of clothing, some of it fashioned of skins by the squaws, much of it trade goods he had gotten from the French or, to a lesser degree, the English.

His hair was trimmed in traditional Ottawa fashion—shaved almost to the skin at nape and crown, and then gradually tapering to a brushlike length of an inch or so high above his forehead. Long ago he had learned from his father to cut his hair in this manner, so that an enemy could not grasp him by the hair with one hand and plunge a knife into him with the other. And more than once his own hand had clasped the hair of a Cherokee in just such manner and jerked the enemy off balance while his other hand directed a knife or tomahawk to the Cherokee's breast or head.

As a youth he had gone on the warpath against the Cherokees under the former Ottawa war chief, Winniwok, and few if any of the other warriors had been as aggressive in the battles as Pontiac. And then in January fifteen winters ago, he returned from the Cherokee country riding at the head of the war party. Thirty-three of them had set out under Chief Winniwok and only twenty-two returned, and Chief Winniwok was not one of those who had survived. They brought back with them thirty-seven scalps, and of this number Pontiac alone had taken seven. It was only logical that he should become war chief, and so he had.

From somewhere else in the longhouse a baby began wailing, but the sound lasted for less than a minute and Pontiac took no notice, his eyes still staring unseeingly into the curling flames. Now and then as the fire suddenly flared up a little, the garish tattoos all over him stood out clearly. There were few broad areas of skin where he was not permanently marked by tattoos. In circles, diamond shapes, blocks, lines, diagonals and swirls, they encircled his legs from ankles to groin and his arms from wrists to elbows. They were around his neck and on his chest and back and buttocks. Most were of geometric shape, but there were two that were not. One, apparently the head of an eagle or some other bird of prey, was drawn in the center of his back, and the other, a representation of the sun emitting heat rays—with eyes and mouth but neither nose nor ears—was in the middle of his chest. Two wide circles of white porcelain beads hung from his pierced ears, and heavy bands of beaten silver encircled both upper arms. The most striking ornamentation, however, was the smooth white crescent of polished stone which appended from his nostrils and hung so that the points came down to the corners of his mouth.

The Ottawa were not a hirsute people and, as was common to the men of his tribe, his chest, arms, legs, pubic area and underarms were essentially hairless. He had never shaved his face, yet only occasional wild hairs sprouted from chin or cheeks and these were already yanked away as soon as they became long enough to grasp.

Pontiac was a proud and arrogant man. A strong streak of vindictiveness ran through him and he was extremely quick to anger. At the moment, this anger was directed at the English. He wished they were not here, wished the French had retained their hold on Canada, wished they would return and help drive the English out. He had little use for any white man, but the French he could tolerate reasonably well, so long as it was on his terms rather than theirs. In fact, to be fair about it, there had been a French officer whom he had admired more than any other man, a man beside whom he had fought against the English. The faintest suggestion of a smile touched his lips now as he thought of that day in May two and a half years ago when he had first met General Louis de Montcalm. Never before had any white man shown him such respect, such deference, such friendship. The Marquis de Montcalm had at that time presented Pontiac with one of his own full dress uniforms and even now the Ottawa war chief could hear again the words that the little officer had spoken to him:

"Accept this from me, Pontiac, as a token of my esteem for you. As I am a general among the French, so you are a general among the Indians and you should have a uniform equivalent to this position. I welcome you warmly to my side in whatever shall befall us."

How moved he had been by it! It was by far the most signal honor he had ever received and on the spot he had replied:

"I, Pontiac, give you my word that I shall never desert you so long as the breath of life remains in one or the other of us."

All through the summer-long siege of Quebec he and his warriors had given their strength to Montcalm at a time when the French general was being deserted by virtually all his other Indian allies—the Algonkins and Abnakis, the Nipissings and Caughnawagas and Senecas. But then had come that tragic September 13 when a lead ball from Wolfe's attacking force had struck Montcalm in the back and he had died before dawn of the next day.[51]

It was Charles Langlade who had brought the word to Pontiac's camp of the French general's death and Pontiac had mourned for him with a sorrow greater than he had ever shown for another person. And he had made a vow, too, while still there at Quebec:

"I will not accept English control over Canada," he had told Langlade. "I do not think they can take it, and if they should take it, I do not think they can hold it. If I am wrong and they do take it and hold it, it is *here* at Quebec they will hold it, not in our country. We will return now to our villages and stand firmly there and not an Englishman will be let into our country except by our favor. Quebec may be lost by us to them; Canada may be lost to them. But as long as he breathes, Pontiac will never embrace the English!"

After that, things had gone badly for the French. The heart of their resistance died when the heart of Montcalm stopped beating. Quebec was lost and the next year—a year ago last month—Montreal was surrendered and the French hold in Canada was suddenly England's. The French had been driven out, but the war was not yet over for these European powers. Elsewhere in the world they still fought, and Pontiac yearned for the day when a vast French force would advance up the Mississippi and onto the Great Lakes, thrusting the English back.

But the fact of the matter was, the English were here now and, whether they liked it or not, the Indians here in the western Great Lakes area were dependent upon them for supplies and ammunition. Perhaps if the detested Iroquois had not sent the deputation last spring to encourage the western tribes to rise up against the English, Pontiac might have done so on his own. But the very thought of joining into an alliance with them was as distasteful to him as it would have been to join hands with the Cherokees, and so it was largely by his counsel that the Iroquois deputies had been shamed and sent back east.

Now the English were here, firmly established and bringing in the goods—or at least some of them—that the Indians needed so much. To raise the hatchet against them now would be to destroy their own livelihood. True, ammunition had not been given to them in the amounts desired, nor had they been given enough replacement tomahawks and scalping knives; but perhaps these would come soon now, as all the Indians here had been led to believe. It was obvious that Captain Campbell at Detroit was giving out all the ammunition he could spare, but that was very little. It was not enough for them to send war parties south against the Cherokees again. It was barely enough to hunt with, if one conserved his shots.

Now the season was too far advanced for many more supplies to come, so Pontiac did not really expect any more ammunition now; but it had better come in the spring when trading resumed. Pontiac had permitted the English to come here and take possession of the French forts without opposition, but he had not embraced them as friends, nor did he plan to. And if suitable and sufficient ammunition and other goods were not made available to him and his people in the spring, then there would be time to consider again the offer of the Iroquois.

His lips turned down slightly and his eyes slitted to such a degree that the glow of the fire no longer reflected in his dark eyes. The English had made their promises that the tribes would have what they needed in the spring. Sir William Johnson himself had given his word on it. Either the English would live up to their word or they would suffer the wrath of Pontiac.

There was no other way.

[*November 20, 1761—Friday*]

Wawatam and his entire family left the island of Michilimackinac at dawn, bound for Fort Michilimackinac on the mainland. A great excitement filled the Chippewa's breast, for today was the culmination of the startling vision that had come to him over three years ago.

They were in four large canoes and they made quite a group. In addition to Wawatam there were his two wives and the three daughters and two sons he had had by them. In addition there were eight of his grandchildren, three by his sons and five by his daughters. The husbands of his daughters were there, as was the wife of his eldest son; his younger son's wife had died two years before. Wawatam's ancient mother was there, too. Finally, there was also the widowed and childless sister of one of his daughters-in-law. At the feet of these twenty-two people were a number of bundles that had been wrapped in fine beaver skins at Wawatam's direction. There were also a great many other items—traps and poles, guns and kettles and ammunition—though very little of that—and blankets.

The sun had risen by the time the boats were beached just southeast of the fort and then each person capable of carrying a parcel took up one of the beaver-skin bundles. Leaving the guns, cooking gear, traps and the unwrapped goods in the canoes, they followed Wawatam in single file into the fort and directly to the storerooms of the handsome young English trader, Alexander Henry.

Bobbing his head and smiling broadly, Wawatam tossed his bundle to the floor and advanced to shake hands warmly with Henry. The young man returned the handshake rather mechanically, his mouth slightly agape at the spectacle of so many people coming in and tossing their bundles down until there was a mound of them on the floor. Without being bidden to, each member of Wawatam's family had seated himself on the floor as soon as he had dropped his load and in a moment all twenty-one of them were settled and Wawatam was still vigorously shaking Henry's hand.

Wawatam was no stranger to Alexander Henry, but the trader had never before met any member of his family. Wawatam had been one of the warriors in the group of Chippewas who had come under the leadership of Minivavana to visit him soon after his arrival here—the one he had noted looking at him so strangely. Once or twice a week since then Wawatam had been sure to show up at Henry's store. He did not often buy anything, but he seemed to get great pleasure out of being in Henry's company and according him high esteem. Henry, delighted to make friends wherever possible, had always welcomed him cordially and had even begun learning some of the Chippewa tongue from Wawatam.

Now, as Wawatam finally disengaged the grip he had on the trader's hand, Henry smiled and bade him welcome. Wawatam bobbed his head again and then one by one introduced the members of his family, though Henry only grasped about half of the relationships and hardly any of the names.

When this was finished, Wawatam signaled his sons and sons-in-law and five men began opening the bundles. The beaver skins were beautiful and obviously of the best prime quality. Some were filled with other skins—more beaver, fox, mink, marten, otter, lynx and raccoon—and others contained large quantities of coarse maple sugar. Still others held many pounds of carefully dried meats, especially deer, moose, elk and dog.

When all had been opened, Wawatam indicated them with a wave of his arm and told Henry that these were not trade goods but, rather, gifts that Wawatam wished him to receive. Henry was sure he must have misunderstood. Gifts! Why, there was a small fortune of goods here. Such an amount had taken no little time and effort to amass. He listened carefully as Wawatam went on.

"Three summers ago," the Chippewa said, speaking slowly and clearly and obviously taking pains to use words he knew the trader would understand, "when I observed a long fast, as is my custom, and removed myself to a high place on our island, the Great Spirit came to me in a vision. He made His presence felt upon me and in the vision He showed me a man who was not greatly above being a boy. The Great Spirit told me that one day I would meet this man and that when I met him I would know him and that I must at once make preparations to adopt him. I was to adopt him as a son. More, I was to adopt him as a brother. More, I was to adopt him as a friend. I was to take him into my heart and into my family and make him one of us.

"For all these many moons I have watched and waited and then, as this late summer was closing, I came here with our great chief, Minivavana, to see this Englishman who had so bravely come among us. I found this Englishman to be you. More, I found you to be he who was given to me in the vision of the Great Spirit."

Alexander Henry was startled and his eyes widened but he said nothing. After only the slightest pause, Wawatam continued. Once again the minor chief swung out an arm to take in the mound of presents.

"These are for you. They were given to me by the Great Spirit and I give them out of my heart to you. When I first saw you in this room I recognized you as the one of my vision, but I was careful and came back often to watch you and talk with you and to allow the Great Spirit time to reveal it to me if there had been some change or if you were not, after all, the one. But you are he and now I have come to offer you my heart and my hand, my lips and my eyes and my arm, my family and my house. With these gifts, which I hope you will accept, you will be a friend to me, yet more than a friend; you will be a brother, yet more than a brother; you will be a son, yet more than a son. I will be bound to honor you and love you, to trust you and help you as I would the dearest friend, the finest brother, the most beloved son. If you accept these things, I will forevermore regard you as a member of my family and they, too, will so regard you. Tell me now, will you accept?"

To say that Alexander Henry was overwhelmed would be to put it mildly. He was stunned. He felt that he really should not accept so large and expensive a gift, yet he feared that to refuse might do irreparable damage. He was also a little concerned over what might be expected of him if he accepted. He did not know if this adoption into Wawatam's family was just a title of friendship or if it really meant what Wawatam said, but he could see no harm in accepting and possibly there would be considerable benefit in doing so. Who could tell when it might not be greatly to his advantage to have a close friend among the Chippewas?

Now he reached out and took Wawatam by both shoulders and looked him straight in the eyes. For a long moment he said nothing, but then he smiled, dropped his arms and grasped one of Wawatam's hands in both of his.

"Though I feel unworthy of them," he said, "I accept your gifts with much pleasure. With even greater pleasure I accept your offer of friendship and brotherhood and paternity. As you have offered your heart and hand to me, so too I offer mine to you and I thank you."

Wawatam grinned hugely and there was an approving murmur from the rest of the family and smiles on their faces. Realizing that he should, in turn, do something for them, Henry presented them with a number of gifts—calicoes and needles, vermilion and other powdered paints, tobacco, twenty good steel otter traps and a bear trap. He also gave them some shirts and other items of clothing, a blanket for each person and, though the prohibitions against it were very strict and he warned Wawatam to hide them against discovery, he gave him two kegs of gunpowder and equivalent lead, eight skinning knives, eight tomahawks, a keg of rum and a quantity of white wampum. These latter items were carefully tied up out of sight in buckskin before being removed from the store. He also gave them each a cupful of rum and toasted their health.

Wawatam was greatly pleased and as soon as the rum was drunk and the goods gathered together that Henry had given him, he shook hands with the trader again and bade him farewell.

"We go now," he said, "to our winter hunting grounds, from which we will not return until early next summer. We take you along in our hearts. Farewell."

[November 30, 1761—Monday]

With winter rapidly closing in on the Detroit area, Captain Donald Campbell was certain that these dispatches he was just finishing writing to be sent eastward would be the last to leave here until spring. Nor was there much likelihood of any further supply boats arriving from Niagara before communications were interrupted by the weather.

For two days Campbell had been writing letters and reports, summing up to General Amherst and Sir William Johnson, Lieutenant Colonel Bouquet and George Croghan, as well as others, the events of this first year of occupancy of the western Great Lakes country by the English. On the whole, things had gone much better than he had anticipated, but he was still concerned about what the future would bring. An aura of almost palpable uneasiness overhung the area and, though he hated to admit it even to himself, Campbell was convinced that Indian troubles were bound to come. Spring was certain to be the dangerous time. The Indians suspected that ammunition, instead of just being in short supply as they had been informed, was actually being withheld from them. As yet they had not confirmed these suspicions, but when trading opened up again next spring, the fact could no longer be hidden. Campbell shuddered at the implications this brought to mind. His comments to Henry Bouquet reflected his concern in the matter:

. . . and everything is now quiet, though I am certain if the Indians knew General Amherst's sentiments about keeping them short of powder, it would be impossible to keep them in temper. . . . If you could send us some ammunition it would be doing a good thing, though it is against the general's orders . . . All the Indian nations have gone to their hunting and by that means it will be quiet here till spring. I hope the general will change his present way of thinking with regard to Indian affairs; as I am of the opinion if they were supplied with ammunition, it would prevent their doing mischief . . .

Campbell sighed. There was little real hope that enough surplus ammunition would come in so that he could continue giving some to the Indians on the sly. An edict like Amherst's in this respect just could not be kept secret for very long, and again he shivered at the thought of what would happen when the Indians discovered what the English policy really was now in regard to them.

One thing was certain: the outlying forts had been garrisoned just in time. With all outlying posts now occupied by English troops—with the exception of the tiny outposts at the Sault Sainte Marie and Fort La Pointe on Madeline Island in Lake Superior—at least a relatively firm grip on the country had been established. Campbell had been more than delighted when Captain Henry Balfour had successfully accomplished his mission and returned here to Detroit earlier this month.

Twelve extremely strategic frontier posts were now firmly under English control. Five of them guarded the important passes to the east of Detroit: Fort Pitt controlled the head of the Ohio River; Fort Niagara, now under command of Major John Wilkins, controlled the gateway to the upper lakes, that greatly important portage around the falls between Lake Ontario and Lake Erie; Fort Presque Isle commanded the eastern portion of Lake Erie and the portage route to the Ohio River tributaries, and was aided in this respect by the smaller posts of Fort Le Boeuf and Fort Venango.[52]

Under his own immediate control from the fort here at Detroit, which itself controlled the passage between the upper and lower Great Lakes, were Detroit's dependency forts. In mid-October, Campbell had sent off Ensign Robert Holmes with a detachment of fifteen men to Fort Miamis at the head of the Maumee River to relieve Lieutenant Butler of Rogers's Rangers, who was still holding the place. This had been accomplished without incident and the garrison there could now be considered permanent. This was an important portage post between western Lake Erie and the lower Ohio River valley. Positioned at the confluence of the St. Joseph and St. Marys Rivers where they merged to form the Maumee,[53] this was the point from which the portage would be made to the waters of the Little Wabash River, which in turn connected with the Wabash—or *Ouabache*, as the Indians called it—and then with the Ohio.

Twenty-four days ago Campbell had sent Lieutenant Edward Jenkins with a detachment of twenty men to relieve another of Rogers's men, Ensign Waite, at Fort Ouiatenon, which was about midway down the length of the Wabash River.[54] That fort guarded the southwestern extension of Canada, for just below it on the high land—or *terra haute* as the French called it—was the boundary between the territory that was Louisiana and that which was Canada. Waite had returned to Detroit only a short time ago with word that the transfer of command had been successfully accomplished and that the permanent garrison was in control.

Now Balfour had returned and his news was just as good. Having left Lieutenant Leslye and his garrison of twenty-eight men at Fort Michilimackinac, he had proceeded to Green Bay and found Fort La Baye had been abandoned by the French long before. The post was important not only in control of the trade with the Wisconsin Indians—the Winnebagos, Sacs, Foxes, and Menominees—but it controlled the portage between Lake Michigan and the upper Mississippi River. Here Balfour had immediately renamed the post, calling it Fort Edward Augustus, and leaving Ensign James Gorrell in command with a garrison of seventeen men.[55]

Without incident Balfour and his remaining seventy men continued down Lake Michigan to another river called St. Joseph, though not the same stream as the one with that name which joined the St. Marys to form the Maumee. This particular St. Joseph River was a relatively short stream which emptied into the southeastern quadrant of Lake Michigan. Following the river about thirty miles upstream from the lake, Balfour and his men had come to the abandoned Fort St. Joseph, in the heart of the Potawatomi Indian country.[56]

The Indians had produced; foolhardly enough and without
immediately result Pontiac sent a Ojibwa in command and
left him with a garrison of fifteen men Fort St. Joseph also
commanded an important portage that lay between southern
Lake Michigan and the upper St. Joseph River which, in turn,
ran into the Illinois River and subsequently into the Mississippi.

his original force, diminished and twenty, in-
minished to fifty-four, commanding himself. Before he
men far behind and struck out overland almost due east.
For the most part he had arrived safely back, free without
any leisure. He had been an arduous mission of Capt.
Dalyell Yet, on his pleasant with the captain in command again, wished it.

THE THIRTEEN
NORTHWESTERN FRONTIER
OUTPOSTS

1 PITT	**6** NIAGARA	**9** SAULT SAINTE MARIE
2 VENANGO	**8** SANDUSKY	**10** EDWARD AUGUSTUS
3 LE BOEUF	**7** DETROIT	**11** MIAMIS
4 PRESQUE ISLE	**9** MICHILIMACKINAC	**12** OUIATENON
		13 ST. JOSEPH

For the second time now it was hooked by the
visit of Pontiac. First it had for the William Johnson who
had come for it. The Indians who had come
from to the place of peace and had seen
as it had now been before. The place being
inspired by the fame the doctor recover at the past faster.
men education and an inventions streak who planned to
spend the entire winter here before heading out on a triad
tour of the upper Great Lakes in the spring.

There was an extremely marginal person of about forty.
He was devout and good-looking and had one of those personalities which could only be termed as being clever veal.

The Indians had greeted them cordially enough and Balfour immediately placed Ensign Francis Schlosser in command and left him with a garrison of fifteen men. Fort St. Joseph also commanded an important portage—that between southern Lake Michigan and the upper Kankakee River which, in turn, ran into the Illinois River and subsequently into the Mississippi.

With his original force of one hundred and twenty men now diminished to fifty-four, including himself, Balfour left his batteaux behind and struck out overland almost due eastward for Detroit and had arrived safely back here without problems. It had been an arduous mission and Captain Campbell was highly pleased with the way Captain Henry Balfour accomplished it.

And now, just today, had come word from Lieutenant Elias Meyer at Sandusky Bay that the fort which he had been building there to form a communications link with Fort Pitt and the other posts to the east, was completed and had been named Fort Sandusky. Meyer was staying on as commander and Ensign Christopher Pauli was his second-in-command. The total English force there was sixteen men.

Early in October, still bedridden with his malaria, Major Henry Gladwin had sent the majority of his detachment back to Fort Niagara under Captain Norman McLeod, and then Gladwin himself, fully recovered, returned east in the middle of that month.

With the forts all well occupied, it appeared that the English were in solid control of the western Great Lakes country, but Captain Donald Campbell knew only too well that appearances can often be deceptive.

[December 1, 1761—Tuesday]

For the second time this year Detroit was honored by the visit of a baronet. First it had been Sir William Johnson who had come to treat with the Indians and who had caused Detroit to bloom in a spate of parties, balls and meetings such as it had never known before. And now the place was being honored by a visit of Sir Robert Davers, an English gentleman of education and an adventurous streak, who planned to spend the entire winter here before heading out on a grand tour of the upper Great Lakes in the spring.

Davers was an extremely engaging person of about thirty. He was dapper and good-looking and had one of those personalities which could only be termed as being effervescent.

Anyone who met him almost instantly felt that he had known him a long time. He was not in the least stuffy about his title and was as much at ease and as cordial with traders and Frenchmen as he was with the English soldiers and their commander.

Like the rest, Captain Campbell was delighted to have him here and went out of his way to provide him with the finest quarters available and everything else possible for his comfort and enjoyment. With good-natured amusement, Campbell and his officers considered Davers to be one of those wealthy and harmless English aristocrats who turn up at remote parts of the world bringing the aura of breeding and gentility into the most primitive of areas.

No one questioned his purpose or background. There was no need to. Was he not on a first-name basis with General Amherst? Did he not intimately know almost everyone of importance in England? Had he not often partaken of royal hospitality from King George himself? No, Sir Robert Davers was not a man whose credentials are questioned.

The fact of the matter was, Robert Davers was an imposter.

A master of passing himself off as something more than he actually was, he had long ago learned that if people think you are someone important, they will treat you importantly. Early this year he had boarded a ship at Plymouth, England, and sailed to New York. In a matter of hours he had won over the captain of the ship, who had not even raised an eyebrow when the well-dressed passenger casually introduced himself as Sir Robert Davers of Suffolk. As the imposter had counted upon, the captain had vaguely heard of the Davers title, but he had no way of knowing that there was no one in the Realm by the name of *Sir* Robert Davers. There was, in the baronetage of England, a Sir *Richard* Davers who was something of an eccentric and recluse and who, in fact, had a son named Robert; but the son was ill with an incurable disease and it seemed likely that he would die very soon and perhaps never come into his father's title.[57] Of all this, the imposter was well aware. With his realization that the very eccentricity of the real baronet would preclude his having many friends or even acquaintances, he felt secure in his present guise as Sir Robert Davers.

He had *some* money—an inheritance—of his own, though not a great deal. It didn't matter that there was not much. When judiciously utilized here and there with a seemingly flamboyant disregard, it gave the impression of enormous wealth in reserve. And, strangely, the more he appeared willing to spend, the less he actually *had* to spend. People delighted in giving him things. In New York the word of the arrival of "Sir Robert" had spread rapidly and he was immediately the object of numerous social invitations, particularly when it became known that he was a bachelor. His personality, his innate likability, his carefully practiced charm and grace made him very popular and, with scarcely the expenditure of a shilling on his own, he was housed and fed and entertained in style.

Sir Robert Davers was, if nothing else, a clever man. He was quite cognizant of the danger of remaining too long in one place, especially where there was a constant turnover of new faces from England. The real Davers might be a recluse but there was always that remote chance that someone would turn up who knew him. To avoid that, the imposter moved about frequently. He accepted with great aplomb the favors bestowed on him in New York and then drifted off to Boston for more of the same. He became popular there and, subsequently, in Philadelphia. He noted with some concern, however, that ever more frequently he was being asked why he was in America. At first it was easy for him to glibly appear to give an answer while adroitly maneuvering the conversation to other channels. Sooner or later, however, he might be pinned down and, to avoid this, he decided this would be a golden opportunity to see this great wild land of which he had heard so much.

From post to post he went, exuding affability and graciously permitting influential people to do him favors. Somehow, no one ever really realized that he spent virtually nothing. Where Captain Donald Campbell was concerned, for example, it was an honor having him here; a pleasure to have the gaiety and charm he brought along with him; a delight to while away long evenings in stimulating conversation; and an honor to help him in any way possible in exchange for the very gift of his presence.

Campbell soon promised that in the spring he would provide Davers with boats and a party of men to aid him in his tour of the upper lakes, and he would look forward to the time when he would come back to Detroit again. He also expressed the sincere hope that Sir Robert Davers's mission would be a complete success. And Davers, thanking Campbell, assured the officer that with his so generously offered help, it would be bound to be attended with success. He did not care in the least that he himself had no more idea of what his "mission" was than did the commander of Detroit.

Freeloading could be most enjoyable if one did not give in to worrying about possible ramifications. Sir Robert Davers had no intention of worrying.

[December 31, 1761—Thursday]

The bitterly cold winter which brought the year 1761 to a close carried with it murmurs of rising discontent from all quarters, but where it counted, they were unheeded. Sir Jeffrey Amherst, snug by his fireplace in New York, managed not only to shut away the winter storms, he also effectively shut away any concern over what the Iroquois or the Ohio country Indians or those of the western Great Lakes might be feeling or contemplating. He was good at shutting away consideration of things which might tend to run counter to his way of thinking. He had had much practice in it all year in his dealings with Sir William Johnson and George Croghan and even with such of his officers as Lieutenant Colonel Henry Bouquet and Captain Donald Campbell.

To put it plainly, Lieutenant General Sir Jeffrey Amherst had had more than his fill of talk about Indians and their feelings or rights, or about what the English should do to improve relations between them. Never having suffered an Indian attack, he habitually underestimated their prowess in battle. What little contact he had shared with them had only served to increase his dislike for them generally. They had moved with him as allies down Lake Ontario and the St. Lawrence on that final drive of the war, as they went against Montreal, but the very fact that they had not arrived there with him only served to increase his contempt for them.

Even now, after well over a year, he could still feel the sting of their comments about the incompetence of the English soldiers in the attack on Fort Lévis; could still visualize their anger when he had refused to give them the presents they had demanded as their due for aiding in the taking of that French installation. It was then that they had deserted him and gone back to their villages, refusing to fight with either an army or a general who were, to the Indian way of thinking, so poorly trained.

Their opinion of him meant little to him now but, since then, his opinion of them had greatly affected all the tribes. Shortly after the capitulation of Montreal and Canada he had magnanimously proclaimed that there would be a free and open trade with the Indian nations, but the promise had been essentially hollow. Trade had come, true, but little of it was of any significant benefit to the Indians.

More than anyone else, however, it was Sir William Johnson who had become the irritating thorn in Amherst's side. It seemed that every messenger brought another request from Johnson, another demand, another plea in regard to the Indians. It became almost a contest of wills and, as commander in chief in America, General Sir Jeffrey Amherst was determined that it would be *his* will which would prevail.

The general was heartily sick of the Indian supervisor's letters; letters which were so frequently filled with vague or subtle warning. The French, Johnson had told him soon after the victory, had always provided the Indians with ammunition and goods to suit their needs. For the English to withhold such items that they had been accustomed to receiving would cause grave hardships for the Indians. He asked that Amherst expand the Indian Department in both manpower and funds, as it was not a matter of luxury; the Indians had grown dependent upon goods from the whites. Without them they would suffer and they would greatly resent being denied them. Johnson was none too tactful when he boasted of the value of the Indians as allies. He had written to Amherst:

Without derogating the known bravery of our troops, without their being aided by the Indians we could not have won the war that has given us Canada. I flatter myself that I could, in a short conference, render this clear to your Excellency.

Amherst was angered at this. That Johnson actually believed the English troops could not have defeated the French without Indian allies, Amherst considered an insult. Besides, it was ridiculous. He did not, of course, give Johnson the audience so broadly hinted for. Nor did he give even a passing thought to expanding the Indian Department. Contrarily, almost as if in spite, though ostensibly in the name of economy, he ordered Johnson to discharge much of his staff—Croghan alone had to cut back from seven assistants to only two—and he further directed that Johnson sharply limit or, better yet, altogether curtail the practice of giving the Indians the customary presents of ammunition and goods at the annual Indian congresses. He reiterated the point that he had already made, which was that he thought it unwise to purchase the good behavior of the Indians and that the red men should be forced to barter with furs for whatever they got. In this way, Amherst reasoned, they would have to keep busy with their hunting and therefore would have no time to create mischief. He conveniently overlooked the fact that without the ammunition they so sorely needed, their hunting success would be severely limited. Without sufficient ammunition they could not get the furs and without the furs, how then could they barter?

Over and over in his management of Indian affairs, Sir William Johnson was being hamstrung by the tightening policies established by General Amherst. Where trade was concerned, Amherst had told Johnson to establish trading regulations, which was done, but then the general promptly enacted such restrictive policies that most of Johnson's regulations were hampered or even negated. No provisions were made to adequately prosecute the English perpetrators of trading abuses and the already impoverished Indians were being subjected to frauds with alarming regularity. Johnson learned of many of these abuses and he was infuriated by them. Still hopeful that he might nudge Amherst into tighter control of the English traders, he wrote of some of the incidents:

An Ottawa chief of great influence, with his family, brought his packs to a trader at Oswego in order to try the market there. The trader, after the usual practice of deceiving him in the weight, hurried the peltry into a private room, telling the Indian that all the merchandise was very dear, owing to the severity of duties (a stale but dangerous artifice still practiced) and desired him to choose out what goods he wanted. The Indian, having made a choice, was astonished to find that his skins produced not one-third of what he had been accustomed to receive from the French for like quality, for the trader had, besides his extortion on the goods, reckoned the peltry at only one-third of its real weight.

[The Indian] went away discontented, but on returning said he was ashamed to go back with such small returns and begged for a small keg of rum, which the trader gave him, as he said, as a high favor. But on opening the keg soon after his departure, it proved to be water.

Another trader, for some valuable furs he received from an Ottawa chief of great influence who came likewise to try the new English market and desired to have his returns in rum for a general feast, gave the Indian 30 small kegs with directions not to open them by the way, otherwise the trader would be punished for letting them have so much; but the In-

dian, before his return to Niagara, being desirous of some liquor, opened them and found them all water.

Who, Johnson asked, could the Indians turn to in such cases? Where could they find recourse? Yes, these were frauds where alcohol was concerned, but the frauds were just as bad, if not worse, where necessary goods were concerned. How could these Indians possibly support their families through the winter if such abuses continued?

Amherst supplied no answers, nor did he pay any heed whatever to Johnson's complaint that, as he had learned it from Daniel Claus, his agent at Montreal, all of the tribes gathered there had not received during the winter thus far what the French would have given to four Indian families.

In desperation, earlier this month, Johnson made another appeal to Amherst in an effort to avert the catastrophe he felt would surely come if restrictions against the Indians were not eased and regulations controlling the traders were not tightened. Despite the firmness of Amherst's earlier edicts against supplying any ammunition to the Indians, Johnson wrote:

There is, in my opinion, a necessity for putting some clothing, ammunition, &c., into the hands of the commanding officers at Oswego, Niagara, Detroit, &c., to be occasionally given to such Indians as are found deserving and serviceable, and as they have been accustomed heretofore to receive presents in great abundance. I submit it to your Excellency whether it will be thought convenient to break off that expense all at once, until everything is settled throughout the country.

But again the general had replied that he did not think such presents were necessary. As a matter of fact, in the fifteen months since the capitulation of Canada, Amherst's dislike for the Indians had only increased. He made no secret of it that he considered them as being something less than human, often referring to them as "disgusting creatures" or "insatiable animals." Whenever there arose a question about which should prevail, the rights of the Indians or military expediency, there was absolutely no doubt that the latter course would be chosen.

In a word, Lieutenant General Sir Jeffrey Amherst was smug. That the Indians might somehow pose a threat was inconceivable to him. It was with the greatest of distaste that he even read the reports he continued to receive about the Indians from Johnson, Croghan, Bouquet and Campbell. All these men had passed on the news to him of rumors being circulated among the Indians about the western posts that a French plot was brewing. The Indians, they reported, were apparently being told by Canadians that the English, no longer afraid of French intervention on behalf of the Indians, were going to destroy the tribes without warfare, simply by withholding vital supplies from them. They were also advising the Indians that they should not despair, but that they should keep their knives and tomahawks sharpened and themselves in readiness to join the army that was soon to be sent to their rescue by their father, the King of France.

Even long before he had gone to the grand council at Detroit, Johnson had sensed this in the wind and had written to Amherst:

I am very apprehensive that something not right is brewing, and that very privately among them. I do not only mean the Six Nations. I fear it is too general, whatever it be.

Then had come exposure of the plot in detail when Kyashuta, the Seneca, had carried the war belt to Sandusky and Detroit. The amazing and wholly unexpected thing had been the rejection of that proposal by the western Indians. Amherst had almost chuckled upon receiving the news. Of the possibility that the Indians might really be a threat to English interests, he wrote Johnson,

. . . never gave me a moment's concern, as I know their incapability for attempting anything serious . . . I had it in my power not only to frustrate them, but to punish the delinquents with entire destruction, which I am firmly resolved on whenever any of them give me cause.

Just as he paid little heed to Johnson's continued pleas that good relations be promulgated with the Indians in the matter of supplying them with goods and ammunition and a fair trade, so Amherst had blandly ignored Johnson's strong warning that no fort should be built at Sandusky Bay, that the Indians were objecting and that to do so without their permission would be to court disaster. Again military expediency had won out. As Amherst wrote to Johnson after the Indian supervisor had returned to his home on the Mohawk River:

With regard to their objection against our erecting a block-house at Sandusky, that has no manner of weight with me. A post at that place is absolutely necessary, not only for the purpose of keeping up the communication, but also to keep the Canadians in proper subjection. I must and will, therefore, say what they will, have one at that place! . . . The disposition you left the western Indians in leaves me no doubt but that everything in those parts will remain quiet, as there can be no fear of their being irritated or provoked by any of his Majesty's subjects . . . The Indians may be assured that I shall always use them as they deserve; reward them as far as is in my power, if they merit it; and punish them if they deserve it.

For his own part, as this year drew to a close, William Johnson was about ready to give up. Never before in his career—not even when his office was dictated to by the bigoted New York Assembly instead of the Crown—had he faced such unwavering resistance to all his efforts to effect good Indian-English relationships.

"I find management of Indian affairs so very difficult and disagreeable now," he told Daniel Claus, "that I heartily wish I was clear of it."

And now, as if Indian relations had not deteriorated enough through matters of trade and policy and lack of ammunition and necessary presents, the problem of encroachment was growing. With the French driven out and peace ostensibly having been settled upon with the Indians, settlers were pouring out of the East into the frontier districts of Virginia and Pennsylvania and little determined effort was being made to officially stem this tide.

Amherst could have clamped down on it without difficulty but he did not, and Sir William Johnson thought he knew why. Amherst almost certainly felt, as did so many other Englishmen of authority, that when you came right down to the crux of the whole business, the Indians didn't really have any right to the land in question anyway. This feeling was strongly supported by an already famous treatise written only three years ago—late in 1758—by that esteemed Swiss jurist, Emer de Vattel. In commenting upon the family of nations who were bound by the duties and enjoyed the rights of international law, he had written that:

The uncertain occupancy by wandering tribes of the vast regions of the New World cannot be held as real and lawful taking possession; and when the nations of Europe, which are too confined at home, come upon lands which the savages have no special need of and are making no present and continuous use of, they may lawfully take possession of them and establish colonies in them.

With that kind of material to back up their claims, who was to care about the rights—if such existed in the first place—of Indian tribes? Had it been in his power to do so, Sir William Johnson would gladly have destroyed any memory of Emer de Vattel's fateful words.

Only recently had come word of two widely separated but disturbing incidents. In Virginia a force of sixty militiamen had been ambushed by a party of Indians, presumably Shawnees and Delawares, and many had been killed; and only a short time after that, on October 3, Captain Donald Campbell at Detroit reported that one of his detachments had been attacked on Lake St. Clair. They were the only Indian attacks that had occurred since before the end of the French and Indian War. Everyone—Sir Jeffrey included—seemed to think they were strictly isolated and unconnected affairs.

Everyone, that is, except Sir William Johnson. He saw them as an evil augury. More than ever now, he was firmly convinced that there were very bad times coming.

[March 30, 1762—Tuesday]

"You know, of course," General Amherst said, smiling, "that you have my congratulations, Major, and my very best wishes."

Henry Gladwin smiled and nodded in return. "Thank you, sir. I'm sure we'll be very happy. Frances and I have both looked forward to this for a long time."

"Will Miss Beridge—" Sir Jeffrey broke off with a chuckle and then began again, "I mean, will the new Mrs. Gladwin be returning to America with you in June?"

Major Gladwin shook his head. "I really don't know yet, sir. Her father, the Reverend John Beridge, is rather elderly and not at all well. I think she fears if she left she might never see him again. Actually, I really wouldn't mind if she preferred to stay in Stubbing with him until his health improved. He has indicated a desire to see America and perhaps he could come then with her to join me. Of course, if he doesn't get well again . . ." The officer shrugged.

Sir Jeffrey made a sympathetic sound. "Well," he said, "I hope everything will work out to your satisfaction. I will miss having you here. Good officers are never abundant and I consider you one of my best." He glanced at his desk and then looked at Gladwin again. "I have a few letters and reports to seal which I'd like you to take to London with you for delivery there, if you don't mind waiting a few minutes?"

"Of course not, sir," Gladwin said, settling back in his chair more comfortably to wait. "Take your time. There are still several hours to go before we sail and I am all ready now, so there is no rush."

Amherst nodded and turned his attention to the papers, sealing some and glancing through others. Several times he made small, exasperated sounds and Gladwin felt a wave of sympathy for him. What an enormous responsibility it must be to be commander in chief. He thought again of the things they had discussed since he appeared here at Amherst's New York office about an hour ago. The general had showed him a number of communications he had received from his officers and Indian agents at the outposts. Almost without exception they were pessimistic. Amherst had ruefully commented that they had been that way ever since he had become commander and he supposed they always would be. Now Gladwin could understand a little better why the general refused to become terribly alarmed every time a disturbing report was received; to do so would be to worry oneself into an early grave.

The major recalled with some chagrin the similar warning letters that he himself had written to the commander back in February. Though Fort William Augustus on the St. Lawrence was no longer the remote frontier post that Niagara and Detroit and Pitt were considered to be, still a large number of alarming reports of French and Indian hostile activity had reached him there. Spain had allied herself to France at the beginning of the year, thus forcing England to declare war on the dons as well, and ever since the news reached America, there were strong whispers that the two powers—French and Spanish—were instigating among the Indians, especially those of the western Great Lakes, Ohio country and Illinois country, urging the tribes to rise up against the English. Being particularly blamed for such instigation were the French residents still living at Detroit and Montreal—the native Canadians. Numerous war belts were being circulated, of this there was no doubt, but it was next to impossible to determine who actually started them. Gladwin had made determined efforts to learn the truth, but had been essentially unsuccessful except in confirming the belief that something serious was afoot. It was this intelligence that he had sent in two detailed letters to Amherst in February. The commanding general's replies—the last of which Gladwin had just received while he was en route to New York— were characteristic. This last one, still in the major's inner pocket, had said:

New York, 21st March, 1762

Sir:

Your letter of the 24th and 25th February, containing some further discoveries you had made concerning the Indian plot, came to my hands last night.

You will see by mine of the 17th Instant, in answer to yours of the 4th Ultimo, that I could not give credit to the Indians intelligence; and I must confess I am still of the same way of thinking, and imagine the whole will appear to have arisen from some drunkenness among themselves.

I, however, approve of your using of all means in your power to come to the truth of this affair; and of your reporting everything you learn to Governor Gage, who, I am persuaded, will be able to discover if there is any foundation for the accusation of the people of Montreal. I am, sir,

Your most obedient servant,
Jeff. Amherst

Gladwin smiled now. He and Amherst had laughed about the reports and Amherst dismissed them easily. Strangely, here in the general's New York office, it was easy to do so; the reports and rumors seemed almost childish when viewed from this vantage. Though he was thirty-four and had been in the English army for almost a decade, Gladwin decided he still had a lot of learning to do before he could qualify as a general officer.

"One must not," Amherst had told him earlier, "casually dismiss every ill report which arrives, but neither should one fly into excitement on the instant. Most alarms, I find, resolve themselves into little more than talk. I really do not believe that the French or Spanish are firing up the Indians against us, but even if I should be wrong and they are, what could tomahawks are no match against rifles and cannon; and this is such scattered bands of savages do against us? Bows and why I no longer permit the giving of ammunition to the Indians. Without it, and without a strong European ally to back them, they are under our control. It is as simple as that."

Amherst had shaken his head and a dusting of powder from his wig settled on the shoulders of his scarlet uniform coat. "Nor," he added, "are these the only problems. I have a terrible time holding down the costs incurred by our Indian Department. Apparently Sir William and Mr. Croghan believe they should have access to unlimited funds and goods for the benefit of the Indians. The congress they held with the western Indians at Detroit last summer cost the Crown £4,400. I was appalled at this expense. On Sir William's advice, I approved the account, but I have cautioned both these gentlemen to exercise the most rigid economy in the future.

"Another thing which bothers me," Amherst continued, "is the way Sir William continues to bypass me and report Indian matters directly to the Board of Trade in London. He has alarmed them unnecessarily with his reports and only a week ago I received a copy of orders that have been sent to all the royal governors of colonies here that no further grants of Indian lands should be valid until approved in England by the Board of Trade. They also said—and of course I approve—that all squatters on Indian land and insistors of dishonest claims should be prosecuted by the Crown in colonial courts. These are good measures, but instigation of them should have gone to the Board through me, not directly from Johnson."

Amherst had shrugged then and finally continued with a smile. "It isn't all so bad. Often, Major, there are moments of great pleasure in this position. Just last month I was allowed to bestow two well-deserved promotions—full colonelcies to both Lieutenant Colonel Bouquet at Fort Pitt, making him colonel of the 60th Foot, and to Lieutenant Colonel John Bradstreet, who is our quartermaster general. I hope soon to have another great pleasure—that of confirming your own temporary rank of major to permanent rank."

The talk had continued about the Indians, the colonies, homeland politics, and finally Gladwin's forthcoming wedding to Frances Beridge in Stubbing, Derbyshire. Gladwin and Miss Beridge had been betrothed for quite a few years now and the major was very pleased that at last they would be married. He wished he could believe that Frances would return here with him in June, but he had little real hope of it. Certainly he would not demand it, for what sort of life could it be for a gentlewoman to live in the crude quarters offered at frontier outposts, simply to be with her husband? No, rather than encourage her to come back with him, he would probably thrust his own desires down and instead urge her to remain in England to await his return.

An increase in the rustling of papers drew his eyes to Amherst again and his thoughts back to the present. He saw that the commander in chief was putting the various sealed letters and dispatches into a pouch. Gladwin stood up and Amherst handed him the packet, then shook his hand with genuine warmth.

"Major," Amherst said, "I wish you Godspeed and good fortune. I shall strongly anticipate your return."

A moment later Major Henry Gladwin was directing his steps toward the wharf where the large sailing vessel was berthed which would carry him to England.

[May 1, 1762—Saturday]

The large batteau was just a speck in the distance upriver before Captain Donald Campbell gave up watching it and headed back for his quarters inside the fort at Detroit. He was genuinely sorry to see Ensign Hutchins and Sir Robert go. Their leaving would create quite a gap in the interest of life here, and already Campbell was looking forward to the time when, five or six months from now, the two would return. Hutchins wouldn't stay, of course, as he'd have to get back to George Croghan and Colonel Bouquet with his report, but Davers had promised to spend another winter here at Detroit and Campbell was very glad of it.

Over this past winter he had grown extremely fond of the engaging Sir Robert Davers. The man was remarkably intelligent and there seemed to be scarcely a subject upon which he could not converse at length and in depth—and ordinarily in a most entertaining fashion. Campbell couldn't recall ever meeting anyone before whose interests were so varied, whose memory was so keen, and whose conversation was so animated. He was an excellent reader as well and had such control over his inflections that when he read aloud from a beautifully bound volume of Shakespeare which he owned, his voice would change for the different characters and one could always tell which character was speaking simply by his modulations of tone, without it becoming necessary for him to announce the name. Twice during the course of the winter Sir Robert had read the entire volume aloud in Campbell's residence, where he was a guest, and both times he had held his audience of officers, English traders, young Frenchwomen and older Frenchmen entranced by his control. It was, to Daver's way of thinking, one way in which he could to some degree repay some of the favors he was receiving.

All through the winter his presence had been a warm glow at Detroit, taking the edge from some of the persistent worry Captain Campbell felt over the Indian situation, which had steadily degenerated. Then, not too long ago, a second rather interesting individual had arrived—a thirty-two-year-old ensign named Thomas Hutchins.[58] A very talented man, Hutchins had been an officer of the Pennsylvania militia until last March 2 when he entered the regular army as an ensign in the Royal American Regiment. He had been working as something of a liaison between the Indian Department and the military at Fort Pitt, represented by George Croghan on the one hand and Colonel Bouquet on the other. His greatest talent, however, lay in the field of cartography; he was highly skilled as a surveyor and the maps he drew were absolutely superb.[59] Croghan had recently given Hutchins—with the approval of Bouquet—the mission of mapping the upper Great Lakes country. Such maps would be invaluable both militarily and for Indian trading enterprises. Delighted with the opportunity, Hutchins had set out at once.

While not quite the raconteur that Davers was, Hutchins nonetheless was a gifted conversationalist and many long and delightful evenings were spent in talk at Campbell's house, in which not only Sir Robert, Captain Campbell and Tom Hutchins joined, but very frequently a young English trader named James Sterling, who had arrived at Detroit with the first group of traders and quickly established himself as the most adept of the lot.

Davers was intrigued when he learned of Hutchins's mission and in his own inimitable way, quickly drew an invitation out of Hutchins for him to join the party which on this trip, would concentrate on running the shorelines of Lake Huron, Lake Superior and Lake Michigan, at least insofar as they could be covered in the time available. Donald Campbell volunteered to detach a few of his men to go along and Sterling contributed two of his employees so that they might take notes and make recommendations regarding the trade on their return.

In more than one way was Davers pleased at the arrival of Hutchins here at Detroit. He himself was very nearly talked out and it was good to let someone else have the floor for a while. Besides which, Hutchins had brought along quite a bit of interesting gossip and information.

The dislike which Amherst held for Indian agents, especially Sir William Johnson and George Croghan, Hutchins said, seemed to grow all the time. And both Croghan and Johnson were practically beside themselves with regard to how they could keep the Indians in check when Amherst continually became more rigid in his rulings in this respect. The staff of the Indian Department had been cut down so severely that many necessary matters could not adequately be taken care of, and the budget had been so slashed that both Croghan and Johnson had been using considerable funds out of their own pockets to supply the Indians with what they needed. Croghan, Hutchins added, had become downright livid at the insinuations directed at him personally—and which Croghan was sure that Amherst had started—that he was not only extravagant but dishonest to boot. Croghan had told Colonel Bouquet that he had never put a dirty sixpence into his pocket and that he would be more than pleased if Amherst would relieve him to install a more economical person. In fact, Hutchins commented, Croghan was even threatening to resign in the fall in order to see to his own affairs.

Conversation about the Indians occupied many of the evenings these four men spent together in Campbell's house. Hutchins told of the growing difficulty with the Delawares and Shawnees in the Susquehanna River valley and westward beyond it, because of an influx in settlers. Further, it seemed that the Quakers in Philadelphia were deliberately doing all in their power to undermine everything done by either Sir William or Croghan in respect to keeping border warfare from breaking out. Apparently it was all part of the continuing feud between the Quakers, who dominated the Pennsylvania Assembly, and the Pennsylvania proprietaries. The other three men listened soberly and then Captain Campbell shook his head and commented that the Indian situation here, too, could hardly be considered good.

"We keep getting reports," he said, "of the French inhabitants lighting fires under these Indians against us, all the way from Presque Isle to the Mississippi. Seems as if they've been telling the Indians—especially those around Detroit—that King Louis is coming back to help them take the country away from us, and apparently there are a lot of them who believe it. I've questioned some of the leading Frenchmen here—Jacques Baby and Mini Chene[60] and Antoine Cuillerier, for example—but they all lay the blame for it on Beaujeu's men and those few of Belêtre's down at Fort de Chartres in the Illinois country. Add that to the fact that we can't give the Indians the supplies they were used to receiving from the French and the whole situation becomes downright explosive. I've heard that new war belts are circulating and I don't like it a bit. Maybe it's all talk, but I'll say one thing for sure: the Indians, all of them, suffered badly this past winter because of lack of ammunition. If we don't provide them with some damned soon, there will be big trouble. I've tried to get this across to the general—and so have Bouquet at Pitt and Wilkins at Niagara and some of the other commanders, to say nothing of Sir William and Croghan—but, as we all know, our general has strong feelings in the matter and he's determined that his will is going to prevail."

Nodding in agreement, James Sterling spoke up. "The Indians are angry, no doubt about it. Right now they don't seem to know who to blame the most—the military or the traders. What can we tell them when they come in wanting lead and powder and hatchets, and all we can give them are blankets and mirrors and paint? Amherst has people going through our shipments before they leave Schenectady to make certain we're not slipping any contraband goods through."

"The whole situation's pretty bad, all right," put in Hutchins, "but maybe some good news will come out of this big Indian congress Johnson's going to hold at Easton in June."

"Easton?" Davers said.

"In Pennsylvania," Hutchins explained, "on the Delaware River. They've held some pretty powerful congresses there before and now they're going to have another one to try to settle differences and smooth matters out between us and the Indians. Croghan's planning on attending and I hear some of the govenors'll be there, too. The whole problem looks insurmountable to me, but I guess if anyone can straighten things out, Croghan and Johnson can. And if they *can't*, then by God, we're really in trouble!"

Night after night the conversations had continued; discussions of politics and policies, art and articles of trade; literature and law. Too soon the time had come for the party to go and now, having seen them off at the Detroit water gate, Captain Donald Campbell walked back to his quarters, steeped in thought. He hoped they'd be all right. It was a dangerous journey they were undertaking, and not only from the elements. If the Indians decided to cut loose, the party just might not make it back at all.

The Detroit commander shuddered at the mental images he suddenly had of their fresh scalps being stretched on willow hoops.

[*May 19, 1762—Wednesday*]

In his nine months of trading activities at Fort Michilimackinac, Alexander Henry had picked up a considerable education—not only about this business of trading with the Indians and Canadians, but equally about the people of this far land themselves. He could now speak understandably in the Chippewa and Ottawa tongues and had even learned French from Etienne Campion. And, because he was unusually observant, he had learned a great deal about the culture of the tribes here, the nature of the terrain and the things he should or should not do.

Despite the troubles he had originally had with the Ottawas under Chief Mackinac, he now engaged in a rather lively trade with the Indians and scattering of French inhabitants—or, more properly, Canadians—at L'Arbre Croche, twenty miles west of Michilimackinac, where Chief Mackinac's village was located. This was, in fact, the seat of the northern Ottawa Nation and a rather substantial village. Only a small percentage of the population of it, however, was there over the winter; the remainder were away at their winter hunting, and there were always some coming or going.

Few occurrences, large or small, escaped Henry's scrutiny. He found it fascinating and invaluable to watch how the Ottawas prepared hominy from the stunted variety of corn which they called maize. The dried kernels were first boiled in a caustic solution made of wood ashes and a small amount of animal fat mixed with water. In only a short time this made the outer husks of the kernels easy to remove, after which the grain would be crushed and then dried on large pieces of bark. At this point it would have the consistency of soft, cooked rice. Most important, it would keep almost indefinitely. When mixed with a small amount of prepared fat it became a highly nutritious and surprisingly tasty dish.

Henry found that a bushel of this hominy and two pounds of the prepared fat was all that an adult warrior—or one of his Canadian assistants—needed for a full month's subsistence. They did not use salt on it, nor did they eat bread with it; the hominy and fat alone were enough. What particularly interested the young trader about it was the fact that this method of victualing was the only practical way his assistants could be fed and therefore it was essential to the trade. Setting out on their rounds in canoes, his men would normally be gone for at least fourteen months and there was no other form of food which could be reasonably carried along, due to space limitations. If, for example, the men tried to carry enough pork and bread to sustain them for such a length of time, the canoes could not hold all they would need and certainly there would be no room for trade goods. As a matter of fact, the Canadians apparently doted on this hominy concoction and neither asked for nor required anything else insofar as victuals were concerned.

Throughout the winter Alexander Henry had found himself frequently in the company of Lieutenant William Leslye, the fort's commander. They enjoyed talking together and Leslye was quite inclined to be sociable, but by winter's end Henry was more than sated with Leslye's complaints on being stationed at such a remote outpost. Leslye felt that if he died at Fort Michilimackinac, the odds were that it would be from simple boredom. The lieutenant's greatest wish—and a request he had already made on several occasions in messages to Captain Campbell at Detroit—was that he be relieved of this command and ordered back to Detroit, or even to the more civilized East.

There really wasn't much to do here for entertainment. The garrison gambled among themselves, but even that grew tiresome. About the only interesting activities that occupied them, and at which Henry often joined them, were shooting matches, hunting, and fishing. However, there was precious little ammunition to waste on the first two pursuits, even though the abundant grouse, deer and varying hares were delightful table meats, so fishing was about all that was left.

This was ice fishing and Alexander Henry, unlike most of the soldiers, enjoyed doing it. Large holes would be cut in the ice with axes and then setlines would be baited and lowered into the water, sometimes to depths of three hundred feet. The soldiers and most of the Frenchmen who were inclined to fish only checked their lines once in every two or three days, but Henry methodically checked his lines daily. Now and then he would catch one of the huge long-snouted and bewhiskered sturgeon in excess of two hundred pounds, but normally the catch was lake trout or whitefish—the former averaging between ten and sixty pounds apiece, the latter from three to seven pounds each.

As the winter passed Henry became acquainted to some degree with every French inhabitant there, as well as with quite a number of Indians. He had had both good and not-so-good experiences with the Indians. Most of them were off hunting but a few remained and one of these, a Chippewa warrior named Owl, made a habit of asking for goods on credit, always promising to pay the next time he came. He came, but the payment never did and when at last Henry demanded it, Owl became so angry that he jerked his tomahawk from his waistband and raised it threateningly and for an instant Henry thought that it was the end for him. After that he avoided Owl and on the few occasions that he saw the Indian from a distance, Owl always fingered his tomahawk handle and gave Henry an ugly look.

This incident, however, was offset by another Chippewa named Muvarron, who lived about ten miles to the south along a stream and who came to Fort Michilimackinac often, especially to visit Henry. It was he who had taught Henry most of what the young trader now knew of the Ottawa and Chippewa languages. It was obvious that he liked the English.

"I was taken prisoner," he told Henry and Leslye during a visit early in February, "by the white chief called by the name of Warraghiyagey—the one you call Johnson—at the time when he captured Fort Niagara. When he saw that I was prisoner, he set me free. He is a good man. He gave me a medal, which I have hidden, and a little flag of your country, and he told me I could go home."

Muvarron shook his head sadly. "When I came again to this place here, I told of the goodness of the English and I put the little flag on a stick over my lodge, but some of our warriors came and pulled it down and tore it to pieces. They broke my lodge down, too, and I was threatened with death. Look here!"

The Chippewa opened a small medicine pouch hung about his neck and, after glancing around to see that no one else was watching, extracted from it the tattered remains of the torn British flag. Leslye immediately offered to give him another in good condition, but Muvarron rolled his eyes and shook his head.

"To take it," he said, "would be to bring down the hatchet on my head."

Although there were severe drops in the temperature at intervals during the winter, the snow on the ground never became more than three feet deep. And then, on the second day of April, the ice in the Straits had broken up with a grinding roar and once again navigation became open. Almost immediately Indians began drifting in with large numbers of wild fowl and they were a welcome change from the primary diet of fish.

For many weeks Alexander Henry had looked forward to visiting the little post at the Sault Sainte Marie, some sixty miles distant. So far as he could determine, the buildings were still there but it had not been regarrisoned since the French had deserted it several weeks after the capitulation of Canada. Since it was the natural pass between Lake Superior and Lake Huron, Henry thought it would probably be an ideal place for a trading post.

He had asked for permission from Lieutenant Leslye to go there and, when Leslye agreed, set about getting his things ready. Four days ago, leaving his business behind in Etienne Campion's capable hands, he set off for the place in a canoe with some of his Canadian employees. It was a pleasant journey. They had crossed the Straits of Mackinac first and then paddled eastward along the north shore until reaching a point of land called by the Canadians *Le Détour*. Here they turned to the north and continued up the shoreline, passing many islands of large size along the way. At last, after ascending a rapids called the Miscoutinsaki—which Henry noted was well adapted for mill sites—the water spread out into something of a long narrow lake. The Canadians called this Lake Nicolet and the southwest shoreline all the rest of the way to the Sault was pleasantly meadowed and fringed some distance back by great groves of sugar maple.

Now, with today's sun approaching the meridian, Henry spied far ahead of them on the south shore of the half-mile-wide strait the small stockaded fort in the midst of a grassy plain perhaps two miles in circumference. The canoe pulled up just below the fort and here was where the portage path began around the harshest rapids and ended at the mouth of Lake Superior.

There was a Chippewa village of perhaps forty conical tents, structures called *wickiups,* scattered about without pattern. Their inhabitants were mostly gone, still out on the winter hunt, though evidently they would soon be returning. From the fort itself, Henry saw a tall, pleasant-appearing Frenchman coming from one of the four houses within the stockade to greet him. The man raised a hand when he came within speaking distance.

"Welcome," he said in the Chippewa tongue. "I am Jean

Baptiste Cadotte, I was once interpreter here when my countrymen still maintained this fort. You are . . . ?"

"Alexander Henry," the young trader supplied, then added, also in Chippewa, "I have been in the trade at Fort Michilimackinac since last summer."

"Ah," said Cadotte, extending his hand and gripping Henry's firmly, "I have heard of you. It is said you are a brave young man. I had wondered when you would come here, although I expected the English soldiers first. It seems you may be as brave as it is said, since you seem to lead the way for them rather than vice versa. Come."

He began leading Henry toward the fort and continued talking: "There is now no one here any longer. Only my wife and myself and our two sons. They are first, Jean Baptiste, named after me, and second, Michel. They are fine strong boys. My wife is Chippewa. When I first came here to trade twelve years ago, she was given to me by her father. She is a good woman. She has kept my home and cooked for me and she has borne me two sons. Six years ago we went together to Michilimackinac and there we were legally married in the church by the Jesuit priest, Father de Jaunay."

Henry nodded, not surprised that Cadotte should have a Chippewa wife. Many of the Canadians at Fort Michilimackinac had Indian wives and now even some of Leslye's men there were breaking regulations and slipping out on the sly to pay nighttime visits to certain Indian women. The trader swiftly filled Cadotte in on his background and told of his own hope of establishing a trading post here at the Sault in time to come.

Cadotte grunted in approval. "It is a wise choice of locations. Many Indians from all over and from many tribes come here in the summer to fish. There is need for a good post here. This, as you see," he indicated the stockade they were now entering, "is all that remains." Only four houses, and three of them are empty. Mine is that one. Beside it, the larger one, was where the governor stayed. He was not really a governor, but was only called so. Actually, he was merely an officer who was a clerk and who managed the Indian trade here on the government account. He had with him a small garrison of soldiers who stayed in those two little houses, which they called barracks. All those men have been gone for a long time."

Cadotte smiled and put an arm around Henry's shoulders. "Come, enter my house and dine with us. We can talk of

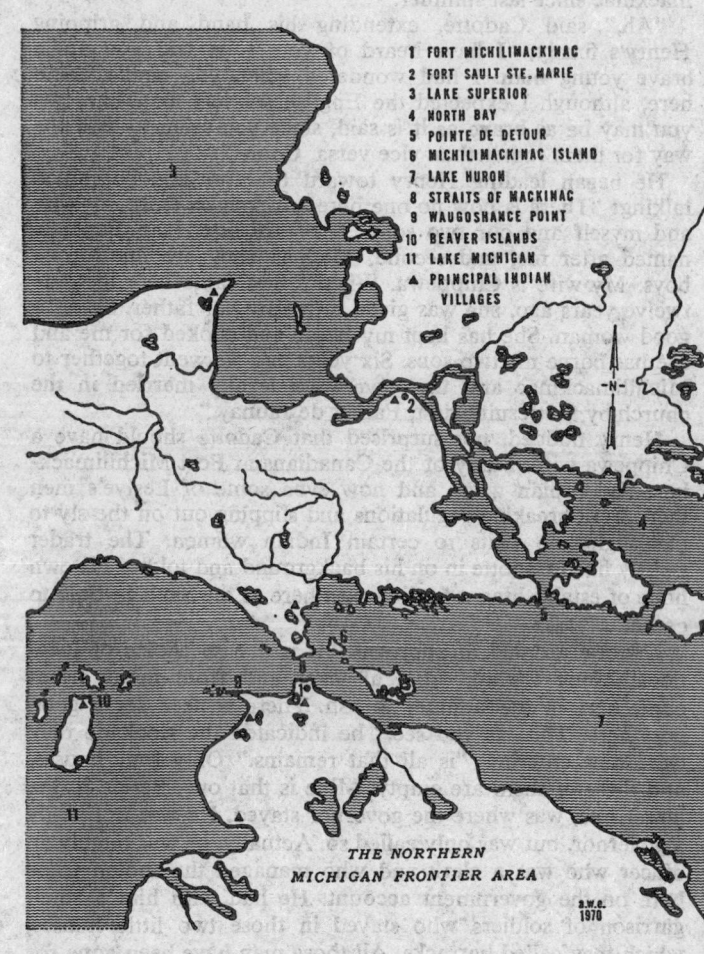

1 FORT MICHILIMACKINAC
2 FORT SAULT STE. MARIE
3 LAKE SUPERIOR
4 NORTH BAY
5 POINTE DE DETOUR
6 MICHILIMACKINAC ISLAND
7 LAKE HURON
8 STRAITS OF MACKINAC
9 WAUGOSHANCE POINT
10 BEAVER ISLANDS
11 LAKE MICHIGAN
▲ PRINCIPAL INDIAN
   VILLAGES

THE NORTHERN
MICHIGAN FRONTIER AREA

a.w.c.
1970

many things. It will be good to have someone to talk with. This is a lonely place. I am glad you have come."

Alexander Henry was just as glad.

[*June 28, 1762—Monday*]

The Easton Council was ended and there was every reason to believe that far more harm than good was resulting from it. A great many men of influence, both Indian and white, were in attendance when the meetings began on June 17. The Iroquois were represented by Canassatego and Rozinoghyata of the Onondagas, Hanging Belt and Monakaduto—better known among the English as Half King—of the Senecas, Steyawa and Scarroyaddy of the Mohawks, Torach of the Oneidas and Shikellimus and his son, Tal-gah-yee-tah—called Logan by the English—of the Cayugas. Of the non-Iroquois tribes, the Delawares were represented by four of their most powerful chiefs: White Eyes, Shingas, Tollema and Beaver. On hand for the Shawnees were Ki-kusgow-lowa, Pucksinwah, Moluntha and their principal chief whom the English knew as Cornstalk, but whose Shawnee name was Hokolesqua. The principal chief of the Miami tribe, Michikiniqua—Little Turtle—was here, too.

With such an array of Indian leaders on hand, it seemed incredible that most of the talking for the Indians was being done by a Delaware without tribal rank, a self-proclaimed prophet called Teedyscung, but it soon became clear why this was so.

The council had been established to justly settle, if possible, a recurrent land-claim question in Pennsylvania which had been undermining English-Indian relations for many years. Sir William Johnson, with orders directly from King George III, was in complete charge of the royal investigation, with Croghan acting as his chief assistant. Pennsylvania's governor, James Hamilton, was in attendance, as were the representatives of the Pennsylvania proprietors, Richard Peters and Benjamin Chew. Allegedly on hand to "see justice done to the Indians" was a large representation of Quakers led by the fiery Israel Pemberton, and the Pennsylvania Assembly was represented by John Hughes and Joseph Fox who, by and large, supported Pemberton.

From the outset it became obvious that more than anything else, this was a political squabble between the white factions, using as a basis the question of the legality of the old "Walking Purchase" as it was called, wherein many years ago the

Delawares had surreptitiously sold to the English some land in Pennsylvania which belonged to the Iroquois. This problem had ostensibly been resolved some years ago when, in public council, the Iroquois had chastised the Delawares and proclaimed that the English had acted in good faith and so the land was theirs.[61]

It was immediately apparent to Johnson and to both Governor Hamilton and the Penn family representatives that the Quakers could hardly care less about the claims of the Delawares, except that they saw in the situation an opportunity to use Teedyscung as a lever in helping to undermine and destroy Pennsylvania's proprietary rule, against which they had been fighting for years.

To drive in the opening wedge for their own attack, the Quakers had gotten the talkative but rather alcoholically foggy-thinking Teedyscung to one side and encouraged him to reopen the whole matter of the Walking Purchase legality. He had done so and, because English-Indian relations were already well deteriorated, the issue of fraud raised by Teedyscung was creating a growing bitterness, especially among the Delawares and Shawnees.

Normally, Teedyscung would not have been listened to seriously, as he was without rank, but because the Quakers exalted him, listened with grave concern to him, and praised him highly for fighting for the rights of his people—while all the time covertly manipulating him—the self-proclaimed prophet was lifted to a position of some prominence in the eyes of many of the Indians in attendance.

But the hopes of the majority of the Indians in attendance that the greater problems of the day could be amicably settled—such problems as continued English encroachment, establishment of new forts unwanted by the Indians, poor trading practices, broken promises, mistreatment and the like—were lost in the quagmire of verbiage stirred up by the garrulous Teedyscung.

Day after day, while the majority of the Indians generally sat in quiet bewilderment over what was going on, the controversy raged. Teedyscung, almost continuously drunk, continued to scream that fraud had been perpetrated against the Delawares and Shawnees, and not even the denial of this claim by the Iroquois chiefs could silence him. The Quakers and assemblymen lambasted Johnson with bitter accusations and abusive language and the whole affair teetered precariously close to erupting into an old-fashioned Donnybrook.

In an effort to smooth matters, Johnson explained the position—and legality—of the claims of the proprietors of Pennsylvania. When he was finished he asked if Teedyscung understood or had any questions. The Delaware said that he fully understood and had no questions. At the very next meeting, however, when it seemed that they could go on to more important things, Teedyscung abruptly presented a paper he had been given by the Quakers, which claimed that he had understood nothing and feared Johnson did not intend to do the Indians justice. When Johnson, flushing with ill-contained anger, asked Teedyscung to explain what he meant, the Delaware simply stood there looking confused.

Pemberton shot to his feet, pointed a trembling finger at Johnson and, on behalf of the Quakers, claimed that Johnson was putting words into the mouth of Teedyscung and that he would complain to the King. When Sir William pointed out that he had been appointed as sole arbiter for the English by the King in this matter and that Pemberton had no right to interpose, a fierce argument developed and degenerated into such personal character assassination that Johnson finally drew his sword, demanded silence and adjourned the meeting.

But then, yesterday, the Quaker cause was abruptly punctured. Apparently wearied of the ruckus being caused by Teedyscung, the Iroquois chiefs met with Teedyscung in private. When the Delaware prophet emerged, he was visibly shaken and this morning, he had announced quite meekly that he was now convinced by the proprietors' show of proof that his own ancestors had misinformed him and that the land in question had been legally purchased by the English. He was therefore willing to drop the entire matter and withdraw his charge of fraud.

The Quakers were stunned; they had lost their bid for control and, worse yet, it was now clearly evident that they had used Teedyscung as a pawn to create trouble for their own purposes and they had besmirched the integrity of the King's skilled Indian representative. By their actions, Indian-English relations had been greatly worsened.

Now the Easton Council was breaking up and no one was pleased, the Indians least of all. They were still confused and angry, not entirely sure what had happened here but certain that they had in no way benefited from it. The Iroquois and the few representatives of the more westerly tribes, such as the Miamis and the Wyandot Hurons, headed for their villages to further consider matters in privacy. The majority of the Shawnees and Delawares headed west toward their homes, but also to stop on their way, as they had promised they would, for another council at Lancaster.

Croghan, too, headed westward toward Fort Pitt, determined to acquire more land for himself in that area and also planning to stop en route at Lancaster for that council. He hoped at that place, free of the disruptive influence of Teedyscung and the Quakers, to be able to appease the Shawnees and Delawares in a more concrete fashion than had been accomplished here in Easton, by giving them gifts of some things they so badly needed.

Johnson, heading north again toward his residence in the Mohawk River valley, was intercepted by a messenger with a letter for him. It was from Captain Donald Campbell and it contained news about the steadily degenerating Indian situation around Detroit, which did not surprise the Indian supervisor, and it also mentioned, in a rather oblique way, Angelique Cuillerier. Campbell had written:

> *I gave a ball on the King's birthday* [June 4], *where a certain acquaintance of yours appeared to great advantage. She never neglects an opportunity of asking about the general.*[62] *"What" says she, "is there no Indian council to be held here this summer?" I think, by her talk, Sir William had promised to return to Detroit. She desired I would present you her best compliments.*

But long ago William Johnson had placed the Angelique Cuillerier episode into what he considered its proper perspective. It was now a closed door and he had no intention of reigniting the affair.

[July 25, 1762—Sunday]

Colonel Henry Bouquet, forty-three-year-old commander of Fort Pitt, was more concerned than he cared to admit about the developing Indian problems. Why, he wondered, could not General Amherst see the folly of treating these people so abysmally? And how could he blandly consider them to be no threat to English interests?

No threat indeed! More than once Bouquet had seen their anger and the havoc wrought by it and he did not relish the thought of possibly witnessing it again. Perhaps they did not fight as the English fought, but this was no sound reason for underestimating their fighting capability when they were aroused to it—and they were rapidly approaching that point.

Bouquet was aware that sometimes the Indians had to be dealt with sternly, but to do so without good reason or for reasons that were pitifully inadequate was little short of criminal. The policy now seemed to be to kick the Indians while they were down, since they had not the supplies necessary to fight back with, nor anyone to come to their aid; but by what conceivable stretch of the imagination could this be considered a sensible policy? They were, after all, human beings and deserving of treatment as such. And not very long ago they had helped the English to win a war that might well have been lost without their alliance.

Bouquet thought fleetingly of what changes he might make if he were commander in chief, but then he sighed and shook his head. There was no possibility of that. As a Swiss mercenary he had now reached the end of the promotional line. Further advancement would be denied him. Even his promotion to full colonel last February had greatly surprised him. Mercenaries, regardless of their value to the English army, regardless of their professional military skill and experience and past achievements, simply did not become generals in the English army.

Henry Bouquet was a good officer—a *very* good one—and, though he knew it, he did not flaunt the fact. About a score of years ago his first command had been in the Dutch service, followed by a commission in the army of Sardinia. Fourteen years ago he had returned to the service of Holland with the rank of lieutenant colonel of Swiss Guards. In that position he had seen service for another eight years before entering the service of His English Majesty, George II, with the same rank.

He had been second-in-command under General John Forbes in the successful expedition to take Fort Duquesne[63] four years ago and, among other assignments since then, he had rebuilt Fort Presque Isle and commanded there as well as here at Fort Pitt. And now, with the certainty bred of his years of experience, he could sense great trouble coming. The only questions remaining were when and where. The pity of it all was that the trouble didn't *have* to come. It could be so easily avoided simply by acting a little more decently toward the Indians. Right now, for example, the Shawnees were being decimated by a devastating epidemic of smallpox and just a little assistance to them at this time when they so sorely needed it could be of inestimable value in future relations with them. Deliberately adding to their already severe hardship could only end in disaster for all concerned, but Amherst's policies permitted little else.

The Fort Pitt commander now riffled through some communications on the desk before him. His brow furrowed as he stopped to read here and there and he sighed again. Sir Jeffrey was an inordinately hard man to understand. Undoubtedly his problems, in view of his responsibilities, were manifold; often, though, it seemed that he went out of his way to compound them. An order he gave one day might be negated in the very next dispatch from him, with no reason given, and even in oral orders he was prone to contradict himself. Yes, Amherst was a difficult man to understand and an even more difficult commander beneath whom to serve.

Bouquet paused in his inspection of the papers and glanced at two different letters recently received from Amherst. The first told of Major Henry Gladwin's rank being made permanent and that this officer, back in America again after getting married while in England, was being named to succeed one of Bouquet's officers, Major Hugh Walters, in the Royal American Regiment. Almost immediately had come this second letter stating that the former order was canceled and that Amherst was, instead, sending Gladwin to take command of Detroit.

This bothered Colonel Bouquet. Though he knew Major Gladwin to be a good man, yet he was far more familiar with Captain Donald Campbell and considered him a most able and perceptive commander who had proven himself well at Detroit and who had a keen grasp of the Indian situation there. Though the Indians and Frenchmen generally disliked and mistrusted the English, yet it was evident that those in the Detroit area trusted Campbell and held him in high regard. Why, then, remove him from his command? Bouquet was perplexed by it.

He shuffled through the correspondence quickly and found the last letter he had received from Captain Campbell, dated July 3, and he reread portions of it. Obviously, Donald Campbell was as confused by General Amherst's policies and orders as everyone else. In one paragraph he commented:

The General says the Crown is to be no longer at the expense of maintaining the Indians, that they may very well live by their hunting, and desires to keep them scarce of powder. I should be glad to know what you do in that respect. I am certain if the Indians in this country had the least hint that we intended to prevent them from the use of ammunition, it would be impossible to keep them quiet. I dare not trust even the interpreters with the secret. The Indians are a good deal elevated on the news of a Spanish war and daily reports spread amongst them that the French and Spaniards are soon to retake Quebec, etc. This goes from one nation to another, and it is impossible to prevent it. I assure you, they only want a good opportunity to fall upon us if they had encouragement from an enemy.

General unrest, it seemed, prevailed in this western wilderness and Bouquet shook his head. He looked up from his reading as there was a sharp rapping and then the door opened. George Croghan entered, greatly agitated, and with his free hand he slapped at a letter he was holding.

"By damn, Colonel," he said angrily, "just what's goin' on? Ain't the Indians already riled up enough as it is?"

"What's the matter, Mister Croghan?"

"Everything, that's what!" Croghan snapped. "Things have been goin' from bad to plain damn terrible. First the general cuts down so much in our budgets that we have to do the King's work among the Indians almost entirely out of our own pockets. Then we're ordered to cut down on our help to such extent that I was left with only two assistants to help do a job that it'd be tough for ten t'do. Then comes the Easton Conference, which blows up in our faces because of stupid politics and when I try to unruffle Indian feathers at Lancaster with gifts—*out of my own pocket, by God!*—the Shawnees and Delawares are so mad about everything that they drop their gifts on the side of the road and walk away in an even bigger huff . . . an' I ain't never seen 'em turn down gifts before. Now this!" He slapped the paper fiercely again.

When Bouquet silently held out his hand, Croghan handed the letter to him and the Fort Pitt commander read it through swiftly. Little wonder that Croghan was upset. The letter was from Sir William Johnson and informed Croghan that General Amherst had just sent down another order directing that there be yet another cut made in the Indian Department budget. Croghan was being told to cut down to only one assistant—Alexander McKee—and to slash his budget far more severely than before. And *nothing at all* was to be given to any Indian except in payment for furs.

"All right, Colonel," Croghan demanded when the officer handed the letter back to him, "now what? Just what are we supposed to do now?"

"Persevere, Mister Croghan. Persevere."

And there was really nothing else Colonel Henry Bouquet could say.

[*August 23, 1762—Monday*]

In a way, Major Henry Gladwin found a certain enjoyment in being back at Detroit again. The debilitating fever he had had the last time he was here, a year ago, had prevented him then from really becoming familiar with the post and its surroundings. Now he would evidently have plenty of time to do so.

That, of course, would come in time. At the moment there were things to do which should not be put off, and these were the things he was now discussing with Captain Campbell. He looked across the desk at the rotund officer sitting in the chair on the other side, holding close to his face a sheaf of orders brought here by the major. Gladwin studied the former Detroit commander as that officer's nearsighted eyes moved swiftly from line to line over what he was reading.

Gladwin liked Campbell and he was more than pleased that the officer had not been upset or taken offense at the fact that he was being superseded in command here. Gladwin always worried about such things; he cared about what people thought, whether they were superior officers, subordinate officers, or even the rank and file. That was largely the reason why, on the way to take over the command here, he had taken advantage of a rest stop at Fort Niagara to write something of an explanatory letter to Colonel Bouquet at Fort Pitt:

Niagara, July 29, 1762

Sir:

Ere this, I am persuaded you will have heard that the General had been pleased to appoint the Major to the battalion you commanded; but as it appears to me no way to my advantage, I thought it best to decline accepting it; not that I have any objection to the corps . . . on the contrary, I can assure you that I have a very good regard for all the gentlemen with whom I happen to be acquainted and for none more than for Colonel Bouquet. I shall proceed for Detroit tomorrow with Captain Etherington's company and thence I shall send him with proper parties under his command to Lake Superior in order to take post at Sault Sainte Marie, . . . Gamenestaquia, and Chaqumigon [Chequamegon]. *If I can serve you any way, I shall be happy in executing your commands.*

> *I am, Sir,*
> *Your most obedient and very humble servant,*
> *Henry Gladwin*

I desire you will present my compliments to the gentlemen with you.

As he had told Bouquet, he and Captain George Etherington and the company of Royal Americans, including Lieutenants John Jamet and Jehu Hay, had left Niagara the next day for Detroit; and all the way here he had wondered what Campbell's reaction would be to the news that he, Gladwin, was taking command. However, instead of being offended, Donald Campbell had evidently welcomed the change, greeted Gladwin effusively and seemed genuinely pleased to be shed of the responsibility of his command here. Gladwin smiled slightly and shook his head. All his worries had been in vain.

Campbell had now finished reading the orders and placed them on the desk. He turned his attention to Gladwin and the major's smile widened.

"Any questions, Captain?" he asked.

"No," Campbell replied, "no questions, Major, but a few comments."

Gladwin nodded him to continue and Campbell cleared his throat.

"I see," he began, "that the general's orders are for you, at your discretion, to send myself and Lieutenant Hay to garrison the forts at Lake Superior—Hay at Gamenestaquia and myself at Fort La Pointe on Madeline Island up on Chequamegon Bay. Unfortunately, sir, according to the reports I've received, both of those places were destroyed by the French garrisons before they abandoned them. It will be necessary to rebuild and without the necessary supplies for that here right now, I really don't see how it could be accomplished this late in the summer."

Gladwin considered this and nodded. "Just as well," he said. "We'll get around to them early next summer. I think I'd prefer keeping you here as second-in-command, anyway. I think I'm going to need your help and advice in dealing with the inhabitants here—both French and Indian—and since they know and seem to respect you so, you will undoubtedly be far more valuable here. What about the other posts?"

"Well, there's a small one up at Sault Sainte Marie which we should garrison, and Lieutenant Leslye has been pressing for a transfer ever since he was appointed to command at Fort Michilimackinac. As a matter of fact, his complaints about the place, which he calls 'a very disagreeable station,' have become rather annoying. Do you intend to keep him in command there?"

Gladwin frowned. He had encountered the complaints of Lieutenant William Leslye before and rarely were they justified. "I think not," he answered slowly, "but I do think it would be good for him to remain there a while longer. I'll send Captain Etherington up to take command and Leslye can act as second. At the same time I'll have Jamet accompany Etherington and then take a small detachment the rest of the way up to Sault Sainte Marie where he will be in command. Anything else?"

"Yes, sir. Lieutenant Meyer—Elias Meyer—in command at Fort Sandusky, has received news of some severe illness in his family and has requested he be relieved to go home and help temporarily. He's done a good job and I see no reason why his request should not be honored. Ensign Christopher Pauli is second-in-command and I'm sure he could take over well enough, unless you wish to place a different officer in command there?"

"No, I agree with you. Have Pauli relieve Meyer and request that Meyer come here first to take dispatches back east with him. What about the other posts?"

"All seem to be in good shape. Jim Gorrell's doing a fine job at Fort Edward Augustus up at Green Bay and Jenkins has had no problems worthy of note at Fort Ouiatenon. I've had a couple of rumors come my way that Ensign Francis Schlosser, commanding at Fort St. Joseph, has been drinking quite a bit, but I've had no opportunity of looking into it yet. Bob Holmes is doing fine at Fort Miamis. Oh, they've all reported Indian unrest, but nothing really serious that they couldn't handle. Holmes reports that the number of our traders going up the Maumee and into the Indian territory to the west is increasing, but the Indians are still wondering why they're not bringing any ammunition to trade with them. I'd hate to say what's going to happen. Sooner or later they're going to realize that the powder and lead's deliberately being withheld from them and then I think we'll have troubles."

"I think you're right, Captain," Gladwin said. "All we can

do is hope the general will relax a bit in his policies toward the Indians. Do they have any ammunition at all?"

"As a matter of fact, sir," Campbell replied, flushing faintly, "on being encouraged by Sir William to do so when he was here with you last year, I've been giving them some from time to time. I must admit, they've used it sparingly. I've also heard that occasionally they've been getting some from the Illinois country—though whether it comes from the French or the Spaniards, I don't know. Probably the former, if the story's true. Anyway, regardless of which, they need much more than they have. Last winter was very hard on them, but this one will be even worse."

"I'm sure it will. Well, it's a problem we'll have to face when the time comes, I suppose. Will you please inform all the officers that we will have a general inspection of the post and troops tomorrow morning, followed by a meeting of all officers. In the afternoon I would like to have separate meetings with the English traders and the principal French inhabitants. I believe that's all for now."

He returned Campbell's salute and watched him leave, then leaned back and closed his eyes. It had been a busy time and he was sure it would be busier.

[September 2, 1762—Thursday]

To the Englishman known as Sir Robert Davers, it was a real delight to be back in Detroit again. He was a bit surprised, of course, to find that there was a new commander now and that Captain Campbell was second-in-command, but in his inimitably charming fashion, he soon had Major Gladwin just about as fond of him as Campbell was.

The summer's journey about the upper Great Lakes had exhilarated him as had few other experiences in his life. As a matter of fact, the country was so beautiful that he was, for the first time, seriously considering settling down and perhaps building a fine mansion at one of the many breathtakingly picturesque spots he had seen in the company of the map maker, Ensign Thomas Hutchins.

Hutchins had proved himself to be a stimulating companion and the two had gotten along famously on the expedition, without even the first incident of bad feelings rising between them. Hutchins had mapped as much as he could, but the enormity of the job precluded finishing it in this one season and he hoped to be back again next year for another go at it. He was every bit as taken by the beauty of the lake country as was Davers, though he did express some perplexity as to how Davers was intending to possibly settle and build in the area when no such settlement was yet permitted. This worried Davers not in the least. Closed doors somehow always seemed to have a way of opening for him when he talked to the right people in the right way.

One of the surprises of the trip had been in meeting, at the Sault Sainte Marie, an intelligent and engaging young English trader named Alexander Henry, who was living with a Frenchman named Cadotte, his Chippewa wife and their two half-breed children. Hutchins and Davers had spent several days with them, during which time Henry talked almost constantly about his plans for a trading post at the Sault. His next move, he told them, was to go back to Michilimackinac to await the return of some of his men who were due back from the interior, and then to return to the Sault to establish the store.

Hutchins, having mapped the Sault in a preliminary manner, suggested that Henry accompany them back to Michilimackinac, where he wanted to map the Straits there as well. Delighted, Henry accepted. They had bade their farewells to the Cadottes, Henry promising that he would be back again before long, and boated back to Fort Michilimackinac. There Davers had met and, as usual, been entertained in the best manner possible by the post commander, Lieutenant William Leslye.

As soon as Hutchins was finished at the Straits, the expedition had continued and Davers was so completely enchanted by all they saw that it had come to him as a shock to realize the summer was nearly gone and it was time to return to Detroit.

Now they had returned and, back in his same quarters in the commander's house, Davers was enjoying the first real solitude and privacy he had experienced in a great many weeks. He was very tired and for a few days he just wanted to rest. Besides, Gladwin and his officers were under something of a strain at the moment. From what Davers could gather, some kind of Indian trouble was being brewed and there was talk of war belts being circulated. This, however, concerned him little. They had seen many Indians during the journey on the lakes and had met with no difficulty whatever. Davers doubted that there would be any, although in truth he had to admit that there was extreme disappointment among them that no gifts had been brought for them.

He was sorry, though, that Hutchins was leaving so

quickly. The cartographer had talked privately with Major Gladwin for almost an hour and, though earlier he had said he would not be starting back to Fort Pitt for a couple of days yet, as soon as he came out he began stowing his gear for immediate departure. He seemed somewhat worried, but he hadn't confided in Davers.

And Davers, at peace with the world, luxuriated in the comfort of his room on the first really good bed he'd been in since he'd left Detroit. Almost immediately he went to sleep.

[September 15, 1762—Wednesday]

Pontiac looked out over the dimly visible sea of faces watching him intently in this huge council chamber in his village on the Detroit River. Whatever emotion surged in him was carefully masked beneath the set, expressionless visage he showed them. He stood there quietly, naked but for a breechcloth which hung fore and aft from his thin rawhide belt.

He was painted in a strange manner. A large pasty-white circle had been drawn in the middle of his forehead, bisected horizontally by a line of royal blue paint. Three red lines painted diagonally on each cheek gave the impression that he had suffered deep scratches from the claws of some wild animal, and a small circle of white with a blue spot in the center of it was on his chin.

His constantly worn crescent of polished white stone pendulating from his nostrils could be seen easily, but none of the many tattoos on his body or limbs were visible. His entire body, from just under the point of the chin, had been painted. From neck to crotch on the left side, including arm and leg, his skin was a deep purplish blue, while on the right side he was similarly painted in a brilliant garish red-orange. He was the only Indian in the room painted in this fashion, although a number of others had designs painted on their cheeks and foreheads.

Pontiac swung his gaze toward the doorway of this council longhouse and saw that the chiefs were still arriving, pausing at the door to be recognized by the squad of guards posted there before being permitted to enter. Already there were over sixty men in the room, seated on the floor. They watched him and waited.

Seated nearby on Pontiac's left was one of the two French soldiers who had been at the first meeting like this in June. As he had been then, so now he was dressed in Indian garb—buckskin leggings, a blanket draped over his shoulders, a pair of feathers fixed to his hair and a few painted lines on his face. The flicker of firelight now and then reflected from his eyes and he seemed tense and excited.

Before this meeting began assembling, Pontiac was told by this Frenchman that a second Frenchman, who had accompanied this one to the June council, was sick and could not attend this time, but he had asked his companion here to tell Pontiac that all had gone well since that June secret meeting—that the war belts started on their rounds then had gone from village to village, and everywhere they had stopped, the fuel of hatred for the English had been ignited and now burned brightly. All warriors, he said, awaited word of the grand war council. They would come from everywhere and they would follow Pontiac.

With the French officer here tonight were three French residents from Detroit. The first was a beefy, sallow-faced man of about thirty-five whose name was Elleopolle Chene, though he was better known by the nickname of Mini. The other two men were father and son—Antoine and Alexis Cuillerier—and their demeanor was serious, intent, expectant. They were father and elder brother of the beautiful Angelique Cuillerier.

All three of the Frenchmen on hand had been personally invited by Pontiac to attend this council. The war chief had cautioned them to say nothing unless they were spoken to, and he approved the idea of the elder Cuillerier that they all come in Indian guise.

Again Pontiac looked out over the faces before him and he was well satisfied. Rarely had such an assembly of Indian power met in council. All of the western Great Lakes tribes and many from beyond were represented here by the chiefs in attendance. There sat Pucksinwah, war chief of the Shawnees and principal chief of the Kispokotha sept of that tribe, accompanied by his second chief, She-me-ne-to—Black Snake. There sat Michikiniqua—Little Turtle—principal chief of the Miami tribe, with his young son, Pacanne, beside him. There, too, were the Seneca chiefs, Grota Younga and Keneghtaugh. Old Shingas was there, representing the Delawares, along with Tollema and Eagle Claw, White Eyes and Buckangehela. Takee of the Detroit Hurons was here, but his brother chief of the same village, Teata, was absent, as was Orontony of the Sandusky Hurons, the Wyandots. Chiefs Winnemac, Ninivois, and Washee of the Potawatomies were here, as were Wabacumaga—also known as Wabbicomigot—and Sekahos of the Mississaugi, Wasson of the Saginaw Bay Chippewas and the most powerful Chippewa chief of all, Minivavana, along with his son Kinonchamek, a young chief rapidly growing in influence.

There were more, many more, from tribes as distant as the Weas on the Wabash—represented by Chief Wa-pa-man-qua, who was known to the English as White Loon—and the Eel River Miamis under Chief She-nock-in-wak, the Kaskaskias under Chacoretony and the Peorias and Cahokias of the Illinois country under, respectively, Chiefs Makatachinga—Black Dog—and Tamerois. Still others were entering and taking their places here in the council longhouse.

The fact that few Ottawa chiefs of influence were on hand pleased rather than annoyed Pontiac. It was a good sign. The ancient and dying former principal chief, Messeaghage, was physically unable to come all the way from L'Arbre Croche and the fact that his successor, Chief Mackinac—The Turtle—was not here signified a tacit consent for Pontiac to go ahead with his plans without, thus far, tribal disapproval. Had disapproval been planned, Mackinac would certainly have been here, along with such other powerful Ottawa chiefs as Macatepilesis, Manitou, and Okinochumake.

At the secret meeting in June, not even half this many chiefs had shown up and the fact that this meeting now was so well attended—especially since such attendance was almost entirely chiefs—was an extremely good sign. Pontiac was now determined to go ahead with the second stage of the plan which he had taken most of the spring to draw up.

No one had entered the council longhouse now for a quarter hour and so, with guards both inside and out at the doorways, Pontiac faced his audience of eighty or more chiefs and subchiefs and began to speak. He greeted them in the customary manner and thanked them for honoring him with their presence here. Then, briefly, he went over the details of the secret meeting held here in June.

The Indian-clad officer to his left, he told them, was one of two such soldiers who had come to that meeting with the stirring news that now the French and Spaniards had joined hands in the continuing struggle against the English; that the French King Louis had not forgotten about his Indian children in this country and was angered by the mistreatment they were receiving at the hands of those Englishmen; that the French King was, with the Spaniards, at this time mounting a great army which would converge here in two waves—one up the St. Lawrence River and Lakes Ontario and Erie, the other up the Mississippi—and on the way they would take back Quebec and Montreal and all the English posts encountered; that the English would be driven back east of the eastern mountains and that there the French and the Spaniards would fall upon them and destroy them and establish once again the brotherhood that had existed between the French and the Indians before Canada was taken. The conquerors would be conquered.

But, Pontiac continued, the Frenchmen were wondering where the western Indians were. The French King wondered if they had all crawled into holes, because he heard nothing from them or about them. Could it be that they would allow the Englishmen to walk into their country and take it without fight? No, the French King could not entertain such a far-fetched thought as this; he believed that they were merely awaiting his return with great armies so that they could then rise and help him wipe out the English. But the King would need strong evidence that this was true; if his Indian children were not able to rise up and strike by themselves, how then could he justify coming to their assistance? It would be well for the Indians to rise and strike the English and then, at this sign, the armies of French and Spanish soldiers would come and while the Indians destroyed the English at the heart of their country, the armies would come and fall upon their flanks and their rear and wipe them out utterly. The French King was aware that his Indian children needed ammunition to carry out such a plan and, though English blockades kept much of what he wanted to send here away, yet he would still manage to get some through to Fort de Chartres in the Illinois country and it would be distributed from there to his Indian children. As soon as he heard that his Indian children had risen against the English conquerors in their country, then he would come to help them.

"This," Pontiac said, his voice filling every corner of the large chamber and touching every ear, "this was what the French officer beside me and his companion told us in the secret council in June. Some of you here now were here then and you know what I have said is truth.

"Some of my brothers here," he continued, his talk becoming suddenly more animated, his gesticulation more frequent, "fear that we are not strong enough and that if we rise against these white conquerors in our land this will bring destruction upon ourselves and our families. To you I say now that yes, this might be true if just one tribe or another rose up against the English and struck at them. But with our tribes joined together as one against them, how then could they stand against us? And remember this—once having struck, we will further be aided by our French father and the Spanish King and there will be no way the English can stand against us!"

He paused for a long moment and then pointed a steady finger at the two Seneca chiefs who were seated together a short distance from him to one side. Grota Younga and Keneghtaugh stared steadily back at the Ottawa war chief, their expressions unreadable.

"From the east," Pontiac continued, "have come again among us deputies from the Iroquois. Six seasons ago, in the spring before the last spring, two of their chiefs came among us. They were then Kyashuta and Teantoriance who came to ask that we bury the bitterness between our peoples and theirs and join hands with them against the English. We refused then, because the English were only just come to our country and they filled us with great promises which we foolishly believed. Now Chiefs Keneghtaugh and Grota Younga have come and extend again the hand of friendship and the desire for alliance. They do not ask that we come to the east to join them in a rise against the English in their country near the great falls. No! This they will do by themselves. They wish to know only will we here rise in our own lands and strike the English, too, so that the Iroquois may not be struck from behind by the English from here while bloodying their tomahawks on the English from there. Now it is time for us to consider carefully the answer we will give them.

"Brothers, think! What, besides hurt and empty promises, have the English given us? Which of their many promises to us have they kept? Who among us can now believe it is to our benefit to have them here in our land? All of us have suffered hurts of different kinds from them and there is no sorrow in them for any of us.

"Brothers, look at what happened to the Iroquois: when the English would have perished without their help, they gave it. The English built forts in their lands but, as they said, only to wage war against the French, about whom they filled us with lies. They said the forts would be used only for that purpose and when the French had been driven away, the forts and the lands they were using would be given back to the Iroquois. But, brothers, what has happened? The French are gone, but the English are still in the forts and they have built new forts. They claim now as their own the land upon which the forts stand and they mock the demands that the lands and the forts be given up as promised."

Every eye in the longhouse was riveted to Pontiac, every ear keenly attuned to his voice and each inflection of it. No sound of any kind could be heard within the chamber except that which bound them so hypnotically, the powerful, commanding voice of Pontiac. Now the strangely painted chief swung his pointing finger first to the Delawares and then to the Shawnees.

"Brothers," he said, "look at what is happening to the Shawnees and to the Delawares: the English have often promised the Delawares that no settlement will be made in their lands, yet even now new forts are built on their Susquehanna River and to the westward of it and like white ants the men flow in a stream from the east to claim the land of the Delawares as their own and to sink white roots into it. The Shawnees, since the last spring, have lost two out of every ten of their people to the spotted sickness brought by the English and though they have appealed for help, the English have turned their backs and refused to give even what it is customary to give.

"Brothers, who among us has not suffered from the English? All of us suffered badly last winter for want of ammunition for our hunting, but though we have asked and asked again for it, it has been withheld from us except for small amounts which mean nothing. Another winter is coming and we will suffer even worse, and our families even more, if we are not provided, as we should be, with the means to do our hunting; but I do not believe we will be given any. Was there ever a time that our French brothers withheld ammunition from us? No! And why is this ammunition being withheld from us? The reason, as my French brothers have told me and I believe, is because the English fear us and they desire what we have, and for this they mean to come against us and destroy us completely as soon as they feel they have made us too weak to any longer be able to defend ourselves."

He paused for a long moment to let this sink in and then continued, his voice a bit calmer but no less disgusted with the English. "And what of the trade, my brothers? We were promised that we would have more trading posts and more traders and more goods and at less expense than ever before. This is what they told us, but it has not happened. Yes, the English traders have come, but they do not provide us with what we need, as the French did. Bears cannot be taken with hoes! Otters cannot be caught with mirrors! Beavers cannot be taken with shirts! Where is the gunpowder we need, and the lead? Where are the traps and the skinning knives and the tomahawks? We are not permitted to buy such items and even those less-needed goods that they will sell to us are sold at prices we cannot afford to pay.

"Brothers, when the French controlled these forts, the English came to us in secret and gave us rum and told us that when the French were gone and the forts were English, then would the rivers run with rum and every Indian would have his fill of it at any time. Now even this small pleasure is withheld from us and when we sometimes find a trader who will sell us at dear price a single keg, it is best to check it at once lest by some magic it turns to water before it is opened.

"What, my brothers, has happened to the presents we always received as rent for the use of our lands or as payment for our friendship and services? Our French brothers gave us such presents often and in abundance, even when it was hard for them to do so because they had little for themselves. The English told us they would give us even more when they came, but now their general sees that we have no army of white men to aid us and he orders that we be *given* nothing, but that we must hunt for furs with which to *buy* what it is our right to expect to receive without charge. But even in this manner he tries to hurt us further; he tells us to hunt furs to buy what we need, but then he keeps our guns quiet so we cannot get furs and are not able to buy and therefore the bellies of our wives and children grow pinched with hunger. We can think of this as nothing but revenge being taken upon us for our support of the French early in the war.

"Even were we blind, my brothers, we could see that the English do not like us. The French came among us as friends, even entering our families as the husbands of our daughters; the English soldiers do not often come near us and if we come near them, we are insulted and sometimes hit with the wooden ends of their guns and we are told that by the orders of their general they are not *allowed* to make friends with us. They mock us in our customs and, unlike with the French, we are not welcomed into their forts; instead, we are allowed inside only long enough to state our business and then we are made to leave."

Pontiac stopped speaking, shook his head sadly and slapped his hands to his side. For some time he stood there with his eyes down, but then he raised them again and they were flashing angrily and his hands had become fists knotted at his sides.

"All of these things, my brothers," he rasped, "are bad things and they light the flames of anger in our hearts. When they are put together as one, they are too much! Worst of all is that we are growing to learn a terrible truth, and hear you well what I say now, for this is the truth we have learned: *the English now claim this land, all of it, as theirs!* They believe, because they pushed the Frenchmen from it, that it has therefore become theirs, because what belonged to the Frenchmen belongs now to them. But this land of ours never *belonged* to the Frenchmen; they were our tenants! We gave them the right only to use some of our land, to build trading posts and forts from which they profited and which were a convenience and benefit to us. *But it was not French land which they could lose if defeated and the land then become the property of the conquerors!* No! We thought at first that the English understood this, that we *let* them come into our land to take the place of the French as tenants to continue for our convenience and their profit the trade which the French had begun with us. They told us that they understood this. But now they do not think this at all. Now they think this is their land! It is not, and we must convince them that it is not!"

Again Pontiac stopped abruptly and a deep silence fell over the council room. The fires had burned low and now were little more than mounds of glowing embers in the gloom. Features could not be seen of the numerous Indians seated here and no man in the assemblage made a sound. The words of Pontiac gripped and held them as no words had ever gripped and held them before. For fully five minutes Pontiac stood silently and then, when at last he spoke again, his voice was low and determined and filled with repressed anger.

"My brothers, when I learned in June that the Spaniards and the French had joined hands against the English and that they would help us, I called a secret meeting with some of you and I sent belts to all of you that you might know of it. Now I will send belts again to all the tribes, so that those who will join with me in what I plan may prepare to rise when it is time to do so. Take back with you in your hearts the words I have spoken here; take them back and let your own mouths speak them to your own warriors and to all of your people, so that when you are finished, they may say to you what is in their hearts.

"Brothers, a winter is coming and our families will need all our efforts to provide them with food, so we should do nothing now. But return to your villages and wait for the word to come to you that another—and final—grand council of all the chiefs will be held in the spring. *Then*, brothers, will we decide what must be done. Then will we do it!"

ing have. But return to your villages and wait for the word in council by you they another—and here—grand council of the chiefs will be held in the spring. Then brothers will we decide what must

CHAPTER III

[*December 8, 1762—Wednesday*]

AS far as Sir William Johnson was concerned, there was no occupation in the world so fraught with frustration as this business of being head of the Indian Department. It seemed that he was continually being pulled apart; by the Indians on one side and by Lieutenant General Sir Jeffrey Amherst on the other. There seemed to be no middle ground whatever where they could meet, and the fault lay not with the Indians but with that fool in military command—and he *was* a fool! No one but a fool could so confidently and consistently ignore the multitude of deadly warnings that were afloat; and no one but a fool could consider the Indians as not being dangerous when goaded too far.

With an exasperated, unintelligible grunt, Johnson read through George Croghan's report a second time and still found it almost beyond belief. Croghan reported first that Ensign Tom Hutchins had returned to Fort Pitt from doing some mapping on the upper lakes and he brought with him the disturbing intelligence that the western Great Lakes Indians were extremely uneasy and that there was evidence of French agitation among them against the English. Reports had it, though Hutchins himself had seen none, that war belts were circulating. Further, the Indians he had encountered were all in very great need and they had fully expected to receive gifts of ammunition and goods. As Hutchins had stated it in his report to Croghan:

> *They were disappointed in their expectations of my having presents for them; and as the French have always accustomed themselves, both in times of peace and during the late war, to make these people great presents three or four times a year and always allowed them a sufficient quantity of ammunition at the posts, they think it very strange that this custom should*

be so immediately broken off by the English, and the traders not allowed even to take so much ammunition with them as to enable those Indians to kill game sufficient for the support of their families.

Croghan went on to say that practically on the heels of this report from Hutchins he had had a visit—late on the night of September 28—from a Detroit Indian, a Huron. This Huron told him that while he had not been allowed to attend it, since he was not a chief, there had been a highly secret council held in June at the village of the Ottawa war chief, Pontiac. Both civil chiefs and war chiefs from a number of tribes had attended and it was whispered that there had been at this council, dressed as Indians, two French officers from the Illinois country. Croghan's informant had admitted he did not know exactly what was said, but he was certain a plot was being fomented against the English and that the French officers were urging the tribes into an uprising. The Huron also said that with his own eyes he had in June seen deputies with belts being sent to tribes in the Illinois and Ohio countries and that another council was said to be scheduled for September, which was probably being held right then, as he had seen numerous parties en route toward Detroit.

Then, as if this were not enough, two days later when Croghan mentioned this to a trio of Iroquois he trusted, they informed him that they knew of it and had heard the same from a Shawnee. This in itself was verified when one of Croghan's associates came in from a trading trip into the Shawnee country with the news that the Shawnees had received a war belt from the Weas and that the Weas had gotten it from the French at Fort de Chartres. Croghan reported that he had then immediately sent all this information to Amherst in the hands of an experienced express messenger, who was to return at once with the general's reply. The man had returned to Fort Pitt from New York in record time, but hardly with the answer Croghan had expected. Amherst had replied:

I look upon the intelligence you received of the French stirring up the Western Indians to be of little consequence, as it is not in their power to hurt us. They are without ammunition and they would not dare to anger us, for before a regular army the Indians are helpless.

Stunned beyond measure, Croghan had thereupon written this report to Sir William. It was obvious that George Croghan was entirely disgusted and Johnson's heart sank at the thought that he might lose the services of his most able assistant. Croghan had concluded:

The Indians are a very jealous people and they had great expectations of being very generally supplied by us, and from their poverty and mercenary disposition, they can't bear such a disappointment. Undoubtedly the General has his own reason for not allowing any presents or ammunition to be given to them, and I wish it may have its desired effect, but I take this opportunity to acquaint you that I dread the event, as I know the Indians can't long persevere. They are a rash, inconsistent people and inclined to mischief and will never consider consequences, though it may end in their ruin. Their success at the beginning of this war on our frontiers is too recent in their memory to suffer them to consider their present inability to make war with us, and if the Senecas, Delawares and Shawnees should break with us, it will end in a general war with all the western nations, though they at present seem jealous of each other. For my part, I am resolved to resign if the General does not liberalize our expenditures for Indian affairs. I don't choose to be begging eternally for such necessaries as are wanted to carry on the service, nor will I support it at my own expense. There are great troubles ahead. How it may end the Lord knows, but I assure you I am of opinion it will not be long before we shall have some quarrels with them.

Slowly William Johnson refolded the letter and pushed it to one side. The thought of an Indian uprising sickened him. Too long had he been close to the Indians not to realize their temper and what would happen if they set out on the warpath. He had seen it time and again—the misery, the atrocities, the paralyzing fear, the death and destruction. To know that one man had it in his power at this moment to prevent this from happening—or, for that matter, to *allow* it to happen—very nearly caused him to tremble, for that one man was General Sir Jeffrey Amherst.

Wearily, fearful that it would do no good, yet desperately hopeful that somehow, in some way, he might find the right words to open the general's eyes to the peril looming, Sir William began to write to Amherst. It was a long letter and it went again over the need to relax policy where the Indians were concerned and to provide them with the materials they so desperately needed. The continued holding back of ammunition from them was a very grave error; instead of preventing an Indian uprising, it would almost certainly precipitate one. The signs were all there that such an uprising was forming now, but there was yet time to avert it if proper actions would be taken swiftly. He continued:

. . . and tragedy, your Excellency, is on the point of breaking. It is true that through your orders the Indians are now very short on ammunition, but this will not prevent their uprising. However short of it they are kept in peace, these Indians will not in war lack for ammunition, as they will certainly capture military supply trains in the woods and overrun depots where ammunition is stored. They will also find powder in the frontier houses they will overrun. Nor, your Excellency, can warriors used to living off the woods be starved out by any blockade or strategic cutting of their supply lines. The forts on which the General relies to hold them back, if not captured, will simply be passed by and the warriors will cut off and destroy a number of families, destroy their houses, effects, and grain, all within the compass of a very few hours, and then return by a different route to some of their places of rendezvous. The surviving inhabitants, together with all those near them, immediately forsake their dwellings and retire with their families in the utmost terror, poverty, and distress to the next towns, striking panic into the inhabitants who then become fearful of going to any of the posts. Trade becomes at once stagnated, nothing can be carried to any of the posts without an escort and, unless 'tis a very strong one—which is not always to be procured—the whole may fall into the hands of the Indians. This picture of a state of a country under an Indian War, however improbable it may seem, will be found on due examination not to have been exaggerated.

Late into the night Sir William continued writing until at last he was drained. He signed the final sheet with a flourish, folded and sealed it and then placed it into a waterproof pouch. At the front door, curled up and sleeping on a rug there, he found his Mohawk messenger, Oughnour, and prodded the warrior with his toe. Dressed in some of Johnson's castoff clothing and with his hair grown long and tied in a small queue in back in English fashion, Oughnour looked far more like a Mohawk Valley settler than an Indian.

"Daniel," said Johnson, using the Mohawk's Christian name as the Indian came alertly to his feet, "this is very important." He tapped the pouch. "Carry it to the big general at the mouth of the Hudson, where you have taken messages to him before. Go as fast as you can. Wait for his reply and then come back safely."

Oughnour dipped his head once, took the packet and an instant later the door had clicked shut behind him.

[December 10, 1762—Friday]

Well established now as the foremost English trader of both Fort Michilimackinac and Fort Sault Sainte Marie, Alexander Henry was rather pleased with his lot and the way things had gone for him. The nervousness over the potential danger his savage customers might be to him had gradually dwindled until now he was rarely bothered with it. All signs pointed to the fact that the Indians had indeed fully accepted the English now and were happy with the trade—or at least as happy as they could be when still being deprived of ammunition and liquor.

He had spent a large portion of this year at the home of Jean Baptiste Cadotte and they had become rather good friends; and since Cadotte, in deference to his wife who could speak no French, preferred to converse in the Chippewa tongue, Henry had by now become quite fluent in the language, though he was still learning more of it every day.

Cadotte was something of an enigma. While he seemed genuinely pleased at the presence of Henry here and the reopening of trade, yet there was a side of the man's character which Henry could not seem to penetrate—an aloof reserve into which Cadotte retreated on occasion. On such occasions, Henry had several times discovered the Canadian staring at him in an uncomfortably penetrating manner; and under that gaze the young trader would experience a little inexplicable shiver of omen at his nape. It was not a pleasant sensation.

But then, on September 19, had arrived a small detachment from Fort Michilimackinac to regarrison Fort Sault Sainte Marie. Five soldiers under the command of a thin, sharp-faced officer. This commander was Lieutenant John Jamet of the 60th Regiment, recently promoted from the rank of ensign, and a rather engaging young man with whom Henry got along well from the very beginning. The presence of the garrison here at the Sault was beneficial for Henry, as the soldiers were eager to buy various trade goods from him.

Beginning in early October the whitefish run began and for weeks Henry had been occupied with the Indians in the taking of them, spearing great numbers as they swam the rapids. Each of the fish, when caught, would be nearly gutted and then with the head also removed, split in half down its length until within an inch of the tail. They would then be hung for drying on a rail resting on two forked sticks, the tails sticking skyward and the slablike sides hanging below and the raw meat exposed to the air. By the middle of October Henry alone had caught and dried over five hundred of the fish and, though he tried to sell some to the garrison, Jamet declined to buy. The young officer had shaken his head and wrinkled his nose.

"Never was much of one for eating fish," he told Henry, "even when they're good and fresh. But when they're like this," he indicated the dry fish with his thumb and made a sour expression, ". . . well, I'd hate to think of being stuck here all winter with nothing to eat but that. I don't think I'll have any trouble trading some of our liquor supply to the Indians for all the venison and other food we might need throughout the winter. Of course," he added hastily at Henry's look of surprise, "that's not something I'd like my superiors to know about. The general frowns on giving them liquor almost as much as he does about giving them powder and lead. But, what little I give them can't be of any consequence."

Henry had shrugged and simply sent several loads of dried fish by boat back to his store at Fort Michilimackinac for his assistant, Etienne Campion, to use in the trade. Now, with winter rapidly closing in and the navigation likely to close any day, Henry began to think about heading back with the remainder of his dried fish to his more comfortable quarters at Michilimackinac—a nice frame house he had rented, standing on the lot beside that belonging to Charles Langlade. It had been a busy time for Henry here and he could do with a few weeks of rest and change.

He had fallen asleep almost instantly upon retiring last night and slept deeply until a few moments ago when shrill cries had penetrated from outside and caused him to sit groggily erect in bed. It was still very dark and he frowned, thinking he had been dreaming, but then the calls came again:

"Fire! It's on fire! Fire!"

He bolted to his feet, hastily dressed and then raced out of the door of his little house, which was fairly close to Cadotte's. The Canadian was already outside, silhouetted by the roaring conflagration which was sweeping through the commander's quarters and even now spreading to the barracks of the garrison. Soldiers, some only partially clad, had spilled out the door of the latter structure. It was their shouting which Henry had heard. The trader ran to Cadotte's side and grasped his arm. He pointed to the front of the commander's house, where the door was little more than a wall of flame, and shouted to make himself heard over the roar of the blaze:

"Jean! Where's the lieutenant? Is Jamet still inside there?"

Cadotte nodded and then shook his head sadly. "There is no way to get to him. He is lost. The fire started there," he pointed at the chimney of the soldiers' barracks, "and fell over onto the front of the officer's house. He couldn't get out."

Henry, familiar with the interior of the officer's quarters, shouted and waved to several of the soldiers to follow him and ran around to the other side of the building. There a small window, broken now, belched great volumes of smoke. With the help of two of the men, both coughing and choking nearly as much as he, Henry smashed the crossrods of the window sash and thrust the upper part of his body inside. The heat and smoke were suffocating.

"Jamet!" he screamed. "*Jamet!* Where are you?"

A gagging, strangling cry reached his ears and the sound of shuffling. An instant later, one of Jamet's outstretched arms touched Henry's hand and the trader snatched it, then caught Jamet's wrist. With a strength bred of panic Henry lunged backward and literally pulled Jamet halfway through the opening. The officer was naked and large areas of his skin were burned and shriveled. Some of these tore free as he was dragged through the narrow opening and dumped to the ground outside.

Immediately, even while the soldiers were continuing to pull Jamet away, Henry was back at the window, leaning inside. He was blinded by the smoke boiling past him, gagging and choking, feeling desperately with out-stretched hands for anything that could be saved. He touched a small keg and with great effort managed to lift it up and carry it some yards off before slumping to the ground. It was a half-keg of gunpowder—a portion of the ammunition supply stored in Jamet's quarters.

An instant later there was a tremendous whooshing explosion as the powder still inside ignited. The entire roof of the burning house lifted and then disintegrated and the pieces flew off in great arcs of cometlike brilliance. Several large chunks struck Henry's own quarters and in a few minutes that place was engulfed in flames. Even the stockade was burning now and in a very short while one whole wall had collapsed. The soldiers were doing all they could to extinguish the fire and keep it from spreading, but their efforts were mostly useless. In less than an hour virtually all of Fort Sault Sainte Marie was destroyed. Only Cadotte's house had by some miracle been spared.

Henry watched his own quarters being destroyed, along with the soldiers' barracks. Everything he and they had was gone—food, clothing, ammunition, supplies, equipment. His face was blackened by smoke and his throat raw from breathing it. White lines channeled down his cheeks from the tears which ran from smarting eyes and he stumbled to the doorway of Cadotte's house and entered.

Jamet, moaning with pain, lay on Cadotte's bed, his bare legs and buttocks and back badly burned. The Chippewa woman who was Cadotte's wife was already carefully rubbing a thick coating of bear grease all over the injured man. Cadotte, standing by the bed, saw Henry and came over to him. He clucked his tongue and shook his head sadly.

"My friend, it does not look good. She will do what she can for him, but he is very badly burned. He may not make it."

[December 31, 1762—Friday]

Pontiac had risen to a considerable height of power and influence during the course of last summer, gradually winning the support not only of many of the chiefs of his own Ottawa tribe, but those of neighboring and even distant tribes as well. Yet, there were still many who were reluctant to cast their lot with him, reluctant to take up the war hatchet against so formidable an enemy as the English without some good sign that they would emerge victorious. This was particularly true with the tribes close to Detroit, where the English strength was most evident in the Great Lakes country.

After the two secret councils, Pontiac had held smaller council after council with these nearby chiefs, assuring them that they would not be in this alone if they joined him. He told them that the Detroit Frenchman who was their good friend, Antoine Cuillerier, had told him that a messenger from the Illinois country—a man named Sibbold—had come to him with word that right now a large French army was being readied and would be here at Detroit in the spring to help the Indians in their endeavor to drive out the English. Cuillerier, Pontiac declared, was one white man who could be trusted and since he said the French army was coming, Pontiac had no doubt of it. Further, the war chief promised the assembled Indians that there would come a sign, that in a manner evident to all, an omen of evil for the English would manifest itself. When it did, he told them, they must divorce themselves from the English and prepare to destroy them all at a given time.

Pontiac was no seer, no prophet, but he was a shrewd leader and he knew that somehow, some way, something was bound to occur sometime that could be construed as an evil omen for the English. He hardly expected the meteorological phenomenon which occurred on October 5, but he was swift to claim it as the manifestation of his prediction. On that Tuesday morning ugly black clouds hung low over the whole area. More and more dense they became until even the chickens of the Frenchmen around Detroit went to roost. It was very nearly like night and the fearful eyes of both Indians and whites were almost continuously directed upward.

At one o'clock in the afternoon the rain began and it was a rain such as no one here had ever before experienced. The rain was black. As if a great reservoir of ink had suddenly been released, the ugly liquid slashed downward in torrents, running off roofs in streams of black, turning the ground dark, collecting in black puddles in every depression, staining the creeks and rivers and lakes with each drop. With the rain came an oppressive smell, similar to that of burning sulphur. It was so strong and offensive that it caused some people to gag and hold kerchiefs to their mouths and noses to breathe through. It caused the eyes to smart and tears to form in them.[64]

To the majority of the English it was simply an unexplainable phenomenon. Some were uneasy about it, but most were merely curious or amused. Some of the soldiers caught the fluid in empty inkpots as it runneled from the eaves, determined to use it for ink, and laughing and joking about it.

To the Indians, however, the black rain was a very powerful omen, a foreboding of evil directed against the English. Pontiac, as much awed by the black and smelly rain as anyone else, was nonetheless swift to snatch up the opportunity and claim it as the sign he had predicted would come; and the Indians who had hesitated in giving their allegiance to him, now were very strongly swayed by the greatness of this

Ottawa chief who apparently knew the future. Many now came and said they would do as he asked.

Pontiac immediately sent runners to carry the news of what had happened here to the far distant villages of numerous tribes and thus increase his renown and prestige. Other runners he held in readiness while under his direction a bevy of squaws worked night and day making numerous long, broad belts of red and black war wampum.

He called for another council to be held in late November and that one was attended by representatives of no less than twenty tribes. This time there were no white men in attendance—neither French nor English. The council was held at Pontiac's village, only recently relocated on the narrow *Isle aux Pêches*[65]—Fish Island—which was hidden from the view of the Englishmen at the fort by the bulk of the thickly wooded island called by the French *Isle aux Cochons*.[66] During the preliminaries before counciling began, medicine men of the various tribes made small fires and removed sacred objects from their medicine bags and mumbled odd incantations. They created magic protective charms out of rocks and twigs by urinating on them, drying them out over the fires and then passing them out to all who were assembled that they might be protected from evil beings who moved through the darkness.

On the fifth day before the council was to begin, Pontiac stained his body black and, naked, disappeared into the woods of the island in order to fast and commune with the Master of Life. Even as the medicine men continued their mumbling over more charms, Pontiac returned and walked among them as if he were possessed. The black stain still covered his body and though it was bitterly cold out and he was unclothed, he gave no sign of being discomfited. His eyes were filled with a feverish brightness and in his right hand he carried a tomahawk stained with vermilion.

As practically everyone watched, he walked to where a cedar post painted black had been sunk to stand upright to a height of six feet. He stopped before it and then, with a wild, incoherent cry he slammed the red tomahawk into it with such force that much of the head of the weapon was buried in the wood. Then he entered his longhouse, had his squaws repaint him in garish blue, red and white paints, attached a cluster of vermilion-stained feathers to his scalp, tossed a blanket about his shoulders and returned to the assemblage.

He moved among them wordlessly to his own place, sat down and quietly smoked a red clay pipe while a score or more Ottawa squaws passed out portions of cooked dog meat from platters to all in attendance except Pontiac. Though it was whispered that Pontiac had not eaten for five days, the chief showed no desire to eat now, but merely sat and puffed on his pipe without expression, the large crescent-shaped nose pendant of smooth white stone reflecting the light of the small fires.

At last, when the assemblage had eaten and smoked, Pontiac stood up again and then he began to speak. His voice was strange, deep and compelling, and they clung to his words. He told them that he had communed with the Master of Life and that he had seen a vision in which a great war eagle had dropped from the skies and crushed Detroit in its grasping talons. He talked to them, chanted to them, sang of his own prowess and exploits, hammered a litany of war into them until it spread to a raging fire in every warrior's breast; and one by one the chiefs in attendance had stood and danced and chanted and then buried their own tomahawks into the war post.

All night they danced and pounced and sang until exhaustion overcame them and they slumped to the ground. Only the Hurons, of all the tribes in the Detroit area, were not fully in agreement. They watched as the Chippewas and Potawatomies, the Ottawas and Mississaugis, Miamis and Delawares and Shawnees sunk their hatchets into the post, but they themselves were split. Half of the Detroit Hurons under Teata—a band largely proselytized by Jesuits—and half of the Sandusky Wyandot Hurons under Orontony rejected the plea of Pontiac and walked out, returning to their village. But the remainder of the Detroit Hurons under Chief Takee and those of Sandusky under Chief Odinghquanooron accepted the belt and hatchet and struck the post. What this all boiled down to was that in the Detroit area alone, Pontiac had now become the head of an alliance of no less than four hundred and sixty proven warriors.

In the morning the messengers who had been held in readiness were given the completed belts of red and black beadwork in intricate design; they memorized the message they contained. They would take them to every tribe and village to the east of the Mississippi and north of the Ohio and west of the Alleghenies; they would sing the message of war and throw down the red hatchet that it might be picked up and ceremoniously driven into the war post; they would tell of the great and final prewar council which would be held on the fifteenth day of the Green Moon—April—on the banks of the River Ecorse near where it emptied into the Detroit River to the south and west of the English fort.

The messengers had gone and already, in these weeks that had passed since then, many had returned from their missions and almost without exception had reported to Pontiac that the hatchet had been picked up and the war post struck, the war belt accepted and the promise given to attend the great council on the fifteenth day of the Green Moon.

And now, to one of his most trusted messengers, Pontiac gave another long, wide belt of wampum woven with a maze of intricate red and black designs. It was a belt that was more than just a war belt; it was a belt that would heal an old wound and which would bind two former enemies together in alliance; it was a belt in reply to a belt of similar construction just received from a runner who had come directly from Chief Kyashuta.

With a savage satisfaction, Pontiac watched his own messenger and the Iroquois messenger, each with his own small party, paddle away downstream on the Detroit River in two canoes. They would follow the river to its mouth and then continue southward and then eastward along the shore of the not-yet-frozen Lake of the Erighs—Lake Erie—until at last they came to the head of the Niagara River. Here they would conceal their boats and strike off overland toward the upper reaches of the Genesee River to the village of Chenusio, seat of the Seneca government.

There, Pontiac had no doubt, the Chenusio Senecas under Chief Kyashuta would accept it—as he had already accepted Kyashuta's belt—and ally the Senecas to his new confederacy. They would help, when the time came, to destroy the English. And possibly—just possibly—that powerful Seneca chief might be able to persuade the entire Iroquois League to join in the uprising.

The dark eyes of the Ottawa war chief glittered at the thought.

[January 24, 1763—Monday]

Captain George Etherington was a long, lanky sort of individual. He had joined the army a decade ago at the age of twenty and in doing so had found his niche. He was a reasonably good officer, though by no means outstanding. He followed orders well, commanded his men well, but rarely projected his thoughts to the future. He was content to accept things as they came. He personally did not like his command of Fort Michilimackinac any more than his predecessor, Lieutenant Leslye, now his second-in-command, had liked it. Etherington, however, would never consider complaining about it as Leslye had done. Long ago the captain had learned to accept without complaint whatever came his way in the military, knowing that eventually, whether he liked it or not, the situation would change. And anyway, things could always be worse. He could, for example, have been named commander of Fort Sault Sainte Marie instead of Michilimackinac, and it could have been he who was at death's door rather than Lieutenant Jamet.

Sitting at his desk in the little office preparing the monthly returns of his company—a copy each to be sent to Major Gladwin at Detroit and Colonel Bouquet, now in Philadelphia—Etherington reflected on what had happened at the Sault and shook his head. Poor Jamet was in a pretty bad way. Eleven days after the fire and explosion there, a messenger had reached Fort Michilimackinac with a letter from Jamet containing news of the disaster. And ten days after that—on December 31—the entire garrison of Fort Sault Sainte Marie, with the exception of Jamet, arrived at Michilimackinac with more details, having completed the hazardous water journey to this post just in time, as navigation closed on the very next day.

Jamet, the returned soldiers told Captain Etherington, was too badly injured to be moved at the moment. He and the trader Alexander Henry were staying in the house of Jean Cadotte, the Frenchman. It was the only structure, other than the scattered wickiups and tepees of the Indians there, left standing after the fire. Since the lieutenant hadn't died of his burns in the first few days, Cadotte was reasonably convinced that Jamet would recover. However, the young officer would have to do a good bit of recuperating before he'd be able to move about. With the barracks destroyed, there had been no other choice for Jamet than to send his men back to Fort Michilimackinac in the two remaining batteaux. He hoped to survive his burns and to follow the men himself before too long, when the lakes and straits had frozen over solidly enough to travel across on foot.

Again Etherington shook his head. From what the returned soldiers told him, Jamet was in a very bad way and they still doubted he would live, despite Cadotte's optimism, much less be able to walk the fifty miles or more through deep snow all the way to Michilimackinac. Etherington sighed and picked up his quill pen again, dipped it into the ink and began a letter to his regimental commander in Philadelphia:

Michilimackinac
24th January 1763

To Colonel Henry Bouquet
Sir:

I have here enclosed you the monthly returns of my company to this day. On the 21st of December I received a letter from Lieutenant Jamet, who commands at the Falls of St. Marys, wherein he informs me that about 1 o'clock in the morning of the 10th of the same month, a fire broke through the soldiers' chimney, which communicated itself directly to Mr. Jamet's house, where the provisions and ammunition were lodged. The latter prevented the soldiers at first from attempting to extinguish the flames, but in a little time the powder took fire and blew the roof off the house, after which the soldiers did everything in their power to put out the fire, but it was all to no purpose; for in less than an hour from the time that the sentry discovered the fire, one of the curtains of the fort, with the officers and soldiers' barracks, was burnt to the ground and all the provisions and ammunition entirely consumed; which obliged Mr. Jamet to send his garrison here, where they arrived safe. Mr. Jamet lost everything he had in the world and made a very narrow escape for his life by getting naked out of a window. He is now, if alive, in a very miserable condition, being burnt to such a degree that he was not able to come in the batteaux with his men and is now at St. Marys without either coat, shirt, shoes or stockings; but as the lake is fast, I intend sending an Indian sleigh for him tomorrow. The other day I had one of my men killed by the fall of a tree. I am, dear sir,

Your most obedient, humble servant,
George Etherington
Captain Commanding

[February 4, 1763—Friday]

Despite the parties and dances held every Saturday night, winter occupancy of Fort Pitt was hardly the most desirable duty. True, the new commander, Captain Simeon Ecuyer, a Swiss mercenary, was a rather lighthearted character and encouraged merriment and levity and casually overlooked numerous infractions of military discipline, but at best the social life at the fort was drab and the weekly dances only emphasized the routine sordidness of duty here.

The barracks were drafty and cold, the men plagued by lice during the day and by bedbugs at night, their tempers short and fistfights common. Sudden torrential flooding came and went from the Monongahela on one side or the Allegheny on the other, and the muck from it collected everywhere. The soldiers had to stay at the post because it was their duty to do so, but why anyone would remain here who was not required to was something of a mystery to every soldier. Yet the fort and the sprawling little town of Pittsburgh around it were crowded with settlers, trappers, Indians, scouts, schemers and drifters. On the whole, they were a coarse and rowdy lot, more often than not drunken and immoral and quite frequently criminals seeking to escape the law.

Some attempt at decorum was made by Captain Ecuyer, but it rarely succeeded. Inevitably he would have a gaggle of old women on hand to act as chaperons at the Saturday night dances, but theirs was a feeble effort at best. George Croghan, who vied with Ecuyer at being the life and wit of each of these sessions always made it a habit to quickly fill the glasses of these women, and fill them often, so that before half the night was over they could scarcely mumble their own names much less perform their charge.

The dances started modestly enough with a dozen to a score or more couples swirling to the tunes played by the garrison's musicians, but as far as most of the men in attendance were concerned, there were only three activities worth engaging in: drinking to excess, gambling for anything, making love with anyone. Liquor flowed in abundance and was consumed by the women almost as much as by the men. The debauchery usually began with toasting, and more often than not it was George Croghan who would leap up onto a chair and tower over the crowd, shouting out toasts and belting down a hefty jolt of liquor for each one. The toasting started innocently enough each time, with glasses raised and then their contents quaffed to such comments as:

"May the friend we trust be honest, the girl we love be true, the country we live in be free!"

"The heart of friendship and the soul of love!"

"Motherhood, friendship, and country!"

"May we kiss whom we please . . . and please whom we kiss!"

Gradually, though, as drink after drink was downed, the

toasts became more ribald. Croghan, thrusting his glass high, would bellow such suggestive toasts as:

"Days of ease . . . and nights of pleasure!"

"Days of sport . . . and nights of transport!"

"May the lady of the night have crossed eyes, but never crossed legs!"

Gales of drunken laughter would sweep over the assemblage at each toast and soon the couples would begin drifting off in search of quieter quarters for activities of a more penetrating nature. Captain Simeon Ecuyer was not at all backward in joining in such measures, nor was he particularly concerned over who knew about it. While well in his cups during the Saturday dance of January 8, he retired to his quarters with a very pretty young lady, and with both braggadocio and indiscretion penned a swift note to Colonel Bouquet in Philadelphia, telling him that:

. . . thus, the prettiest ladies attend these dances and are regaled with punch; and, if that fails to produce an effect, whiskey. You may be sure that we shall not be completely cheated.

Of all the officers, soldiers and civilians connected to Fort Pitt, only three did not have regular Indian mistresses. Neither Croghan nor Ecuyer were of these three. The Indian women, mainly Delawares or Senecas, for presents of bright cloth or powdered paints or mirrors, would service any man and quite often they brought along daughters as young as only eleven or twelve to do the same. There was not an ordained minister at the post at this time and Sunday prayers were led by one of the local traders, but they were of little conviction and not only frequently interrupted by drunken hiccoughs, but tempered by each man's knowledge of the fact that the man who was delivering them was living with Fort Pitt's most prominent prostitute. The doctor hired by Croghan to look after his Indian employees seduced and impregnated the daughter of the blacksmith and then fought a duel with an officer of the Royal Americans over his right to her.

An air of hollow gaiety overhung all activities. It was as if each person there suddenly felt that his life would soon be over and now was the time to throw inhibition to the winds and do things which heretofore had only been shadowy, shameful thoughts. A common, undiscussed knowledge was in every man; a knowledge that before long, perhaps very soon, all hell was going to break loose on the frontiers again and that if anyone at all was to blame, it was none other than the commander of all the English military forces in America, Lieutenant General Sir Jeffrey Amherst. Indicatively, of all the multitude of toasts drunk at Fort Pitt, there had never been one drunk to him.

Secure in the haven of his own quarters in New York, Amherst continued handing down directives which seemed to be deliberately calculated to offend and deprive the Indians. Croghan had pleaded with Amherst in letter after letter to alter his instructions for harsh economy, to ease up on the unbearable pressure he was placing on the Indians, to help alleviate the suffering being undergone by many of the tribes because they were being denied the very means of survival. Amherst continued deaf to all such pleas and Croghan became more and more convinced that the only sensible course for himself to follow was resignation of his office and a trip to London in an effort to get some measure of restitution for his personal financial losses in the handling of Indian affairs for the Crown.

And the prevailing impulse at Fort Pitt continued to be to eat, drink, and make merry . . .

[February 10, 1763—Thursday]

Peace!

With the scratching of pens on parchment in the city of Paris this day, the war between England and France, which was already being called the Seven Years' War, was ended. The Treaty of Paris was signed and enemies in Europe had now become friends. The terms of the treaty were both noteworthy and audacious, for France had bought her peace by giving up to England what she had never owned in the first place.

By the dictates of the treaty, France now ceded to Great Britain all her territories in North America to the east of the Mississippi River, with the exception—by special provision—of New Orleans and its suburbs, from whence she declared she would continue to govern her immense Louisiana Territory.

And so now by this act, England not only had possession of Canada and the territory to the north and west of the Ohio River—the Northwest Territory—but also what she felt was the rightful ownership of the land and control of the inhabitants of it.

But Paris is a long way from the valleys of the Ohio and Mississippi and St. Lawrence Rivers. Sxity-five thousand French residents of Canada, plus several thousand more in the Michigan, Indiana and Illinois countries still knew nothing of this declaration of peace. Nor did the conquerors in residence—the English—know of it.

Nor did the Indians whose land it was.

[March 16, 1763—Wednesday]

Ensign Robert Holmes, commander of Fort Miamis at the confluence of the St. Joseph and St. Marys Rivers, where these two substantial streams met to form the Maumee River, sat in his chair and tried hard to concentrate on the report he was writing to Major Gladwin at Detroit. Concentration was difficult at best and his eyes kept deserting the paper before him and swinging to the bed where the bare-breasted Miami Indian woman lay outstretched, her dark eyes locked on him and waiting patiently. Her only covering was a loincloth, and even as his eyes met hers, she smiled and untied the waist-cord knot, raised her hips slightly to free the material and then tossed the flimsy garment to the floor.

With herculean effort, Holmes turned his attention back to the report. Much as he wanted to put it off, he simply *had* to get this report written tonight to send off to Detroit with that damned war belt first thing in the morning. There might not be much to it, but then again it could be very important, perhaps even vital.

The last express from Gladwin had brought word that peace negotiations were in progress in Paris and that a cessation of arms had been called while the talks went on. The only problem here was that neither the French nor the Indians whom Holmes told about it in this area seemed inclined to believe it. The war belt was evidence of what they were thinking and feeling. Well, he would send it to Gladwin and that officer could be the judge of its importance. The major would probably talk it over with Captain Campbell and together they'd reach some conclusion and pass it on to the general.

A faint smile curled Holmes's lips as he thought of the general. What would that officer think if he could see Ensign Holmes now, writing an official report while not fifteen feet away an attractive, naked Indian woman lay waiting for him. He stifled a giggle. Amherst ought to know better than to order no friendly contact between his officers and the Indians. Men were only human, after all, and had fundamental hungers which had to be satisfied. Besides, rumor had it that even Major Gladwin had a little Chippewa filly to romp with, so why should Ensign Holmes be concerned?

Robert Holmes had first bedded with this Miami maid a couple of months ago. She was perhaps five or six years younger than he, which made her about eighteen, and the tanned coppery skin covered a body that was lithe and firm and showed no trace of the plumpness so common among many of the somewhat older women of her tribe. A rather striking angularity of facial features kept her from being truly beautiful, but she was indeed attractive and, as Holmes already knew well, extremely fulfilling. She had told him her name—Ouiske-lotha Nebi—but he was unable to pronounce it well and so he had simply called her by the first two syllables of it—Whiskey—and she seemed pleased with the nickname. During these weeks past she had virtually moved into his quarters, providing him not only a carnal release but also cooking meals for him and washing his clothing. In return, he provided her with food from the garrison's stores and even gave her occasional pouches of powder and lead. After all, the poor devils had to hunt, didn't they?

As Whiskey made a slight noise behind him, he turned and watched with admiration as she yawned and stretched luxuriously, then turned on her side facing him and smiled again. Holmes swallowed and blew out a deep breath, averted his gaze reluctantly and began writing again hurriedly.

In the letter he explained to Major Gladwin how he had heard from an Indian—he did not mention that it was Whiskey who had told him—that a war belt had arrived and was circulating in the Miami nation. He told how he had then summoned Chief Little Turtle, the one who called himself Michikiniqua, who had come to him early this morning and readily admitted the truth of the rumor. The chief went even further; from a pouch slung over one shoulder he extracted the long, broad war belt and gave it to Holmes, saying that he had received it the day before from a party of Shawnees. It was a belt, Michikiniqua had said, that directed him to gather his warriors together and wait for a prearranged signal, at which time they were to rise and strike down all the English. But Michikiniqua, having always been far more inclined toward the English than toward the French, did not care to do so.

"This belt," he told Holmes, pointing to one end of it, "says to me, 'The English seek to become masters of all and will put all Indians to death. Brothers, let us die together, since the design of the English is to destroy us. We are dead one way or the other.' This is what the belt says at its beginning, and it says much more."

For nearly two hours Holmes had questioned Michikiniqua, until he was sure he had all the information. Then he directed the Miami principal chief to bring all his lesser chiefs into council so that he could speak with them, and this Michikiniqua had done. All afternoon Holmes had spoken to them and listened to what they had to say in return. It had not been until early evening that the council had ended and the Miamis had gone their own way.

Holmes had returned to his own quarters and mechanically ate the meal Whiskey had prepared for him and then started this report. Now he finished it with a flourish and quickly reread what he had written, to be certain he had left nothing out. After explaining to Gladwin how he came to acquire the belt and information, the ensign reported on the meeting with the chiefs and concluded with a transcription, as nearly accurate as possible, of what Chief Michikiniqua had said to him at the close of the council. He wrote:

I made notes as it was given and the following is a reasonably accurate copy of the speech of Chief Little Turtle:

"My Brother, according to your desires and treaties with us I have consulted with our chief warriors in respect to this belt of wampum which you discovered to be in the village. We all think it best to deliver it to you so that you may send it to your general, though we were not to let this belt be known of till it arrived at Ouiatenon; and then we were to rise and put the English to death all about this place and those at the other places. This belt we received from the Shawnee Nation; they received it from the Delawares; and they from the Senecas, who are very much enraged against the English. As for the Indian who was the beginner of this, we cannot tell him, but he was one of their chiefs and one that is always doing mischief. And the Indian that brought it to this place was our Chief Michikiniqua, who was down at the council held in Pennsylvania last summer. We desire you to send this down to your general and George Croghan and let them find out the man who was making this mischief. For our parts, we will be still and take no more notice of their mischief; neither will we be concerned in it. If we had ever so much mind to kill the English, there is always some discovery made before we can accomplish our design. This is all we have to say,

only you must give our young warriors some paints, some powder and ball and some knives, as they are all going to war against our enemies, the Cherokees."

I think, to the best of my knowledge, this is the contents of what was said at the delivery of the belt now sent. This affair is very timely stopped, and I hope the news of a peace in prospect will put a stop to any further troubles with these Indians who are the principal ones of setting mischief afoot. I send you the belt with this packet, which I hope you will forward to the general.

I am, Sir, etc.,

> *Robert Holmes*
> *Ensign 1, B.R.A.R.*
> *Commanding at the Miamis*

True Copy and Endorsed of Indian Speech.

Satisfied, Holmes placed the folded belt of wampum atop the letter, ready for dispatch in the morning. He then lowered the lamp flame to a dim glow and turned toward the bed, swiftly stripping off his clothing as he went. By the time he reached Whiskey he was as bare as she and thoughts of Amherst or Gladwin or anyone else were suddenly very far away.

[April 4, 1763—Monday]

Henry Gladwin, ever since taking command of Detroit, had made it a practice to meet with all his officers once each month to discuss anything that required attention and, in general, to learn the views of his subordinate officers. But the meeting he had called for today was not one of those regularly scheduled affairs and a spark of uncommon interest was alight in the eyes of most of the young officers as they assembled.

Captain Campbell and Captain Joseph Hopkins entered together, conversing quietly between themselves, and they were followed by Lieutenants Jehu Hay and James MacDonald. Moments later a half-dozen more junior officers entered, with Lieutenant George McDougall in the lead. All took seats on the chairs provided and fell silent as they waited expectantly for the commander's opening remarks.

"Gentlemen," Gladwin began, "I have just received some reports which I would like to read to you and discuss. I would like to know your opinions in regard to their contents."

Gladwin raised a large black and red wampum belt from the desk and let it fall open. It was so long that although he held it near the middle over his head, both ends were still on the floor. He then bunched it together and placed it back on the desk and picked up a letter. It was the communiqué he had received, along with the belt, from Ensign Holmes at Fort Miamis. The assembled officers listened attentively as he read the letter, including Holmes's transcription of the speech made to him by Michikiniqua.

Without pause after he finished it, Gladwin put it down and picked up a second letter. "This one," he told them, "is from Lieutenant Jenkins, dated a week ago at Fort Ouiatenon, which I have just received. I read as follows:

Sir:

The bearer arrived from the post last Sunday, with two more deserters and his wife. They have not heard yet below of the cessation of arms, and I am acquainted by Monsieur La Bond that we have attacked or at least blocked up some place near the Mississippi; indeed, I don't well understand him, as he has an odd way of talking, but Captain Campbell will understand him better. Mr Hugh Crawford, the trader, acquainted me this morning that the Canadians that are here are eternally telling lies to the Indians, and tells me likewise that the interpreter and one La Pointe told the Indians a few days ago that we should all be prisoners in a short time [and he adds parenthetically here] (showing them when the corn was about a foot high) that there was a great army to come from the Mississippi; and that they were to have a great number of Indians with them, therefore advised them not to help us; that they would soon take Detroit and these small posts, and that then they would take Quebec, Montreal and all Canada and go on into our country. This, I am informed, they tell them from one end of the year to the other, with a great deal more that I cannot remember. I am convinced that while the French are permitted to trade here, that the Indians here never will be in our interest, for although our merchants sell them a stroud for three beaver, they will rather give six to a Frenchman. It is needless inquiring into the affair as the French had so much influence over them that they will deny what they said, for the other day I had the express before me saying we should all be fighting by and by; but could make nothing of it as the Indians were afraid to

*own it before him, although the Indians that heard them talk
of it stood to it. I am, Yours, et cetera.*

That, gentlemen, is the end of Mr. Jenkins's letter. Now I would like your feelings in the matter. Do you think there is an actual plot afoot, or do you think this is all just so much talk calculated to keep us on the defensive?"

Donald Campbell was first to reply. He raised his rotund figure from his chair and straightened his wig slightly. "It seems to me, sir," he began, "that it may be a little of both. Certainly there is no doubt that the stories being fed the Indians that an army is coming to help them are lies. Yet, it appears that the Indians are beginning to put some credence in it. Though they have been very quiet lately, I feel sure I've detected a fundamental change in the attitude toward us recently. I have noticed a distinct coolness in them and there's a possibility that, acting on this misinformation, they may indeed be planning some sort of mischief. I've heard from some of the French here that Pontiac has been holding numerous councils and is gaining in prestige, but no one seems to know—or will *admit* to knowing—what they have been about. The general feeling is that he's stirring up the tribes."

Campbell paused and seemed about to say more when Captain Hopkins indicated a desire to comment and Campbell yielded to him.

"I agree," Hopkins said to Campbell, then addressed himself to the major: "Sir, I've heard a lot of reports that the French inhabitants here at Detroit—*some* of them at any rate—are growing continually more bitter at having to pay taxes for our support. They are angered, apparently, that they should have to help support with increased taxes, a garrison much larger than their own king had maintained here, and they complain that the outlying posts are always sending for more supplies. Men such as Antoine Cuillerier are said to be actively stirring up a heated resentment against us among the Indians and promising them with every breath that King Louis is going to send them help. They've passed the word that the report you gave out, sir, on the cessation of arms while peace talks are progressing, is a lie to hold them in check until we are ready to destroy them. The Indians believe them, but they're angry and frightened. At the moment they are quiet, but if they *should* happen to rise against us, we'll be in great trouble. The new policies have kept the tribes desperately in want, and yet they see here at Detroit and the dependencies goods worth in value somewhere around half a million pounds sterling, and they are envious. If only we could provide them with the gifts they are accustomed to . . ."

Hopkins's voice dwindled away and he shook his head and sat down again, knowing it was unnecessary for him to finish.

"Unfortunately, Captain," Gladwin said, "our directives from the general are clear: we may not *give* the Indians anything. What they have need of, they can barter for with the traders, bargaining with the skins they have brought in. It is a policy we are required to uphold, regardless of our own personal feelings and whether or not we approve."

For over an hour they continued discussing the situation before finally breaking up. Gladwin returned at once to his own quarters and wrote a letter to Amherst, enclosing the Wampum belt and the letters from both Holmes and Jenkins. Pointing out that the sum total of Detroit's defenses were three cannon—two six-pounders and a three-pounder—and several small mortars, along with one hundred and twenty-two men and eight officers, their position here was none too strong if the Indians decided to rise against them. The forty English traders and their engagees now at Detroit might be of some help in such a case, but this was offset by the likelihood that many of the French would either do nothing to help the English, or might even actively aid the Indians. Nevertheless, mentally crossing his fingers and praying he was right, he concluded the letter by expressing the opinion formed from his staff meeting today: that there was a general sense of irritation among the Indians near the dependency forts but that the affair would probably blow over, and that in the neighborhood of Detroit the Indians were perfectly tranquil, as they had been for some months. The Indians, he added, apparently did not relish the idea of the war between England and France possibly coming to an end, but that if he could have seventy or eighty medals to bestow on their chiefs as rewards and distinctions, he was sure they would be mollified.

In less than half an hour after Gladwin finished his writing, the packet for Amherst was on its way east by express courier.

[April 27, 1763—Wednesday]

A sense of power such as he had never known before surged through Pontiac as he looked out over the great sea of faces before him, patiently awaiting his words which they had come so many miles to hear. Never before in the memory of any person present had so many Indians gathered at one spot to listen to the words of one man. Never before had one Indian had such influence among this many tribes as did Pontiac on this day and he was filled with an exultation and pride beyond anything previously experienced.

Seated on the ground before the little knoll upon which he stood were nine thousand warriors, representing at least two dozen tribes; and beyond them on both sides and at the rear were easily that many or more women and children. Perhaps eighteen or twenty thousand Indians were gathered here and with the morning sun not yet halfway to its zenith, they waited patiently to hear the words of the war chief of the Ottawas.

This was the fifteenth day of the Green Moon and many of those in attendance had been traveling for weeks to arrive here for what promised to be one of the most important Indian councils ever held on the continent. For days they had been arriving here and as far as the eye could see there were hastily erected clusters of quonsets and wegiwas, tepees and wickiups, longhouses and cabins and various other types of shelters, while the air roundabout was filled with the bluish-white haze of smoke from a thousand or more campfires and nine times that many pipes.

The site Pontiac had chosen for this council was well selected. At his back as he faced to the north was the broad expanse of the Ecorse River and, in front of him, the broad grassy valley which so handily accommodated such an assembly.[67] Less than a quarter mile up-stream the Ecorse River split into north and south branches, and about the same distance downstream the watercourse emptied into the swiftly moving Detroit River at the foot of a nearly mile-long treeless island.[68]

Most populous among the tribes on hand were the Chippewa, with about four thousand warriors, plus another thousand from the subtribe, the Mississaugi. The Delawares and Shawnees present from the Ohio country numbered six hundred and five hundred men respectively, while the Ouiatenons—also called the Eel River Miamis—had four hundred men here. The Miami and Potawatomi tribes were represented by three hundred and fifty men each and there were another three hundred each for the Hurons and Kickapoos, plus two hundred and fifty Piankeshaws. Another fifty men were on hand representing such tribes as the Seneca, Peoria, Fox, Muncee, Sac, Menominee, Mascouten, Sioux, Osage, Winnebago, Cahokia, Nipissing, Caughnawaga, Abnaki, Algonkin, and Kaskaskia.

The air quivered and thrummed with the muted sounds of ankle bells and rattling beads, pebble-filled gourds and shell horns, crude string instruments, small drums attached by rawhide thongs to the outer thighs, and smooth sticks of varying sizes tapped together to produce a wide range of tone. There was a pervading murmur of thousands of private conversations and soft laughter interspersed with raucous chatter from the squaws and children.

There were Frenchmen on hand, too—some of the most prominent Canadians from Detroit; men such as Antoine Cuillerier and his son Alexis and daughter Angelique, Mini Chene, Jacques Godefroy, two of the Campeau brothers, Baptiste and Chartoc, Pierre Cardinale, Thomas Gouin, and many others. They had been specifically invited here by Pontiac and had been escorted by a special squad of the war chief's men. They had all been shocked and more than just a little frightened by such an enormous gathering of Indians.

Incredibly, though Fort Detroit was less than six miles distant and inhabited by no less than one hundred and thirty men and officers, not one Englishman was here at the Ecorse River. As a matter of fact, not a single individual of Major Henry Gladwin's garrison even suspected that such an Indian council was convening here. Secrecy had been maintained in exemplary manner and now guards were stationed on the perimeters to intercept and hold or turn back any Englishman, whether soldier or trader, who might accidentally come this way.

Over an hour ago a half dozen or more elderly Indian men acting as heralds under the orders of Pontiac, had wound their way through the makeshift shelters of the sprawling encampments calling in loud voices every so often that it was time to assemble for the council. And assemble they had, until now all were on hand who were expected and Pontiac stood before them, visible to all on the steep little knoll beside the river.

The crescent-shaped pendant hanging from his nostrils glistened whitely against the darkness of his skin and the swirling lines of paint and tattoos which decorated him. The loops of white porcelain beads hanging from his ears clicked softly as he moved his head back and forth, studying the assemblage. Broad beaten-silver bands were around both his arms just above the elbows and, from a silver disk an inch in diameter which was attached to his right temple, three eagle feathers—one bleached white and two dyed red—hung down and over his right shoulder. He was naked except for a loincloth perhaps eight inches wide which hung to his knees in back and front, and a pair of soft doeskin moccasins upon his feet. Though not especially large in stature, he was nonetheless a commanding figure with a well-muscled body and stern, self-assured features. Around his neck and hanging down his sides so far that the two ends were on the ground was a broad belt of wampum, its black characters and symbols afloat in a field of deep red.

He raised both arms now and, as if by magic, a profound hush fell over the audience. His voice when he spoke was strong and far-carrying, audible clearly even to those farthest removed from him. Even as he spoke there came the murmur of many interpreters of the various tribes softly transposing the Ottawa tongue into that of their own people.

"Friends and brothers," Pontiac began, "it is the will of the Great Spirit that we should meet together this day. He orders all things and has given us a fine day for our council. He has taken His garment from before the sun and caused it to shine with brightness upon us. Our eyes are opened that we may clearly see; our ears are unstopped, that we may distinctly hear; our minds are open, that we may understand."

He paused and as the voices of the interpreters gradually died away after him, there came the rumble of a number of deep, guttural sounds of agreement and approval. When there was silence again, he continued:

"Friends and brothers, now do we know in our hearts what the great antlered moose feels when he is pulled down in the snow by wolves, and his body devoured even before he is dead. Now do we know this, because now we are that moose and the wolves are the white men in red suits who call themselves Englishmen. They have worried us and kept us from our sustenance until we are become weak, and even now they crouch with tightened muscles, ready to spring and throw us down and devour us while still we live. *It shall not be!*

"Brothers! These Englishmen are not as the French who are our friends. The Frenchmen wished to be our brothers, to live with us in peace, but not the English. No! The Frenchmen wished to do business with us and provide for us what we needed in exchange for what they wanted, but not the English. No! Yet now the French soldiers who protected us have been driven away and the English soldiers have taken their place and our lot grows unbearable. They take from us our land, our game, our forests, devouring them in great bites, always taking more than they can use and destroying that which is left; and when we request them to leave, they snap at us as will a mad dog snap at the hand of he who has nurtured and protected it. They deny us the means by which we survive. They are full of pride and they are constantly grasping for whatever they can reach, and there is no way by which we can obtain justice. Their highest general treats us with neglect and contempt, withholding from us those necessaries without which we grow weak, so that one day soon he may merely puff out his cheeks and blow us off the land. His officers in command of the posts on our lands abuse us, laugh at our misery, kick us away from them and call us names. When we come to their forts to council, we are made to state our business too quickly and then we are ordered away like little children whose minds are not complete and must be told what to do; and if we do not leave at once, we are struck by hard fists or the wooden ends of their guns until we run away for our own safety. Look at what they have done to us, my brothers. They have taken our game. They have taken our furs. They have taken our weapons. They have taken our pride and our self-respect. Still they reach out for more that they can take from us and only two things are left—our land and our lives—and now it is these they seek to grasp. They have swept away the French forever, so they think, *but such is not so!*"

He stopped and pulled the wampum belt away from around his neck and held it high over his head in outstretched hands, turning from side to side several times so that all who were present could see it.

"Friends and brothers," he shouted passionately, "*it is not so!* This belt I have only recently received from an emissary of the French King, in token that he has heard the voice of his red children. It says that he has been asleep for many seasons, but now he is no longer asleep and his great war canoes will soon come up the big river of the lakes from the eastern sea, and he will pluck Canada back out of the English hands, and he will lay against them a great punishment for their misdeeds against his red children while he slept. At this time the Indians and their French brothers will again fight side by side as they have always fought. We will then strike the English down as eight summers ago we struck down their strong army under the General Braddock on the Monongahela when, as many of you who were there remember, we watched them walk up to where we were hidden and then we shot them down like empty-headed pigeons who are too slow-witted to flee. So again we will destroy them!"

There was a prolonged roar of approval punctuated by shrill war cries as he paused and several minutes passed before it became silent enough for him to continue. In the interval he glanced at the Frenchmen in attendance who were obviously very nervous. Before the meeting had begun, one of his chiefs who had helped escort the Frenchmen here had come to him. He reported to Pontiac that many of the French feared that an uprising, if it came, would be directed against all white men, including themselves, and they wished reassurance that this was not so. Now the war chief of the Ottawas directed his gaze toward them.

"The French," he said loudly, "have always been our brothers, and it is not necessary for brothers to fear brothers. I wish no harm to come to my French brothers here or elsewhere in this land. As a proof that I do not desire it, just call to mind the war with the Foxes and the way I behaved as regards you seventeen summers ago. When the Chippewas and Ottawas of Michilimackinac and all the northern nations came with the Sacs and Foxes to destroy you, who was it that defended you? Was it not I and my men?

"When Mackinac, then great war chief of all these nations, said in his council that he would carry the head of your commander to his village and devour his heart and drink his blood, did I not take up your cause and go to his village and tell him that if he wanted to kill the French, he would have to begin first with me and my men? Did I not help you rid yourselves of them and drive them away? How does it come then, my brothers, that you would think me today ready to turn my weapons against you? No, my brothers, I am the same French Pontiac who helped you seventeen summers before."[69]

Pontiac at this time handed the war belt to one of his chiefs sitting nearby and directed his gaze once again over the huge audience. Now that he had stirred their anger and resentment, it was time to appeal to their religious beliefs and superstitions. Some months ago when he had visited a Delaware village he had listened to the words of an alleged prophet of that tribe who told of an encounter he had had with the Great Spirit. Not sure in his own mind whether or not he believed the story, Pontiac had nevertheless been greatly moved by the vocal picture the ancient Delaware had painted. Such a story, turned to his own devices, could be just what he needed to weld the Indian nations together under his leadership. Word had already spread through this assemblage of the vision Pontiac had claimed to have had last autumn. It had laid the groundwork for what was to come now. Ten days before this council convened, Pontiac had made a show of mysteriously striking out into the woods in a straight line, his movements trancelike. On the ninth day he reappeared and hinted broadly of the great meeting he had just concluded with the most powerful deity, the Master of Life. Rumor of this flashed to every ear as the Indians had assembled here. Now Pontiac meant to profit from the seeds he had planted.

The Indian audience was sitting with quiet attendance, waiting for him to continue, and so he did, his voice still carrying clearly but filled now with a new and stirring tonal quality. He told them of how he had heard the Delaware prophet—noticing the Delawares in attendance nodding in support—and how he had learned from the old man the secret of direct communication and confrontation with the Great Spirit. He told them that he had then returned here and set about achieving a similar meeting. He now raised both arms until every eye impaled him, every tongue was mute.

"Friends and brothers," he continued, "let your ears hear well what now I have to say to you. As that Delaware Indian had, so had I a great desire to learn wisdom from the Master of Life. In order to find Him that I might learn from Him, I did as the Delaware prophet advised and took to fasting and dreaming and the saying of magical songs. By these means it was revealed to me that if I would travel straight ahead in a course as true as the good arrow's flight, I would in time reach the lodge of the Great Spirit. I told my vision to no one, but set out on my straightforward journey, having first equipped myself with gun, powder horn, lead balls, and a kettle for preparing my food. For some time I journeyed on in high hope and confidence.

"Some of you here," he added, "have told me that you witnessed my leaving, but I saw no one and heard nothing as I departed this place. On the evening of the eighth day of my travel I stopped by the side of a brook at the edge of a meadow and there I began to prepare my evening meal. Suddenly looking up, I saw in the woods before me three large openings and three well-beaten paths entering them. I was much surprised and my wonder increased the more when even after darkness had fallen the three paths were more clearly visible than ever. Remembering the important object of my journey, I could neither rest nor sleep and so, leaving my fire, I crossed the meadow and entered the largest of the three openings. I had advanced but a short distance when a bright flame came out of the ground before me and I could go no farther. In great amazement I turned back and entered the second opening, and in a little while I encountered the same strange fire again and was forced to go back. Now, though afraid and puzzled, I yet resolved to persevere and I followed the last of the three paths into its opening. On this I journeyed a whole day without interruption and at last, emerging from the forest through which the path had been winding, I saw before me a great mountain of dazzling whiteness."

Pontiac paused to give the straining interpreters time to catch up. As they did so, a satisfied murmuring arose from the assemblage who had been listening intently to his story. There was absolutely no doubt that they believed implicitly every word he was speaking.

"So steep was the climb, my brothers," the Ottawa war chief continued, "that I thought it hopeless to be able to go farther and I looked about myself in despair. My eyes searched the woods and the meadow and then the mountain and in that moment they stopped on a beautiful woman all in white who was seated some distance above. She stood up as I looked upon her and said to me thus: 'How can you hope to succeed in your design when laden as you are? Go down to the foot of the mountain, throw away your gun, your ammunition, your provisions, and your clothing; wash yourself in the stream which flows there, and you will then be prepared to stand before the Master of Life.' I obeyed her and began to climb among the rocks, but it was very difficult and the woman, seeing me still discouraged, laughed at my faintness of heart and told me that if I wished for success, I must make my climb using only one hand and one foot. After great effort and suffering, I at last reached the summit, but the woman had disappeared and I was alone. A rich and beautiful plain lay before me and at a little distance I saw three great villages far superior to the homes of my own people. I walked to the largest and hesitated before it, wondering whether I should enter. A man superbly dressed stepped out, took me by the hand and welcomed me to the abode. He then conducted me into the presence of the Great Spirit and I was awed to silence at the unspeakable splendor about him. The Great Spirit told me to sit and spoke to me thus: 'I am the Maker of heaven and earth, the trees, lakes, rivers, and all things else. I am the Maker of mankind, and because I love you, you must do my will. The land on which you live I have made for you, and not for others. Why do you suffer the English men to dwell among you? Your people, my children, have forgotten the customs and traditions of your forefathers. Why do you not clothe yourself in skins as they did? Why do you not use the bows and arrows and the stone-tipped lances which they used? You have bought guns, knives, kettles and blankets from the white men until you can no longer do without them. What is worse, you have drunk the poison firewater which turns you into fools. Fling all these things away and live as your wise forefathers lived before you. Take to you no more than one wife and do no longer practice the use of magic, which is a way of worshipping the spirit of evil. And as for these English, these dogs dressed in red, who have come to rob you of your hunting grounds and drive away the game, you must lift the hatchet against them! Wipe them from the face of the earth and then you will win my favor back again, and once more be happy and prosperous. The children of your great father, the King of France, are not like the English. Never forget that they are your brothers. They are very dear to me, for they love the red men and understand the true manner of worshiping me. Go back now to your people, gather them together and those of other tribes and explain to them what I have explained to you. Direct them each tribe to rise as one in their own land and strike down the intruder of your lands who wears the red coat. Do not give him warning. Do not let him suspect. Catch him unawares and destroy him, and when you have done so, then you may discard his clothes and his weapons and his food and return again to the way of life that I directed for you in the beginning.' This," Pontiac added, "is what he said to me and then at once he was gone and the beautiful house and white mountain were gone and I was in the woods near here and returned to my village to tell my people what I had seen and felt and experienced and heard. I told them and now I have told you."

Abruptly his voice became harshly passionate again and his arms spread as if to encompass the whole of the assemblage. His body was shiny with perspiration and the flesh of his chest and thighs and upper arms quivered and trembled as if from a great chill and he appeared to be a man possessed.

"My brothers!" he shouted. "My friends! My children! Hear me now: we must now, from this time forward, cast out of us the anger for whatever ill has risen up between ourselves in the past. We must cast it away from us and we must let ourselves become one people whose common purpose it must be to drive from among us the English dogs who seek to destroy us and take our lands!"

There was a wild, shrill, thunderous roar of approval which grew in volume until the mind and ear were dazed by it; a fantastic, fierce, frightening, unforgettable sound which only gradually died away. Here was a man possessed of the Great Spirit. They could see it! Before their eyes the Great Spirit was using the voice of the war chief Pontiac to command them and a riotous blood-seeking fever swept through them. There was no need for Pontiac to ask them if they were with him. It was self-evident that they were. Fully five minutes elapsed before Pontiac found it quiet enough again to continue.

"Go now," he said to them. "Return to your homelands. Study the English in your lands and see how best to fall upon them and destroy them utterly before they can prepare to meet you. Deceive them! Let them accept you as friends and when the moment is right, strike them all in the same instant. Leave here at once, and when the word comes to you that Detroit has been struck by Pontiac, raise then your own war clubs to crush the English in your own land. You will not be alone. We are united to this cause and we will have coming to us the great army of men from our good father in France. Go!"

And go they did, swiftly and silently. In less than two hours' time, the only humans left in the great clearing on the north side of the Ecorse River were the Detroit Potawatomies and Hurons, along with a substantial number of Ottawas who clustered around their war chief, wanting to see and hear and touch this man who was the instrument of the Divine; this man who had received commands directly from the mouth of the Great Spirit!

A delegation of the chiefs of the Potawatomi and Huron factions came up to Pontiac now. These were the Hurons under Takee and only a few of those under Teata. The latter chief was disapproving of Pontiac's plan and he had kept himself and most of his people away from the council. But Takee, along with Washee of the Potawatomies, declared fealty to Pontiac in the strongest of terms and both chiefs asked what they could do.

Pontiac, greatly buoyed by the success of his oration, shook his head. "Say nothing to any Englishman of this. Return to your villages and remain quiet, except to prepare your weapons for war. After four more days have passed, I and some of my young men will go into the fort to dance the calumet and let Major Gladwin and his men think we are there only to entertain them. But as some of us dance, others will spread out inside the fort to determine the strength of the garrison—the number of men and rifles and cannons, the number of traders and stores, and the location of the goods we will need to take at once when the attack is begun. When we have learned what we need to learn, we will leave, and then I will summon another council of the tribes here and we will determine among ourselves the best method of attack."

[April 30, 1763—Saturday, Noon]

"Letter for you, Colonel."

The sergeant stepped through the doorway into George Croghan's quarters and handed the Indian agent an envelope, then added: "It's from Sir William."

Croghan took the letter and smiled at the sloppy salute the sergeant tossed off to him. It was with considerable amusement that he was allowing his friends and acquaintances to keep on addressing him with the lofty title they had recently begun using. Though in his own career with the military he had never been higher in rank than a captain of the militia, somehow almost everyone here at Fort Pitt had suddenly started calling him *Colonel* Croghan. He had been a bit taken aback by it at first and was on the point of asking that such a title not be used, as he was not of that rank. Before he could do so, however, the feisty little commander of the fort, Captain Simeon Ecuyer, had accosted him like an angry rooster. He abruptly accused Croghan of both initiating and promoting the fictitious title in an effort to undermine Ecuyer's own authority here and demanded that he have it stopped.

George Croghan had never been very appreciative of either accusations or demands and so he had merely smiled and settled back and said nothing at all. The captain was furious but there was really nothing he could do. Croghan suspected that the unearned title had been given to him because of his growing fame and seemingly endless and fascinating speculations in any number of fields—prospecting for silver or copper, trading with the Indians, acquiring vast tracts of wilderness land, and so on. Even his large and now very well appointed house a little way upstream on the Allegheny from the fort was being called Croghan Hall and though at first the Indian agent thought that both titles would soon die out, they hadn't. Several months had passed and it was evident that from now on he was going to be known as Colonel Croghan of Croghan Hall.

It *did* amuse him and, to be frank about it, there was precious little else to be amused over at Fort Pitt these days. Numerous prisoners of the Indians who were supposed to be given up this spring, in accordance with the terms of the Easton Treaty last year, had not been turned over to him. In fact, only five prisoners given up by the Shawnees had been released. There should have been fifty or sixty of them from both the Shawnees and the Delawares and the whole situation, as Croghan saw it, boded ill.

The trace of the smile still on his face disappeared as he opened the letter dated April 8 from Sir William Johnson. Among other things, his supervisor had written:

> *From all quarters on the frontier and from virtually all traders and most of his subordinate officers, his Excellency has received the pleas that his Indian policies be relaxed. From this place I have repeatedly sent pleas that the Indians be provided with what necessaries and ammunition as they are accustomed to receive. Unfortunately, Sir Jeffrey is inflexible in his decision. I agree with you that his policy is wrong, but it is not in my power to convince the General thereof.*

Growling deep in his throat, Croghan tossed the letter down on his desk. All he could hope now was that the letter he had sent to Amherst would succeed where all others had failed. Rumors were flashing across the frontier that in Paris the French were turning over all their North American real estate to England and, though no official word had been received on it, it was putting the Indians into an ugly mood. As he had written to Amherst:

> *By letters from Major Gladwin and Captain Campbell at Detroit, which I have received, I understand that the Indians in those parts seem uneasy in their minds, since they have heard talk of so much of North America being ceded to Great Britain. And the Indian Nations this way seem somewhat dissatisfied since they heard it, and say the French had no right to give away their country as, they say, they were never conquered by any nation; and I am of opinion the accounts of the peace and hearing so much of this country being given up to Great Britain has thrown them into confu-*

sion and prevented their bringing in all our prisoners this spring as they promised.

Now, as George Croghan turned to go out the door, he almost ran into the same sergeant who had given him the letter from William Johnson. The noncom grinned and held out another envelope.

"Sorry, Colonel," he said. "Here's another one for you that was under some others. It's from the gen'ral."

Croghan nodded and took it from him, cracking the heavy seal with his thumbnail as he tore it open. As he read the expression on his face changed and the sergeant's grin faded as he quietly backed away and then disappeared from view. Discussing the Indians, the general had written, in part:

Whatever idle notions they may entertain, in regard to the cessions made by the French Crown, can be of very little consequence . . . I regard fears of any supposed plots they might hatch as mere bugbears. So long as the military keeps its guard up, the Indians cannot cause any serious harm.

George Croghan sat down slowly in his desk chair and buried his head in his hands for a long while. At last he looked up, grasped his pen and, after dipping it into the inkpot, began writing boldly on a fresh sheet of paper:

> *From every generous, noble passion free,*
> *As proud and ignorant as man can be;*
> *Revengeful, avaricious, obstinate is he,*
> *Malicious, stupid, and obdurate will ever be;*
> *A fleeting consequence, he's dully grave . . .*
> *Rest here, my pen, enough—the man's a knave!*

[*April 30, 1763—Saturday, 3:00* P.M.]

When the word had spread that a pair of batteaux were in sight, heading this way, Alexander Henry immediately thought it was one of the trading parties he had sent out. He joined one of the newer traders here, John Tracy, and sauntered with him to the Fort Michilimackinac landing to await their arrival. He was surprised they were coming in so soon, since none of the fur-trade boats were expected until late May, perhaps not until June.

A sizable crowd of Indians, English and French had already gathered at the landing by the time he and Tracy arrived, but the two batteaux were still too distant to determine who they were. The two traders gravitated toward a group of four or five men off to one side and joined them. They were traders and their engagees and their expressions were sober as they listened to what Henry Bostwick was saying.

Bostwick was the only English trader who had been at Michilimackinac longer than Alexander Henry and, while he may not have been quite as energetic as Henry, he was nevertheless a good trader and had established himself well here. He did not do quite as much Indian business as Henry did, simply because he couldn't force himself to enjoy working or associating with Indians very much and adamantly refused to learn their language. He preferred catering to the needs of the English garrison and the French inhabitants.

Bostwick nodded a greeting at Henry and Tracy, but did not stop talking. "And the way I look at it," he continued, "there's trouble ahead. Bad trouble."

"I got to go along with you there," put in Ezekiel Solomon, the Jewish trader. "They's a smell in the air I don't like."

"They ain't a whole hell of a lot t'be done about it, though," added Stanley Goddard. Except for Alexander Henry, he was the youngest of the English traders at this place.

"What trouble?" Henry asked. "What's the matter?"

Bostwick shook his head. "Don't really know for sure. Nothing you can really put your finger on, but there's something in the wind. The Indians are acting queerly, 'specially the Chippewas. I don't know, I ain't dealt with 'em enough to read 'em right yet, but it seems to me they're gettin' hostile toward us. You're pretty close to 'em, Alex. What do you think?"

Henry gave a deprecating grunt. "Not that close. I don't know. I guess I have detected sort of a cooling off between them and us, but I don't know that it amounts to much. There's always those we haven't been able to get along with. Look at the trouble I've had with Owl, for example. I think he'd slit my throat if he had half the chance. But he's an exception. As for the rest, I just don't know. I think probably they're still mad about the fact that we can't sell 'em lead and gunpowder. They're really hurting for it."

"Wouldn't surprise me none," Solomon interjected, "if they took a notion to explode on us one of these days an' just help themselves from our stock."

"Oh, I doubt it, Zeke," Henry said quickly. "It wouldn't be worth the risk to them. At least not with Captain Etherington and his men here to hold the lid on; and Etherington says they wouldn't dare to make trouble. Wait a minute, here comes Jamet. Let's see what he has to say about it."

Lieutenant John Jamet, leaning heavily on a makeshift cane, was moving slowly toward the group and the traders began walking toward him. Henry smiled as he saw how well Jamet was doing. After the fire at the Sault he hadn't thought the young officer had much of a chance to survive. But the care and Indian remedies administered by Cadotte's Chippewa wife had worked wonders. By January 20 he was well enough to travel slowly and so he and Henry and Cadotte, along with four or five Indians, had strapped on snowshoes and set out southward along the shoreline in an effort to reach Fort Michilimackinac. It was slow going; much slower then they'd anticipated. Jamet's legs and feet were in such bad shape that they were quickly chafed raw. They had expected to reach the fort in four or five days but as it turned out, they had only reached Pointe de Détour—approximately the halfway mark—after a full week had passed and by then their provisions were nearly exhausted. Worse yet, there was still open water toward the center of the Straits of Mackinac and, without a boat of any kind, there would be no way to cross over to the fort until the remainder of the water froze solidly.

There was nothing to do but camp there and send the Indians back to the Sault at once for more supplies. Henry had carefully rationed what they had remaining into three parts—for Jamet, Cadotte, and himself—and they settled down to wait. Four bitterly cold days later, with the provisions all but gone, the swiftly traveling Indians had returned with more. By now a coating of ice had formed on the previously open surface of the Straits, but it was still too thin to trust, so once more they had started toward the fort on land, and again Jamet's condition slowed them dangerously. Soon the supplies were nearly gone again. That was when they made the decision to camp where they were and wait, Cadotte taking care of Jamet, while Henry struck out alone for the fort to get help. He left them at daybreak and traveled swiftly until opposite the fort and then, gritting his teeth, took the chance and crossed the new ice. It held beneath him and he reached Fort Michilimackinac and reported to Captain Etherington late that afternoon. An earlier rescue party sent out by Etherington had been forced back, but now another was readied and set out the following morning with a sleigh.

On the second day after that, the party brought Jamet and Cadotte in safely.

Since then Jamet had been recuperating, but he was still far from well. Not only had the fire damaged his legs badly, but his feet had been severely frostbitten on the trip here. Henry was surprised Jamet could even stand, much less walk with the aid of a cane.

The traders gathered around the lieutenant and repeated much of what they had been discussing, asking his opinion. Jamet pursed his lips and then shook his head.

"I don't know," he said. "You men have certainly been having closer contact with the Indians than I. However, I do know that Captain Etherington has received a couple of warnings from French inhabitants that there's some sort of trouble brewing, but he doesn't believe it. I rather suspect he's right. Whose boats are coming?"

The group turned their attention to the advancing batteaux and now they were close enough to see that these were not the boats belonging to Henry or any of the other traders. Moving slowly down to the waterfront with Jamet, they were there when the two large open boats dropped sail and scraped to a stop on the rocky shore.

It was Sergeant Patrick Shaw with a detachment of nineteen soldiers and a woman. He had been dispatched from Detroit on April 17 by Major Gladwin with supplies for the fort here at the Straits. Now, while his men were unloading the boats and carrying the goods into the fort, the traders and Lieutenant Jamet questioned Shaw. The sergeant grinned, delighted at the attention he was getting, and answered the questions as rapidly as they were asked. Yes, he had a packet of mail and dispatches from Detroit and the east, but so far as he knew it was all routine matter. No, the Indians were very quiet at Detroit. No, there hadn't been any hostilities at all, though a couple of messengers were overdue in arriving. No, the general had not yet relaxed any of the trading restrictions. Yes, Sir Robert Davers was still at Detroit, but was planning to go on a sounding tour of Lake St. Clair with a party Major Gladwin was going to send out to determine whether or not a schooner could negotiate the river connecting Lake Huron to Lake St. Clair. Yes, Sir Robert was planning to come back to Michilimackinac again after that. No, there were not any new promotions to announce.

On and on the questions went as they walked back to the fort. When finally they had reached the parade square inside,

Alexander Henry nodded to Jamet and started back to his own store. The voice of the lieutenant followed him.

"From the looks of it, Alex, I'd say there was nothing to worry about. These Indians can't keep a secret. If they were planning something, you can be sure we'd know all about it far in advance."

But Alexander Henry was not as convinced of this as Lieutenant Jamet seemed to be. He decided he'd keep eyes and ears open. Something just didn't *feel* right.

[*May 1, 1763—Sunday*]

The churning excitement within Pontiac's breast was not reflected in the least degree in his expression or actions. Behind him as he approached the west gate of the fort at Detroit were strung out forty of his warriors, including Macatepilesis, second war chief to himself over the southern Ottawas. All of the men had been given their instructions before crossing the river and now they acted their roles perfectly.

The warriors laughed and joked among themselves, sometimes leaping and prancing about to the merriment of the others as they moved along. Most of them were bare-chested. Some wore buckskin leggings, while others had on only a loincloth. They were not painted, and so their tattoos—circles and lines, diagonals and spirals and odd faces etched on arms and legs, back and chest and buttocks—stood out in marked contrast against their coppery skin in the bright midafternoon sunlight. Pontiac and Macatepilesis and several of the minor chiefs had skinning knives in their waistbands, but this was not abnormal. Most of the men were without weapons and each carried a tobacco pouch and the red calumet clay pipe.

From ahead of them a sentry sang out loudly, "Indians approaching the west gate, sir!" and in a moment a small squad of soldiers and a Frenchman had positioned themselves at the gate to bar entry until instructions were received. Pontiac did not slow his pace, but moved directly to the men and addressed himself to the Frenchman.

"We have come," Pontiac said agreeably, "as is our custom each spring, to smoke and dance the calumet before your chief to reaffirm to him our friendship for the English."

Pierre LaButte, head interpreter for Detroit, nodded and told them to wait, that he would inform the major. A few minutes later at the east end of the Rue St. Louis, LaButte knocked at the door of the house of the commanding officer.

It was opened by Captain Campbell, who was joined in a moment by Major Gladwin and Sir Robert Davers.

"What is it, LaButte?" Gladwin asked.

"The Ottawas, Major. They've come to the west gate, led by Pontiac. They've asked to be allowed to come in to smoke and dance the calumet for you. There are about forty or fifty of them."

Gladwin frowned and glanced at Campbell. The captain nodded. "Usual custom, sir," he told the major. "Each spring they come to smoke and dance in front of the house here to attest their continuing friendship for us."

Gladwin shook his head. "Not this year. We still don't know what went on at that big council on the Ecorse last Wednesday, I don't like it. Tell them to leave."

LaButte was shocked and protested at once. "Sir, you mustn't! Excuse me, sir, but they would take it as a great insult if you turned them away when they've come to honor you like this. They're not armed. All they have with them are their pipes."

Campbell backed him up. "I believe he's right, Major. They'd be sure to take offense if we turned them away now. Might cause some serious problems."

Gladwin hesitated and then gave in. "All right, lead them in, LaButte, and let them get it over with. Captain, pass the word for the guard to remain alert. Sir Robert, you may find this interesting."

By the time LaButte and Campbell returned to the gate, a sizable crowd of people had gathered—French inhabitants, men, women and children, from both inside and outside the fort, those soldiers who were not on guard duty, many of the traders, and a fair number of English women and children who were dependents of the soldiers. The captain nodded to the sentries, who backed out of the way respectfully, and then greeted Pontiac, shaking hands and expressing his pleasure at seeing him again. Pontiac responded in kind and then allowed Campbell to lead him and his warriors and chiefs—followed by a mass of onlookers—along the Rue St. Jacques to the east end of the street where they turned to the right in front of Ste. Anne's Church and proceeded to the commander's house. There were now so many people in the streets that no one paid particular attention as one by one Macatepilesis and nine other Ottawas lagged back and then disappeared among the buildings inside the fort.

Major Henry Gladwin and Sir Robert Davers were seated in chairs on the front porch of the major's house. Davers seemed most interested, but Gladwin watched without expression as they approached. When the group stopped before his house, he nodded once. Pontiac detached himself and came forward and Gladwin stood and moved to meet him. The two men shook hands and, with LaButte doing the interpreting, exchanged greetings. Pontiac presented Gladwin with a pipe and then raised his hand as a signal for the dancing to begin. A long wooden stake was pounded into the ground in the middle of the Rue St. Louis and, while the majority of the Indians followed Pontiac's lead and just sat and smoked, a handful of warriors pranced and leaped and whirled around the post, chanting phrases unintelligible to the English.

For nearly an hour the dancing and smoking continued and the crowd watched with interest. At intervals the ten Indians who had separated themselves from Pontiac's party quietly and unobtrusively came back one by one to take their places with the seated smokers. Finally Pontiac stood and the dancing ceased. He stepped to within five feet of Major Gladwin and in a loud voice spoke rapidly and at some length. When he paused, La Butte interpreted for the commander.

"He says, Major, that the Ottawas wish you to know that they are your friends now and will ever more be so, as long as the grass shall grow and the rivers run. He thanks you for whatever favors you have done him and his people in the past. He apologizes that this calumet dance party is so small, but says that many of his nation are still at their winter hunting, though he expects them to return in a few days from now. He says when they do so, then he and they will return here to pay a formal visit to the English commander. He asks that now, as a token of your friendship for him, that his party here be provided with a little bread, tobacco, and rum."

"Tell him," Gladwin replied, smiling slightly, "that we are honored by his visit and appreciate the expression of his friendship for the English. Tell him that whatever friendship he holds for us is returned by us in like measure to him and his people. Tell him we look forward to the formal visit he intends honoring us with soon. Tell him that bread and tobacco will be distributed, but that the general does not permit the Indians to have rum, and that instead they may have beer to drink."

As LaButte translated for Pontiac, Gladwin ordered the bread, tobacco and beer brought and distributed. The Indians accepted the portions gravely and in a short while, Pontiac again having shaken the hands of both Campbell and Gladwin, the party filed back out of the fort. They proceeded casually back to where their canoes were beached, took their places in them and then paddled across the river, angling upstream toward Pontiac's village.

Not until he reentered his own town did the set expression on the Ottawa war chief's face change. The lips spread in a satisfied smile and the dark eyes took on a gleam. He ordered Macatepilesis and the other nine Ottawas who had disappeared within the fort to report to him and they did so, each man contributing his portion of keen observations. The ten had spied thoroughly, observing where the cannon and mortars were placed, noting how the guard was mounted on ramparts and in bastions, describing in detail where the various traders' stores were located and, as near as could be determined, what was in each, and noting in particular that the fort's powder magazine, its door locked and guarded by a sentry, was the first building to the north of Ste. Anne's Church, making it the last building to the east on the south side of the Rue St. Joseph.

The fort was not especially strong, it seemed. Though the wooden stockade was subject to fire, this danger had been considerably reduced when the French were in occupancy here by banking earth several feet high against the inside of the cedar picket walls. There were three bastions, one each on the corners closest to the river and one in the center of the north wall. There were also a couple of blockhouses apart from the fort to the north perhaps one hundred and fifty yards. As luck would have it, though, there was only one cannon—a three-pounder—mounted in the north bastion. The two six-pounders were on the parade ground and therefore useless until moved. The twin-masted schooner *Huron* had six guns and was anchored at the upper end of the fort, while the slightly larger eighty-ton sloop *Michigan* was anchored at the lower end, a little farther out in the river. As for soldiers, the garrison strength was not more than one hundred and twenty men, plus perhaps twenty or thirty traders presently on hand. Best of all, some Frenchmen had volunteered the information that supplies in the fort were very short. The first spring shipment had not yet come from Fort Niagara and there was within Detroit provision enough for only about two weeks.

By the time the conference was over, Pontiac had a remarkably good mental picture of the interior of Detroit, its strengths and weaknesses. In the gathering darkness of the evening, Pontiac sent out two parties of five men each, one under Chief Macatepilesis and the other under Chief Mehemah; the former to carry a summary of the day's activities and intelligence to Chief Washee in the Potawatomi village a mile or so downstream from the fort on the northwest bank of the river, the latter to carry the same news to Chief Takee's Huron village just slightly upstream across the river from Washee's village.

"In addition to telling them what you have told me, and about what we did within the fort," Pontiac instructed the two chiefs, "tell them that we will all meet for secret council at Washee's village when the sun is straight up on the fourth day from now. Tell them to send away all squaws and children and to let no one near who might betray us. At that time we will set the date and time of our attack on Detroit and discuss the best way that place can be taken."

And the smile on Pontiac's face broadened as the two parties turned away and were quickly swallowed up in the deepening dusk.

[May 2, 1763—Monday, 9:00 A.M.]

"Sir," the young soldier stood at the door he had just opened, and saluted. "There's a man here to see you. A Frenchman, sir."

Captain George Etherington looked up from the letter he was writing and then lay his pen aside. "Who is it, Private?"

"Said his name is Ducharme, sir. Laurent Ducharme."

Etherington nodded, hoping this was not another wide-eyed gossip with a warning for him. There had been several already and he had had his fill of them. The private stepped back and showed the visitor in. He was a lean man, though not tall, who bobbed his head in a birdlike manner in greeting and then looked all around the room nervously. Etherington stood and motioned the man to a chair before the desk. He glanced at the soldier.

"Private, close the door behind you when you leave." His gaze moved to the Frenchman as the soldier departed and he added, "Sit down, Monsieur Ducharme. You wish to tell me something?"

The visitor perched on the edge of the seat and, though he seemed relieved when the door was closed and he was alone with the commander of Fort Michilimackinac, there was still an abundant nervousness about him. He licked his lips and coughed lightly. Etherington said nothing more and when the man finally spoke, his voice was hardly above a whisper.

"Captain, you are in danger here. Very great danger."

Etherington's brows pinched. "Tell me about it," he said flatly.

Laurent Ducharme coughed again, wiped his mouth on his sleeve and then said rapidly, "I have been in the woods for a long time. I have seen many Indians. I stayed with many and talked with them. There is a plan being made now to absolutely destroy you and your garrison and all of the English in this country. You cannot hope to stand against them. For the sake of your life and the lives of your men you ought to prepare to leave this place now. You ought—"

As Ducharme had spoken, the frown grew deeper on Etherington's face and now the officer slammed his hand down on the desk with a crash, interrupting him. "By God, sir," the captain said, rising, "I've had just about enough of you people running around with tales like that. What do you expect to accomplish by spreading such lies? Do you think we'll get frightened and desert the fort so you can walk in and take over again?"

Etherington's voice had risen angrily and now Ducharme looked even smaller than he seemed before as he sat on the edge of his chair. He opened his mouth to say something, but Etherington cut him off with a slashing movement of his hand.

"Ducharme, that story has no foundation in fact. You're not even the first to tell it. You're one of these men around here so ill-disposed to the English that you'll do anything to cause us mischief. Don't say one more word to me. Not one! I'm tired of hearing such lies. Now get out!"

Ducharme slid from the chair and walked swiftly toward the door, but Etherington's voice halted him just as he began opening it.

"Ducharme! Don't let me hear that you've been spreading that story around among the garrison or the other French inhabitants here. But here's a message you *can* carry along with you and spread. The next one of you people who comes to me with that kind of a story will be put into irons and sent down to Detroit. Is that clear?"

The Frenchman bobbed his head and almost ran out, quickly closing the door behind him. George Etherington grunted and sat down, shaking his head. That was what he should have done a long time ago. Maybe now these stupid senseless rumors would cease.

It had been a long, rather tedious winter and Sir Robert Davers could not have been happier than he was to get away from Detroit for a while. When Captain Campbell had told him of Major Gladwin's decision to send a large batteau up into Lake St. Clair and the connecting river to Lake Huron, Davers had instantly requested permission of Gladwin to accompany the expedition, and Gladwin had agreed.

The purpose of the voyage was to make soundings of the bottom and determine whether or not the schooner *Huron*, which lay anchored at the fort, could safely negotiate both the small lake and the river above it. The ship drew seven feet of water and if it could be determined that the channels on the connecting waterways were deep enough and wide enough, further supplies for Fort Michilimackinac could be sent by schooner from Detroit rather than by batteaux, thereby saving much time, effort and manpower.

Both Captain Campbell and Major Gladwin had walked down to the water gate of the fort this morning to give final instructions and see the party off. The batteau they were taking was a good-sized craft, with ample room for the dozen men aboard and their supplies. They did not anticipate being gone from Detroit for more than a couple of weeks.

The boat's party, under command of Lieutenant Charles Robertson, consisted of six soldiers, a young trader named John Rutherford, who was the nephew of Detroit trader James Sterling's partner, Samuel Rutherford, a Pawnee slave of Rutherford's from the far west, two sailors, Sir Robert Davers and, of course, the expedition's commander.

Davers shook hands warmly with Gladwin and Campbell and then climbed eagerly into the boat and took a position standing up in the bow, holding the fine new rifle given to him recently by James Sterling. His eyes flashed with excitement and he leaned forward, as if in so doing he could help push the boat along faster.

The lines were slipped and the rowers bent to their task. Within mere minutes the batteau had moved out into midstream on the Detroit River and was already dwindling in size to the eyes of the two officers watching the departure. Davers could still be seen standing in the bow and leaning forward and Gladwin chuckled and shook his head.

"By God," he said, "I swear I don't believe I ever encountered anyone anywhere who enjoys life as much as Sir Robert does."

Both the commander and Captain Campbell were still laughing when they reentered the fort and the water gate closed behind them.

[*May 5, 1763—Thursday*]

Though the sun was at its highest point, the windowless interior of the council longhouse at the Potawatomi village just downstream from Detroit was dim and gloomy. A sense of tension permeated the atmosphere within and though nearly twelve hundred Chippewas, Hurons, Ottawas and Potawatomies were gathered here, there was scarcely a sound from among them.

The village itself was practically empty of life, since all the women and children had been sent away into the woods at the order of Pontiac. A cordon of young warriors had been stationed at intervals around the entire town to intercept anyone who might approach and perhaps interrupt the important council ready to begin.

Over one hundred chiefs were present inside the longhouse and the most important among them, besides Pontiac himself and Macatepilesis, his second, were Chief Washee of the Potawatomies, Chiefs Wasson and Perwash of the Chippewas, and Chief Takee of the Hurons. Pontiac wasted no time in getting to the point of this council.

"My brothers," he began, "we have come now to the most important moment. The time has come now when I must know where you stand and whether or not you will support your brothers in the work that is ahead of them. I will speak to you, and then you will give me your answers.

"It is important, my brothers, that we should exterminate from this land these English, whose only object is our death. You all know, even as I know, that we can no longer fulfill our wants in the way we were accustoned to do with our fathers, the French. The English sell us their goods at double the price that the French made us pay, and yet their merchandise is good for nothing, for no sooner have we bought a blanket or other thing to cover us than it becomes necessary to procure others against the time of departing for our wintering ground. Neither will they let us have them on credit, as our brothers the French used to do. When I visit the English chief and inform him of the death of any of our comrades, instead of lamenting as our brothers the French used to do, they make game of us. If I ask him for anything for our sick, he refuses and tells us that he does not want us, from which it is apparent he seeks our death. We must therefore, in return, destroy these Englishmen without delay."

At this there was a guttural drone of approval from his listeners and when at length it had quieted down a little, Pontiac continued:

"There is nothing to prevent us. There are but few of them and we shall easily overcome them. Why should we not attack them? Are we not men? Have I not shown you the belts I received from our great father, the King of France? *He* tells us to strike! Why should we not listen to his words? What do you fear? The time has arrived. It is here! It is now!"

The response now was more tumultuous, with shrieks rising in the throats of the listeners, hands clapping together and feet thudding on the earthen floor. It was two or three minutes before the outcry dwindled enough for Pontiac to go on.

"Do you fear that our brothers the French, who are yet among us, will hinder us? Hear me now: they are not yet acquainted with our final designs and if they *did* know them, could they prevent them? You know as well as myself that when the English came upon our lands to drive from them our father, Belêtre, they took from the French who remained here all the guns they had, so that now they have no guns to defend themselves with. Therefore, *now is the time: let us strike!* Should there be any French to take their part, let us strike them as we do the English. Remember what the Giver of Life desired our brother the Delaware to do; this regards us as much as it does them. Hear me now: I have already sent belts and speeches to our friends the Chippewas of Saginaw and Michilimackinac, and the Ottawas, our brothers, of L'Arbre Croche, and to the children of the Chippewas, the Mississaugi of the valley of the *Rivière à la Tranch*,[70] inviting them to join us and I have been told they will not delay. Everywhere the tomahawk is raised and ready to fall as soon as ours falls here. Therefore, let us strike! There is no longer any time to lose, and when the English shall be defeated, we will stop up the way so that no more of them shall ever return again upon our lands. *We must destroy them now!*"

A wild, raucous shrieking burst from the throats of his listeners and everywhere in the assemblage the chiefs leaped to their feet brandishing tomahawks and they slashed and struck the air with them at an imaginary English foe.

It was a declaration of war.

One by one then, the chiefs pledged their tribes not only to join in the war against the English as proposed by Pontiac, but to accept him as the principal leader of all the Indians, irrespective of tribe. They clamored to know what they should do and when, and Pontiac was not hesitant in telling them.

"Three days ago," he said, after a semblance of order had been restored, "a boat filled with English left the fort and went into the little lake above. There they are measuring waters so that they can know how to send great ships against us. They are in the country of the Chippewas and I now give it to Chief Perwash of that tribe to see to them at once, that what they have learned does not come to the ears of their chief, Gladwin.

"Two days ago I received messages that Chief Takee and his Huron chiefs met at Sandusky with their brother Wyandots, and those of that tribe under the leadership of Chief Odinghquanooron are with us. Also there were many of the Shawnees and Delawares, who are all in full agreement with us and who have received a present of three barrels of gunpowder from the French in the Illinois, with the encouragement that they use it to go against the fort called Pitt at the head of the *Spay-lay-wi-theepi*—the Ohio River—and if they should not be able to take it by treachery, they shall pass it by and go instead against the English people who have disobeyed treaty lines and have moved into Indian lands where they are now sinking roots and building their cabins made from tree trunks.

"Now," he continued, pointing to the Potawatomies in attendance, "I say to you, Chief Washee, to take your men to the west of here to the place of the English called Fort St. Joseph and when you hear that we have struck here, do you the same there."

His pointing finger swung to the Hurons. "And to you, Chief Takee, I say the same: go to Sandusky, but leave some messengers to run after you, and when they bring you word of our strike here, you will join with Chief Odinghquanooron and strike Fort Sandusky at once. I am assured that Chief Minivavana and Chief Mackinac will likewise lead the northern Chippewas and Ottawas against the fort at Michilimackinac, and so it will go at all the other forts of the English which are in our country.

"As for us here, we will strike Detroit the second day from now. With sixty strong warriors, I will go into the fort of Detroit to talk, as their chief Gladwin supposes, of peace. Some of our women will go in first, with guns cut short and hidden beneath the blankets they wear. While counciling is being done, others of our warriors will enter and spread themselves out into good places inside the fort. And when, during that council, I lift my voice in the death cry, then will each warrior strike on that instant the Englishman closest to him and then all others he can reach and destroy. Take care that no French are struck by mistake, for they are still our brothers and, even though without weapons, they are with us and will help us."

On and on the refinement of details in this war planning went on. Not until late in the afternoon did the council end and the Indians separate to go to their proper locations. For his own part, Pontiac and a number of the other chiefs went at once to the house of Antoine Cuillerier and talked long into the night with him and other such Frenchmen as Jacques Godefroy, Chartoc Campeau, and Elleopolle "Mini" Chene. The interpreter, Pierre LaButte, was there, as was the French trader of such influence, Jacques Duperon Baby.

It was obvious that Pontiac had gone over much of this before with Cuillerier. The Ottawa and the Frenchman had had numerous meetings in this house in the past days and weeks. Certainly he was the only Frenchman on hand who was not startled by the news of the planned attack so soon. Even his son and daughter, Alexis and Angelique, gasped aloud when they heard what was planned. Jacques Duperon Baby turned absolutely ashen and no word of support for Pontiac left his lips, but his lack of enthusiasm was lost in the abundance of it from others on hand. No Frenchman on hand gave a disapproving word on the plan and most of them promised they would help Pontiac all they could, while at the same time pretending to remain neutral.

"It is enough," Pontiac said, well satisfied. "The time for you to rise actively beside me will come when your King sends his army here as he has promised. In the meanwhile, we will strike and take Detroit, and when it has been taken," he placed his hand on the shoulder of Antoine Cuillerier, "then my friend, will you take command of Detroit and hold it until such officer will come who is sent by your great King?"

"I will do it," Cuillerier agreed, nodding. "I know it will come to pass as you have said. There is but one thing I would ask: that the life of Captain Campbell be spared. He always treated us and you well, understood us and sympathized with us. He is a good man and I would not want to see him slain."

Pontiac shrugged. "Who is to say who may be killed or who may be saved when battle is undertaken? This I will say: he will not fall by my hand if I see him to know him. That is all I can say."

[*May 6, 1763—Friday, 3:00* A.M.].

François Clairmont was one of five Frenchmen in the little camp who jerked erect out of his sleep at the loud halloo which came from the darkness around them. Instinctively as he sat up he felt for the knife at his belt and then joined the other four men of his camp who were getting to their feet. They were all from Detroit, these five, looking for good timber for boats. They had camped in this spot last night, not far from where the Huron River[71] empties Lake Huron into Lake St. Clair.

Now, as the Frenchmen stood nervously by the glowing remains of the campfire, a party of twenty-five or thirty Chippewas came into view out of the darkness from the west, their right hands held palm forward in the sign of peace. Clairmont recognized the leader, a chief named Perwash.

Baptiste Campeau, leader of this French party, moved forward to greet the chief and shook his hand. As the warriors squatted in a wide ring around them, the five Frenchmen crouched near the hastily rebuilt fire and listened while Perwash spoke. He told them of the plan that had been laid to take Detroit by treachery during a formal council and said further that he had been sent by Pontiac with a belt to invite all Indians encountered to fall upon the English wherever they found them. Especially was it his mission to find and destroy a party of boatmen sent out by Major Gladwin four days ago. These men would soon be moving upstream on the Huron River and it was there that Perwash intended to surprise and take them.

Clairmont was shocked. He had heard talk of an uprising forming, but such rumors had floated about periodically for years. Now, apparently, it was becoming reality and he felt sickened. He glanced at the other members of his party. Henri Massac, like himself, seemed stunned. Baptiste Campeau and Henri Dunoir were grinning, obviously pleased by the news. Charles Dusette was suddenly eager and he gripped the Indian's arm.

"Chief Perwash," he said, "I'll go with you. *Sacré bleu!*

There is nothing I would like more," and he drew his knife from his waistband, "than to stick this into the throat of an Englishman!"

Perwash grunted his approval for Dusette to join him and the men continued talking with the chief in low tones. Massac and Clairmont got up and drifted off to one side until their voices could not be heard by the others.

"My God, Henri," Clairmont whispered hoarsely, "it'll be slaughter. We've got to do something, warn somebody."

"No!" Massac whispered back. "No! Don't talk like that. They'd kill us if they thought we'd do that. Leave it alone! I want nothing to do with it, nothing! I am going into the woods. I do not want to hear what is being said, François. I am afraid."

He jerked his arm from Clairmont's grasp and faded into the predawn darkness. Clairmont swallowed and drifted back toward the fire where Campeau, Dusette and Dunoir were still talking with Perwash. Though he wanted to hear no more about it, he was powerless to move out of hearing and so he listened and his mouth became dry and his stomach rolled as he heard what they were going to do at the fort and with the boat party.

Not until Perwash and his warriors—Charles Dusette with them—silently padded away to the northeast in the first light of dawn did Massac return to the camp. When Clairmont went to him and began to tell him what had been said, Massac shook his head and drew away.

"No!" he said. "I told you before, do not tell me. Even though I do not like the English, I do not want to hear such things. What happens to them is not my concern. Leave me alone!"

Clairmont went back to his blanket and lay down, rolling himself in it. He was very still and it seemed he had gone back to sleep.

But François Clairmont was very much awake.

[*May 6, 1763—Friday, 8:00* A.M.]

"Look, Lieutenant," said Sir Robert Davers, pointing toward the shore.

Charles Robertson looked in that direction and saw four men beside a small fire, apparently eating. He motioned to the rowers to put in and the boat angled toward shore at once. Davers was first to alight when it scraped ashore and he greeted the Frenchmen cheerfully. Their leader, who introduced himself as Baptiste Campeau, brother of Chartoc and Matthieu, greeted them affably enough and invited them to have something to eat. The other three men with them were peculiarly quiet.

The boat crew had spent the night on an island some miles away and had embarked again at first light to continue the sounding they had been engaged in ever since leaving Detroit. Thus far they had found the water to be plenty deep enough for the schooner, but the river ahead, connecting Lake Huron with Lake St. Clair, was where they were apt to encounter some dangerous narrows and shallows. It would, therefore, be a good idea to make a rest stop here before continuing with the journey.

The boat party, unwilling to deprive the Frenchmen of their supplies, ate from their own provisions and even passed out some of what they had. Davers, as usual, chattered on about the beauty of this country, affairs at Detroit and elsewhere until finally Lieutenant Robertson announced it was time to leave. The Englishmen filed back to their boat and one of the Frenchmen sauntered casually back with them.

It was François Clairmont.

Suspicous, Baptiste Campeau followed a dozen feet farther back and now a wild look come into Clairmont's eyes.

"Listen to me," he hissed through clenched teeth as he walked between Robertson and Davers. "Listen! You're in danger, Indians. Go back to the fort quickly. Warn them. Attack coming!"

Both Davers and Robertson looked at the man in surprise and Clairmont, seeing Campeau coming up on them, burst into hoarse laughter and slapped the lieutenant on the back and turned away from them. The two Englishmen joined the other members of the party already on board the boat and shoved off. Davers looked at Robertson and frowned.

"Now what do you suppose that was all about?" he asked softly.

Robertson hunched his shoulders and grinned. "Who knows? I didn't see any rum, but I'll bet he had a bellyful of it." He nodded to one of the sailors. "All right," he said loudly, "start sounding and be on your toes. The hard part's coming up now."

Davers, still frowning slightly, moved up to the bow. There he picked up his new rifle and checked its priming. Suddenly he was very glad that he had it with him.

The current pouring through the Huron River into Lake St. Clair was so strong that it took every bit of strength of the rowers to move the batteau along at a slow pace. Less than a mile back, Lieutenant Robertson's boat had entered the river mouth heading north. Even though the current had been swift there and the channel relatively narrow, he had been pleased to see that the soundings remained more than amply deep enough for the passage of a schooner having a brisk enough wind behind to shove her through. He hoped it would continue this way. The water was very clear and became a deep green color where it deepened with the main channel; a channel which sometimes swung so close to the west shore that the oars of the rowers very nearly hit the shoreline.

All six soldiers and the two sailors were manning the oars, four to a side, while Lieutenant Robertson and the Pawnee slave kept the tiller under tight control. In the bow, John Rutherford stood beside Sir Robert Davers. The former was bent over, looking at a fish moving along under the bow when Davers caught a glimpse of movement on the shore not thirty feet away. A three-pronged grapnel with rope trailing from it sailed through the air from behind some rocks. Even as Davers stared at it in amazement, a half dozen or more shots rang out.

A ball of lead more than half an inch in diameter caught Davers just above and between the eyes, slamming him backward, blowing out the whole back of his skull, and showering young Rutherford with bloody residue. In the same instant, another ball tore through the heart of Lieutenant Robertson, dropping him into the bottom of the boat. The two sailors, who were on port oars were killed in the same moment.

So swiftly had all this happened that those four men were dead before the grappling hook thumped into the bottom of the boat. It slid for an instant, then caught as the craft began falling back with the current. The shoreward end of the rope was snugged around a huge boulder and as it tightened, it forced the batteau to veer sharply shoreward and then slam into the rocks. Those still upright were sent flying by the impact and the screech of a score of wildly exultant voices filled the air as the Chippewas surged toward them. Charles Dusette, with them, leaped from a rock into the bow, bowling young Rutherford over in the process. The Frenchman swiftly snatched up Davers's new rifle and then raced down

201

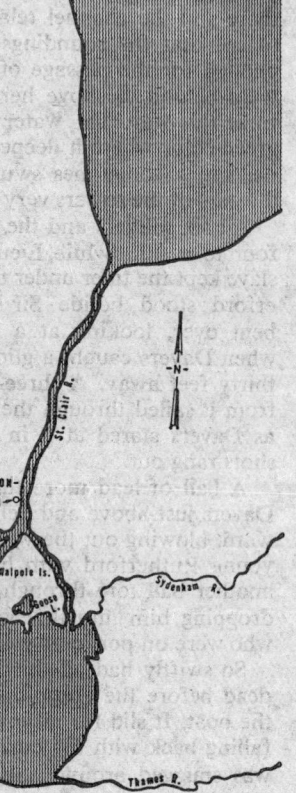

THE
LOWER LAKE HURON,
ST. CLAIR RIVER,
AND
LAKE ST. CLAIR
AREA

the length of the boat, clubbing two soldiers with the butt of the weapon as he did so, and finally smashing the barrel across the temple of the Pawnee slave, who fell beside Robertson. Dusette then snatched up the lieutenant's powder horn and slung it around his own neck.

By this time the boat was filled with Indians. Each of the remaining six soldiers had at least two men holding him and John Rutherford, still dazed by it all, stared into the muzzle of the rifle which Chief Perwash held to his face.

It had all happened so suddenly there was no opportunity for resistance. One minute they were busy rowing upstream and the next they were dead or captive. It was that simple. The scalps were taken from the four dead men at once. Lieutenant Robertson's body was tossed out onto a rocky shelf and there it was stripped of its clothing and great chunks of flesh hacked away with tomahawks. These chunks the Chippewas thrust into their mouths and ate raw, chewing and tearing while a frothy, bloody spittle ran down their chins and stained their chests.

Chief Perwash himself slashed open the lieutenant's chest with his scalping knife and tore the heart free. He ripped a great bite out of it with his teeth and then laughed as he threw it to his warriors, who did as he had done with it. Then the chief cut a circle around the undamaged left upper arm of Robertson and stripped the skin backward, peeling it off like a stocking all the way down to the wrist. There he severed it so that it came free intact as a cylinder of skin. He intended making a tobacco pouch of it.

It was the most grisly scene young John Rutherford had ever witnessed and his eyes turned upward in his head and he fell to the ground in a faint. It was just as well that he did so; it saved him from having to witness the no less grisly butchering of the remaining six soldiers.[72]

[May 6, 1763—Friday, 3:30 P.M.]

François Clairmont could not recall ever having been so afraid as he was now. Ever since about ten o'clock this morning when the faint poppings of gunshots were wafted to the camp by the breeze from the north, he had felt sick. Now he sat waiting, hoping desperately that his reasoning was wrong, yet knowing with a sickening certainty that it was not.

Nor was it. He looked up now at a slight noise to see Perwash and his Chippewas coming back into the clearing they had left at daybreak. Dusette was still with them and now he was carrying a fine new rifle and powder horn and his eyes glittered wickedly as he grinned.

It was almost anticlimactic to see what they were carrying with them—the equipment and provisions from the English boat, the two kegs of gunpowder and eleven rifles, the food . . . the scalps. They also had two men from the boat prisoners; Rutherford, who walked as if in a trance, and the Pawnee slave.

Campeau and Dunoir, only momentarily startled, welcomed the party, but Massac and Clairmont looked at one another with horrified eyes. Massac's whisper was barely audible to Clairmont as he repeated time and again, "I didn't think they'd do it . . . My God, I didn't think they'd do it . . ."

Clairmont nudged Massac and jerked his head toward the woods. The two men eased out of sight of the rest of the party, ran a short distance and then stopped, panting.

"One of us," Clairmont said, "has got to tell Major Gladwin. He's *got* to be told."

Massac nodded. "I'll tell him," he said, "but you've got to go with me."

"No!" Clairmont was aghast. "I have a wife and child to think of in Detroit, and a home. You are alone and you do not have to fear for any but yourself. You do it."

"Massac is no fool," the second Frenchman muttered, his face pale and his lips beginning to tremble. "You wish me to bear the burden and take the risk. No, I will do nothing now. I should have done something to prevent this while I could. I didn't. Now it is done. Now it is too late. I did nothing then, I will do nothing now. Don't talk to me any more, Clairmont. You are not my conscience. I will not listen to you. Go away."

He spun around and headed back to the camp. Clairmont angrily watched him go and then struck out westward toward Detroit. He started with the idea of going directly to Gladwin and telling him what happened, but the more he thought about what happened, the more afraid he became. By the time he had gone half a mile, he was trembling and he had made a decision. He would report what happened, but not to the major. He would tell Chief Pontiac. Gladwin would learn of it soon enough, but not from him.

François Clairmont had just abruptly realized that he was very much a coward.

Major Henry Gladwin was normally not a man to worry about things, but he was worried now and it bothered him. Something was brewing, possibly something very grave, and yet he couldn't quite piece it together. He had intended writing letters this evening but for the better part of an hour now, ever since James Sterling had stopped by briefly, he had been sitting here at his desk just thinking. The more he thought, the more concerned he became. It was not one thing in particular that gnawed at him but, rather, several unrelated occurrences.

The first had come in the form of the old Chippewa woman who came to the fort so frequently to sell her handiwork. No one seemed to know her by any other name than Catherine, but she did uncommonly beautiful work in the making of moccasins, which she sold to the garrison and traders. Gladwin, in fact, had some time ago requested her to make a pair of moccasins for him and the delivery of them was what ostensibly had brought her to his quarters this afternoon.

The handiwork on the footwear had been superb; elkhide worked to a marvelously soft pliability, with intricate designs interwoven on the sides and over the arches in blue beads and porcupine quills, some of which had been dyed red. Gladwin had expressed his unqualified admiration for them and paid her more than she asked, but even then she had hesitated about leaving the room. She lingered with downcast eyes and something evidently on her mind; but then when the major had asked her what was wrong, she had merely looked at him with a frightened glance and hurried out without replying.

Not very long after she left, the sentry at his door rapped to announce a visitor. Gladwin nodded and the soldier stepped aside. Thomas Gouin, a well-known French inhabitant of Detroit, entered and shook hands with the major, but said nothing until the soldier left them in privacy. Then he looked at Gladwin for a long moment before speaking.

"Major," he said at last, "I have heard something peculiar that perhaps you should know about."

"Yes?"

"I went on some business to the shop of Monsieur Peltier, the smith, this afternoon. He told me that last night the wife of Gabriel St. Aubin, his neighbor, mentioned to him that she had crossed the river to the Ottawa village to buy some venison and maple sugar. There, according to Madame St. Aubin, she happened to see several of Pontiac's warriors busily shortening their guns—sawing off part of the stock and filing off part of the barrel, so that instead of five feet long or more, the guns were cut to only three feet. Monsieur Peltier said that answered the question in his mind of why so many Indians had recently been borrowing saws and files from him. I do not know what this means, but it is very strange."

It *was* strange and Gladwin continued to ponder about it after Monsieur Gouin was gone. For what conceivable purpose would the Indians cut their rifles down to only three feet in length? It was puzzling.

About an hour after Gouin departed, the sentry again knocked and entered and mentioned that though it was almost time for the fort's gates to be closed for the night, the old Chippewa woman, Catherine, was still loitering close by and had been there ever since leaving Gladwin's office. The major looked out to where the soldier indicated and saw her still there. He called her to him and the old squaw came hesitantly, rather fearfully. At first when he asked again what was wrong, she refused to answer; but after repeatedly coaxing her and telling her she had nothing to fear from him or anyone else, she moved close to him, looked around carefully and then swiftly whispered:

"You are in great danger, Major. Be watchful!"

Before he could say anything, she was hurrying away and he shook his head and frowned as he watched her go. She disappeared in the direction of the east gate and Gladwin returned to his quarters. It had been just over an hour ago that James Sterling had stopped by briefly and said just enough to contribute to the concern that was already beginning to gnaw at Gladwin.

It was no secret in Detroit that Angelique Cuillerier had been deeply enamored of Sir William Johnson; nor that Johnson, once having left here, had blandly turned his back on her despite whatever his promises had been. It was not long after she realized this that Angelique had apparently switched her affection to James Sterling. The tall, rugged-looking young trader was not only handsome, he was one of the most successful traders at Detroit. It was no surprise to anyone that the most beautiful woman at Detroit should fall in love with him. Rumor had it they would soon be married, but no formal announcement of it had yet been made. It was hinted that she feared her father, who disliked the English intensely, would oppose any such marriage.[73]

Now Sterling shook his head and frowned. "Don't know quite what to make of it, Major," he said, "but Angelique came to my trading house today acting very peculiar. She said she had to tell me something, but made me promise first that I wouldn't ask her any questions. I promised and then she said the strangest thing; she said I should not open for business tomorrow, but rather keep my doors locked and shutters closed and stay indoors, not even to show myself at a window. She said I'd be all right if I did that, and then she left. I don't understand it."

Neither did Henry Gladwin, although now the concern he felt was becoming a tangible thing. He continued pondering about it after the trader left. More than once in the past rumors had come to him that the Indians were planning mischief, but nothing had ever materialized and he was inclined to believe there was really nothing to it now. He might even have just shrugged the incidents away except for the rapping which came on his door now. The man on the porch was dressed in dark clothing and it was hard to make him out against the darkness outside. Then the visitor stepped into the glow of the lamplight and Gladwin recognized him as Jacques Duperon Baby, the only French resident here whom Gladwin could honestly call a good friend. Even before the major could say anything. Baby quickly stepped in and shut the door.

"Henry," he said, "Detroit's going to be attacked by the Indians tomorrow. I was there when the plans were made. Pontiac'll lead them. Everything's ready for it."

Shocked, Gladwin offered Baby a chair and poured him a brandy, then listened while Baby gave him the details. The Ottawa war chief had told Gladwin on his last visit here that he would be back again soon for a formal council when his people had come in from hunting. This, Baby said, is what he would allegedly be doing tomorrow. Early in the morning more squaws than usual would enter the fort and stroll the streets. Each of them would have, hidden beneath her blanket, a rifle that had been shortened enough for it to be concealed, a tomahawk, a war club, and a knife. They would scatter and position themselves at various points throughout the fort. Then Pontiac would lead about fifty of his best warriors in, supposedly for a council. Those men with him who wore blankets would have sawed-off rifles under them, and those who wore only loincloths or leggings would be given weapons by the squaws who had already entered with them. When Gladwin and his officers were assembled in the council house within the fort and only the normal duty force of guards at the gates, Pontiac would make a speech professing friendship for the English. He would move close to Gladwin, supposedly to present him with a wampum belt, but then he would suddenly give vent to the piercing death cry and strike Gladwin with his war club. That cry would be the signal for all others elsewhere to take out their own weapons or get them from the nearest squaw and strike instantly at the nearest Englishmen. Not expecting it, the garrison would be badly crippled in the first moments, with most of the officers dead or wounded. The fort would then fall easily to the attackers. Ammunition stores would be taken first, and then each trading house would be plundered of all its goods and the traders themselves would be slaughtered.

The pieces fitted now and Gladwin's face was set in harsh lines as the Frenchman finished. He thanked Jacques Duperon Baby with great sincerity and promised, as Baby insisted he do, that he would never tell anyone who had revealed the plot to him.[74] The two men shook hands warmly and the lamp was turned low before Baby slipped out of the door and disappeared into the night.

Now Henry Gladwin had an important decision to make. He could easily deny Pontiac and his Indians entry to the fort on the morrow, but to do so might well place the sounding party under Lieutenant Robertson in jeopardy, as well as those English traders or others living here outside the confines of the fort. There was also the supply party under Sergeant Shaw, which was very probably on its way back here by now from Fort Michilimackinac. All these people would be jeopardized if he acted too hastily.

Even if he openly accused Pontiac and the chief denied it, that might only result in the attack plan being put off until a later date when suspicion had been dulled. Might it not be best to allow Pontiac to enter and then let him see, with a show of strength, that the garrison was aware of the plot and could not be taken by surprise? In so doing, perhaps Pontiac could be so disgraced in the eyes of his followers that he would lose his influence and the whole affair would blow over. It was, Gladwin decided, worth a try.

Within five minutes a messenger was racing about the fort, alerting the garrison and telling all officers to report immediately to Gladwin's quarters for an emergency meeting. Within a quarter hour, all the officers were there, and by a half hour after that, the meeting was over and preparations were already being made. Half the garrison was ordered under arms for the remainder of the night and all officers were to spend the night on the ramparts, in case some wild impulse should make the Indians launch their attack sooner than planned.

Throughout the night a fearful tenseness gripped the officers and men of Detroit.

[May 7, 1763—Saturday, 9:00 A.M.]

Captain Donald Campbell rubbed his eyes with the heels of his hands and stifled a yawn. He felt dirty and tired and his eyes were gritty from having had no sleep all night, but he made no complaint. Just about everyone else was in the same boat. The unaccustomed weight of the heavy pistol holstered on his right hip and the sword sheathed on his left made him feel just a little bit ridiculous. A faint smile touched his lips as he thought of what Pontiac's reaction would be when he saw everyone armed to the teeth like this.

The deployment of men at the gates, in the bastions and on the ramparts had been carried into execution without a hitch. Half the garrison had been up all night manning these positions, including all of the officers, and the rest of the men would be taking their positions on the drum roll.

He paused at the west gate and noted that the two chiefs and fifteen warriors had now approached to within several hundred yards and were still coming, moving along as carelessly as if nothing at all was wrong. Campbell shook his head. He wondered fleetingly what he would do if he were still in command here. Would he let these approaching Potawatomies come in? Knowing what he knew, would he allow Pontiac and his men to come in when they arrived? He doubted it. He hoped Gladwin was acting wisely, but he just didn't know.

Perhaps if the commander hadn't been warned—and none of the officers seemed to have any idea who it was that had warned him—perhaps then the things that had happened this morning would not even have seemed noteworthy. Knowledge of the plot, however, gave them a different perspective and ordinary things carried ominous undertones. There was the fact, for example, that though it was Saturday morning, not a single French resident from outside the fort had made any attempt to enter it thus far, and that a number of French women and children inside had already casually wandered outside and vanished. Then, too, there was the fact that at sunrise the lookouts had spotted thirty or forty canoes crossing from Pontiac's village to this side of the river with two or three men each in them, yet the boats sitting so low in the water that it was obvious that eight or ten more must be lying in the bottom of each. It was another fact that might well have gone unnoticed.

Since then an abnormal number of Indians—both men and women—had casually come to the fort and entered. This was a practice not unusual on a Saturday morning, when trading always seemed more active than at other times. The women and many of the men were wearing blankets draped loosely about themselves and they were scattering themselves around the interior of the fort, nodding pleasantly and smiling at everyone encountered, but mainly staying out of the way. Again Campbell doubted the wisdom of letting them come in like this. Already they numbered as many or more than the entire garrison. It was risky to say the least.

He looked up at the sound of voices and watched with interest as the two Potawatomi chiefs—Winnemac and Nontenee—entered, followed by their warriors. Campbell smiled as he walked up to them and shook the hands of the two chiefs. He didn't know Nontenee very well, but Winnemac was a powerful chief, next in rank in the tribe only to Washee and Ninivois.

"Welcome," he said in the Potawatomi tongue. "Our chief, Major Gladwin, is honored that you visit. He wishes you to come see him that he may pay his respects."

Winnemac and Nontenee glanced at one another and nodded. Winnemac said something in an undertone to the warriors and they began dispersing, to meander about within the fort. Campbell pretended not to notice and led the two chiefs toward Gladwin's house. A squad of six soldiers unobtrusively fell in behind them.

Past Gladwin's house Campbell led them, to a low, sturdy-looking building not far from the fort's water gate. There was a soldier standing at the heavy wooden door and at a nod from Campbell he opened the door, saluted and stepped aside. Campbell motioned the chiefs to enter ahead of him and they did so. He followed them inside, the squad of soldiers behind him. It took a moment for the eyes to adjust to the dimness of the interior, but then the chiefs both looked startled when they found no one waiting for them inside and the windows heavily barred.

"Disarm them," Campbell ordered, stepping back. He watched calmly as the shock in the eyes of the Indians changed to outrage as their knives and pipe tomahawks were lifted from their belts. "I'm sorry," he told them softly. "Major Gladwin's orders. He will explain to you later."

He and the soldiers left the Indians standing in the middle of the room and bolted the big door shut from the outside. The soldier on guard there snapped a large padlock through the latch loop and five minutes later Campbell was reporting to his commander.

Gladwin nodded when Campbell finished. "Good. They may come in handy. How many Indians inside the fort right now?"

"Three or four dozen women," Campbell replied. "Easily twice that many men. They've scattered. Several have asked when the trading houses are going to open, but we've only told them 'Pretty soon' and let it go at that."

"The traders?"

"They're all over at Sterling's place and all armed. They'll come outside at the drum roll. Half the garrison's on post alert now and the rest ready to take position at the drum. Drummer's been told to give the roll and then maintain a tapping without pause after that. If the tapping stops, everyone's to open fire instantly. Sir . . ." He paused briefly, uncomfortably, and then said, ". . . do you really think this is best?"

"I do, Captain. I do indeed. Sergeant Shaw's detachment is probably on the way back here from Michilimackinac right now. Lieutenant Robertson and his party, along with Sir Robert, are still sounding. Sergeant Fisher and his family are over on the island tending the King's cattle. All these people are at this moment in jeopardy. As I see it, the plan I've laid out places them in the *least* amount of jeopardy. Hopefully it will work out well. Hopefully," he added with feeling, "by handling it the way we are, this whole thing will collapse quietly."

Abruptly a prolonged drum roll filled the air and there was a flurry of activity as every soldier not previously on duty moved swiftly to his assigned post. Captain Joseph Hopkins, third in command of Detroit, moved among them, checking them. Gladwin smiled faintly.

"I'll be at the council house, Captain. You may escort our visitors there as soon as they arrive."

Gladwin walked away confidently and gave no sign of even noticing the chill of a trickle of perspiration which abruptly ran down the small of his back. Campbell's final comment still echoed in his mind. Was what he was doing the best action to take? He didn't know, but he hoped to God that it was.

Pontiac walked at the head of a single file of some fifty or more of his chiefs and warriors. The majority of them, like Pontiac himself, were wrapped in blankets which shrouded their bodies. The feathers of eagles hung from the temples of eight or ten chiefs directly behind him and many of the warriors wore the feathers of hawks or crows attached to the tuft of hair rising from the front of the head, the rest of the skull shaved smooth. Their faces were lined and circled with vermilion and ochre pigments, with pasty white and black soot. Bones and stones and beads and bells hung from their ears and noses, and jangled about wrists and ankles as they walked.

Pontiac glanced neither to right nor left, but kept his eyes locked on the distant fort they were heading toward. He could see the east gate, through which they planned to enter, and felt an exultation grow in him as he saw it was still open and there were small, casual groups of Indians still entering. Everything was going as planned.

At the narrow bridge crossing Parent's Creek, a Canadian Pontiac recognized as Luciene Beaufait stepped aside in order to let them pass. Pontiac paid no attention to him, nor did any of those following, except for the very last warrior in line. He was an Ottawa who knew Beaufait well and he grinned at him and briefly opened his blanket to show the gun and tomahawk hidden there, then closed it again and jerked his head toward the fort. Beaufait paled and the Ottawa's grin widened.

Very faintly from ahead Pontiac heard a staccato drum roll, but it did not bother him. Such sounds were not uncommon from the fort. The important thing was that the gates were still open and everything appeared normal. His eyes glittered as he envisioned how that would soon be changed. He continued the steady pace toward the portal.

When he was still fifty feet or more from the gate, he saw the interpreter, LaButte, and Captain Campbell coming forward to meet him. An honor guard of a dozen or more soldiers in full dress uniform stood at attention on either side of the interior of the entryway. It was with something of a start that he saw fixed bayonets on the ends of the rifles.

When Campbell and LaButte fell in on either side of him,

he nodded in greeting but said nothing, nor did they. In another moment they were passing through the gate and into the fort. Immediately some of the aloof disdain fell away from Pontiac and his eyes widened. A harsh expulsion of breath began leaving him and was instantly silenced. Everywhere he looked there were soldiers armed with bayoneted rifles—on the ramparts, in the bastions, at the street corners, on some of the roofs, in many of the windows and elsewhere. A company of about forty soldiers stood at the edge of the drill field, their weapons at the ready and a captain standing before them. Both of the six-pounder cannon were manned and aimed in strategic directions, and officers were calling orders to their men. Every officer was armed with sword and sidearm.

Here and there as he walked Pontiac could see clusters of Indians pretending to pay little attention to him; but down the street of the trading houses, where bustling Saturday morning crowds should have been busy at the business of trading, every building was locked and the shutters drawn. The traders themselves, armed with rifles, stood in small attentive groups here and there. Behind the unshuttered windows of houses, people stood looking and waiting. The Ottawa chief's face was frozen in sour lines as he allowed Campbell and LaButte to lead the Indian column toward the council chambers. The steady tapping of a drum paced them all the way and it was an ominous sound. It paced them through the little town, west on the Rue St. Joseph to the center street and then south past the Rue. St. Jacques, the Rue Ste. Anne, and the Rue St. Louis to the council house near the river front.

Major Henry Gladwin, wearing pistol and sword, was already in the chambers and he nodded casually at Pontiac and the chiefs directly behind him—Mukeeta, Pinaasee, Neewish, Waubinema, Macatepilesis, Chavinon and Greton—as each entered. Campbell and LaButte joined the commander as wordlessly the chiefs filed in and sat in a semicircle and the rest of the warrior party took their places behind them. They all looked nervous and worried, muttered among themselves and frequently glanced at Pontiac for a clue from his expression for how they should act. Pontiac's features were unchanging.

When all the Indians had entered who were going to, about sixty of them, Gladwin ordered the distribution of some bread and tobacco, as was customary. Neither by expression nor action did he give any indication that everything was not normal. In an undertone he asked Campbell how many Indians were in the fort now and the captain whispered back that, including these assembled here, there were now about three hundred on hand—almost three times the strength of the garrison—and that the gates were now closed.

The Indians gnawed on the bread until it was gone and then pipes were lighted and smoked in sullen silence. All the while the steady monotonous tapping of the drum could be heard outside. It was a tense situation to say the least. Gladwin, Campbell, the two French interpreters—including Jacques St. Martin as well as Pierre LaButte—and a sergeant posted at the door, all stood quietly, saying nothing. It was very nearly an hour before Pontiac finally rose to speak. His expression was still ugly.

"We have come, as is our custom," he told Gladwin, "to profess our friendship for the English and to smoke the pipe of peace with our good friends. Why," his voice became suddenly harsh, accusatory, "do I see so many of your young men outside with guns? Why should this be? We are greatly surprised, brother, at this unusual step you have taken, to have all your soldiers under arms and that all of your young chiefs are not here for this council, as they have always been before. We would be very glad to know the reason for this. Could it be that some bad bird has sung in your ear ill news of us? If so, we advise you not to believe it, brother, for as you know, there are bad birds who would like to see you rise up against your Indian brothers who have come in peace and who have always been in perfect friendship with their brothers, the English."

When LaButte completed interpreting, Gladwin looked at the chief calmly and spoke without any hint of irritation or anger, without any sign that he had any knowledge of the proposed treachery.

"Pontiac," he said, "should not be concerned by what he has seen of my young men armed and ready outside. Often this takes place for the sake of exercise and drill and discipline. In addition, today I have heard that some other Indian nations are on their way to council here and since I do not know them well and perhaps should not trust them, I intend to have the garrison under arms when they arrive. Yet, I would not wish these strangers to be affronted by a reception such as this, so I resolved to begin the custom with our greatest friends, the Ottawas, as I am sure you would not take offense at it; and if you did not take offense, then how could strangers who came?"

The scowl on Pontiac's face deepened as LaButte transformed the message into the guttural Ottawa tongue. It was quite obvious that both men were well aware of what the other was doing, yet each continued to pretend ignorance. Pontiac remained silent for a long moment after LaButte finished interpreting and then he dipped one hand inside the blanket wrapped around him. Casually, the hands of both Gladwin and Campbell moved near the butts of the handguns they wore. Pontiac appeared not to notice and he removed from inside the blanket a wide belt of wampum, white on one side and green on the other. A sudden electric tension seemed to flow through the room. This, as Gladwin understood it, was the prelude to the signal for the attack to begin. The Ottawa war chief was holding the belt with the white side up, but the signal for attack was to be when he turned the green side up and raised his voice in the eerie death cry.

Pontiac now held the belt out, white side still up, and abruptly broke into a rather long speech about the misfortune that had been visited upon the Ottawas by the death of six chiefs over the past winter. He expressed the hope that the English chief would give them presents that might help to banish their grief. As he said this, he raised the belt slightly and seemed about to flip it over.

Gladwin made a small motion with his hand, which was relayed by the sergeant at the door to someone outside. Instantly the tapping of the drum changed to the rolling din of the charge and there was the clash of numerous weapons from outside. Pontiac stopped as if struck and then, after a long pause, stepped closer to Gladwin and handed him the belt, white side up. He made no sound.

With an outward calmness belying the hammering of his heart, Gladwin thanked Pontiac for the belt, expressed sorrow at the news of the death of the six chiefs over the winter and ordered that six suits of clothes and more bread and tobacco be presented in their memory to these Ottawas under Pontiac.

"It is good to know," he concluded, "that we English have such good friends as the Ottawas in this land. I can assure Pontiac that our friendship and protection will always be extended as long as it is deserved. The strange tribes which are coming will soon be made aware that this is our way; but that at the first act of aggression against us, we will retaliate with a crushing vengeance."

The innuendo was not lost on the Ottawa chief and for an instant Gladwin was sure that Pontiac was going to give the signal anyway. His stomach muscles tensed and he was prepared to move fast, but then the moment passed and Pontiac spoke again.

"It is not fitting," he said, "that we should have come to you with so few to honor you. We will go now, and in a few days we will come back with our entire nation, including even our women and children, and hold a council in which we will properly express to you the friendship between the Ottawa and English."

To this Gladwin made no reply and in a moment Pontiac stalked out of the chamber, followed by his chiefs and warriors. Again the drum was tapping a moderate cadence and the Indians walked directly back to the gate. It was opened as they approached and they filed through it to the outside. The Indians still scattered about on the streets suddenly drifted toward the gates, too, and began leaving. Within a very few minutes there was not an Indian left in the fort except the two hostages Gladwin was still holding, as yet unbeknownst to the tribes.

As the gates were closed again behind the last Indian to leave, Captain Donald Campbell leaned against the picket wall and blew out a deep breath. His mouth was dry and his heart was still beating much too fast and the underarms of his uniform were soaked. It was several minutes before he could trust his own legs to carry him again.

[May 7, 1763—Saturday, 7:00 P.M.]

The council held at the Ottawa village immediately upon the return of Pontiac and his warriors there lasted the remainder of the afternoon and well into this evening, and it was a bad time for the war chief. The young chiefs and warriors were angry and much of the confidence they had had in Pontiac seemed to have melted away.

Why, they asked bitterly, had Pontiac not given the signal? Why had he not turned the wampum belt and why had not his voice been lifted in the death cry? Why had they not attacked as planned, when it was apparent that they outnumbered the enemy perhaps as much as three to one?

And Pontiac replied just as angrily: "Would you have us throw away Indian lives one for one in exchange for English lives? What kind of a victory would it be if, for the cost of it, our whole nation was thrown into mourning for the losses of its young men? Yes, you would have attacked had I given the signal, but give thanks that I did not. Could you not see the preparation that had been made? Did you not see every man there with gun loaded and bayonet attached? Did you not reach behind the innocent words of the Major Gladwin? We went to Detroit to destroy Englishmen, not to be ourselves destroyed, which would have happened had the signal been given. My children, it was far more difficult for me *not* to give it than to give it. Reflect and you will see that I acted wisely. You say that you would have been willing to lose some of our men to destroy those dogs, but look in your own hearts. Ask yourself the question, 'Should I sacrifice my life in such an attack when it is not necessary and when it can be done at another time without risk?' If you answer truthfully, the answer must be no."

There was some easing of the tension then, but Pontiac was well aware that he had been shamed, that he had lost some of the esteem in which they had been holding him and he needed to reestablish himself as leader at once or his whole plan could crumble. He directed discussion toward attempting to ascertain how Gladwin had become suspicious of their plan. Obviously someone had given a warning, but who? At once a warrior stood and said he thought he knew who it was. On the evening before, he said, he happened to see coming out of the fort the old Chippewa squaw who made moccasins to sell to the English—the squaw who had been proselytized by one of the Detroit Jesuit priests, Father Simple Bocquet, and who had been named Catherine by him; the old woman who, though she was Chippewa, now lived at the Potawatomi village on the same side of the river as the fort. It was nearly dark when he had seen her come out, he declared, acting frightened and hiding herself as much as possible from anyone who might look toward her.

Instantly Pontiac appointed six warriors to go fetch her. "Take her first to the fort," he said, "and show her to the major. Tell him it has come to us that some bad bird has been telling him lies about us and ask him if she was the one, because if so, then she must be punished. Then bring her here."

The six warriors raced off and the council resumed. As best he could Pontiac soothed their anger and frustration, promising them that they would have their chance to destroy the English, but at less risk than they would have undergone today.

"I have another plan," he said, "which will put them off their guard. Tomorrow I will go to the fort again, taking with me only Macatepilesis, Breton and Chavinon. We four will talk with the Major Gladwin and smoke our pipes with him and convince him that he had been deceived in whatever it was he heard about what we intended. We will be friendly and give our promise of good behavior. When he is convinced, then we will promise to return again for formal council of all the tribe. It will be as if nothing had happened and a fresh surprise will be possible."

They discussed at length how they would do it, until suddenly there was a disturbance at the doorway to the council chamber. In a moment a young chief swiftly picked his way through the crowd to Pontiac and spoke softly but excitedly to him. For the first time since the affair at the fort, a smile appeared briefly on the chief's face.

"My brothers," he said loudly, and when all attention was centered on him he continued, "there is good news! The Frenchman Clairmont has just come from the head of the little lake above us. He brings word that yesterday morning the boat party of twelve who left the fort was taken. All have been killed except the one young trader called Rutherford and his Pawnee, which two were kept by Chief Perwash as his slaves. No one escaped. English blood has been drawn, but no Indian blood lost. It has begun, and it is a good sign for us!"

There were wild, exultant shrieks from the assemblage and it was a long while before the hubbub abated. Just then there was a signal cry from the river and the party of six which Pontiac had sent out after the woman returned. They beached their canoe and dragged the frightened Catherine out of it. Pontiac and the others had moved outside to meet them and now they brought her before him.

They had taken her, they told the chief, in the Potawatomi village and brought her at once to the fort, where they were met at the gate by the Major Gladwin. They had shown her to him and asked him if she was the bad bird who had brought false information to him about the Ottawas. The major, they said, declared she had never given him any information, but that the person who had done so was one of themselves, whom he had promised not to name.[75]

Pontiac's expression was ugly. He reached down and picked up a lacrosse racket leaning against a rock nearby and approached her. With his free hand he snatched her hair and twisted until she moaned and her eyes bulged with fear.

"You betrayed us to the English, didn't you?"

Catherine's mouth worked but she could not speak. Pontiac repeated, "Didn't you?" and swung the lacrosse racket viciously. It thudded on her head, stunning her, and she fell to her knees.

"Didn't you?" Pontiac repeated, and swung again. There was a meaty thud as the stick hit her again. She was on hands and knees now, but still she said nothing.

One more time the war chief slammed the stick across her head and this time blood gushed from the wound and her eyes turned up in her head and she rolled over unconscious.

"Kill her! *Kill her!*" The Indians crowded around, chanting the words savagely, but Pontiac struck her no more. He tossed the stick across her still form and walked away.[76]

[*May 8, 1763—Sunday*]

"Well, they don't act as if they have murder on their minds, do they?" Donald Campbell nodded toward the Indians roisterously playing ball in the huge open field nearby the fort. Faintly the cries of the players could be heard and often the meaty smacks of rackets connecting with flesh instead of the ball. The game they were playing was commonly called *baggataway* by them, but was more familiar to the English by the French term for it, *lacrosse,* so named after the shape of the racket. It was not a game for the faint of heart. Rarely did the blood not flow freely, and bones often got broken during the course of the game. Campbell looked back at the commander and added, "What do you think, Major? Do you think the danger's past?"

Henry Gladwin shook his head slowly. For the past quarter hour, as early evening shadows were lengthening, he and Captain Campbell had stood here on the west rampart and watched the distant Indians. Certainly they seemed innocuous enough now.

"I wish I knew," he replied. "Frankly, I don't think so. I get a feeling that something's cooking and if we don't watch out, it's apt to be our own goose. That meeting today with Pontiac, for example. It just didn't feel right."

Donald Campbell nodded. This morning when the sentry had announced the approach of Pontiac and three of his chiefs, Campbell had been at the gate to meet them and informed them that at the request of Major Gladwin, he would speak for the English. Though such an act might well have been taken as an insult, the chiefs accepted it with understanding nods and they had thereupon smoked the pipe of peace and had even presented a beautifully carved and feather-decorated calumet to Campbell as a token of friendship and esteem. They said they were very sorry about the reports Major Gladwin had apparently received of the supposed bad intentions of the Indians, and that these were false reports which they wished to bury now, once and for all.

"Tomorrow," Pontiac told Campbell, "I will come back here to council with Major Gladwin and I will have my whole nation with me to honor him and you and to assure you both in formal manner of our wish for nothing but peace between us and you. Evil birds have sung lies in your ears, my father, for there is no bad blood between us. We who stand before you are friends of the English. We love them as brothers and it is to prove this love that we have come today to smoke peace with you."

Campbell had shaken his head and replied that the major might give audience to Pontiac and his chiefs on the morrow, but that he was sure Pontiac's whole nation would not be allowed to enter the fort. Pontiac appeared unconcerned, stressed again his undying friendship and then he and his three chiefs, who had said nothing, filed out of the fort.

In the late afternoon, as if to show that all reports had been errors or lies, the Potawatomies, Hurons, and Ottawas engaged in the game of *baggataway*, which lasted throughout the afternoon and was only now drawing to an end as darkness approached. A sudden loud shrieking by the victors indicated the finish of the game and in a short time all of the Indians had withdrawn to their respective villages.

Again Gladwin shook his head, as he and Campbell began descending from the rampart. "We will not relax our caution, Captain," he said. "Order a thirty-man captain's guard for the night and everyone else to see to their weapons and be prepared for alert at a moment's notice. All we can do now is keep on our toes and see what tomorrow brings."

[May 9, 1763—Monday, 11:30 A.M.]

Realizing that little could be more demoralizing to his command than simply waiting for an unknown evil—and perhaps an imaginary one at that—to manifest itself, Major Henry Gladwin had put most of the garrison to work early in the morning. The defenses within Detroit were improved, the cannon moved to better commanding positions in the bastions and loaded for firing, personal weapons seen to, fire-fighting tools readied and water barrels placed at intervals along the interior of the wall for use in dousing, if necessary, blazes caused by fire-arrows. Several parties of soldiers, well-armed, left the fort and visited each of the houses outside the fort where Englishmen were lodged, inviting them or any French families so inclined to come to the sanctuary of the fort until the trouble, if any, should blow over.

Few accepted the offer. A small number from the more outlying districts did come in, but they were the exception. The reaction of Mrs. Edgar Turnbull, who lived in a small farmhouse about a mile to the rear of the fort with her two sons, was more typical.

"Leave here?" she sniffed scornfully. "Not on your life, son." She jerked her head toward the fort and glared at the ensign and his little squad. "Go back and tell the major that here we live and here we'll stay. Mr. Turnbull built this house, lived in it and—God rest his soul—six months ago he died in it. We aren't going to walk off and turn it over to a bunch of thievin' redskins. Just tell the major to mind his own house and me and my boys'll mind ours!"

Even some of those who had accepted sanctuary began to wonder with nervous embarrassment if perhaps they hadn't been too hasty. Everything seemed perfectly normal. This was the first of three Rogation Days in the Catholic calendar and in the morning, while some of the residents were taking sanctuary, Father Simple Bocquet led his congregation in an innocuous, chanting procession. Things couldn't have been calmer.

Then, just before 11:00 A.M., a loud call was directed to Gladwin from the watch on the ramparts.

"Sir, they're crossing over from the other side. Indians! A lot of 'em!"

Gladwin and Campbell climbed to the rampart on the eastern wall and studied the movement carefully. Far above the fort a flotilla of canoes was coming across the river from the direction of Pontiac's village. Campbell's nearsighted eyes counted fifty-six of the boats, while Gladwin put the number at sixty-five. Each craft had seven or eight Indians in it.

"Have the drummer sound alert, Captain," Gladwin said crisply. "Every man to his post. All gates barred. Looks as if we're going to have some company. Pass the word again to the men to be careful about exposing themselves unnecessarily. Hard to say what's going to happen."

Gladwin climbed back down and sent a runner to fetch LaButte and St. Martin. When the two interpreters hurried up to him, he told them to step outside the east gate and wait there for the approach of the Indians. He also gave them a message for Pontiac. Then he returned to his own chambers.

Within twenty minutes, something over four hundred Indians—Potawatomies, Chippewas and Hurons, as well as Ottawas—with Pontiac at their head approached the fort. LaButte and St. Martin moved slowly forward to meet them.

"I and my people have come, as we said we would," Pontiac said, coming to a halt before the pair and eyeing the closed gate behind them, "to council with the English and set aside what bad news is in the air. We have come to smoke the pipe and then, to remove all suspicion from the minds of our English friends, we will immediately disperse and go about our business. But first we must enter and council with all the English chiefs."

Both interpreters shook their heads, but it was LaButte who relayed the message Gladwin had given them.

"The major," he added, "asks Pontiac to remember that yesterday he was informed by Captain Campbell that the whole nation would not be let inside the fort. Major Gladwin is willing to council peaceably with you if you wish, but not above sixty of your men will be allowed to enter the fort with you."

An expression of great anger swept across the features of the Ottawa war chief. Tossing aside any remaining hope of taking the fort by surprise, he pointed toward the place and spoke in a chilling voice:

"Go! Return to your major and tell him this: tell him that if *all* the Indians have not free access to his fort, *none* of them will enter it, and we will throw away the belt of friendship we received from Sir William Johnson. Tell your major that *he* may stay in his fort, and that I will keep the country!"

He spun about and began marching back the way he had come, toward the beached canoes, his followers on his heels. Before the two interpreters had reentered the gate, harsh yipping cries were issuing from many of the Indians who were beyond effective gun range. And by the time the two interpreters were repeating to Major Gladwin and Captain Campbell what Pontiac had said, sentries on the ramparts announced that the canoes were recrossing the river.

"What do you think, Major?" Captain Campbell asked when the two Frenchmen were gone.

Gladwin smiled without humor. "I think," he said, "we are about to see the Indian uprising that our esteemed general said could not possibly occur."

CHAPTER IV

[*May 9, 1763—Monday Noon*]

PONTIAC said nothing all the way back to his village on the opposite side of the river from Detroit and somewhat upstream. The fact that the element of surprise had been irrevocably lost, and that the initial shocking value of such a factor was equally lost, was galling. It was one thing to fall upon a garrison and take it by surprise, but quite another to come up against it when its defenses were ready and the men alerted to danger. His own power as leader of the confederacy of tribes, however loose a confederacy it was, hung in the balance now. Almost the whole warrior population was spoiling for battle and to delay it again would be to jeopardize his leadership. By the time his canoe grounded on the opposite shore, he had made up his mind.

In the center of his village—only recently reestablished here after a short stay on the river island—without even repairing to the council longhouse, he ripped off his blanket and raised his voice in a stirring, far-carrying cry. From his waistband he jerked out his tomahawk and instantly broke into the formal war dance of his nation. In a loud voice he recounted his past exploits, his burning hatred of the English, the long list of complaints the Indians held against the English. More and more frenzied his actions and words became. His body soon glistened with perspiration under the early afternoon sun, and one by one his watchers divested themselves of their own blankets and joined him in the wild, savage dance.

For nearly an hour it lasted and, when it ended, Pontiac made his first offensive moves. Two large marauding parties were sent out at once to move against any Englishmen not in the fort. A huge detachment of Hurons was sent downriver to take up a position on Turkey Island[77] and the shores adjacent to it, where the river was narrowest, there to cut off any En-

223

glish parties who might be on their way to the fort from the east. And realizing that it was now too difficult a burden to wage war across a river as broad as this, Pontiac again issued orders for the village to be moved at once to the same side of the river as the fort, but about two miles upstream from it, on the east side of the little stream known as Parent's Creek. It was to be rebuilt on the farm of the Frenchman Jean Baptiste Meloche. There was a touch of irony to it, as this was the same site where an Ottawa village had stood over two-score years ago and where Pontiac had been born of a Chippewa mother and Ottawa father.[78]

The remainder of the day was a flurry of activity everywhere except within the fort itself, where a nervous alert was maintained. For now, however, the Indians kept out of effective rifle range of the fort. One of the war parties sent out by Pontiac also recrossed the river, giving the fort a wide berth and landing about a mile below it. Instantly they spread out with wild cries and their first target was the house of Mrs. Edgar Turnbull.

The widow heard them coming and stood with her back against the far wall, her two young sons beside her, an ancient musket in her grasp pointed at the closed door. Her lips were moving silently as the door was smashed open and Indians poured into the room. She jerked the trigger and the weapon misfired. She didn't get another chance. A tomahawk thunked into her forehead, burying itself deeply and she was dead before her body struck the floor. Both sons followed her an instant later and now the triumphant death halloo was uttered by the warriors as they removed the three scalps, ransacked the house of its pitiful few supplies and valuables and then set it afire. The Turnbull cattle were driven off into the woods.

In the fort the Indians' death halloo reached the soldiers faintly and they looked at one another soberly. Any hope that a fight might be avoided was now gone. The vocal declaration was made that English blood had been spilled. It was now an open war and the order was flashed from man to man to withhold fire no longer, but shoot to kill whenever targets presented themselves.

The second marauding party was at the same time landing on the large *Isle aux Cochons*—Hog Island—where Detroit's cattle were kept. These animals were under the care of a recently retired English sergeant named James Fisher, plus two privates who acted as his helpers. The old sergeant had a small house there in which he lived with his wife, four children, and a maid. In addition there was a soldier from the fort visiting Fisher and also a French sawyer named François Goslin, who was there squaring some timbers. Unaware yet that anything was afoot, the men cared for the two dozen cattle and were not especially watchful for anything else. They should have been.

Even before they realized the island had been invaded, there was a sudden shrieking attack and murderous onslaught. Within five minutes Fisher, one of his children, the visiting soldiers and one of the privates had all been slain. Goslin, frightened out of his wits and fearing that he, too, was going to be killed, broke and ran, trying to escape. The Indians thought he was another Englishman, and before the error was recognized the woodworker had been cut down. All the rest at the place were taken captive.

Fisher's wife was hysterical and beat with her fists at the chests and faces of the two Indians trying to hold her. It was her undoing. The leader of the Indians rasped out a command and a long rawhide thong was looped around her neck. Even as the remaining little Fisher children, all girls, the private and the servingwoman watched in horror, Mrs. Fisher was led to a tree and the rawhide thong tossed over a low branch. One Indian held the woman up a couple of feet off the ground while two others tied the trailing end to another tree. Then she was released and the loop bit deeply into her throat. She kicked and thrashed and tore unavailingly at her throat while the Indians howled with laughter. The woman's tongue protruded, swelling ever larger and turning very dark. Apparently she bit it for blood ran from her mouth-corner and drooled down her neck. It was fully five minutes before she stopped moving and, though her bugged eyes were still open, it was obvious that she was dead. Then the King's cattle were all killed, the house ransacked of weapons, ammunition and anything else of value, and the house set afire. As the weeping Fisher girls were led away, along with the other two prisoners, several warriors busied themselves taking the scalps of the dead, including Mrs. Fisher.

By the time both marauding parties reported back to Pontiac, the new Ottawa camp had taken root on the farm of Jean Meloche and it was now late afternoon. Pontiac ordered the fort itself put under fire and bands of warriors slipped up as close as possible, taking advantage of the out-fort houses of the French inhabitants and other natural barriers for cover. A scattering of shots began which gradually picked up in tempo until a relatively hot firing was going on from both sides. One band of Indians had penetrated as far as the King's gardens at the southeast corner of the fort and there, hiding in the gardener's house, which belonged to LaButte, they fired on both the fort and the schooner *Huron*. Little damage was done to either and every now and then the *Huron* artillery blasted back at them.

Pontiac sent messengers to all the French residents, warning them to stay indoors and not take up arms against the Indians, so that no harm would come to them. He also passed word to them that any Frenchman found taking provisions into the fort or helping the English in any way would be put to death. French informants had already assured him that the garrison had no more than two weeks' worth of provisions inside the fort. If kept bottled up tightly, they would soon be forced to surrender or starve.

In late afternoon the Chippewas under Chief Perwash appeared at Pontiac's new camp with their trophies and reported in detail on the attack against the boat party of Robertson and Davers, about which the Frenchman Clairmont had only sketchily filled Pontiac in. It was good news to the Indians and they listened eagerly to the account as Perwash told it. These Chippewa had brought back with them a French carpenter named Peter Desnoyers, whom they had encountered in the woods. The man was badly frightened, but Pontiac told him he would not be harmed and directed him to approach the fort under a flag of truce and tell the commander that already nineteen had been killed without even one Indian being injured.

Fearfully, waving his flag energetically with every step and constantly calling out "Don't shoot!", Desnoyers approached the west gate. It was opened just enough to allow him to enter and he was taken at once to Gladwin. Grim-faced, the major heard him out. It was confirmation of what he had feared.

"LaButte," he told the interpreter, "I want you to act as emissary between us and Pontiac. Go to him now and ask him just what he wants and what he expects to accomplish with this idiotic action. Try to find out what his immediate plans are. Tell him if he does not end his attack at once, he and his people will be destroyed."

Obviously not relishing the job, LaButte did as ordered, but he returned with precious little information and Pontiac's counterthreat that it was the English who would be destroyed. Pontiac, he added, was momentarily expecting the arrival of another large body of Chippewas from the Saginaw Bay area.

As near as could be estimated now, Pontiac's whole force of Ottawas, Chippewas, Hurons and Potawatomies amounted to somewhere between 900 and 1500 warriors. It was not an encouraging report for Gladwin to hear. Several times during the course of the evening, the interpreter went back and forth between the two commanders until at last, tiring of this business of threat and counterthreat, Pontiac sent LaButte back a final time and told him not to show his face again at this camp in Gladwin's behalf.

Within the fort, Gladwin was confused. He had never heard of Indians maintaining a seige against a proper fortification. It just wasn't their way of fighting. They preferred to hit and run, exposing themselves in the least manner possible to their enemies, taking advantage of natural cover and never attempting to openly attack and take such a strong fort. He was suddenly frighteningly aware of the fact that no spring shipments of supplies had arrived as yet from Niagara and Detroit's remaining provisions were at an ominously low point. There was food enough for perhaps two weeks, but no more. He hoped Pontiac did not realize this.

With a sigh he climbed to the ramparts and began to walk them as the shooting died away with the approach of darkness. There would be no sleep for any English soldier at Detroit tonight.

[*May 10, 1763—Tuesday, 10:00* A.M.]

Disdaining the chair which had been offered him, Pontiac stood along one wall in the parlor of Antoine Cuillerier's house and listened to the continuing conversation. Though he could speak French only in a broken manner, yet he could understand it reasonably well. A number of Frenchmen present spoke the Ottawa tongue fluently, so there was no real problem in communication.

The room was crowded with men, both French and Indian. In addition to Pontiac there were three or four minor chiefs present who thus far had contributed nothing more than their presence to this council. There were also about two dozen Frenchmen scattered about the big room, some seated, some standing.

To the west of them, in the direction of the fort, came the continuing rattle of gunfire, punctuated every once in a while by the throaty rumble of cannon or mortar shot. Ever since four o'clock this morning when the combined Indian forces here began attacking the fort in earnest from three sides, the firing had been fairly steady, though without a great deal being accomplished by either side. Within the fort five soldiers had been slightly wounded. On the outside, three Indians had suffered minor bullet wounds and one had been rather badly injured by shrapnel from an exploding cannon shot. In at least two cases the fort's cannon had been loaded with red hot spikes which were then fired into nearby houses from which the Indian gunfire had become rather deadly. The resultant conflagrations had driven the Indians out, but the firing had not eased off to any appreciable degree.

It was Pontiac who had asked Cuillerier early in the morning to assemble the most influential—and sympathetic—Frenchmen at this house for a council with Pontiac by 10:00 A.M. Now they were on hand in sufficient number for that meeting to begin. Antoine Cuillerier was there, of course, as was his son, Alexis. The arrogantly anti-English Baptiste Campeau was there, and so was Mini Chene, whose views were identical. Pierre LaButte was present, carefully establishing at the onset that while he was interpreting for the English and acting as go-between for them and the Indians, this did not signify that his sympathies were with the garrison. Dr. Jean Chapeton was there, as were Laurence Gamelin. Thomas Gouin, all three of the Meloche brothers—Baptiste, Matthieu, and François—Charles Parent, Jacques Godefroy and some others.

Now Pontiac wasted no time in clarifying the purpose of the council. He wanted to know whether the French community was going to be with him or not, and he wanted to discuss means for the swift reduction of the fort. He was not terribly pleased with the comments which followed. While some of the Frenchmen apparently leaned heavily in support of him and a few hesitantly implied they thought the war a mistake the consensus seemed to be that while they were not sorry Pontiac had declared war against the English, they could not openly support him—at least not yet; not until some word came from the French King that they should do so.

"There is talk," Pontiac said, "of the Frenchmen and Englishmen across the great waters setting aside their fighting while they discuss peace. Is this true?"

"No!" Cuillerier slammed his hand down on the table with the sound of a shot. "Never! There can *never* be peace between us until what has been taken from us is returned. Talk of peaceful negotiations is nothing but lies!"

"You have told me," Pontiac said, looking at this excitable Frenchman, "and others have told me as well, that the

French army will soon be coming. When is soon? When will they be here? I have hit the English for them and I have these Englishmen stopped up in their fort. When will your army come to help?"

Cuillerier shrugged. "Soon, but who can say when for certain? Perhaps as soon as they learn you have struck; perhaps that is what Captain Neyon de Villiere at Fort de Chartres is waiting for. When he hears you have moved against them, then he will probably send you from Fort de Chartres the army you wish to have aid you."

Young Alexis Cuillerier could no longer hold his silence. A hot-tempered, arrogant, decidedly militant individual, he seemed angered at the lack of French support for Pontiac and now he stood and addressed Pontiac in the Ottawa tongue:

"The others may hold back, but not I! I have eaten the same bread as you and I have drunk from the same cup; therefore, I will fire out of the same gun at the English!"

The outburst caused some murmuring among the French and Antoine Cuillerier's expression showed guarded approval of his son. For the first time since this council began, a smile touched Pontiac's lips fleetingly, but it was to the elder Cuillerier that he continued addressing himself.

"You said before that when we took the fort, you would act as commander until the French army came. You will still do this?"

"I will still do it," Cuillerier replied firmly.

"It is good. I will not," Pontiac added, flicking a glance at the younger Cuillerier, "ask you French to support me openly yet. But you must not support the English in any way. Now, how best can we quickly reduce the fort?"

Pierre LaButte spoke up. "Major Gladwin is most anxious for peace. He wants to know the reasons for your conduct and he wishes you to know that he is willing to give redress for any real complaint against the English which you may have. He is poorly provided and cannot hold out for long. Perhaps if you offered to let him and his men go without harm, they would leave and return to Fort Niagara."

Pontiac made an impolite sound. "He knows the reasons for my conduct. He need not ask if I have complaint. And why should we let them go when we have them in our hand and have only but to squeeze to destroy them?"

"Are you willing, at least," LaButte persisted, "to call a temporary halt to hostilities while some peaceful discussions are engaged in? It wouldn't hurt to try."

Pontiac considered this for a while and at last he nodded. "Yes. Carry word to the fort that we wish the English to be represented here for talks in the persons of Captain Campbell and one other officer. Then we will see what we will see. You will carry a letter to him from us."

"I won't order you to go," Henry Gladwin said.

Donald Campbell grinned at his superior and shook his head. "You don't have to, Major. I'm volunteering. Look, most of the French people here and quite a few of the Indians know me pretty well. We've had pretty good relations for a couple of years, which is apparently why they want me to represent the English for the talks. It can't hurt anything to try."

"I still don't like it," Gladwin said. "I don't trust them even a little bit."

Campbell shrugged. "It's not only the word of Pontiac. La-Butte brought the note from Dr. Chapeton. All of them gave their word—Cuillerier, Godefroy, Gouin, Gamelin, to say nothing of Pontiac and his chiefs."

For a long while Henry Gladwin said nothing. The silence outside was pleasant after the all-day gunfire and he wished it could stay that way. Nevertheless, he counted on Campbell more than he could say and he didn't like the idea of the captain being unnecessarily exposed to jeopardy.

It had only been a bit over an hour ago that the firing had abruptly ceased from the Indians and the major had in turn ordered his men to hold their fire. For a while nothing happened, but then a small party of Hurons led by Chief Teata boldly walked toward the fort on the west road and, when they got to the gate, Gladwin ordered that they be permitted to enter. LaButte was out somewhere, so it was the younger Jacques St. Martin who acted as interpreter. Teata spoke soberly for a while and then St. Martin turned to face Gladwin.

"He says, Major, that he has no part in this war; that he did not wish it, that he spoke against it, and that he has not supported it. He wants you to know that. He says that part of the Hurons, under Takee, have joined with Pontiac, but that he himself and his followers have not. He says Pontiac has summoned him and he is on his way now to council with him. He promises to do all in his power to solicit Pontiac from committing further hostilities. He wishes you to know this."

"Tell him," Gladwin replied, "that I appreciate his concern and his efforts and that I applaud his refusal to join Pontiac in this action. Ask him to assure Pontiac that there should be no strife between us and that I am willing to listen with an open heart to any complaints he might have against the English and do what it is in my power to do to help. Tell him that I will also transmit his complaints and comments to General Amherst and to Sir William Johnson and that whatever troubles there are can be settled amicably."

St. Martin told Teata these things and the Huron chief nodded and shook hands with Gladwin, then led his small party out the east gate toward Pontiac's camp. At the same time, approaching, was a group of Frenchmen and four Indians. They were being led by Pierre LaButte. The two groups paused and spoke to one another briefly and then continued on their respective ways. Gladwin ordered that LaButte's group be allowed to enter.

Without wasted words, LaButte told of the council being held at the house of Antoine Cuillerier and the desire of Pontiac that Captain Campbell and another officer be sent out to represent the garrison. That this was the wish of all the tribes involved here was ascertained by the fact that one chief from each of the four Indian nations had accompanied LaButte. Further, LaButte handed Gladwin the note written in French and signed by Dr. Chapeton, Jacques Godefroy, and Laurence Gamelin, guaranteeing the safe return of the two officers. A strictly adhered-to truce was to be observed by both sides while the talks went forward.

Now, while the party of Indians and Frenchmen waited out in the street, Gladwin had closeted himself with Campbell and four others of his officers—Captain Joseph Hopkins. Lieutenant Jehu Hay, Lieutenant George McDougall, and Lieutenant James MacDonald. Their discussion was lively and almost immediately Lieutenant George McDougall volunteered to accompany Campbell. Campbell himself was eager to go, feeling that it might be their only real opportunity to settle this thing before it got completely out of hand.

"Major," he said, "it looks like this is a pretty local thing brought about by Pontiac and if we act properly, perhaps we can keep it from spreading. We have the word of some of the most prominent Frenchmen in the community that we'll be safe. Personally, I've always had good relations with the Indians and I think there's a pretty fair chance some good can come of it. Besides, even if nothing is settled, there'll still be a truce in effect while we're gone. It'll soon be dark and maybe we can take advantage of the lull to get some provisions in; enough, at least, to tide us over until the first shipment of the season from Niagara."

It was against his better judgment, but Gladwin allowed himself to be swayed. Indeed, supplies were perilously low. It was not normal Indian tactics to hold a fort under siege, but if these Indians just happened to do so, the garrison would quickly be in a bad way. Some further discussion went on regarding what concessions Campbell might offer and then both the captain and Lieutenant McDougall shook hands with their fellow officers and rejoined the group of Frenchmen. Gladwin and Hopkins watched the men until the gate shut behind them and then Hopkins exhaled deeply.

"I *still* think we should have detained those four chiefs, sir," he commented.

Gladwin shrugged. "Perhaps, Captain, perhaps. But it certainly wouldn't have shown our good faith very well, would it? We want to give them every reason to believe that we are as peacefully inclined as we say we are. Certainly we want to give them no excuse for detaining or harming Campbell and McDougall, or any cause for building more fire under their resentment. Well, it'll be interesting to hear what they have to say when they get back. Right now, Captain, would you ask Mr. Baby to come to my quarters. We've got to see about getting some provisions in."

[*May 10, 1763—Tuesday, 3:15* P.M.]

From a distance of perhaps thirty yards, Captain Donald Campbell recognized the two men running toward his little party. Both were workers in the employ of the French merchant, Thomas Gouin. They were coming from the direction of the meeting toward which Campbell's party was heading and the several Frenchmen and four Indian chiefs accompanying Campbell and Lieutenant George McDougall murmured uneasily among themselves as the party stopped to wait.

Behind him some forty or fifty yards, Campbell noticed, the east gate of the fort had been closed now and half a dozen or more heads showed above the stockade walls as men stood on the ramparts watching them go. Turning his attention back to the approaching men, Campbell watched them thud to a stop before the group and nod nervously at the party in general; then one of them, a man Campbell knew only as Gerteau, spoke to the officer.

"Captain," he said, panting heavily, "we have a private message for you and the other officer."

Campbell nodded and, touching McDougall's arm, the two moved about twenty feet away from the French and Indians, who were showing some irritation at the delay. As soon as they were relatively out of earshot, Gerteau began speaking rapidly.

"Monsieur Gouin has sent us to you," he explained in a hoarse whisper. "He wishes to warn you to return immediately to the fort—that you are walking into a dangerous situation. He says to tell you he overheard some things after these men left," he indicated the other group with a jerk of his head, "which make him believe you will be in jeopardy if you continue."

Campbell shook his head and whispered back. "Thank you, Monsieur Gerteau, for delivering Monsieur Gouin's warning. But we have said we will come and so we will do so. I don't really believe anyone would try anything in such circumstances. Besides, as you probably know by now, Major Gladwin is holding two Potawatomi chiefs in custody as something of a guarantee. It is not likely that Pontiac would do anything to jeopardize us when retaliation would be apt to take place on those two. No, we'll go on to the meeting."

Gerteau shook his head and continued to whisper protests in a rather agitated manner, but when Campbell continued to declare they would go ahead, he at length shrugged his shoulders and, nodding at the other messenger to follow him, set off to the north away from the group.

Campbell and McDougall casually rejoined their escorts and the walk toward Cuillerier's house resumed. A little over a mile from the fort the party crossed over a narrow wooden bridge spanning Parent's Creek. On the other side they could see the Ottawa encampment and almost at once they were seen from it.

There was a wild screeching as the natives caught sight of the scarlet-coated officers and immediately a rush was begun toward them, the men, women and children snatching up clubs, sticks, switches and other things to use as weapons. Evidently they thought two captives were being brought in and were already moving to set up a gauntlet for them to run.

A loud, authoritative cry, however, abruptly silenced and stopped them. Virtually all eyes turned to the muscular Indian chief with the crescent of white stone hung from his nostrils and the long loops of white porcelain beads hanging from his earlobes. It was Pontiac and his single command had produced a pronounced effect upon them. Without hastening, he came up to the group and, paying no attention to the others, he walked directly to the officers and shook the hands of both.

"You need have nothing to fear from them, my father," he told Campbell. "I have you wrapped in my blanket and my hand is on your shoulder. I am pleased that you and your officer have arrived. We are waiting for you there."

He pointed toward the large, sprawling structure on the other side of the Indian camp, which was the house belonging to Antoine Cuillerier. Without saying more he turned and began walking in that direction. Campbell and McDougall glanced at one another—the latter silently blowing out an exaggerated breath of relief—and they fell in behind the chief. The other chiefs and the Frenchmen brought up the rear.

It was rather dim inside the house and even though a couple of lanterns were burning, it took a little while for Campbell to realize that at least three dozen men were here and that perhaps a third of them were French. A large, beautifully finished wooden table dominated the center of the room and at its head sat Antoine Cuillerier. He wore a dark, rather dressy coat over a ruffled white shirt and on his head there was a large black hat upon which were some embroidered gold lace designs. He barely glanced up at the entry of the party and gave neither a nod of recognition nor a greeting to either officer. He did not rise, nor did he remove his hat. The insults were not lost on the two soldiers, but they said nothing.

Before Cuillerier on the table was a long loaf of bread from which, with a heavy butcher knife, he was cutting slices. One of these he picked up and commenced eating. Then he passed out the rest among the Indians gathered. One of the Potawatomi chiefs, taking offense at this, demanded to know why Cuillerier had insulted them by eating first. Cuillerier grinned, dropped the knife onto the table with a clatter and belched.

"Because, my friend," he replied, "I wish you to have no fear now or ever that you are in danger under this roof—neither by hand," he held up a fist, "by weapon," he flicked the knife with a finger, causing it to spin in a circle, "nor by poison." He took another mouthful of the bread, chewed and swallowed it, then grinned again.

Pontiac had now walked to one side of the table, a few feet from it. The only person closer to Cuillerier than himself was young Alexis who, a look of naked hatred for the English on his face, stood at his father's left and slightly behind him. Pontiac now addressed the elder Cuillerier:

"I look upon you as my father come to life and as the commanding officer of Detroit until the arrival of my brother, Captain Belêtre."

Cuillerier looked genuinely pleased and dipped his head at this, but said nothing. Pontiac now swung his gaze to the two officers who stood across the table from him. Behind them the doorway was now blocked by three or four Indians who stood with their arms crossed, faces without expression.

"If peace is to be made between us," Pontiac began in the Ottawa tongue without preamble, "it can only be on the same terms that you English gave my brother, Belêtre, when he was my father here. You will be allowed to leave Detroit without harm, leaving behind all your baggage and arms. You will be escorted by warriors to the English settlements beyond the mountains to the east and you must promise that you English will never return here again."

Antoine Cuillerier now got to his feet and, walking around the table, took George McDougall by the hand and said enthusiastically in English, "My friend, this is my work. You might now be dead, were it not for my concern for you. Rejoice that I have obtained such good terms for you. I thought Pontiac would have been much harder." Though he spoke in a genial manner, it was evident that he had hoped Pontiac would indeed have been much harder.

"We now," Pontiac continued, an edge of anger in his voice over Cuillerier's interruption, "have many more warriors than you have soldiers. You are like the tree at start of winter, with branches that break easily and with only a few leaves remaining; but we are like a strong young tree filled with the new lifeblood of spring and our leaves are unnumbered. You may not again have a chance to consider such a proposal, so consider it well now. The Ottawas are against you, as are the Potawatomies and the Chippewas and their nephews, the Mississaugi. More than half of the Hurons are with us, and those remaining have just now said they will be of us. You have in your fort no more than enough to feed your soldiers small means for less than a moon. You will weaken and be unable to continue against us. Though then I might still be willing to see you go unharmed, I cannot know that I will be able to control those who fight with me and who will, by then, be thirsty for blood and who will not be so friendly. Consider well, father, what your answer will be."

Although Campbell understood the gist of what Pontiac

was saying, he and McDougall nevertheless listened with attentiveness to Pierre LaButte's interpretation. The Frenchman spoke softly, at the same time that the Ottawa war chief was speaking, and he finished only a few seconds after Pontiac. Campbell's round face was set in firm lines and he saw McDougall looking at him inquiringly, but said nothing to him. He watched as Pontiac turned and took a place along a wall near the other prominent chiefs on hand. Still he waited without saying anything and a heavy, uncomfortable silence fell over the room. The room was growing darker and despite the strategically placed lamps there were deep shadows in some areas. At the table, Cuillerier belched again and it was an abnormally loud sound in the stillness. Outside could be heard activities in the Ottawa village; dogs yapped now and then, children occasionally yelled or laughed, squaws called stridently.

Fully fifteen minutes passed before Campbell slowly stepped forward more into the center of the room, his impeccable uniform a striking contrast to the nondescript garb of most of the Frenchmen and what little the Indians wore. His eyes held steadily on Pontiac's and he spoke softly but with strength, inwardly pleased that the people on hand here could not detect the hammering of his heart and the genuine fright which had been causing his back muscles to tighten and his stomach to roll.

"I had thought," he began, "that my brother, Chief Pontiac, would have long before now given up acting as a child might act. I am filled with sorrow to find him raising a war hatchet against his friends, the English. He ought to reconsider and take a look around him. The war hatchet he raises is just a handle; it no longer has a head. His allies, of whom he boasts, are like silly little children playing a game who, wishing sweets, decide to open the bee tree, but first they stand bravely a mile from the hive and shout for the bees to give up and go away, leaving their honey behind. But should they come closer and the bees get angry and begin to sting, like the children they are, they will run away to where they are safe.

"My brother, Chief Pontiac, knows me; he knows that when I speak to him, I speak from my heart and that I have not told him lies. We have had friendship between us and there never was a time when, if you had grievances against us, you could not have come to us to speak of them and let us try to smooth them away. I know that you have had an anger in your heart, but to declare war against us is not the way to settle any differences. For you to consider war against us is foolish and the act of a child, for it can only result in your total ruin. All over this country there are forts in which there are English soldiers, and the farther to the east one goes, the more of them there are. If you continue in the way you have begun, so many soldiers will spill from the east into this country that they could not be counted and one by one they will destroy villages and warriors until peace is made again or there are no Indians left.

"We do not," he added, a note of sympathy entering his voice, "wish to see this happen. For over two years I have lived here among you and I have come to know you. And you have come to know me. You know that when it was possible for me to do so, I gave you what I could spare, often when this was against the orders of my general. Perhaps things have been hard for you, but this is only temporary and will pass if you have patience. That will not happen if you continue this war you have so foolishly begun against us."

He paused for a long period. Even after LaButte had finished quietly interpreting into the Ottawa tongue, he remained silent. Finally, he shook his head.

"No," he sighed, "we cannot accept what my brother, Pontiac, seems to think is a kind offer. We have been sent here by our King to hold this place and this we will do. We are bees with deadly stingers and as long as we are left in peace, we will not bring harm to you. But if Pontiac continues his attack against us, we will lock up our honey and stand at the entrance to our hive and protect it against any who come, regardless of their numbers. Think on it. Will Pontiac now lay aside his tomahawk and once again stretch out the hand of friendship? Does he truly wish destruction brought upon him and his people and upon those who have so foolishly followed him in the way he is going? Will my brother, Pontiac, not now tell me that the fires of anger have cooled; and will my brother, Pontiac, not now come to the fort with us to talk with Major Gladwin and settle whatever difficulties he feels exist between us?"

Campbell stepped back beside Lieutenant McDougall, briefly caught the respectful gaze in that younger officer's eyes, and then looked back at Pontiac. LaButte had concluded his interpreting, and now there was an oppressive silence in the room. Everyone waited for Pontiac to make his reply, but the war chief chose not to do so as yet. He simply stood there, arms folded across his bare chest, expression unreadable.

They waited . . . and waited. An hour passed, and then even more time beyond that. It was growing dark outside and Campbell was hungry and tired. Still he waited without complaint. But at last he grunted and exhaled noisily and shook his head. He was convinced now that Pontiac would no more give in to his ideas than the English would turn over the fort to him. It was a stalemate. He nodded meaningfully at Lieutenant McDougall and the pair turned to leave. Instantly the Indians who were in relaxed postures by the entrance straightened and barred the way. Several knives appeared, as if by magic, and glinted ominously in the lamplight.

Flushing deeply, Donald Campbell spun on his heel, an angry comment already shaping his lips; but it remained unspoken as the Ottawa chief held up his hand and shook his head once.

"My father," he said calmly, "will stay tonight among us."

Beside him, Campbell sensed McDougall tightening like a spring and he unobtrusively reached out and touched the lieutenant's arm reassuringly. Then he addressed Pontiac.

"We came to you," he said sternly, "as emissaries of peace, with your word given as well as that of the other Indians and French here assembled, that we would come to no harm and that we would be permitted to return to the fort safely. Is this how Pontiac honors a promise he gives?"

"My father," Pontiac repeated flatly, "will stay among the Ottawa, and his officer will stay also."

Captain Donald Campbell and Lieutenant George McDougall became, in that moment, prisoners of the Indians.

[*May 10, 1763—Tuesday, 11:00 P.M.*]

Jacques Duperon Baby sat in the chair opposite Henry Gladwin's desk, his breathing still a bit uneven. The night air was rather cool, yet beads of perspiration stood out on his forehead and glinted tiny reflections of the single lamp on the desk. He had worked up a sweat, yes, but the perspiration was more than that. He was honest enough with himself to admit that he was very frightened and for perhaps the twentieth time since darkness had fallen some two or three hours ago, he chided himself inwardly for getting involved as he now was. Yet, he knew there was nothing else he could do.

Gladwin was writing on a scrap of paper, but now he paused and glanced up at Baby. A faint smile tilted the corners of the major's lips and he thought again of how little the Frenchman across from him looked like someone cut out to be a spy or, in a manner of speaking, a blockade runner. The Frenchman was dark and slight and nervous-appearing at first glance. That impression ended, however, with a look at the eyes. They were strong, direct, sincere eyes. At the moment they held in them the light of excitement, as well as a trace of fear.

Seeing Gladwin looking at him, Baby smiled and shook his head. "It is a risky business, Major. My heart," he touched an index finger to his chest, "tells me it is unaccustomed to such jeopardy."

Gladwin nodded. "Again, Jacques," he said earnestly, "there is no way I can fully express my appreciation for what you have done, for the risk you've taken."

Baby shrugged deprecatingly. "It is only what is right, Major," he said. "I may not like to do it, but I would like even less *not* to do it."

Gladwin looked at the notes he had made. It was a listing of supplies—flour, maple sugar, dried corn and peas, jerked meat, dried fish, a small amount of gunpowder and lead—all of which Baby had gathered together from his own supplies and from trustworthy French inhabitants who he knew were opposed to the rash steps being undertaken by Pontiac. There were enough goods to last the garrison for two months or longer. There were barrels and kegs, bales and parcels of goods that he had accumulated in a storage shed he owned across the river from the fort and which, ever since darkness had fallen, he and his men had been secretly ferrying by batteaux to the vessels anchored in the river adjacent to the fort.

He had been reluctantly willing to bring them directly to the fort, but Gladwin had demurred, not willing to have the risks for this valuable ally made even greater. From the two ships, Gladwin told him, his soldiers would have no real difficulty bringing the supplies into the fort through the water gate.

While the land gates on east and west sides of the fort were obviously being carefully watched by Pontiac's men, there was really no effective way to guard the water gate. And with the sky overcast to hide his actions, Jacques Baby and his men had brought the supplies unseen to the ships. For Gladwin it was the relaxation of an enormous strain. With only the eighteen or twenty days' worth of supplies he had had on hand before this, it was evident that some sort of desperate chances would soon have to be taken if Pontiac maintained the siege, which he evidently intended doing. But Gladwin knew, too, that the Indian temperament is not conducive to maintaining long-time sieges. Now, with these supplies Baby had brought—and his promise of more, if at all possible—they would be able to sit tight, not take any unnecessary risks and just let Pontiac's siege die away, as it probably would in a matter of a few weeks if Campbell and McDougall were unsuccessful tonight in convincing Pontiac of the futility of it. Even if the siege didn't end, even if somehow Pontiac managed to coerce his allies to keep it up, these supplies just obtained would surely last the garrison until the regular supply convoy came from Niagara.

"A simple verbal thanks is hardly reward enough for the service you've rendered, Jacques," Major Gladwin said now, "but rest assured that the general will be informed and you will be amply rewar—"

Baby cut him off with an upraised hand and shook his head vigorously. "No, Major! The only reward I wish is a safeguarding of my identity. I do not think they would hesitate to kill me if they knew what I have done. Do not tell the general of me. Such a message might fall into the wrong hands and then I would be done. Besides," he smiled a curiously appealing smile, "I do this not for any reward. I do it because it is right, and what they are doing is wrong. I could not live with myself if I did less."

The admiration Gladwin felt for Jacques Duperon Baby swelled within him and he determined that somehow, some way, after all this business was settled, reward of a more tangible nature would indeed be given to Baby.

They continued talking for another half hour of what had occurred thus far and what the chances were of Captain Campbell and Lieutenant McDougall being able to convince Pontiac that he should become peaceable again. Neither man held much hope of it. Baby was about to make some comment in this respect when there came a hesitant tapping on Gladwin's door. The Frenchman's eyes widened and the fear showed in them again.

"What is it?" Gladwin called out.

"Sir," came the voice of his aide from the other side of the door. "Monsieur LaButte is here. He says he has an extremely important message for you."

"One moment," Gladwin replied. Swiftly and silently he led Baby to a side door and, after shaking his hand warmly, let him out and closed the portal noiselessly. Then he took off his jacket, slightly mussed his hair, rubbed his eyes vigorously to make them red, slid the papers on his desk into a drawer and put a military report he had been writing on the desktop beside his pen. Then he walked to the principal door and opened it.

LaButte, his waspish face tight with repressed excitement or concern, spoke instantly, his words almost unintelligible in his haste to expel them.

"Major," he rasped, "Captain Campbell and Lieutenant McDougall won't be coming back. Pontiac's holding them prisoner. He took them after the meeting. We Frenchmen who were there protested strongly, but he would not hear us. He has put them under guard in the house of François Meloche on the other side of Parent's Creek."

It was a possibility Gladwin had feared, but never really thought would occur. Now he groaned audibly, closed his eyes and pinched the bridge of his nose between finger and thumb. "Damn," he muttered. He sounded ill. "Damn, damn, damn!" He opened his eyes and straightened and the look he gave the interpreter now was not a friendly one.

"All right, LaButte," he said, "come on in here and give me all the details." He glanced at his aide. "Send an orderly around to all the officers except the officer of the guard. He's to tell them there will be a meeting here in exactly fifteen minutes."

"Yes sir!" said the aide, and he was gone even before Gladwin had closed the door to his chambers and turned to question LaButte.

[*May 10, 1763—Tuesday Midnight*]

In his plush quarters at New York City, Lieutenant General Sir Jeffrey Amherst listened to the delicate chiming of the clock as it tinkled out the sixteen notes of four quatrains and then, in a somewhat mellower tone, bonged twelve times. He yawned prodigiously and rubbed a hand through the thin, scraggly, carrot-colored hair covering his pate. His fine powdered wig sat on its ball-stand on the bedroom dresser and he was clad in a comfortable and timeworn old robe.

He scuffed to his desk and glanced quickly over the several pages he had written already and once more he felt the irritation rise within him. He wished these damned frontier diplomats would desist in being so eternally pessimistic about everything. If it wasn't Conrad Weiser or William Johnson warning him about dire events to come from the Indians, then it was Daniel Claus or George Croghan. He was getting very tired of it.

That he, His Majesty's top military commander in this

hemisphere, should feel anything but scorn and disdain for these motley savages was incomprehensible to him. Now Croghan was warning him that with rumors of the French cessions of Canada to England going the rounds of the tribes, the situation had become ugly and fraught with peril. Croghan darkly warned that they might rise at any time.

Amherst snorted. That they should pose a threat to him or to any of the garrisons was laughable. He had no doubt they were angry, but so what? It made little difference. Let them scream and yowl all they wanted. What could they do? Maybe now his detractors would see the wisdom of his preventing their acquiring lead and gunpowder and firearms over these many months. Now what possible threat could unarmed ignorant savages possibly pose to a well-oiled military might such as that which Sir Jeffrey controlled? That anybody might even suggest that they were a threat to him seemed to him to be little short of a slur on his own ability and that of his men, and he was becoming damned well irked at these continuing dire predictions from the frontier Indian agents and, yes, even some of his junior officers. By God, if a commander of one of his forts could not, with the arms and artillery and fortifications at his disposal, keep the savages under control without any difficulty whatever, then that man would not long be in a command position!

Now, having read again the warnings and advice just received today from George Croghan, he tossed the letter down and returned to the one he had not yet finished. He concluded it:

Whatever idle notions they [the Indians] may entertain in regard to the cessions made by the French crown, can be of very little consequence. Imagination can turn a man's insides to jelly if he will permit it to do so. Guard against it.

He signed the letter with his usual flourish, stood, scratched his stomach expansively with both hands and retired to the bedroom. He was exhausted from the day's letter writing.

[May 11, 1763—Wednesday, 6:30 A.M.]

Although it was only around an hour after dawn, Captain Campbell and Lieutenant McDougall had been awake for a couple of hours already. They had breakfasted well at the table of François Meloche, who nervously helped his wife serve them and repeatedly apologized that it was in his house that they were being held prisoner.

Actually, Donald Campbell reflected, if one had to be a captive, conditions could hardly have been better. He had been informed that Pontiac had left two warriors on guard outside the house and their duty was not only to prevent the escape of the captives, but equally to turn away any Indians who might come to humiliate or harm them. Otherwise, the two officers were to be given every freedom possible.

"I don't really think," Campbell told George McDougall over their breakfast of fresh eggs and fried fish, "that we have anything much to worry about. Pontiac and I have always had good relations and the fact that he is protecting us now bears out my belief that no harm will come to us if we just take it easy and don't do anything rash."

McDougall nodded, inclined to agree, but still not at all pleased with the idea of being kept against their will. Nevertheless, as Campbell had pointed out, it did give them something of an opportunity to keep their eyes and ears open and perhaps gather some information which would be beneficial to the English when the two of them did somehow get back inside the fort. They continued chatting about their situation until, about eight o'clock, Pontiac showed up with a number of his chiefs, plus a half dozen or more Frenchmen, including Pierre LaButte. While most of the men waited outside, Pontiac entered Meloche's house, bade Meloche bring pen and ink and, when he had done so, told Campbell to sit at the table and write what he dictated as a message to Major Gladwin.

It took about half an hour to complete writing down the Ottawa war chief's demands to the English commander. Gladwin was told that fifteen hundred Indians were now poised to attack and that another fifteen hundred would be here within a few days. Gladwin and his garrison would be allowed to leave aboard batteaux, taking with them enough supplies to see them through to Fort Niagara. However, they must leave behind all other effects, all weapons—their own as well as the remaining French artillery—and everything else that was in the fort. They must also leave behind the *Huron* and *Michigan*, still anchored in the river adjacent to the fort.

Campbell shook his head as he finished writing. In his halting Ottawa tongue he told Pontiac that such a demand was ridiculous. "For one thing," he said, "Major Gladwin would not even *consider* giving up everything in the fort as well as the two vessels. For another, I am sure he will not negotiate in any way, so long as the lieutenant and I are being detained as hostages like this."

Pontiac was abruptly angry and snatched the paper away from him. He glanced briefly at the English writing, which was quite foreign to him, and then folded the paper twice and stared at the two officers in an ugly manner.

"Do not think," he warned, "because I have so far seen that you are well treated, that I am particularly concerned about your health. You are useful to me as tools for bargaining, but no more. If your commander will not bargain now, perhaps when he receives the ears of you and the other officer, and then your right hands, and then your left feet—perhaps then he will be willing to make terms. You would be surprised how many parts of you can be taken and still you be kept alive. An eye gouged out with a thumb will not kill you; nor will a tongue slit off with a sharp knife. So do not think Pontiac is so greatly concerned for your health!"

With that he wheeled and strode outside, clutching the paper Campbell had written, while the captain sat staring at the door, his face grown ashen.

[May 11, 1763—Wednesday, 8:45 A.M.]

Having slammed the door of Meloche's house behind him as he left, Pontiac strode up to the cluster of waiting French inhabitants and Indian chiefs. His expression was still ugly, but in spite of his threatening words to Captain Campbell, he had no intention of seeing the two officers come to harm. He would, in fact, do his utmost to protect them if anyone else bothered them—at least for now—because they were the key to his own security.

From all outward appearances, excluding only Chief Teata's band of sixty Huron warriors, the Indians everywhere around Detroit were solidly behind him and eager to obey his commands. Yet, ever since the failure to surprise Detroit and take it by storm in one fell swoop, a niggling doubt over just how strong their loyalty was had ridden Pontiac. He had to admit that even though he held the fort under siege at present, there was always the possibility that it could hold until reinforcements arrived. Either that or else his own Indians, unaccustomed to maintaining sieges and preferring to strike and leave, would tire of such warfare as this and drift away. In either case, if such came to pass, it was going to be necessary to have some sort of insurance for his own survival. At such a juncture he would be able to use Campbell and

McDougall to bargain for his own safety and escape retribution.

It was time now, however, to give Gladwin the note he had had Campbell write and if the major refused its demands, as Pontiac was almost sure he would, then it was also time to give a display of force that would strike a note of fear into the hearts of the men inside the fort and perhaps cause them to bring pressure to bear on their commander to accept the terms while they could still be taken and retreat to Fort Niagara.

His mind made up, he handed the note to Pierre LaButte, the leader of the small group of Frenchmen, giving him instructions to take it to the commander of the fort and, under the guise of solicitude, to urge him in the presence of his officers to leave the fort at once because of the large force being readied against him. LaButte and his men were to await Gladwin's reply and then bring it at once to Pontiac. The Ottawa war chief would be somewhere to the southwest of the fort, tending to some business he would have there with outlying French residents. LaButte nodded his understanding and set off with his men.

Pontiac turned and surveyed the remaining Indians. There were about twenty of them, along with eight or nine of his ablest subchiefs. He pointed to four of them in turn.

"You, Macatepilesis, as well as Breton, Chavinon and Golletah—you four will come with me. The rest of you alert everyone else. Every man to take position around the fort and remain hidden until my word is given, at which time you will then rush forward and attack the fort, doing all in your power to enter it."

Without another word Pontiac moved off, following a path which would allow him to circle the fort at a safe distance to approach the French dwellings on the other side. Macatepilesis and Breton strode side by side behind him, while Chavinon and his nephew, Golletah, brought up the rear.

In less than half an hour the four had split away under Pontiac's order and were calling the heads of all the French houses to come and hear Pontiac at once. In another few minutes a score or more French inhabitants had gathered and were standing in a wary and somewhat apprehensive cluster. Pontiac faced them with hauteur.

"I call you together to tell you this," he said: "We are sorely lacking in supplies, especially powder and ball. You have such supplies and you will turn them over to me. If you do not do so willingly, then you will suffer the pain of having them plundered from you, and I would not wish to see any of you hurt. Don't hold back or keep supplies from me, but give them freely. You will be paid for their worth; but if you try to hold them back from me, you will be paid in another way."

He pointed to a two-wheeled cart beside one house. "I will use that," he said, "and it will be returned. We will go from house to house and you will place in it your ammunition, for which few of you have guns anyway."

The Frenchmen grumbled audibly, but did not resist. That the powder and lead were to be used against the English did not bother them. It was the imperious, dictatorial manner of Pontiac which rankled. But there was not a man among them who dared to stand and refuse the order of the chief.

[*May 11, 1763—Wednesday, 9:30* A.M.]

With the majority of his officers standing at ease behind him, Gladwin listened to the words of the Frenchman, LaButte, who had brought the note in Captain Campbell's handwriting. The commander had inwardly chuckled at the way Campbell had worded some of Pontiac's demands, making it evident without actually saying so that he thought Major Gladwin should do nothing and that he and McDougall were, thus far, perfectly all right.

The demands, of course, were utterly ridiculous. The major had begun shaking his head even while reading the note and continued to do so at intervals as he read it aloud a second time to the assembled officers. But Pierre LaButte had begun speaking at once when he finished and Gladwin heard the fort's interpreter out courteously.

"Major," LaButte said earnestly, "you are in a much worse position than you know. At this moment there are fifteen hundred Indians all around the fort waiting to attack should your answer offend Pontiac. Nor are they all. An equal number are on their way here—from Saginaw Bay and L'Arbre Croche and from near the forts of St. Joseph and Michilimackinac and Miamis. You are bottled up here without many supplies and you cannot hold out long against such a force. It is foolishness to try to maintain what you no longer have the strength to hold onto. For your own safety and the safety of your men, I implore you, sir, leave! You have enough batteaux to transport your garrison and I have the word from Pontiac himself that if you leave at once, taking nothing with you but what supplies it will be necessary to have to carry you to Fort Niagara, you will be allowed to leave in peace."

Again Gladwin was shaking his head.

"Tell Pontiac," he said, "that I was not sent here to hand this fort and all its contents over to him. Tell him that if he and his men are foolish enough to attack, many of his men will die. Tell him further that even were I inclined to surrender this fort to him, which I am not, I would never do so as long as he was holding my officers prisoner. He gives me his word, you say, that he would let us depart in batteaux, but I recall only too clearly that he also gave his word when he sent for Captain Campbell and Lieutenant McDougall to attend the meeting, that they would be treated as emissaries of peace have a right to be treated. Instead, they have been held captive. Is this how Pontiac honors his promises? Is this how he shows the value of his given word? I will not treat with any Indians until those two officers are returned safely to the fort!"

There was a murmur of approval from the officers gathered behind him, at which LaButte shrugged and resignedly slapped his hands against his sides. He had done what he was sent to do and there was no more to be said. He dipped his head toward Gladwin and the officers and went away.

Henry Gladwin watched the interpreter go and then nodded at Joseph Hopkins. "Captain, double all guards. See that every rifle is readied for firing. Prime the cannon and mortars. There is a full alert again, as of now. I wouldn't be surprised if we see some action pretty quickly."

[May 11, 1763—Wednesday, 10:30 A.M.]

A half dozen warriors pulled the heavily laden two-wheeled cart along the encirling path around Detroit. Kegs and half-kegs of gunpowder were piled helter-skelter upon it and there were sacks and bars of lead, a few firearms and numerous bullet molds. Pontiac and his four subchiefs walked ahead of the wagon, angling toward his camp. It was as they were within a mile of their destination that LaButte and his small party intercepted them.

Pontiac stopped the procession as the whites approached, and waited. He had noted with approval the placement of warriors under cover all around the fort. He had little doubt that they would now be used in an attack. Until this moment many of the Indians who had paid him lip service had been

247

obviously reticent about engaging in open warfare against the English. It was evident that they were willing to see the English run out and eager to have the French return, but as to openly supporting an actual attack against the English, that was another matter. Still, Pontiac was shrewd enough to realize that once they had been goaded into making such attack, the line would be drawn and they would be committed beyond withdrawal.

The force prepared to attack now was almost equally made up of Ottawas, Potawatomies and Chippewas. The Hurons were less numerous; some of them Wyandots from the Sandusky area, the remainder from Takee's band here near Detroit. The fact that Teata's Hurons directly across the river from the fort had refused to gather for the assault was galling and Pontiac determined to force the issue at once.

Without change of expression he listened to the report of this interpreter who had gone to see Gladwin. When LaButte was finished, Pontiac made a grunting sound and turned his gaze on Macatepilesis.

"Spread the word for the attack to begin now."

Macatepilesis moved away at once and Pontiac continued with the loaded cart to his campsite near Parent's Creek. There he divided the goods into three large piles and one small one. One of these he gave to Chief Washee of the Potawatomies and another was pointed out for Chief Sanpear of the Chippewas to distribute among his own warriors. The third large pile he kept and the smaller allotment was given to a pair of Huron warriors to take to Chief Takee.

By this time Macatepilesis had returned and at a nod of Pontiac's head, joined Chavinon, Breton and Golletah to follow the war chief as he walked to the riverbank and stepped into a canoe. They pushed off and the methodically dipping paddles thrust them cross-stream toward Teata's village. When they were about in midstream they paused briefly as the wind carried to their ears the sounds of shrieking and the rattle of gunfire and, after a few moments, the thudding at intervals of the fort's artillery. For the first time this day, Pontiac's sour expression dissolved into a grin.

The sourness had returned, however, by the time the slender craft was beached on the river shore adjacent to Teata's village. The Huron chief, accompanied by the gowned Jesuit priest, Father Pothier, came forward slowly to greet them. Pontiac ignored the greeting and pierced Teata with a stern glare.

"You will now fight the English," he said flatly.

Teata glanced nervously at the priest and swallowed. He shook his head faintly and his voice quavered somewhat as he spoke. "It is your war, Pontiac, not ours. From the beginning I have said that we Christian Hurons did not wish war against the English and would not fight them. Our priest has told us that it is against God's wish that we take up arms to kill them. We cannot do it."

As if he had not even heard the words, Pontiac continued: "Because if you do not fight the English beside us now, we will destroy you along with them. Hear! The guns bark now and the fort will soon fall. Perhaps not today or tomorrow, but very soon. But though we are busy fighting them now, we will take the time if necessary and leave off fighting them and bring disaster on you and your people if you do not join us."

Father Pothier now spoke up. He was a chubby little man and, with the cowl of his robe hanging loosely in back of him, the glistening beads of perspiration could clearly be seen on his bald pate above the circlet of very curly, almost kinky hair.

"Chief Pontiac," he said slowly in the Ottawa tongue, "Teata does not hold the hatred for the English that is in your breast. He does not wish to kill them and I have told him he is right in feeling this way. But he and his warriors and their families are my flock and I wish to see no hurt come to them; so now I say to him that it is upon his head what he will do. Better, my children, that you should join hands in what you do, rather than lift the hatchet among yourselves. Only this do I ask of you, Pontiac: tomorrow is Holy Thursday, which is one of God's most sacred days. I ask that Teata and his people be allowed to attend the Mass I will sing tomorrow in observance. After that I will not interfere and Teata may do whatever it is in his heart to do."

"And what will Teata do?" Pontiac asked, his black eyes still boring into those of the Huron chief. "Will he then again say no and cause us to stop our important business across the river to come here and attend to him? Or will he, as his brothers under Takee have done, join us in our fight to drive these Englishmen from our lands? Speak, Teata!"

"After the Mass tomorrow, Pontiac," Teata said, his voice hardly more than a whisper, "my warriors and I will come under your wing and do as you ask of us."

And for the second time this day, Pontiac's lips screwed up into a savage smile.

Throughout the afternoon Henry Gladwin had detected the change in attitude of his officers. Before the fighting had broken out in earnest they had been resolute in their determination to thrust back any attacking force. But that had been this morning. Now it was half past seven in the evening and the air inside the fort had been acrid all day with the smoke of gunpowder. Their eyes were bloodshot and their ears still ringing with the day-long thunder of artillery and cracking of rifles.

The Indians had fought with admirable bravery, rushing the fort in wave after wave in the face of withering fire, taking advantage of every possible bit of cover available. Occasionally had come an outcry as an Indian was apparently struck by a bullet but, despite the heavy fusillade laid down, such times were few indeed and gradually the early resolution of Gladwin's garrison began to fail. Now, as twilight approached, seven privates with wounds of varying degrees of severity were moaning or sobbing in the makeshift hospital quarters and there was the stark realization among the other soldiers that the next bullet might take them. No longer were they so eager to show themselves, however briefly, to fire at the attackers—and now, to a man, they were remembering with some degree of wistfulness that had Pontiac's offer been accepted this morning, they might at this moment be on Lake Erie, moving steadily toward the stone sanctuary of Fort Niagara. They were not cowards, they were merely afraid; many were new men who not only hadn't fought in any battles of the so recently ended French and Indian War, but had never in their lives fired a weapon at another human being or, more importantly, themselves been fired upon.

"Sir!" The voice of a soldier on the ramparts came to Gladwin dimly over the gunfire. "The enemy's stopped firing and there's a party approaching under a truce flag. Looks like Mister LaButte's with 'em."

Gladwin acknowledged and ordered the firing to be halted and the party be allowed to enter. At the same time he gave an order for a party of soldiers to man batteaux and go out under cover of the cease-fire to the two vessels and bring into the fort another supply of the provisions that had been gathered and deposited aboard the ships by Jacques Baby and his men. Ten minutes later there was a very similar reenactment of the scene of this morning when the French emissary delivered Pontiac's terms as dictated to Campbell. Once more the terms of the war chief, virtually identical with those offered earlier, were given and once again Pierre LaButte pleaded with Gladwin to consider the lives of his men, now obviously in great jeopardy.

"Pontiac is willing to do all he can to prevent further bloodshed," the interpreter added. "He has now said that he is even willing to allow you and your men to take the two ships and go, leaving behind your arms and supplies. Major, these are good terms and I strongly urge you to take them. The only other term he asks is a guarantee that the Negro boy who is a servant of the merchant James Rankin be turned over to him as his own personal servant. On the whole, sir," he reiterated, "these are very good terms which I recommend you take while the offer holds. Others of my countrymen, many of them very sympathetic to you, think the best thing now that you English can do would be to give up what you must eventually lose and save yourselves and the vessels."

Gladwin did not reply at once, but merely stood beside his desk steeped in thought. Finally he looked directly at LaButte and said, "Wait in the other room while we discuss this."

LaButte, trailed by the small French party, nodded and allowed himself to be escorted into another room. A guard was stationed at the door while the officers went into a conference among themselves. The proposal was discussed from all standpoints and Gladwin was more than a little disturbed when it became evident his officers were almost unanimous in their desire to accept the terms, board the ships and abandon Detroit. The commander, though as yet he had said nothing, was appalled and angered by the realization that he stood essentially alone in a determination to hold the fort. The rest talked so animatedly about boarding the *Huron* and the *Michigan* and sailing for Niagara that it almost seemed a decision had already been made to do so. The officers discussed the dire results if fire arrows set Detroit ablaze and the massacre that was sure to result if the enemy continued its present attack and managed to burn or cut its way through the pickets.

Gladwin had not let the possibility of the Indians using fire arrows go unheeded. Early this afternoon he had ordered every available empty tub, barrel or keg to be filled with water and placed strategically around the fort for use in immediate fire extinguishing, but he seriously doubted that Pontiac would order such an attack. There were too many traders' goods stored in the fort, goods which Pontiac desperately needed, for the chief to wantonly destroy them if it could be avoided. Gladwin, however, kept his thoughts in this respect to himself and continued to listen with set expression to the general discussion among the officers in favor of abandoning the fort.

Gradually the talk died away until all the officers were waiting mutely and rather self-consciously for the major to make known his views. He surprised them. Instead of talking to them, he merely told the guard to show the French party back in. When they assembled before him, Gladwin addressed LaButte.

"Go back to Pontiac and tell him this," he said. His voice was low and even and gave the impression of unwavering strength. "Tell him that my officers and men are of one mind and one accord: that Captain Campbell and Lieutenant McDougall must be returned to us before we will give him any answer. When they are returned to us, we will release our two Potawatomi prisoners. Tell him that until then, we will defend this place, if necessary to the last man, before making any agreement with him. Tell him that as soon as General Amherst hears of what has happened here, his fury will be unquenchable and he will send great numbers of men against all the Indians here and he will wipe them out utterly. Tell him that we are not foolish chickens who will run because he screeches like a hawk. Tell him that he has raised his tomahawk against *men*, and that he had best take care when he brings it down that he does not, in his rashness, bury it in his own head. Above all else, tell him that I demand the *immediate* return of Captain Campbell and Lieutenant McDougall; that until they are returned safely, my ears can no longer hear any word he speaks. Go and tell him all this now!"

As the French party left without speaking, Gladwin's officers shuffled their feet and murmured uncomfortably among themselves. He shot a stern glance at them and the murmuring ceased.

"Any comments, gentlemen?"

There were none.

An hour or so later, Major Gladwin was once again closeted in his chambers with Jacques Duperon Baby and was gratified to learn that almost the same quantity of supplies as last time had been quietly ferried to the two vessels anchored adjacent to the fort. This time the supplies were principally barrels and half-barrels of corn, peans, and bear grease. In addition, Baby brought some satisfying news:

"It may interest you to know, Major, that there were some Indian casualties in the fighting today. I'm told there were three warriors killed and twelve wounded. Some of the chiefs are angry with Pontiac."

"If they keep on attacking as they did today," Gladwin observed, "there'll be a good many more to add to those statistics."

But while he spoke with conviction, he felt a deep disappointment. It was a very small casualty ratio, indeed, from the force of six hundred Indians who had attacked all day.

[May 12, 1763—Thursday, 9:00 A.M.]

The word had spread swiftly among the French and Indians in the vicinity of Detroit about the council Pontiac was to hold this morning and by the time it convened a great many of the more sympathetic French and nearly all of the chiefs had assembled. Present, too, at the Ottawa village where the council was being held were the two English hostages, Donald Campbell and George McDougall. They sat on the ground beside one another with a Frenchman on either side of them and two warriors close behind them. Neither officer had any idea what the council was about, but both were very curious as to what would be said.

Occasionally from the distance toward the fort could be heard the popping of rifles, but only in a sporadic way, as the relatively small Indian force around it kept the garrison on alert and prevented any detachments from making a sally. Ignoring these sounds, Pontiac addressed the crowd before him and Campbell, in a low voice, kept McDougall informed in English in a general way.

Pontiac, fully regaled in his ornamentation and fresh paint, was a fearsome figure as he stood before them and directed his first remarks to those Frenchmen in attendance:

"My brothers, the French, you are ignorant of all the reasons that have induced me to act, although I have spared no pains to keep you informed of my sentiments. But, as I fear that our father, the French King, will not come and take possession of the fort soon enough after I have expelled or killed the English, and that the Indians gathered here may turn and insult you if there is no French commandant here to prevent this difficulty, I have therefore resolved to send to the Illinois some of our French brothers, along with some Indians, to carry our war belts and our words to our father at Fort de Chartres, Captain Neyon de Villiere. In my message I will ask him to send us a French officer for a commandant to guide us and replace the English. You, my brothers, will do me a pleasure to write our father there in this matter, joining your words with mine."

Although it was apparent that many of the French in attendance took these words at face value, there were a good number who did not. Some of them were well aware, as were both English officers, that the words were deceptive to the extreme. A certain number of them already knew that Pontiac had appointed Antoine Cuillerier to take command for the French here when the fort was taken, so there was no need to send for another officer to take command. It took no great degree of logic to read behind Pontiac's words. The Ottawa war chief had now come to the inescapable conclusion that, having failed to take the fort by surprise and having tested the defenses of the fort and found them not lacking, the only way he was going to be able to bring the garrison to its knees was by laying siege and starving them out. Yet Pontiac, whose way of fighting this was not, was aware that he needed particular direction for carrying out such a siege and so what he was seeking from the French military at Fort de Chartres was, in essence, an officer skilled in waging siege warfare. Besides, there was no doubt in his mind that the arrival of such an officer from Fort de Chartres would not only encourage his own Indians, it would tend to swing those French still vacillating in their allegiance to the Indian side.

"I have asked five of your French to carry the messages for me, escorted by some of our warriors, and these five have agreed." Pontiac indicated a quintet of Frenchmen seated to one side of him. The chief continued: "These men are Elleopolle Chene, who is known to us and to you more often by the name of Mini; Jacques Godefroy, Philippe Beauban, Maurice Chauvin, and Pierre Labadie. I ask now that they take down what I say as a message to Monsieur Neyon de Villiere."

Immediately Mini Chene took out paper and pen, uncapped a large ink-pot and poised himself to write. Pontiac began slowly dictating, pleased that the entire crowd clung to his every word.

"Listen, you French, our brothers, who are prisoners as well as we: it is an anger to us that the English, who at first we were willing to adopt as brothers, should deceive so many nations. All that the Delawares and Shawnees told us in seasons past is now come to pass. They warned us that we should not trust the English, as they sought only to deceive us, and so it has happened; we have been deceived. Except for the help of some of the French merchants here, who gave us credit when the English would not, and except for some small reserves of supplies that we have held back for our use at such a time as this, we would have before now been undone in our aims.

"Since the French father who had commanded here, Monsieur Belêtre, went away, we have had no news; only the English here receive letters. Is it possible that our French father in the Illinois never writes? Not only Indians, but no Frenchmen here receive any letters. Therefore, this message is to let our father Neyon de Villiere, at the Illinois, know our situation and to request him to inform us what is happening, that we may know if we are abandoned."

A note of anger crept into his voice now and he spoke both louder and faster, causing Chene's pen to race without pause across the pages he was writing:

"The English tell us over and over, 'What, you savages, dare you speak of? Do you not see what we have done? We have overthrown your father and the Spaniards. We are masters of all these lands and of all that belonged to your father, for we have conquered him, and we possess all these countries, even to the Illinois, except a small edge, which is but a trifling thing.' This is what they tell us unendingly.

"This very spring, the Delawares told us that the English sought to become masters of all and would put us to death. And so they told us also, 'Our brothers, if this is their plan, to destroy us, then let us join hands and die together. We are dead one way or another.' This is what they said. When we heard this, we decided to say to all the nations who are your children, to assemble here at Detroit, and they have done so. We have raised our hand against them and now they hide behind their walls, afraid to show their heads. We can continue to hold them, as bees in a tree whose hole has been stopped up with mud, but beyond this what are we to do? We pray our father at the Illinois to hasten to our assistance, that he may have pity upon us, notwithstanding that the English keep telling us, 'Now who will give you what you stand in need of?' "

Pontiac slapped his thighs resoundingly, angrily, and stood in silence until the scratching pen of Elleopolle Chene caught up with him, and then he continued in a calmer voice:

"When our father, Captain Belêtre, left here he told us,

'My children, the English today overthrow your father. As long as they have the upper hand, you will not have what you stand in need of; but this will not last!' This is what he said and now we pray our father, Neyon de Villiere, at the Illinois, to take pity on us and say, 'These are my poor children, who wish to restore me, to raise me up again.' Therefore, do not ask why we do what we are doing today; it is because we do not want the English to hold these lands, and it is this which causes your children to rise and strike everywhere!

"We beg, my father, that you send us an answer speedily by these couriers. Tell us your thought and your wish. We will place in your hands the one who expelled you from this place, Captain Campbell, who is in our hands now; no harm will come to him. We will give him to you and say, 'Behold! Here he is!' We ask also, my father, that you treat our embassies with kindness, for we are the cause of the fatigue which they are going to suffer. I am finished."

Almost immediately upon Pontiac's stepping down, his place was taken by the most prominent Chippewa chief present, Wasson, who also directed Chene to take his words down. Holding up a small rose-colored belt, Wasson dictated:

"We approve of the Ottawas' speech and we have not forgotten our father. We remember what it was that our ancestors told us—that if our father was overthrown, our lands would be taken from us. We know well the intention of these English people who now crawl over our lands, and this is what makes us do as we have done and are doing. Know you this: we still keep hold of our French father's hands, and we do what it lies in our power to do to draw him unto us and restore him in this place; and if once again we possess it, we shall nevermore let it go. I have said."

Immediately after the talks, Pontiac huddled together with the five Frenchmen who would carry these messages. While they talked and Pontiac handed them not only message belts, but war belts, too, a few feet away from Donald Campbell, François Meloche shook his head and grunted sourly. Leaving Campbell and McDougall well guarded, he approached a group of six or eight other Frenchmen to one side and engaged in an animated, whispered conversation with them. After much talk and considerable gesticulation, the conversation ended in the nodding of heads. Immediately Meloche sat down and began to write a note, which would be given to Pontiac's messengers to carry with them to Neyon de Villiere. It succinctly stated the situation and gave the present point of view of a substantial representation of the French population here at Detroit.

He wrote:

TO THE GENTLEMEN COMMANDANTS AT THE ILLINOIS

Gentlemen: We are obliged to submit to what the Indians exact from us; the English are blocked up and all the passages are shut up; we cannot express to you our perplexity. It would be necessary, in order to judge of the calamities which threaten us and which appear to us inevitable, that you saw with your own eyes what is going on here. God alone can prevent our becoming the victims of the English and savages. These couriers bear to you the talks of the Nations here; we look upon it as a happiness to have it in our power to acquaint you of our deplorable situation. We certainly never have contributed thereto by our conduct; the English on their part never gave us occasion. Instruct us what we can do; we look upon you as protectors and mediators who would be willing to employ themselves efficaciously to pacify two contending parties who threaten us with an unexemplary desolation.

Without signing the letter, Meloche blew on it to dry the ink and then folded it twice. A bit nervously he carried it over to where Pontiac was still giving instructions to the messengers. He arrived in time to learn that Pontiac was instructing them to give war messages at each village they passed, calling upon the resident Indians at each to fall at once upon the English—traders or soldiers—in their areas, especially those in the areas of Fort Miamis and Fort Ouiatenon.

Assuming a casual mien, Meloche handed the folded letter to Jacques Godefroy with the muttered instruction that it be given to Captain Neyon de Villiere or whatever other officer might be concerned. Noting Pontiac suddenly staring at him, Meloche explained:

"Pontiac and Wasson have told their father at Fort de Chartres what it is they have done and of their need for assistance. We felt that it would be well for there to be a letter from the French inhabitants, also, to authenticate what it is you have said and to urge the hasty dispatch of a French force here to aid you and us."

Pontiac nodded slowly and seemed about on the point of inquiring further into the matter when there was an interruption. A messenger came running up from the direction of the river, calling out that Teata's Hurons on the other side of the river had just emerged from their Holy Thursday Mass and had immediately broken into war cries. Already they were pushing out from shore in canoes and heading in this direction.

The Ottawa war chief grunted approvingly, gave final orders for the five French messengers to be provisioned for their journey out of the Ottawa supplies and strode off to meet the boats. His own warriors and Takee's Hurons, as well as the warriors of the Chippewa and Potawatomi, followed respectfully and it was apparent that his prestige had risen a few notches because of the manner in which with only a few words he had whipped the recalcitrant faction into line.

He was waiting on the Detroit River shore when the canoes carrying Teata and his sixty warriors grated to a stop and they alighted. Gravely and with surprisingly friendly demeanor, he shook hands with Teata.

"Now," the Ottawa said with uncharacteristic diplomacy, "with my brother taking my hand, the English will shrivel up before us and be blown away by the wind we will make."

Turning, he pointed a finger at Takee. "Take your men down to the narrow part of the river close to where it joins the lake. Keep yourself there on good watch, to cut off any from the fort here who may try to go to the east with a message for help, as well as to cut off any who might be coming from the east to bring supplies for the English here. The rest of us will now attack the fort again with full strength and perhaps this time we will cause it to fall."

[*May 12, 1763—Thursday, 3:30* P.M.]

Seated side by side in the foremost of the five heavily laden batteaux en route from Niagara to Detroit, the two traders—one rather fat and the other lean and bearded—spied the roof of the house of Gerrieu St. Louis simultaneously. That Frenchman's house was the first sign of European habitation at the mouth of the Detroit River.

"Ah," said the overweight Jewish trader, Chapman Abraham, "our long trip begins to end."

His wiry assistant, Willem Rackman, grunted appreciatively at the sight of the house and scratched his bearded chin. "Ve vill schtop?" he asked.

Abraham nodded, then signaled to the boatmen following and pointed toward the Frenchman's house. "To shore," he called. "It is late and we will stay here for the night and reach Detroit tomorrow forenoon."

There was a small cheer from the weary men who had begun their rowing this day at the first light of dawn. Only twice during the day had the breeze picked up well enough to carry the heavy batteaux by sail-power. That tomorrow's labors would be short and their destination reached early was a delight to them. There would be wine and merriment and women awaiting, they knew.

The five large cargo craft gradually drew near the shore and when they were still a thousand feet away, the traders noted the figure of Monsieur St. Louis coming toward the landing to await them. As always, he would probably ask if there was mail from the east for him and, as always, they would have to tell him no. But it would be pleasant to chat with him this evening and learn what was new in this area while at the same time passing on news of the east.

Strangely, though, instead of coming to the boats as he always did, St. Louis remained a dozen yards or more from the shore as the five boats ground to a halt and the boatmen pulled them firmly ashore and tied them to the limb-studded log that had been long ago placed there for such purpose.

Not until they had straightened from these labors and began walking toward the Frenchman did he give a small signal and the woods around them suddenly erupted with war-painted Hurons. In a moment, wholly unprepared for defense, the entire party was captive.

Furiously, Chapman Abraham glared at Gerrieu St. Louis and demanded, "What is this? Why is this being done?"

St. Louis shrugged unconcernedly. In broken English he replied, "I am very sorry, monsieurs. The fort, she is under attack for three days now. They have no supplies and little ammunition. Soon she will fall. The Indians, they will have their way."

A shriek of triumph suddenly burst from the Indians who were pawing through the cargo of the five boats. Chapman Abraham needed no explanation of what had caused it: among the many other items of the cargo were thirty kegs of rum and brandy, and—the rotund trader groaned softly as he pictured it—seventeen barrels of gunpowder!

[May 12, 1763—Thursday, 9:30 P.M.]

It was just over an hour after darkness had fallen when Pontiac arrived at the house of Gerrieu St. Louis. His dour expression brightened somewhat when, by the glow of firelight, he saw the supplies that had been confiscated, especially the gunpowder. More than anything else, this was what was needed. Already several of the rum kegs had been knocked open and their contents considerably diminished.

Immediately the Ottawa war chief stepped forward and declared there would be no more drinking for the present. He directed that the trading party be taken out of earshot and well guarded and then swiftly described a new plan—one that might result in a substantial victory for his forces and further weaken the fort.

Takee's Hurons, he directed, were to take the majority of the trade goods and some of the rum to their village only a short way downstream from the fort on the opposite side of the river. At the same time, Pontiac would send messages to the other chiefs to leave only a token force around the fort to watch it and bring the rest to the same spot. Word would be sent into the fort by Monsieur St. Louis that Abraham's supply batteaux had been captured and were presently at that village, where the gunpowder was only poorly guarded and the majority of the Indians were already roaringly drunk or unconscious from overimbibing. If luck was with them, Gladwin would send out a strong detachment in some of the fort's batteaux to make an attack on the supposedly drunken Indians, destroy them as much as possible and recover the desperately needed supplies.

It was a good plan and Pontiac watched with satisfaction as the trade goods and some of the rum and brandy kegs were quickly reloaded in the five boats and then, manned by Takee's Hurons, shoved off. The current was strong but the warriors were fresh and they rowed swiftly, soon moving the boats out of hearing. At the same time, having received his instructions, St. Louis set off on horseback for Detroit.

With an intensity unfamiliar to him, Pontiac hoped desperately for the success of this ruse. When and if the English detachment came and put ashore, they would find waiting for them not a mass of rum-befogged Indians, but a savage assemblage in ambush which would wipe them out to the last man.

A victory of this nature was badly needed. All day the fort had been attacked as strongly as his warriors could attack it, but with precious little effect. Four more of his men had been killed and another ten wounded; and there was good reason to believe, considering what LaButte had related to him, that there had been little harm done to the garrison. Only two soldiers were known for sure to have been wounded—one on the ramparts and another aboard one of the vessels. Worse yet, Gladwin had shrewdly fired more red-hot spikes from his cannon at nearby barns and houses which the Indians had been using for cover. Those places had burnt to the ground, thereby making further attack by the Indians that much more difficult and hazardous.

Before leaving the fort area, Pontiac had sent another message in to Gladwin. It had been carried by the Frenchman Laurence Gamelin and asked for a cease-fire while the dead were collected and brought off, plus a reiteration of the demands for Gladwin to surrender the fort and vacate. Pontiac had remained long enough to see forty of his men move out into the open a half hour later without weapons to collect the dead and wounded Indians. They were not fired upon and, satisfied, the chief had then ridden off for the house of Gerrieu St. Louis. What he had found here had been more than gratifying.

Now, nodding toward the small party of warriors and subchiefs sitting astride horses and still awaiting his word, he headed back toward Detroit. There was much to be done to prepare for the ambush.

[*May 12, 1763—Thursday, Midnight*]

Even from this distance Henry Gladwin, standing on the ramparts of the river wall, could see the glow of the huge fire at the downstream Huron village and, with occasional shiftings of the faint breeze, the wildly drunken cries dimly reached him. There could be no doubt of it. The Indians *were* drunk and the story brought by Gerrieu St. Louis of the cargo batteaux of Chapman Abraham and Willem Rackman being taken was true.

Late in the afternoon he had thanked Laurence Gamelin for delivering the message from Pontiac during the cease-fire, but sent him back to tell Pontiac that his answer remained the same: that he would make no decision until the release of his officers and that Pontiac and his warriors had better use their ammunition for hunting rather than against the English.

Then, an hour or so ago had come the Frenchman named St. Louis and Gladwin had supposed it was another of the Ottawa war chief's ridiculous demands he was carrying. Instead it had turned out to be news of the capture of the cargo boats. After St. Louis was gone, Major Gladwin considered the report at length. Beyond any doubt, there would be considerable goods in that cargo which were vital to the continued defense of the fort here—gunpowder in particular—and almost any risk would be worth it to recover the goods. Or, if they couldn't be recovered, then at least perhaps they could be destroyed so that they would not be of benefit to Pontiac.

"It's not an order, Joseph," Gladwin told the officer standing beside him now, who was likewise studying the distant glow of the Huron campfire. "There's apt to be a good bit of danger and we can't afford to overlook the possibility that it's all merely a ruse to draw us out. But there is equally a chance that it is not and we can't very well afford to let that chance go by untested. Still, I won't make it an order. Your taking a detachment out will have to be on a strictly volunteer basis."

Captain Joseph Hopkins grinned tightly, his features barely visible in the wan light of the moon. It wasn't really necessary for him to repeat his earlier eagerness to lead such a detachment, but he did so now in two words.

"I volunteer."

[*May 13, 1763—Friday, 5:00* A.M.]

It was still an hour before dawn when the well-armed sloop, *Michigan,* quietly upped anchor and swung neatly with the current and breeze and headed downstream. Aboard her, in addition to her crew of eight, were Captain Joseph Hopkins and his twenty-five volunteers, plus three of Detroit's English traders—James Sterling, John Watkins and Caesar Cormick.

The cannon aboard the vessel were all primed for firing and the port rail was lined with soldiers armed with rifles. The ship handled well under the skillful hand of her skipper, Captain Jacob Newman, for the first half mile or so, but then the breeze died and current alone carried the ship along, making steering difficult.

The glow of the Huron fire could be seen more clearly now and, using Captain Newman's fine brass telescope, Captain Hopkins studied the scene intently. In clusters around the fire he could see the sprawled forms of numerous Indians, apparently in drunken sleep, while about half that many still pranced and whirled in orgiastic delight in the illumination from the gradually dying blaze. Though he studied the dark shoreline carefully and the deeper shadows of the trees around the village, he could detect no sign of life. He was positive now that this was no ruse and what excited him considerably was that he could just barely make out the five captured batteaux drawn partially up on the bank, bundles and barrels of merchandise forming deeper shadows within them.

"Take her right in, Captain Newman," he directed firmly. They were now only about a half mile from the village and in midstream.

"Aye," Newman said and spun the helm to angle the ship in that direction.

Abruptly and unexpectedly a breeze touched their faces and gently popped the limp canvas. Within moments it grew to considerably more than just a vagrant gust. It became a wind blowing directly into their faces and it grew steadily stronger every minute. Within five minutes the ship was almost at a standstill, current and wind equalizing one another and the vessel growing more and more difficult to keep under control and hold. For another five minutes beyond that, the skipper strove to advance or even just hold place, but now the wind was blowing at eighteen or twenty knots, kicking up whitecaps on the water's surface and picking up sparks from the Huron fire and hurling them through the air like fireworks. The *Michigan* turned lumberingly with it and there was no way, short of dropping canvas and anchoring, to hold her. Jacob Newman shook his head regretfully.

"No use, Captain," he told Hopkins. "Can't do it. We'll have to head back."

Gritting his teeth in disappointment, Joseph Hopkins stood silently as the ship heeled about and began a slow push against the current toward the fort. He was inwardly cursing the caprice of Mother Nature when the eastern shoreline suddenly came alive with the flashes of rifle fire. There were shrill howls of anger and frustration which were borne to them on the wind. All along that shore, even up this far—a couple of thousand yards above the village—guns were being fired in great number.

The men aboard the ship took cover instantly, but the range was too great for any kind of effective shooting. Except for a few balls passing through the shrouding or smacking ineffectually against the side of the ship, no real damage was done. But it was obvious that if the wind had not risen as it had, in another few minutes the vessel would have glided neatly into a vicious—and very likely successful—ambush.

"It looks, Captain," Jacob Newman commented, still manning the helm, "as if we have a rather powerful ally."

His face pale and lips narrowed to a tight line, Hopkins looked at Newman in befuddlement, not understanding his meaning. Newman grinned.

"God," he said simply. "Looks like we've got God on our side."

Taking his command position in the leading boat, Lieutenant Abraham Cuyler[79] of the Queen's Rangers stood and watched the jockeying of the other seventeen batteaux as they fell into loose formation behind. A deep sigh of relief escaped him with the knowledge that the demanding labors of the past days were now behind him and that they were embarking.

A young, thin-faced officer with narrow black moustache and peculiarly bright blue eyes, Cuyler was reveling in this, his first major expedition of any kind in a command position. The fact that it was merely the command of the year's first of several supply convoys to Detroit from Niagara and apt to be as mundane a trip as the many convoys that had preceded it over the past two summers, made little difference to him. It was, after all, his first real opportunity to act in an independent command capacity and he was greatly buoyed by the realization of the responsibility being invested in him. He had long ago determined to do an exemplary job in every respect.

The transportation of one hundred and thirty-nine barrels of provisions and eighteen massive batteaux[80] from Fort Niagara at the head of Lake Ontario, around the falls to Fort Schlosser[81] and then the rest of the way up the Niagara River to the foot of Lake Erie was no little job, but at least now the worst of it was over. First the batteaux had been loaded at the big fort and rowed upstream against the strong current to the small portage post called Fort Little Niagara a few miles below the falls. Here the cargo had to be unloaded from the boats, loaded aboard wagons and carted to Fort Schlosser above the falls where navigation was again practical. With the cargo all stacked at Fort Schlosser, then the cumbersome batteaux themselves had to be laboriously hauled along the rocky portage road to be relaunched at the upper fort and the cargo reloaded. Not only was the portage road bumpy, it was often narrow and at times precipitous and extremely difficult to negotiate, despite the extensive use it had seen. Cuyler had escorted wagonload after wagonload of goods and boats around the falls, marveling each time he passed them at the grandeur of the two great cataracts and the rampaging river in the gorge far below, where each great whirlpool seemed to stare malevolently with its single swirling eye.

At length the portage had been completed and the batteaux all relaunched and reloaded. They were unwieldy craft with flat bottoms and pointed bows and sterns, their sides very high in order to hold the maximum safe load. Each was equipped with eight oars to the side and sails to be used when possible.

Now, with cargo in place and his detachment of ninety-six men aboard, Lieutenant Cuyler nodded to his noncommissioned officer. Sergeant Geoffrey Cope, of the Royal Americans, cupped his mouth with both hands and bellowed out the order to proceed. In a few moments the oarsmen had fallen into a methodical cadence on their oars—dipping, pulling, raising, pushing—and the boats sliced through the current until it gradually diminished, the expanse of water widened and they entered the smallest of the Great Lakes. A fairly stiff following breeze soon enabled them to raise the sails and coast along the northern shoreline of Lake Erie, heading westward.

Eyes shining with excitement, Abraham Cuyler watched the western New York shoreline behind them diminish and then turned his gaze to the Canadian shoreline. Not only had he not seen it before, but very few of the ninety-six men in this detachment—of which only eighteen, under Sergeant Cope, were of the Royal Americans, and the remaining seventy-six belonged to the Queen's Rangers under Cuyler—had ever come this way before. Those few that had previously made the journey told glowing stories of the beauty of the lakeshore all the way and of the delightful trip it would be, especially if favorable winds lightened their workload. Each night they would camp on shore and if the winds were charitable they ought to reach Detroit in fifteen to eighteen days, perhaps even less.

Cuyler was certain they would be given a warm welcome at Detroit. This year's first supply convoy to the west was weeks overdue because of difficulty in getting the supplies from Albany to Niagara, and the last dispatches received from Major Gladwin had urged that the goods be sent as expeditiously as possible, since supplies were running low. Adventurous by nature, Cuyler allowed himself the luxury of indulging in a continuing string of brief fantasies in which he became the daring commander leading his detachment into the very teeth of savage Lake Erie storms or through attacking hordes of hostile Indians to bring the much-needed goods safely to their destination. He was, however, realistic enough to realize that this was just wishful thinking. The spring storm season on Lake Erie was well-nigh past and they were not apt to run into any difficulty in that respect. And as for the Indians, how hostile could any of them be—despite vague rumors to the contrary—when they had no ammunition with which to fight?

Lieutenant Abraham Cuyler chuckled lightly as he pictured a handful of naked, war-painted Indians attempting to attack this convoy of eighteen sturdy boats protected by nearly a hundred trained and well-armed soldiers. It made a ludicrous image and he chuckled again.

[*May 14, 1763—Saturday, 1:00* P.M.]

Until yesterday morning's fortunately abortive ambush on Captain Joseph Hopkins's detachment, Major Henry Gladwin had been subconsciously striving to convince himself that this uprising of the Indians around Detroit was a rather local thing which he could handle and which would, after a short burst of energy, burn out the accumulated angers of the Indians and fade away. The fact, however, that traders bringing supplies from the east had been captured and their goods confiscated—providing the Indians with a bountiful supply of ammunition—and that a very nearly successful ambush, thwarted only by nature, had been set up against the English, had now convinced Detroit's commander that this was no small or brief affair. It was time now to cast all reluctance aside and advise the general of what was occurring and ask that reinforcements be sent to put down this uprising.

There had been one advantage to these days of waiting in which Major Gladwin was pleased. The initial reticence of his officers to defend the fort and their desire to accept Pontiac's offer to allow them peaceable withdrawal had now all but disappeared. An anger was growing in them instead. They were resentful over the hardships Pontiac was causing them, over the senseless killings that had already been perpetrated, over the imprisonment of Campbell and McDougall who had been peace emissaries with Pontiac's given word of their guaranteed good treatment, safety and return. They were angry, too, over the taking of the traders, Chapman Abraham and Willem Rackman and their party, for the goods they had been bringing could have been put to urgent use here in the fort; the fact that these supplies would now be used *against* the garrison was galling. But for some reason, more than for anything else that had yet occurred, they were furious over the attempted ambush of Hopkins's detachment. With their anger came a growing determination to hang onto this place in spite of anything Pontiac would do, and the conviction that these Indians who outnumbered them so greatly had neither the brains nor the ability to take them.

In essence, the morale of the entire garrison had taken a surprising upswing to the point where now Gladwin seriously doubted that very many of the men would elect to leave even if given the choice. It was a point he meant to stress in the letter he was now preparing to write to General Amherst.

Sharpening his quill and slitting the end, he dipped it carefully into the inkpot, gently shook off the blobs and then put his hand to the paper on the desk before him. For a moment he paused, reflecting on where best to begin the report, and then he began to write swiftly:

Detroit, May 14, 1763

General Sir Jeffrey Amherst
Headquarters at New York
Sir:
On the first instant, Pontiac, the chief of the Ottawa Nation, came here with about fifty of his men and told me that in a few days, when the rest of his Nation came in, he intended to pay me a formal visit. The 7th he came, but I was luckily informed, the night before, that he was coming with an intention to surprise us; upon which I took such precautions that when they entered the fort, though they were by the best accounts about three hundred and armed with knives, tomahawks, and a great many guns cut short and hid under their blankets, they were so much surprised to see our disposition that they would scarcely sit down to council: however, in about half an hour, after they saw their designs were discovered, they sat down and Pontiac made a speech which I answered calmly, without intimating my suspicion of their intentions, and after receiving some trifling presents, they went away to their camp.

Page after page the letter continued, telling about the return of Pontiac, Gladwin's refusal to allow him to reenter the fort with his whole nation, of Pontiac's rage and hatred which had broken out at this point and the chief's statement that while Gladwin could keep the fort, he, Pontiac, would keep the country. Matter-of-factly he told about the attack in which Robertson and Davers and their party were killed, of the attacks on the other English outside the fort and then of the taking of Campbell and McDougall as hostages, followed by the all-out assault on the fort, the capture of the traders and their goods, and the attempted ambush of Hopkins's detachment. The body of Indians attacking the fort, he reported, was larger than the garrison by anywhere from ten to fifteen times and, since Pontiac claimed that another body of warriors of equal size was on the way here, it was important that reinforcement and supplies arrive quickly. A normal shipment of provisions was expected soon from Niagara, but Gladwin was concerned for its safety since it was unlikely that they had yet learned of the outbreak.

He concluded:

. . . but the garrison is in high spirits and I am in hopes of being able to defend this place until I receive succor from Major Wilkins at Niagara, who shall have heard about our difficulty before you.

I am, Sir,

Your most obedient, your most humble servant,
Henry Gladwin

The problem remaining now was getting the letter out and safely to its destination. Though he hated to take the risk of possibly losing the ship, there was no other way than to send one of the vessels anchored beside the fort. Its absence would weaken the defenses of the fort to a certain degree, but there was no help for it. If word did not get back to the east quickly, it could be disastrous. Though he hated to admit it even to himself, Major Henry Gladwin had no illusions about their situation here: without solid reinforcement and supplies coming soon, there was the very viable possibility that Detroit would fall.

[*May 14, 1763—Saturday, 9:30* P.M.]

Pontiac sat alone before his fire, staring unseeingly into the glowing heart of coals. It was the first time since before dawn that he had had a moment to himself and he was glad to be undisturbed. Though the day had been warm, a dank chill had crept in with the night and he had a trade blanket tossed lightly over his back, the front of it open to catch and contain the warmth of this little blaze.

Though night had fallen an hour or so ago, still he could hear the occasional poppings of guns from the direction of

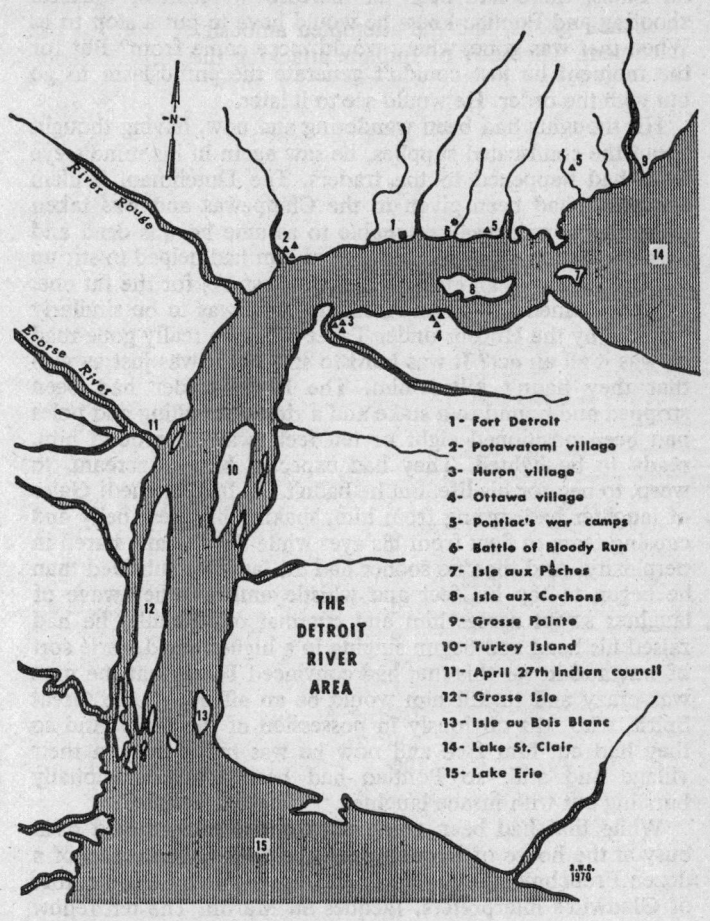

THE
DETROIT
RIVER
AREA

1 - Fort Detroit
2 - Potawatomi village
3 - Huron village
4 - Ottawa village
5 - Pontiac's war camps
6 - Battle of Bloody Run
7 - Isle aux Pêches
8 - Isle aux Cochons
9 - Grosse Pointe
10 - Turkey Island
11 - April 27th Indian council
12 - Grosse Isle
13 - Isle au Bois Blanc
14 - Lake St. Clair
15 - Lake Erie

the fort as his warriors sniped at soldiers who showed themselves briefly above the pickets. Because of the supply of ammunition confiscated from the traders at the house of Gerrieu St. Louis, there had been an increase in reckless, wasteful shooting and Pontiac knew he would have to put a stop to it. When that was gone, where would more come from? But for the moment he just couldn't generate the enthusiasm to go out with the order. He would see to it later.

His thoughts had been wandering and now, having thought about the confiscated supplies, he saw again in his mind's eye what had happened to the traders. The Dutchman, Willem Rackman, had been given to the Chippewas and was taken away. By now it was reasonable to assume he was dead and perhaps the torturing and burning of him had helped to stir up the Chippewas to an even greater war lust. As for the fat one, the Jew named Chapman Abraham, who was to be similarly tortured by the Hurons under Takee—had he really gone mad or was it all an act? It was hard to say, but it was just as well that they hadn't killed him. The heavy trader had been stripped and bound to a stake and a ring of kindling and poles had been positioned eight or ten feet away all around him, ready to be lighted. They had expected him to scream, to weep, to beg for his life, but he hadn't. He had laughed! Gales of laughter had sprung from him, shaking his great belly and causing tears to flow from his eyes while the Indians stared in perplexity. And then no sooner had the laughter subsided than he began to tap his feet and whistle until another wave of laughter swept across him and cut that off. Finally, he had raised his head and begun singing in a high-pitched, eerie sort of way and it was this that had convinced Takee that the man was crazy and to kill him would be an affront to the Great Spirit, who was obviously in possession of the man. And so they had cut him free and now he was being held in their village and still, so Pontiac had been told, occasionally bursting out with insane laughter.

While that had been going on, Pontiac himself had been busy at the house of Baptiste Meloche with a deputation of a dozen Frenchmen led by Jacques Duperon Baby and another of Gladwin's interpreters, Jacques St. Martin. The ten fellow Frenchmen they had brought with them had been among the most influential in the whole Detroit community, and all of them were angry.

"Before coming here," Baby had said, "we met with Father Pothier and learned of how you have forced the Christian Hurons to support you in this affair. He has asked us to solicit you to stop this business and to send your warriors away and reinstate peace here. Many of the Hurons of Teata's band, including Teata himself, have gone back to their village and will fight no more. Father Pothier has immobilized them by refusing to administer any further sacraments to them unless they remain neutral and now they are determined to do just that. Many of them have already moved away from Detroit to avoid inducement by you or in fear of harm coming to their families at your hand."

Baby paused, expecting some comment from Pontiac, but the Ottawa war chief said nothing and so Baby continued: "This is between you and them, but there is a matter closer to us and more important. We wish to know, Pontiac, what exactly are your aims in this business? What do you hope to achieve?"

As if surprised that they should still have to ask this, Pontiac replied, "My aim is to expel the English from this fort and from this country in preparation for the arrival of the French commandant who is on his way here from the Illinois country with a little army, and who will be followed here by a bigger, stronger army."

Now it was St. Martin who interposed with an objection. "That is only rumor, Pontiac—stories told from nothing, which you only *wish* to believe. We cannot believe that any army of our government is coming here at this time."

Pontiac said nothing, but the look he gave St. Martin was scornful, withering. It was Baby who spoke again, indicating the rest of the Frenchmen with a sweep of his arm.

"It is your war, Pontiac, but it is we who are being ruined by the stopping of the trade. We must have relief from this."

"If you wish relief," Pontiac observed, "then you have only to join me and all the fighting will end that much faster."

There was a mutter of opposition from the French and Baby shook his head in exasperation. "We cannot," he said. "We swore English allegiance in 1760 when they came here and as long as we remain here, we are bound by our oaths."

"There is then," Pontiac said with finality, "nothing more to say."

They had tried to talk more, but he had refused to listen and finally they had gone away. All during their talk the sound of shooting from the area of the fort had continued, just as now, in the darkness, the gunfire still sounded sporadically. He thought again of St. Martin's comment and grunted softly. By this time, he knew, the five Frenchmen and detachment of Indians he had sent to escort them to Captain Neyon de Villiere should have reached the mouth of the Maumee River, perhaps even starting the more difficult journey upstream on it. He hoped they would move rapidly. He had no more believed the rumor than St. Martin did, that a French army was on the way here right now, but it was important to keep that story alive to encourage his allies to continue the fight, to maintain the siege. He had no doubt whatever, though, that the Illinois commandant would indeed send such an army as soon as he learned what had happened here. And there should be good news soon from other quarters: Chief Washee would soon lead his Potawatomies against Fort St. Joseph; Cold Foot and his Miami warriors would rise up against Fort Miamis; Minivavana with his Chippewas and Mackinac with all the northern Ottawas would hit Fort Michilimackinac. Soonest of all, Odinghquanooron and his Huron Wyandots would take Fort Sandusky. In fact, the party of warriors Pontiac had sent to assist Odinghquanooron should have arrived there by now.

As a matter of fact, Pontiac's reasoning was accurate. That party's shore-hugging canoe journey of just over one hundred miles behind them, they had arrived at Sandusky Bay just at sunset and since that time had been in secret council with the Wyandot and his minor chiefs.

Odinghquanooron—known to the French traders as Chief Babi and to the English as Big Jaw—listened attentively to the plan for the taking of Fort Sandusky. From the onset the Wyandot chief was assured that all plunder from the fort, both military and trade goods, as well as whatever horses might be there, should be his property when the place was taken. All that the party from Detroit wanted was the commander, in order to take him back alive to Detroit with them as living proof of the fall of this fort. With these ground rules established, Odinghquanooron grunted and then, except for an occasional nod of agreement, he said nothing more as Pontiac's plan was outlined. When explanations were over, he nodded again and gave his opinion that there would be no great difficulty involved in taking the fort. Its commander, Ensign Christopher Pauli, had only fifteen men and there were no more than a dozen traders on hand at the moment who had been carefully—though surreptitiously—watched to see that they did not set out for Detroit.

With the plan now completely laid out, Pontiac's party placed themselves wholly under Odinghquanooron's orders. The Wyandot chief spoke briefly, instructing his own and Pontiac's men in the role each would play. When he was sure that they understood fully, he emitted another approving grunt.

"It is good," he said. "Speak of it to no one who might betray our plan. We wish none of our own people hurt. We will take the fort on the second day from now."

[May 15, 1763—Sunday]

It was shortly after the Sunday Mass in the little Catholic Church at Fort Michilimackinac that the commander, Captain George Etherington, looked up from a book he was reading. The light tapping at his door that had interrupted him was repeated and he sighed and set the book down.

"Come in," he said.

The young trader, Alexander Henry, entered the room and quietly closed the door behind him. Etherington nodded and smiled. He liked Henry reasonably well, but he didn't much care for the way he came trotting to him with every new rumor which came up. He supposed it was another one now and he waited, masking his impatience.

"Captain," Henry said, "sorry to disturb you on a Sunday, but I'm getting a little bit concerned about some things I've noticed lately."

Etherington said nothing and after a moment Alexander Henry continued in a slightly apologetic manner.

"I hope you won't take this as idle criticism, sir," he said, "but do you really think you ought to let the Indians have as much freedom in roaming about the fort as they have?"

"Haven't we always permitted them to come in for trade when they cared to, Mr. Henry?"

"Well, yes," Henry agreed, "but surely you've taken notice of the increase in their numbers lately, haven't you? Every day there are more Indians in the fort than there ever were before and I've heard some of the French saying that there are upwards of four hundred of them in little camps just out of sight all around us. Mostly warriors. It bothers me a little. Quite frankly, sir, I've come to know them pretty well and, except for a few individuals, I don't have much confidence in them."

"Have you personally seen these four hundred who are supposed to be hidden around us, Mr. Henry?" There was a glint of amusement in the commander's eyes which Henry detected and he flushed faintly.

"No, I haven't, Captain."

"Have you heard of any planned attacks against us?"

"No, sir."

"Isn't it true that our relations with them have improved considerably since the garrison's arrival here? Since I took command from Lieutenant Leslye?"

"Well, yes sir, but . . ." Henry hesitated.

"But what, Mr. Henry?"

"It's just that I have this *feeling*, sir. A sense of things not being quite right."

George Etherington's amusement could no longer be contained. He grinned broadly and then broke into laughter. He put an arm around Henry's shoulder and adroitly turned him toward the door.

"I hope," he said, still chuckling as he opened the door and showed Henry out, "that you'll soon be *feeling* better. I do indeed."

Even after the door had closed behind him, Alexander Henry could hear Captain Etherington laughing.

[May 16, 1763—Monday]

Ensign Christopher Pauli was, at age twenty-four, an intelligent and dependable young officer. Not too often was an ensign given the responsibility of commanding one of His Britannic Majesty's forts, regardless of how remote or small. He was proud that this early in his military career—to which he was determined to devote his life—he had achieved this degree of recognition already.

When he had taken command of Fort Sandusky upon the departure of its builder, Lieutenant Elias Meyer, it had been with a glow of achievement that still thrilled him. It was a very small post, to be sure, with a garrison of only himself, a sergeant and fourteen enlisted men, but the fact remained that it was a vital link in His Majesty's chain of forts into the western wilderness. It was the only Lake Erie fort between Fort Presque Isle and Detroit and was therefore an important stopping point. In addition, next to Detroit itself, it was probably the most important trading stop—at least for the current trade—west of Fort Niagara. Right at this moment, for example, there were twelve traders on hand here—some of them were permanent at this post, or at least reasonably so, but the majority were transient between the east and Detroit, Fort Miamis or Fort Ouiatenon. The flow of furs along the upper reaches of the Sandusky River to the stores here— brought by the Indians from the Ohio country heartland— was heavy and constant and this fact alone increased the fort's importance and permanence. One day, Pauli supposed, this fort would become very nearly as important as Detroit itself.

Now, walking from his quarters, where he had breakfasted, to his small headquarters cabin, he paused to breathe deeply of the gloriously warm and fragrant air on this beautiful mid-May morning. Already the gate had been opened and through it, perhaps sixty yards away, he could see the husky Sergeant Delton puttering in his garden.

Pauli grinned. It was unusual to see a tough noncommissioned officer tenderly caring for his growing things like this, but ever since Jim Delton had put the garden in, several weeks or so ago, he had made it a point to carefully water it, cultivate the soil, pluck out weeds and otherwise nurture the newly sprouting plants every morning, not trusting anyone else to do it properly.

The incongruity of it tickled Pauli and he chuckled aloud. Continuing his leisurely walk he remembered how Delton had calmly and methodically whipped two privates who had decided to goad him about his "pretty little sprouts." No one had dared show open amusement in them since that time.

Pauli was only a few yards from his headquarters cabin when the gate sentry abruptly called to him.

"Sir," the private said, "there's a party of Indians here. They want to come in and council."

Pauli turned and walked back more briskly toward the gate. It was the first council the Indians had requested in a couple of weeks and he supposed they were going to repeat their often voiced need for ammunition. He felt sorry for them, wishing he could help them out, but orders were orders and he knew he would have to reject their appeal. The important thing was to do it in such manner that your genuine sympathy was sensed by them and they did not take offense. Thus far he had been markedly successful in his diplomacy, mollifying Big Jaw, even though sometimes the chief tended to provoke an issue over it. Pauli hoped it was something else this time instead of a reiteration of the old demands.

At the gate he was startled to see not a small handful of minor chiefs under Big Jaw, but upwards of forty Indians. Big Jaw was there, indeed, along with a number of his lesser chiefs whom Pauli recognized, but there were also several chiefs—two of whom appeared to be Ottawas—and a number of men he was certain the had never seen before.

As the ensign approached them, Big Jaw stepped forward, smiled expansively and greeted Pauli with a warm handshake.

The chief wished him good health and then gravely introduced him to five other chiefs he did not know—chiefs whose compounded Indian names were so involved that he was unable to retain the pronunciation of even one of them.

"We have come in friendship to our good friend and brother, the commander," Big Jaw told him, "to speak of things which are important to us. Will you council with us now?"

Obviously, with these strangers on hand, something of an important nature was brewing and Pauli nodded slowly. An indefinable disquiet arose in him and he decided to proceed cautiously. He pointed to a small cabin near his headquarters. It was hardly more than eight feet square, without windows and having only one door.

"Yes," he told Big Jaw, "but as you know, our council chambers are not large and there is room for only a few. You may come in, along with your second chief and these five others whose faces I do not know, but there will be room for no others."

"It is as we expected," Big Jaw replied, bobbing his head.

A number of Indians behind the chiefs were chattering cheerfully among themselves, often laughing, some of them already squatting to wait and others moving casually about. Beyond them Pauli could see Sergeant Delton still plucking weeds from his garden plot and a wash of irritation swept through him. Delton knew full well that standing orders called for any soldier outside the fort to return to it at the approach of any group of Indians, however peaceful their intentions. Obviously there was no danger here—an assessment apparently already made by Delton—but it still rankled that the noncom should flaunt the fort's regulations. The commander decided he would have to talk with Delton about that as soon as the Indians left.

Indicating to the sentry that it was all right to let them pass, Pauli led the way to the tiny council chambers. Quite a few of the garrison, as well as some of the traders, were now watching curiously. Pauli beckoned one of the privates to him and told him to bring some tobacco for distribution to these chiefs. Then he stood to one side, allowing the seven Indians to enter first, after which he followed them in. Perhaps another twenty warriors had sauntered into the fort behind them and were now separating into casual little groups.

The chiefs were still standing when Pauli entered and he motioned them to sit, taking a cross-legged sitting position himself on the packed earthen floor toward the wall opposite the door. Two of the chiefs took seats on either side of him and the rest fanned out in a sort of crescent shape in the center of which was Pauli. Big Jaw's second chief remained standing at the doorway, but he moved courteously aside when the private brought the tobacco.

As the soldier left, Pauli personally distributed the tobacco to the chiefs and then resumed his place with his own pipe, watching silently as they packed and lighted theirs. It was the usual way and Pauli knew no business would be discussed until the final pipe was finished.

Only once did he break the silence in the next few minutes—when he suddenly realized there was no council fire, which there certainly should be. Aghast at his own blunder, he apologized to Big Jaw and said he would order one built at once but the Wyandot shook his head, smiled and said that neither fire nor apology were necessary.

After another few minutes, by which time several of the chiefs had already smoked their pipes out, Big Jaw's second chief who was still standing, leaning against the doorjamb and not smoking but looking lazily outside, suddenly stiffened, looked back into the room and nodded once. Instantly the Indians on either side of Pauli dropped their pipes and seized him. Though he called out and struggled furiously, they tied his wrists tightly behind him with strips of rawhide. From outside Pauli heard a couple of shrieks and yells and some thudding of bare feet, but hardly enough to indicate any sort of engagement was coming. Why, then, had no one responded to his calls? He opened his mouth to shout again, but a small war club one of the chiefs jerked up from somewhere struck glancingly against his temple. He was momentarily stunned, though not knocked unconscious. Had not the two Indians at his sides been holding him, however, he would certainly have fallen.

It took only moments for his reeling senses to settle again and by this time he was being led outside. Close at hand the soldier who had brought the tobacco lay still upon the ground in an enormous and still-spreading pool of blood. His throat had been slit and his scalp was gone. Dazedly, Pauli looked around as he was forced toward the gate. There, where he had left the sentry standing, the man lay dead on the ground, the side of his head crushed and his scalp, too, missing. Blinking with disbelief, Pauli now realized that all around them soldiers lay similarly in death and he could see a number of the traders who had also been killed. Among the latter he could still recognize Slim Callender, whom he knew very well and who had formerly been a captain in the Pennsylvania Regiment. The trader had been very nearly decapitated.

The whole scene had a macabre, dreamlike quality to it, enhanced by the utter silence with which it had been accomplished and which strangely still prevailed. Beyond any doubt the plan had been for the Indians to position themselves close but unobtrusively to every man in the fort and, at a given signal, to strike. The fact that outcry or scuffling had been practically absent attested only too well to the plan's success.

As he was hustled through the gate, a faint hope welled in Pauli's breast that Sergeant Delton, being outside, had managed to escape. A moment later he saw him, still in the garden, lying face down while blood from the great gash across his throat stained the tender green shoots of his treasured plants.

Now and then Pauli was struck or kicked as he was hustled along until at length he was viciously thrown to the ground and staked face up in a spreadeagled position. In addition to each wrist and ankle being securely tied to individual stakes, a rawhide loop was placed around his neck and snubbed tight to a sapling so that he could barely turn his head without choking.

Throughout the day he lay there, mostly with his eyes closed, still not able to fully comprehend the enormity of what had occurred. On the occasions when he did open his eyes at sounds and turn his head what little distance he could, he saw horseload after horseload of provisions being removed from the fort. In an almost childlike way he tried to count the packhorses as they were led away to Big Jaw's nearby village, laden with all the traders' goods and military stores from the fort. When he reached one hundred his eyes suddenly filled with tears and he could no longer see to count. For a long while he wept silently.

It was growing dark when his bonds were loosened, his arms tied behind him again and he was forced to walk toward the shore. There he was directed to enter a large canoe and sit while the strange chiefs conferred a final time with Big Jaw, calling him Odinghquanooron and shaking hands with him. Then they parted and the Wyandot chief disappeared in the gathering gloom. The two Ottawas entered the boat in which Pauli was captive, while other members of the party boarded three other canoes and all were shoved off into the water. By the time they had paddled a quarter mile it was full dark and from where he sat facing backward, Pauli could see first a glow and then the bright light of sheets of flame rising high into the air as Fort Sandusky was burned.

He had had no food or water since his breakfast and his throat was raw, his lips parched. For the first time since being taken prisoner he tried to speak and his voice came out in a croak.

"Where are . . ." he coughed raspingly, then tried it again. "Where are you taking me?"

The chief sitting behind him grasped his hair and twisted it in his fist painfully. He barked a short ugly laugh and said, "You are going to Detroit. When they have seen you, the commander of the fort of Sandusky, and the scalps we bring, then a great celebration will be held and then you will be roasted." He laughed again.

"How many scalps were taken?" he asked, surprising himself that he had asked the question.

"Twenty-seven," the Ottawa replied, then jerked his hair again and added, "and with this one, twenty-eight!"

Twenty-seven! Beside himself, the garrison had had fifteen soldiers and twelve traders had been there. That made twenty-seven. As he realized that he was the only survivor, a violent trembling struck him, and when it had passed, Ensign Christopher Pauli's chest still heaved with the uncontrollable sobs which wracked him.[82]

CHAPTER V

[May 17, 1763—Tuesday]

ALTHOUGH the squaws, some of them his wives, moved about him quietly or hovered solicitiously just within range of the dying fire's glow, Pontiac paid them no heed. He had not touched the several wooden bowls of food that had been placed close to him on the ground, nor had he any desire to at the moment. He could not recall when last he had eaten and knew he should, but for the moment he continued to sit hunched here close to the fire. The infrequent popping of the burning wood punctuated his thoughts as he reviewed the events of the past couple of days and revised his future plans accordingly. Perhaps tonight he would sleep, but not yet.

Except by the garrison itself, there had been little activity today. Having heard that a sizable party of the Saginaw Bay Chippewas were en route to join his forces, Pontiac saw no need to recklessly expose his warriors to gunfire from the fort. A ring of warriors continued to surround the place, occasionally during the day throwing shots at the fort, but mostly keeping under cover until the Chippewas should arrive. Pontiac had spent the day conferring with various chiefs and sympathetic Frenchmen and occasionally receiving reports from messengers. He seemed peculiarly unconcerned by the news that a strong party of soldiers had come out of the fort to set afire and destroy the fences and sheds still proving to be suitable cover for attacking Indians. A few shots had been exchanged but no one was hit and in a short while, its job not completed, the detachment hastened back into the fort.

Nor was the chief perturbed by the intelligence brought to him that two new embrasures had been cut through the fort's stockade timbers and a pair of four-pounder cannon mounted in them. But he became markedly agitated when he visited Antoine Cuillerier and discovered that the crusty old

Frenchman had persuaded the Indians who had killed Lieutenant Robertson and Sir Robert Davers to sell him as a slave the white captive from that attack, John Rutherford. Immediately Pontiac had summoned the chiefs involved, demanded that they return to Cuillerier the £80 worth of goods he had given them for Rutherford—which they did, though reluctantly—and then took the fearful young man back into captivity.

Angrily, Cuillerier had demanded to know why Pontiac was doing this, but the chief did not elaborate beyond quietly and firmly saying, "It is not a good thing for Indians to sell English prisoners to Frenchmen as slaves." Almost immediately Pontiac left, taking Rutherford with him and leaving Cuillerier fuming behind.

The Frenchmen, on the whole, puzzled Pontiac. He had thought, before starting this war, that as soon as the actual attacks began, all of the Frenchmen here and elswhere would flock to join him in his fight against their conquerors, the detested Englishmen. Yet, it had not happened that way. True, there were a number of the French who sided with him— men like Cuillerier and Chene, Godefroy and a few others— but mostly there was an aloofness among them, a seeming fear on their parts to openly commit themselves to him. Some, in fact, he strongly suspected were aiding the English. A few names in this last category had been whispered to him by young Alexis Cuillerier, but there was no real proof. It would not be a good thing to be too hasty in making accusations and possibly alienating men who were neutral or perhaps even leaning toward him. But he intended watching them carefully.

Rumor was strong that foodstuffs had been secretly brought to the English on several occasions and that now the garrison was nowhere near as lacking for food as had been the case when hostilities erupted. Young Cuillerier had told him he thought that either Jacques Duperon Baby or Jacques St. Martin were behind it, but as yet there was no proof.

Already there was considerable grumbling, in fact, from among many of the French residents from whom Pontiac's Indians had requisitioned food. Not only was it a matter of their having to provide for the Indians out of their own meager stores which angered some of the French; they resented very strongly the imperious manner in which their goods had been taken. It had all come to a head yesterday when a large number of the French had come to Pontiac while he was conferring with Captain Campbell at Meloche's house. They had asked Pontiac to summon his chiefs and he had sent runners to fetch them. When they had arrived, the Frenchmen at once began complaining bitterly of the treatment they were being subjected to. It was the esteemed French judge, Robert Navarre, who acted as their spokesman.

"Your warriors," he told the Ottawa war chief, "pass amongst us from house to house, helping themselves to whatever they want, without regard to our own needs or objections. Sometimes they have asked, but mostly they have demanded the provisions and threatened us with harm if we refused. Yet, even when we have given our food to them, we have seen it gobbled down without thought to the future, and sometimes even wasted.

"You, Chief Pontiac," Navarre continued accusingly, "pretend to be friend of the French, and yet your young warriors plunder us of our hogs and cattle and they trample upon our fields of young corn. When they come into our houses, they do so without being invited and with their tomahawks in their hands. You say you are awaiting the French army to come to aid you against the English here, but when your French father comes and hears what you have done to us, instead of shaking your hands as brothers, he will punish you as enemies."

All through Navarre's speech, Pontiac had stared at the ground silently, but as soon as the judge had finished he looked up and let his uncomfortably penetrating gaze move across the Frenchmen, settling momentarily on each of them. At last he spoke.

"My brothers, we have never wished to do harm." His voice was curiously soft, filled with sympathy and with perhaps a trace of contrition. "Nor have we wished that any harm would be done to you. Yet there are among us many young warriors who, though carefully watched, find opportunities to make mischief. For this we are sorry and all that can be done to prevent it in the future will be done.

"My brothers, it is not to revenge myself alone that I make war on the English." An edge of steel crept into his words now. "It is also to revenge you, my brothers. When the English insulted us, they insulted you also. I know that they have taken away your arms and made you sign a paper which they have sent home to their country. Therefore you are left defenseless, and I mean now to revenge your cause and my own together. I mean to destroy the English and leave not one upon our lands. You do not know all the reasons from which I act. I have told you those only which concern yourselves, but you will learn them all in time. You will cease then to think me a fool."

He paused briefly and again let his glance swing over the individual Frenchmen assembled here. A bleakness came into his expression and there were some who thought a sigh escaped him before he continued.

"I know, my brothers," he added, "that there are some among you who take part with the English. I am sorry for it, for your own sakes, for already I know who some of you are and soon I will know of them all. When our French father arrives, I shall point them out to him and we will see then whether they or I have most reason to be satisfied with the parts we have acted."

He smacked his palm resoundingly against his bare thigh. "I do not doubt, my brothers, that this war is very troublesome to you, and made the more so because our warriors are continually passing and repassing through your settlement. I am sorry for it. Do not think that I approve of the damage that is done by them. As proof of this, remember the war with the Fox tribe and the part which I took in it. It is now seventeen years since the Chippewas of Michilimackinac combined with the Sacs and Foxes and came down to destroy you. Who then defended you? Was it not I and my young men? Even Mackinac, great chief of all the Ottawas, said in council he would carry to his village the head of your commandant, that he would eat his heart and drink his blood. Did I not take your part? Did I not, though he was my chief, too, go to his camp and say to him that if he wished to kill the French he must first kill me and my warriors? Did I not assist you in routing them and driving them away?[83] And now you think that I would turn my arms against you! No, my brothers, I am the same French Pontiac who assisted you seventeen years ago. I am a Frenchman and I wish to die a Frenchman, and I now repeat to you that you and I are one—that it is for both our interests that I should be avenged."

He flung his hand out in an angry, chopping motion. "Let me alone! I do not ask you for aid, for it is not in your power to give it. I only ask provisions for myself and my men. Yet, if you are inclined to assist me, I shall not refuse you. It would please me, and you yourselves would sooner be rid of your troubles, for I promise you that as soon as the English are driven out, we will go back to our villages and there await the arrival of our French father. Until now, you French have been allowed to come and go from the fort at your desire, but from somewhere the English are receiving goods. Therefore, from this time forward, except for those whom I allow to go there, none among you will enter the fort anymore. You have heard what I have to say; remain at peace, and I will watch that no harm shall be done to you, either by my men or by the other Indians. Nothing will be taken from you except that you will be paid for it, either at that time or with a note from me by which later you may be redeemed full value for that of yours which was used by us."

Visibly impressed by this long and powerful speech, the Frenchmen had silently gone away. Now, still seated by his fire, Pontiac's hand mechanically went out to one of the bowls and extracted a cooked but cold chunk of *withse*—dog meat—from it, which he gnawed absently, his mind still dwelling on that meeting and the events that had followed it. After the Frenchmen had gone, Pontiac had warned his chiefs to allow no further mistreatment of the Frenchmen themselves. Providing food for the Indians was, however, to be mandatory on their part. Any Frenchman who refused was to have his cattle or hogs butchered in reprisal. The Ottawas were to get their food supplies from the French inhabitants living to the north and east of the fort; the Hurons from the French living across the river; the Potawatomies and Chippewas from the inhabitants south and west of the fort. For when such goods were demanded, Pontiac drew up a large number of promissory notes on which he sketched his totem, the figure of an otter.[84] These were to be given to the French with the word of Pontiac that they would be redeemed in full when possible. Control and distribution of the goods collected was to rest solely with the principal chief of each tribe and Pontiac ordered that all goods collected for—and by—the Ottawas were hereafter to be stored in the house of Baptiste Meloche and issued by himself as required.

Later the same day Pontiac, all by himself, confronted Jacques Duperon Baby. Curiously, though he had been told by the younger Cuillerier that Baby was actively providing the garrison with foodstuffs whenever possible, he did not mention it. Instead he looked at the Frenchman sadly and said:

"I have heard, my friend, that the English have offered you a bushel of silver coins for my scalp."

Baby, nervous with the presence of the war chief, shook his head vigorously. "What you have heard," he said, "is a lie. I would never so betray you."

Pontiac grunted. "My brother," he said, "has spoken the

truth and to show that I believe him, I will stay the night here."

Incredulously then, the Frenchman watched as the Ottawa chief stretched out on a bench, tossed his blanket over himself and promptly went to sleep. The vulnerability of the chief lying there put Baby into a strange state of mind. How simple it would be to kill him on the spot and thus almost certainly end this war. Perhaps he might even hit him, knock him unconscious, bind him and deliver him to Major Gladwin. But at last, shaking his head, Baby himself had gone to bed. Providing foodstuffs for the beleaguered garrison was one thing; betraying such a trust as this was another, and he could not do it.

Pontiac had read his man well.

[*May 18, 1763—Wednesday*]

The party of twelve or thirteen Delawares were camped along the uppermost reaches of the Sandusky River, where that stream was little more than a dozen feet across and mostly shallow except for an occasional pool.[85] Under their chief, Pitwe-owa, they had been camped here for five days, hunting and trapping, and were on the point of heading home.

They had stayed in at least a dozen other camps like this since last fall and although they had seven or eight very large bundles of furs—mainly mink, raccoon and muskrat, but with a scattering of otter—these were hardly more than a fraction of the number they used to get with far less effort than had been expended on this trip. The reason, as each of them knew, was lack of ammunition. It rankled Pitwe-owa to think of how very anxious the English traders were, back at the village of Tuscarawas, to obtain the furs and yet how difficult they made it for the Indians to get them by withholding the ammunition vital to their pursuit. The traders were generally sorry about it, sympathizing with them about the difficulty this caused the whole tribe, but claiming they could not disobey the orders of General Amherst. Each time a hunting and trapping party returned to the Delaware village located on the banks of the Tuscarawas River after having been out for some time, one of the first questions asked was whether or not the traders were again trading ammunition for pelts. Always the answer had been no, and Pitwe-owa expected it would be no different this time. With these furs they would be able to trade for blankets and utensils, powdered paints and cloth and, if they were lucky, perhaps even some skinning knives. But not ammunition. As it always did, the anger in Pitwe-owa's breast grew the more he thought about it.

"Pitwe-owa!"

Swiveling at the call of his name, he saw one of his men pointing to the north across a sprawling prairie which ended about a mile distant in a huge island of trees. At first he saw nothing and he glanced back at the man who had called. The young warrior bobbed his head and, continuing to point, said excitedly: *"Nithese elene pe-e-wah meshewa!"*—Three men coming on horses.

Pitwe-owa looked again and now he could see them. They were a short distance from the trees and following the Indian trail in this direction, apparently heading toward the Shawnee country in the valley of the Scioto River. By this time all the warriors had risen and, seeing that the riders were Indians, cupped their mouths and raised their voices in the far-carrying halloo.

Abruptly the trio reined up and one stood up upon the back of the horse he had been riding, shading his eyes with both hands to see better. After only a moment he waved and dropped back down astride the animal and then all three horsemen began a smart canter toward the camp.

A peculiar excitement welled up in Chief Pitwe-owa as they approached. He quickly recognized them as Wyandot Hurons and one of the three horses—a blotched black-and-white pony with a white head—he recognized as belonging to one of the English traders, the man called Callender. In a few minutes the Wyandots had arrived and halted their horses. Their leader, a muscular man of middle age, nodded his head gravely toward them. His eyes swept over the group and came to rest on Pitwe-owa.

"Okema nema-ta," he said in the Delaware tongue, *"Was he kee sheke. Weshe lah shama-mo?"*—Greetings, Chief. A fine day. Are you well?

Pitwe-owa, pleased at the Wyandot's courtesy in using the Delaware tongue, nodded at the traditional greeting and replied automatically, *"Nema-ta. Ne weshe lah geh shama-mo."*—Greetings. I am very well.

The Delaware chief then made a motion with his hand for the three to alight and join them at the fire. There, though it was obvious that they were as anxious to speak as he was to listen, he first offered them food and drink, which they accepted gravely, then smoked a pipe with them. Not until these ritualistic acts were completed did Pitwe-owa nod his head toward the leader of the little party.

"*Atch-mo-loh,*" he said.—Speak.

The man introduced himself as Ska-ki—Goose—warrior from Sandusky. Then, with rising tempo and excitement, he told of the surprise attack made on Fort Sandusky in which, without the loss or injury of a single warrior, twenty-seven English soldiers and traders had been slain, their scalps lifted, their commander taken prisoner, the fort itself plundered of everything and then burned. The very horses being ridden by these three were part of the plunder. Further, a general uprising against the English had now begun under Pontiac, centered at Detroit, though already spreading to all English forts. Detroit itself had been under attack for at least ten days, perhaps more.

Ska-ki withdrew from his belt a wide band of black wampum. All Indian nations, he said, were urged now to stop whatever they were doing, cast aside any intertribal rivalries or jealousies, take up their weapons and immediately fall upon the English wherever they found them in order to kill them or drive them out of the country. Messengers had been sent in all directions with the news and Ska-ki and his men were themselves on their way now to tell the Shawnees at their principal villages of Kispoko Town and Chalahgawtha[86] along the Scioto River.

Excitement rising sharply in all of the Delawares of this camp, they heard Ska-ki out, then saw him and his two men off with friendly waves and promises. The promises were that they would return at once to their own village of Tuscarawas and from there, armed as strongly as possible, they would head for the Fort Pitt area and the Pennsylvania border country to bloody their own tomahawks and war clubs.

Pitwe-owa's dark eyes glittered at the thought. At last the time had come! Now would the English pay dearly for all the woes and insults they had heaped upon the Delawares. Like a ravaging fire they would spread across the frontier and Pitwe-owa would be in their very front, leading his men to strike the English wherever they found them.

Not at all unappropriately had this Delaware been named Pitwe-owa—The Wolf!

[*May 20, 1763—Friday*]

"You understand your instructions upon reaching Niagara, Captain?"

Jacob Newman flashed a toothy grin at the Detroit commander and nodded. "Yes sir."

"Repeat, please," Henry Gladwin said.

"To personally deliver the three dispatch pouches to Major John Wilkins,[87] the commanding officer, instantly upon arrival there. To advise that the one so marked be sent by express to Captain Simeon Ecuyer, commander of Fort Pitt, immediately. To advise that the one so marked be sent by express, also immediately, to Lieutenant Colonel Jeffrey Amherst in New York. To advise that Major Wilkins open and read immediately the contents of the pouch addressed to himself; that after doing so, he dispatch messengers at once to Forts Oswego, Stanwix, Presque Isle, Le Boeuf and Venango with the news and strong warning to prepare for defensive measures and in no case to trust any body of Indians approaching any fort, whether or not they are professing friendship. No Indians to be admitted inside any fort except for small parties of chiefs who are first disarmed and kept constantly under guard. To reiterate vocally the great need for immediate supplies and reinforcements here at Detroit, as outlined in your dispatches."

"Good," Gladwin said, smiling slightly. "Now, what about when you leave here?"

"I'll proceed downriver aboard and in command of the *Michigan* to a point just outside the mouth of the river. There, finding protective anchorage if possible, we are to wait until June 6 or until in our measured judgement it becomes hazardous to wait any longer; the object being to alert and divert the expected supply convoy of batteaux from Fort Niagara and escort them until such time as they will be reasonably safe to proceed on their own."

Major Gladwin shook Captain Jacob Newman's hand. The Detroit commander smiled wryly. "That's it. You'll leave a little after midnight. Don't take any chances. Good luck, Jake—you'll need it."

[May 21, 1763—Saturday]

For the first time since he had been taken captive, Captain Donald Campbell caught sight of the fort. With his hands tied behind him and a long rawhide tether attached to his neck, he had little opportunity to gaze around him, however, as he was led by the party of a score or more of Ottawa warriors. Yet he did glimpse the stockade once or twice through the trees and felt a deep yearning grow in him to again be within the sanctuary of those walls.

He had no idea why he had been separated from Lieutenant McDougall who, as far as he knew, was still back at Meloche's house. Nor had he been told where he was being taken, even though the interpreter, Pierre LaButte, was beside him. In fact, though they had treated him well enough, none of the party even spoke to him as they circled the fort and then headed first west and then south along the river trail.

It was near the Potawatomi village below the fort where he was led to the river shore and put aboard a canoe. The downstream journey continued until finally they came ashore just a mile or so below the mouth of the Ecorse River on the northern tip of the long Grosse Isle. Here a camp was made and they waited, though Campbell still had no idea for what. Continually more canoes arrived until there were about thirty of the long craft beached here and perhaps four hundred warriors assembled. Though all of the Detroit area tribes were represented, the Potawatomies seemed to be on hand in the greatest number.

From the last canoe to be beached stepped Pontiac, the white stone crescent hanging from his nostrils identifying him to Campbell even before his features were visible. At once he went into a huddled conference with LaButte. Occasionally the two men looked or pointed downstream and twice the entire group of Indians near them looked at Campbell and nodded in agreement to something Pontiac said. At last they broke apart and both LaButte and Pontiac—the chief newly painted like the rest of the Indians—came to him.

"Captain Campbell," Pontiac said slowly, "one of the big boats has left the fort and its rope is now tied to the bottom of the river just below this island. There are not many men on it and they cannot hope to stand up to as many men and canoes as we have. We intend to float down to it, make a circle around it and demand its surrender. If it will surrender, no one will be harmed. If we are forced to attack, I cannot promise that any on board will live."

Campbell sensed what was coming now but he waited silently and in a moment Pontiac continued.

"At first we will stay far enough away from them so there will be little danger to us from whatever guns they have. But you, wearing this red coat of yours, will be standing in the front of one of the boats, so that if they shoot, it will be you who will draw the bullets and your blood will be upon their hands, not ours. When you get close enough that they can hear your voice, you will call to them and order them to surrender. I do not give you a choice. You will say to them what I have said or you will die. I will not be there to protect you, as I have other business, so your life is in your own hands. Do not try to trick us or you will die. I have no more to say."

There was little point in arguing about it and so Campbell merely shrugged. In a short while he was in the bow of the canoe moving downstream and the twenty-nine other canoes —one having carried Pontiac back upstream—clustered in a formless grouping some distance behind. He was pleased to learn that the ship had been sent away from the fort, but was at a loss to understand why it had anchored at Grosse Isle's southern tip near the mouth of the river when by now it should have been well out into Lake Erie. He wondered if perhaps a stop had been made to repair a leak before venturing out into the lake. Whatever the reason, he decided, it was hardly worth the risk.

It was midafternoon when the downstream end of the miles-long island was reached and he caught sight of the ship, immediately identifying her as the eighty-ton *Michigan*. He knew her to be a sturdy craft, well cared for under the hand of her master, Captain Newman, and his wonder at her anchorage here increased. LaButte, in the canoe with him, ordered him to get ready to call out his message from Pontiac. Campbell stood up and even before they had come within earshot he saw that the advancing canoes had been sighted and the rails of the ship were lined with armed men.

Campbell's scarlet coat had obviously been seen and as his canoe came ever nearer, no shots were fired from the ship. Campbell noted that the sails hung limply. If the vessel tried to run, as he hoped she would, she'd have to maneuver almost solely by the force of the current and the canoes could run her down easily. Not daring to wait any longer, since the canoes behind were already beginning to spread out, Campbell cupped his mouth with both hands. He had an idea that these might be the last words he would ever speak.

"Ship ho!" he shouted. "Is Captain Newman aboard?"

"Newman here." The reply was faint but audible.

"This is Captain Campbell. I've been obliged by Pontiac to demand that you stay where you are and surrender. But as second-in-command of the fort, I this moment order you to weigh anchor and move away at once!"

"You'll be killed!" Jacob Newman's voice was strained but more audible now.

"Concern yourself with the ship," Campbell shouted angrily. "Do your duty and get away now if you can. You are going to be surrounded and attacked. Weigh anchor!"

Even as he spoke he could see the big vessel begin to drift as the anchor left bottom and began raising. There came an immediate howl from the Indians and Campbell was suddenly snatched around the neck and pulled off his feet by LaButte, who snarled a vile oath at him.[88] The *Michigan*, its anchor now coming clear of the water, swung ponderously with the current and began moving downstream, but its speed was considerably less than that of the canoes which darted forward toward it. Already, even though they were not yet in effective range, the Indians in the five leading canoes were firing at the ship. There was no answering fire.

Narrower and narrower became the gap which separated them. Abruptly the water rippled as a little breeze sprang up and the sails began to fill their bellies. At the same moment there was a sharp command from aboard and a volley of shots was fired. A Potawatomi warrior standing in the bow of one of the closest of the five pursuing canoes was struck in the chest, knocked off his feet and out of the boat. For an instant his head could be seen on the surface and then it disappeared.

Now the remaining canoes held back some, trying the impossible feat of remaining out of range of the riflemen aboard the big craft while at the same time getting in range to fire effectively themselves. The ripples became a light chop and the ship picked up speed. Soon it began widening the gap and the paddlers gave up and swung around to rejoin the other canoes. Together all of them began moving slowly upstream.

A lump forming high on his cheekbone where he had struck the gunwale when jerked backwards, Captain Campbell now sat facing astern, watching the diminishing ship. It was now well into the widening waters of the lake and suddenly Campbell sucked in his breath. There had been a momentary white splash near the ship's bow. Her sails were dropped and once again the ship turned and faced upstream as the anchor bit and held.

In a moment the Indians, too, had noticed it. They shouted back and forth to one another hesitantly, wondering if they should attempt a second attack. But with a bonny breeze blowing now and the vessel well out to where the water was more lake than river, it was obvious that the big craft would have the advantage and it was decided not to go at it again.

And now, at last, comprehension dawned for Campbell regarding the boat's peculiar actions. The regular first shipment of goods for the year was already long overdue at Detroit from Niagara. It would be a string of clumsy batteaux which could well fall into the enemy's hands if not alerted and protected. Major Gladwin had undoubtedly ordered Newman to wait at the river's mouth to head off the convoy. Otherwise they couldn't help but be taken.

Donald Campbell, not a particularly religious man, closed his eyes now and, for the first time in a very long time, prayed devoutly.

[May 22, 1763—Sunday, 10:00 A.M.]

Antoine Cuillerier's mocking laughter rebounded cheerlessly from the walls and he slammed his fist down upon the table with such impact that the glasses in a nearby cupboard clinked together.

"So this is how the brave Indians fight, eh?" The Frenchman gave another bark of sarcastic laughter. "You send thirty boats—*four hundred brave warriors!*—to fight a single small ship and what happens? Twenty-five of the canoes do not even get close enough to begin shooting and the other five turn and run when a single Potawatomi gets himself killed. Only five boats attack; but why not the thirty? Is this how Indian fighting works? You only fight when no one can get killed? Pah! Twenty Frenchmen in two canoes could have taken that ship. Now the opportunity is gone and for that we can look forward to reinforcements coming soon from Fort Niagara. Perhaps Pontiac is not so much the general that he would have his followers believe."

Slowly, almost casually, Pontiac reached out and gathered the front of Cuillerier's ruffled shirt in his fist. His free hand hovered dangerously near the big knife in his waistband. When he spoke, his voice was tight, ominous.

"The French could learn from us in fighting the English. Do not laugh again. It would not be wise to push against me too hard. We will fight to the death at any time it is necessary—more so than will you French!—but at no time when it is unnecessary will we throw away our lives. It is not our way. No ten white lives are worth that of one Indian. No other English ship will go safely down the river. No other ship will safely come up from the lake!"

Cuillerier had indeed pressed his luck and now, his face pale, the Frenchman stepped back when Pontiac released him. He smoothed out his shirt and stammered an apology of sorts. Pontiac merely looked at him and then turned and left the house. Had not the chief been almost as disgusted as the Frenchman over the retreat of the canoes, things would have gone badly for Cuillerier. But if criticism was to be made, Pontiac intended to be the one to make it. Already he had severely tongue-lashed the returned party, fortunately taking out so much of his anger on them that he had little left for Captain Donald Campbell.

The rotund officer apparently expected to be killed, but Pontiac had no intention of slaying him. The man was too valuable to him to just throw away. He had other plans for him. Above all else, Campbell was still his insurance. If worse came to worst, as now it might, he could trade Campbell's life for his own. With a scowl he had sent the captain back under guard to Meloche's house.

Now, striding back toward his camp, Pontiac considered the matter and gradually the lines of anger in his face gave way to thoughtfulness. The big ship was still there at the mouth of the river. Why? Why had it stopped near the southern end of Grosse Isle in the first place? Why, when attacked there, did it move only to the more open waters for safety and then anchor again?

Throughout the night and well into the morning his men had watched the ship. Only moments before Pontiac had seen Cuillerier he had received a report that the ship was still there and showed no sign of preparing to leave the area. The logical mind of Pontiac pursued the thought relentlessly now. Abruptly the tension seemed to go out of him and, when he entered his camp a few moments later, he might not have been smiling, but at least the angry scowl was gone. His mood improved even more when he learned that while he had been closeted with Cuillerier, Chief Sekahos had come to join him, bringing with him one hundred and twenty of his Mississaugi warriors. Within ten or fifteen minutes of his return, Pontiac stood before upwards of two hundred and fifty warriors and spoke to them at length in a voice which carried well enough to their ears, but no farther. To Sekahos and to Ottawa Chief Mehemah of his own village he spoke further in private, giving them clear instructions, and when, after a little while more the council broke up, there was considerable activity as weapons were checked, medicine bags hung about necks or tied tightly to waistbands, faces and bodies repainted.

As darkness fell, the entire party boarded canoes and, with Chief Mehemah leading them, disappeared toward the other side of the river. In less than an hour the canoes had returned, empty except for paddlers. Perhaps now there would be something to show Cuillerier about which he would not laugh in scorn.

[*May 22, 1763—Sunday, 9:00* P.M.]

At this very moment, two meetings were going on at Michilimackinac. One was in the fort and it was very small but the other, in the main council house of the Chippewa village, was quite large.

In the latter place, guards were posted not only inside and out at the doors of either end of the long council house, but other guards stood in the darkness farther out from the structure, watching and listening to prevent any unwanted persons from hearing what was being discussed. Now and then to these guards would drift faintly the sound rather than the words being spoken by the principal chief of the nation, Minivavana.

Two Indian messengers—an Ottawa and a Chippewa—had arrived late in the afternoon bearing with them the secret and important news of Pontiac's attack on Detroit. It was the word that the more northern tribal factions had been alerted to wait for, and now it had come.

Minivavana was taller than most of his followers. He was big-boned and heavy-jawed and his voice had a rich timbre which filled the council chambers easily. He spoke to his audience, mostly Chippewas but also with perhaps a score of Sac Indians in attendance, for almost an hour without interruption, telling them of the attack on Detroit, of the scalps already lifted there, of the fact that now it was time to plan decisively here for the attack on Fort Michilimackinac.

"It was said at first," Minivavana told them, "that when the time came for us to strike the English, it would be with Chippewa and Ottawa acting together, as one. Yet, the Ottawa of L'Arbre Croche are not here now and Chief Mackinac has not given us any word of himself and his warriors. With so little regard on his part for us, there is little reason for us to wait on their favor. Pontiac and his Ottawas struck Detroit without the aid of many of our tribe. So then, we will strike Fort Michilimackinac without the aid of the L'Arbre Croche Ottawas. Pontiac would not share the plunder of Detroit with us; therefore we will not share the plunder of this fort with Chief Mackinac unless he should come here with his men to join us in the attack. And unlike Pontiac, we will give the English no opportunity to hide themselves within their walls."

In detail then, with attending chiefs given leave to interject their ideas, the entire plan was laid out. It was a good plan, which seemed without flaw, and it was to be put into operation on the day following the next full moon—June 2.

Hardly more than a mile away, in the commanding officer's chambers of Fort Michilimackinac, Captain George Etherington stared angrily at Alexander Henry and the two traders he had brought with him here, Ezekiel Solomon and John Tracy. He had heard them out silently, but with his temper fraying at each word they uttered.

All three of the traders, independently of one another, had learned of a growing hostility for the English among the Indians. Talk had reached them of attacks being planned on each of the forts. There was a rumor even purporting Detroit itself to be under attack. And it was said that very soon Fort Michilimackinac's entire English population, soldiers and traders alike, would be slain. On and on the three went with their stories until finally they began repeating themselves and then George Etherington exploded.

"By damn!" he shouted. "Silence! All of you! What are you, a bunch of old women? Ever since I came here all I've heard from you and others is gossip. You're as bad as these Frenchmen. They've been in here half a dozen times with these warnings of impending danger and I'm damned well sick of all the wild stories about how the Indians are going to attack. My God, gentlemen, think! How in the name of heaven could these Indians—without ammunition, with guns that wouldn't work if they *had* ammunition, with nothing but flimsy bows and rabbit-skinning knives—how, I ask you, could they possibly attack us even if they had the desire to, which I don't believe they have? I want you to leave now. I'll tell you three just what I told Laurent Ducharme and his French cronies: I refuse to hear any more of this. In fact, spread this word to everyone, since you are so good at word-spreading: the next man who comes up with any such story in my hearing will be punished severely. That is all!"

[*May 23, 1763—Monday, 10:30* P.M.]

Not since the fighting first broke out here at Detroit a fortnight ago had such a peculiar restiveness gripped Henry Gladwin. Nor was it something brought about by word of the attack on the *Michigan* at the mouth of the river. From several Frenchmen he had learned details of the attack, of Captain Campbell having been used as a shield, of the Potawatomi warrior having been killed. The ship, so he was told, still hovered near the river's mouth and Gladwin could imagine Captain Newman's growing concern as he waited, on the commander's orders, to warn off the expected supply convoy.

But this was not what was causing the restlessness Gladwin had been experiencing since nightfall. It was a very still night and he attributed his ill feeling to the strangely excited, almost exultant cries occasionally reaching the fort from the Huron, Ottawa and Potawatomi villages. It was as if something of considerable moment was looming and would suddenly manifest itself in some way. Certainly if it was, indeed, something that was giving the natives excitement and pleasure, it boded no good for the garrison.

It was only a few minutes after the little clock on the fireplace mantel had chimed its eight notes to indicate 10:30 P.M. that there came a tapping on his door. Almost as if he had been expecting it, though he had not been, Gladwin strode to the door and opened it. His aide stood there.

"Sir, Mr. St. Martin's just arrived with several Huron chiefs. They're at the west gate. They were afraid of being seen and so we let them in and have them under guard. They seem very excited and they want to see you right away."

Gladwin nodded and crossed the room to get his uniform coat. As he shrugged into it, he wondered what was in the wind now. Strangely, he felt relieved that it was Jacques St. Martin who had come. Of all the Frenchmen at Detroit, there were none he trusted so implicitly as St. Martin and Jacques Baby. Now he left the room and strode briskly toward the west gate, having indicated with a jerk of his head for his aide to come along. High overhead a fat crescent of moon shone weakly, almost lost in the aura of light shed by the lantern his aide carried.

At the gate, Gladwin and the Frenchman shook hands warmly and then St. Martin introduced him in turn to the three chiefs—Teata, the principal chief, and two others introduced only as Thomas and Andrew. All three appeared very nervous and kept their faces out of the direct lantern light. Even St. Martin seemed rather agitated and he suggested to the major that they speak in privacy.

Gladwin immediately led them to a nearby storage shed without windows. Stationing his aide at the door, he showed the four men in, closed the door behind himself and set the lantern on a pork barrel. He then screwed the lantern wick high and, turning, was shocked to see that not only were all three Indians stripped except for loincloths, but that none wore any symbol of rank and all had smeared ashes and charcoal liberally on their bodies and faces.

St. Martin spoke briefly to them in the Huron tongue and all three nodded. Then he returned his attention to the major.

"Sorry, sir. Just explained to them that I wanted to tell you briefly what has happened and then I'll interpret for them and you as you talk together." He cleared his throat nervously and then hurried on. "First of all, sir, Fort Sandusky has fallen."

"What!"

"Yes sir. No doubt in my mind about it. They have Ensign Pauli down near the river mouth. They're going to give him a chance to recover a little before they bring him in, because they want him to be able to run a gauntlet. I talked with some of the Ottawas who were in on the taking of the fort. I couldn't get many details, but the news is all bad. They told me they surprised the fort a week ago—on the sixteenth; a few of them were Ottawas, but mostly it was done by the Sandusky Wyandots." As if he sensed Gladwin forming the question, St. Martin hastened to add, "No survivors, sir. Only Pauli. All the traders killed, too, and everything plundered. When it was all over and they'd cleaned out the fort, they burned the place down."

A sick helplessness washed through Gladwin and for some time he could not speak. When the pause became uncomfortable, St. Martin added: "Pontiac's heard about it, of course, and he's jubilant. They all are. You've probably heard them celebrating. All except Teata's band. Now he wants to talk to you."

The interpreter stood to one side and nodded at Teata and immediately the stocky Huron chief began speaking, pausing as he was accustomed to after every sentence or two in order to allow St. Martin to interpret.

"He says to tell you," St. Martin began, assuming the monotone he always seemed to adopt when interpreting, "that he and his people were largely responsible for the taking of the traders named Rackman and Abraham, but that they were forced to do so by Pontiac. They also took a canoe yesterday near the west side of the lake in which were five Englishmen but few goods. Among them is one who calls himself Thomas Smallman and who says he is a cousin of George Croghan. There are also a couple of Jews in the party. Teata says it is lucky for them that they fell into his hands, for if they had fallen into the hands of any other Indians, even his brother Hurons under Chief Takee, it would have gone hard for them. None of them have been killed. He says—"

"Say it in his words, Jacques," Gladwin interjected. It was a hurdle of interpreting that St. Martin always seemed to have difficulty with. The Frenchman bobbed his head and continued almost without pause:

"I would not let my men harm them, though I do not think they would be alive now if others had them. The Hurons do not want this war. They have never wanted it, but they have been forced into it. Now I desire to know the father's opinion of us. If you will make peace with us, we will give up to you our prisoners and pay the trader Abraham for that part of his merchandise which it fell to us to receive in the division of the goods with the other Indians. If you will make peace with us, we promise to cause the English no further harm, to remain quiet, and to make every effort to convince other tribes and bands to separate themselves from Pontiac. We had no part in the destruction of Fort Sandusky and are ashamed of our brother, Odinghquanooron, for so misleading his children to do such a thing. We wish peace with you."

Teata, and then St. Martin after him, stopped speaking and Gladwin tugged at his chin as he thought. Then he addressed the Huron and St. Martin echoed him in their tongue.

"Chief Teata, under the conditions you state, I will take it upon myself to make peace with you and recommend your band to General Amherst, whom I have no doubt will make it a lasting peace if your future behavior merits it."

All three chiefs murmured in apparent relief and then Teata spoke up again.

"Our future behavior will be good and your general will see that it is so. If you wish it, we will help you by hiding ourselves on Isle au Bois Blanc"—Whitewood Island—"which is closest to the mouth of the river and there we will intercept and protect from other Indians all merchant boats which should arrive there."

Gladwin shook his head. "No. For several good reasons which I will not go into here, Chief Teata, I will not ask that of you. Rather, I ask that you should faithfully perform the other promises you have made and remain quiet and, where it is possible for you, to use your endeavors to try to separate Pontiac's followers from him."

Teata, Thomas and Andrew all nodded in unison and each, in turn, gravely shook the commander's hand. Gladwin dipped his head at St. Martin and the interpreter turned the lamp down until it was only a dim glow. Almost without sound the door opened for a moment and then closed and all four men were gone.

So already some of the Indians were getting nervous. At any other time Gladwin would have been elated, but now that he was alone in the semi-darkness, the full impact of the bad news brought by St. Martin threatened to engulf him.

Fort Sandusky gone and all but one man dead! Gladwin buried his face in his hands and a small groan escaped him. Fort Sandusky gone . . . and now, what next?

[*May 23, 1763—Monday, 11:45* P.M.]

Although it was close to midnight now, Ensign Robert Holmes was not especially sleepy. In a little while, he supposed, he would get out of bed and pad over to the table to blow out the guttering little stub of candle glowing there, but not yet. In the faint, flickering light he could see the gentle rise and fall of the uncovered breasts of the girl asleep beside him.

For some peculiar reason he thought of home and a faint flush touched him, causing his cheeks and neck to tingle. How far away it was, in time as well as miles. When he had left there he was little more than a boy, intensely proud of his new ensign rank and determined to be a fine soldier and to rise in the ranks step by step until he became a great commander whose men would eagerly follow him anywhere. In farewell he had shaken hands with his father and kissed his mother, noting the cool dampness of her tear-stained cheek. To them he was a little boy yet, heading uncertainly into an unknown future.

He wondered what they would think if they could see him now; if they would still consider him their "little boy." He doubted it. Now he was commander of Fort Miamis and its garrison of fifteen men, guardian of His Majesty's interests in the Far West. And what remnant of little boyhood that had remained when he arrived here was gone now, melted away in the heat of the passion of this young woman asleep beside him.

He still called her Whiskey, which was his shortening of her Indian name—Ouiske-lotha Nebi. It meant, in the Miami language, Water Bird or, more literally, Bird-of-the-Water. He no longer had any difficulty pronouncing the full name, but to Holmes she had become just Whiskey and he rarely even thought of her full Indian name anymore. He grinned at the irony of it, remembering how on his departure from home he had solemnly promised his mother that he would avoid whiskey.

Angular features or not, in his eyes she was a beautiful girl. Her hair was long and black and fell freely down her back except when she was working, when it was braided. Loose and spread out as it was beneath her head now, it framed her face and gave her a charming, innocent look and made her appear even younger than she was.

Ensign Holmes had been captivated by her at first encounter and became even more so as time passed. During those first passionate weeks he had begun to wonder if he was truly in love with her. Now he had no doubt of it and he knew only too well the problems it would eventually engender. Sooner or later he would be reassigned and have to leave here. Would he then take her with him, or would they part? He could not imagine adapting himself to live in her world and wondered if she could make the transition to his. It was a painful thought and now, as on past occasions when it occurred, he pushed it out of his mind. It would have to be a matter decided when the time came, not now.

His eyes moved across her, studying her, and he wondered how anyone could be vicious or cruel to Indians. If only people could get to know them like he knew Whiskey, all the hatred and ugliness directed against Indians would vanish. They, like her, were a gentle and thoughtful people, inclined to great friendliness if given half a chance. It rankled him when people spoke against them, as had those two Frenchmen earlier today.

The pair were traders, en route from Detroit to Fort de Chartres on the Mississippi, and they had come to him immediately upon their arrival here. They had, they told him, left Detroit fifteen days ago, on May 8. They had heard considerable talk before that of possible hostile intentions on the part of the Indians but had not put too much stock in it. On the next day after leaving, however, just as they were breaking camp near the mouth of the Detroit River, they heard the muted booming of the fort's cannon far to the north, leading them to believe the installation was under attack. Rather than returning, they had continued on their journey, following the western shore of Lake Erie to the mouth of the Maumee— which the Indians called the *Omee*—and then up the Maumee River to this place where the larger river was formed by the confluence of the St. Marys River from the southeast and the St. Joseph River from the northeast. The two men seemed genuinely concerned and commented that the Indians couldn't be trusted.

At first when he heard the story, Robert Holmes had been angry. He accused the men of being *provocateurs,* of spreading fear and distrust with such malicious tales, and he ordered that they cease such talk or he would place them under arrest. Angered themselves at such reaction, the pair had left in stiff silence.

It took a while for Holmes to cool down after they were gone and then he began to reconsider what they had said. He had to admit that there was a certain amount of Indian unrest prevailing in this country, but he could not bring himself to believe it was a prelude to uprising. Nevertheless, he was too conscientious a commander to ignore the faint possibility of truth to the story. All afternoon, therefore, he had kept his men busy making cartridges, warned them to keep alert and issued orders restricting them to the confines of this post until he could determine the facts. He commended himself on the actions he had taken.

Beside him he felt Whiskey stir and glanced at her again. She had opened her eyes and was looking at him sleepily, a faint smile tilting the corners of her lips. He leaned over and kissed her gently on each eyelid, on the tip of her nose and then on her mouth. Earlier he had been exhausted, but now he felt the heat rising in him again and he pulled her to him.

The little candle across the room eventually burned itself out.

[*May 24, 1763—Tuesday, 7:00* P.M.]

Chief Washee of the Potawatomies had not touched the bowl of food that had been placed on the ground beside him as he sat quietly before the fire. He had no intention of eating it. He felt that it dulled the faculties to eat before a very important occurrence, whether that occurrence be a battle or a council or whatever. He always prayed to the Great Spirit on the eve of something so important.

He was praying now.

Even though weeks before he had fully agreed to Pontiac's plan of surprise attack against all English forts in this country, Washee was worried. It was not the English at Fort St. Joseph that bothered him, but rather the fact that while he had agreed with Pontiac, there was more than a reasonable likelihood that the Potawatomies of this area far to the west of Detroit and not many miles from Lake Michigan would not be in favor of the plan.

Washee knew Chief Kioqua only too well. Kioqua was disenchanted with the English, true, but he was also a very cautious man and more often than not reluctant to lead his people into difficulties if they could in any way be avoided. Therefore, the closer Washee had come to the village where Kioqua presided, the more certain he became that not only would Kioqua refuse to help him and his small band of Detroit Potawatomies in the taking of the fort, but that he might even try to prevent it. Worse, he would be almost certain to attempt to prevent any attack if he learned that Major Gladwin was presently holding Chief Winnemac and another Potawatomi as hostages—a fact Washee himself had only verified a short time ago.

It had been late this afternoon when Washee motioned to the score of warriors following him to halt. They were on the bank of the St. Joseph River[89] not more than a mile above the fort, which was also on this side of the stream. A little fire was built and the plan discussed. There were only sixteen soldiers at the little fort, including their commander, Ensign Francis Schlosser, but if the surprise was not complete and they managed to fortify, Washee would have trouble taking the place with even three times as many warriors as he had. Too, there were bound to be a number of traders there as well, who would have to be taken.

Washee would have liked it better if he had not cause to use some of the men of Kioqua's village. The fact remained, however, that his own Detroit Potawatomies were not known to the garrison here and without some familiar faces of Fort St. Joseph's Potawatomi neighbors, suspicion might be aroused at the outset. No, he would have to recruit the help of some of Kioqua's men.

One of the warriors in his own band, who until just recently had lived in Kioqua's village, mentioned that there were many young warriors like himself there who were eager to fight the English and would gladly join in an attack with Washee. They were resentful, he said, over Kioqua's easygoing manner and he felt sure he could convince a select fifteen or twenty of them, perhaps even more, to give their help.

The idea sounded promising and Washee had sent him on alone to the village to carefully sound out the right men. He was to emphasize the fact that there would be much plunder and the majority of it would go to them. Those men the young warrior found willing he was to send to council with

Washee here this evening, just across the river from the village and about a half mile upstream from it, where they would be neither heard nor seen. If, as Washee had been told, the fort's commander was almost always tipsy with brandy, it would make the surprise that much easier to pull off. And once it had been pulled off and the fort taken, then regardless of whether he liked it or not, Chief Kioqua would be committed.

Now, in the subdued glow of the setting sun, Washee hunkered by the little fire that his men had built and fingered the smooth red stone hanging around his neck by a thin strand of rawhide. His lips moved silently as he called upon the Great Spirit to make them successful in what lay ahead. After a while, a serene expression on his face, he turned his attention to his warriors and the handful from Kioqua's village who had already drifted in and told them that they would make their attempt to surprise the fort in the morning. And then, in considerable detail, he went over what each of them must do.

[May 24, 1763—Tuesday, 9:00 P.M.]

About two miles from Fort Miamis was the village of Chief Cold Foot, a Miami. He was one of the few of his tribe who had attended the great council held by Pontiac on the bank of the River Ecorse a month ago. There, as others did, he had caught the war spirit and agreed that when he was informed that Pontiac had indeed attacked Detroit, he would in turn make his attempt to surprise and take Fort Miamis. Now that word had come.

Earlier today two Frenchmen and a small number of Ottawas had arrived, carrying with them war belts and the exciting news that Pontiac had struck and Detroit was under siege. The men met with Cold Foot in his lodge and told him what had transpired, then called upon him to make good his promise and take Fort Miamis. The Miami chief, his ardor somewhat cooled since the River Ecorse council, was not too pleased.

The Frenchmen were Mini Chene and Jacques Godefroy. With them, their hands bound behind them and rawhide halters around their necks, were a trader, two of his helpers and a soldier. Cold Foot recognized them, as well he should, since they had left Fort Miamis only days before. The trader was John Welch[90] and the soldier was Private Robert Lawton of the 60th Regiment.

When they had left Fort Miamis, Welch's party was laden with furs and trade goods which they intended taking to Detroit. Ensign Robert Holmes had detached Private Lawton from garrison duty both to carry messages to Major Gladwin and to act as escort for Welch. He was supposed to return to Fort Miamis as soon as possible with whatever dispatches and mail which might be waiting there for delivery here. The four men had set off in two canoes and made good time paddling downstream with the Maumee River current.

They were still considerably above the mouth of the river, however, when they met the party of five Frenchmen and Ottawas coming upstream. The Frenchmen had hailed them with apparent friendliness, but as soon as they had all gone ashore to chat, Welch, his men, and Private Lawton were seized and disarmed, then bound. Their goods were plundered and three of the Frenchmen—Chauvin, Beauban, and Labadie—agreed to take the goods back to Detroit while the other two—Chene and Godefroy—would continue westward with the prisoners and the Ottawas to fulfill the mission Pontiac had sent them on.

Now, by the light of the fire in Cold Foot's lodge, the French pair pressed Chief Cold Foot for information about Fort Miamis and its garrison. What the village chief told them was not encouraging. Until just recently the commander, Ensign Holmes, had been quite friendly; but suddenly he had become suspicious, although Cold Foot was not certain why. Perhaps it was due to another pair of Frenchmen who had passed through here and stopped in briefly to see him. At any rate, there was in this village now a young Miami woman named Ouiske-lotha Nebi who had been sleeping with the commander. It was she who had reported to Cold Foot that Holmes had become suspicious of hostility on the part of the Indians. He had, as a result, alerted his men, restricted them to the fort and set them to making cartridges. Cold Foot shook his head morosely.

"I see no way now," he said slowly, "that he might be taken by surprise."

"But are you willing to try?" Chene pressed.

"My word was given to Pontiac that I would do so, but perhaps it would be better to wait until his suspicions have melted away."

Chene shook his head. "No. If you wait, he will learn of Detroit. It must be soon; as soon as you can prepare for it. A few days only, no later. But I think there is a way yet that we can surprise him and his men. Pontiac has sent us to the Illinois country, but we will pause here and help you. What about this girl who beds with Holmes? Will she help?"

Cold Foot considered this and then nodded slowly. "If," he said, "it is a matter of choice between her own people or him, Ouiske-lotha Nebi will stay by her own."

Chene grinned broadly and winked at Godefroy. "Good! Then send for her and we'll tell her what she has to do."

[*May 25, 1763—Wednesday, 9:00* A.M.]

Less than an hour ago Ensign Francis Schlosser, commander of Fort St. Joseph, had groggily climbed out of bed, splashed cold water over his face from the basin on the washstand in his room and dressed. As always on arising, he moved about in a half-stupor until he poured a healthy jolt of brandy into a cup and downed it. Now, at nine o'clock, with the sun shining brightly, birds singing their hearts out beyond the stockade walls and three more helpings of brandy warming his interior, he began to feel a bit more human.

As frequently happened, the thought struck him again that he wished he could be reassigned. What he yearned for was to be attached to some post like Detroit or Niagara or Pitt. Or, better yet, perhaps in some major eastern city where there would be plenty of young ladies and an abundance of alcoholic beverages.

He moved across the room to a large trunk and opened it, knowing he would find in it only one bottle of brandy remaining unopened, but somehow hoping that maybe he had miscounted last time. He hadn't. He shook his head gloomily. If he severely rationed himself, he might make it last for two or three days. He hadn't heard from Detroit in weeks, but the supply convoy from Niagara must have arrived there by now. He'd have to send some men there to pick up some badly needed provisions, such as more brandy. The very thought of it made him thirsty and he recrossed the room and poured himself another measure from the nearly empty bottle on the desk. He was just raising it to his lips when there was a knocking on his door and the voice of Sergeant Dawson Moody drifted in.

"Sir, there's a good-sized party of Indians at the gate. They're asking for a council with you."

"All right, Sergeant. Tell them I'll be right out. Show them to the council chambers."

He finished his drink and shook his head, wondering what Kioqua wanted now. Probably asking for powder and lead again. Damned nuisance, that's what these Indians were. He opened the trunk again and removed from it a two-foot belt of white wampum—friendship wampum—about three inches wide. A few geometric figures in red had been woven into it which, so he had been told, were supposed to represent the lasting chain of friendship between English and Indians. As he draped it over his arm, the door was suddenly flung open and Louison Chevalie, a resident Frenchman, burst in.

"Monsieur Schlosser," he said hurriedly, "watch out! I think they mean trouble. They have been detaining me outside for over an hour, but I managed to get past them."

Without a word, Francis Schlosser dropped the wampum belt on the desk, ran past the Frenchman and headed toward the barracks. Arriving there he found the place crowded with Potawatomies mingling with eight or nine soldiers. They were smiling and chattering good-naturedly, but Schlosser silently cursed the gate sentry for letting so many enter. Some of these Indians he recognized as residents of Kioqua's village, but there were a number he had not seen before. All, he noted, had tomahawks or war clubs in their waistbands.

"Sergeant!" he called sharply as he caught sight of Moody in the milling throng. The grinning noncommissioned officer detached himself and came to him. Schlosser took him by the arm and pulled him just outside, then spoke in an urgent whisper:

"Watch out for trouble. Alert the men, but don't start anything. I'll find Kioqua and see what this is all about. For God's sake, keep on your toes."

Dawson Moody, very sober now, nodded and disappeared back into the barracks, Schlosser, abruptly realizing himself to be unarmed, began heading back to his quarters. He saw that seven or eight Indians were talking to the sentry at the gate and three other soldiers standing close by. He groaned but continued toward his room. Halfway there he was intercepted by a chief he did not recognize and six or seven other Potawatomies. Utilizing what little he knew of the language, Schlosser greeted them cordially and shook hands with the chief, whose name he now learned was Washee. He told them he had to go to his quarters for a moment, but that the council house—he pointed—was over there and he would join them there very soon. However, as he began to walk rapidly they fell in behind.

They entered the room after him and now, hesitating over the risk of getting his weapon, Schlosser instead scooped up the wampum belt from the desktop and began to formally welcome them to the fort. While he was in the process of doing so, there came a fierce screeching and some screams from the direction of the barracks. He dropped the belt and spun around to get his gun but was instantly seized by several of the men with Chief Washee.

Almost as quickly as it had begun, the uproar died away. Ensign Schlosser, angry and frightened, felt his hands being bound behind him and then he was shoved outside. The three privates who were at the gate near the sentry were being held and similarly tied by a number of Indians. The sentry himself lay on the hard-packed earth in a spreading pool of blood, his scalp missing. From the barracks door a stream of warriors were issuing, many with fresh scalps from which they were shaking the blood. Schlosser thought he recognized Sergeant Moody's among them.

The Frenchman, Louison Chevalie, was arguing with some of the Indians, but they paid little attention to him. In bewilderment, Schlosser wondered why they didn't attack him, too. Of the two English traders at the fort—Richard Winston and James Hambach—he saw nothing.[91] Chevalie, seeing Schlosser and Chief Washee, hurried to them.

"Chief Kioqua isn't going to like this," he threatened.

Washee grunted in derision. "It is too late for his likes now. He has no choice."

Speaking English, which Washee could not understand, Chevalie in a sort of cryptic jargon told Schlosser that the two English traders, whom he referred to only as "H" and "W" were at his house and had hidden themselves in the loft. He added that the Indians said they would not harm the French so perhaps he could keep them safe; at least he would try to help them in every way.

Barely comprehending, Schlosser nodded, his gaze drifting away from the Frenchman to watch the Indians racing through every building, plundering. Even as he and the three privates were led out of the gate he continued watching them as long as he could. When the fort's walls intervened, he faced front and walked along mechanically, eyes downcast, and saying nothing.

At the riverbank the four men were signaled to sit down and they did so. No other prisoners were brought out. The conclusion was inescapable: the other eleven men of the garrison, including Sergeant Moody, had been slain. Abruptly Ensign Schlosser turned his head to one side and vomited violently. When he finished he saw that all three privates were staring at him with naked contempt.

Toward evening, as they still sat in place, the captives watched as Chief Kioqua and several of his older subchiefs approached them. Louison Chevalie was with them to act as interpreter.

"We know nothing of this affair," Kioqua said, addressing Schlosser. Even after Chevalie spoke the words in English, the ensign gave no reply and merely stared at a point slightly over the chief's head.

"This was done," Kioqua continued after a moment, "by our brother Potawatomies from Detroit who are not under our control and who acted under orders from Pontiac of the Ottawas. Some of our young men crossed the river in the night, unknown to us, and joined Washee in his plan. We desire you to tell Major Gladwin that we are not concerned in this war, nor will we be."

Francis Schlosser still said nothing and with a sound of exasperation, Kioqua walked away, followed by the others. And Schlosser, now more than ever in his life before, wished he had a drink.

[*May 25, 1763—Wednesday, 7:30* P.M.]

Behind them the Detroit River reflected the redness of a beautiful sunset, but Ensign Christopher Pauli was unaware of it. His eyes were directed, instead, to Detroit which they were at this moment passing. He was bound and seated in the middle of the leading canoe and wishing with all his heart that he was inside those walls this moment. He imagined he could see Major Gladwin on the water-wall ramparts, watching through his telescope as the three large canoes passed by, close to the opposite shore. The red flag from Fort Sandusky, now gaily flapping at the top of a rod affixed to the prow of this canoe, eloquently announced the fort's fall. The realization that Detroit itself was apparently under siege by the Indians destroyed the last vestige of hope he had harbored for salvation.

Stiff and bruised from the cuffings he had received in the days following Fort Sandusky's fall, Pauli was nonetheless in fairly good physical shape. His hands were tied behind him and the only clothing he wore were trousers. Even his boots and stockings had been taken. His spirits were far more damaged than his body. He had no hope that he would survive the day, the day was already nearly gone.

Half a mile above the fort the canoes began angling across the river and the sun was five minutes set when they touched the shore adjacent to Pontiac's camp and just above the mouth of Parent's Creek. The gauntlet line was already formed, as Pauli had known it would be—a long double row of warriors, squaws, and children, each armed with cudgels or brambly switches, all of them howling and screeching an insane cacophony. He attempted to stand but a short, chopping blow from the pipe end of a tomahawk struck his temple, stunning him. Dimly he felt himself gripped savagely by the hair and literally dragged from the boat and toward where he would have to begin the gauntlet run.

They stood him at the entrance to the line and he was barely able to maintain his balance as they cut the thongs which bound his wrists. From the end of the line an older man bearing a yard-long heavy stick approached. Without a word he rammed one end of it into Pauli's stomach and the young officer reeled but somehow kept his footing. The Ottawa pointed down the slot between the double line of Indians and glared at Pauli.

"*Courir!*" he shouted in French, drawing back his stick, "*Courir!*"—Run! Run!

He swung the club and it struck across the small of Pauli's back, propelling him forward. He stumbled. Blows began raining on him from both sides, bruising, tearing, setting him afire with hurt, and now he ran as never before.

The line was several hundred yards in length and Christopher Pauli was sure he wouldn't make it. He was right. Hardly more than half the distance had been run when his senses began to falter. He stumbled, ran, stumbled, fell, ran again. The blows were no longer individual. They merged into one massive hurt and his feet were great leaden weights which became progressively more difficult to raise from the ground.

About two-thirds of the way down the line he fell again. Incredibly, this time he did not hit the ground. A pair of fleshy arms had snatched him and he felt himself almost smothered in an enveloping softness. Voices shrilled and it took him a while to realize that a grotesquely fat squaw had caught him and was now hugging him so tightly to her that his head was almost lost between her enormous breasts. Her strident words came dimly to him and though he could not understand them all, he caught the gist of what she was saying.

Her husband had been one of the few warriors killed since the siege began and, as was her right if she so chose, she was claiming this prisoner. It would be her choice now whether to torture and kill him as an act of vengeance or, through adoption, let him take her husband's place. And incredibly, as he sensed a blackness enfolding him, the thought struck him that this was a choice of death or a fate worse than death.

A small hysterical giggle escaped him as he lost consciousness.

It was just after the sentries had given their eleven o'clock calls when Jacques Duperon Baby reentered the fort through the secret little port on the east wall near the river and hastened to Henry Gladwin's chambers. The commander of Detroit was waiting for him and once again Baby felt a pang of sympathy for him. The major looked wan and sapped, as if he would enjoy nothing more than simply to collapse into bed and remain there for a week. For the major's sake, Baby wished he could. The man would kill himself if he kept on this way. Since the uprising had broken out he had slept less and worked more than any other man in the fort, but it had taken its toll.

"He's dead, isn't he?" Even the officer's voice was slurred with weariness.

"No," said Baby, shaking his head, "no, they didn't kill him. At least not yet and now I don't think they will. They beat him unconscious in the line, but now a squaw has claimed him. She wants him as an adopted husband to replace her own who was killed outside the walls last week."

For the first time a slight animation returned to the officer. "Thank God," he said softly. "Thank God for that, at least."

Baby shook his head again. "Major," he said, "you must get some rest. No man can do so much and for so long without rest."

The Frenchman thought again of all this incredible officer had done. Everyone came to him with their problems and he shouldered them all. Upon his head as well rested the responsibility for the lives of everyone in this fort. He had been everywhere, doing everything, overseeing every operation, directing every defensive measure, preparing for every conceivable future event. He had fired as many cannon shots as his own artillerists. He had aided in the hazardous job of burning down the nearby houses and fences and breastworks behind which the Indians would hide to fire upon the fort and now, except at the decided risk of his life, no Indian could approach the walls more closely than eighty or a hundred yards.

"I'll rest," Gladwin said. "I'll rest. Thank God Pauli's still alive. I didn't think he would be. I really didn't."

The major's speech was becoming more slurred and rambling. He scuffed to his desk and dropped heavily into the chair. "Must write some reports," he said. "Tell general that Pauli's safe."

Sorry now for what he had to say next, Baby stared at the floor and spoke softly. "The Indians, Major, they were faltering. They were beginning to fall away from Pontiac, blaming him for getting them into this war. Now all of a sudden it's reversed. It was as if they hadn't believed any of the forts could fall. Fort Sandusky has and they're behind him all the way again. It's as if they believe with Sandusky gone, it's only a matter of time until the rest fall, too. His prestige has risen to greater heights than ever. Before, it looked like an end might be in sight, but now that has passed. Now—"

Baby broke off as he looked up and saw that the Detroit commander was lolling in his chair, his head to one side, his chest rising and falling methodically in sleep. The Frenchman smiled. He walked around the desk and roused Gladwin enough to help him to his bed. The officer's heavy breathing resumed the instant he fell onto it. Baby pulled off the boots with some effort and then spread a light coverlet over him.

"Tomorrow, Major," he muttered when he was finished. "It will keep till tomorrow."

[*May 27, 1763—Friday, 7:45* A.M.]

The instant Ouiske-lotha Nebi entered his Fort Miamis quarters, Robert Holmes knew something was seriously wrong. Her lips trembled and her eyes swam in tears not yet shed. Her whole expression emanated a sense of profound grief and he came to her at once. He put his arms around her.

"What is it, Whiskey? What's wrong?"

At his words, his touch, his gentleness, the tears came. Her anguished words were spoken in the Miami tongue, his own understanding of which was limited at best.

"*Meshepshe*," she cried. "*Meshepshe. Neeshematha—*"

Meshepshe was her pet name for him, just as his was Whiskey for her. It meant panther and he had felt a foolish little-boy pride when she had begun calling him that. It felt good to know she thought of him as her strong, fierce, cunning panther. And *neeshematha*—he knew that, too.

"Your sister?" he said "What's happened to her, Whiskey?"

"Neeshematha match-squathi Matchemenetoo."

"Your little sister has an evil spirit?" His brow wrinkled. "I don't understand. Is she——"

"Aghquelogel! Matou-ouisah aghquelogel!"—Sick! Badly sick!

"How can I help, Whiskey? What can I do?"

"Ki-Iuh pe-e-wah, ni-ne-e-meh. Hogthelah."

The first three words he understood: You come, see. He shook his head. *"Hogthelah?* I don't know that, Whiskey. What do you mean?"

She held up her left hand, palm up, and several times ran the nail of her right index finger across her wrist. She was even more distressed than earlier and crying harder now. *"Hogthelah! Hogthelah!"*

Comprehension came to him and he nodded. "Oh, I see. You want me to come and bleed her, like you saw me bleed Private Darrel when he was sick?"

She bobbed her head and he stooped to take a small satchel out from under his bed and quickly left his quarters with her. Sergeant Wesley Williams was at the gate and the commander stopped to speak to him briefly.

"Whiskey's sister is sick," he said. "I'm going to see if I can help. She wants me to bleed her. I'll be back shortly."

Williams nodded, offered his help, which Holmes declined, and then remained standing near the gate as the officer and young woman moved away. Whiskey pointed to a flimsy little cabin made of sticks. It was about three hundred yards distant and she said her sister was inside. They headed that way at a brisk walk, she close behind him at first. As they neared the shelter, however, she drew a little to one side of him and the officer did not even appear to notice.

Ensign Robert Holmes heard the first shot, but not the second. The first sent a lead ball crashing through his shoulder and spun him around. The second, just a moment later, struck midway between his shoulder blades, breaking his back and severing the spinal column. He was dead before his body stopped moving.

Ouiske-lotha Nebi gave a strangled cry and broke into a run. She disappeared around the shelter as the animal hide door-flap pushed to one side and three Indians came out. One ran to the officer and scalped him swiftly and expertly, then held the grisly trophy high and shrieked triumphantly.

Sergeant Williams had been talking to the sentry at the gate when the two shots resounded. He ran outside and instantly was tackled and sent sprawling by an Ottawa who had been crouched against the wall. Two Miamis raced up and helped pin him down. The sentry, who had also started out, now turned back and slammed the big gate closed, shooting the bolt just as something on the other side slammed heavily against it.

"Attack!" he screamed. "They attacking!"

Soldiers boiled out of the barracks and from other buildings inside the fort. Including the sentry, there were eleven of them, all privates. In moments they had climbed the ramparts and were cautiously peering out over the stockade walls. Below on the outside, the three Indians were just pulling the limp form of Sergeant Williams out of sight into the woods. It was not possible to say whether he was dead or just unconscious. No one else was visible outside.

A few minutes of ominous silence passed and then, from the direction of the rickety cabin, a white man approached holding a white cloth aloft in his hand. On either side of him walked an Ottawa. Almost immediately all of the privates recognized the man as the trader, John Welch.

"For God's sake," Welch called out, "don't shoot! Mr. Holmes is dead and Sergeant Williams is prisoner. The two soldiers who left here early this morning to hunt have been taken, too. They took me way down the Maumee. Private Lawton, too. They've sent me out to tell you their demands. They give their word that no one else will be hurt if you'll throw down your arms and come out. If you don't do so right away, they plan to burn down the fort and kill every one of you."

Still on the ramparts, the soldiers held a hurried conference and then suddenly a rifle sailed over the wall and thudded to the ground outside the stockade. Another followed it, and another. Then several at once, until all eleven weapons were scattered on the ground. The stock on one of them had broken when it hit.

Now from all sides, as the gates were opened, Indians moved out from hiding and within minutes the eleven privates were hustled away. Mini Chene and Jacques Godefroy entered the fort, along with some of the Miamis and Ottawas, while the men were being led off. Just before they lost sight of the fort, two of the captives—John McCoy and James Barns—turned and saw the French colors being hoisted to the top of the fort's flagstaff.

"Goddammit," muttered McCoy, who had fought under Wolfe at Quebec against the French, "it's started again."

The captives were led to Cold Foot's village and made to sit in a cluster and wait. Their two companions who had left the fort shortly after sunrise this morning to hunt where there also, as were Sergeant Wesley Williams, Private Robert Lawton, trader John Welch and his two helpers. An angry bluish knot had raised on the outside edge of the sergeant's left eye and the eye itself was nearly swollen shut.

All eighteen of the captives were guarded but not mistreated and after an hour or so they saw numerous Miami squaws and warriors laden with plunder from the fort, bringing it to the village. They were followed by Godefroy and Chene. The two Frenchmen stopped and talked for some time with Chief Cold Foot and then shook hands with him. Godefroy sauntered over to where the captives were seated and looked them over contemptuously.

"Englishmen," he said, "never learn, do they?" He squatted beside Private Barns and removed the silver buckles from his shoes. "I'll take these," he muttered. "I might as well have them as the Indians."[92]

He rejoined Chene then, dropping the buckles into his shirt pocket as he walked. As the captives watched, the Frenchmen prepared to leave.

Mini Chene straightened and now it was he who strolled over to the captives. He spoke softly to the group in general, but there was a maliciously triumphant ring to his words. His gaze settled most frequently on Sergeant Williams.

"Most of you are to be taken to Detroit," he said. "In case you don't know it by now, Pontiac has attacked that place and probably has taken it by now. Four of you will remain here as Chief Cold Foot's guests. You'll be insurance for him. As for us," he indicated Godefroy by tilting his head to one side, "we'll be leaving now. You might tell Major Gladwin, if you see him, that we're still heading for the Illinois country and that we intend taking Fort Ouiatenon as we pass it, just as we took this one. And let him know that when we come back, there'll be a new French army coming with us. Whether you like it or not, the English are done in this country!"

[*May 27, 1763—Friday, 11* P.M.]

The trader named Calhoun squatted by the fire before the lean-to and stared into the dying coals. He was bothered, restless, and thought that how he felt right now must be pretty much how a wildcat felt as it paced back and forth in a cage. For Calhoun, this was an odd thing, because he was a man who rarely worried about anything. But he *was* a man who had the knack of sensing when things just weren't right, and that sixth sense was hard at work tonight. Behind him in the lean-to, their snoring and rhythmical deep breathing audible, were twelve men. They had been asleep for quite a while. A few of them were traders like himself, but the majority were helpers, young men learning the trade who had signed on for a sort of apprenticeship.

Despite claims to the contrary by practically everyone who knew him, Calhoun had a first name. He hadn't used it in so long, however, that at times he himself almost came to believe the stories that he had never been given one. Whoever heard of a frontiersman or a trader named *Dexter?* He'd be laughed out of the country if it ever came out. Thinking about that was a sampling of how his thoughts had been running. He couldn't seem to concentrate on anything for long and that, to him, was a danger signal. Something no good was brewing. He knew it more surely than he knew his own first name, but he didn't know what. Or when.

Beyond the muted glow of the embers he could make out the shapes of several of the nearer lodges. This Delaware village of Tuscarawas[96] was not the largest Indian village he'd ever seen, but it was a respectable one. He'd been trading with the Indians here a long time now, even when it had been damned risky to enter this country, and Chief Shingas was one of the few red men he trusted. They'd had a good relationship over the years, which was something not many of the traders had with important chiefs. Calhoun had never tried to cheat any Indian, and Shingas knew this as well as he.

There he went again, off on another tangent. It must be eleven o'clock or later by now. Why couldn't he sleep? What was brewing? He wished he knew, but he decided he wouldn't worry about it. He reckoned he'd find out soon enough. From near his feet he picked up a tiny dried twig, tossed it onto the coals and watched it blacken and then burst into a tiny flame which died away almost immediately.

"Calhoun!"

He started violently at the whisper, having heard nothing prior to it. He reached for his rifle automatically, but it was no longer standing against the upright of the lean-to where he had propped it within arm's reach. Abruptly he relaxed as he recognized Chief Shingas standing several yards away. The trader shook his head and chuckled.

"Shingas, you walk just about as noisy as a hoot owl flies. Now where's my gun?"

The chief neither replied nor smiled for a moment. When at length he did speak again, the tension in his whisper was apparent and all sense of levity left Calhoun in that instant.

"Calhoun, leave here now. An Indian war has begun. Detroit is under attack and Fort Sandusky has been burned and all Englishmen there killed. Pitwe-owa, the chief you know as The Wolf, has come for men to go with him against the English to the east. He has brought a war belt that came from the Ottawas at Detroit. He plans to kill you—all of you—first. In the morning before you wake. I warn you because we have been brothers. We are no longer. When next we meet, you must kill me or I will kill you. Go. You have little time."

With no more sound than he made on his approach, Shingas melted into the darkness. Calhoun swallowed and found his mouth and throat were dry. Just as he was a man who rarely worried, so too he was a man who rarely became afraid. But suddenly he was very much frightened.

Quickly but softly he moved to the closest of the sleeping men and placed a hand firmly over his mouth. Instantly the man jerked erect, one hand reaching for the rifle he had placed beside him. Like Calhoun's, it was gone. Calhoun's lips were an inch from his ear.

"Not a sound," he hissed. "We got to get out of here."

One by one he woke them in the same manner until all thirteen men were huddled in a compact group, heads together, all of them painfully aware that there was not one of their guns left amongst them. The knowledge that whoever took each man's gun had been close enough to just as easily slit a throat caused back muscles to tighten in reaction and fear. In the same hissing whisper inaudible more than a few feet away, Calhoun explained briefly the warning.

"We got to get the hell out of here right now," he added. "Take only what you're wearin'. That an' your belt knives. Make up your blankets to look like you're still in 'em. Use your packs, furs, extra blankets, anything. Do it fast an' then let's move."

They did. In less than three minutes they were thirteen silent single-file shadows moving rapidly along the trail which led ultimately to Fort Pitt—almost exactly one hundred miles due east.

[May 28, 1763—Saturday, Noon]

Captain Simeon Ecuyer, commander of Fort Pitt, had never liked Indians. True, he was forced to deal civilly with them on occasion and he even sympathized with them to a certain extent in their problems. But he didn't like them. He didn't think he ever would.

Now he watched those Shawnees and Delawares who had come into the fort this morning, viewing them with a growing suspicion that all was not what it seemed to be. They pretended to be on a trading mission and had the bales of furs and preserved meats and fish and fowl to prove it, but somehow Ecuyer felt something was wrong.

First of all, why had they not come in last night? This party of twenty-six men with laden packhorses had appeared on the other side of the Allegheny about sundown yesterday. They had moved slowly out of the woods and down the hill to the rocky shoreline of the river, but there they had stopped to make camp. Knowing, as they must have known, that there was good food available here and that, prohibitions aside, they could undoubtedly find traders here who would have no scruples about covertly selling them rum and ammunition, why then had they not come in? Why had they waited till morning?

Throughout the morning today after they came to the fort the trading had gone on and now, with the sun at its meridian, they were leaving. Ecuyer watched until they disappeared into the woods upstream on the east side of the Allegheny and then, still troubled, he returned to his quarters. It was not until about an hour later that a sudden disturbing thought struck him. He called his aide, gave him instructions and sent him away. In less than an hour the young man returned.

"Sir," he reported, "you were right. I talked with about a dozen of the traders. Not one of them sold any blankets or cloth or kettles or anything like that. In fact they didn't admit to selling anything except some paint, knives, and tomahawks. And, sir, every man I talked to said that he knew some of the traders—naming no names—had made some of the best trades they'd ever made before, selling them powder and lead. Apparently they were getting three to five times more in trade for the ammunition than anyone ever got before, and without one Indian complaining about the prices. Frankly, sir, I think every one of the traders sold some ammunition to them."

Ecuyer's lips had tightened as his aide spoke and he dismissed him with a curt nod when the recital was finished. Suspicions confirmed, he paced his room, his brow furrowed. Suddenly he stopped and sucked in his breath. There was one last question that remained to be answered: when they left here, why had the Shawnees and Delawares gone northeast along this side of the Allegheny instead of crossing back in the direction of their villages? And the answer came simultaneously with the question: because they were not returning to their villages. Now they were well equipped with paint for their faces, knives and tomahawks in their belts and with plenty of ammunition for their guns.

With a sudden sick feeling, Captain Simeon Ecuyer realized that all of Fort Pitt had just witnessed the genesis of a war party.

[May 28, 1763—Saturday, 7:00 P.M.]

The northern shoreline of Lake Erie had been every bit as beautiful as Lieutenant Abraham Cuyler had been told it was, perhaps even more so. This was the evening of their fifteenth day afloat since leaving the Niagara portage and thus far the weather had been absolutely ideal. In fact if anything, it had been almost too good. Strong winds had been absent and the breezes had been very gentle. On numerous days there had been so little wind that the sails had hung limply and the men had been forced to row. They grumbled, of course, but as Cuyler pointed out to them, better to have no wind at all than one of the savage tempests for which Lake Erie had received such a bad reputation. It might be the smallest of the Great Lakes but it was still an extremely large lake and such a shallow one that it did not take much of a blow to kick up waves of dreadful proportions.[94]

Today's weather had been equally nice and as the evening had drawn nigh the slight breeze that had been blowing all day tapered away and then died altogether. Now the surface of the water was glassy calm and ahead of his flotilla of eighteen batteaux only a short distance away was the welcome sight of Point Pelee, that long tapering finger of land stretching almost due south into the lake from this northern shoreline. Here, as was customary with regular supply convoys running this route, they would camp for the night, and this was the point which marked the beginning of the end of their journey. From here it was only a dozen miles or a little more to the mouth of the Detroit River and a similar distance upstream to the fort. With luck and favorable weather, Detroit was only a day and a half or two days away. It was almost with a sense of regret that Cuyler considered the end of such an idyllic cruise.

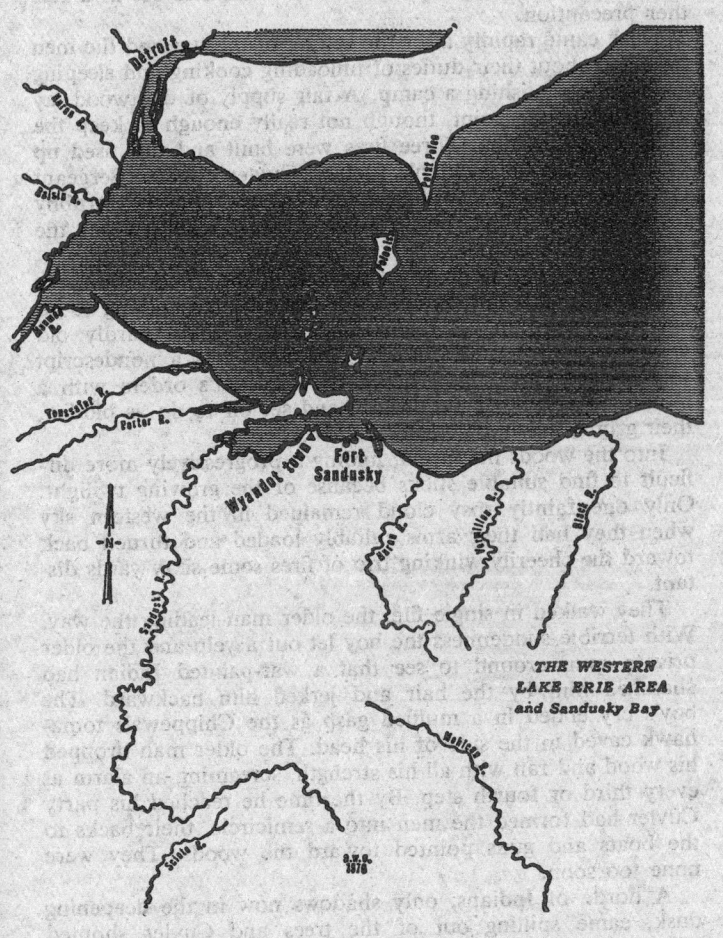

THE WESTERN
LAKE ERIE AREA
and Sandusky Bay

Eagerness to be done with their rowing brought reserve strength to their arms as the oarsmen sent the big batteaux hissing over the smooth surface toward a beach. As the boats scraped to a stop, the men leaped out and pulled them up firmly onto the sand so that a sudden wind during the night would not set them adrift. Land lines were also set as a further precaution.

Dusk came rapidly after the setting of the sun and the men hastened about their duties of unloading cooking and sleeping gear and establishing a camp. A fair supply of driftwood lay scattered on the point, though not really enough to keep the fires going for long. Three fires were built and this used up practically all the available fuel, so Cuyler directed Sergeant Cope to send out a wood-gathering party into the scrubby forest growth which began some forty yards up from the water.

Geoffrey Cope spotted two privates of the Queen's Rangers who had chosen this unlucky moment to have nothing to do and he homed in on them. One was a youth hardly old enough to be in uniform and the other was a nondescript middle-aged man. They heard the sergeant's orders with a monumental lack of enthusiasm and set off to do as bidden, their grumbling audible behind them.

Into the woods they went, finding it progressively more difficult to find suitable sticks because of the growing twilight. Only one faintly rosy cloud remained in the western sky when they had their arms suitably loaded and turned back toward the cheerily winking trio of fires some sixty yards distant.

They walked in single file, the older man leading the way. With terrible suddenness the boy let out a yelp and the older private spun around to see that a war-painted Indian had snatched him by the hair and jerked him backward. The boy's cry ended in a muffled gasp as the Chippewa's tomahawk caved in the side of his head. The older man dropped his wood and ran with all his strength, screaming an alarm at every third or fourth step. By the time he reached his party Cuyler had formed the men into a semicircle, their backs to the boats and guns pointed toward the woods. They were none too soon.

A horde of Indians, only shadows now in the deepening dusk, came spilling out of the trees and Cuyler shouted "Fire!" It was the last clearly audible word for a good while. The guns of the soldiers erupted in a ragged explosion of sound, but it was as nothing compared to the gunfire returned their way from the trees. It seemed like a thousand rifles spitting fire and lead at the same time, but actually it was only a quarter that number. These were the Chippewas and Ottawas and Mississaugi warriors under Chiefs Sekahos and Mehemah who had been so shrewdly sent by Pontiac to this customary landing point to set up their ambush. It was superbly executed and in that first return fire, a score or more of Cuyler's men were killed and many others wounded.

Lieutenant Cuyler himself gasped as a ball angled through his right breast and exited out of the armpit, creasing the muscle of his underarm as it left. Almost at the same moment there was a chorus of fierce shriekings and the whole body of Indians charged the center of the formation. In that instant the gallant defense degenerated to abject panic. The men dropped their guns and ran screaming, those who were able, to the boats.

Now the wisdom that had predicated beaching the batteaux so high had become folly. Those most heavily laden could scarcely be moved and the men sobbed aloud and moaned in anguish as they strained and shoved. Only five of the boats could be launched before the Indians were among them. Cuyler found himself being abandoned and he ordered six men toward a batteau and told them to launch it. They could not and abruptly they ran off in panic.

Out in the water Cuyler saw one of the boats afloat and he plunged in, reaching it when the water was neck deep. He felt several pairs of arms grab him and haul him aboard. This batteau had only five other men in it and the lieutenant was unable to account for its launching, which no five men could accomplish, despite the fact that this one had carried mostly men and camping goods so that now it was relatively empty. Still, it was a very heavy, cumbersome craft. Now, wincing with the pain of his wound, he manned an oar along with the others and gradually they formed a rhythm and pulled away from shore. Other boats were having difficulty, their oars out of cadence, bumping into one another and wallowing drunkenly in circles.

Ashore the shrieks and moans continued and then two more of the batteaux were launched, but this time their crews had painted faces. In rapid succession they closed on three of the overcrowded batteaux and the men in them surrendered. Cuyler's boat and one other pulled even farther from shore and the two Indian-manned batteaux took up the chase as soon as the three captive boats were grounded again. They closed the gap quickly, their freshness and strength telling against the already sapped oarsmen. Five hundred yards separated them, then half that. Soon the Indians were only fifty yards behind and it seemed that the bid for escape had failed.

And then there was a wind.

Suddenly it was there, not gradually growing but having come on strong and fresh and directly off the shore. With frenzied haste oars were dropped and sails raised and they bellied full with the pregnant promise of safety. The Indians had moved up to within thirty yards but now the two fleeing batteaux were holding their own. In fact now they began drawing away and the frustrated cries of the Indians were music to their ears. The Indians fumbled with the sails in their own boats, but were unable to properly set them. The gap between the two pairs of boats widened even more. The pursuers followed only a short while longer and then turned back.

The soldiers slumped in exhaustion on their seats and from far behind them they could still hear occasional agonizing screams and see the glow of the two fires—the third having been extinguished by the body of Sergeant Geoffrey Cope falling across it after a bullet passed through his heart.

The two escaping boats drew together and Abraham Cuyler took stock. There were twenty-nine men in the second craft, some of whom began transferring to the less crowded boat in which Cuyler sat. In these two boats there were only nine barrels of provisions and a very small amount of gunpowder and lead. One hundred thirty barrels of provisions had been lost, including an enormous amount of powder and lead intended for distribution from Detroit to all the western posts.

Worse yet, sixty-one men were dead or captured and of those who were aboard these two escaped batteaux, at least a dozen were wounded, some of them grievously. And sixteen out of eighteen batteaux had been lost.

In the darkness a man from the second boat suddenly asked aloud, "Well, Lieutenant Cuyler, where do we go now?"

The commander had been using his handkerchief torn in half to form makeshift compresses to cover the badly bleeding holes in his breast and armpit. It was a long moment before he replied but even he was surprised at the measured calmness and strength in his voice.

"We have no choice. Steer due south. We'll head directly for Fort Sandusky."

Calhoun and the twelve traders or traders' helpers in his party had rested little and traveled far since fleeing the Delaware village of Tuscarawas. Accustomed to the hardships of frontier life, they were in good condition physically. Throughout the remainder of that first night, all of yesterday and most of last night they had alternately trotted or walked swiftly. As a result, now, with the sun just ready to rise, they were approaching the mouth of Beaver River, which emptied into the Ohio only twenty-five miles or a little more below Fort Pitt; and if they kept up the pace they had been setting, they could reach the fort tonight.

Early this morning they had been joined by another trader with one packhorse who had been en route to Tuscarawas from Fort Pitt. After Calhoun briefly explained what had happened there, he wisely elected to turn around and accompany them back to the fort, he and his laden packhorse bringing up the rear.

The very fact, though, that they were now so near to Fort Pitt without having seen even a sign of danger made some of the men relax a little. Several of them began to have second thoughts. Every man here, except for the newcomer, had lost a great deal in this precipitous flight—gun, baggage, gear, provisions, trade goods, packhorses, peltry. The loss for each represented a substantial investment of both time and funds and now a growing anger was replacing their fear. What, they began to wonder, could have possessed them to flee as they had simply on the word of Calhoun that an attack by the Indians was imminent? Was not Calhoun a friend of Shingas? Was it not possible that he was working in collusion with Shingas? Could it not have been Calhoun, rather than the Indians, who took their guns while they slept? And might not Calhoun, at his leisure, go back to Tuscarawas to divide up this booty between himself and Shingas?

They began to mutter about it, first to themselves and then aloud to one another. Calhoun ignored them, concerned with his own thoughts. Always before when warned by his odd sixth sense of danger, the feeling passed away as soon as the danger was exposed and steps taken to preserve and protect. This time it hadn't happened that way. If anything, Calhoun was bothered even more right now by a sense of something not right than he had been at Tuscarawas. He couldn't quite put his finger on why and, as a result, all his senses were sharply alert.

The fourteen men were only a hundred yards or so from the mouth of Beaver River when Calhoun abruptly jolted to a stop with a hand upraised and head cocked to one side. A vague sound had come to him, familiar yet inappropriate at this time and place. Had he imagined it? No, there it was again. From the distant trees to the right it was repeated—the faint nicker of a horse; a sound cut off in the middle as if someone had cupped his hands over the animal's muzzle.

"Scatter!" Calhoun shouted, at the same time plunging off the trail and into the heavier cover to their left in headlong bounds. The two traders directly behind him followed his lead instantly, instinctively. The remaining eleven, startled by the suddenness of it all, reacted too slowly. Even before the undergrowth had swallowed up the three men there came a fusillade of shots. Every man still on the trail was hit by at least one bullet and several of them by three or four. All eleven died in that moment.

General Jeffrey Amherst yawned and sighed, feeling more than just a passing twinge of self-pity. If only people realized what a commander had to go through in dealing with people they might be a little more considerate. It was no easy matter to do your job in the best way you saw possible if you constantly had to be explaining away someone else's fears or in some manner mollifying them. The colonial governors, assemblymen, clergy, dignitaries of all kinds, Indian agents and others just had to keep meddling and poking their noses into matters which didn't concern them. He sighed again, supposing that many of them had nothing better to do—but it did make his job more onerous.

He was still clad in the robe he had put on a short while ago when he arose and had not yet donned his wig. On the desktop before him was the latest letter from Sir William Johnson, again expressing his fears of Indian plots against the English over a wide front. Beside that letter was his own reply, begun last night but which he had become too sleepy to finish. Now, determined to get this chore out of the way, he dipped his pen and concluded:

I realize that being as close to the Indians as you are, you obviously hear many stories that alarm you. Is it not probable that you are so close to the situation, that you are unable to view it in the proper perspective? Rest assured, Sir William, that I am as aware as anyone of supposed schemes on their part, but they concern me very little. Fears of their plots are mere bugbears and you may rest content in the knowledge that as long as the military keeps its guard up, the Indians cannot cause any serious harm.

[May 29, 1763—Sunday, 7:30 P.M.]

The Delaware chief named Pitwe-owa had been furious at the ruse that had been pulled off on him by the traders. In the predawn, at which time the Englishmen would be most deeply asleep, he and his warriors, supported by Chief Shingas and his men, had inched toward the lean-to with utmost silence. Everything had looked favorable for their surprise attack. The campfire before the lean-to had burned down so far that there was no longer any glow from the embers and only the scent of the wisp of smoke drifting in the darkness indicated it was still alive.

As the sky began graying, the shapes of blanketed figures outstretched on the ground within the open face of the lean-to became visible. Abruptly a dozen of the attackers sped forward silently and flung themselves onto the figures, their knives and tomahawks thrusting deeply. The howls of anger and frustration that filled the air a moment later resounded in the river valley.

How had the traders learned of the planned surprise attack? How had they gotten away without a sound, especially since at the last checking before the middle of the night they were all still there—twelve of them asleep and one sitting hunched by the fire? Obviously they had been warned, but by whom? Pitwe-owa and Shingas both loudly proclaimed that death would be the reward of the traitor if his identity were discovered, but no one seemed to know who it had been.

Studying the traders' camp and the goods left behind, including even their packhorses, Pitwe-owa determined that the Englishmen had left in such haste that all they had taken with them was their guns. They were afoot and had struck out toward Fort Pitt, but it was a long way to that post and they were still vulnerable.

In a way, this fitted Pitwe-owa's plans. He was preparing to head that way to make border attacks anyway. Now he would simply combine the two. There was plenty of time. Since the traders had taken their guns and were undoubtedly extremely alert to danger, it would be better to let them go a good distance unmolested, to let them grow weary and drop their guard. To risk the life of any Delaware in order to take these thirteen men would be foolish.

They took their time preparing themselves and their horses for border warfare, but even so they arrived at the mouth of the Beaver River long before the traders and had had ample time to set up their ambush. Pitwe-owa had deduced the Englishmen's line of travel with remarkable accuracy and felt elated when they first saw the file of men coming. To have figured this out so neatly raised Pitwe-owa's prestige among his followers another notch. And there was a bonus, in that another trader with packhorse had joined them.

It had been a disappointment, of course, that only instants before the ambush was to be sprung the man Calhoun had shouted an alarm and he and a couple of others had escaped; but this disappointment was minor when considered beside the fact of eleven scalps, one gun and a laden packhorse being acquired. Only one point confused the Delaware chief. Where were their guns? Except for the man with the packhorse, the traders had no weapons except for knives and a few tomahawks. It was inconceivable that they had cached their rifles somewhere along the route—not when they were obviously in such peril. It was then that Pitwe-owa first began to consider that perhaps the men had been warned by none other than Shingas, who was known to be a longtime friend of Calhoun. The more he considered it, the more he realized that this had to be what happened. Shingas had warned them, but he had also cleverly taken their guns. There are few forms of humor that the Indians appreciated more than the practical joke, even when it was played upon themselves. Obviously Shingas, who had played his role so perfectly in the surprise attack back at Tuscarawas, had known that Pitwe-owa could easily overtake the traders and massacre them. How the belly of Shingas must have ached to contain the laughter that was bursting to get out! Pitwe-owa was a stern-faced individual who rarely even smiled, but now he slapped his sides and howled with laughter which would not stop until at last he sank weakly to the ground and held his stomach as the laughter kept rolling from him and the tears from it ran down his cheeks and melted his war paint.

His confused followers clustered around him, torn between amusement and fear, not knowing whether the laughter was genuine or if their chief had suddenly become possessed of an evil spirit. But gradually, between further bursts of laughter,

Pitwe-owa told them of Shingas's trick and of how he had not only pulled off a superb practical joke on all of them here, but had gained for himself all of the guns of the traders and saved himself from having to witness the death of a man who had been his friend. By the time he was finished his warriors, too, were convulsed with laughter. This was a story that would be told around council fires for years to come, warming the heart on cold winter evenings.

It was some time before the war party sufficiently collected itself to go on with their mission. Probably the three escapees could have been tracked down, but it would have taken more time than Pitwe-owa now cared to spend on them. Therefore, as soon as the scalps and knives of the traders had been taken, he had ordered his men to mount up and the journey toward the Pennsylvania border country was resumed.

Before noon today the war party was in the vicinity of Fort Pitt. Pitwe-owa had a deep respect for the strength of this fortification and he gave it a healthy berth. At a sawmill just upstream of the Allegheny, however, they encountered three soldiers cutting wood into lumber and killed two of them. The third escaped on his horse and thundered off toward the fort to give the alarm. Knowing there would probably be a strong detachment sent out after them, and preferring to fight on his own terms rather than the army's, Pitwe-owa wasted no time vacating the area.

The alarm spread by the soldier had been effective indeed. Though the war party passed a number of outlying cabins, all were empty and each was set afire by the Indians as they went by. One very large and fine home was encountered, also empty, and the blaze it made as they left it behind was a stirring thing to witness. This was the home of George Croghan.

Angling sharply to the southeast, since if a military detachment did come after them it would undoubtedly head northeast toward the sawmill first, Pitwe-owa moved his party rapidly. When, after several hours had passed, there had been no indication of pursuit, the chief correctly reasoned that they had no further cause for worry from the Fort Pitt soldiers at present. They would have been given orders not to go too far, in order that they could return to the fort quickly and help protect it if the attack happened to presage a general uprising. Chief Pitwe-owa knew his enemy well and fully deserved to be named after the wolf. He was cunning, savage, merciless.

In midafternoon, when they were about twenty-five miles southeast of Fort Pitt, the war party surprised the little settlement established by Colonel William Clapham, on land which the colonel was developing in a partnership of sorts with George Croghan.[95] It was a hit-and-run massacre.

Now, as they rode on while the sun was just setting, they had in addition to the scalps of the eleven traders and two soldiers, five fresh ones—from one of Clapham's men, two of his women, one from a ten-year-old girl, and the thick black scalp of none other than Colonel Clapham himself. Three attacks, eighteen scalps, and still the war party had not suffered a single injury among themselves.

The Wolf intended to keep it that way.

[May 29, 1763—Sunday, 7:45 P.M.]

In the glow of that same sunset but over two hundred miles to the northwest of where Pitwe-owa was now preparing to camp for the night, the two remaining batteaux of Lieutenant Abraham Cuyler's defeated convoy worked their way slowly into the mouth of Sandusky Bay. It was flat calm again, as it had been most of the afternoon, and the men worked the oars mechanically, painfully.

Cuyler, very pale and holding onto the gunwale to keep from falling, got to his feet again for perhaps the tenth time in the past quarter hour. He stood there in the lead canoe, swaying dizzily from loss of blood, his teeth tightly clenched against the deep throbbing pain emanating from his wound and spreading across his chest and down his side. His right arm was practically useless now, each movement of it causing lightning streaks of agony to his whole right side, and so he had had one of his men bind it securely to his waist in a makeshift stationary sling.

Again he peered ahead, watching for movement, firelight, horses, men, boats—anything that would indicate they were nearing Fort Sandusky and safety; but again he saw nothing and his brow furrowed. Surely they should have seen something by now.

He could imagine the shock their appearance would have on the garrison of the fort and how this shock would deepen to alarm as Cuyler explained to the commander, Ensign Christopher Pauli, about the attack at Point Pelee and what followed. It was all like some awful nightmare.

Even after the two pursuing batteaux had turned back, the surviving soldiers had remained keenly vigilant and it was not until the light from the two fires was no longer visible that they relaxed a little. The northern breeze was still blowing well and, fearful lest they become separated in the darkness, Cuyler had ordered the two boats linked with a long rope which had been coiled in the stern of his batteau.

After they had traveled perhaps ten or twelve miles from Point Pelee, a faint glow of firelight caught their attention off the starboard side and just vaguely they could make out the suggestion of a large island perhaps a mile or less distant. His order being passed from man to man in whispers, Cuyler cautioned against any sound whatsoever and stationed uninjured men beside those most seriously injured so that they could cut off any inadvertent groan of pain which might escape them and be heard. They maintained their course and soon the island and twinkle of firelight disappeared behind them. Cuyler had no doubt that it was an Indian camp, recalling that he had been told before leaving Fort Niagara that there was a large island off Point Pelee—called Pelee Island[96]—where Indian parties crossing the lake often camped.

Again darkness had enveloped them and it was about another twenty miles later, in the predawn hours, when another island, smaller than the first, loomed ahead and Cuyler ordered that they land there.[97] The party needed rest and food badly and the injured, himself included, required treatment of their wounds.

They landed, beaching the boats lightly, and disembarked. It was only then that they discovered that two of the soldiers most seriously wounded had died during their passage. Cuyler told the men to forget them for now and see to themselves, care for their wounds, eat their fill of cold rations, maintain silence, build no fires and sleep if they could. The possibility that there were Indians on this island, too, was naggingly present, but there was no help for it. They just could not possibly go any farther right now. And so here they had spent the remainder of the night, with half-hour guard shifts established to prevent their being surprised again.

Even when dawn came, then sunrise, they were too fatigued to go on right away and, though he was anxious to reach Fort Sandusky, Cuyler permitted them to rest. In truth, he wanted and needed it as much as they. It had not been till noon today that some animation returned to the party and the first order of business was the burial of the two dead soldiers. When this had been seen to and a brief prayer spoken over the common grave in which the blanket-shrouded pair had been buried side by side, Cuyler gave the order for reboarding and the passage to Fort Sandusky had been resumed. It was then almost midafternoon and once again the lake had become glassy smooth.

With sails furled, the men rowed slowly, the two batteaux abreast and no longer joined by the line. And now, at last, with twilight coming, they were approaching the fort.

Less than half an hour later, his stomach knotted within him and the fear returning in an almost overpowering wave, Lieutenant Abraham Cuyler stared with shocked disbelief through the dusk at the ashes and rubble and blackened timbers where once Fort Sandusky had stood.

Mechanically, Cuyler stooped and felt the ground, noting it was not hot and deducing that the burning had taken place at least three days ago, but probably more than that. Behind him he heard one of his men give out a little whimper and some of the others were murmuring in voices sharp with a growing hysteria. He knew he must not let it envelop them, for panic could become a worse enemy than any mortal foe. Whole armies had been lost because of it and he had no intention now of letting it get out of hand. He swung about sharply and stared at them in stern silence until the muttering ceased and they waited mutely for him to speak.

"There will be no point whatever in our making any further attempt to reach Detroit," he said. He stretched out his uninjured arm to indicate the ruins and added, "In view of this, there's no telling what has happened there. We'll start back to Niagara at once."

As the men turned wearily to obey, another lancing of pain raced through Cuyler's chest and side and for the first time since he was a little boy, he wished that he could just sit down somewhere and cry.

[May 30, 1763—Monday, 7:30 A.M.]

Major Henry Gladwin picked unenthusiastically at his unappetizing breakfast of fried peas, dried fish and hard biscuits, mulling over the events of the past few days. There was little to be pleased about.

The worst thing, of course, had been the news brought by Jacques Duperon Baby a couple of days ago of the capture of Sergeant Shaw's detachment which Gladwin had sent to Fort Michilimackinac with supplies on April 17. Apparently the supplies had been delivered without problem and Shaw's party of nineteen men and a woman were en route back to Detroit when they were surprised and captured in the Huron River not far from where the Robertson-Davers party had been massacred. The capture had taken place two mornings ago, without deaths, but Baby morosely informed Gladwin that the Indians seemed to be waiting for something and that when it occurred, whatever it was, then the entire Shaw party—being held now at Pontiac's camp—was to be tortured and killed. Gladwin prayed that Baby was wrong.

The trader James Sterling had also come to Jim a couple of days ago with a letter he had received from his nephew, John Rutherford, the only white survivor of the Davers attack. In it Rutherford told the details of that attack, of the deaths of Sir Robert and Captain Robertson and the others, along with the fact that he had been bought as a slave by Antoine Cuillerier but that the sale had been revoked by Pontiac. He pleaded with Sterling to help arrange his escape.

Jacques St. Martin had told Gladwin yesterday that despite the destruction of Fort Sandusky, the Hurons under Chief Teata remained firm in their promise to stay neutral. In fact, the interpreter had added, Teata declared to him that if Pontiac tried to make them fight he would take his people and go off into the woods. And the chief had added that if that portion of their nation at Sandusky under Chief Odinghquanooron—Big Jaw—would not desist in their hostilities against the English, Teata's people would disarm them. Gladwin strongly doubted this.

Over the past few days hardly a shot had been fired at the fort or at the *Huron* which was still anchored in the river beside it. Largely this was due to the cavalier Gladwin had ordered to be built by a detachment of five men under Ensign Watkins. Soldiers on the ramparts had stood watch over the men while they worked, in order to drive away any Indians intent on harassing them.

The cavalier was a mound of earth that had been thrown up to flank the riverbank between the fort and St. Martin's house, and from whence detachments of soldiers could better defilade a position from which the Indians had been annoying them. Obviously the successful completion of the defensive works had been in part responsible for the slackening of enemy fire against both fort and vessel.

Yet, Gladwin admitted, there seemed to be more to it than that. It seemed that there were fewer Indians around and only a minimal force was being kept on hand to keep the fort bottled up while the remainder were engaged in . . . what? Gladwin wished he knew. Another attack on the *Michigan* at the mouth of the river? The Detroit commander hoped not. He had learned, with anger, of Captain Donald Campbell having been used as a shield for a canoe attack on the vessel and he hoped that, having successfully beaten it off, Captain Newman had come to the conclusion that it was wiser to head at once toward Niagara for reinforcements than to wait for the expected convoy until June 6, as Gladwin had initially ordered.

The major had the annoying suspicion that the Indians were far better informed of his own plans than he was about theirs. And, though as yet he had no real proof of it, he rated the fort's chief interpreter, Pierre LaButte, high on the list of probable informers to Chief Pontiac.

It was in the middle of this thought that Gladwin heard a wild cheering from his men and the single boom of a cannon on the south wall. Instantly he dropped his work and raced out the door. An aide came running to him, greatly excited.

"The supply convoy, sir!" he gasped. "It's coming!"

Elation blossoming in him, Gladwin ran to the southeast corner of the fort and climbed to the ramparts. Yes, they were there! Fourteen, fifteen . . . sixteen batteaux, flags fluttering in the breeze, coming upstream close to the opposite bank. Their nearness to that shore and its adjacent Huron village was hazardous and he muttered an urging for them to begin angling across the river. They did not. In a short while it became obvious why not and the happy, excited cries of the garrison slowly dwindled away.

Most of the batteaux were crowded with Indians and each craft had two or three or even more English prisoners in it. The convoy had been taken! Henry Gladwin groaned and then cursed bitterly. Aboard the *Huron* the crew was lining the rails, hurling insults at the victorious Chippewas, Mississaugis and Ottawas as the batteaux came up opposite them. They shouted in unison for the prisoners to make an escape attempt and, incredibly, the second batteau, which was being rowed by four soldiers who were guarded by only two Indians aboard, abruptly sheared off toward midstream.

Instantly there was a scuffle with the Indian guards. One of the Ottawas at the front of the craft was heaved overboard by three soldiers who jumped him and then he was clubbed with an oar when he surfaced. He sank at once. At the rear of the boat the fourth soldier was locked in mortal struggle with the other guard and in moments they had fallen overboard together. When they surfaced, the Indian held a tomahawk in his hand and smashed it down with crushing force on the crown of his assailant. The soldier disappeared.

By this time the Indian was twenty feet or more from the

batteau, which was being rowed with frantic haste toward midstream by the three remaining soldiers. He screamed angrily and then turned and began swimming back toward those batteaux closer to shore. From the Indians aboard these boats as well as from those on the shore, a ragged firing of rifles was made at the escapees. Two of the soldiers were wounded at once, but miraculously they drew the boat out of effective range of fire. From both fort and vessel there now came a withering protective firing which discouraged any of the other batteaux from pursuing.

The escaping batteau, carrying seven barrels of provisions, made it safely to the vessel and the three men and supplies were brought aboard. Less than ten minutes later a small boat shoved off from the ship and came directly to the fort's water gate. The three escapees, exhausted, remained on the ship but a sergeant now brought their intelligence to the Detroit commander.

Briefly Major Gladwin was informed of the attack at Point Pelee and the loss of almost all the supplies and a great many men. Only two boats had escaped, but it was not known how many men had gotten away, though the number was estimated to be no more than forty.

Those soldiers who had not been slain at the site of the ambush on Point Pelee had been forced to row the boats here. From the Indians they had gathered that Chiefs Sekahos and Mehemah had sent runners overland to Pontiac to tell of the victory and to prepare for their arrival. All the captives, they reported, were scheduled to be tortured and killed and there was little doubt this would happen, in view of the fact that the convoy had been bringing with it a good supply of liquor. Once the Indians began drinking it they would lose any control and slaughter was almost inevitable.

A veil of despair settled over the Detroit garrison as the news filtered out. To many of the men, it was as if their own death knell had been sounded. Gladwin gave orders setting everyone to work in an effort to keep them so busy they would not have time to wallow in their own fear, but he was deeply depressed himself.

The batteaux still in the hands of the Indians angled across the river a half mile above the fort and landed by Pontiac's camp. Throughout the remainder of the day the shrieks and screams of both Indians and Englishmen there increased in tempo as gauntlets were run and as men were tied to stakes, tortured and eventually killed.

It was about four o'clock in the afternoon when the

scalped and otherwise mutilated naked bodies of both Lieutenant Cuyler's and Sergeant Shaw's men began floating past the fort on little makeshift rafts set adrift so that the garrison would see them and be further horrified. They were. The sickening procession continued at intervals until the fall of night mercifully blotted out the sight.

[May 30, 1763—Monday, 9:30 P.M.]

For four more days after the canoe attack on his vessel by the Indians using Captain Campbell as a shield, Captain Jacob Newman had kept the *Michigan* hovering at the mouth of the Detroit River, still hoping to intercept and save the supply convoy from Fort Niagara which surely must be en route. But as day after day went by and there was no sign of it, Newman grew increasingly nervous.

On the twenty-third, two days after the Potawatomi had been shot out of the canoe, another half-hearted canoe attack was launched, but it was easily beaten off without harm to either the Indians or the men aboard the *Michigan*.

Major Gladwin had ordered Newman to wait at the river mouth until June 6 or until events indicated that further waiting would be too hazardous. On the evening of the twenty-fifth, after yet another unrewarded day of waiting, the skipper had made his decision. The convoy should have been here long ago and the fact that it still had not arrived indicated that either it had been stopped or had never even been sent. The next attack against the *Michigan* could well be an all-out assault and if this ship was lost, Detroit would almost certainly fall. It was imperative to reach Fort Niagara and tell Major John Wilkins of the uprising so that he could both have reinforcements sent to Detroit and alert General Amherst in New York.

On the morning of the twenty-sixth, therefore, Captain Newman had given orders to weigh anchor and hoist sail. The *Michigan* quickly began slicing the water toward Fort Niagara. For half a day it moved along well and then the wind failed and the ship was becalmed. And there it had continued to sit, powerless, until this very moment, and without any end in sight yet to one of the worst becalmings Captain Jacob Newman had ever encountered; at a time when he and every other man aboard the ship realized only too well the urgency of haste.

It was the first time in nearly a year that Alexander Henry had seen Wawatam and he greeted the Chippewa with great warmth as the Indian strode into his trading store at Fort Michilimackinac. Ever since that time so long ago when Wawatam had adopted him as a son, brother, and friend, no further mention had been made of the fact and Henry not unexpectedly, when he thought of it at all, considered the adoption to be a ceremonial thing, nothing more.

Now, although Wawatam had smiled with equal warmth, hugged the trader to him and shook his hand, Alexander Henry detected that something was bothering his Chippewa friend. The man was decidedly melancholy.

"What's the matter, Wawatam?" he asked. "Is there anything I can do?"

The village chief shook his head and denied there was anything at all wrong, but now he seemed even more bothered. Yet, whatever it was that was troubling him, he refused to talk about it and only spoke innocuous generalities. He had, he told Henry, only lately returned from his winter hunting grounds to the south and east of here. Yes, hunting had been good and the game plentiful, but his family's efforts would have been far more rewarding had sufficient ammunition been available. Finally, on the verge of departure, Wawatam paused at the door.

"I was very sorry on returning here to learn that you were still here, my friend," he said. "I had hoped you might have gone elsewhere to take care of your business, perhaps back among the Englishmen in the east."

"But why, Wawatam?" Henry was frowning.

Wawatam did not reply to the question. "I must go up to the Saulte Sainte Marie," he said. "I wish for you to go with me. Today. Now."

Henry shook his head slowly. "I wish I could," he said. "I'd enjoy getting out with you. And I'd like to see Jean Cadotte again. Unfortunately, I just can't get away right now. How about this: I'll be finished with what I have to do here in three or four days. Supposing I follow you then and meet you up there at Cadotte's?"

Wawatam seemed about to say something, but then he pressed his lips together and merely nodded in agreement, gave a little wave and left. Henry shook his head. He wished he knew what was troubling the man. He'd like to help him if he could. But a few minutes later, back at his work again, he hardly even remembered that Wawatam had visited.

He worked steadily for another hour before he was interrupted by the arrival of Lieutenant John Jamet. He grinned and nodded at the officer. The two had formed a strong friendship since that night last December when Fort Sault Sainte Marie had been destroyed by fire and Jamet was so badly burned. The harrowing midwinter journey they had made—he and Cadotte with the injured Jamet—had become a near-fatal thing for all of them.

His burns had very nearly killed the lieutenant and for months he had recuperated, gradually forming new skin where he had been burned shallowly, and scar tissue where the burns had been very deep. The scars insured that he would never again be thought of as the handsome young lieutenant, but at least he was alive and he was well aware that without the efforts of both Jean Cadotte and Alexander Henry—*especially* Henry—he would now be dead.

It was Jamet, more than anyone else, who kept Henry well up to date with what was going on insofar as the garrison here at Fort Michilimackinac was concerned. Captain George Etherington and Alexander Henry now shared a faint mutual dislike and so there was little unnecessary communication between them.

Jamet had come to Henry's store today for no other purpose than just to chat as a friend. He stayed for about an hour and they talked about the trade and the Indians. Whatever tensions had been evident between the English and the Indians here some months ago had seemed to have eased to the point where now they were nonexistent. In fact, as Jamet pointed out, the council that the Chippewa chiefs Minivavana and Matchekewis had held yesterday with Etherington had been merely to tell the commander what a great deal of friendship they felt for the garrison in general and George Etherington in particular. While at first it had been difficult adjusting to the change from a French post here, they had added, now they were very glad that the English had come. And after the chiefs had gone, Etherington was so smug in his prior evaluation of the English-Indian relationship here that he was almost unbearable.

Jamet chuckled and shook his head. "You know, I pity the next man who goes to him with a warning that the Indians are going to rise. The captain'll take his scalp long before any Indian can get at it."

The two men laughed and then, shortly afterward, parted.

Not until the lieutenant was gone, still limping just slightly from his fire injuries, did Alexander Henry remember that he hadn't told John about his curious visit from Wawatam. Well, he shrugged and went back to work, it really didn't matter.

Relatively young he may have been, and sometimes rash or foolish, but Captain Simeon Ecuyer was neither cowardly nor inclined to self-deception. The Fort Pitt commander knew that the Indian attacks which had broken out over the past few days—and the deaths and destruction that were the outcome—had in part been caused by his own carelessness in permitting unscrupulous traders to sell them powder and lead. True, he had not known of the dealings until after the Indians were gone from the post, but he blamed himself sharply for being so lax in his controls that such a thing could have happened at all.

It was up to him now to shoulder what responsibility was his and he did so without hesitation. In all his long service career, he had never had any commander whom he so much admired and to whom he was even a fraction so devoted as to Colonel Henry Bouquet. Like Bouquet, Ecuyer was a Swiss mercenary. He lacked the experience and the strategic ability of the colonel, but in many ways he was as serious, dependable and professional as the older man. It was after Bouquet that Ecuyer patterned himself, always striving in whatever he did to do it as he thought Henry Bouquet might.

He had often thought that it was almost criminal that a man like Sir Jeffrey Amherst should be commander in chief of all His Majesty's forces in America, when such responsibility rightfully should have been placed with Bouquet. Even as a younger soldier years ago, Bouquet had always been far more a professional officer and strategist than Amherst could ever hope to be. To Ecuyer's way of thinking, Colonel Henry Bouquet was at this moment the most brilliant and skilled military man in North America and probably one of the best in the world. Little wonder that he found in the colonel a model to pattern himself after, a goal for which to strive.

As always when Ecuyer wrote to Bouquet, he wrote in French, finding in that language a far greater range of expression than he could command in English. And in the past three days he had written several such letters, doing all in his power to keep the colonel—who was presently in Philadelphia headquarters—closely advised as to what was occurring at and around this outpost.

In the evening of the twenty-ninth, just two days ago, he had written Bouquet to tell him of the party of Indians who had come to the fort to trade and how, without murmur or complaint on their part, they had paid dearly in fine peltry for a surreptitious purchase of gunpowder and lead. It was, he had added, largely his own fault for having permitted conditions to exist where such an exchange could have occurred and he was now taking steps to insure that such a thing could not happen again. Perhaps the traders were right and the Indians had only wanted it for hunting; however, he felt that a grave error had been made and that there would be unpleasant repercussions. He was only too right. The following morning—yesterday—he wrote to Bouquet again:

Sir:

It is as I had feared. Just as I finished my letter, three men came in from Clapham's with the melancholy news that yesterday at three o'clock in the afternoon, the Indians murdered Clapham and everybody in his house: these three men were out at work and escaped through the woods. I immediately armed them and sent them to assist our people at Bushy Run. The Indians have told the settler Byerly there to leave his place in four days or he and his family would all be murdered. I am uneasy for the little posts. As for this post, I will answer for it.

Shortly after sending that letter yesterday, Ecuyer had sent a small detachment to carry an express to Fort Venango and warn the commander of that sixteen-man post, Lieutenant Francis Gordon, of possible danger. He had included instructions for Gordon in turn to relay the news north to Fort Le Boeuf and Fort Presque Isle. Hardly had the detachment left than the trader named Calhoun and two other traders showed up at Fort Pitt and told him of the warning they had received at Tuscarawas from Chief Shingas, their hasty departure and the subsequent attack on them near the mouth of Beaver River. Eleven of the men had been killed and only Calhoun and these other two had escaped.

Soon other traders were coming in with their own stories of attack and plundering by the Indians. Then, later still, the detachment Ecuyer had sent to warn Fort Venango came galloping back badly frightened. Reporting to Ecuyer at once, they told him that a small Indian town up the Allegheny was found to be abandoned, though always before it had been filled with friendly Delawares. Worse, a little way beyond that point they were fired on from ambush and though no one was hit, one horse had its rump creased by a bullet and the party had been forced to retreat. They had come back by way of the little sawmill not far from here and there they found the scalped bodies of two of Ecuyer's soldiers.

A general alert had been ordered by Ecuyer and throughout the night he had not slept as he personally saw to all defenses and made every preparation possible for a full-scale Indian attack. From the way reports were continuing to come in of Indian activity, it was an attack he expected to come very soon.

Now it was noon of this last day of the month and Ecuyer was again at his desk, hastily penning yet another letter to his colonel. He wrote:

Sir:

We have most melancholy accounts here. The Indians have broken out in several places, and murdered Colonel Clapham and his family; also two of our soldiers at the sawmill near the fort, and scalps taken from each man. The horse-driver, Daniel Collette, in charge of the King's cattle, was turned back on his way to Tuscarawas with forty-four horses and declares that an Indian has brought a war belt to Tuscarawas and says Detroit is invested; and that Sandusky is cut off and Ensign Pawley [Pauli] made prisoner. The trader Levy's good are stopped at Tuscarawas by the Indians. Thirteen men being led by the trader Calhoun were attacked by Beaver Creek, eleven of whom, it is said, were killed. And twenty-five of Macrae's and Allison's horses loaded with skins, are all taken.

Sir, I see that the affair is general. I tremble for our outposts. I believe, from what I hear, that I am surrounded by Indians. I neglect nothing to give them a good reception; and I expect to be attacked tomorrow morning. Please God I may be. I am passably well prepared. Everybody is at work and I do not sleep; but I tremble lest my messenger should be cut off.

[*May 31, 1763—Tuesday, 8:00 P.M.*]

There was one particular factor which set Chief Pontiac apart from most other Indians and the majority of chiefs. He usually took the time to think things out far in advance instead of acting rashly on spur-of-the-moment emotional impulse. If there was revenge to take, he generally took it, but at a time and place where he and his warriors would suffer least for it. He was quick to see and benefit from his own mistakes and he was, as few Indians were, his own greatest critic. As any good leader of men must do, he constantly assessed what he had already done, what he was doing, and what yet needed to be done before moving ahead with his plans. As a result, he rarely failed in what he set out to do and it was this aspect of his character which had made of him not only a leader among his own people but that rarity of the wilderness, a chief who could command the respect of other tribes to such extent that their chiefs and warriors would join him and accept him as leader.

He rarely acted rashly, true, but occasionally he did and almost always it was to his later regret. And he had rarely in his life acted as rashly as he had in his anger at the very beginning of this war which was not yet a month old. Because of the failure of his projected surprise attack on Detroit, he rashly opened the war anyway and his prestige had suffered greatly because of the failure of the fort to fall as days had become weeks. But now, in only a matter of days, events had occurred which had caused his prestige and influence to soar to unprecedented heights. He was riding a crest of popularity and devotion among the majority of the western tribes such as no Indian had ever before experienced.

Just as his support had begun to crumble, just as he began being plagued by the defection of important segments of his Indian force, a reprieve had come with the stunning news about Sandusky. The small force he had sent there had not only convinced the Wyandot Hurons to join in a surprise attack on the fort, but they had pulled it off superbly. The fort had fallen, its entire complement of soldiers and traders killed except for the commander alone—who was prisoner here at Detroit—and an abundance of horses and goods taken. The fact that Fort Sandusky no longer existed was a painful thorn plucked from the side of all these tribes.

Then had come the taking of the supply convoy en route to Detroit from Niagara, resulting in a great abundance of plunder and certainly all the ammunition they would need for a considerable while. Until then there had still been a sense of reluctance on the parts of many of his followers, a feeling that perhaps they were making a great mistake. But that had come to a decisive end when the convoy prisoners were brought here. There was much liquor in the plunder and the minds of his followers had been set afire with it. In the orgy of torture and death, every Englishman's life which spilled away had cemented Pontiac's followers more closely to him.

Few of the Indians were vacillating any longer by that time, and then even those few were completely won over by the tremendous news which had just arrived from the south, the west, and the north. Three runners had arrived within hours of each other. The first brought word from the south, that Chief Cold Foot of the Miamis, having received the war belt sent by Pontiac in the care of his party journeying to the Illinois country, accepted Pontiac's plan. He had surprised Fort Miamis, killed the commander and had the entire garrison prisoner. Pontiac's party was now moving down the Wabash toward Fort Ouiatenon, hoping to accomplish the same thing there by convincing the Weas, along with whatever Kickapoos or Kaskaskias or Mascoutens were in the area, to take that fort similarly by surprise.

The runner from the west brought news that Chief Washee of the Potawatomies, even without the aid of the resident chief, Kioqua, had surprised and taken Fort St. Joseph. The commander and three of the garrison were being held prisoner; the remaining eleven had all been killed.

From the north came word from a Chippewa runner that Fort Michilimackinac had been primed for the surprise. The commander had successfully been put entirely off guard and knew nothing of the uprisings elsewhere. The L'Arbre Croche Ottawas were still debating among themselves whether or not to fall in with the plan, but Chiefs Minivavana and Matchekewis of the Chippewas had convinced a large party of visiting Sacs to aid them and so, whether or not the northern Ottawas came to help, the attack was going to be made within the week.

It was a wholesale commitment on all fronts and there was no longer any doubt of Pontiac's supremacy of command. Any tribe or faction of a tribe still not in favor of the war knew better, at this point, than to make a public proclamation of it.

But though riding this crest of prestige, Pontiac did not delude himself. Throughout the night while the orgy continued and the shrieks and screams periodically rent the air, he had sat alone in his quarters thinking, only occasionally being interrupted by his favorite wife, Kantuk-keghun, bringing food or drink. His thoughts were on Detroit and, while he had no doubt of its eventual fall, it would be a long time in coming and only following an extensive siege. It therefore lost its prime importance at this time and attention must be directed to greater efforts elsewhere.

At noon today he had ordered Kantuk-keghun to find the three Ottawa chiefs, Chauvin, Breton, and Mintiwaby, and send them to him at once. Within a few minutes all three had arrived, spatters of blood on their loin-cloths and skin, their eyes bright. They had entered talking and laughing among themselves, their voices slightly slurred from too much drink, but they were still in command of themselves. They squatted in a row before the small fire like three strange apes, staring silently across the coals at their chief while he unraveled more of his plan to them and told them their part in it.

They were to take two hundred and fifty men—Ottawas, primarily, but warriors of other tribes, too, if they wished—and leave at once for the east. Along the way they were to present war belts to any Indians encountered, regardless of tribe, and enlist their aid. They were not to concern themselves with Fort Pitt, which was in the domain of the Shawnees and Delawares and which those tribes were probably at this time already seeing to. No, their mission was to sever the communication between Fort Pitt and Niagara. That communication was represented by three English forts —Presque Isle on the Lake Erie shore; Le Boeuf to the south of that some fifteen miles at the end of the portage road; and Venango, some forty miles south of Le Boeuf on the upper Allegheny River. All three of these were small forts, especially Venango and Le Boeuf. They were to try to take them by surprise if possible, but if that was not possible, then they were to be taken by direct attack. When this was accomplished, then attention could be directed on Fort Niagara itself.

Within half an hour the entire plan had been laid out and the three chiefs and Pontiac went outside. By late afternoon the necessary supplies had been gathered for the enterprise, the weapons seen to, war paint applied and the canoes readied. And before the setting of the sun, eight large canoes each carrying upwards of thirty warriors, glided smoothly down the Detroit River past the fort but far out of range of its guns.

Major Henry Gladwin, standing on the ramparts with Captain Joseph Hopkins, was one of those who watched them go. When they had passed out of sight, the junior officer turned to his commander.

"Strange that they'd be leaving like that when the rest are

still drinking and carrying on like they've been these past couple of days. What do you make of it, sir?"

Gladwin shook his head slowly. "Hard to say, Joseph," he answered. "Whatever it is, it's not to our good. Maybe they've learned of another convoy coming and are going to try to cut it off. I hope to God I'm wrong."

And, of course, he was.

Lieutenant Jehu Hay's face was flushed with excitement when he burst into the quarters of Major Henry Gladwin shortly after sunrise. Gladwin, his powdered wig not yet donned and his own hair tousled, was irked at Hay momentarily, but not for long. In a few minutes a grin as wide as Hay's own had spread across his face and a deep, relieved sigh escaped him.

"You say Captain Campbell sent it in?" the Detroit commander asked.

Hay nodded. "Apparently he was able to talk with some of the men of Cuyler's detachment before they were butchered. One of them had the letter hidden somewhere in his clothes. Captain Campbell asked to be allowed to talk to Mr. St. Martin, and it was St. Martin who brought it to the fort this morning."

Gladwin looked at the paper again and then slowly walked to his desk and put it down there. "Well," he said, "it won't end this uprising right away but at least it eases the pressure a little. Looks like Pontiac's on his own now."

The two men grinned again. It was a nice feeling to have a small piece of good news after the series of blows that had fallen on Detroit and its dependencies. The letter was brief and to the point. It stated that the Seven Years' War was officially ended and that England and France had signed a conclusive treaty of peace in which France had ceded all her claims east of the Mississippi to the English. There would be no reconquest of Canada by the French. More pointedly, Pontiac's dream of a French army coming to assist him had just burst.

As Gladwin so aptly put it, the Ottawa war chief was indeed strictly on his own.

Wawatam of the Chippewas had never been a very complex man. He was accustomed to living with and acting upon simple things. Occasionally he had run up against one problem or another that caused him a little more than the normal amount of consideration, but such problems were rare and even they, once his mind had set to work on them, had been quite readily resolved. But not in his experience had he ever come up against a problem so insoluble as the one that had been plaguing him for a fortnight or more.

Always before he had been able to make his decision on any matter and then philosophically live with it, even on those occasions when the wrong decision had been made. Such was not the case now. Irrespective of what decision he made now, he would be dishonored. How could a man choose in such a situation? In the one case he would betray his family, his village, his tribe, his race; in the other he would betray his most fundamental beliefs in the Great Spirit, the *Manitou,* whose existence he no more doubted than he doubted his own. Five years ago the Great Spirit had come to him in a vision and commanded him to watch for a particular man and, when he saw him, to adopt him as friend, brother, and son—a command which bound him to love, honor and protect this person above all others. The man had turned out to be a young English trader, Alexander Henry. Yet now Wawatam's own people were on the eve of bloody warfare with the English in which, during a surprise attack tomorrow, it was quite probable that all Englishmen at Fort Michilimackinac would die.

Wawatam's honor, his belief in the *Manitou,* demanded that he warn Alexander Henry; but the knowledge was there that if he did so, it was almost certain that Henry would take steps to preserve his own people and, in doing so, the element of surprise would be lost and perhaps the lives of many of Wawatam's people with it. And so, what was he to do?

Yesterday when he had gone into the store of his adopted friend-brother-son, fully intending to live up to the dictates of his beliefs and the command of the Great Spirit, he found that when he tried to give the warning his resolve to do so had fled. He found himself standing there uncomfortable and muttering generalities. He had gone as far as asking Henry to come away with him to the Sault Sainte Marie, but Henry had not been able to accept the invitation then and so Wawatam had left him, more miserable than ever.

Now the time was running out. Throughout this sleepless night just ended Wawatam had mulled the problem until he felt his head must burst. His wife, Oghqua, had remained beside him, knowing his problem and wishing desperately to be able to help, yet unable to do so. The decision, whatever it would be, had to be Wawatam's. And here, in the bright morning light, he was no closer to a solution than before.

Almost involuntarily his steps carried him toward the fort and Henry's store. Oghqua walked with him, unnoticed, determined to back her husband fully in whatever his decision would be. As he walked, Wawatam glumly noted the great numbers of his people, as well as visiting Sacs, who were assembled here now, going about their business with outward nonchalance, with no hint of their plan evident in their actions. For the past week, in fact, they had been playing their favorite competitive sport, baggataway, on the field adjacent to the fort, seemingly at peace with the world. For them it was so simple, as it would have been for Wawatam himself had it not been for young Henry.

The trader was separating bundles of furs and rebaling them according to type and quality when Wawatam and his squaw entered. He looked up as he heard them and a broad grin blossomed on his features. He strode to the chief to shake his hand with genuine pleasure and nodded engagingly at Oghqua, whom he had grown to like.

"Wawatam! Oghqua! You didn't go up to the Sault yesterday after all. Are you going to wait for a few days until I finish up here so I can go with you?"

The Chippewa village chief shook his head. "No, my friend, we go today. But we have come back to beg again that you lay aside what it is you have to do and go with us now. We beg that you do this."

Henry looked startled at the intensity of Wawatam's plea and glanced at Oghqua. Her expression was equally concerned and she moved to him and placed a hand lightly on his arm in a touch that was decidedly maternal.

"You are my husband's friend, his brother, his son, and so you are also mine. I add my words to his and beg you come with us. It is important to him and to me that you come."

To his amazement, Alexander Henry saw tears well in her eyes and slide down her cheeks and he glanced quickly at Wawatam and was even more shocked to see the older man's eyes swimming. He was suddenly greatly concerned.

"My friend, my dear friend, what is it? Something is bothering you. Tell me. Is there nothing I can do to help you?"

"Only that you go with us," Wawatam said softly.

Now it was Henry who was in a quandary. If it meant this much to them, perhaps he should go; yet, at the same time he knew he simply couldn't right now. There was just too much that needed to be done. These furs had to be shipped to the east and some of his trading parties that had been gone since last fall were expected back here momentarily. Surely Wawatam's reasons for wanting him to go to the Sault were not that important. He decided to treat the whole matter lightly and he laughed.

"What, go now and miss the big game tomorrow? Everyone has been waiting to see it played."

He was referring to the Indian game of baggataway—*la crosse*—which the Indians had announced they would play as a final international competition tomorrow in the great open field adjacent to the fort. It would be quite a spectacle and practically everyone who could, was going to be on hand to see it; which was another reason why Henry couldn't understand why Wawatam and Oghqua were so adamant about leaving now. It was only logical to assume that they, too, would want to see the game, since it would be the Chippewas pitted against the Sacs in a contest which might last from early morning until darkness came.

"No," he continued, squeezing Wawatam's shoulder, "I can't go with you now. With all this work," he indicated the interior of the store, "I very much doubt I will be watching the game myself. But I promise you that as soon as my men get in and I get matters straightened out and send a large shipment to the east, then I will join you at the Sault without fail."

There was no use in pursuing the matter any further and Wawatam knew it. Silently he shook Henry's hand again and walked out of the store, followed by the dutiful Oghqua. Neither of them looked back and they left the fort proper and were proceeding toward the Chippewa village when they were intercepted by the principal chief of their tribe, Minivavana.

"You have been to see the English trader again," he said. It was not a question. "You saw him yesterday as well."

Wawatam nodded, his eyes unfalteringly on Minivavana's.

"You have not told him of our plan for tomorrow during the heat of the game?"

"I have not told him," Wawatam replied, "though my heart tells me that I should have. He is my son, my brother, and he is my friend."

Minivavana nodded his head sympathetically. "It is well known, your love for this Englishman. It is why you have been watched and why it was important for me to know if you had told him of our plan. The burden you wear grows heavier and now I will take that burden from you and wear it myself that you may no longer be troubled. I will send you away now, across the narrow water here, you and your family. You have no choice. You will go at once and not come back until it is done. The matter is then beyond your control and you need no longer be torn within you in your loyalty or what you believe to be right."

"And the trader Henry?"

Minivavana shrugged. "I will see that he is not harmed. I promise this for myself, but who can say what will be? It is not possible that I be in all places at one time. But you have the promise of your chief: I will try to see to him."

It was the best that Wawatam could hope for, but his concern grew no less and his heart remained heavy within him.

[*June 1, 1763—Wednesday, 3:00 P.M.*]

Lieutenant Edward Jenkins, commander at Fort Ouiatenon, rubbed his wrists and winced a little. The rawhide had been snugged so tightly around them that circulation had been cut off and now that they had been temporarily removed, his hands were tingling and there were angry red welts on the wrists. He was having trouble flexing his fingers and he knew it would be a little while yet before he would be able to control them enough to write.

He and his twenty men had, he thought, been treated quite well considering what had happened. He had had decided qualms about ordering a surrender, despite the assurances of both the Frenchmen and Indians here that they would not be mistreated if he did so. Circumstances being what they were, however, there had really been little choice in the matter. Happily, they had lived up to their word, as evidenced by the fact that they now had even granted the request he made— they had removed his bonds and provided him with pen and paper with which to write to his commander, Major Gladwin.

Jenkins flexed his fingers again, found them responding well now and the tingling nearly gone. The pair of Indians on guard at the door held their tomahawks casually, but he could see they were tense and prepared to move swiftly if he attempted anything foolish. He had no intention of doing so.

Slowly and carefully he dipped the newly sharpened and slitted end of the turkey quill into the inkpot and began to write:

To Major Henry Gladwin
Commanding at Detroit

*Sir: I have heard of your situation, which gives me much
pain. Indeed, we are not a great deal better, for this morning
the Indians sent for me to speak with me, and immediately
bound me when I got to their cabin, and I soon found some
of my soldiers in the same situation. They told me Detroit,
Miamis and all these posts were cut off and that it was folly
to make any resistance; therefore desired me to make the few
soldiers I had in the fort surrender, otherwise they would put
all of us to death in case one man of theirs was killed.*

*They were to have fallen on us and killed us all last night,
but Monsieurs Maisonville and Lorrain gave them wampum
not to kill us all. And when they told the interpreter we were
all to be killed, and he knowing the Canadians of the fort,
begged of them to make us prisoners. They have put us into
the French houses and both Indians and French use us very
well.*

*All these nations say they are very sorry, that they were
obliged to do it by the other nations. The belt did not arrive
here till last night about eight o'clock; Mr. Lorrain* [98]*can inform you of all.*

*Just now received the news of St. Joseph's being taken,
eleven were killed and three taken prisoners with the officer.*

*I have nothing more to say but that I sincerely wish you a
speedy succour, and that we may be able to revenge ourselves
on them that deserve it.*

I remain, with my sincerest wishes for your safety, &c.,

Edwd. Jenkins

N.B. We expect to set off in a day or two for the Illinois.

348

CHAPTER VI

THE day dawned beautifully and the air seemed almost to drip with the fragrance of wildflowers. For a while, just before the sun came up, the Straits of Mackinac were almost mirror smooth, as hardly a breath of breeze was stirring. Here and there the water dimpled enticingly as fish came to the surface to feed. With the sunrise came the very gentle wind now blowing, creating a slight rippling on the water. It was a perfect day for the game and most of the Fort Michilimackinac garrison was looking forward to it.

Already in the fine, mile-long meadow adjacent to the fort new goalposts were being erected by the Indians. These were fir logs about eight inches in diameter and there were only two of them, a half mile apart. Each was sunk in the ground until it stood firmly upright about fifteen feet high. The post which was a quarter mile to the east of the fort's gate was the goal to be defended by the Chippewas, while that which was equidistant to the west of the gate belonged to the visiting Sacs.

For nearly a week the seventy or more Sacs from across Lake Michigan in the area of the Wisconsin River had been here visiting the Chippewas, trading with them, playing baggataway, and renewing old friendships and alliances. This time, as they did nearly every time they visited, they brought a few slaves with them to trade to the Chippewas for goods they wanted. The slaves were usually women or boys who had been taken on raids made by the Sacs to the west among their mortal enemies—the Sioux, Pawnee, Oto, Mandan, and Dakotah tribes.

It was only after the Sacs had been here several days that an announcement was made by the chiefs of both tribes that a great international competition was going to take place. The stakes, according to the chiefs, were going to be very high, though no one seemed to know exactly what these stakes were. The competition was to be in the favorite athletic sport of these tribes, baggataway—an exciting but extremely brutal game. Rarely was it ever played that blood did not flow freely, that bones were not broken, that injured players did not crawl off the field or have to be carried off. And not infrequently players were killed.

Every player—and there might be as many as thirty or forty to the side, each gaudily painted with vermilion—is armed with a stout four-foot stick, at the end of which is a sort of little webbed racket. The ball is relatively small, about the size and shape of a turkey egg, and carved from wood. At the beginning of the game it often has a cluster of dyed feathers attached to it, but these are always quickly knocked off as the game progresses.

The object of the game is to move the ball to the opponent's territory and hit his goalpost with it. At no time can the ball be touched with the hand. It can be scooped up and thrown with the racket, hit like a golf ball, kicked, or even grasped between the feet and hopped toward the post. A game might last from dawn till darkness if no goal is made.

The opponent does everything in his power to prevent his post from being touched by the ball. Tripping, hitting, clubbing, kicking and other assorted forms of mayhem are permitted. Extreme roughness is standard procedure. If one of the Indians on the opposing team has the ball between his feet and is hopping with it, a defender has every right and obligation to rush up and, with all his strength, strike the man with his racket on the feet or legs, sometimes on the body or head. The man attacked is protected, if possible, by his own teammates. He also tries to ward off any blows with his own racket while at the same time continuing to move the ball. The game becomes an incredibly extended brawl, with broken arms and legs extremely common and broken heads not rare.

Surprisingly, considering all this conflict, no personal animosity develops between players. Whatever injury occurs is accepted as the luck of the game and the injured, if at all possible, try to keep on playing despite broken limbs or whatever. It becomes a mark of honor to be permanently crippled during the course of a game of baggataway.

In this game preparing to begin between the Sacs and the Chippewas, each team had about twenty men on the field. In addition, there were dozens of other Indians on the sidelines near the fort who would, very soon, be adding their own howls and shrieks to the din created by the players. Adding to the many Chippewas under Chief Minivavana were those of Chief Matchekewis, whose village was almost twenty miles away on a small bay fronting on Lake Huron.[99] All in all, there were somewhere around a hundred Indian men present, plus almost as many squaws heavily swathed in blankets despite the growing warmness of the day. Surprisingly, few children were to be seen anywhere.

The squaws gravitated toward the fort and many of them squatted to watch near the gate, while a score or more others, apparently not too interested in the contest, strolled into the fort proper and casually walked about among the picturesque French homes with their rude porticoes and bark roofs with elongated eaves. Numerous slender birch canoes lay about here and there beside the dwellings and a dozen or more large fish nets were spread out on wooden racks to dry in the sun.

The blanketed squaws stopped occasionally to greet or briefly speak with the soldiers or Frenchmen sauntering about while they waited for the game to began. Three hundred French were still living here at Fort Michilimackinac and it seemed that at least a third of them were out roaming about. Of the garrison of thirty-five, which included the three officers, practically all were outside wandering around with the exception of those having duties to perform, such as the sentries and the Officer of the Day.

From near midfield, when the sun was about an hour high, came a peculiar ululation from Minivavana who stood with hands cupping his mouth and head thrown back. This wail was the signal for the game to begin. And begin it did, with a vengeance, as soon as Minivavana reached the sidelines by the fort's gate. There were yells and screams, the banging of heavy rackets together, and the meaty sound of bodies colliding violently or being hit with the sticks.

Immediately there was a general movement of Frenchmen and soldiers toward the sidelines to watch. Only rarely could the little oval ball be seen, such as when it would suddenly bounce free and be scooped up in a racket and hurled toward a teammate or toward the goalpost. Then the whole howling mob of players would surge after it, converge on it and again begin their kicking and hitting and shrieking.

Of the fort's five resident English traders, only one was not on hand. James Stanley Goddard had left for Montreal nearly a month ago and did not expect to return until late in the summer. The other four—Alexander Henry, Ezekiel Solomon, Henry Bostwick, and John Tracy—had all seen baggataway played many times before and had other things to do now, so they were not spectators of the game. Bostwick and Solomon were busy tending to their business. Alexander Henry, now living in a little cottage beside the much larger house of the Frenchman Charles Langlade, had been told that a canoe would be leaving for Montreal tomorrow and so he was hurriedly writing letters to friends, these letters to be taken east by the boat and relayed to their destinations from Montreal. Only John Tracy was not closely occupied at this moment. He stood near the water's edge looking toward Lake Huron, maintaining a vigil he had begun several days before in anticipation of a shipment of goods arriving from Detroit.

Of the officers, both the commander, Captain George Etherington, and his second, Lieutenant William Leslye, joined the general movement out of the gate toward the sidelines as the game began. With them was a nondescript English drifter named Samuels who had arrived at the fort alone in a canoe just a few days ago. Etherington had placed a substantial wager on the Chippewas emerging the victors and now he, too, occasionally cheered or loudly lamented to Leslye at the fluctuations of the game. It was evident that he was enjoying the whole affair immensely.

Lieutenant John Jamet was Officer of the Day and seeing to his duties methodically. His slight limp was still evident but he felt quite fit. Occasionally now when there was an especially loud cry or laughter or applause from the spectators, he would pause and look in that direction longingly. He always enjoyed seeing a baggataway competition and regretted having to miss this very important one. As regulations required, he wore his complete uniform, even to having his sword buckled to his belt.

Back and forth the players moved the ball, grunting, yelling, clashing, throughout the morning hours. Many of the French spectators began drifting away toward their homes, ostensibly to eat lunch, knowing the game would probably last until evening. More of the squaws, too, seemed to be losing interest and mingled with the Frenchmen, clutching their blankets around them and sauntering with them into the fort.

At about this time a large canoe appeared in the distance. It was a party of Indians from the Detroit area approaching, but still so far distant that John Tracy mistook it for his supply boat. He made a satisfied sound and then turned and strode toward Alexander Henry's cottage. He knocked at the front door and then entered at Henry's bidding and found the

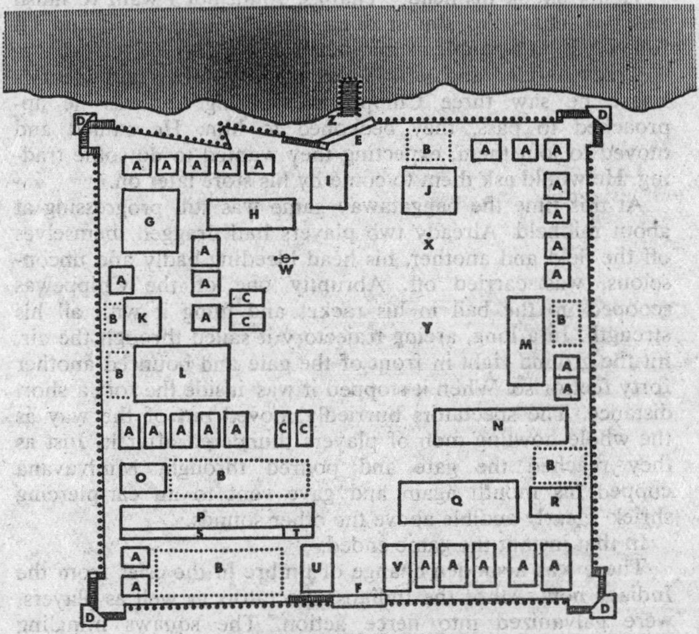

FORT MICHILIMACKINAC

A • Residences	J • Commanding Officer	S • Stables
B • Gardens	K • Priest's Quarters	T • Blacksmith
C • Stores	L • Church	U • Transient Traders
D • Blockhouse Guardposts	M • Trading House	V • Sentry Quarters
E • Water Gate	N • Traders–Soldiers' Barracks	W • Wells
F • Land Gate	O • Guardhouse	X • Flagstaff
G • Indian Council House	P • Soldiers' Barracks	Y • Parade Ground
H • Officers' Quarters	Q • Transient Military	Z • Dock
I • Quartermaster	R • Magazine	

a.w.g.
1970

younger man sitting at a desk, a pile of letters stacked to one side and presently working on yet another. Tracy grinned.

"You're working too hard, Alex," he said. "Why don't you quit for a while? My boat's coming in at last. Come on, walk down to the landing with me and we'll see what the news is from Detroit."

Henry shook his head. "Thanks, John, but I want to finish this last letter. I'm almost done now. You go ahead and I'll follow you in a couple of minutes."

Tracy nodded and left. About twenty yards from Henry's house he saw three Chippewas standing and, as he approached to pass, they beckoned to him. He smiled and moved to join them, expecting they wanted to do some trading. He would ask them to come by his store later on.

At this time the baggataway game was still progressing at about midfield. Already two players had dragged themselves off the field and another, his head bleeding badly and unconscious, was carried off. Abruptly one of the Chippewas scooped up the ball in his racket and flung it with all his strength. In a long, arcing trajectory it sailed through the air, hit the ground right in front of the gate and bounced another forty feet or so. When it stopped it was inside the fort a short distance. The spectators hurriedly moved out of the way as the whole howling mob of players thundered after it. Just as they reached the gate and poured through, Minivavana cupped his mouth again and gave vent to an ear-piercing shriek clearly audible above the other sounds.

In that instant the game ended.

There was a sudden change of timbre in the cries from the Indians now. All of the Indians, spectators as well as players, were galvanized into fierce action. The squaws mingling among them suddenly threw open or dropped their blankets, exposing knives, tomahawks, war clubs, even a few spears and guns. The warriors dropped their baggataway rackets, snatched the weapons from their women and leaped toward the nearest English soldiers. Few if any of the soldier spectators were armed and the carnage was horrible. The two sentries at the gate were first to die, brained by tomahawk blows before they could have realized anything was amiss. Following them in death moments later were seven or eight other soldiers nearby.

Even as Minivavana's signal scream was given, both Captain Etherington and Lieutenant Leslye were grabbed from behind and held while their wrists were swiftly bound behind them. Samuels, a few yards away at this time, was similarly seized and bound. Soldiers were still kicking their lives away near the gate when the three men were hustled off toward a wooded copse.

Inside the fort, John Tracy was still talking with the three Chippewas who had stopped him and at the cry he paused and looked toward the gate. As he did so a tomahawk appeared as if by magic in the hand of one of the warriors and the narrow blade of it plunged deeply into the trader's chest. He died almost immediately.

Alexander Henry, just finishing his letter, heard Minivavana's cry too and then, an instant later, a considerable cacophony of anguished screams and war cries. He leaped to his feet, rushed to the front window and saw, not more than twenty paces away outside, John Tracy lying on his back on the ground, his shirtfront scarlet with blood and one of the three Indians by him already removing his scalp. Toward the gate he could see soldiers running wildly and some being struck down.

Racing back across the room, Henry snatched up his fowling piece loaded with swan shot and returned to the window. He clenched the gun tightly, expecting every instant to hear the to-arms drum roll, but it didn't come. There were few French in sight now, but the dozen or so he could see were standing back out of the way, neither hindering the Indians nor helping the soldiers. The Indians paid no attention to them.

Two of the running soldiers were struck tomahawk blows which wounded but did not kill them. As they scrabbled along on hands and knees trying to get away, both were straddled by Indians who gripped their heads between their knees and began scalping them. The screams were wrenching, chaotic, hideous.

Suddenly Henry's attention was caught by the sight of Lieutenant Jamet holding a circle of Indians at bay with his sword. He fought with tigerish frenzy, slashing, jabbing, thrusting, crying out hoarsely in his anger. Always the Indians managed to stay out of reach of that questing blade, darting in when the officer's back was toward them, striking swiftly and then jumping back again. Time after time the knives or tomahawks found their mark on him and yet somehow, staggering, he continued to keep his feet, continued to slash and thrust. His arms, back, buttocks, legs and neck were all a mass of wounds bleeding freely and staining him and the ground where he fought. Everywhere he stepped he left behind a little scarlet pool. It could not last and it didn't. A tomahawk blow—the thirty-sixth wound he received in this fight—caught him solidly between the shoulder blades, severing the spine and ending his life. It was the Chippewa chief, Matchekewis, who snatched the sword from the limp grasp and shouted an order. One of the warriors grabbed Jamet's hair and lifted until his head and part of his torso were off the ground. Matchekewis swung the sword with both hands and the body fell back to the ground while the warrior did an insane jig with the dripping head still clenched in his grasp.

The heavy, florid-faced trader Henry Bostwick had been walking between his house and his store when the attack broke out. Stunned, he watched the sentries and the unarmed soldiers being cut down. He ran to a nearby house but the door was locked and he flattened his back against it and stared as a private raced past in the street. Two Indians, ten yards behind, were chasing him. Seeing the Frenchman Sans Chagarine standing in his open doorway watching the slaughter, the soldier headed that way.

"Help me!" he gasped, "Help me!"

Chagarine quickly stepped back inside and slammed the door in the private's face just as he reached it. The young soldier was beating on the door and still crying "Help me!" when the Indians caught up to him and a tomahawk blow smashed through the back of his head. He slammed forward against the door, knocking it open. Bostwick waited to see no more. Vaulting a low porch railing, he ran between houses to look for a place—*any* place—he could hide.

Less than five minutes had passed and Henry, still clenching his fowling piece, was rooted at the window. The to-arms drumbeat had never sounded. There was hardly any resistance and the fort was overrun by savages. To expose himself with the gun would be certain death and so now he flung it aside and ran out of the back door of his house, one dominant thought in his mind: the Frenchmen were not being attacked. If he was to escape at all, it would have to be with a Frenchman's aid.

With a single bound he cleared the waist-high fence separating his yard from Langlade's. He entered the back door in a rush and, running through the house and into the front room, found the entire family—Langlade, his wife and three young sons—standing by the window watching what was going on outside.

The relationship between Henry and Langlade had never been warm, though equally it had never been hostile. They had always gone their own separate ways with only an occasional nod of the head passing between them. A half-breed himself, Langlade had married a Chippewa woman many years ago. She was very unusual in that with that marriage she had virtually divorced herself of any further contact with her tribe, adopted an entirely European form of dress and manner, and had quickly learned French from her husband and spoke it almost exclusively. Her hair was cut in the French manner and she had raised her sons thus far as Frenchmen rather than as Indians. To one who did not know her lineage, she was French through and through.

Now, as Alexander Henry burst in among them, the family turned and Madame Langlade gave a harsh gasp and clasped her husband's arm. Langlade himself stared at the trader from under pinched brows.

"Monsieur Langlade," Henry pleaded, "for God's sake, hide me! They're killing all the English. Please man, hide me, at least until the heat of this slaughter is over."

Langlade looked at him coolly for a long moment and then, with a shrug of his shoulders intimating he could hardly care less about what happened to the trader, he turned his back and again looked out the window.

"Que voudriez-vous que j'en ferais?" he said—What would you have me do?

Acting on Langlade's example, the whole family turned their backs to him and resumed their watch of what was occurring outside. Henry, mouth agape with disbelief, backed away. He turned to leave then but had not quite reached the back door when Langlade's housegirl, a Pawnee slave in her midtwenties, beckoned urgently to him from a doorway. He went to her.

"Follow me," she whispered in French, taking his hand. She led him down a narrow hallway to an equally narrow door, opened it and motioned for him to enter. There were steps leading upward just inside. "It is the garret," she hissed, close to his ear. "Go up and hide yourself. Make no noise! Maybe you'll be safe."

He started up, tiptoeing, and heard her close the door gently behind him. The key turned, locking the door, and then there was silence. He continued up the stairs to the rather large attic and found it to be quite dark, since there were no windows. A feather ticking lay to one side of the stairwell and here and there were boxes and trunks and other stored items. In one corner was a huge mound of oddly-shaped birchbark vessels of the type he knew were used to collect sap when the maple trees were tapped. At the wall toward the front of the house he could see daylight coming in through some small holes in the chinking and he moved over there quietly and stooped to put his eye to one and look out. It gave him a rather good view of the fort's interior grounds and what he saw caused him to shudder uncontrollably, yet he could not force himself to stop looking.

A few soldiers were still writhing and shrieking under the knife and bodies were scattered all about, especially close to the gate. He counted eighteen of them—more than half the garrison!—but the only officer among them was Jamet. He could see nothing of either Etherington or Leslye, nor of Bostwick or Solomon or the English drifter, Samuels.[100]

Even as he watched, Henry saw the bodies of several of the dead soldiers laid open with knives or tomahawks. Numbers of the Sacs and Chippewas squatted or kneeled beside them and placed their hands inside the body cavities. When the cupped hands filled with blood, they raised them to their lips and quaffed it and then shrieked with this climactic ceremony of their blood lust. Elsewhere Indians were moving about from house to house, through stores and barracks and offices, looking for more Englishmen.

Just as a call was raised from outside in the Chippewa tongue—"All is finished . . . All is finished"—and then repeated numerous times from different points, Alexander Henry heard some Indians come to the front door and then enter the room below him. With his muscles straining almost unbearably with the effort of remaining absolutely still, the trader managed to stop much of the trembling that was wracking him.

This attic floor was mere thin planking over beams, with similar thin planking nailed to the bottoms of the beams acting as the ceiling of the room below. He could hear the downstairs conversation clearly, which made him only too painfully aware that they could hear the slightest sound he might make, too. Yet, fearful of missing anything said, he very carefully kneeled and placed his ear to the flooring to listen.

"Are there any Englishmen in your house?" he heard one of the Indians ask.

Langlade's reply was calm and pleasant. He knew he had nothing to fear from these warriors. Was not his own mother a Chippewa? And his wife? Had not he himself led these very warriors into battle two or three times before when they had offered the strength of their arms to the great French general, the Marquis de Montcalm, before his untimely death at the battle for Quebec?

"I can not say," he replied. "I do not know of any. Take a look around and see, if you like."

"We will," the Indian told him and then added, to his companions, "Look everywhere."

As he heard them beginning their room-by-room search, Henry could feel a rivulet of perspiration run along the hollow of his breastbone and he looked around himself carefully. His eyes had adjusted to the darkness and he could now see surprisingly well, but there was no place to hide which looked reasonably safe. His dark clothing might help conceal him but, except for two trunks, there was nothing big enough to get into or behind. He stepped quietly to the trunks, which stood together in the middle of the floor and tried to lift the lids. They were locked. Frantically his eyes swept his prison. No place else to hide, unless . . . that mound of birchbark vessels! Swiftly but very quietly he began moving toward them. When he was opposite the stairwell he heard someone grasp and rattle the door handle.

"Locked," came Langlade's voice faintly. "This leads to the garret. Wait. I'll get a key."

Again Henry moved quietly, slipping to the back side of the waist-high mound of vessels. On his stomach, then, he began to burrow his way in, gently thrusting the containers aside and little by little getting under the pile, dreading the possibility of the whole mound shifting and some of them falling, even if the noise would be slight. He was only halfway under when he heard the key turn in the lock and the door open. Immediately they started up the stairs.

With a desperate gamble that they wouldn't topple, Henry drew himself up in inchworm fashion. His feet and lower legs were still sticking out, but there was no help for it; he dared not move anymore. The movement just made had already caused a small sound, but fortunately it was lost in the louder noise of the men coming up. Now, through a cup-sized gap in the vessels in front of him, he could see the stairwell clearly, and the men as they reached the top. Langlade was in the lead and he was followed by four Indians—a Sac and three Chippewas—all of them clad only in loincloth and each with tomahawk in hand.

The four spread out at once, moving among the trunks and clutter, poking into every dark corner, moving things, occasionally making guttural comments. Though he knew their eyes were not yet accustomed to the darkness, still Henry was sure he would be seen. Langlade, who had remained at the head of the stairwell, abruptly said in Chippewa: "You see? There is no one. I would have known it had any Englishman come up here. How many are missing?"

"No soldiers missing," one of the Chippewas replied, "only three traders. We have killed many soldiers and we will kill the three traders when we find them. One trader we have already killed, and eighteen soldiers. All the rest are prisoners except the three traders and we will find them."

Several times already one or another of the Indians had come past the mound of birchbark vessels and Henry could see their legs and tomahawks were darkly spattered and streaked, apparently by blood. Now one of the warriors stopped beside the pile and shoved at it with his bare foot. He was so close that if he had stooped, he could have placed his hand upon Alexander Henry's head. The trader was virtually positive that the thudding of his heart would be heard. In a moment, however, the Indian moved away and then all five men were going down the stairs. The door was closed and locked again and at that sound a deep, shuddering exhalation puffed from Henry's mouth. His clothing was drenched with perspiration.

The house became quiet. So quiet, in fact, that Henry was sure the Langlade family must have gone outside with the Indians. Carefully he eased his way backward out of the mound and returned to the front chinking holes. Except for a handful of Indians and groups of Frenchmen milling around—he saw Charles Langlade with one of them—and three bodies from which the heads and one or more of the limbs had been hacked, he could not determine what was happening now. As he watched, those three remaining mangled bodies were dragged toward the gate and passed out of sight.

Incredibly, less than an hour had gone by since the attack began. It was not yet one o'clock in the afternoon, but still an enormous weariness settled over the young trader. It was due, he knew, to shock and fear and the intense emotional strain he had experienced and was still suffering and he tried to shake it off, but could not. At length he abandoned the chinking hole and returned to where the rumpled feather-bedding lay on the floor near the stairwell.

He sat down on it and thought fleetingly about the signs he had ignored which had resulted in his being in such a sorry fix. *This* was the reason why Wawatam had come to him, why he had acted so queerly, why he and Oghqua had begged him to go away with them, even to the point of weeping. Henry shook his head foggily at his own stupidity for failing to comprehend and then lay back on the bedding. He tried to think, but couldn't concentrate. He didn't know what would happen now and didn't even want to guess. He had no plan, no idea, nothing. His mind seemed a vacuum and his eyes closed.

Amazingly, he slept.

It was so dark when Henry awakened that he thought night had come. Actually it was dusk, but heavy clouds had come up, darkening the sky, and now a steady rainfall was drumming on the roof of Charles Langlade's house.

It took a second or so for him to realize that it was the opening of the attic door which had awakened him and that someone was already on the way up. There was no possibility of hiding again and so Henry merely stood and watched the rectangle of light in the stairwell grow brighter as the lantern-carrying person neared the top.

It was Madame Langlade, the lantern in one hand and a small basin in the other. She did not see him until she reached the top and then, when she did, she started so badly that Henry thought she was going to fall backwards down the stairs.

"Madame," he whispered, "please don't be frightened. I hid here from the Indians. I beg you, don't give me away."

"I . . . came to fix a leak," she said, her voice high-pitched with lingering fear. "Don't be uneasy. They are no longer my people. I won't tell them you are here. It has been terrible. They have killed so many! They will kill you if they can find you, but the worst is past and perhaps now you may escape with your life."

She held the lantern out, noted a puddle on the floor where the roof was leaking and set the basin down to catch the water. When she straightened again she repeated, "No, have no fear. I won't tell them."

"What has happened since the attack?" he asked.

She rolled her eyes. "Thirteen soldiers were killed at once, mostly near the gate. Five others were chased down or found in hiding, and they were killed also. Eighteen soldiers killed and Monsieur Tracy. All the rest captured—all but you. They have all the Englishmen, traders and soldiers both, at the house of the priest, Father de Jaunay. All afternoon they plundered. Everything in the fort and everything in your store and house and the stores and houses of the other traders—all has been taken. Now they are drinking. They found much liquor and they are getting drunk. That is why the prisoners were put in the priest's house, so that he can turn away any drunk Indians who might try to take them. It is a bad time. A bad time."

"The officers?" Henry asked.

"Yes, they are there, too, but they would not be except for my Charles. The Indians came here to search after you left. It is a good thing you were not up here then, or they would have found you. But my Charles, he went with them to their camp where the two officers were tied and he found the Indians trying to decide in what manner they would kill them, but in the name of the friendship that he has had for them for so many years, he made them promise not to harm them. He told them that if things went badly in this war—did you know Detroit is surrounded and Fort Sandusky and others taken?—that if things went badly, they might find the officers of great value in bargaining."

Henry was shocked. Detroit! Sandusky! Others! Then it was an all-out war and not just an uprising here at Michilimackinac. He groaned.

"I must go down," Madame Langlade told him.

"Madame," he said quickly, "can you send some water to drink? I am very thirsty."

She bobbed her head. "I will send some, but I will not come back up here tonight. Tomorrow, perhaps, I will come again. Adieu."

Three minutes after she had gone the door opened softly again and the Pawnee girl came up hesitantly in the darkness carrying a jug filled with water. He reached out and touched her and felt her start and suck in her breath, then relax. He took the vessel from her and put his hand on her arm and squeezed gently.

"*Merci*," he whispered.

"*Oui*," she whispered back, and then she was gone.

He heard the door click quietly and the key turn and then he drank deeply, greedily. He was so thirsty! And now he was realizing that he was hungry, too, and he wished he had asked for food as well. He sat back down on the bedding and tried to think. If only he had agreed to go with Wawatam! Now what should he do? Where could he go from here? Montreal? Too far, too hazardous a journey. Detroit? Under attack, and even if he could get into the place, he doubted his ability to travel through nearly four hundred miles of wilderness peopled with hostile Indians. Where then? Stay here? No, that was just as bad. Sooner or later he would be found.

Jean Cadotte's house at the Sault? No, not with Cadotte's house right beside a Chippewa village. But where? *Where?* He *had* to get away to somewhere, but he didn't know how ... or when ... or where.

He drank again, set the jug aside and lay back down. The rain continued drumming on the roof and dripping into the basin and within minutes he was once again asleep.

[*June 3, 1763—Friday,* 10:00 A.M.]

For many months the commander of Fort Bedford[101] had been expecting Indian trouble. Now that it had apparently arrived, Captain Louis Ourry[102] was neither surprised nor greatly concerned for his fortification. Even though this fort, along with Fort Ligonier[103] was one of the most advanced and exposed of the chain of small forts between Philadelphia and Fort Pitt, it was nevertheless sturdy and quite defensible. What concerned Ourry considerably, however, was the terror running rampant in this country, against which the settlers were essentially defenseless. If one were to believe the rumors—and there was every reason to, the way things looked—then already scores of them had been driven from their homes or massacred, their cabins burned, cattle slaughtered, possessions lost. And the result was that now there was a veritable flow of refugees coming to this fort for sanctuary; far more of them than provisions were adequate for maintaining.

None of these forts, despite the faith of the settlers in them, were above being attacked. Several half-hearted attempts, quickly beaten off, had already been made against this very fort and Ourry knew as well, from dispatches sent by Lieutenant Archibald Blane, commander of Fort Ligonier, that it had been hit as well. Even Captain Ecuyer at Fort Pitt had reported several minor attacks thus far and gave the prediction that these were just preliminaries and that tougher onslaughts would be forthcoming. How the forts to the north of Pittsburgh were doing—Venango, Le Boeuf and Presque Isle—was anyone's guess right now, and Ourry shook his head gloomily when he thought about what must be happening at the far western posts, of which Detroit was the hub.

Lieutenant Blane, judging by the tenor of his messages, was badly worried. His garrison at Fort Ligonier was quite small and not terribly well equipped. Ecuyer, on the other hand, had a garrison of three hundred and thirty soldiers and could tap, from adjacent Pittsburgh, scores of traders and backwoodsmen. The only drawback was that he probably also had well over two hundred women and children in Pittsburgh and the fort, mainly soldiers' dependents and the families of settlers.

That same problem here was giving Ourry his own private little hell. What was he going to do with all these refugees? They certainly couldn't stay here indefinitely. His supplies were vital for maintaining his own garrison and holding this post. How could he be expected to protect, feed and house an additional two or three hundred civilians? He had all but ordered them to return to the east until the present trouble was settled but, except for a very few, they were not so inclined.

Actually, many of them were really not so terribly alarmed right now as they had been on first arriving. Already there was talk among them that if no more attacks came during the next few days, they would probably go back to their cabins—or go back to where they had been, if they were burned, and rebuild. Still, the fact remained that they were here, demanding protection as their right and, until orders to the contrary came, he was duty bound to provide it.

Like everyone else, Captain Ourry hoped that yesterday's very brief hit-and-run attack on the fort by a small Indian war party signified the ending of the trouble. They were Delawares and Shawnees who had first appeared from the west, struck at the fort very ineffectually and then quickly fled back to the west again. This, so the rumor went, had all the earmarks of being a last defiant gesture on the Indians' part before heading home. But though he hoped the story was true, he strongly doubted it. If another body of Indians should attack in force, he could envision severe problems. With its extra burden of people, the fort just couldn't withstand any sort of protracted siege.

Thinking again of that attack yesterday, he decided that those Indians must have been the same party that had hit Fort Ligonier earlier. On the desk before Ourry right now was the latest express from Lieutenant Blane for Colonel Bouquet. Blane had requested that Ourry read it and then relay it at once to Philadelphia along with whatever comments he might wish to add. The captain picked it up and read it again:

Sir: Thursday last my garrison was attacked by a body of Indians about five in the morning; but as they only fired upon us from the skirt of the woods, I contented myself with giving them three cheers, without spending a single shot on them. But as they still continued their popping on the side

*next the town, I sent the Sergeant of the Royal Americans
with a proper detachment to fire the houses, which effectually
disappointed them in their plans.*

Captain Ourry took up his pen and on a new sheet he
brought Bouquet up to date on what had happened here at
Fort Bedford and the steps being taken to preserve and protect both the garrison and its refugees. Then he added:

*No less than ninety-three families are now come in here
for refuge, and more hourly arriving. I expect ten more before night. Most of the men and older boys who have come I
have formed into militia companies. My returns amount already to 155 men. My regulars are increased by expresses,
&c., to three corporals and nine privates; no despicable garrison!*

He paused, wondering if he should complain about the
drain the refugees were making on his supplies, then decided
against it. It was possible that the whole problem was a temporary one and there was no sense in getting too quickly
alarmed. If matters persisted, he could advise his commander
in a later message.

He added a few more details, folded and wax-sealed both
his own letter and that of Blane's and was already calling for
an express to be readied as he slipped the dispatches into a
pouch.

[June 3, 1763—Friday, Noon]

His handsome young face set in unhappy lines, Ensign John
Christie walked about within the confines of Fort Presque Isle
and studied the installation's defenses with a new perspective.
Around him his garrison worked silently, grimly, a decided
aura of fear enveloping them. The young officer, too, felt the
continuing churn of his stomach and the sour taste in his
throat which had been instilled by this morning's early arrival
of Lieutenant Abraham Cuyler and the gaunt survivors of his
supply convoy. As Cuyler had told about the attack, the pursuit, the flight across the lake, the finding of Fort Sandusky in
ashes and the subsequent retreat to this place, the sick feeling
had grown within Christie.

Now the commander of Fort Presque Isle shook his head
as he reviewed the situation in the light of Cuyler's incredible
report. It was reasonable to assume, under the circumstances,

that this place also would soon be attacked, and very likely Fort Le Boeuf and Fort Venango as well.[104] Could any of them hold out? Christie knew too little about the defenses of those two smaller forts to judge accurately, but he doubted it. He did know that Presque Isle was the strongest by far of the three and yet he worried about his own ability to stand in the face of a concerted attack. He also knew that it was his responsibility to try and he was determined to do so, which was why he had immediately set his men to seeing to the defense of the place.

Ever since the time Colonel Bouquet had been in command here and improved the then-faulty defenses, it was assumed that Presque Isle could withstand almost any attack, but now John Christie was not so sure. Granted, the blockhouse *was* very strong and supposedly impregnable to Indian attack. Constructed of massive logs, it stood at an angle of the fort's stockade walls. The upper story of it projected so that defenders could fire almost vertically, if need be, upon the heads of attackers through gunports in the floor as well as in the walls. It also had a sort of bastion from which two of its out-facing walls could be covered by a flanking fire. True, the roof was shingled and might possibly be set afire, but there was also a sentry's lookout box up there with a supply of water which could be thrown on any blaze started. The lake was on one side and a small stream on the other, but there was a flaw here in the defenses which Christie recognized but was powerless to correct; the bank of that stream rose in a high steep ridge within forty yards of the blockhouse and there was a similar bank at the lakeshore. Both these places could afford assailants ideal cover from the fort's fire.

Again Christie studied the activities of his men. Counting himself, he had a garrison of twenty-one soldiers. It wasn't much and he was glad that Cuyler had agreed to leave six of his men here when he left for Fort Niagara tomorrow. That would jack his total manpower to twenty-seven, but ammunition was far from adequate and they'd soon go through it all if attack came, and then where would they be? He sighed, unwilling to dwell on such an eventuality.

Ensign Christie was not an engineer but he had a good eye for what needed to be done and his gaze now flicked approvingly across his working men. The doors of the blockhouse and the sentry box at the top were being lined to make them bulletproof; the roof was being covered with sod to help make it more impervious to fire arrows. Even with that he was not satisfied and had ordered gutters of bark to be fashioned so that water could be directed down them to any part of the roof from the sentry box to douse fires. He doubted very much that the blockhouse could now be set afire, but he still had strong reservations about the other outbuildings of the fort. It was for this reason that one of his first orders of the day had been for everyone in the fort to move inside the blockhouse.

It was important, too, that Forts Le Boeuf and Venango be warned and so now Christie returned to his own quarters and began hastily writing letters. One would be sent by express immediately, via Fort Le Boeuf where Ensign George Price was commanding, to their immediate superior, Lieutenant Francis Gordon who was commanding at Fort Venango. The other would be carried to Major John Wilkins at Fort Niagara by Lieutenant Cuyler when he left for that place in the morning.

It was on the letter to Gordon that Christie concentrated first, writing:

> *Presqu' Isle*
> *3rd June 1763*
>
> Sir,
>
> *This morning Lieut. Cuyler of the Queen's Company of Rangers came here and gave me the following melancholy account of his whole party being cut off by a large body of Indians near the mouth of the Detroit River the 28th of May . . .*

Briefly but thoroughly he reported what Cuyler had told him of the attack, the losses, Fort Sandusky's destruction and other details up to the point where the survivors had reached Fort Presque Isle early this morning. Then he concluded:

> *He is to return to Niagara tomorrow with the two batteaux he has saved and the remainder of his command. I have sent to Niagara a letter to the Major desiring some more ammunition and provisions and have kept six men of Lieut. Cuyler's as I expect a visit from the Hell-hounds. I have ordered everybody here to move into the blockhouse and shall be ready for them, come when they will.*
>
> *I am, Sir,*
>
> > *Your very humble Servant*
> > *John Christie*
>
> To Lieut. Gordon

It was midafternoon when the Indian runner came panting out of the woods from the northeast and padded into the principal northern Ottawa village of L'Arbre Croche. When he first came into view the scene was a normal one—men moving about casually seeing to their nets and fish spears, women cleaning and drying on great long wooden racks the abundant catch of whitefish, children and dogs racing about intent on their games and fun. But the normal activity ceased at the appearance of the runner and by the time he had reached the longhouse dwelling place of Chief Mackinac, he was being followed by a considerable crowd.

In matters of everyday discourse, it was improper to plunge into immediate council without first observing the amenities—the silent sitting and smoking of pipes, the partaking of food and drink, the expressions of good health and happiness and full bellies. But on occasions where it was a matter of urgency, proper procedure was cast aside. There was little doubt that such would be the case now, though the decision on that score would be Chief Mackinac's.

The runner disappeared into Mackinac's lodge and was gone from view only a matter of minutes when a warrior came out and sounded the eerie, high-pitched wail which called the chiefs and subchiefs to assemble at once. Within a quarter hour of the runner's arrival in the village, all the Ottawa chiefs and subchiefs were assembled with Chief Mackinac and listening with great surprise to the account of yesterday's completely successful attack and taking of Fort Michilimackinac by the Chippewas, aided by the Sacs. An outrage blossomed and grew in them as the story was told and when the runner finished, Mackinac stood and addressed his chiefs:

"We have long known that a time would come when a rising would be made against the English. Word has already come to us that Pontiac has struck at Detroit and that several other forts of the English have fallen. But," the anger and bitterness became very evident now, "when attack was to be made here in our country, it was to be made by *our* direction and none other. By this act of moving alone against the English, aided only by the Sacs, our neighbors, the Chippewas have insulted us. They have also cheated us by their act of

368

having taken for themselves all that the English had there, leaving nothing for us, which it was our right to have."

His glare swept the small assemblage and fastened on the tall, brawny figure of the second chief of this village, Chief Okinochumake, at whom he pointed.

"Okinochumake, you will pick your men and prepare them, having them see to their weapons. Leave only twenty men here. The rest are to go with you tomorrow when the sun is straight up. You will go to Michilimackinac and you will confront Chief Minivavana. You will demand in my name, in the very strongest of terms, that those goods and English captives be turned over to us which it would have been our share to have had if we participated in the attack. If they are not given willingly, then they are to be taken by force."

The eyes of Chief Okinochumake glittered malevolently as he nodded and the council broke up at once.

[June 3, 1763—Friday, 4:00 P.M.]

The express from Ensign John Christie at Fort Presque Isle to Lieutenant Francis Gordon at Fort Venango had arrived at Fort Le Boeuf only a few minutes ago. Already the entire garrison of fifteen men under Ensign George Price was teetering on the thin edge of panic. There was not a man among them who didn't realize that Le Boeuf was undoubtedly one of the weakest of the frontier posts and that against a strong attack it would have virtually no chance at all. It was only through showing firmness and strength that Price was able to keep them under control. As Christie had done, he immediately ordered an improvement of the defenses, such as they were.

With a sense of despair he read Christie's dispatch through a second time, swiftly wrote a note of his own and re-enclosed the messages in the pouch. He returned it to the express.

"I suppose you realize there's no time to waste," he said. "Get going at once for Venango and make sure these are delivered into the hands of Lieutenant Gordon and no one else. He'll undoubtedly dispatch his own express from there to Pitt."

The messenger nodded, saluted, and turned to go but stopped as Price raised a hand. "And, Private," the Le Boeuf commander added sternly, "don't make the mistake that you did here. You've just about thrown this place into a panic.

When you get to Venango, keep your mouth shut about what's going on until you are in private with the lieutenant. He'll inform his men soon enough and in his own way, without any help from you. That's an order!"

The private flushed, nodded again and raced out of the room. Within one minute he had left Fort Le Boeuf behind and was on the makeshift road to Fort Venango.

It was the murmur of voices from somewhere down below which awakened Alexander Henry in the garret of Charles Langlade's house. The words were indistinct and even though he held his breath and placed his ear to the floor in an effort to hear what was being said, it was to no avail. The talkers were apparently in a distant room downstairs rather than the main room directly beneath him, because he could clearly hear the chimes of the dainty clock on the Langlade's front room mantel striking ten.

Henry lay back down on the bedding and stared unseeingly upward, wide awake now. Ten o'clock at night already! He shivered a little as he recalled the events of the day, marveling that he was still alive in view of what had happened. The whole thing seemed like some monstrous nightmare and if he were not at this moment dispossessed of his coat and shirt, he thought he might have imagined the whole thing.

Throughout the previous night, after the departure of Madame Langlade and the Pawnee woman, he had slept undisturbed up here and at dawn he had awakened and spent the first half hour peering through the chinking holes to see what was occurring below. Strangely, there was hardly a person to be seen; a Frenchman here or there, but no Indians whatever. Apparently they had retired to their village to spend the rainy night and Henry had felt a sudden resurgence of hope that he might escape after all, though he still had no idea of how, nor where he could head to if he did manage to get away.

At the rising of the sun he had heard the Langlade family below beginning to stir. He wondered if Madame Langlade had told her husband of his presence here in the attic, but then shook his head. It wasn't likely or Charles Langlade would probably have come up to see him. But how long could he remain hidden like this?

Not five minutes more passed when there came to him the sound of Indian voices speaking in the Chippewa and, from the amount of slurring of words, he was sure they were drunk. Carefully, cautious against making the slightest suggestion of sound, Henry stretched out on his stomach on the floor, pressed an ear to the planking and listened. There was the sound of the front door being opened and Langlade greeting them, but their response was surly.

"We have found all but one of the English," one of them said. "All but the trader Henry who lives in the house next to yours. We have looked at all the bodies and he is not among them, and so he must be hidden. We wish to have him. Your place is close to his, so maybe he has come here for safety."

"I have not given him refuge," Langlade replied in the Indian tongue. "I know the man you mean, but I have not seen him."

Almost at once the nearly hysterical voice of Madame Langlade came in a harsh whisper, speaking in French.

"Charles! You know he is up there! You can't let him stay there any longer. Give him up to them. My God, Charles, if you don't and they find him, what will they do to us? Listen to me; I know them! Suppose they decide to make an example of us and take out their revenge on the children?"

"No," Langlade replied, also in French, "we cannot just give him to them to be killed. He—"

"Charles, stop! I won't hear it! He is not our concern, can't you understand that? We didn't invite him here. We owe him nothing. Better he should die than our own children. Turn him over to them. I swear to you, Charles, if you don't, I will!"

Henry felt his heart pounding heavily as he listened and, after a momentary pause he heard Langlade again, addressing the Indians.

"I am told," he said wearily, "that the man Henry is in this house, hidden in the garret. He has come here without my knowledge and I will give him to you. Come."

The trader heard the sounds of their footsteps leaving the room and then soon the rattle of the garret door being unlocked and opened. He stood up slowly, facing the stairwell. It was over. There was nowhere to go, no hiding place, no way out. His last moments had come and he determined to meet his end calmly.

Langlade came up the stairs first. In the dimness of the filtered garret light, Henry could see that the Frenchman was glaring angrily at him. The Indians were right behind him, six of them, led by a Chippewa whom Henry recognized in spite of his distorted appearance, a subchief named Wenniway. As

Langlade reached the top of the stairs and stepped out of the way, Wenniway came charging at Henry, a large skinning knife clenched in his right hand. Even without the knife he would have been frightening. He was naked except for a loin-cloth and his face and body had been heavily smeared with a foul black coating of charcoal powder mixed with grease. Only at his eyes was there any difference; each eye was the center of a circle two inches in diameter of pasty white paint. He looked absolutely hideous. Little wonder that Madame Langlade had been frightened.

In two great bounds the Chippewa reached Henry and bunched into his left fist the throat of Henry's coat and shirt, forcing the trader's head backwards. He raised the knife to plunge it home and then paused in this position, his gaze locked on Henry's widely staring eyes. For a fragile moment they stood like this, Henry unresisting and awaiting only the thrust which would kill him. But then, incredibly, Wenniway's knife arm dropped and he released his hold on the garments.

"I won't kill you," he said. "I have often fought against the English and killed many who could have killed me, but never one who stood unarmed before me. The English in battle killed my only brother, Musinigon, but I will not kill you. I will take you under my wing and call you after his name. To me, you are now Musinigon and under my protection. Now you will come with me to our village. I will keep you there in my house."

Hardly daring to believe he had been reprieved and trembling very badly, Henry moved as directed down the stairs. But they were not yet to the front door when the fear began building in him again and he turned and spoke imploringly to both Wenniway and Langlade.

"The Indians have had so much liquor," he said, "that they will be crazy with it. If you take me to the village, they will take me from you and kill me. I know it. Monsieur Langlade, I beg you, tell him that this is what will happen. Allow me to stay here, please!"

Langlade nodded with surprising sympathy and said to Wenniway, "He is right. You would not be able to prevent his being killed if you took him there. If you will leave him here, I will see that he remains here for you."

Wenniway considered this for a moment and then he too nodded. To Henry he said, "You will stay up where I found you, until I can find a better time to come and take you away with me."

In a daze, Henry was returned to the garret and locked in

once more. His haven was now a prison, his presence known and he had no idea what to expect next, but he *was* alive. He sat down on the bedding and buried his face in his hands and for a long while was overcome with great shuddering sobs.

He was still in the same position just over an hour later when the door was suddenly unlocked and opened and the voice of Charles Langlade came up to him.

"Monsieur Henry, come down here!"

The young trader did as bidden and found that another Chippewa whom he recognized was in the house. It was Owl, the warrior who had so often bought from him on credit and then had refused to pay and even threatened him when he asked for payment.

"You come with me," Owl said. "Wenniway has sent me to fetch you to him."

"Monsieur Langlade," Henry protested, once more afraid, "I don't think that's true. I think he means to kill me. Keep me here!"

Langlade shook his head. "You are no longer your own master, Monsieur Henry. You must do as you are ordered to do."

At that, Owl grinned. "Take off your clothes," he demanded. "They will look better on me than on you."

Helpless to resist, Henry did so, handing the removed apparel to Owl. The Indian removed his own loincloth, filthy with grease and bloodstains, and gave it to Henry to wear if he chose to. It was either wear the cloth or go out naked, so Henry put it on and watched as Owl shrugged into the European clothing. Henry was becoming increasingly alarmed and he addressed Langlade again.

"Monsieur Langlade, can't you see what he's doing? He wanted the clothes off me so they would not get bloodstained when he kills me. For the love of God, sir, please keep me here."

The Frenchman shook his head. "You are ordered to go. I can do nothing."

At a motion from Owl, Henry went out the door and, with the Chippewa just a little behind him and to one side, proceeded across the parade ground to the gate and then outside. Automatically he turned in the direction of the Chippewa village, but Owl snatched at his arm and jerked him savagely around and thrust him in the other direction toward a cluster of bush-cloaked sand dunes. They were not quite there when Henry stopped and faced Owl.

"I'm not going any farther," he said flatly. "I think you intend to kill me and if so, you might as well do it here in the open."

Owl nodded and withdrew a knife he had put into the waistband of the trousers he was now wearing. "You are right," he said, grinning. "You remember I said long ago I would pay you for the goods? Now I will make that payment."

Still holding Henry's arm with his left hand, he drew the knife back, but this time the trader did not stand calmly. With a violent jerk he pulled himself free of the grasp and then shoved the Indian hard, sending him staggering backward and almost falling. Henry raced off toward the fort and Owl came close on his heels, shrieking and waving the knife.

Maintaining the gap between them, Henry sped into the fort and there he saw Wenniway in the midst of the parade ground talking with a Frenchman and two other Indians. He ran toward him. Wenniway watched them come and called to Owl to stop, but made no move against the warrior when he refused. For a moment it was like something out of a comic play, with Henry running in circles around Wenniway's group and Owl chasing him, brandishing the knife and spitting out flecks of foam in rage. At last, seeing that the door to Langlade's house was open, Henry sprinted for it and ran inside. Owl chased him that far, but stopped at the door at a barked command from Wenniway. There was no mistaking the menace in the subchief's voice this time. In a surly manner, Owl put the knife away and walked out of the fort, still muttering.

Henry allowed Langlade to lead him back to the garret once more, where he threw himself down on the bedding and gradually his breathing came back under control. He lay on his back and stared up at the roofing timbers and then, after a long while, he whispered aloud:

"God, I think you're overruling these Indians. I don't think you're going to let me be killed by them, no matter what. God . . . thank you."

He closed his eyes and that was all he remembered until a few moments ago when he awoke to the murmured voices below and the sound of the clock striking ten. Still he could not hear what was being said down there or identify the voices, but the enigma was solved for him. Langlade called him to descend again.

In this utter darkness he felt his way carefully to the stairwell and came down again, momentarily blinking against the light of the three lanterns in the kitchen, to which he was led. There, sitting around the table, were four more men—Captain Etherington, Lieutenant Leslye, Henry Bostwick, and the Jesuit, Father de Jaunay. Henry's relief at seeing them was so great that he could not speak and tears slid silently down his cheeks. Langlade left the room, saying he would see about some food.

The two officers and the trader Bostwick, like Henry, were all clad in Indian garb, their own clothing having been taken from them. George Etherington filled Henry in on the details of what had happened since they were captured—how first they had been taken to the woods and then to the Chippewa village; then, after the Indians and some of the French had plundered the English goods, how the Indians had returned and had begun drinking heavily. Chief Minivavana, knowing the prisoners would be killed if kept in the village when the Indians became roaring drunk, had ordered them taken to the residence of the priest where the fifteen captive privates, along with the trader Solomon and the drifter Samuels, were being sheltered. Then, this evening, having learned of Henry being held in Langlade's garret, the three Englishmen and the priest had come here at Langlade's invitation, where the accommodations would be a little more comfortable. Now, Etherington concluded, the Indians were still working on their consumption of the liquor at their village over a half mile distant and there was no one inside the fort except the French and themselves.

"Then, Captain," Henry said, standing up, "I think it's time we took some definite action. With no Indians inside, not even guards on us, there's no reason at all why we couldn't just close and lock the gates, repossess the fort and maintain it against them until some reinforcements come."

Bostwick nodded and Lieutenant William Leslye added his voice to Henry's in approval of the idea. Etherington, however, was shaking his head all the while and Henry slapped his hands to his sides in exasperation.

"But why not, Captain?" He was surprised and not a little angry. "We still have fifteen privates over at Father de Jaunay's house, plus us here, plus Zeke Solomon and that fellow Samuels. That makes a total of twenty-one men. Surely we can find enough guns and powder, and the artillery's still on the ramparts. Why not?"

"Because it would be stupid," Etherington replied mildly. "The Indians have plundered everything and what they haven't got their hands on, some of these French have taken. I saw our gallant interpreter, Farli, for example, plundering English goods with every bit as much enthusiasm as the Indians, and he wasn't the only one. The Indians have about fifty barrels of powder, and lead in proportion, from our stores. Just how could we possibly hold out against them? It would be idiocy to try. Look," he added reasonably, "we who are still alive stand a relatively good chance of staying alive if we don't rile them. But just as sure as we start getting ideas, we'll eliminate our chances."

The Jesuit de Jaunay nodded in agreement. "The captain is right," he said. "It is a sad thing, but he is right. Yes, you could close the fort and perhaps hold it for a little while, but there are many Frenchmen here who do not like the English—who have *never* liked the English—and who would think nothing of opening the gates to the Indians again. Then they would surely kill you. No, I think our commander is right. Wait and see what happens."

In the silence which followed this, Langlade came back into the room, saying, "The food will be here in a moment, gentlemen. I know all of you must be very hungry."

"Monsieur Langlade," Etherington said, "for all of us, I thank you. I don't know what will happen now, but whatever it will be, there is no doubt in my mind that His Majesty will soon reclaim possession of this fort. In the interim, however, I would like you to accept temporary command of the place, to be in charge of all affairs until the situation is resolved. Will you do this?"

Langlade shrugged. "I will do what I can."

Etherington nodded, satisfied. "It is all I ask."

Now the Pawnee housegirl belonging to Langlade came in. She was carrying a large tray upon which was heaped smoked fish, bread and wine. The sight and smell of it was almost overwhelming to these men who had not seen food for so long and without further discussion they fell upon it. When it was all gone and their appetites sated, the two officers and two traders were led back to the garret and locked into it by Langlade, who apologized for having to do so. In the light of a single fat candle given to them by the Frenchman, they talked until long after midnight of their individual experiences in this incident, but not again was the idea to retake the fort discussed.

What would be, would be.

[*June 4, 1763—Saturday*]

Alexander Henry was jerked erect by his name being called loudly. In the darkness he could hear the other prisoners stirring near him. The call came again and he recognized the voice of Charles Langlade, ordering him to come downstairs.

Still drugged with sleep, Henry felt his way to the stairs and descended, unable to comprehend why he was being summoned. At the bottom he found out. Wenniway was there, waiting for him.

"Musinigon you were," the Chippewa told the trader, "but Musinigon you are no longer. You follow me."

Langlade had relocked the garret door and now he followed the pair to the front door of the house and let them out. The door closed and as the bolt slid behind the Indian and trader, all of Henry's apprehensions returned in a rush. The ominous ring of Wenniway's words had finally penetrated.

In the first faint light of the dawn, Wenniway directed Henry to a small house and ordered him to enter a narrow dark room there. Here he found himself in the company of his fellow trader, Ezekiel Solomon, the English drifter named Samuels, and a private who said his name was Robert Wayne. They, too, had been brought here only a short while before, but no one knew why and all were frightened.

For several hours they remained here and then the door was unbarred and opened by an unfamiliar Indian. He addressed them in broken English.

"English come. Follow. Come."

The four men left the room and followed the Indian out of the fort to the shore of the Strait. Here a canoe, laden with plunder, was waiting and they were told to enter it, sit down and man paddles. Private Wayne had a rawhide rope placed around his neck and tied to a cross-member of the canoe, but the others remained untied. In a little while seven Indians had gathered and now the canoe was pushed off. Four of the seven Indians manned paddles and the prisoners were ordered to stroke in time with them. They were all Chippewas, though Henry did not recognize any of them. The canoe headed due west.

"Where are you taking us?" he asked in Chippewa.

The Indian who was apparently the leader of this group grinned. He was obviously pleased to find that Henry could speak the language.

"You are our share," he said. "We are taking you to the Beaver Islands, where you will be safe."

At this remark the other Indians in the canoe burst into harsh laughter, but when Henry tried to ask another question he was thumped painfully in the back with a tomahawk handle and told to paddle, not talk.

It was a gray day with a clammy northeast breeze and before they had been gone two hours a fog began rolling in, first shutting away from view the far-distant northern shoreline hills and then coming in quickly to blanket them. It became difficult to see more than twenty or thirty yards ahead and the prisoners, clad in practically nothing, were soon shivering and miserable. The canoe hugged the shoreline and every half hour the leader of the party would give vent to a far-carrying whoop, four times in succession. Henry recognized it as the customary cry given to announce to any Indians within hearing that there were four captives aboard.

At one point, when it was nearly noon, Ezekiel Solomon complained that he and the others were hungry and needed food if they were to keep up with the paddling. Henry interpreted and the leader of the Indians nodded and dug into a pack, from which he produced a long loaf of bread and, from his belt sheath, a knife which was literally caked with dried blood. He broke off four small chunks of bread, spat upon the knife blade to moisten the blood, smeared it around and then wiped some of it onto each of the pieces of bread. He tossed them into the canoe at the feet of Solomon and laughed in an ugly way.

"You hungry?" he said in English. "You eat blood of English. Make you strong!"

Again the Indians laughed and the four chunks of bread remained untouched on the canoe floor.

By this time they were approaching Waugoshance Point, about eighteen miles west of Fort Michilimackinac. This was the mouth of Lake Michigan and beyond this point the shoreline they had been following turned south. Dead ahead was the open lake until, twenty miles out, they would encounter the Beaver Islands, or *Iles du Castor* as the French called them. As they neared Waugoshance Point now, the leader again gave his whoop four times repeated. This time it was answered once from shore and a moment later they saw an Ottawa Indian there, gesturing for them to land.

The boat swung toward him and, as they approached, the Ottawa asked what the news was and who these prisoners were. Unsuspecting and filled with pride, the Chippewas boasted of their attack on the fort and its fall, of all the men killed, the plunder and prisoners taken. But as the canoe was just beginning to scrape into the shallows within a few yards of land, there came a fierce screeching and upwards of a hundred Ottawas thundered out of hiding in the bushes on shore, rushed out to the canoe and bodily dragged all four prisoners to shore. Each of the four was sure his last moment had come but, instead, all were stood on their feet and given immediate reassurance by none other than the second chief of L'Arbe Croche.

"You are safe with us for now," Okinochumake announced. "We are your friends. We are Ottawas, who have been insulted by our neighbors the Chippewa, who have destroyed the English without consulting us on the matter."

"They told us," Henry said slowly, not so familiar with the Ottawa dialect but still making a stab at conversation, "that they were taking us to the Beaver Islands where we would be safe."

Okinochumake snorted. "If you believed that, you are a foolish man. I will tell you why they were taking you there. It is where the remainder of their own village people await them and they were going to kill you when they got you there, and then cut you up and boil you into broth and then eat you. That is how safe you would have been! No, we heard them coming with you and we knew what they would do. You are now our prisoners, not theirs, and the goods that they have with them which were taken from the English are ours, not theirs. And there is more, much more, back at Michilimackinac, which is ours, not theirs. We will go back there and see what our neighbors, the Chippewa, will do about this."

Throughout the exchange the seven Chippewas, though at first startled, made no complaint nor offered resistance. They watched calmly as the Ottawas dragged their own canoes out of the bushes and launched them, and obeyed when they were told to head back for Michilimackinac, surrounded by Ottawa canoes. Once again, it seemed, Alexander Henry had been snatched away from an untimely end.

The sun had already set when they got back to the fort and their arrival created a stir. Minivavana's Chippewas were obviously confounded at seeing the Ottawas and learning what they had done. But the Ottawas, except to say they would council with the Chippewas tomorrow, offered no explanation. Boldly, Chief Okinochumake took possession of the fort, lodged the prisoners in the commander's quarters, set a guard up over them and remained silent.

It was, at the very least, a strange situation.

General Jeffrey Amherst was positively sick and tired of North America in general and the native inhabitants in particular. He would have liked nothing more than to be able to board the first ship sailing out of this harbor of New York City and head back for mother England. There, perhaps, he might be given an assignment he considered worthy of his ability, instead of sitting in this distant land listening to his commanders complain. Long before this he had applied for permission to return to London, but the Crown had not yet deigned to give him an answer.

Sitting at his desk now, he stuck a forefinger under the front of his wig, raised it a little and then delicately scratched an itch in the sparse rusty hair which covered his pate. He sighed as he thought of England. How nice it would be to go home again, and how unfair that he was being kept here as commander in chief of His Majesty's forces in North America. There was no good *reason* to keep him here. There hadn't been a military campaign for nearly two years and he was decidedly tired of this continent. Five years was a long time to be in the field and he felt he most assuredly deserved relief. And why not? Hadn't the war been won under his command? Hadn't the peace been signed months ago? Hadn't he taken possession of Canada for His Royal Majesty? Again he sighed.

A light tapping on the door interrupted his thinking and he straightened, tugged his wig into place and then bade the caller to enter. It was his aide, an overeager young captain named James Dalyell.[105] He was a young man who was positively obsessed with the dream of becoming one of the greatest military leaders in history. This could not be done, of course, by acting as a general's aide, but by judiciously hinting now and then of his desire for battle action and a command position, he hoped one day that events might develop which would encourage Amherst to give him what he wanted.

Now, as if sensing he might be the bearer of news toward this end, Captain Dalyell bobbed his head and smiled broadly.

"Dispatches, sir," he said, "from Colonel Bouquet."

He handed two letters to the general, did an about-face and, still smiling, exited precisely and closed the door gently behind him. Amherst smiled slightly himself. He always enjoyed hearing from Bouquet. Swiss or not, he was a good man; as good or better than any commander he had in the field; a man with a level head and a keen mind and a man who was, in every respect, a truly professional soldier. He wished he had more commanders like Bouquet.

Breaking the seals, he found that inside there were four letters. Two of these were short notes from Bouquet and the other two were rather excited letters that Bouquet had received from Captain Simeon Ecuyer, which the Fort Pitt commander had written on May 29 and 30. As he read them, Amherst's lips pinched together and his nostrils began to flare. Ecuyer's first letter told of the first attack of the Indians, which resulted in the killing of four persons. The second letter reported the killing of two men just outside Fort Pitt and details of the attack on the Calhoun party of traders, who had been all but wiped out. Ecuyer also had written that there were unconfirmed reports that Fort Sandusky had been taken and that Detroit itself was under siege. The captain felt certain the uprising was general and that all the western posts were in jeopardy.

With an irritated sound, Amherst dropped the letters onto the desktop and thoughtfully massaged his facial wart. Ecuyer, he knew, was inclined to be gullible and easily frightened. How could he possibly put any credence in such reports? And if there had been a few killings around Fort Pitt, it was probably because some fool had done something to upset the savages and they had struck out in anger. By now they were undoubtedly regretting anything they might have done. The possibility of a general uprising was absolute rubbish and Captain Ecuyer should know better than to spread such tales and get everyone in a lather about it. Admittedly, *something* must have happened around Fort Pitt and just on the chance, however far removed, that it was a prelude to a serious outbreak, he supposed he would have to take some preliminary precautions, but it was irksome to say the least to have to be bothered with things like this.

The reports, if any were to be sent, should have been directed not to him but rather to the Indian supervisor and his assistants. Of course, as Amherst knew, Sir William Johnson was at the seashore in Connecticut at the moment, recuperating from an illness, but there was always Croghan, wasn't there? The Shawnees and Delawares were in his bailiwick anyway. He would have to see to it that the deputy Indian supervisor was notified at once and took some action.

Amherst called in Captain Dalyell and gave orders for Croghan to be notified of the developments outlined by

Ecuyer, and then the general dictated an order to Major John Campbell[106] of the 42nd Regiment. That officer was to assemble the light companies of his own regiment as well as the 17th and 77th and take them over to Staten Island to be held in readiness there should anything serious develop. If it did, they could move at once to Colonel Bouquet at Philadelphia and then on to Fort Pitt under the colonel's command. Dalyell's frost-colored eyes lighted at the thought of serious trouble developing, but he said nothing.

Having taken care of this matter, Amherst directed Dalyell to take down another letter, this one to Colonel Bouquet in reply to the alarming dispatches received today.

Genl. Headqtrs. New York
6 June 1763

Sir,

I am in receipt of your two letters and those inclosed by you in the hand of Captain Ecuyer. I regret that a disturbance of sorts had occurred, but strongly doubt the seriousness of it as so depicted by the Fort Pitt commanding officer. Nevertheless, I have begun inquiry into the matter and have ordered that Mr. Croghan be advised and instigate his own inquiry at once.

I gave immediate orders for completing the light infantry companies of the 17th, 42nd, and 77th Regiments. They are to assemble without loss of time and to encamp on Staten Island, under Major Campbell of the 42nd . . .

Although I have thought proper to assemble this force, which I judge more than sufficient to quell any disturbance the whole Indian strength could raise, yet I am persuaded this alarm will end in nothing more than a rash attempt at what the Senecas have been threatening and which we have heard of for some time past. As to their cutting off defenseless families, or even some of the small posts, it is certainly at all times in their power to effect such enterprises; particularly while we ourselves supply them with powder and lead, as appears from Captain Ecuyer's letter of the 29th May to have been the case with those villains who are suspected to have committed the mischief. The post of Fort Pitt, or any of the others commanded by officers, can certainly never be in danger from such a wretched enemy as the Indians are at this time, if the garrisons do their duty. I am only sorry that when such outrages are committed, the guilty should escape; for I am fully convinced the only true method of treating those savages is to keep them in proper subjection and pun-

ish, without exception, the transgressors . . . As I have no sort of dependence on the Assembly of Pennsylvania, I have taken such measures as will enable me to chastise any nation or tribe of Indians that dare to commit hostilities on his Majesty's subjects. I only wait to hear from you what farther steps the savages have taken; for I still think it cannot be anything general, but the rash attempt of that turbulent tribe, the Senecas, who richly deserve a severe chastisement from our hands, for their treacherous behavior on many occasions.

I am, Sir, Yrs., &c.
Jeffrey Amherst

Colonel Henry Bouquet
Commanding at Philadelphia

[June 6, 1763—Monday, 11:00 A.M.]

For two days the councils had gone on at Michilimackinac between the Ottawas and Chippewas. They were days filled with tension and poorly veiled threat. At times there was the distinct likelihood that there would be a most serious and permanent rupture of relations between these two northern tribes; a rupture which would almost certainly have resulted in war.

The Ottawa, for their part, were deeply disgusted with the Chippewas for taking it upon themselves to attack and take the fort without notifying the Ottawas of their intentions to do so. This they attributed to the Chippewas' greed for the plunder and men captured at the fort.

The Chippewa, on the other hand, objected that the Ottawas had long known an attack was in the offing and that much time had passed while the Chippewa had waited for them to come and join such an attack. When they had not done so, it was assumed that they did not intend to, and so the plan had gone forward. They declared that they had had no intention of trying to cheat the Ottawas out of their just deserts.

It was Chief Okinochumake, who presided at the councils for the Ottawa tribe and Chief Minivavana who spoke for the Chippewa nation. And even though here at Michilimackinac the Chippewas outnumbered the Ottawas considerably, it was clearly evident that they wished no breach to occur between themselves and the Ottawas and that they were, in fact, more than just a little frightened of the latter tribe.

Early in the morning yesterday the council had opened in the council house within the fort. A great heap of plunder had been stacked up on the middle of the floor and beside it were placed Lieutenant William Leslye and two privates, all three of the men looking frightened. Minivavana spoke first and he addressed his remarks to Okinochumaki as if he were the only Ottawa present.

"We are much surprised and saddened," he said carefully, "at the actions of our neighbors from L'Arbre Croche, who have betrayed the common cause and opposed the will of the Great Spirit, who has decreed that every Englishman must die. How is it that the Ottawas take it upon themselves to rob us of our prisoners which we risked our lives to take? How is it that not only those prisoners being taken away by our people were taken away from them by the Ottawa, but that they should be brought back here and then the remaining prisoners still here should also be claimed by the Ottawa? By what right do our neighbors do this to us? We do not understand. Do the Ottawas of L'Arbre Croche not realize that all of the tribes are at war with the English except themselves? Do they not realize that even their war chief to the south, Pontiac, has led an alliance of these tribes against Detroit and has directed the taking of several of the smaller forts already? Yet, is not Pontiac an Ottawa? Does the Ottawa tribe see out of a different eye on each side of its head and hear out of a different ear? How is it that the Ottawa are not one, as it is with all other tribes?"

He paused and then pointed a finger at Okinochumake, and when he spoke again there was almost a righteous whine to the tone of his voice: "Okinochumake comes here to act as the eyes and ears and mouth of the great chief Mackinac, but what have those eyes seen, what have those ears heard, and what now will that mouth say? Do the Ottawa not know that the King of France has awakened himself from his long sleep and taken back to himself his place at Quebec and Montreal? Do the Ottawa not know that the English are meeting destruction, not only here at Michilimackinac but all over this country and in every part of the world? From this, do not we, the Chippewa, have every right to believe that it becomes the responsibility of the Ottawa to return to us the prisoners which they took from us and also to join in the war? We wish no strife with our neighbors from L'Arbre Croche. It is the English who are our enemies, not the Ottawa. Therefore, to the Ottawa we make a present of these goods . . ." he pointed at the heap of plunder ". . . and these men . . ." his finger swung to indicate Leslye and the two soldiers ". . . which it is felt by all of us here is a just share of what has been taken. Now I have spoken and now it is the turn of my ears to hear what the Ottawa will say."

For now, the Ottawa said nothing. It was customary at intertribal councils for no answer to be given until the following day and this was a custom maintained here. But it was considered a definitely ominous sign by the Chippewas when the Ottawas refused to even inspect the pile of plunder and three prisoners.

Early this morning, then, the council had resumed and much time was taken up with pipe-smoking ceremonies and simple silent sitting. But now, at last, Okinochumake arose to speak and his voice was flat and emotionless as he made his reply.

"The Chief of the Chippewas has asked many questions, but they are questions to which he knows the answers. To them all we reply with a question: why is it that the Chippewas took it upon themselves to attack this fort without informing us of their plan and without inviting us to participate? The answer is before our eyes. It is because they wished for themselves all the English goods that were here and all the English soldiers and traders as their own prisoners. Already they have killed more soldiers than are now left alive, and yet they wish to keep those who remain and offer us but three men and a few items to soothe us. This we do not accept! We demand *all* of the prisoners and that portion of the plunder which we, the Ottawas, deem to be our share, and we will not settle for less!"

It was, in effect, the starting point of a bargaining session which lasted throughout the day. The upshot was that a settlement was made and before long the Ottawas were on their way back to L'Arbre Croche with fifteen of the prisoners—Captain Etherington, Lieutenant Leslye, Henry Bostwick, Ezekiel Solomon, and eleven privates.

The remainder—including Alexander Henry—were the property of the Chippewas, to keep or to butcher as they saw fit.

[June 6, 1763—Monday, 3:00 P.M.]

It was a rare thing indeed when the war chief of the Ottawas smiled, but he was smiling now. Pontiac sat in the Potawatomi council house downriver from Detroit, smoking his pipe and listening with pleasure to the assembled Indians continuing to discuss his plan for striking the English schooner *Huron*, still anchored adjacent to the fort.

Not very many days had been good ones for Pontiac lately, but this had been one of the better ones. A great new surge of confidence in him had come as the result of the news which came from four widely separated points. Runners arrived at almost the same time from the south and the east with the stirring news that the Shawnees and Delawares had raised the war hatchet and struck at Fort Pitt and, while they had not taken that place, they had killed several soldiers and a large number of traders and settlers. At the same time it was reported that a party of Mississaugi warriors had captured eleven traders and their three bargeloads of goods at the mouth of the Grand River.[107]

Now, more than at any time before, Pontiac's war strength was solidified. Right here at Detroit he had firmly under his command one hundred and fifty Potawatomies under Chief Ninivois, two hundred and fifty Chippewas from the Saginaw Bay area under Chief Wasson, his own Ottawas to the same number, one hundred and seventy Mississaugis who had been brought here from the south and east of Lake St. Clair by Chief Sekahos and, not even counting the more or less defected Hurons under Chief Teata, fifty warriors of that tribe under Chief Takee, plus whatever number of Wyandot Hurons Chief Odinghquanooron had under his command in the Sandusky Bay area. A total of at least eight hundred and seventy warriors here around Detroit, plus the two hundred and fifty that he had sent against Fort Presque Isle.

In addition, there were a great many anti-English Indians now hovering around Detroit's dependent forts, plus the addition of Delawares and Shawnees and possibly even some of the Iroquois. At a moderate estimate, certainly there were two or three thousand Indians rallying to the cause and more joining it every day. That he was the driving force which had caused this to be was a source of great satisfaction for the Ottawa war chief.

The one great source of frustration, however, was the continued holding-out of Detroit. If that place could be taken, what then could stop the Indians? Yet the fort held on and now, almost a month after the siege was begun, it seemed no nearer capitulation than it had been in the first days. Obviously some of the Frenchmen must be providing them with goods and he determined to put an end to this quickly, for once and all.

There was no doubt, of course, that he could take Detroit by storm. The Indian numbers were far greater than the English under Gladwin and, once inside the walls, the massacre could be completed very speedily. There was, however, more to this than met the eye. In order to take it by storm, many Indian lives would have to be sacrificed and not even Pontiac, farsighted though he was, could bring himself to so singularly break the traditional method of Indian fighting. True, warriors would fight demonically in a surprise attack and they would also allow themselves to suffer severe privation in order to take revenge; but in no case would they even consider undertaking a stratagem which they knew in advance must result in the death of many Indians. The Indian mentality was simply much too individualistic to blandly accept sacrificing a few of their numbers for the sake of many others. Expendability was an unknown term. Therefore, if Detroit was to be taken at all, it would be by the fort capitulating for lack of supplies and reinforcement.

And Pontiac was determined to see this dream become reality.

[June 6, 1763—Monday, 4:00 P.M.]

Though he would never have admitted the fact to anyone, the commander of Fort Niagara was a very frightened man. He was glad that his Iroquois visitors of half an hour ago were gone; they always made him very nervous. Now, for the third time in succession, Major John Wilkins read the report submitted to him by Lieutenant Abraham Cuyler. As he read he belched softly and rubbed his stomach to alleviate the discomfort he felt there, then automatically reached into a drawer of his desk for a paper-wrapped sweet from the box of fudgelike candies he so favored. He paid no attention to the cockroaches which scurried away from this unexpected intrusion.

Having finished his third reading of it, Wilkins folded and sealed the report and then, to enclose with the packet soon to leave here, began his own letter to General Amherst, writing swiftly and with a pleasing but fragile penmanship:

Niagara, 6th June, 1763

Sir:

Just as I was sending off my letter of yesterday, Lieutenant Cuyler of the Queen's Rangers arrived from his intended voyage to the Detroit.[108] *He has been very unfortunate, having been defeated by Indians within 30 miles of the Detroit River, with 56 known dead and 130 barrels of provisions taken. I observed that he was wounded and weak and desired* him to take the surgeon's assistance and some rest and recollect the particulars of the affair and let me have them in writing, as perhaps I should find it necessary to transmit them to your Excellency, which I have now done.

At the same time with the arrival of Lieut. Cuyler came the few survivors of a trading party which left here for the Detroit about a week or so ago, which was attacked by Indians in the vicinity of Grand River. Eleven traders killed and all their goods taken.

Various are the opinions at this place concerning the cause of what has happened; some say the want of ye rum trade, others that a squaw was put to death at the Detroit; others will have it that the French are concerned.

It is probable that your Excellency will have heard of what has happened, by way of Fort Pitt, as Ensign Christie, commanding at Presque Isle, writes me he has sent an express to acquaint the commanding officer at that place of Sandusky's being defeated and of Lieut. Cuyler's defeat.

Some Indians of the Six Nations were just with me. They seemed very civil; the interpreter had told them I was writing to your Excellency for rum, and they were very glad. However, their actions are suspect, as I have it from Mr. DeCouagne here, assistant to Sir William Johnson, that a squaw living with him, who is the daughter of old Betts, had been warned by some Iroquois just leaving Fort Niagara, to go back to her people because they, and all the Indians in America, were just going to war with the English. They further told her, as Mr. DeCouagne relates to me and that she told him in turn, that they have received a belt from the Indians about Pittsburgh to take up the bloody hatchet and that all the surrounding Indians in those parts are absolutely determined thereupon.

You may depend upon me to give you the most timely notice of everything that pertains to his Majesty's service, in the most distinct manner that my capability will permit, & I never shall fail meriting, honored Sir, to be

> Your most humble & faithful servant
> J. Wilkins

To Genl. Sir Jeffrey Amherst
New York

P.S. Your Excellency, the belt received by these Indians here was accompanied by a scalp said to be that of a soldier killed beneath the very wall of Fort Pitt.

The sourness of George Croghan's disposition steadily deepened the farther west he traveled and the more often he heard reports of attacks against individual settlers and frontier outposts.

He had heard, for example, that Colonel Clapham was murdered on the very land that Croghan had sold to him—land in which he and Clapham had entered into sort of a quasi-partnership agreement on. Further, that his own residence up the Allegheny from Fort Pitt—Croghan Hall—was burned; that Forts Pitt and Ligonier and Bedford were being attacked; that the scalping knife was out and already very bloody and that the Indian uprising was a reality.

He was appalled, and the fact that it was no more than he had expected and predicted did not act as a balm. There was a deep anger in him that such incidents had occurred at all, when they could so easily have been prevented. Now only God knew where it would end.

Although the sun was just making its appearance on the eastern horizon, already he was preparing to continue his journey toward Fort Pitt. Before him stretched the broad expanse of the Susquehanna River and, beyond that, a brooding, forested land through which blood had begun to flow and would undoubtedly become a gushing torrent before it could be checked.

Edward Shippen, influential Pennsylvanian and a sometime business associate of Croghan's, stood with him now in the early morning light here at Harris's Ferry.[109] He looked unhappy.

"Be mighty careful, George," he said. "They've only been scattered attacks, but there could be danger for you till it blows over."

"Blows over!" Croghan snorted derisively. "Ed, you still don't see the picture, do you? Believe me, this ain't gonna be no small war. Sure as God made little green apples, it'll be a general war all over the whole frontier and it's gonna involve every western tribe. By damn, I seen it coming a long time ago and it all could've been prevented if a certain great man in New York had heeded my advice and Sir William's. I'll send the high-an'-mighty general another dispatch from Carlisle and this time, by damn, it'll not bear laughing at as usual! There ain't no wind strong enough to make this

389

business blow over. Like it or not, you're seeing the door open to a major uprising."

Croghan left then and Shippen, watching him, shook his head. He didn't want to believe the Indian agent, but he was terribly afraid that George Croghan was absolutely right.

[*June 8, 1763—Wednesday, 7:00* A.M.]

Throughout this whole affair, Alexander Henry had heard some terrible sounds. Nothing, however, had been as ghastly and frightening as the prolonged hideous screams which jolted him out of his sleep this morning. On and on they went, and only after a long while did they degenerate into a blubbering whimper and then silence.

Cautiously, Henry peered out of the doorway while the sounds were at their peak. He felt the hair at his nape prickle and against his will he envisioned in his mind's eye what must be occurring in the lodge nearby which was being used as a prison for the soldiers still in possession of the Chippewas here at Michilimackinac. Henry had moved the animal hide covering the door just a little to one side and, unable to tear himself away, the young trader kept his eye to the small opening he had made. Through it he could see the structure from which the cries were continuing, but for the moment he could see no more. Whatever was happening there, he knew that but for an incredibly fortunate circumstance, his own voice would have been added to that unholy din.

This was the second morning since the Ottawas under Okinochumake had left Michilimackinac after making the settlement with the Chippewas. With a dreadful foreboding, Henry had watched them go, taking with them the fort's officers, most of the soldiers, and the traders Bostwick and Solomon. Their chances with the Ottawas might be no better than his with the Chippewas, but Henry had nearly wept with his desire to be with them.

Instead, he and the man Samuels, along with the four remaining privates, had been retained by the Chippewas and throughout the night they had huddled together, strongly guarded and tied by the neck to the center pole of the lodge. None of them slept and in the morning, yesterday, a council was called by Minivavana. The prisoners had been brought to the council house and ordered to sit, and throughout the morning hours the Indians had talked. Dully, hopelessly, Henry interpreted as best he could for his equally miserable companions. It soon became clear that the matter being so seriously discussed was in what manner all the prisoners should be put to death. To Henry it was like a weird nightmare, sitting here and hearing men discuss his forthcoming death and whether they would burn him, boil him, dismember him or in some other ghoulish way end his life.

At just about noon, however, there was an interruption of the proceedings. Chief Matchekewis, directing his remarks to Minivavana and Wenniway who sat in front, was just finishing expounding on his ideas of how the prisoners should be disposed of, when the council house door flap was opened and in strode Wawatam.

The relief which swept through Henry at the sight of this man who had adopted him was indescribable. Since the attack on the fort first took place, Alexander Henry had thought of Wawatam numerous times, wondering where he was and wishing desperately that he could be with him. And now the village chief had presented himself!

Wawatam moved toward the front with all eyes upon him. As he passed by Henry, he gave the young trader's shoulder a reassuring squeeze but continued without saying anything. The Indian moved directly to a place beside Minivavana and Wenniway and took a seat there. Then began a long, unbroken silence as pipes were lighted and smoked. When they were finished, Wawatam looked at Minivavana. The principal Chippewa chief returned his gaze levelly and then nodded once. Immediately Wawatam got to his feet and left the council house. Again as he passed Henry he touched his shoulder, but this time he murmured, "Take courage!"

Another full hour of silence ensued as pipes were again filled, lighted and smoked. More Indians—some of them chiefs—arrived during this interval and took their places near the front. At last Wawatam reentered, followed by his wife, Oghqua. Both of them were heavily loaded with merchandise of all kinds—knives, furs, traps, bows, arrows, blankets, a gun, powder horn, paint pots, silver ornaments and other items. Many of these were gifts Henry had given Wawatam over these many months. All of the material was placed on the floor a few feet from Minivavana.

The chief looked them over without moving or speaking. He turned his gaze upon Oghqua, who lowered her eyes, and then looked directly at Wawatam, again nodding as he had done before. At this sign, Wawatam turned and faced the large audience and began to speak.

"Friends and relations," he said, "what is it that I shall say? You know what I feel. You all have friends and brothers and children whom, as yourselves, you love; and you—what would you experience did you, like me, behold your dearest friend, your brother, your son, in the condition of a slave; a slave exposed every moment to insult and to menace of death? This case, as you all know, is mine. See there . . ."

He stretched out an arm and pointed a long finger at Alexander Henry and continued without pause:

". . . my friend and brother among slaves—himself a slave! You all know that long before the war began I adopted him as my brother. From that moment he became one of my family, so that no change of circumstances could break the cord which fastened us together. He is my brother! And because I am your relative, he is therefore your relation, too. And how," his voice rang out now with a trace of anger, "being your relation, can he be your slave?"

Wawatam paused and then turned his head so that he could look at Chief Minivavana. He continued:

"On the day on which the war began, you were fearful lest on this very account I should reveal your secret. You requested, therefore, that I would leave the fort, and even cross the lake. I did so, but I did it with reluctance. I did it with reluctance, notwithstanding that you, Minivavana, who had the command in this enterprise, gave me your promise that you would protect my friend, delivering him from all danger and giving him safely to me."

The village chief's voice became stern now, and demanding: "The performance of this promise I now claim. I come not with empty hands to ask it. You, Minivavana, best know whether or not, as it respects yourself, you have kept your word, but I bring these goods to buy off every claim which any man among you all may have on my brother, as his prisoner."

It was the end of Wawatam's speech and Alexander Henry's vision was blurred by the tears which filled his eyes. He did not know if Wawatam's plea would be heeded but, whether or not it was, he felt a gratitude to his Chippewa brother that he had never felt for any other human being. He also felt humbled and unworthy of it because of his tendency in the past to consider the adoption with amusement or flippancy. How much deeper it went than he had even begun to realize!

As soon as Wawatam sat down beside Oghqua, pipes were again lighted and smoked in silence. Not until the last of them had been smoked and laid aside did Minivavana rise to speak, directing his remarks to Wawatam.

"My friend and brother," he said, "what you have spoken is truth. We were acquainted with the friendship which existed between yourself and the Englishman, in whose behalf you have now addressed us. We knew the danger of having our secret discovered, and the consequences which must follow; and you say truly that we requested you to leave the fort. This we did out of regard for you and your family, for if a discovery of our design had been made, you would have been blamed, whether guilty or not, and you would have been involved in difficulties from which you could not have extricated yourself.

"It is also true," he continued, his voice surprisingly gentle, "that I promised you to take care of your friend; and this promise I performed by desiring my son, at the moment of assault, to seek him out and bring him to my lodge. He went accordingly, but could not find him. The day after, I sent him to Langlade's, where he was informed that your friend was safe; and had it not been that our people were then drinking the rum that had been found in the fort, he would have brought him home with him, according to my orders. I am very glad to find that your friend has escaped. We accept your present and you may take him home with you."

Wawatam rose slowly and Oghqua stood beside him. He looked at Minivavana and then at the other chiefs in the assemblage and nodded, a small smile on his face.

"I thank Minivavana and all the chiefs of my tribe for their thoughtfulness and generosity in this matter."

With that he walked to Alexander Henry, took him by the hand and led him out. With Oghqua following, they had gone directly to Wawatam's lodge which was only, to Henry's surprise, a dozen yards or so from the prison lodge in which he had spent the previous night. Inside, he had found Wawatam's whole family waiting and all of them gave expressions of great joy and relief at the young trader's deliverance. Food was prepared for him in abundance and, for the first time since the attack broke out, Henry ate a meal without similarly swallowing fear with each mouthful. He was filled with a gratitude which knew no bounds but, despite the words of Minivavana, he still walked in dread of the other Chippewas.

It was a fear decidedly justified, as evidenced by the shrieks of agony that had awakened him and were just this moment dwindling away to silence. Henry returned to his pallet and sat there, deeply troubled, but his fearful curiosity drove him back to the doorflap and he peered out again. He was just in time to see the flap of the prison lodge doorway thrust open and one by one the naked, scalped, and badly mutilated bodies of the four privates and the man named Samuels were dragged outside by their feet.

Several of Wawatam's family were in the lodge with Henry. They had turned their eyes away from him while all this was going on and would not speak to him, seemingly embarrassed by what was happening. It was not until several minutes later, when Wawatam himself returned, that the incident was explained.

"It is a regrettable thing for them," Wawatam said, shaking his head, "but I am glad you were not still among them. A great chief of our tribe, Kolopesh—he whom the French here call *Le Grand Sable*—had just returned from his winter hunting grounds. Having been absent when the war began, and his hatred of the English strong, he desired to show all the Indians his complete approval of what had been done. He has done this by what you heard and saw. It was understandable that he would wish to do so, but not wise of him. The council had planned another end for them and now Minivavana must be very angry when he learns what has happened. Still, my people will continue as well as can be done with what was planned for them."

Henry was deeply disturbed at the nonchalance of Wawatam's comments and at the implication that more was yet to be done to those pitiful victims. When Wawatam turned to attend to other matters in the lodge, the trader returned to the doorway to peer out unseen at the bodies. It was not until about an hour after they had been dragged out of the prison lodge that he saw two warriors approach the bodies and walk among them, studying them. In a moment they stopped before that of one of the soldiers, a rather fat young man whom Henry had known only as Private Walter. Swiftly and with a skill belying previous inexperience at such things, the two cut off the head and then divided the body into five parts. These they carried back toward the prison lodge and now, for the first time, Henry saw that five campfires had been built outside the structure and over each of them was suspended a steaming, soot-blackened iron kettle. One part of Private Walter's body went into each of the kettles and a crowd began assembling. Sickened and at last unable to watch anymore, Henry threw himself onto his pallet and buried his face in his hands.

After the passage of another half hour or so, a warrior came to the door of the lodge and summoned Wawatam, as a village chief and head of his family, to come and partake of the feast. Wawatam said he would come, took a dish and spoon of wood which was handed to him by the silent Oghqua, and left the lodge. He was gone about twenty minutes and when he returned he was carrying on his plate a boiled human hand and a large piece of body flesh. This he carried to a corner and squatted there.

Unbelieving and horrified, filled with an unspeakable revulsion, Alexander Henry watched as Wawatam ate all of it without apparent enjoyment. When he was finished he wiped his hands on a piece of old shirt while Oghqua picked up the dish containing the bones and carried it outside. Barely able to contain the loathing welling up within him, Henry confronted Wawatam.

"There is no one in this world," he said, "to whom I owe more than to you, Wawatam. You have saved my life and I am grateful. No possible words can convey what gratitude I feel. You are my brother, my father, and my friend. But, dear God, Wawatam, how could you possibly have done what you just did? How could you actually *eat* a fellow man?"

Wawatam seemed surprised at first at Henry's concern, but then he shrugged his shoulders. "I do not like the taste of such meat," he admitted simply, "but it is now and always has been the custom among my people and the peoples of other tribes to do so. When returning from war or after overcoming an enemy, it is our custom to make a war feast from among the slain. This inspires a warrior with courage in the attack. It adds to him the strength of his enemy and it enables him to meet death with fearlessness. It is our way."

[June 8, 1763—Wednesday, Noon]

That Colonel Henry Bouquet clearly expected more of an emphatic and definitive reaction from General Amherst in reply to the letters he had sent to the commander—both those of his own and those he enclosed which were written by Captain Ecuyer—was obvious. That he muffled his dismay and resorted to no backbiting comments about his superior was typical of his character. There was only the faintest flaring of his nostrils as he read the general's words while the express rider waited, and then he smiled at the messenger and thanked him, telling him there was no reply at the moment.

A few minutes later he was himself writing a somewhat more encouraging letter to Ecuyer than he had just gotten from Amherst:

Philadelphia, 8th June 1763

My Dear Ecuyer,

The General has taken the necessary measures to chastise those infamous villains, and defers only to make them feel the weight of his resentment till he is better informed of their intentions.

I give you joy of the success of our troops at the Manilla, where Captain George Ourry hath acquired the two best things in this world, glory and money . . .

Bouquet

P.S. The General expects that Mr. Croghan will proceed directly to Fort Pitt, when he will soon discover the causes of this sudden rupture and the intentions of these rascals.

Hardly, however, had the express carrying this letter gotten out of sight than another showed up, bearing yet another letter from Ecuyer with even worse news than before. Holocaust was breaking out all over the western frontier and it seemed that the report of the loss of Fort Sandusky was regrettably true. Worse yet, there had been absolutely no word from Detroit, indicating something amiss there. Forts Pitt, Ligonier, and Bedford were being fired upon with ever-increasing frequency and it was daily becoming more apparent that the affair was both general and serious.

Sighing, Bouquet returned to his desk, ordered his aide to have another express stand by to carry Ecuyer's letter and another by himself to the general within the hour.

[June 10, 1763—Friday]

Although assured that he was now safe from harm, Alexander Henry was still extremely uneasy. Of all the things that had happened since the attack began on Fort Michilimackinac, it was the sight of Wawatam sitting in the corner calmly and methodically eating human flesh which most haunted him. He knew Wawatam as a kind and gentle individual and the knowledge that such a person could have done as he did made Henry wonder just how well any person could ever get to know any other.

Matters had taken an unexpected turn since that grisly feast. Late in the afternoon there came into view a large trading canoe, approaching from the direction of Montreal and it was loaded with Englishmen and supplies. The Indians sounded an alarm and by the time the unsuspecting occupants beached the craft at the fort, some two hundred Chippewa warriors were waiting for them. Evidently the Englishmen thought they were simply friendly natives waiting for news of the east, but at the stopping of the craft the Indians dashed out, grappled with the Englishmen and dragged them screaming and struggling through the water to shore. There they beat them unmercifully and reviled them in numerous ways, confiscated all their goods, stripped them of their clothing and held them bound in the prison lodge.

Early yesterday morning, though, there seemed to be a change in the Indians. By this time the alcohol had long been consumed and now a certain amount of thought was being given by many of the Indians to what they had done and what the ramifications might be of their acts. They were becoming apprehensive lest there be a retaliatory strike by the English and a council was called during which it was decided that for the sake of safety and better defensibility, the whole population would move to Wawatam's island, also called Michilimackinac, six miles distant. This place, Wawatam told Henry, was the very island upon which the Great Spirit had revealed to him that one day Henry would come here.

By noon yesterday the village near the fort was broken up and over fourscore canoes—one of them containing Alexander Henry, Wawatam and his family—were on their way to Michilimackinac Island. The new English prisoners were also being taken. Halfway to the island, however, a sharp wind sprang up and the Indians, fearful that it would turn into a gale, grasped one of their dogs, bound its legs together and pitched it into the water as an offering designed to appease some angry god of the wind or water. To Henry's amazement, the wind died as quickly as it had risen.

Just as they approached the island, Oghqua and another squaw in Henry's boat broke into a series of hideously melancholy cries and the fear welled up in the trader again as he stared around him anxiously to ascertain the cause of it. Wawatam, smiling, reassured him. He pointed to a large tree near the shoreline.

"There is nothing to fear, my brother," he said. "Beside that tree are buried two men who were members of our family. It is the custom of our women on passing the burial place of any relative to always give voice to the grief first experienced at that place. By this means the dead are not just forgotten."

Not long after that they came ashore and Henry was greatly impressed at the swiftness with which the men and women, working together, erected new lodges from the bundles of poles that had been taken from the dismantled lodges on the old village site. By nightfall a new village had sprung into being. A strong guard patrol was mounted to keep watch and the rest, greatly wearied by their efforts of the day, quickly went to sleep for the night.

It was at about ten o'clock this morning that one of the guards shrilled an alarm and the word spread in the village that a canoe was approaching. The alarm was unjustified. In the canoe was a party of warriors from Pontiac, who had come at their chief's order to try to persuade the Michilimackinac Chippewas to return with them to Detroit to help bring about the downfall of the fort there.

The Chippewas adamantly refused, their apprehension by now grown too strong. Minivavana sent them away with instructions to tell Pontiac about the fall of Fort Michilimackinac, along with his promise that he and his Chippewas would prevent any further Englishmen from entering this country, but beyond that they would do nothing. The disgruntled Ottawas shoved off and headed westward, apparently for L'Arbre Croche. They were not yet out of sight when Minivavana raised his arms for silence.

"The guard will be maintained," he announced, "during the day as well as during the night. A keen watch will be kept at all times. If an English force approaches us, all Englishmen among us here will be put to death at once."

And Alexander Henry felt himself shrink inwardly as scores of heads were turned his way and a multitude of dark eyes impaled him with their stare.

[*June 12, 1763—Sunday, 9:00* A.M.]

Every soldier and every officer at Detroit clearly showed the effects of the strain of existing under the state of siege laid down against the fort by Pontiac. Food supplies were severely rationed and there was not an individual here who had not lost weight and vigor. Probably none looked the worse for wear than Major Henry Gladwin, but this was not surprising, since none worked quite so hard, ate quite so sparingly, or slept quite so little.

The situation about the fort remained pretty much as it had been for the past few weeks. Usually there was some desultory firing at the fort or ship by the Indians during the day and sometimes at night, but with little real damage being done. Occasionally Gladwin sent out sorties to burn down

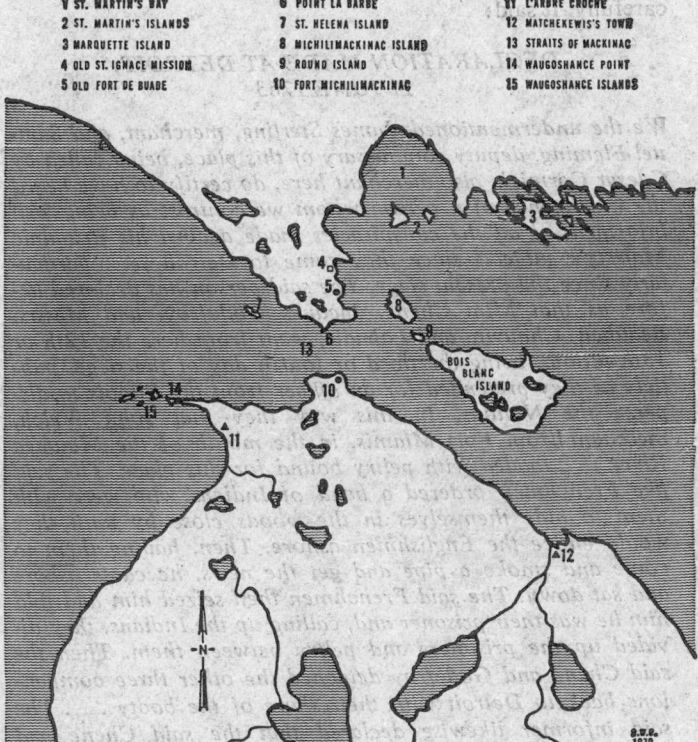

THE
STRAITS OF MACKINAC
AREA

1 ST. MARTIN'S BAY	**6** POINT LA BARBE	**11** L'ARBRE CROCHE
2 ST. MARTIN'S ISLANDS	**7** ST. HELENA ISLAND	**12** MATCHEKEWIS'S TOWN
3 MARQUETTE ISLAND	**8** MICHILIMACKINAC ISLAND	**13** STRAITS OF MACKINAC
4 OLD ST. IGNACE MISSION	**9** ROUND ISLAND	**14** WAUGOSHANCE POINT
5 OLD FORT DE BUADE	**10** FORT MICHILIMACKINAC	**15** WAUGOSHANCE ISLANDS

houses from which the enemy would fire on the fort or vessel. But while the situation had remained static, the news received had been one jarring blow after another until Gladwin dreaded seeing a new day dawn. Today was no improvement.

The first thing that caught the Detroit commander's eye this morning was a deposition that had been placed on his desk by his aide, who had received it from the fort's deputy commissary, Samuel Fleming. He read it swiftly, realized that it was something of a confirmation of his own suspicions that the French were instigating, aiding and abetting the Indians in this uprising, and then he read it a second time more carefully. It said:

DECLARATION MADE AT DETROIT, 11 JUNE 1763

We the undermentioned, James Sterling, merchant, and Samuel Fleming, deputy commissary of this place, being called by Caesar Cormick, also merchant here, do certify to have heard the intelligence of a person whom we contrast as being well informed, of all the conspiracies made against his Britannic Majesty's subjects since they came to Detroit . . . particularly since the present siege. The said person has declared before us that Mini Chene, Jacques Godefroy, and Messrs. Beauban, Chauvin, and Labadie, went from here the 12th or 13th ultimo, being the third or fourth day of the siege, publicly as they pretended for an officer from the Illinois to disperse the Nations. In this way they met John Welch, merchant from Fort Miamis, in the mouth of the Maumee River . . . loaded with peltry bound for this place. The said five Frenchmen ordered a band of Indians who were with them to hide themselves in the woods close by until they would entice the Englishmen ashore. Then, hailing them to come and smoke a pipe and get the news, he came ashore and sat down. The said Frenchmen then seized him and told him he was their prisoner and, calling up the Indians, they divided up the prisoners and peltry between them. Then the said Chene and Godefroy detached the other three companions back to Detroit with their share of the booty . . . The said informer likewise declared that the said Chene and Godefroy took also four of the said prisoners along with them, saying they would take them to the Illinois and make soup of them to spirit up the Indians to war and come against the English, which they now daily expect here. And that the said Chene and Godefroy, proceeding with the same

Indians to Fort Miamis, with whom they acted in conjunction to destroy that garrison. Then they parted for Ouiatenon, intending to act the same barbarous part there, being in their way to Illinois. We then questioned the said informer if we could depend on the abovesaid intelligence, or from whence they were derived. He answered that Ninivois, a Potawatomi chief, sent for Isadore Chene, brother of the said Mini Chene, the evening that he, Ninivois, arrived with Ensign Schlosser, Commanding Officer of Fort St. Joseph, and acquainted him of what his brother Mini had done at Fort Miamis. The said Isadore, in tears, replied that he wished to God his brother might die in that place, for as soon as he arrived in Detroit he would be hanged. And that the said informer declares to have been present when all this was told by the said Ninivois in the house of the abovesaid Mini Chene.

Signed,
Caesar Cormick

Witnesses,
   James Sterling
   Samuel Fleming

Henry Gladwin pursed his mouth into a silent whistle and shook his head. Somewhat garbled though the deposition might be, it nonetheless pointed a strongly accusatory finger at the French, particularly Chene and Godefroy. He made a mental note to have these men arrested the moment they returned to Detroit. The deposition itself he filed with other notes and writings which made up the conglomerate of bad news which had filtered to him since the siege began.

Many of the messages—though more of them vocal than written—had filtered in from Captain Donald Campbell and Lieutenant George McDougall, who were still being held captive at Meloche's house on orders of Pontiac. Insofar as Gladwin had been able to determine, neither man had been harmed and, as a matter of fact, they were proving themselves invaluable in the role of spies. Whatever material they were able to gather was generally given, either in spoken word or writing, to Jacques Duperon Baby or Jacques St. Martin who, in turn, delivered it to Gladwin.

It was the two captive officers who had managed to have Gladwin informed about the fall of Fort Miamis and the death of its commander, Robert Holmes, as soon as they learned of it. Likewise, it was they who sent in word about the subsequent fall of Fort Ouiatenon and Fort St. Joseph.

Fortunately, the Fort Ouiatenon garrison under Lieutenant Edward Jenkins had apparently been treated reasonably well and were taken to Fort de Chartres in the Illinois country to be turned over to the French. Ensign Schlosser's garrison at Fort St. Joseph had not been so lucky. Most of the men had been killed.

Another report from Campbell and McDougall had been delivered this morning. It was equally important, and equally depressing. Pontiac's strength, they said, was constantly increasing with the arrival of new bands of Indians from all directions. Only today another band of Mississaugi Chippewas from the Saginaw Bay area had come and pledged to the Ottawa war chief their services. This was apparently as a direct result of the taking of Fort St. Joseph and the arrival of the surviving prisoners of that garrison—including Ensign Schlosser—here at Detroit several days ago.

It had been a bad time for the prisoners to arrive. Almost on their heels had come the party of Mississaugis who had captured the trading party near the mouth of Grand River, bringing with them a few prisoners and considerable plunder, including rum. With bellies and brains set afire by the alcohol, the Ottawas had gone on another rampage. Prisoners were made to run the gauntlet until beaten into insensibility or killed, several were scalped alive and then tomahawked, and at least one of the latter had been quartered, boiled and eaten.

Now, as he tried to foresee what new complication the future might bring, Major Gladwin was interrupted by Captain Joseph Hopkins.

"Sir," the acting second-in-command said, "Chief Washee of the Potawatomies is outside the gate under a flag of truce. He has several of his chiefs with him and the Frenchman Laurence Gamelin is acting as interpreter for them. Washee claims he has had nothing to do with the taking of Fort St. Joseph and wants to talk with you. He also says he wishes to talk with that Potawatomi chief we're holding prisoner, Winnemac. I gather that he wants to work out a trade with you—Schlosser for Winnemac."

Gladwin considered this and then nodded. "All right, take them to see the two Potawatomi prisoners first, so they'll know they are all right. Give them ten minutes together, but guarded well and no passing of anything between them but words. Then bring them here."

Hopkins nodded and left. It was close to twenty minutes later that he returned with Chief Washee, three of his subchiefs and the Frenchman, Gamelin. Gladwin's greeting of them was cool. Washee responded without rancor.

"We," he told Gladwin through Gamelin, "dislike this war and have been forced into it by Pontiac. Our chief at St. Joseph, Kioqua, knew nothing of the plan to take the fort there. Yet, you hold here in a locked room two of our men. One of these is Winnemac, one of the greatest chiefs of the Potawatomi, who has done you no ill. Why, then, do you hold him?"

"Are you Potawatomies slaves of Pontiac?" Gladwin replied, still no warmth in his voice. "Are you bound to do as he orders you? Are you not a nation in your own right? If so, how then is it you do as he bids? You say you had no part in the taking of Fort St. Joseph. Yet, I am told from unimpeachable sources that it was the Potawatomies who took the fort, not the Ottawas. I have even heard it said that you led this attack, Washee. How do you answer this?"

Washee looked startled as Gamelin interpreted. It was clear that he was not expecting Gladwin to have any knowledge of his attacking Fort St. Joseph against the wishes of Chief Kioqua. Now he merely clamped his lips together and refused to speak.

The Detroit commander shrugged. "I speak sincerely when I tell you this, Washee; the day will come when the Ottawas themselves will kill Pontiac for starting this war which, in the end, is bound to ruin them. I advise you to disperse and mind your hunting and planting. If you persist in the way you are going, it will end in your ruin also.

"Now then," he continued more briskly, "you came here to make a deal, I take it. All right, you have Ensign Schlosser and three of his men. Release them to us and we will release a prisoner to you. Until you do, I have nothing further to discuss with you."

He turned his back to them and in a moment he heard the door open and then close softly behind them as they left.

[June 12, 1763—Sunday, 10:00 A.M.]

When the Ottawas had demanded of the Chippewas what they considered their share of the plunder at Michilimackinac, Captain George Etherington had been more than surprised at the manner in which the Chippewas had given in. Though they greatly outnumbered the Ottawas here, yet they seemed to harbor an abundant fear of the tribe ruled by Chief Mackinac. That by far the greater majority of the prisoners, including Leslye and himself, had become the "share" of the Ottawas was reassuring. Etherington had not held out much hope for their survival while in the hands of Minivavana and his people. This was not to say that, at the onset at any rate, he had expected anything better from the Ottawas. The fact remained, however, that the L'Arbre Croche Indians had not taken part in the massacre and might well lend themselves to being convinced that great rewards would be theirs in return for good treatment of the prisoners.

When Etherington and his men, along with the two traders, had been herded away from Michilimackinac by the Ottawas immediately after the Indians had come to agreement in their dispute, the commanding officer had thought they would be taken to L'Arbre Croche. This had not happened. A few miles west of Michilimackinac a camp was established along the south shore of the Straits of Mackinac by Chief Okinochumake's men and runners were sent on to L'Arbre Croche to inform Chief Mackinac of what had transpired and to receive his instructions. Until then, Etherington had been informed by Farli, the interpreter, they would remain in this camp.

Farli was a hard one to figure out, Etherington decided. Though the man had liberally helped himself to the English plunder following the massacre, yet he had gone out of his way to help Etherington and Leslye and the remaining men. He had, in fact, come with them this far and was still acting as interpreter between the captain and the Ottawa chief. It was through Farli that Etherington had apparently convinced Okinochumake that great would be the rewards given to the L'Arbre Croche Ottawas if the English prisoners in their hands were well treated. Such rewards would become even greater if the Ottawas would escort all the captives safely to Montreal.

A fortunate circumstance occurred then which tended to underline Captain Etherington's promise. A party of French *voyageurs* in the employ of English traders hove into view in two canoes. At Etherington's hail to them they came ashore and reported that they were on their way from Montreal to Fort Edward Augustus on the west side of Lake Michigan at Green Bay. They had planned to stop at Fort Michilimackinac, but two days before getting there they had heard of the massacre and, fearful of what the Indians might do with them because they were transporting a large shipment of trading goods belonging to the English, they had detoured around the fort.

Promising them in the name of the King that their employers would be compensated for what he must now do, Etherington conscripted all the goods in the shipment. Then, with Farli interpreting, he spoke to Chief Okinochumake:

"Our friends, the Ottawas, are good friends and good friends deserve reward. I therefore give to you of my own free will, all these goods you see here and assure you that they are only a small part of what Chief Mackinac's people will receive as reward for our continued safety and for aid in returning us to Montreal."

Okinochumake was decidedly impressed. "For myself," he told Etherington, "I promise to keep you safe from harm, but I cannot promise to deliver you to Montreal. That must be a decision of our great chief, Mackinac. I will send a runner off to him with this news."

Etherington nodded and then, with Farli's aid, convinced Okinochumake that it would be a good idea if he, Etherington, was to write a letter to Lieutenant James Gorrell at Fort Edward Augustus, which Okinochumake knew better as Fort La Baye, and instruct that commander to abandon that fort and meet them at L'Arbre Croche, hopefully to return to Montreal. Not only was Okinochumake agreeable to this, but he insisted upon supplying one of his men to carry the message to Gorrell.

Farli had privately told Etherington that there were rumors to the effect that Detroit was under attack and that several of the smaller forts had already fallen. For this reason it would be useless, even dangerous, for Etherington to try to make it to Detroit. Etherington nodded and, bearing this in mind, wrote the letter yesterday and watched with satisfaction as several of the L'Arbre Croche warriors boarded a canoe with it and set off to the west. He had written:

Michilimackinac, 11 June 1763

Dear Sir—

The second instant this place was taken by surprise by the Chippewas, at which time Lieutenant Jamet and twenty more were killed and all the rest taken prisoners; but our good friends, the Ottawas, have taken Lieutenant Leslye, me, and eleven men out of their hands and have promised to reinstate us again. You will, therefore, on receipt of this (which I send by a canoe of Ottawas) set out with all your garrison and what English traders you have there with you and come with the Indian who gives you this, who will conduct you safe to me. You must be sure to follow the instructions you receive from the bearer of this, as you are by no means whatever to come to this post before you see me at the village [L'Arbre Croche] twenty miles from this . . . I must once more beg you'll lose no time in coming to join me and, at the same time be very careful and always on your guard. I long much to see you and am, Dear Sir,

> *Your most humble servant,*
> *Geo. Etherington*

To J. Gorrell, Lieut.
Royal Americans

Now another night had passed and this morning the runners sent ahead to Chief Mackinac had returned with encouraging news. Farli was on hand when they reported to Okinochumake and, a few minutes later, the Frenchman came to where Captain Etherington and Lieutenant Leslye were waiting with their men. He grinned as he approached.

"The news, Captain," he said, "is good. Chief Mackinac is very pleased with the way Chief Okinochumake has handled this whole affair. He is also very impressed by your gifts and promises of further reward. It would seem that he plans to help you get to Montreal, but only after a delay. He wishes all to come first to L'Arbre Croche until the war fervor of the Chippewas has somewhat cooled. He is not afraid of them, but he does not wish to needlessly precipitate a war between his people and Minivavana's. We will leave in a few hours for L'Arbre Croche. I will not go there with you. I may go down toward Detroit with Father de Jaunay."

"The priest is going to Detroit?"

Farli nodded and then left to speak again with Okinochumake. Looking around the encampment, Etherington soon spotted the Jesuit missionary and went to him at once. After a few minutes of earnest conversation, he entered the priest's shelter and, with writing materials supplied by de Jaunay, hastily wrote a letter to Major Gladwin:

> *Michilimackinac, 12 June 1763*
Sir:
> *Notwithstanding that I wrote you in my last that all the savages were arrived and that everything seemed in perfect tranquility, yet, on the 2nd instant the Chippewas, who live in a plain near this fort, assembled to play ball as they had done almost every day since their arrival. They played from morning till noon. Then, throwing their ball close to the gate*

and observing Lieutenant Leslye and me a few paces out of it, they came behind us, seized and carried us into the woods.

In the meantime the rest rushed into the fort where they found their squaws, whom they had previously planted there, with their hatchets hid under their blankets, which they took and in an instant killed Lieutenant Jamet and fifteen rank and file, and a trader named Tracy. They wounded two and took the rest of the garrison prisoners, five of whom they have since, I am told, killed.

They made prisoners of all the English traders and robbed them of everything they had; but they offered no violence to the persons or property of any of the Frenchmen.

When that massacre was over, Messrs. Langlade and Farli, the interpreter, came down to the place where Lieutenant Leslye and I were prisoners, and on their giving themselves as security to return us when demanded, they obtained leave for us to go to the fort under a guard of savages, which gave time, by the assistance of the gentlemen above-mentioned, to send for the Ottawas, who came down on the first notice and were very displeased at what the Chippewas had done.

Since the arrival of the Ottawas they have done everything in their power to serve us and, with what prisoners the Chippewas had given them and what they have bought, I have now with me Lieutenant Leslye and eleven privates; and the other four of the garrison who are yet living remaining in the hands of the Chippewas.

The Chippewas, who are superior in numbers to the Ottawas, have declared in council to them that if they do not remove us out of the fort, they will cut off all communications to this post, by which means all the convoys of merchants from Montreal, La Baye, St. Joseph and the upper posts would perish. But if the news of your posts being attacked (which they say was the reason they took up the hatchet) be false, and you can send up a strong reinforcement with provisions, &c., accompanied by some of your savages, I believe the post might be reestablished again.

Since this affair happened, two canoes arrived from Montreal, which put in my power to make a present to the Ottawa nation, who very well deserve anything that can be done for them.

I have been very much obliged to Messrs. Langlade and Farli, the interpreter, as likewise to the Jesuit, for the many good offices they have done on this occasion. The priest seems inclinable to go down to your post for a day or two, which I am very glad of, as he is a very good man, and had a great deal to say with the savages hereabout, who will believe everything he tells them on his return, which I hope will be soon. The Ottawas say they will take Lieutenant Leslye and me, and the eleven men which I mentioned before were in their hands, up to their village, and there keep us till they hear what is doing at your post. They have sent this canoe for that purpose.

I refer you to the priest for the particulars of this melancholy affair and am, Dear Sir,

> *Yours very sincerely,*
> *Geo. Etherington*

To Major Gladwin

P.S. The Indians that are to carry the priest to Detroit will not undertake to land him at the fort, but at some of the Indian villages near it; so you must not take it amiss that he does not pay you the first visit. And once more I beg that nothing may stop your sending him back and next day after his arrival, if possible, as we shall be at a great loss for the want of him, and I make no doubt that you will do all in your power to make peace, as you see the situation we are in, and send up provisions as soon as possible, and ammunition, as what we had was pillaged by the savages.

> *Adieu,*
> *Geo. Etherington*

[*June 12, 1763—Sunday, 11:00 A.M.*]

Lieutenant General Sir Jeffrey Amherst was one of those individuals who, even in the face of the most overwhelming evidence, refuses to acknowledge that matters may not be as he wishes them to be and confidently believes them to be. For months past the reports from the west had been worsening and the warnings received from officers and Indian agents had increased and grown more forbidding. But up until last night, Amherst had blandly sloughed them off as ridiculous. To his way of thinking, there was no band or tribe or even confederation of savages who could possibly cause anything more than the merest inconvenience to any western fort under the command of one of his officers.

The day before yesterday, Amherst had become extremely annoyed when his aide, Captain Dalyell, placed a June 9 copy of the Pennsylvania *Gazette* in his hands and he read an extract of a letter from Fort Pitt which was something of a bombshell. It told of scalpings and attacks on merchant convoys, of settlement burnings and even of attacks against Fort Pitt itself and smaller installations as far eastward as Fort Bedford.

Amherst had slammed the paper down with a heart-felt "Damn!" and then paced the room furiously. He could envision what was going to happen now. Every major newspaper on the coast—The New York *Mercury*, The Boston *News-Letter*, the Newport *Mercury*, probably even the South Carolina *Gazette*—would pick the story up and the whole populace would be thrown into an attack of palpitations. Worse yet, their reporters would undoubtedly start to besiege the families of soldiers and officers for permission to print extracts of the letters received from their loved ones at the frontier posts. And leave it to these newspapers to find and print those extracts which showed the situation in its most exaggerated light. Couldn't these fools see that whatever was happening had to be only minor incidents and that the whole affair would simply peter out after a few outrages had been committed against the inhabitants before assistance could be sent to them?

Amherst decided he would not lower himself to abet such newspaper garbage by making any sort of public statement. So lightly did he consider it, in fact, that he did not even send on the intelligence he had received to John Stuart, the superintendent of Indian Affairs in the South, who was the counterpart of Sir William Johnson in the North. The likelihood of any disturbances spreading that far, or even to Virginia, which was in Stuart's jurisdiction, was laughable.

All that had been on the day before yesterday. But then, last night, the complexion of matters changed suddenly. Just as Amherst was thinking of turning in, James Dalyell showed up with urgent expresses from Philadelphia. Bouquet had written again with even graver news from the west and enclosed letters not only from Captain Ecuyer at Fort Pitt, but also from Lieutenant Archibald Blane at Fort Ligonier and Captain Louis Ourry at Fort Bedford. The words contained in them struck Amherst with the impact of physical blows: Fort Pitt surrounded, practically under siege, unable to make contact with Fort Venango eighty miles to the north; Fort Ligonier attacked four or five different times and also practically under a state of siege; settlers literally swarming into Fort Bedford for military protection and the fort itself several times fired upon; Detroit seemingly cut off and good, though not conclusive, evidence that Fort Sandusky was destroyed and its garrison slain.

Captain Ourry, for example, had written in his most recent letter to Bouquet:

. . . as to myself, I find I can bear a good deal. Since the alarm I never lie down till about twelve, and am walking about the fort between two and three in the morning, turning out the guards and sending out patrols before I suffer the gates to remain open . . . My greatest difficulty is to keep my militia from straggling by twos and threes to their dear plantations, thereby exposing themselves to be scalped, and weakening my garrison by such numbers absenting themselves. They are still in good spirits, but they don't know all the bad news. I shall use all means to prevail on them to stay until some troops come up. I long to see my Indian scouts come in with intelligence; but I long more to hear the Grenadier's March, and see some more red-coats . . .

Obviously, even Colonel Bouquet was taking the whole matter very seriously. He was not one to cry wolf without good cause, yet in his accompanying letter to Amherst, which the general read with more than a trace of nervousness, he had written:

. . . and I cannot impress too strongly upon you, your Excellency, the gravity of the situation. If the reports that Sandusky has been destroyed are true, then it may be a portent of what is in store for others of the smaller outposts. I would suggest, Sir, that it might be wise to order the immediate abandonment of those posts too distant for swift reinforcement and too small for withstanding concerted attack. Might it not be wise if Venango was abandoned and Lieutenant Gordon led his garrison to Fort Pitt; and might it not be just as prudent for Fort Le Boeuf to be likewise abandoned and the garrison under Ensign Price to move up to Fort Presque Isle?

Jeffery Amherst had sat quietly at his desk for long minutes after finishing his reading of all the letters and reports. Could it really be that this situation was more serious that he believed? Rubbish! Obviously certain people were letting their imaginations blow a small matter all out of proportion to its true importance. Nevertheless, it might be wise to at least concede, albeit grudgingly, that a major uprising could *conceivably* occur, however unlikely, and consider what might be done if it did. With this decision having been made, Amherst felt much better. He dismissed Captain Dalyell, retired for the night and slept quite well.

Now, with the morning already well spent and having thoroughly reread each letter and report, Amherst reluctantly admitted to his delighted aide that there just *might* be some truth in what was reported. He carefully dictated a number of orders, sending two of the companies—the 42nd and 77th Regimental companies—of the detachment under Major Campbell at Staten Island to join Bouquet at Philadelphia and await the colonel's orders there. He also sent out orders which now disbanded a portion of the Royal Americans, all of Hopkins's Ranger Company and all of the 80th Regiment and assigned these men to fill out the ranks of other corps which were below prescribed strength.

Well aware of Captain Dalyell's desire for action and independent command, Amherst smiled at his aide and murmured, "I'm saving you in case something really important comes up, Jim."

All this having been done before noon, Amherst felt very pleased at his own steps, realizing that the people always respected a commander who swiftly made the necessary moves to maintain military preparedness. Should something untoward actually develop in the western Great Lakes, he could expediently push these troops forward in two wings— one going up the valleys of the Hudson and Mohawk to Oswego on Lake Ontario and thence to Fort Niagara, possibly under command of Dalyell; the other down to Philadelphia and then west to Fort Pitt and north to Presque Isle on Lake Erie, probably under John Campbell. From these locations— if the need arose of course—they could be hurled against any offending Indians.

To Colonel Bouquet, General Amherst replied in a manner designed to ease that officer's fears, indirectly chide him for putting too much stock in what Ecuyer, Blane and Ourry were reporting, and at the same time intimate that he was really becoming much too upset over what must be a relatively simple situation. He wrote:

I find by the intelligence enclosed in your letters, that the affair of the Indians appears to be more general than I had apprehended, although I believe nothing of what is mentioned regarding the garrison of the Detroit being cut off. It is extremely inconvenient at this time; there are many other matters which demand my attention, but I cannot defer sending you a reinforcement for the communication . . . If you think necessary, you will yourself proceed to Fort Pitt that you may the better be enabled to put into execution the requisite orders for securing the communication and reducing the Indians to reason. As for the smaller outposts which you suggest abandoning, I cannot think of giving them up at this time, if we can keep them, as such a step would give the Indians room to think themselves more formidable than they really are; and it would be much better we never attempted to take posts in what they call their country if, upon every alarm, we abandon them . . . It remains at present for us to take every precaution we can, by which we may put a stop, as soon as possible, to their committing any farther mischief, and to bring them to a proper subjection; for, without that, I never do expect they will be quiet and orderly, as every act of kindness and generosity to those barbarians is looked upon as proceeding from our fears.

Having thus dispensed with the problem to his satisfaction, Amherst now dictated a final letter—this one to Sir William Johnson, still recuperating on the Connecticut shore. It gave Amherst a decided pleasure to dig Johnson a bit on the unruliness of his charges. It also, he felt, might inspire the Indian agent to cut short his stay on the coast and return to his duties. In part, Amherst wrote:

You will no doubt have heard that the Indians near Fort Pitt have been doing mischief; and it would seem that the affair is more general than I had once apprehended. I herewith enclose you copies of what I have received from Colonel Bouquet. The last part of the intelligence seems to be greatly exaggerated, as I cannot entertain a thought that they have been able to cut off the garrison of the Detroit, or any of the posts where officers are stationed . . .

CHAPTER VII

[June 13, 1763—Monday]

LIEUTENANT FRANCIS GORDON, commander of Fort Venango on the line of communication between Fort Pitt and Fort Presque Isle, considered himself to be a very levelheaded officer; a man who was prudent and disinclined to jump to conclusions. This being his frame of mind, he was not terribly tolerant of impulsiveness in other officers, considering it a grave weakness of which no officer of the Crown should be guilty.

He considered Ensign Christie, who commanded at Fort Presque Isle, to be just such an impulsive person. When John Christie's message had arrived here at Venango a week ago, telling about the attack on Abraham Cuyler's convoy and subsequent details up to the point where the survivors reached Presque Isle, Gordon just couldn't buy the story in its entirety as apparently Christie had. It was just too farfetched. He had no doubt that Lieutenant Cuyler's party may have been attacked, but it was his studied conclusion that Cuyler had panicked, abandoned the majority of his men and fled. He also doubted that Cuyler had come anywhere near Fort Sandusky. If Sandusky was burned, as he claimed, then logic dictated that Detroit, too, had been taken and this was simply inconceivable. Therefore, when the message from Christie had come, Gordon had dutifully relayed it on toward Fort Pitt, but with a message of his own expressing his doubt about the situation and suggesting that matters were not as grave as some young officers believed.

He was bolstered in his assumptions early this morning as a party of Shawnees and Senecas, showing the usual signs of friendship, approached Venango. There were over fifty of them and they were being led by Chief Kyashuta, the Seneca with whom Gordon had councilled many times. The lieutenant was pleased to see him. If anyone knew the truth

413

about what the western Great Lakes Indians were up to, it would be Kyashuta.

Smiling genially, he met the party at the gate and escorted Kyashuta and fourteen other chiefs and subchiefs of both the Seneca and Shawnee tribe toward the council chambers. The fifteen rank and file of the fort stood about casually and watched with interest as the remaining thirty-five or more Indians entered a short distance behind their chiefs. The scene was not a new one to them; they had witnessed similar ones many times before and Chief Kyashuta himself had become a reasonably familiar figure here. It was, however, a break in the monotony of life at this outpost and so they looked on curiously while their commander led Kyashuta and the other chiefs toward the council house while the rest of the Indians spread out, little groups of them converging smilingly upon each of the soldiers.

As they neared the door of the council house, Lieutenant Gordon moved politely to one side in order that the chiefs might enter first. He was just in the process of beckoning to one of his soldiers to bring tobacco for the visitors when several things happened simultaneously.

Three of the chiefs had moved up until they were hardly a pace behind Gordon. Abruptly Kyashuta jerked his tomahawk from his waistband and brandished it high with a threatening aspect. Startled, Gordon wheeled about and was immediately grasped by an Indian putting an arm around his neck and two others snatching his arms. As he struggled to free himself, an inarticulate screech erupted from Kyashuta and at that the warriors struck.

In no more than ten seconds the entire garrison, with the exception of Lieutenant Francis Gordon, were on the ground, dead or dying. In less than a minute, all fifteen of the soldiers had been scalped.

Unbelieving, virtually paralyzed with shock, Gordon offered no resistance as his clothing was stripped from him, his hands tied tightly behind his back and a tether six feet long snugged around his throat and tied to a post on the edge of the parade ground. He watched numbly as the goods of the fort were gathered and carried outside. When his hands were freed, it was with almost childlike obedience that he accepted the writing materials handed to him by Kyashuta and wrote down in English, as directed by the chief, a list of grievances which the Seneca dictated. These complaints covered the scarcity and dearness of gunpowder and lead over the past couple of years, plus the fact that the English were keeping possession of so many forts which they had occupied only with the understanding that as soon as the French were defeated, they would vacate the premises and turn the forts over to the Indians. That they had not done so and obviously had no intention of doing so was evidence in the eyes of the Indians that the English meant to possess themselves not only of these forts but the entire Indian country if not stopped. It was a relatively long and relatively accurate statement of complaints and when Gordon was finished, the document and the writing materials were taken from him.

And then the torture began.

[June 14, 1763—Tuesday]

The nearly two hundred and fifty Chippewas, Ottawas, Mississaugis and Hurons under such chiefs as Sekahos, Mintiwaby, Breton and others, had made their camp just up from the shore of Lake Erie about four miles to the west of Fort Presque Isle. The many canoes which had brought them here from the Detroit area to carry out the plan conceived by Pontiac had been dragged far ashore and hidden. Even the drag-marks in the sand had been smoothed away so as not to give away their presence before they themselves wished it known.

They sat now in their fireless camp, gnawing on bits of dried fish and jerked meat and listening avidly while Chief Kyashuta of the Senecas told them how he and his men had taken Fort Venango without the faintest suggestion of resistance. They grunted in pleased approval when he told them of the swiftness with which the garrison had been cut down in the early morning hours yesterday.

He had left a small party there, he added, to finish a ritual torturing of the commanding officer, after which the fort itself would be burned. The plunder had been divided with the Shawnees who had helped his men in the attack and another segment of his people were at this moment carrying the Senecas' share of the loot back to their village on the Genesee River.

Some earlier covert observation, Kyashuta went on, indicated that the commander of Fort Presque Isle was alert and suspicious, so that place would not be taken as easily, perhaps, but it *would* be taken; and, after that, the little Fort Le Boeuf, fifteen miles to the south.

Kyashuta voiced his pleasure at finding Pontiac's men here at the appointed time, as the runner had said they would be. Now, with the Iroquois at last joining hands with the western Great Lakes tribes, the English would be uprooted from this land and never allowed to return. Kyashuta failed to mention that the Iroquois League tribes—the Mohawk, Onondaga, Oneida, Cayuga and Tuscarora, as well as his own Seneca tribe—had not, as a confederation, given sanction to joining with the western tribes in any uprising against the English. For the most part, they were in the dark about it and the only ones actively involved—and completely without League approval—were a few bands of the Senecas.

Now, as discussion continued at this Lake Erie lakeshore camp, the plan of attack against Fort Presque Isle was discussed in detail. It was a simple plan but one which should meet with success if all went well. As soon as darkness had fallen this evening, they would move quietly overland and take a position behind two hills near the fort, which would provide them protection. At dawn they would launch their attack and if gunfire and arrows were not enough, then perhaps fire would do the job.

Not a man among these Indians had the slightest doubt that they would quickly wipe out Fort Presque Isle.

[*June 15, 1763—Wednesday, 7:00* A.M.]

Trembling with the cold, Alexander Henry crawled stiffly out from beneath the dense foliage of the bush he had used as a shelter for the night. His muscles ached from being so long drawn tight against the dank chill of the night and he slapped his arms to his sides and stamped his feet to get the circulation moving, wishing all the while that he had a fire at which to warm himself. Even more than that, he wished Wawatam would come back soon.

Uncomfortable it might have been up here on this mountain, and cold as well, but he was well aware that it probably would have been a great deal more uncomfortable had he remained in the village on the other side of this island called Michilimackinac. It had been wise, indeed, for Wawatam to have secreted him up here. With that much liquor to be drunk, who could tell what might happen.

The exile from the village had its genesis shortly after sunrise the day before yesterday, when an alarm had echoed through the village from the guards still on watch. Henry had not been sure what was happening, but in a little while upwards of twenty canoes, each with a dozen or more men in it, had shoved off from the shore adjacent to the village and glided out onto the open face of Lake Huron. Not until they had set their course to the northeast did the young trader see the object of this activity. Two large trading canoes were approaching.

In less than an hour the whole party was back. The canoes had been surrounded and brought to the island. Manned by Frenchmen, they contained a great amount of goods consigned to an English trader named Levy. This made them fair game for the Chippewas and everything was confiscated and the Frenchmen sent on their way, bewildered by it all but delighted at having escaped with their lives. In addition to the usual trade goods among Levy's things there were a number of new rifles, a quantity of powder and lead, and a dozen or more kegs of liquor.

It was a dangerous acquisition and both Wawatam and Henry knew it. Like most Indian nations, the Chippewas did not hold any member of their tribe responsible for anything he did while intoxicated. Drunken brawls were common whenever liquor was available. A fair proportion of the men of the tribe were missing an ear or a nose—favorite targets for the fiercely biting teeth of warriors in drunken fights with their fellows. The hazard was generally much greater for anyone on hand who was not a fellow tribesman—including even those who had been adopted into the tribe—and it was almost certain death for any captive on hand.

By late afternoon many were already drunk and Wawatam was becoming progressively more nervous on Henry's behalf. Finally admitting that he, too, wanted to join in the imbibing, Wawatam suggested that Henry allow himself to be hidden until the liquor was all consumed, the debauchery ended. Henry consented with alacrity and they left immediately, heading inland. They went directly to the principal mountain of the island, at its center. At the base it was very thickly forested and at its top it was extremely craggy. After they had walked a considerable distance, they came to a massive rock at the base of which was the opening of a cave.

"My brother," said Wawatam, "it would be best if you remained inside there until I come back for you."

"I will," Henry replied, shaking Wawatam's hand. He watched the Indian descend until he was lost from sight, then set about gathering some willowy, heavily leafed branches to spread as a bed. It was already dusk when he carried them inside the cave. The entrance was about ten feet wide, but it

417

expanded into a rather spacious room inside, perhaps forty feet long and thirty wide. It was now too dark to see much, but by feeling along the walls, Henry determined that there was an aperture at the wall opposite the entrance but so small that he dared not try to explore it lest he become wedged.

In the darkness he spread out the branches, lay upon them and covered himself with the single blanket Wawatam had given him. He fell asleep almost at once and did not awaken until morning, feeling uncomfortable because there was something gouging his back. He felt beneath him and removed the object. It was a bone and he thought it was probably that of a deer or some other large animal, but it was still too dark inside to be sure. He lay back and dozed restlessly for another hour, occasionally rolling over and feeling more bones, which he shoved away with his hands. When at last he fully wakened again, it was bright daylight outside and vision was reasonably good inside the cave here. He looked around himself and then suddenly cried out involuntarily at the start he got. There were a multitude of bones all over the cave floor and at least half a hundred of them were skulls. *Human* skulls!

Just for a moment the revulsion and horror of it nearly caused Henry to gag, but then he brought himself under control, demanding his own mind to realize there was nothing to fear. In fact, after a while he looked them over rather closely and spent several hours so engaged. When, by late afternoon, Wawatam had not returned, he went outside to sit and watch, but the sun went down without any sign of the Chippewa. Reluctantly, Henry reentered the cave, tried to lie down and sleep, but could not. The bones, which he had studied all day with clinical detachment, now loomed forbiddingly in his imagination, stirring up such frightening fantasies that he finally gathered up his blanket and left the cave. It was then that he had made his bed under the bush.

Now, feeling very hungry and thirsty and still quite chilled, he turned at the sound of footfalls and broke into a smile as he saw Wawatam returning. The Chippewa was somewhat bleary-eyed, but he snapped out of it quickly enough as Henry explained what was in the cave. Together they went inside and viewed the contents.

"What do you suppose happened to them?" Henry whispered.

Wawatam shook his head, awed by the sight. "I did not know they were here. I know of no one who has ever seen them before. We do not often go into caves, because of the evil spirits said to dwell in them. It was why I thought you would be safe here. How did the bones get here? I don't know. Perhaps it happened when, just after time began, the great waters overflowed all the land. Perhaps the people who lived here then came up and took refuge in this cave and were drowned here. Or perhaps it was the same inhabitants who hid themselves here when the Hurons came to make war on them, as tradition says they did, and they were discovered and massacred here."

Henry listened and nodded, but he had his own idea about the origin of the boneyard. He felt it very likely that this was the depository for the bones of prisoners sacrificed and devoured at war feasts in ancient times. Once again the vision of the private who had been butchered, quartered, boiled and eaten near the fort came surging back and he shuddered. Whatever the source, he was thankful when Wawatam told him that the liquor was all gone, the drunkenness over and it would now be safe for him to return to the village.

[June 15, 1763—Wednesday, 9:00 A.M.]

Lieutenant James Gorrell squinted slightly against the rippled sunlight reflecting off Green Bay and spoke in a voice which betrayed none of the nervousness he felt. He addressed himself to the Indian chiefs and numerous warriors who had assembled here outside the gate of Fort Edward Augustus at his bidding. Mostly they were of the Menominee tribe—meaning the Wild Rice People—led by their chief, Oshkosh,[110] but there were also a good many Winnebagos on hand under Chief Taychee, plus a fair number of Sacs and Foxes. In attendance too, to Gorrell's surprise, was a single Dakotah chief, Sahagi, newly arrived from the west. There were also three Ottawa warriors.

Now, though he spoke to them all, protocol demanded that since the Menominees were in the greatest number here, he direct his remarks to them, and so Gorrell did so.

"The Menominees," he began, "have always been good friends of the English. You who have come here at my request to listen to my words, know in your hearts that we have been concerned with your welfare and have tried to help you whenever and however we could. Sometimes supplies have been abundant, sometimes they have been scarce, but in either case we have always shared with you whatever we had. Even our powder and lead has been shared with you, though this was against the orders of my general, because I know full well that you must have them in order to live and provide for your families. For this reason I have disobeyed my general and have not kept them from you. You have told me that you are grateful for this and many times you have come to reaffirm your friendship for me in particular and for the English in general. Now has come the time when we will know the depth of that friendship.

"You see my men standing here under arms," he added, pointing to the formation of seventeen soldiers behind him. "Perhaps you wonder why this is so, but perhaps you already know. I will not keep it from you. This morning word was brought to me by these three Ottawa warriors from L'Arbre Croche," he indicated the trio with a dip of his head, "that the Chippewas, aided by some of the Sacs, have taken up the war hatchet against the English."

Gorrell looked sharply now at the contingent of Sac and Fox on hand. The chiefs and warriors stared back at him with open hostility, but Gorrell continued with no more than a slight pause.

"They have risen against Fort Michilimackinac and have massacred more than half of the English there. Those they did not kill were taken prisoner. When our good friends, the Ottawas, learned of this, they were very angry and they went to Michilimackinac and held council with the Chippewas; and when they returned to L'Arbre Croche, these Ottawas brought back with them in protective custody the commander of that fort and his first officer and eleven of his men, along with two traders.

"The three Ottawas who have brought me this word brought also a letter to me from that commanding officer, Captain Etherington. He has asked me to bring my men and our English traders and come to him, to help restore order, and this I must do. This means that our fort here, which you still call Fort La Baye after the name given to it by the French, must be temporarily abandoned. We are not giving it up entirely, but only leaving it for a little while, and now we will test your friendship for us. All of the goods in the fort, except those that we will need for our journey, will be distributed as presents among you with the understanding that you, on your part, will act as guardians of this fort and hold it for us for our eventual return. It is not to be given over to the French or to any other Indians or to anyone else except the English. Neither is it to be burned after our departure or in any way damaged, although you may have the use of it as you see fit. We wish to leave it in the trust of the Menominees, our friends. Are they agreeable to do this, in the name of the friendship we have shared?"

With great insult to the Menominee chief and marked insolence toward the English, a young Sac chief named Osa leaped to his feet and spoke up.

"The English," he said contemptuously, "are soft like women. Now that they know what has happened across the big water, they grow afraid and they hope to buy their safety by giving us gifts. They even offer to give us this fort, but only because they know now that we are on the eve of taking it ourselves. They think that by giving us the fort in trust they will become immune to our weapons. No!" He shouted the last word and pointed a finger at Gorrell, continuing: "Do not be so sure of this, Englishman! It may be that you will *never* depart this land!"

There was a mumble of agreement and ugly looks from the assembled Fox and Sac, but before either Gorrell or Chief Oshkosh could reply, the lone Dakotah chief stood. He dipped his head gravely at Gorrell and then spoke softly to the Menominee chief:

"Does Sahagi have the permission of Chief Oshkosh to speak before the chief of the Menominees makes his own answer to what has been said here?"

At the nod which Oshkosh gave him, Sahagi folded his arms across his chest and stood looking at Chief Osa of the Sacs for what seemed an interminable time without speaking. The young chief glared back, but after a few moments the glare began to die and Osa shifted his gaze to the ground between them. When Sahagi finally spoke, it was coldly, all trace of softness gone.

"The Sac and Fox," he said, "are the enemies of the Dakotah, just as the Chippewa are. They would like nothing so much as to kill me as I stand here, yet I stand here without fear. I know they do not dare, for it is *they* who are women. They and the Chippewa do not call us Dakotah; they call us *Nadouessioux*, or sometimes just Sioux, because this in their language means adders and, therefore, enemies. Yes! We are enemies, but I fear them not! The adder has long fangs. It is they who fear its poisoned bite and the destruction that would rain down upon them if the least of us was harmed."

Sahagi now dropped his arms and deliberately, insultingly, turned his back to the Sac and Fox and addressed his next remarks to Gorrell.

"The Dakotah have sharp ears," he said. "They hear many things from far places. Long before this time our ears heard of the bad conduct of the Chippewas toward our friends, the English. That is why I have come here with a message from my people. It is this: we hope that the tribes of this country will not follow the example of the Chippewa, but that instead they will protect these English. Unless they do so," the threat was quite pronounced in his tone now, "the Dakotah will fall upon them and take a suitable revenge. I have said. I say no more."

Shamed by the remarks, the Sac and Fox contingents shot furtive looks of fear and hatred at both Sahagi and Gorrell, then abruptly turned and stalked away. Now it was Oshkosh who spoke, and his voice was singularly gentle.

"The Dakotah chief is our friend and our guest. We thank Chief Sahagi for what he has said. All nations greatly fear the sting of the Sioux and there is not likely to be trouble for our English friends from anyone in this country."

He turned now to face Gorrell and continued: "What you say is true. The English have been good to us and we are your friends. Our hearts weep tears at the news of the misfortune of your brothers and it is with regret that we will see you leave here. Yes, we will gladly be the guardians of this fort until you return. We will keep it safe for you and we will welcome you when you come back with as much joy then as we have sorrow now at your leaving. You are going at once?"

"As soon as possible," Gorrell replied, "but it will take some days to prepare."

Oshkosh nodded. "Little birds have sung softly in our ears that bands of Chippewa move about nearby and it is likely that they and their Sac and Fox allies mean you harm, despite the warning of Sahagi. This shall not be. As long as you are here we will guard you; and when you leave, I will take a party of my best warriors to go with you across the lake and deliver you safely to your destination."

Gorrell was moved by the gesture and accepted it with thanks, shook hands with each of the Menominee and Winnebago chiefs and with the Dakotah, then marched his men back inside the fort to prepare for departure. As he did so, he could not help but wonder if such devotion from the Menominees and Dakotahs would have been forthcoming had he not consistently disobeyed General Amherst's orders and provided them with ammunition.

He doubted it.

It had not come as an especially stunning surprise to Ensign John Christie when the Indians attacked Fort Presque Isle without warning at dawn yesterday. Ever since the sloop *Michigan* from Detroit had passed by here seven days ago, he had been anticipating some sort of move by the savages.

The ship had first been seen by the rampart guard shortly after sunrise that day. At first sight it had been perhaps five or six miles from shore, just a sail standing toward Niagara. Christie had been summoned and he, along with a good many of his men, had gazed out over the ramparts of the fort at it. Christie expected the ship to turn in to the fort, but when it became obvious that it was not going to deviate from its heading, he dispatched a detachment under command of a corporal to row a batteau out on an interception course and find out what the news was from Detroit. It was imperative to know whether or not the Indians had attacked it, as feared.

The interception had been made and after an interval the batteau returned while the sloop continued its journey. As soon as the corporal reported to him, Christie realized that the fears had indeed become reality. The commander of the ship—Captain Jacob Newman—had told the corporal of the siege placed on Detroit by Pontiac and confirmed the belief that the uprising was general. He, in turn, was shocked to hear of the destruction of both Cuyler's convoy and Fort Sandusky. Having been first becalmed on the lake for nearly a week and then further detained a fortnight by consistently strong contrary winds, he knew nothing of these details. Now he was en route to Fort Niagara with dispatches from Major Gladwin about the outbreak and he cautioned the corporal to tell Christie to be on guard constantly and expect almost anything. He felt sure that Major Wilkins at Niagara would send Christie a reinforcement as soon as possible.

In the meanwhile, all twenty-seven of Christie's men, including those six of Cuyler's men who had been kept here, were ordered by the fort commander to remain in the blockhouse as the only truly secure place in the fort. The lone woman at Presque Isle—wife of a sergeant—also stayed in the blockhouse. Christie had immediately sent a messenger with word of Newman's report to Fort Pitt, via Fort Le Boeuf and Fort Venango.

Since then they had waited, but no reinforcement had

come from Niagara and now they were under full-scale attack. Thus far they had held out, but Christie was beginning to wonder just how long they could do so. Though this place was reasonably well built, its shortcomings were making themselves only too evident.

They had spotted the Indians yesterday morning before the attack began, silently crossing the mouth of the little creek where the fort's batteaux had been drawn up. They were shadowy figures in this first light, not only at the creek mouth but also crawling along to reach the protection of the lake bank and the sawpits adjacent to it, but there was no doubt they were Indians. Unwilling to begin the fight if it could be avoided, Christie had sternly forbidden his men to shoot unless the Indians started it. Unfortunately, it was a gamble that did not pay off, as it allowed the Indians to get quite close to the blockhouse before they opened fire on the fort and, when the fire was immediately returned, they were able to take cover in the well-sheltered ditch only a dozen yards or so from the fort walls. From this vantage they maintained a casual fire at the portholes of the fort and some of the Indians even took to throwing rocks at the gunports to conserve their ammunition. A number of balls of flaming pitch were also lobbed at the walls.

Almost immediately some of the Indians had gotten into the fort and took cover behind the bakeshop and other buildings. From there, too, they kept up a steady firing at the blockhouse. One enterprising group of ten Indians pulled down a small outbuilding made of planks and used it as a sort of movable breastworks, pushing it in front of them as they advanced. At the same time a great many of them were keeping up a running fire at the gunports from the creekbed and lake bank, making it extremely hazardous for anyone inside the blockhouse to expose himself even momentarily at one of the ports in order to shoot.

As the hours passed, new ideas were tried by the Indians. Burning arrows were shot into the sides of the blockhouse and onto the roof. Those on the sides rather quickly burned a small hole and then fell out; those on the roof had been anticipated by Christie, planned for, and quickly extinguished with water.

In three different places the Indians rolled logs up atop the southern ridge to form breastworks from behind which they could shoot with greater effectiveness and less exposure of themselves. Occasionally an individual or two would attempt to sprint across the intervening space from the ridge to join

THE NORTHERN
FRONTIER OUTPOSTS OF
PENNSYLVANIA

his companions in the ditch close to the fort, but this practice was soon abandoned when several Indians were killed or wounded by gunfire from the blockhouse ports.

For more than half the day the garrison seemed to be holding its own quite handily. The rumbling blasts of the few small cannon were effective in holding the Indians outside the walls in place. Those inside the fort, however, were safe from the light artillery and it soon became clear from the amount of earth and stone being thrown out from behind the nearest breastwork that the Indians were beginning to tunnel the short remaining distance to the blockhouse. Even worse was the discovery that the water supply in the blockhouse barrels had already been nearly depleted through extinguishing fires—and the well, outside in the parade ground, was now exposed to enemy fire. The only hope was to start doing some digging themselves and hope to tunnel to the well in time.

While part of the men kept up an answering fire from the gunports the rest, Ensign Christie included, put their backs to the labor of tearing up the floorboards and beginning to dig. Before the tunnel had been dug halfway to the well, the roof was set ablaze again and every last bit of water remaining had to be used to put out the fire. Only minutes later another blaze began on the roof and one of the soldiers risked his life to climb out on it and, with bullets spattering all around him, ripped the burning shingles off and threw them to the ground.

Suddenly darkness was upon them and it came as a shock to the whole garrison to realize that they had been fighting steadily since sunup. The firing from the Indians diminished somewhat, but did not altogether stop. All through the night came the flashes and poppings of guns.

This morning, soon after daybreak, the gunfire from the Indians mysteriously stopped. When it had not resumed after three or four hours, the men within the blockhouse were heartened, believing this signified that the enemy was running out of ammunition and would soon be withdrawing, but Christie shook his head at this.

"I doubt it," he said. "Much more likely that they're working on their trenches or figuring out some new way to get at us. Keep working on that tunnel."

He was quite correct. A little while after noon the firing recommenced and at about two o'clock a new hazard flared up. The digging of the Indians had taken them to the commander's house, which stood adjacent to the blockhouse. Now, shrieking like madmen, they set the place afire and withdrew from it as the flames raged fiercely through the sap-laden planks and pine logs of the building. In a short time the flames were roaring against the side of the blockhouse and a great pall of smoke rose blackly over the fort and wafted eastward along the shoreline.

"Dig on that well tunnel!" Christie shouted. "For God's sake, *dig!* We'll be on fire in a few minutes. *Dig!*"

Two miles off shore, unseen by the embattled garrison, the sloop *Michigan*, fresh from Niagara with a reinforcement for Detroit, floated quietly. It had come to this spot last night and, hearing the gunfire, had anchored far out to await the dawn. Now its crew and the reinforcement soldiers lined the shoreward rail and watched the pillar of black smoke rise from beside the blockhouse. They had almost gone in when the firing had not resumed in the morning, hopeful that the attackers had withdrawn; but now, even from this distance, they could see the orange of the flames licking the blockhouse wall.

"Looks like they'll be goners if they don't get some help," Captain Newman said. "What do you think, Lieutenant? Shall I put in and see what we can do?"

Lieutenant Abraham Cuyler straightened from leaning on the rail and winced as a streak of pain from his not-yet-healed wound shot through him. He shook his head regretfully.

"What could we do? There's no way to get the garrison to the boat and we're not half the Indians' number. Besides, we have all these supplies and a reinforcement of fifty men which Major Wilkins ordered me to take to Major Gladwin at Detroit. If it comes to a choice between the two, Detroit is the more important fort. It'll fall without what we're bringing. I'm sorry for them over there," he glanced at the burning Fort Presque Isle again and shook his head regretfully, "but there's nothing we can do. Weigh anchor, Captain. There's no joy in watching the defeat of our own men."

Within the fort's blockhouse the entire garrison was gagging and coughing from the smoke which now filled the structure, and the heat was intense. Grimly, faces muddied with soot and dirt and sweat, the men dug on. Suddenly there was a shout.

"We're through! Mr. Christie, we're through!"

A bucket brigade was formed right away. Even the sergeant's wife and the men at the gunports pitched in to help as bucketful after bucketful of water sloshed down the side of the blockhouse and, incredibly, the fire of the outside wall was extinguished. By this time the commander's house was so completely consumed that the flames remaining from it no longer were able to lick the walls of the blockhouse. The garrison had won this round, but the fight was not yet over.

Fatigued almost beyond endurance, hardly able to lift and fire and reload their weapons, choking on the gun smoke which was again displacing the wood smoke in the close confines of the blockhouse, the garrison doggedly fought on. Throughout the remainder of the day and into the night they fought until now, at last, just before midnight, the Indians ceased firing again. The exhausted soldiers inside the blockhouse slumped to the floor or leaned against the walls, gasping for breath, heads hanging, eyes bloodshot and burning and the tears from them carving light grooves in the facial grime.

The silence was eerie, almost overwhelming. For five, ten, fifteen minutes there was no sound and then came a voice calling in French from outside.

"Attention! Attention! You men inside the blockhouse. You have no chance. We give you warning to surrender now, as you have no chance at all. If you do not surrender, we mean to set fire to the blockhouse above and below at the same time *and keep it burning! You will be roasted!"*

Ensign Christie understood only a little of the French and the others could not understand it at all. He moved to a gunport, cupped his mouth and shouted hoarsely, "Is there anyone among you who speaks English? We don't understand French."

In a moment there came another voice which sounded almost rusty from disuse in the English tongue. It repeated essentially the same thing. The speaker, dressed in Indian garb, came into moonlit view from behind one of the log breastworks on the ridge.

"Who are you?" Christie demanded.

"Don't make no never mind who'm I. Nobody you ever heered of. Got myself tooken whilst fightin' fer that dunderhead Braddock in 'fifty-five. Ottawas patched me up an' 'dopted me. Iffen you cain't fight 'em, j'in 'em, thet's what I allus say. But me, I don' matter none. What matters is thet you'uns is gonna git fried in there 'lessen you give up. Hell, they don' want you—they jist wanta destroy the fort. Give it up an' they promise y'all kin go anywheres y'like."

In the dimness of the blockhouse, Christie looked around him. Every man was staring at him, their eyes unseen except as deep shadows in the somewhat lighter smudge of face. No one said anything and Christie turned back to the porthole.

"A soldier of the King does not give up his fort without considerable thought," he called. "Will you give us till morning to give our answer?"

There was an extended pause as the man disappeared, but then he returned and his voice drifted up to them. "Reckon y'all got till sunrise. But no longer."

The man turned and vanished quickly around the log breastwork and Christie stepped away from the port, half expecting the gunfire to resume. When, after several minutes had passed, it didn't, he sat heavily on the floor and leaned back against one wall. It was fully ten minutes more before he spoke again.

"Well, men, what'll it be. To misquote our interpreter out there, do we surrender or fry?"

[June 16, 1763—Thursday, Midnight]

At the very instant that Ensign Christie and his men were deliberating their decision in the blockhouse at Fort Presque Isle, important letters were being written at three widely separated locations: at Fort Bedford, Captain Louis Ourry was writing to his immediate commander, Colonel Henry Bouquet, at Philadelphia; in Philadelphia, Bouquet was writing to his immediate commander, General Jeffrey Amherst, at New York; and in New York, Amherst was writing to both Sir William Johnson at Johnson Hall on the Mohawk, and Major Henry Gladwin at Detroit.

The letter being written by lantern light in his quarters at Fort Bedford by Captain Ourry was, in essence, a continuation of the running report this Swiss officer had been supplying to Colonel Bouquet. Three days ago he had written:

> *I am now, as I foresaw, entirely deserted by the country people. No further incident having happened here, they have gradually left me to return to their plantations; so that my whole force is reduced to twelve Royal Americans to guard the fort and seven Indian prisoners. I should be very glad to see some troops come to my assistance. A fort with five bastions cannot be guarded, much less defended, by a dozen men; but I hope God will protect us.*

Yesterday, Ourry had written again, with constrained excitement:

This moment I return from the parade. Some scalps taken up Denning's Creek yesterday, and today some families murdered and house burnt, have restored me my militia . . . Two or three other families are missing, and the houses are seen in flames. The people are all flocking in again.

Now, with midnight at hand and his eyes scratchy from lack of sleep, Louis Ourry was again writing, his weariness evident in the poor penmanship and even in the effort it caused him to dip his pen and return it to the paper. He was writing:

. . . and even while the country men were at drill on the parade here, three Indians attempted to seize two small girls close to the fort; but they were, I am pleased to report, driven off by a volley. This had greatly added to the panic of the people. With difficulty I can restrain them from murdering the Indian prisoners . . . I can't help thinking that the enemy will collect, after cutting off the little posts one after another, leaving Fort Pitt as too tough a morsel, and bend their whole force upon the frontiers.

For his own part, Henry Bouquet, despite his prolonged efforts to convince Amherst of the gravity of the situation, found himself suddenly wondering if perhaps it was not Amherst who was correct in playing down the significance of the multitude of reports, most of them entirely unverified, emerging from the frontier. His change of attitude was extremely temporary, but it was reflected in the letter he had written two days ago to Ecuyer at Fort Pitt, in which he said, in part:

The savages have blundered so much in not attempting to surprise our posts that we must entertain the most contemptible opinion of their courage and intellects.
Their lies about Detroit give me some hopes that Sandusky is not lost. I flatter myself that we shall be able to disengage Venango and Le Boeuf if they have provisions for some time . . .

But Bouquet's pendulum swung back swiftly and the conviction that the uprising was general and severe descended upon him with even greater impact. Carelessness and underestimating an enemy's potential was a grievous fault of any commander, just as was overabundant caution and undue fear. But of the two, Bouquet had rather be guilty of the latter, for in that case he would be prepared, but in the former it could well be the forerunner of great disaster. Despite Amherst's blunt rejection of his suggestion to abandon Venango and Le Boeuf, Bouquet still considered this a wise move under the circumstances and so decided to suggest it again as if he had never mentioned it before. With Amherst's letter of June 12 before him on his desk, he began his carefully worded reply:

Philada. 16th June 1763

Sir:

I received your Excellency's letter of the 12th and have required Major Campbell to proceed to this town with the two companies.

We are yet too much in the dark to form a plan, but if things are as represented, I propose to march these two companies to Fort Pitt, with a convoy of flour, sheep, and some powder, which be kept ready at Shippensburg: and in escorting back the horses and drivers, clear the forts of all useless people and have sufficient garrisons on the communication to keep it clear and open to further supplies. Any alteration you think proper to make in that disposition will come in time. In the supposition that the communication with Niagara from Montreal and Albany can be depended upon, I beg you would be pleased to take in consideration whether the blockhouses at Venango and Le Boeuf ought not be abandoned and their small garrisons, when disengaged, sent to Fort Pitt or Presque Isle, keeping only this last post, which can be conveniently supplied from the lake, whereas to support the other two is very precarious and would require more men than we can spare, without visible advantage.

The communication from Ft. Pitt to the Detroit by Sandusky appears to me impracticable during a war with the savages, from the too-great distance, through a country full of swamps and cut by rivers and creeks, some of which are seldom fordable.

The panic appears general on the frontiers, which will soon be deserted. Should these Provinces raise troops, permit me to submit to you whether they would not be of more service if formed in ranging companies composed of hunters and woodsmen, who may be had on the frontiers of this Province, but particularly on those of Maryland and Virginia; and if those levies were under the inspection of an officer, to reject the rabble too commonly received, which occasions great ex-

pense in pay and provisions without doing any service. We have no powder here. I shall get some from the traders in Cumberland County. The magazine at Fort Pitt being liable to be overflowed, would you approve of building a small one of the bastions? Bricks are ready made; a few bricklayers might be wanted. I shall join Major Campbell at Carlisle and proceed to Bedford to forward what is wanted, and be in the way to act as circumstances may require.

I am, &c.
H. Bouquet

His Excellency
Sir Jeffrey Amherst

Meanwhile, in New York, the bubble of complacency General Amherst had so laboriously blown around himself had just been pricked and the general was drenched in his own wrath. James Dalyell, his face flushed with ill-contained excitement, had just rushed into the general's quarters with both a letter from Sir William Johnson and Major John Wilkins's letter of June 6 from Fort Niagara, telling of the return of Cuyler's shattered survivors.

Amherst read Sir William's letter first, while Dalyell waited, and then, still in a placid fame of mind, turned to that of Major Wilkins. Suddenly his eyes widened and his face paled. Incredible as it was for him to believe, not only was the report of the destruction of Fort Sandusky true, as confirmed by Cuyler, but a major convoy of the King's supplies to Detroit had been cut to ribbons, with two-thirds of its near-hundred men killed and nine-tenths of its cargo lost to the savages. The initial pallor on the general's face was quickly replaced by a deep flush and his rage was a fearsome thing to witness. His aide stepped discreetly back out of the way and for once made himself relatively unobtrusive. Amherst didn't let it stay that way.

"Dalyell!"

"Sir?"

"By God, you've been itching for action. Well, all right, sir, you've got it! Collect whatever reinforcements are available—the 17th Regiment for one—and leave immediately for Albany. Collect more reinforcements there and at every step along the way. Major Robert Rogers ought to still be there in Albany. I'll give you a letter ordering him to accompany you under your command. He's to bring as many of his men as he can get. Move up to Oswego as soon as possible and then directly on to Niagara for that fort's protection."

Dalyell nodded. "And the Detroit, sir?"

"I still can't believe anything's happened there. We'd've heard by now. But just in case it becomes necessary, you have authority to proceed to the Detroit and take whatever action is required."

"I'm to be in command, sir?"

"Yes, by God, you're to be in command. Responsible directly to me. It's what you've been hinting around for, isn't it?"

"Yes, sir!"

"All right then, get moving. *Now!* I've got some letters to write."

Dalyell practically ran out of the room and within moments the general was at his desk hastily penning the letter to Sir William:

New York, 16th June 1763

Sir:

I am to thank you for your letter of the 6th instant, which I have this moment received, with some advices from Niagara concerning the motions of the Indians that way, they having attacked a detachment of the King's under the command of Lieut. Cuyler of Hopkins's Rangers, who were on their route toward the Detroit, and obliged him to return to Niagara with (I am sorry to say) too few of his men.

Upon this intelligence I have thought it necessary to dispatch Captain Dalyell, my aide-de-camp, with orders to carry with him all such reinforcement as can possibly be collected (having at the same time a due regard for an attention to the safety of the principal forts) to Niagara and to proceed to the Detroit if necessary and judged proper.

Hurriedly completing that letter, Amherst now began another, this time to Major Gladwin at Detroit, explaining the steps he had taken essentially as he had explained them to Sir William, and then adding:

. . . but I flatter myself, notwithstanding the reports we have heard, that I shall have the pleasure to find you and your garrison are all well, and that you have been able to defeat the weak attempts of the Indians, if they have been so rash as to make any.

A prognosticator Lieutenant General Sir Jeffrey Amherst certainly was not, but where an idea of his own was concerned, he cherished an almost unbounded tenacity.

[*June 17, 1763—Friday, 3:15* A.M.]

It was a rare occasion when George Croghan did not sleep well at night. There were those who claimed he could "sleep right through the stampede of a herd of buffalo if one of the critters didn't tromp on him whilst passing." Yet, here it was with dawn now only a couple of hours away and Croghan was still unable to sleep. A disturbing uneasiness seemed to perch on his shoulders and peck at him each time he closed his eyes and for hours, tired though he was, he had lain awake thinking of what had already happened on the frontier and wondering what yet lay ahead.

By June 11 he had reached Shippensburg, some thirty-five miles west of Carlisle and still over sixty-five miles east of Fort Bedford. Not unexpectedly, he found the whole countryside in turmoil, with the populace scared out of its wits by the murderous hit-and-run attacks being launched against the settlements and individual cabins farther to the west by the Indians; and equally by the prevailing rumors that it would be their own turn next.

Immediate inquiries by Croghan showed that practically no defensive measures had been taken by the people. Too far from either Carlisle or Fort Bedford for protection, even had armies been available at either place, they simply milled about like ants in a disrupted anthill, with everyone excited and no one knowing what to do. Fort Lyttleton, which might have been of some benefit, lay deserted and it was with some agitation that Croghan rounded up twenty-five men to pool their strength and act as a garrison for the tiny post. With an effectiveness which far overshadowed any efforts thus far by the country magistrates, he did what they couldn't, wouldn't, or had not the authority to do. In addition to manning Fort Lyttleton, he also hired a party of men to escort a supply of ammunition from where it was stored at Fort Loudoun on the west branch of Conococheague Creek, doing no one any good, to Fort Bedford, for which it had long been intended. More than anything else, perhaps, even though he was thoroughly detested by a great many persons, his very presence here seemed to have a calming effect on the people.

By June 15 he had reached Fort Bedford, only to find Captain Louis Ourry and his seven-man garrison practically beside themselves in their efforts to calm the one hundred or more fear-ridden families who had flocked to the little post for military protection. Within mere minutes of his arrival, the whisper that "Croghan's here" had sped through the crowd, carrying with it a peculiar security which soothed the people and encouraged them to listen to reason and pull together instead of everyone seeing to the safety only of himself and his own. There was the prevailing feeling that Croghan was some sort of guardian spirit and so long as he was on hand, they were safe from attack. Even Ourry felt it, as evidenced by the brief comment made in a letter to Bouquet:

His company, as you may well imagine, is a great relief to me, as his generosity has been to many a starving family.

Yet, despite the good he was doing, there were those who were the backbiters, who nipped and snarled at his heels and tried to use him as a scapegoat for their problems. Prominent among these—and quite outspoken in their criticism—were the Quakers in Philadelphia, who now heaped blame for the uprising on George Croghan's shoulders, claiming that it was the settlements Croghan had begun in the valleys of the Youghiogheny and Allegheny Rivers which had sparked the bloodlust in the Indians. There was just enough truth to the statement to make the sting very sharp; all settlements west of the Susquehanna, Croghan's included, were in part responsible for the anger of the Indians, though his were neither first nor anywhere near the most extensive.

Yet, long jealous of Croghan and Sir William because of their influence with the Indians, and because the two Indian agents had more than once effectively blocked intrigues engaged in with the Indians against these two men by the Quakers, the Society evidently hoped that by branding Croghan as the cause of the war they could reduce his effectiveness and influence among both Indians and settlers. Even Henry Bouquet, who usually remained calm in such matters, became ruffled over the charges and angrily refuted them in public.

But the Quaker charges provided ammunition for some. Only a month ago, a shrewd land office character named William Peters, along with a Philadelphia merchant named Daniel Clark, who also happened to be Croghan's cousin, sensing a get-rich-quick scheme in land near the Carlisle-Fort Bedford Road in Cumberland County, purchased thirty thousand acres of it from Croghan. Now, with the Indians on the warpath, the pair found that instead of being able to break up the land and sell it in small plots at a handsome profit, they would have had difficulty even giving it away. For this they bitterly blamed Croghan, accusing him of selling lands to them when he knew the Indians were about to attack.

At this Croghan exploded. Was it possible, he asked with scathing contempt, that if he had known the Indians were about to attack he would have entered into a land partnership with Colonel Clapham at a cost to himself of £2,500? Land, he added, which was now gone, along with his murdered partner? Further, if he had known the Indians were rising, would he have left Croghan Hall on the Allegheny, with its new stock of equipment and furnishings and livestock—which cost him another £2,000—for the Indians to burn, destroy and kill?

But these matters, though troublesome to him, were not the cause of Croghan's sleeplessness. What was bothering him was something he could not quite put his finger on and so now, with dawn still a long way off, he sighed and got out of bed, lighted his lamp and sat at the desk to write to Bouquet of how matters stood at this time:

Fort Bedford, June 17th 1763
Dear Sir:

I wrote you from Shippensburg the eleventh, to which instant I refer you for my opinion of the Indians' behavior at this time, till I hear from Fort Pitt. As no express has come down this twelve days, I have reason to think the place is invested so that none can safely escape them. But they can no longer continue there, in my opinion. The fine cattle there which may fall into their way can support them. The Delawares, in my opinion, are the people who have begun this sudden war, and if the Ottawas and Chippewas have attacked Detroit, I believe it will be found that the French were acquainted with their designs. I imagine the Delawares will remove over the . . . Mississippi. Perhaps this may be a stroke of policy in the French to get as many Indian Nations as possible to go to the country over the Mississippi, which they have to people, as well as to make themselves respectable with their Indian allies as to secure as much of the Indian trade as they can.

As for what the Quakers accuse me of, it is of little concern to me, as I know from whence it stems. Perhaps somehow their eyes will be opened to what they are doing. I wish the Quakers might find that their interfering with Indian affairs may have done more hurt to His Majesty's Indian in-

terest—and given them a greater dislike to his troops—than any settlement.

> *I am dear sir,*
> *Your most humble servt*
> *Geo. Croghan*

To:
Col. Henry Bouquet

[June 17, 1763—Friday, 5:30 A.M.]

An aching weariness settled over Ensign John Christie as the light of dawn began to seep through the gunports into the still faintly gunsmoke-acrid interior of the Fort Presque Isle blockhouse. Throughout the night, sometimes spiritedly, sometimes with considerable heat, more often with resignation, he and his twenty-seven men and the wife of his sergeant discussed whether or not they should give up the fort. The greatest stumbling block was whether or not the Indians would honor their word to let the garrison go.

A few of the soldiers, such as Privates Benjamin Gray and David Smart, were for continuing a defense of the blockhouse, regardless of the threats. There were equally a few who, wearied beyond further endurance from the battle already fought, were strongly adamant in favor of giving up the place unconditionally, even if it meant becoming prisoners of the savages. The majority, however, felt that it would be best to proceed cautiously, hear what terms they offered, study what further onslaught they might be able to make against the blockhouse, and then come to a decision.

It was the latter course which seemed wisest to Christie and therefore a plan had been established. Two men would go out first to hear the terms. At the same time they would study the enemy's potential against the fort if the attack were renewed. If, in their judgment, there was no chance that the blockhouse could withstand such an attack, they were to give a secret signal with their hands to Ensign Christie, who would be watching from the blockhouse. At that point Christie himself would come out to negotiate.

This plan agreed upon, the garrison lapsed into silence. Some of them slept, others merely sat and stared. Thus they remained until, with the first light of the sunrise, a voice from outside hailed them and the two volunteers looked at one another wordlessly, then rose and left the blockhouse, hearing the awful finality of the sound as the bolts were shot behind them and they were locked out.

They moved slowly, looking about themselves carefully, gradually approaching the two Indians who stood exposed on the parade awaiting them. By the time they came to a stop before them, neither of the privates had any doubt in his mind: the blockhouse was doomed. Preparations had been made during the night to virtually layer the walls of the blockhouse with fire arrows, pitch balls, wagons of kindling and the like. It was also evident that the roof of the installation would be struck by dozens of fire arrows at the same time. There was simply no possibility that the place could hold out.

Attempting to converse with the two Indians in sign language, both men surreptitiously gave the prearranged hand signal that surrender was the only course remaining. A moment later, Ensign John Christie emerged from the blockhouse, leaving the door open behind him. The Indian-dressed white man acted as interpreter as Christie conversed with the Indians and assured him that he and his men would not be harmed if they surrendered; that they could go to Fort Pitt or Fort Niagara or wherever they cared to go, unmolested. The main object of the Indians here, it was claimed, was to destroy the fort, which was offensive to them. It was to be burned.

Christie capitulated and called an order for his men to lay down their arms. Several of the soldiers had already emerged from the doorway of the blockhouse when a horde of Indians broke from cover. One of the soldiers was seized and held while twenty or thirty of the Indians poured into the blockhouse. At the same time well over a hundred others began ransacking all other parts of the fort, seeking whatever plunder was available.

Abruptly the sergeant's wife still in the blockhouse gave a piercing scream, which was followed by shouts and scuffling sounds. Immediately Christie and his two men who had been talking with the Indians were seized and bound, while others of the garrison were dragged, struggling, from the blockhouse.

Only two men escaped. Benjamin Gray and David Smart, taking advantage of the confusion in progress, raced to the ditch the Indians had dug and then followed it to the little creek, crossed it safely and then disappeared into the woods beyond. Everyone else, including the woman—who was frightened but not injured—was quickly bound and led outside the fort.

Christie was furious, demanding loudly and angrily that

they be turned loose and the word of the capitulation terms be lived up to. The Indians paid no attention. The entire fort was ransacked of anything worth taking and then every structure left standing was put to the torch.

The prisoners were then divided up among the Indian factions on hand. Some were taken by the Shawnees, some by the Senecas, others by the Ottawas and Chippewas, the few Delawares and Hurons, and the two Sacs who had taken part in the attack.

As for the commanding officer, Christie and four of his soldiers, along with the sergeant's wife, were taken by the Hurons who, with their prisoners in tow, immediately set out on their own for Detroit.

Fort Presque Isle—the connecting link in the communication between Detroit and both Fort Pitt and Fort Niagara— no longer existed.

[June 17, 1763—Friday, 1:00 P.M.]

Major Henry Gladwin looked better today than he had at any time since the siege of Detroit had begun. His eyes were still badly sunken and his face gaunt, but today he carried himself better, as if the enormous weariness that had so long enshrouded him had dissolved. The rims of his eyes were no longer so inflamed and he seemed more alert.

The whole answer was simply *rest*. Until last night, Gladwin had not slept more than a few hours at a time since May 9. But after the delegation of Indian chiefs left the fort yesterday afternoon just after two o'clock, Gladwin had collapsed on his bed and slept a deep, undisturbed, thoroughly rejuvenating sleep. For almost eighteen hours he had scarcely moved. At eight this morning he had awakened briefly, feeling logy and doped, removed his clothing and got back into bed and slept again undisturbed until noon. The twenty-two hours of sleep had answered the long unheeded demands of his body and now, an hour after rising, he felt wonderfully fit and alert.

He thought again of the events of yesterday and a smile creased his lips. It had been the first truly encouraging development of the siege for this garrison; for the whole English cause, as a matter of fact.

"The rats are beginning to desert the sinking ship," he muttered aloud, and his smile broadened.

The encouragement had begun two days ago, on the fifteenth, when Chief Washee of the Potawatomies, along with several of his warriors, came to the fort under a flag of truce, bringing along with him Ensign Francis Schlosser and two of his privates from Fort St. Joseph, plus a private from Fort Miamis. His object was to trade them for the two Potawatomies still being held by Gladwin, including the important chief named Winnemac.

There had been little talk on that occasion. Gladwin had accepted the captives, hustled them out of sight and sent for one of the Potawatomi captives, specifically ordering, however, that Winnemac remain locked up. When the less important Potawatomi was delivered to Washee, the chief was extremely dissatisfied.

"We brought you four of your men to trade for two of ours," he complained, "which we considered to be more than fair. Yet, you have taken those four and given us back only one of our own, and not he whom we most desired to be freed."

Gladwin shook his head. "These are not the only English captives you and the Ottawas, the Hurons and Chippewas— all of you!—have prisoners from this or other forts. Is not Captain Campbell still being held, as he has been from the very beginning? Is not Lieutenant McDougall also being held? And what of Ensign Pauli? No, Chief Washee, with the four men you have brought in to us, you have bought the release of this one only. For Chief Winnemac, a good many other captives must be released."

"But I have no more," Washee objected.

"Some of your people have more, and all of your allies have. Go see them."

Washee and his men had gone then and for long hours after that, Gladwin and some of his officers questioned Ensign Schlosser and the privates who had been released and learned from them the details of how both Fort St. Joseph and Fort Miamis had been taken.

Then, yesterday at noon, Washee had returned. He brought along with him not more prisoners for liberation but rather two other Potawatomi chiefs and two chiefs of the Mississaugi Chippewas from the Saginaw Bay area. One of the latter pair was Chief Mindoghquay, known well to be one of the most influential chiefs of that tribe. They wished to hold council and Gladwin directed that they be taken to the council chambers. The major arrived there only moments after they had taken their places, and he was attended by Captain Joseph Hopkins, Lieutenant Jehu Hay, and the interpreter, Jacques St. Martin. Pipes were filled, lighted, and

440

smoked in silence and then it was Washee who arose first to speak. Holding out a small string of wampum to emphasize his remarks, he spoke deliberately and with surprising directness.

"What we have already told you on our first two visits here has been true. What we are going to say now is from our hearts."

He stepped forward and handed the wampum to Gladwin and then stepped back to his place and continued:

"My two brothers from Saginaw who are here with me have also been sent in the name of their chief to speak for their whole nation. Their hearts, like ours, are inclined toward peace with the English. Hear now my words of truth: I say to you that the Potawatomies knew nothing about the commencement of this present war between us. It had begun before we knew of it and we were hurried into it by the Ottawas under Chief Pontiac. It was never the strong wish of our chiefs; it was only the wish of some of our young men, to seek your blood. Now we have talked long on it among ourselves and, for ourselves only, I can tell you now that we have buried the red hatchet in a place where it can never be found and raised up again."

With this he handed another small string of wampum to Gladwin and continued:

"To the rest of our people we have sent messages running, telling them that whatever English prisoners they have must be delivered up to you, and this will be done as soon as they come to Detroit. It is the word of Washee."

With this he turned and resumed his seat and now it was Chief Mindoghquay who rose smoothly, a string of wampum in his hand, and then stood quietly for a long moment before beginning to speak softly.

"I have been sent here to speak for my people and for the Chippewas in the name of Wasson, chief of all the Chippewas of the Saginaw, and in the name of all the other chiefs of our people there. My words are straight and true and I desire that you will hear them in your heart as well as in your ears. Our hands and yours have always been joined, ever since the English took possession of this country, and they should never be parted. I have not entered into the war against you at all, nor have most of our chiefs. Those who have raised the tomahawk against you, besides Pontiac, are but a few and they act for themselves only, not for the Chippewas of Saginaw. Our hearts are the same as the Potawatomies and we intend that they will remain so. I speak the real sentiments of the hearts of all our chiefs who desire that you English should believe us, knowing that if I told lies the Great God would be offended at me."

With this declaration he presented the wampum string to Gladwin and resumed his seat beside Washee. Gladwin gave the strings into the care of Lieutenant Hay and then, from Captain Hopkins, he took one of his own—a slightly broader and longer belt—and held it in his hands as he looked at the Indians before him.

"Before I give you any answer to what you have said here," he began, "I must know one thing." His gaze flicked to Washee. "Do the Potawatomi chiefs here speak only for their own bands in particular, or do they speak for their whole nation?"

Without rising, Washee replied: "For our nation!" and the two chiefs of his tribe who were with him nodded their heads in agreement.

"That is good," the major said. "I am glad that you have opened your eyes and do not intend to persist in a thing that must end in your ruin. Still, the only thing you can really do to convince me of your good intentions is to give up the rest of your prisoners, go back to your villages and tend to your corn and your hunting. I have not the authority to make a peace with you independent of General Amherst, but if you do remain tranquil, if you do return to your villages and give no further support to Pontiac, then I will recommend you to the general and you will find that everything I have told you is true—that a peace has actually been made between the French and English people, and that if you persist in this kind of thing, not only the English will fight against you, but the French—the very people you think you are fighting for—will also take arms against you. I, too, speak from the heart and my words are straight. I therefore say to you that the white people are now all one and that if the Indians make war against one, they are making war against all. I know that you have been made to believe that there is no peace between French and English, and that there is an army of French soldiers coming from the Illinois country to help you. This is what you have been told, but those who told you so have told you lies and are your enemies, which you will soon see. If you take my advice and do as I desire that you do, you may live for the future in tranquility as before and you will then see around you the Ottawas starving in the woods for want of the necessaries of life that you can in no way get except from the English."

He then presented the wampum belt and asked Mindoghquay whether or not he spoke for the many Chippewas up at Michilimackinac as well as for those of Saginaw Bay. Would they, he asked, refrain from striking Fort Michilimackinac? Chief Mindoghquay replied with less assurance than before.

"I have come here to speak for the Chippewas who are my people at Saginaw. The Chippewas who are at the Michilimackinac, they are the people of Minivavana and Matchekewis and they must speak for themselves. Yet, I have heard nothing from them and I do not believe they will strike your fort there; and I promise you this, that if Pontiac tries to go from here toward that post, we will stop him!"

Gladwin believed Mindoghquay was speaking the truth and he smiled faintly. "I am very glad," he said, "to hear that you are so well inclined and that you have more sense than to be led into a thing by the Ottawas which would be your ruin. The Ottawas have been misled badly, for I never intended anything but peace with them, and they have begun this war without any good reason. As for the Chippewas of Saginaw Bay, I am well pleased with your behavior and will recommend you to the general if you continue at your villages in the same tranquility you say you are in. You may be sure that everything I have said to you here is true, which you will find to be the case in the end. I strongly advise you not to listen to any lies which may be spread among you."

To each of the chiefs Gladwin now gave another string of wampum, along with a few token gifts of blankets and tobacco, and all of them moved toward the door to leave, the major walking with them. At the doorway, Mindoghquay paused and turned. He held the string of wampum Gladwin had given him and he looked satisfied.

"I am glad to receive this from my English brother," he said. "When I return to my people, I will show the chiefs this wampum, which will be my mouth as I speak, and they will believe that they are pitied by you."

The entire group left the fort after that and when finally the gate had been closed behind them, Gladwin had given word that he was not to be disturbed except in the direst emergency and with that he returned to his quarters. It was then that he had collapsed onto his bed in his first real rest for weeks.

Reviewing what had happened at the council yesterday, Gladwin was pleased. He did not try to fool himself into believing that this marked the end of the war, or even the beginning of the end, but it was nonetheless a good sign. It was entirely possible, of course, that these wavering Indians would flock to support Pontiac if there was any good indication that he was winning the war, but for now at least perhaps they would remain idle long enough to undermine some of Pontiac's prestige.

Abruptly he was jarred from his thoughts by an excited rapping on the door. He bade the caller enter and one of the rampart guards, his face flushed and his breathing rapid, entered and gave his commander a hurried salute.

"Sir," he said, "it looks like maybe the *Michigan* is coming back. We just heard a cannon roll from far down the river."

"Are you certain?"

"Well, it certainly sounded like one, sir. Several of us heard it. Sounded like maybe they were trying to signal us."

"Let's hope you're right," Gladwin said. "Have a cannon fired in return at once in that direction. If it is the ship, it'll let them know we're still in possession here."

[*June 18, 1763—Saturday*]

It was just after nine in the morning when the private standing guard at the door of the small blockhouse suddenly straightened and called, "Mr. Price, some Indians are coming. Corporal Fisher's out there with them."

Ensign George Price, commanding officer of Fort Le Boeuf, came to the doorway at once and looked out. Forty yards from the blockhouse the young, mustachioed Jacob Fisher was shaking hands in turn with five Senecas. The Indians all carried rifles and even from this distance it was evident that Corporal Fisher was very nervous.

Price turned his head and whispered a crackling command to the other corporal and the eleven privates of the garrison in the room behind him:

"Get your guns ready. Hop to it!"

Since having received that devastating express from Ensign Christie telling of the siege on Detroit, he had held his men under constant alert and, as Christie had done, moved them all into the blockhouse. The messenger had been fed and sent on his way toward Venango and Fort Pitt.

Now, studying what was happening outside, Price saw that Fisher, unarmed and being closely followed by the five Senecas, was walking toward the blockhouse, his back rigid as if expecting at any moment to feel the shock of a lead ball or tomahawk blade crashing into him. The Indians were smiling, but Price thought that they too, looked a little nervous.

He made a sign with his own gun for the Senecas to put down their weapons before coming any closer and was more than a little surprised when they complied, although he noted that all of them still carried knives and tomahawks in their belts.

The commander remained at the door, his stomach knotting within him but showing no outward sign of it. Instead, he smiled pleasantly and held the door open until Fisher got to him and then, with a small movement of his head, motioned the corporal inside. Expelling a great sigh as he passed the officer, Fisher slipped inside.

By now Price was greeting the Indians who had stopped a yard or so away. In reasonably fluent Iroquois speech, he asked them what they wanted.

"We are on our way," said the leader of the party, "to make war on the Cherokee. We need powder and ball. We do not have enough. You will give us some?"

"No." Price shook his head. "I have orders to give no powder or lead to the Indians."

The Seneca evidently expected such an answer. He shrugged and, still smiling, continued: "It makes no difference. We come from a long way off and we are very tired. Will you let us make camp and sleep there?" He pointed to the smooth open ground of the parade adjacent to the blockhouse.

"It will be all right," Price replied, nodding, seeing no way of preventing them from doing so without trouble.

The Indians stepped off a few paces and muttered among themselves. One of them bobbed his head and ran off toward the north on the makeshift wagon road which connected Fort Le Boeuf and Fort Presque Isle. Price, taking advantage of the moment, stepped back inside, quickly closed the door and shot the bolts, then ordered the heavy timber bar dropped in place and the heavy wooden shutters to be closed on the three windows as a further precaution.

"Sir!" It was Corporal John Nash in the lookout perch just under the roof. "He's coming back, sir. An' there's maybe thirty more Injens with 'im."

"Watch them," Price cautioned and then, to all of them, he warned: "No shooting unless they start it. Maybe there won't be trouble, but I wouldn't count on it. Corporal Fisher, there was no excuse for you being out there without your weapon."

Fisher, chagrined, lowered his eyes and mumbled, "Yes, sir."

"Well, never mind that now. You're supplies keeper. How do we stand on ammunition?"

Fisher shook his head morosely. "Not good, Mr. Price. 'Bout twenty rounds apiece. Powder's been damp, too. May not fire so good."

"Sir!" It was Nash again. "They're coming up to the blockhouse. Every one of 'em's armed."

"Keep that door locked," Price ordered over his shoulder. "Don't open it under any circumstance."

He strode to one of the small side windows and raised the shutter. Immediately the Senecas came crowding around it and begged for the loan of a kettle in which to cook their food. Still hopeful of averting trouble, Price agreed and ordered a couple of privates—John Nigley and Uriah Trunk— to give them one through the window. The two men lifted it, but it was too large to fit through the opening. Immediately the Indians began clamoring that the door be opened so that it could be handed to them. Price smiled and nodded, but suddenly reached out and slammed the shutter into place and locked it. The result was howls of anger from outside and a drumming of fists and gun butts on the door.

"I think," Price said slowly, "we can consider this the beginning of an attack. We'll wait it out and see what happens."

Through small ports they watched as the Indians milled about outside, insolently careless of exposing themselves to view. Within a few minutes they went to a neighboring storehouse only thirty feet from the blockhouse, dislodged and pulled out some of the foundation stones and crawled into the cellar. At once they began knocking out some planking above the sill of the building and Price grunted with reluctant admiration. They had chosen the spot well. From there they could fire on the blockhouse with great effect, yet in complete safety, as they were below the range of shot from the blockhouse loopholes.

Price looked around in the dim interior and was not heartened. Thirteen men besides himself, with extremely limited ammunition and damaged gunpowder. Not much with which to fight off almost three times as many Indians. The blockhouse, too, left much to be desired, as did the whole fort. The few buildings outside were just of planking and not defensible. Only this log blockhouse, ill-constructed at best, could provide any protection, and not much at that. Its dimensions were only twenty-four by thirty-two feet, its water supply almost nonexistent, its roof disturbingly vulnerable. Matters did not look good at all. Worse yet, some of the men were already showing signs of approaching hysteria.

"Do you think they really mean to attack, sir?" asked Private John Dogood, a thin and rather squirrel-faced young man.

"I wouldn't bet against it," Price said. "But as I said, we'll just wait it out."

Through the remainder of the morning and all afternoon long the Indians moved about outside, obviously getting themselves well prepared and situated for the opening of their onslaught. The first shots from them, however, did not come until early evening. At that time there came a considerable amount of shooting and the men upstairs in the blockhouse crouched out of line of the loopholes, through which the bullets were spanging and ricocheting or burying themselves in timbers.

Darkness was coming on rapidly when the first fire arrows were shot. They thumped into the walls of the blockhouse and three of them ignited the dried timbers. Each time, by battering out the chinking and pouring limited amounts of water through to run down the outside wall, the fires were extinguished, but the situation was becoming progressively precarious.

Suddenly the men above were crying out and stamping around and then a few moments later they hurried downstairs, calling out despairingly that the roof was afire and they could not extinguish it. There was no more water and even if there were, it had gone considerably beyond that point now. The place began filling with smoke and already sparks were falling on the plank flooring above and starting to set that afire.

"For God's sake, Mr. Price," one of the men cried out, "let's get out of here or we'll all be burnt alive!"

"We've got to fight together," Price replied in a strained voice. "We've got to hold out as long as we can and if it means dying together, then that's what we'll do."

"We've *already* held the place as long as we can, sir. God Almighty, let's get out!"

A chorus of assenting cries followed this and now Price, reluctantly convinced of the uselessness of trying to remain here any longer, agreed.

"All right," he said, "let's do it fast. We don't have much time. If we manage to get out, stick together if possible, but if that's not possible, then everyone see to himself and head for Fort Venango. They'll probably go there next and we'll have to help Lieutenant Gordon."

"What about Presque Isle? It's a lot closer. Why not go there?"

Price shook his head. "That's the direction these Senecas came from. It's probably under attack or already been taken."

Appointing five men to continue shooting occasionally from the front and side loopholes, Price indicated the rear window, which was much smaller than the heavily shuttered side windows, and directed that the shutter be ripped off. It was, but the window was so small that no one could possibly get through it. An axe was snatched up and as swiftly as possible the window framing was knocked away and the opening enlarged somewhat. The sound of this activity was completely lost in the fierce crackling of the fire raging above them, the continuing gunfire from both inside and out, and the shrieking of the attackers. Even as the flooring above the soldiers began burning through and caving in, sending showers of sparks and clouds of gagging smoke through the small room, the chopping ended and one by one the fourteen men—Ensign Price waiting to be last—squeezed out headfirst and then rushed into the dark woods beyond. There was no sign of Indians outside the wall in back of the blazing blockhouse. Undoubtedly the little window had been dismissed by the attackers as being far too small to permit escape. The howling and gunfire in front continued as the Indians waited for the door or window shutters to be opened very soon now and the defenders to come streaming out.

Within five minutes, Price was a thousand yards away in a dense thicket, huddled with all his men and taking a last look back toward the conflagration lighting the sky.

"Wouldn't've believed we'd make it," he said, his voice choppy as he, like the others, panted heavily from the long run. "At least not all of us. All right, our chances are better now. Who knows the trails? Who knows them well enough to lead us to Venango in the dark?"

A private named John Dortinger spoke up. He had been assigned to Fort Le Boeuf sixteen months before and said he knew the surroundings pretty well. He had, on several past occasions, carried messages to Fort Venango and thought he could find the way easily despite the darkness.

"Good," Price said, "then you're our guide. Lead on and we'll follow. The rest of you, stay close. It's overcast, so it's going to be a dark night and we don't want to get separated.

Above all, move quietly, watch your step and keep your mouths shut. Absolutely no talking; not even a whisper. That's an order! Let's go."

And in single file, silent as the shadows they walked in, the fourteen men disappeared into the blackness of the woods to the south, with the yips and cries and shots from the Senecas still hanging in the air behind them.

[June 19, 1763—Sunday, 5:45 A.M.]

All night the men from Fort Le Boeuf had pushed on, doggedly following the lead of Private John Dortinger as he bulled his way through tangled forests and slogged through mucky, waist-deep swamps. They climbed steep hills and tumbled down the sides of deep ravines. They forded murky creeks and they ripped their way through great stretches of blackberry briers.

All night they kept moving without a pause to rest. They had no water, though some of them drank from the muddy streams, and for food they had only three hard biscuits apiece, of which Ensign George Price permitted them to nibble on only one.

All night they walked and stumbled and staggered and an hour before dawn the discovery was suddenly made that the final six men in the file were missing. No one knew how long they had been separated from the rest. Fearful of calling out, lest they be heard by the Indians, Price whistled and coughed softly in the hope of attracting their attention if they were still close by, but they were gone and no one knew how or why or where.

All night they walked, covering mile after dogged mile of territory until, by the time dawn came, they had walked twenty miles or more. And in this first grayness before the sun came up, they saw a deep gray smudge of smoke rising in the still air not more than two miles ahead of them. Corporal Nash volunteered to climb a tall tree to see what it was, and when he came back down his face was contorted with anger and he strode up to Private Dortinger and struck him full in the mouth with his fist.

All night they had walked, twenty miles or more through unbearable terrain and now, clothing ripped, feet blistered, skin badly scratched and bleeding, mosquito-bitten, and with a deep exhaustion settling upon all of them, they found that they had been circling—and the pillar of smoke so short a distance ahead was the deserted, still-burning remains of Fort Le Boeuf.

Whatever small comfort Major Henry Gladwin had gleaned from the fact that some of the chiefs were beginning to talk of peace with him was shattered this morning with the arrival at the fort of the Jesuit priest from the north, Father de Jaunay.

Swiftly, mincing no words, the missionary told him of the massacre which had taken place at Fort Michilimackinac more than a fortnight ago. He told of the ruse that had been employed to allay the suspicions of the garrison—of how the Indians had staged a baggataway competition just outside the fort; of how, in one fell swoop, the major post had been taken; of how an officer, Lieutenant Jamet, and a trader named Tracy and about two-thirds of the garrison had been slaughtered. From within his flowing robe, de Jaunay produced the letter written by Captain Etherington to Major Gladwin. He handed it to the Detroit commander and then sat quietly while Gladwin read it. When the major was finished and had let the letter drop to the desktop, the priest shook his head sympathetically.

"I am sorry, my son," he said, "that it fell upon me to have to bring you such sad tidings as this. I know the pain it gives you, just as I know too well the pain it gave them. There is little of a heartening nature that I can tell you, but there are two points . . ."

His voice trailed away but, at Gladwin's nod to go on, he continued: "I have every confidence that Chief Mackinac fully intends to have a party of his men escort your remaining men up there to Montreal in safety as soon as those soldiers from across the lake at Green Bay arrive. Further, I detect that there is a serious rift developing among the tribes because of the manner in which Pontiac has forced this war upon them and for the way he has conducted his portion of it."

Father de Jaunay went on to tell Gladwin how he had arrived at Detroit yesterday morning in the company of seven of Chief Okinochumake's Ottawas from L'Arbre Croche and eight of Chief Minivavana's Chippewas from Michilimackinac. Unable to leave the Indians immediately upon his arrival here, the priest had gone from village to village in the Detroit area with the northern party while they questioned the Indians here and grew progressively more agitated with Pontiac's conduct thus far in the war.

"Apparently," de Jaunay went on, "they feel that Pontiac has taken too much power upon himself, that he has set himself up as the commander of all the tribes, which they do not consider him as being. Even the L'Arbre Croche Ottawas are very angry with him, though he is that nation's war chief, for moving ahead with his plan without the unanimous concurrence of his own people. At any rate, a major council is set to be held among them in the midafternoon today. Delegations from tribes as far south as the Ohio River and eastward to the Allegheny will be there—Shawnees, Delawares, some of the Iroquois, as well as the tribes from this area. Though I do not know it for fact, I suspect that many of the chiefs are jealous of Pontiac and not a little afraid of the power he has assumed. I believe they mean to castigate him publicly. For their spokesman in this, though they certainly are no less guilty than Pontiac himself of cruelty and viciousness, the Chippewas have sent along Minivavana's son, Kinonchamek, who speaks in the name of his father."

"Will you be attending?" Gladwin asked the priest.

De Jaunay shook his head. "No white men will be; not even those who have long been adopted into the various tribes. The council is open to all tribes, but closed to all whites."

"Do you intend to remain here?"

Again the priest shook his head. "I will talk again this afternoon with Father Pothier and then I am expected to go back north again with Kinonchamek's party tomorrow. I will go first to Michilimackinac and then to L'Arbre Croche, where my mission is located."

"You'll be seeing Captain Etherington again, then?"

"Yes, if he is still there."

"Will you carry a private letter to him from me?"

"It would not be a wise thing for me to do so, Major. It is known that I have come here. If the Indians should ask me whether or not I had a letter from you to him, I would be obliged to say yes, as I have never told a lie in my life. However," he added, at Gladwin's look of disappointment, "I have a very good memory and I will make mental notes of anything you wish said to them and pass it along when I see them."

Though he had some reservations regarding the priest's comment on his own truthfulness, Gladwin nonetheless agreed and went over in detail with de Jaunay what he wished the Jesuit to tell not only Etherington, but the French at Michilimackinac and the Ottawas at L'Arbre Croche. He first gave de Jaunay a wampum belt which was to be delivered to Chief Mackinac and the Ottawas at L'Arbre Croche, expressing his pleasure in him and them at their not meddling in an affair which would be ruinous for them, and adding that if they did indeed send their English prisoners to Montreal, it would go far in convincing General Amherst of their good intentions. Further, Major General Thomas Gage, second-in-command under Amherst and the present Canadian governor at Montreal, would probably reward them well for their help.

"Secondly," Gladwin continued, "please extend my compliments to Monsieur Langlade and Monsieur Farli, along with my sincere thanks for their good offices in this affair, which I beg them to continue. Say that it is my desire for them to prevent, as much as possible, all commerce with the enemies of the English, above all in the matter of arms and ammunition. Tell Monsieur Langlade that I authorize him to continue commanding the fort according to the orders given to him by Captain Etherington, until further ordered.

"Finally, tell Captain Etherington of our situation here and extend to him my regrets that I am unable to send for the assistance he has asked for. Tell him as well, that—provided he gets to Montreal—he is to report immediately to General Gage, giving him the full details of what has happened. Any French or English traders he encounters en route who are on their way west, he is to turn back to Montreal. Give him all the information we have discussed about the fall of the various posts dependent upon Detroit and also inform him of the treaty of peace that has been confirmed between France and England. I believe that's all, except that to you, sir, my deepest gratitude for your help."

The two men stood and shook hands. At the door, de Jaunay turned, "Major," he said, "you have my most heartfelt sympathy in this entire matter. I only wish I could do more to help. Good-by."

[June 19, 1763—Sunday, 3:00 P.M.]

The assemblage of Indians at Pontiac's camp along Parent's Creek was extensive. In addition to his own men, there were chiefs and warriors on hand from all the villages near Detroit, plus contingents of Miamis, Shawnees, Delawares, and a scattering of Iroquois. There was also the party of Ottawas and Chippewas from the north.

Already two distinct insults had been ladled out to Pontiac and he was in an ugly frame of mind because of that. The Indians under Kinonchamek had visited every village in the Detroit area after their arrival here yesterday, but they had not given Pontiac the courtesy of paying their respects to him, which was the first thing protocol demanded.

Then, this morning, while Kinonchamek was listening to the grievances of a delegation of Detroit Frenchmen about Pontiac's treatment of them, two more large canoes filled with Shawnees and Delawares arrived at the Huron village downstream from the fort. They paused there for a while and then went directly to the camp of Kinonchamek, pointedly bypassing Pontiac's camp without paying their respects. These were not good signs.

Now, still without any greetings having been extended to him by the visitors, Pontiac watched silently, without expression, as the council members arrived and took their places and the proceedings began. Pipes were lighted and smoked, but without much of the ceremony normally connected with this act. As soon as the smoking was concluded, Kinonchamek rose and a deep hush fell over the assemblage. The son of the principal chief of the Chippewas got straight to the point with a complete absence of the amenities.

"I come," he said, "in the name of my father, the great Chief Minivavana, to speak to the Detroit Ottawas under Chief Pontiac. We have learned at home, my brothers, that you are waging war very differently from us. Like you, we have undertaken to throw the Englishmen out of our land. In this we have succeeded. There are now no English at Fort Michilimackinac and none in our whole country except those who are prisoners. We killed many of the English in the taking of the fort, but we threw the English out of our territory without glutting ourselves with their blood after we had taken them, as you have done.[111]

"When we made war on them," he continued, "we kept our plans to ourselves and did not tell the French there, knowing that if we did so, word of it would somehow reach the English and they would have been suspicious of us and prepared for us when we came. Such prudence was not used at Detroit and now we see the result—all other forts have fallen, but not this one, though this one was in the hands of him who would lead all tribes to victory.

"Our surprise over the English was complete; we surprised

453

them while playing a game of baggataway, at a time when they were least suspecting of danger from us. Our brothers, the French, knew nothing of our plan and when the English found out, too late for them to do anything, that they were the ones we held the grudge against, they surrendered. We made prisoners of them and will send them unharmed to Montreal. Yes! The soldiers tried to defend the officers and we killed them, but it was done in battle. Nor did we harm our friends, the French, as you are doing here. No! Instead, we made them guardians and custodians of our captives."

Up to this point Kinonchamek was speaking to the Detroit Ottawas generally, but now he turned and locked his gaze upon Pontiac and continued, his manner cold and his words filled with contempt.

"But as for you, Pontiac, you have taken prisoners upon the lake and upon the river, and after having brought them to your camp you have killed them and drunk their blood and eaten their flesh. You did it not in the manner of our—and your!—custom, immediately after battle, when the flesh of the enemy is devoured so that we may take onto ourselves his strength and courage. No! You did it deliberately, when the time for custom was past. Is the flesh of men good for food? No! One eats only the flesh of deer and other animals which the Master of Life has placed on the earth for that purpose.

"Furthermore, Pontiac, in making war upon the English, you have made war upon the French, our friends, by killing their cows and pigs and by devouring their provisions. I have been told that if they refused you what you demanded of them, you had your followers pillage them. Is this how one treats a friend in war? We have not done so. We have not relied upon provisions from the Frenchmen to make our war. No! We took care, when planning to attack the English, to first gather up provisions for ourselves and for our wives and our children. If you had done likewise, Pontiac, you would not be in danger of experiencing the disfavor of our great father, the French King, when he shall come. You await him, and we, too; but he will be satisfied with us and not with you."

Pontiac was both surprised and furious that he would be taken to task publicly this way by the son of a Chippewa chief, yet he said nothing. Kinonchamek glowered at Pontiac for fully a minute after finishing, but when the Ottawa war chief made no effort to respond, he sat down. There was a wondering murmur of conversation from those in attendance, but it died immediately as Pluk-ke-motah, a secondary war chief of the Shawnees, arose to speak.

"My brothers," he began, "we have also fallen upon the English, because the Master of Life came in a vision to one of our brother Delawares and told us to do so. But it was forbidden for us to attack our brothers, the French. In the war belts which we sent you, this was made clear to you and we knew that you understood it. Yet you have, in your own way, attacked them and hurt them. Is this your answer to what we had told you by means of the belt which we have sent you? Ask our brothers, the Delawares, what the Master of Life had told them; they will tell you it is this: that it is all right to kill during battle, but afterwards, and when one has taken prisoners, it is no longer of any value unless for a specific vengeance. Nor is it of value then to drink the blood or eat the flesh of men. Since you are French as well as we, ask the French, our brothers, if, when they make war and have taken prisoners, they kill those they have brought home with them. No! They do not! But they keep them to exchange for their own men who are prisoners among the enemy. By eating them, you are eating your own flesh!

"We understand very well," Pluk-ke-motah continued, "why you have treated our French brothers as you have. It is because you began the war ill-advisedly, without proper preparation and with too much dependence upon others and not enough upon yourself! Now you are in a rage at not having been able to take the English in this fort, and you take out this rage on your French brothers, by stealing from them what you need to sustain you, and which you should have laid aside for such use before you began. So it is our brothers, the French, who feel your bad humor. We had thought to supply you with some of the things you need, but now we shall not do so because we suspect you would then lay at our feet the blame for all the harm that you and your followers have caused our brothers, the French. For this reason we do not desire to put ourselves in a bad light with our great father."

Pluk-ke-motah sat down, and now it was Pontiac's turn. His expression was hard, cold, unpleasant. The smooth white stone pendulating like a crescent moon from his nostrils quivered slightly with the pent-up emotions within him. Yet, when he spoke, it was more with sadness than with anger.

"My brothers," he began, "have seen fit to lay at my feet all the wrongs they feel have been committed. It is a surprise to me that they have done so. I would remind them that we are at war with the English and that if we lose this war, we lose our homes and our lands and all that we have. The object of a war is to fight and the object of the fighting is to win. Never was there a war fought in which both sides did not suffer inconvenience. Yet I am berated by the Chippewas and by the Shawnees because I have inconvenienced the French at this place. Yes, they are our brothers! Yes, I wish to see them back here among us in place of the English. They wish this too, for they have told me so. But they are unwilling to sacrifice their comfort for a little while to have this come about. They wish the road to be cleared for them, but are unwilling to help provide axes for the task. It is for them, as well as for ourselves, that we are fighting. Yet, when I asked them for provisions, which we could not stop the war to go seek, they refused them. I was left with no choice but to take what should have been gladly given!"

He paused for the space of several breaths and then continued bleakly, "As for those prisoners who were killed after they were brought here, this was the work of the evil spirit of rum, not of my desire. Those whom I myself have taken prisoner, such as the two officers of this fort, have not been harmed, nor will they be. No! They have been treated well."

Pontiac expelled a noisy breath and made a slashing motion with his right hand. "I do not," he concluded, "wish to discuss this more. Only this much I will say, and mark me well: the war is here and we must fight it to win. If we do not, we will perish!"

The council ended immediately after that, long before the sun had set. Not much had been accomplished at it, but this much was clear: if the Indians lost the war, it would be more from internal discord than from any other single source.

[*June 20, 1763—Monday*]

All through the day yesterday and into the night, still without any real rest and with nothing to eat but their remaining two biscuits per man, the seven soldiers following Ensign George Price pushed on toward Fort Venango. A defeating weariness enshrouded them and they moved mechanically. For almost thirty hours they had been on the move and their exhaustion was mental as well as physical. Their minds had been numbed by a persistent dread that the Senecas who had destroyed Fort Le Boeuf were on their trail and that every moment, every step might be their last.

The shattering blow of having found themselves at dawn

yesterday back where they started after a grueling night's march, had done much to damage their morale. In the mind of each man present was the same thought: they could very easily have wandered right back into the hands of those Indians. They very fact that they hadn't, George Price concluded, was little short of a miracle.

Private John Dortinger, presently missing one of his front teeth and nursing a split and badly swollen lip, now dejectedly brought up the rear of the silent, slowly moving file. He had not uttered a word this entire day. What he had done—as well as what he had *nearly* done—weighed heavily upon him.

Ensign Price had cautioned his men to keep scanning the woods and hills and valleys around them, not only to watch for Indians with the hope that they might see them before they were themselves seen, but also in the hope that they might spot the six missing privates who had somehow gotten separated from them the night before. But the day passed and night had fallen again without their having seen any of them.

They did, however, see something that unsettled them even more. For nearly an hour prior to sunset they had been following a trail which Price was sure led eventually to Venango. Suddenly a ghastly odor had assailed them and a great swarm of flies buzzed angrily about when disturbed. Beside the trail was the nude, bloated, scalped body of a white man. There was a great hole in the stomach which literally seethed with maggots. They quickly passed on, leaving the nauseating sight, but now Price was haunted by a new fear. Though the corpse had been badly decomposed, he was almost sure he recognized the man as being the messenger from Presque Isle who had brought him Christie's message about Detroit; the man he had fed and then sent on his way to take the same news to Fort Venango and Fort Pitt. Still not positive of the identification, however, Price kept his thoughts to himself. He pushed grimly on and his men followed dutifully.

It was a cloudless night tonight with a three-quarter moon and visibility was good. In fact almost an hour ago, just after midnight, Price had seen a familiar landmark and realized they were less than an hour from Fort Venango. It had been an encouraging announcement for him to make and the flagging spirits of the men were given a much-needed pickup. And now, at one o'clock in the morning, they were entering the valley where French Creek emptied into the Allegheny—the site of Fort Venango.

They pushed on with renewed energy, but not until they were almost upon its ruins did the realization strike them with sledgehammer force that the fort was no longer there. Dazed, unbelieving, they moved about the gray and lifeless ashes of the fort and stared down sickened at the bloated remains of sixteen men. All of the corpses were without scalps. Some were partially burned and some were mutilated in one respect or another. None, however, was as ghastly in appearance as that of Lieutenant Francis Gordon.

It was obvious that the fort commander had not only been tortured, but that the torture must have extended over a period of several days before he died. He was hanging by one wrist tied to a post which had apparently been on the parade ground of the fort. All of his fingers had been severed and his feet had been mangled to pulp by chopping blows of tomahawks. That both the hands and what remained of the feet were enormously swollen indicated that all this had taken place before he died. A great circle of skin had been cut off his back and his nipples and genitals had been severed. His stomach had been opened and residue of ash there indicated that hot coals had been poked inside him. He had been decapitated and the head, minus the scalp, was impaled on a stake a short distance away. The eyelids, lips and ears had been cut away.

Sickened and frightened, Ensign George Price tonguelashed his men into movement, leading them away from this terrible place and along a trail running parallel with the river, heading downstream toward Fort Pitt, which was still another eighty miles or more distant. Some of the men were crying, two were still vomiting, but they all followed him for another mile or so until they were unable to go any farther and then they all collapsed for the night in a fireless camp, cold, hungry, haunted with dread and horror.

[*June 21, 1763—Tuesday, 9:00* A.M.]

Lieutenant James Gorrell looked back across the choppy waters of Green Bay toward Fort Edward Augustus. He could still just barely make it out in the distance behind them and he wondered if they would ever see it again or, for that matter, if the English would ever possess it again. A deep melancholy had infected him and his men upon abandoning the fort. It was as if, in the very process of leaving it, they were also abandoning something of themselves with it.

"It's a strange feeling," Gorrell had commented to his sergeant as the canoes were being loaded. "A commander can defend his fort and still lose it in a fight, but at least feel when it is all over that he did what he could, that he stayed with it to the end. But there's something wrong, something *degrading,* about just abandoning a fort. I don't think I'll ever feel right about this, regardless of the outcome."

Around him now, in this and other canoes of the flotilla, were the seventeen men of his garrison with all their personal effects, equipment and provisions. And with them, too, was an escort of ninety warriors, mainly Menominees under Chief Oshkosh, who would see them safely to L'Arbre Croche to be reunited with Captain Etherington's party.

The waters of Green Bay had been nearly flat calm when they set out, but in a short while a breeze had sprung up which had increased in strength until now it was a rather cold, brisk wind out of the northeast. Whitecaps were beginning to form on the water and everyone was becoming wet and chilled with spray.

By midafternoon, pummeled by the waves, they saw the expanse of Lake Michigan before them. The water was very rough and gray-green, frothed with foam and decidedly menacing in aspect. To attempt to go straight across the lake via the Beaver Islands would have been foolhardy in the extreme, and so now the prows of the canoes were turned to the north to follow the shoreline in more protected waters all the way around to the Straits of Mackinac, then south across the Strait and down the western shore of that long spit of land called Waugoshance point and eventually to beach themselves before the Ottawa village of L'Arbre Croche.

It would take eight or nine days to get there with the weather like this, but at least they would be reasonably sure of reaching their destination without loss of anything more dear than time.

Once again Lieutenant Gorrell looked back, but he could make out nothing familiar. Fort Edward Augustus was gone . . . in more ways than one.

[*June 21, 1763—Tuesday, Noon*]

This was the forty-third day of the Indian uprising and there was little about it to encourage any Englishman. The Indians, whom General Sir Jeffrey Amherst persisted in styling as "stupid barbarians" and "ignorant savages" who "do not have it in their power to substantially harm the English" and who

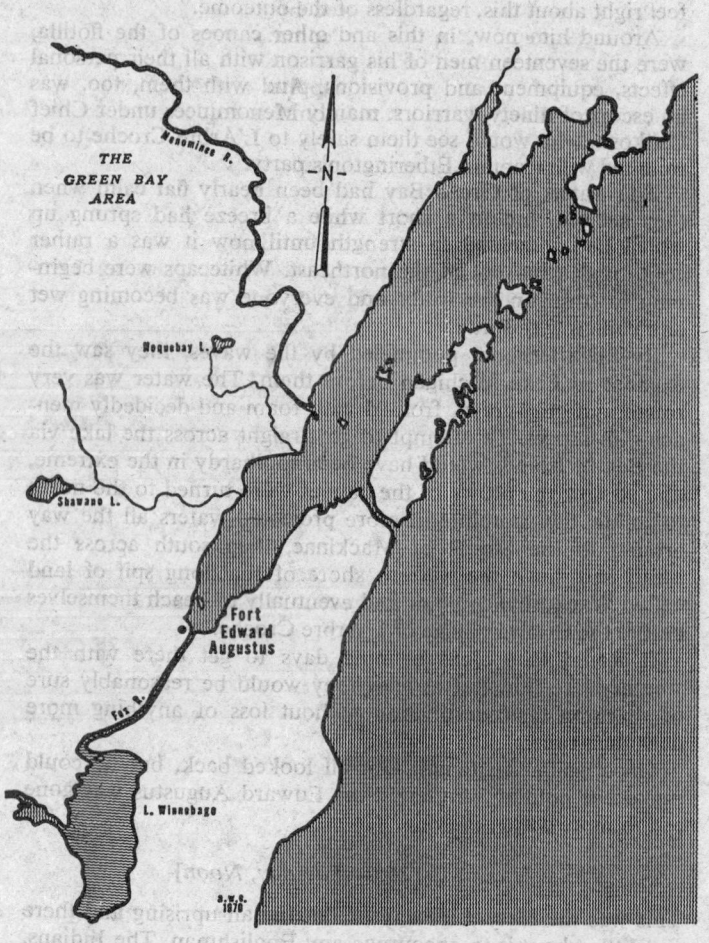

would "never be so rash as to attack any English forts," had already racked up an impressive score.

Fort Sandusky was lost—consumed by fire, its supplies all plundered, most of its garrison and traders killed, its commanding officer, Ensign Christopher Pauli, in captivity.

Fort Miamis was lost—captured by the Indians, its goods taken, its garrison prisoners, its commander, Ensign Robert Holmes, dead.

Fort Ouiatenon was lost—all supplies and equipment plundered, all its men, including its commander, Lieutenant Edward Jenkins, prisoners.

Fort St. Joseph was lost—pillaged, partially burned, most of the garrison killed, its commander, Ensign Francis Schlosser, captured and already exchanged.

Fort Michilimackinac was lost—military and trade goods plundered, most of its garrison massacred, including Lieutenant John Jamet and trader John Tracy; its commander and second-in-command, Captain George Etherington and Lieutenant William Leslye, in captivity along with the surviving soldiers and traders.

Fort Presque Isle was lost—looted, burned, the entire garrison, including the commander, Ensign John Christie, held captive.

Fort Le Boeuf was lost—destroyed by fire, plundered, half its garrison lost in the woods and perhaps dead, the other half and its commander, Ensign George Price, still struggling afoot through the wilderness and in dire jeopardy.

Fort Venango was lost—plundered, burned, the entire garrison butchered, its commander, Lieutenant Francis Gordon, tortured to death.

Fort Edward Augustus was lost—abandoned to the Indians by its garrison and the men themselves heading toward an unknown and possibly hazardous future under their commander, Lieutenant James Gorrell.

Fort Lyttleton was lost—abandoned only yesterday to the Indians on order of Captain Louis Ourry of Fort Bedford. It had been garrisoned by only three men, who must surely have been killed had it been attacked.

Fort Detroit—under command of Major Henry Gladwin, still grimly holding on at the forty-third day of siege, its communications severed, its second-in-command and previous commanding officer, Captain Donald Campbell, a captive, along with Lieutenant George McDougall.

Fort Pitt—under Captain Simeon Ecuyer, under intermittent siege, with attacks growing more frequent, a number of his men already killed.

Fort Ligonier—under Lieutenant Archibald Blane, under attack and the installation in grave danger of falling.

Fort Bedford—under Captain Louis Ourry, under attack and also apt to fall.

Two-thirds of the men of a major military convoy under Lieutenant Abraham Cuyler lost, along with nearly all the goods, including a great supply of ammunition.

Traders all over the Indian territories being slain, their goods and horses plundered.

Settlers everywhere on the Pennsylvania frontier being massacred, their cattle butchered, their horses stolen, their goods plundered, their homes burned, their wives and children killed or taken captive.

Ten forts lost. Three forts being attacked and in jeopardy. One fort under prolonged siege. The English toehold in the Northwest Territory virtually lost. The frontier terrorized. Conflagration. Disaster. Death. All this and more in just forty-three days!

Lieutenant General Sir Jeffrey Amherst had a great deal yet to learn about these "ignorant savages" who were his adversaries.

[*June 22, 1763—Wednesday, 1:00 P.M.*]

The anger with which Jeffrey Amherst had greeted Major Wilkins's letter detailing the loss of Cuyler's supply convoy and the destruction of Fort Sandusky was as nothing compared to the towering rage now consuming him. Before him was the detailed letter from Major Henry Gladwin, written on May 14, five days after the siege against Detroit began, and a fury burned in the general now such as he had never before experienced.

At last the commander in chief of His Majesty's North American military forces was beginning to view the whole picture. It was not a minor incident or series of incidents; it was not a resentment manifesting itself in a few scattered attacks which would soon die away; it was not just a single tribe rising and shaking an angry but weak fist at the English giant. No, this was a major uprising of the majority of the western and Great Lakes tribes banding together to thrust the white encroacher from their lands.

It was war!

This was the greatest Indian uprising against white men that had ever occurred till now on the North American continent and Amherst was trembling so badly that his penmanship was at first very shaky, almost illegible, as he dashed off an immediate reply to Gladwin:

New York, 22nd June, 1763

Sir:

The precautions you took when the perfidious villains came to pay you a visit were indeed very wisely concerted; and I approve heartily and entirely of the steps you have since taken for the defense of the place, which, I hope, will have enabled you to keep the savages at bay until the reinforcement, which Major Wilkins writes me he had sent to you, arrives with you.

I most sincerely grieve for the unfortunate fate of Sir Robert Davers, Lieutenant Robertson, and the rest of the poor people who have fallen into the hands of the merciless villains. I trust you did not know of the murder of those gentlemen when Pontiac came with a Pipe of Peace, for, if you had, you certainly would have put him, and every other Indian in your power, to Death. Such retaliation is the only way of treating such miscreants.

I cannot but approve of your having permitted Captain Campbell and Lieutenant McDougall to go to the Indians, as you had no other method to procure provisions, by which means you may have been enabled to preserve the garrison; for no other inducement should have prevailed on you to allow those gentlemen to entrust themselves with the savages. I am nevertheless not without my fears for them, and were it not that you have two Indians in your hands, in lieu of those gentlemen, I should give them over for lost.

I shall add no more at present; Captain Dalyell will inform you of the steps taken for reinforcing you: and you may be assured—the utmost expedition will be used for collecting such a force as may be sufficient for bringing ample vengeance on the treacherous and bloody villains who have so perfidiously attacked their benefactors. I am, sir,

Yrs., &c.,
Jeffrey Amherst

To Major Henry Gladwin
Commanding at Detroit

Amherst immediately began a second letter, this one to his second, General Thomas Gage, at Montreal, telling him of the letter and outlining the steps he had taken. This was followed by a short, similar letter to the army's quartermaster general, Colonel John Bradstreet, whom he told to be prepared for moving at a moment's notice because, if the Indians were not quickly stopped, Amherst might want to employ him on a command.

Finally, he wrote another but more detailed letter and this one was addressed to Colonel Henry Bouquet:

New York

Sir,

Since my last I have received a letter from Major Gladwin by the way of Niagara, dated the 14th May, wherein he acquaints me of the base and treacherous behavior of the Indians, who had actually invested the fort and were committing hostilities, although he did not doubt but he should be able to defend the place until reinforcements arrived. He writes me that the chief of the Ottawas, who seems to be the principal ringleader of this mischief, sent a message that he, with a considerable number of Indians, intended to pay the major a friendly visit and accordingly, a body of about three hundred came to the fort. But the major, getting information the night before that their designs were bad, made such a disposition that the Indians, who were armed with knives, tomahawks, and guns cut short and hid under their blankets, were confounded; and after making a short speech and receiving a few presents, they went off. That immediately after, they sent out parties who unfortunately were at a distance from the fort, among whom were Sir Robert Davers, Lieutenant Robertson, and their boat's crew—Lieutenant Robertson having been employed in sounding the entrance of Lake Huron and Sir Robert had accompanied him. The villains, after this, had the assurance to come with a Pipe of Peace, desiring admittance to the fort. Major Gladwin refusing to receive any but their chiefs, they immediately commenced open hostilities by killing the King's cattle and murdering the people who had the care of them, and then fired upon the fort, on which, however, they could make no impressions, Major Gladwin being well provided by that time with provisions and ammunition. Everything Major Gladwin mentions to have done on that occasion has my approbation. I only regret when the chief of the Ottawas and the other villains returned with the Pipe of Peace, they were not instantly put to Death. I conclude Major Gladwin was not apprised of the murder of Sir Robert Davers, Lieutenant Robertson, &ca at that time, or he certainly would have revenged their death by that method.

Indeed, I cannot but wish that whenever we have any of the savage barbarians in our power, who have in so treacherous a way committed barbarities on our people, a quick retaliation may be made without the least exception or hesitation. Major Wilkins, on the arrival of the schooner with this news, immediately sent a reinforcement of fifty men, with a lieutenant and noncommissioned officers which I hope may have got very seasonably to Major Gladwin's relief.

This makes not the least alteration to any plan I had fixed upon before I received this advice, as I am determined to take every measure in my power not only for securing and keeping entire possession of the country, but for punishing those barbarians who have thus perfidiously massacred His Majesty's subjects.

To effect this most essential service, I intend to collect, agreeable to what I wrote you in my last, all the force I can at Presque Isle and Niagara, that I may push them forward as occasion may require. I have therefore ordered the remains of the 42nd and 77th Regiments—the first consisting of 214 men, including officers, & the latter of 133 men, officers included—which will march in the morning tomorrow or on the morning of the next day, June 24, under command of Major Campbell of the 42nd, who has my orders to send an officer before, to acquaint you of his being on the march and to obey such further directions as he may receive from you.

Sir John St. Clair, who is here, assured me that the best route is by Newson, Ashton, &ca, and avoid the town of Philadelphia. I have recommended to Major Campbell to pursue that route, as I wish to have these corps at Pittsburgh as soon as possible; and I would not have any of the 42nd, and as few of the 77th as may be, left behind on the communication, for the reasons I have just now given you. You will observe that I have now forwarded from hence every man that was here, for the small remains of the 17th Regiment are already on their march up the Mohawk and I have sent such of the 42nd and 77th as were not able to march to Albany, to relieve the company of the 55th, at present there, who are to march immediately to Oswego. Sir William Johnson, in a letter I received yesterday, gives it as his opinion that turning the Cherokees, Catawbas, &c., against the Indians concerned in the present mischief would answer many good ends. To which I have answered that he is no doubt the best judge of the disposition of the Indians and consequently of the methods most likely to succeed in engaging them to fall upon one another, but that at present our chief attention must be to regain as soon as possible the entire command of country, &ca.

Just as I am writing this, Mr. Franks has come in and has delivered me your letter of the 19th, enclosing the duplicate vouchers of your accounts, which shall be examined when the hurry is over.

I am, Sir
Your obedt. Servt.
Jeff: Amherst

Colonel Bouquet

P.S. The number of officers with Major Campbell bear no proportion to the men, particularly those of the 77th. I am, however, glad to send you the whole, as the officers must be of great service to you on this occasion; for five or six men with a proper officer at their head may often do more than three times the number under a sergeant or corporal.

J.A.

[*June 22, 1763—Wednesday, 4:00* P.M.]

"I don't like it, Joseph." Major Henry Gladwin stood with his hands clasped behind his back, his brow creased by lines of puzzlement. "No sign yet of Mr. St. Martin or Jacques Baby?"

Captain Joseph Hopkins shook his head. "No, sir. The men've been told to keep a sharp eye out for them so they don't fire at them by mistake, but they haven't seen either one of them yet."

"I don't like it," Gladwin repeated. "Something's up and I wish to God we knew what it was. Pontiac hasn't been this active for weeks."

Hopkins shrugged. "We haven't had any word at all from Captain Campbell or Lieutenant McDougall. If it was anything really serious, they'd've gotten word to us by now."

"If they *could*," Gladwin said glumly. "Let's not forget that they're still prisoners, not guests. As a matter of fact, I'm as concerned about how they are as anything else. But I wish I knew what was going on."

The uneasiness felt by both the Detroit commander and Captain Hopkins had built up sharply over the past few days. Until that time the siege had been maintained by the Indians in an almost desultory manner, with occasional rifle fire from long distances which tended to keep the garrison pinned in place, but did no real damage. But then, a couple of days ago, numerous boats—both canoes and batteaux—had been seen moving upstream along the opposite shore of the river. It had been dusk and difficult to make anything out, even using the glass, other than the fact that the boats were manned by Indians and they were loaded with goods and possibly some captives.

During the night, unseen by anyone in the fort, a sizable party of Indians—Gladwin the next morning estimated at least fifty and possibly considerably more than that—moved to within range of the fort and took over the house of Jacques Duperon Baby. Shortly after dawn they had opened up with an extremely brisk fire directed at both the fort and the schooner *Huron,* which still lay anchored adjacent to the fort and was guarded on board by a strong detachment of soldiers, plus the crew. In this firing, one of the men aboard the vessel had been killed and one of the soldiers at the ramparts had been wounded.

Gladwin, not able to know for sure whether or not Baby and his family were being held in the house, was unwilling to lob cannon fire into the place and gave orders for rifle fire only, and then only when the target could be seen and was definitely an Indian. As a result, few shots were returned by the garrison.

It had been just after noon when the attackers pulled away, leaving Baby's house through a back window and then dodging from tree to tree in an orchard behind it until they were out of range. When, after a couple of hours, there had been no resumption of the attack, Gladwin had sent out a sortie under Lieutenant James MacDonald to cut down the trees in the orchard and level a picket fence along one side of it, behind which the Indians had taken cover. The detachment had done so, under fire from a long distance on several occasions, and completed their mission unscathed. But what puzzled Gladwin was why had the Indians left Baby's house at all, when they had such good cover there so close to the fort?

Later in the afternoon, three large parties of Indians had been seen moving downstream—two of them circling widely around the fort afoot, and the third in a large flotilla of canoes moving down close to the opposite shore. Where were they going, and why? Then, today, another party of them circled the fort on foot and disappeared in a downstream direction, and the major estimated that by now somewhere close to eight hundred Indians had gone in that direction. Was an army on the march here; a reinforcement from Niagara or Pitt? Was it the sloop *Michigan* returning? After all, there had been that false alarm four or five days ago that the ship was coming back. Maybe now it really was. Certainly it was more than due. Again Gladwin wished that either Jacques St. Martin or Baby would make an appearance with some news.

Almost as if in answer to his desire, there was a light rapping on the door and a corporal opened it, said, "Mister Baby's here, sir," and then stepped aside for the Frenchman to enter. Gladwin went to him at once and shook his hand warmly, expressing his relief at seeing him.

Baby's expression was grim. "I couldn't come sooner, Major. I'm pretty sure Pontiac already suspects that I'm feeding you information."

"What about St. Martin?"

"He's all right, but he's suspected, too. I think," he added with a fleeting grin, "that our Ottawa friend is beginning to suspect *all* the Frenchmen."

"Were they holding you in your house while they were firing from it yesterday?" Gladwin was concerned. "We couldn't give an adequate return fire for fear you were inside."

Baby shook his head. "No, we were elsewhere. I'm sorry, Major, that they used my house for cover."

"I may have to burn it, Jacques," Gladwin said softly. "I don't want to, but they killed one of my men and wounded another from it yesterday. If they use it for cover anymore, I'll have to destroy it."

"I would regret that," Baby said, shrugging, "but in your place I would do the same. It is my home, however, and I hope you will not have to do it."

"I won't," Gladwin promised, "if it's not absolutely necessary. Now, then, what's the news? What were all those boats that came in the other night, and what's Pontiac up to, moving all those men downstream?"

"Again, Major," Baby replied, "the news is bad. The returning party was part of the war party sent out by Pontiac toward the east a couple of weeks or so ago under Chief Sekahos, Chief Breton, Mintiwaby and some others. They were more than successful. The communication with Fort Pitt has been cut. All three forts—Venango, Le Boeuf, and Presque Isle—have been destroyed and their men killed or taken."

Gladwin and Hopkins both started at the news. Gladwin gripped Baby's arm. "Presque Isle! Are you positive?"

"No doubt whatever. Its commander, Ensign Christie, was

a prisoner on one of those boats you saw come in. They took him first, and some of the others—including a woman—to the Huron town across the river. Now he's being held at Monsieur Labadie's house. I wanted to talk with him, but couldn't get near him without arousing suspicion. But there is no doubt that all three forts are gone. It was a total massacre at Venango, according to the Indians. No survivors. Apparently Sekahos and the others joined up with some Senecas and Shawnees in the area and they took all three forts by surprise.

"As you might have guessed," he added gloomily, "Pontiac's prestige has risen enormously again. Seems he was in trouble for a while there from his own people. The L'Arbre Croche Ottawas, some Shawnees and some of the Michilimackinac Chippewas took him down pretty badly for the way he was conducting the war. Looked for a while like his own people here might desert him. But with the news of the taking of those three forts—and apparently Fort Pitt is bottled up, too—his prestige has gone up and he acts as if he couldn't care less about what Kinonchamek and the other chiefs said. At any rate, he has warriors aplenty behind him all the way again."

Gladwin groaned and leaned against the wall. He fumbled for his pipe and his voice was expressionless as he asked, "What else?"

"The sloop that left here under Captain Newman—the *Michigan*—is coming back. Seems like it was at the mouth of the river for about a week now, waiting for a good aft wind in order to ascend. Pontiac got news of it and began sending men down to Isle au Deinde—Turkey Island, as you call it[112]—where the channel is narrowest. He means to cut them off there in a major attack. With my own ears I heard him order that trees be felled to make breastworks to be used if necessary, but the plan is for the ship to be attacked under cover of darkness by many canoes at once."

"Does he have a strong reinforcement with him? Captain Newman, I mean."

Baby shook his head. "Pontiac does not seem to think so. His men reported that they watched it closely and they saw only twelve men. It does not look good, Major. If they don't get past the island quickly, they are going to be in grave danger."

There was little Gladwin could do. He could not hope to successfully send a detachment afoot to help—not against eight hundred savages! They'd be cut to ribbons. Nor would it do any good to send the *Huron* downstream to meet and escort the vessel. Smaller than the *Michigan* and with less armament, she would be even more vulnerable than the sloop and he could not afford the loss of even one of the ships, much less the loss of both. There was a horrible frustration to the whole business.

"Joseph," Gladwin said, turning to face Hopkins, "go up to the ramparts and have a couple of cannon shots fired. The least we can do is let them know we're still holding on and know they're coming. I hope they make it. My God, I hope they do!"

[*June 22, 1763—Wednesday, 5:00* P.M.]

Even while the military wheels were grinding into movement in the east, the situation in Pennsylvania, from the Susquehanna River westward, continued degenerating. Indians were still attacking with virtual impunity the line of communication stretching from Harris's Ferry to Fort Pitt.

Lieutenant Blane at Fort Ligonier sent dispatches to Colonel Bouquet as often as possible, keeping him advised on what was happening. Little of his news was good. Ten days ago one of his men imprudently left the fort—no one knew why, for sure—and was instantly killed and scalped just outside rifle range of the walls. The very next night, three Indians crept up to the fort and hid themselves beneath an outbuilding. Fortunately, they were discovered before they could do any damage, but they managed to make good their escape in the darkness. Four days ago Blane had written Bouquet of his belief that Fort Pitt was now cut off from communication, as he had received no messages from that post since May 30. Shortly after that express was sent off—at the same moment that Fort Le Boeuf was being destroyed by Senecas—Fort Ligonier was sharply attacked by Shawnees and Delawares and a hot fire was maintained on both sides throughout the remainder of the day until the Indians finally withdrew after darkness had fallen.

Even as far east as on the Susquehanna itself, tiny Fort Augustus was menaced and might have suffered Le Boeuf's fate had it not been for the opportune arrival of a fair body of reinforcements. Scattered shots were fired nearly every day at Carlisle, Fort Bedford and Fort Lyttleton, and so worried had Captain Ourry been over the meager defenses of the latter post that he had ordered the three-man garrison to abandon it and come in to Fort Bedford, and they had done so without incident.

Just yesterday the Indians made their second major attack on Fort Ligonier. It had begun with a ruse. Four Indians showed themselves insolently and, against his better judgment, Lieutenant Blane had allowed himself to be talked into sending out a fifteen-man detachment in pursuit of them. It turned out to be a near-fatal miscalculation. The men, following the four Indians, were suddenly the object of an attack by a hundred Indians who came boiling out of hiding from under a creek bank only four hundred yards from the fort. Only the fact that a section of boggy ground slowed the Indians in their rush, enabled the detachment to make it back to the safety of the fort. Immediately the Indians had begun an all-out attack against the installation and by the time darkness had fallen, they had fired over a thousand shots at the place. Only one soldier was slightly wounded.

Luck was not holding out so well at Fort Pitt. Early this afternoon a group of Indians appeared with shocking abruptness, drove off the garrison's horses which were grazing close at hand, shot the King's cattle and then, as soldiers began lining the ramparts on Captain Ecuyer's orders to drive them off with rifle fire, they were themselves fired upon by an enormous number of Indians hidden at a distance on all sides, even on the far banks of the Allegheny and Monongahela. It was a ridiculous distance from which to be firing, and yet two balls found their marks and two of Ecuyer's defenders fell dead of head wounds.

And now, with the sun rapidly falling, it appeared that even more parties of Indians were joining those already pouring their gunfire at the fort. It was nerve-racking to hear the whine of the balls as they passed close overhead or thunked with menacing sounds into the wall timbers.

The whole situation in western Pennsylvania was, at best, unnerving—and it was growing steadily worse.

[June 22, 1763—Wednesday, 6:00 P.M.]

"If you've ever prayed in your life for anything, Lieutenant," Captain Jacob Newman commented as the anchor was weighed and he pointed the bow of the *Michigan* upstream in the mouth of the Detroit River, "pray now that this wind holds till we reach Detroit. If it doesn't, we could be in serious trouble."

Lieutenant Abraham Cuyler grinned. "You may not know

it, but I've been praying ever since we passed Presque Isle. Looks like this wind'll hold, though." He glanced upward at the bulging sails, billowing with their weight of wind.

Newman shook his head. "Too early to say. Wind has a tendency to die about dusk. Even if it kept up, we'd be lucky to reach Detroit before midnight. Like I say, son, pray."

Already a foamy curl had formed at the prow as the ship knifed neatly through the powerful current of this river which connected two of the largest freshwater lakes in the world. As the river narrowed further upstream, the current would become even more swift and it would take at least as much wind as was blowing now, perhaps even more, to negotiate the passage.

The two officers watched in silence as the wooded shorelines passed. At length, continuing to pay strict attention to his course, Newman spoke again. It was obvious that he was very nervous.

"Your men are all ready down below, Lieutenant?"

"Yes sir." Cuyler had given the fifty-man reinforcement company instructions before the anchor was weighed to make certain their weapons were primed and to stay below decks, out of sight, until further notice. This had been on Newman's suggestion, who had voiced the opinion that if the Indians meant to attack, not so many attackers would come at them if they thought the ship to be lightly manned.

"Better get down below with them, then," Newman said. "Make sure everybody knows the plan and especially that no weapons are fired until the signal is given."

Cuyler nodded and swiftly moved out of sight below decks. To his crew of eleven men Newman now called out, "Easy as she goes, boys. Keep alert, now."

The danger spot, he knew, would be in the narrow, curving channel where the southern tip of Turkey Island was only a few hundred yards or less from the northern portion of the massive Grosse Isle. The closer they came to these narrows, the more nervous he became and the more often he cast a worried eye at the sails. Every few moments he would repeat the order to his men, "Watch, boys, watch!"

From the distance to the north came a faint, muted rumble, almost like thunder. A moment later it was repeated. The Detroit cannon! At least Gladwin still held the place.

It was little real consolation, though, because what Newman had feared might happen, did. The wind began dying. He sensed it first in a growing sluggishness of the ship, a growing difficulty in fighting the current. In the gathering dusk the southern end of Turkey Island slid slowly past off the starboard beam and his eyes burned from the intensity of peering through the gloom to see any possible movement on shore.

Another two hundred yards . . . four hundred . . . six hundred . . . and then there could be no doubt of it: the shore was no longer sliding by. It was stationary. Wind and current were equalizing one another and the ship was no longer progressing. It was a dangerous situation and not only because of the vulnerability to possible Indian attack. If the wind died any more and helm control was lost, the *Michigan* would spin around with the current and float downstream, probably to be smashed against the rocks of the craggy eastern shore of Grosse Isle. Even if some degree of control was regained, it was too dark to attempt to run downstream through the twisting channel. One slight error and the ship would be aground, her bottom being chewed to splinters against the river's rocky teeth.

"Drop anchor!" he ordered, and a moment later there was a heavy splash as the anchor fell, followed by the drumming clatter of the cable playing out. Sails were dropped as soon as the ship was snugged on the cable and the anchor had bitten firmly. And then she sat there like a great wounded duck. It was nine o'clock and darkness was coming on rapidly. Newman went to the hatchway and called down softly.

"All right, Lieutenant, bring 'em up. Looks like we've bought ourselves some trouble. For God's sake, though, keep 'em out of sight. Have 'em crawl to the rails and keep down under 'em. They're not to rise and fire till the hammer strikes."

Led by Cuyler, the men came up in single file rapidly, crawling on hands and knees or squirming along the deck on their stomachs to the rails when they reached topside. Within eight or ten minutes they were all in place, weapons ready, still crouched beneath the rails and well hidden from off the ship. At Captain Newman's direction, the crew now took their posts at the swivels and waited. The nerves of every man aboard were strung as taut as bowstrings.

It was the lookout who saw them first—a dozen, a score, half a hundred canoes being shoved out of hiding in the dense shadows of bushes and into the water a short distance ahead of them. His call to the ship's master was inaudible beyond the ship.

"Here they come, Cap'n."

"Easy. Easy, boys. Keep down. Easy."

473

From the deck beside him, Newman now picked up a large wooden mallet and held it loosely as he watched. Not until the canoes were quite close and the Indians, realizing they must soon be seen, started their attacking shrieks, did he raise the mallet and with both hands bring it down onto the deck with a resounding boom.

A frightful din followed. Rising from their concealment at a harsh cry from Cuyler, the soldiers leveled their weapons and fired, and the barking of their weapons was quickly overridden by the throaty booming of the ship's bigger guns. The tables had adroitly been turned on the Indians and the surprise they had planned for the ship now turned into a surprise on themselves.

Indian after Indian felt the sting of the gunfire and even as the fight continued furiously during these first few minutes, Abraham Cuyler counted fourteen of the Indians who were knocked out of their canoes, dead or wounded, and were swept off into the darkness by the swift current. As many or more seemed to be falling into the bottoms of their boats.

The firepower from the ship was too sudden, too powerful. The sound of it was more like the sound from a hundred or more guns instead of the detachment of fifty men, plus the crew of twelve. Abruptly the Indians were fleeing, paddling madly back toward shore to get out of range of the lead balls and the devastating grapeshot reaching out in the darkness for them. It was an extremely brief battle. Ten minutes after it had all begun, only a few of the soldiers' guns were still rattling, but none of the Indians'. In another five minutes all was quiet.

Lieutenant Abraham Cuyler passed up and down before his men, quietly passing the order for them to make sure their weapons were ready for immediate firing again and, for their own safety, to keep down below the rails whenever possible. Then he joined Captain Newman at the helm.

"Well, by George, Captain," he said, surprised at the dryness of his mouth, "we gave it to them, didn't we? Do you think they'll come back for another try at us?"

"I hope not," Newman said. "I doubt it, really. We hurt 'em pretty bad. Kinda think they'll be going home to nurse their wounds for a while. How are your boys? Anybody hit?"

"No sir, not a man. Everything's just fine. What do we do now?"

"No choice but to keep alert and sit it out here till morning. I said I didn't think we'd be hit again tonight, but there'll be no sleeping. Pass the word. As for the morning—if we make it through the night all right and the wind doesn't come up strong by just after daybreak, we'll have to up anchor and take her back out to the mouth to wait for more favorable conditions. Don't stop praying yet."

Cuyler raised his eyes skyward and held his palms together in a prayerful gesture and both men chuckled, but it was a strained humor at best.

CHAPTER VIII

[June 23, 1763—Thursday]

ALTHOUGH Captain James Dalyell was, by his very nature, an enthusiastic and rather impulsive type of person, he was victim now of a prolonged excitement that surpassed anything he'd ever felt before. His greatest dreams were coming true and he was fully savoring every second of it. For no less than the hundredth time today, he stood up to look behind his leading batteau at the forty other batteaux following. Yesterday they had left Albany, today they were on the Mohawk, tomorrow they would arrive at Fort Stanwix. Before long they would reach Oswego and then Niagara and beyond that would lie the glory and recognition that James Dalyell so yearned for.

It had been a disappointment to him that in Albany he had been able to recruit only twenty-one New York Provincials to add to his force, which was largely made up of companies from the 55th and 60th Regiments. However, he expected to get more men from Major Wilkins at Niagara; and even though the force he had now was not terribly large, his confidence was so boundless that it bordered on the ridiculous.

Beside the captain in this boat—having joined Dalyell in Albany according to Amherst's orders—was Major Robert Rogers, who had won such fame as an Indian fighter during the French and Indian War with his exploits against Fort St. Frederic at Crown Point and Fort Carillon, which was now Fort Ticonderoga. Rogers shared little of Dalyell's confidence and only a small degree of his enthusiasm for what lay ahead of them. He was neither as young nor as fit as he had been during those strenuous days of fighting the French and Indians on their own terms in the wilderness.[113]

Now thirty-two years old, Rogers was becoming a trifle heavy. Had he been given the choice, he would have preferred staying home with his beloved wife, Betsey, but there had been no choice. The orders from General Amherst had been explicit, and not a little disappointing. Not only was he required to go on this expedition to the west, he was not even given command of it. This rankled him badly. With his rank of major and his experience in Indian fighting—to say nothing of the fact that he had created and trained those tough wilderness guerrillas, the famed Ranger force—he felt it only fitting that it was he who should have had command of this force, rather than a still-wet-behind-the-ears captain who had precious little battle experience and who had acquired his rank mainly because he was the son of a baronet, rather than because of any outstanding ability as a soldier.

That was being a little unfair, though, since Dalyell did have a reasonable amount of experience and he was a good soldier, albeit extremely ambitious. It was true that it was because of his father's baronetcy that he himself was given the rank of lieutenant in the Royal Americans in January of 1756. The Royal Americans were at that time a brand-new force, a full regiment, raised for action in the war. They saw a good bit of that action and they accounted for themselves very well. The outfit had, in fact, developed an oversized *esprit de corps* which more than once had led them into brawls with other regular and provincial companies.

When, in 1757, General Thomas Gage—then a colonel—was forming a new regiment to be called the 80th, Dalyell had been quick to accept a captaincy in the unit, but he did so solely for the rank that went with it. Immediately he started some wheels turning and, with some political help from friends and relatives back home in England, he managed to get himself transferred in September of 1760 into the 1st Regiment, one of the oldest units, which had great prestige both militarily and socially. It was with this unit that he also became aide-de-camp to General Sir Jeffrey Amherst.

Now, having finished counting again the forty batteaux coming behind him on the Mohawk with their abundant supplies and ammunition and two hundred and twenty men, Dalyell sat down again beside Rogers. He nudged the older officer with an elbow and chuckled.

"Can't wait to get to Detroit, Major. We'll whip the war paint off those red devils so fast they won't know what happened, won't we?"

"Mebbe," Rogers replied laconically. After a brief pause he added, "Mebbe not."

At least fifteen of his men had reached this spot before him and were looking down over the ramparts and past the outer ditch where the Fort Pitt commander and his interpreter, Alexander McKee, arrived on the scene. The soldiers respectfully gave way for them and in a moment Captain Simeon Ecuyer could also see the two Indians below. He marveled at the temerity of these people in so brashly approaching a fort which they had been attacking off and on for many days now. One of the two Indians he did not recognize, but the other was the Delaware chief Kitehi, more familiarly known to the garrison as Turtle's Heart.

The pair stood with cool confidence on the far rim of the ditch waiting patiently, and now that Captain Ecuyer had made an appearance they recognized him and dipped their heads. Kitehi did not shout, yet what he said now was clearly audible to Ecuyer and the rest of the men on the rampart. McKee interpreted as Kitehi spoke.

"We come as friends to you, my brother," the chief said, "to tell you that we are concerned for you and to give you some good advice that we hope you will take. We have very grave news to tell you. The Iroquois have taken up the hatchet against you and these six great nations of Indians have put themselves against your forts to the north. They have cut them off. Fort Venango and Fort Le Boeuf and Fort Presque Isle, as you call them, have all been destroyed and now these Iroquois are coming here to destroy you as well.

"My brother," he continued, "we who stand here below you are your friends and it is our earnest desire to save your lives. We have no wish to see you and your men, as well as the women and children who are in this place, captured and perhaps killed. You must take them all and go down to the English settlements over the mountains to the east, where you and they will be safe. Already all around you there are a great many bad Indians who wish nothing more than to see you dead, but this is not the wish of Kitehi. I and my warriors will protect you from them if you leave at once, but you must do so quickly. If you wait until the Six Nations arrive here it will then be too late and you will all be killed and there will be nothing we can do to protect you."

When McKee finished interpreting, Simeon Ecuyer motioned a private to come to him, whispered something in his ear and then, as the private nodded and began hurriedly climbing down on some errand, the Fort Pitt commander replied to Chief Kitehi. Again McKee interpreted, in a louder voice now, as Ecuyer spoke.

"My brothers," the captain said, "we are very grateful for the kindness which Chief Kitehi has shown us. I have just this moment sent one of my men to fetch you a present as a reward for your concern for us and in appreciation for your warning. Nevertheless, we are convinced that you are mistaken in what you have told us about the forts to the north of us having been captured. They are strong forts, capable of caring well for themselves and we cannot believe that they have fallen to the Iroquois. Perhaps some bad bird has been whispering false stories in your ear and, if that is the case, then you should punish him.

"As for ourselves, my brothers," Ecuyer went on smoothly, "we have no worry in us about what Indians might come against us. As you must know, already we have been hit and hit again, but it has had no more effect on us than if the Indians had hit their hands against a rock. We have plenty of provisions here, more than we need, and we are able to defend this fort against all nations of Indians that may dare to attack it. We are very well off in this place and we mean to stay here."

He glanced down inside the fort as McKee began catching up with the interpreting. He saw that the private he had sent away was now standing at the gate waiting and in his arms he carried two neatly folded blankets and a large white handkerchief. Ecuyer signaled the guard and the gate was opened just enough to let the man out. The private carried the gifts just to the two Delawares, who accepted them with nods of their heads. Nothing more was said until the private was back inside the fort and the gate again closed and barred. Then Ecuyer continued:

"Take those blankets and the handkerchief, my brother, as a token of our friendship for you and the other Delawares, and listen now to what I have to say to you. Since you have shown yourselves to be true friends in coming to warn us, so we will be friends to you and give you some good advice. Remove yourselves from this area at once so that you and your people are not hurt by what is to come next. I inform you now that an army of six thousand English soldiers will arrive here very soon and that another army of three thousand are already gone to the west on the lakes to punish the Ottawas and Chippewas, and a third army is moving to the frontier of Virginia where they will be joined by your enemies, the Cherokees and Catawbas, who are coming here to destroy you. Therefore, take pity on your women and children and get out of the way as soon as possible. We tell you this in confidence because of our great regard for you, lest you should be hurt; and we hope that you will not tell this news to the other Indians, lest they should escape the vengeance we are planning on them."

For a long moment after that the pair of Indians and the Fort Pitt commander stared at one another and then, abruptly, Kitehi turned and rapidly walked off, followed by his warrior. Ecuyer watched them until they disappeared from sight in the woods and then he moved to return to his own quarters. McKee left with him and kept pace.

"Do you think they believed you, Captain?"

"I doubt it, Mr. McKee," Ecuyer admitted, "any more than I believed them. They could at least have invented something more plausible than three of our forts having been destroyed. I might have been more apt to believe them if they'd just said the forts were surrounded and bottled up. Well, it makes no difference. At least they'll go back and tell the others what I said and it might worry them a little."

"You don't believe what they said about the Iroquois rising up and coming against us right now, sir?"

"Not for a minute. What could they gain by it? They couldn't hope to take this place. Look, McKee, we've got three hundred and thirty-eight men in this garrison now. Supplies aren't plentiful but we can certainly hold out for a good while if necessary—long enough for a reinforcement to reach us, anyway. Besides, in another week or so the Indians aren't going to feel much like pushing any war against us."

McKee frowned. "I don't understand what you mean, Captain."

Ecuyer grinned with a maliciousness uncommon to him and explained. "Mister McKee, how many men do we have down with the smallpox now? Twelve? Thirteen?"

"Fifteen, as of this morning, I understand. I heard that two of the men died during the night."

"I'm aware of that. That's where those two blankets and the handkerchief came from that I gave to Kitehi. They were covering the bodies till burial. They ought to be pretty well infected. A little gift from us to them, and here's hoping they all share it equally."

Ecuyer was chuckling as he left the dumbfounded Alexander McKee and entered his own quarters to send a report of the incident off to Bouquet. If he felt any sense of guilt over this attempt at germ warfare, he showed no sign of it. Captain Simeon Ecuyer was a realist, motivated by logic. Obviously, the English were again at war with the Indians. The Indians were enemies. Enemies were to be killed in any way possible. That was how wars were won. What possible difference did it make? Whether the enemy died from a bullet wound or during a fatal epidemic was of little concern to him. The death was the important thing, regardless of how it claimed its victim.

It was all a matter of logic.

[June 26, 1763—Sunday, 1:00 P.M.]

Occasionally a few shots would be fired at Detroit but over these past few days there had been less really concerted effort against it than at almost any time since the siege began. Henry Gladwin, of course, knew exactly why this was so: Pontiac was otherwise engaged, still trying to somehow get at the sloop *Michigan*.

Jacques St. Martin had brought the highly cheering news that the sloop, apparently with a fair-sized reinforcement aboard after all, had deluded the Indians into thinking it was occupied only by its crew. When the wind had fallen and the ship had been forced to anchor for the night, the Indians tried to attack it and were met with a barrage of gunfire which killed many of their number, wounded a great many others and forced them to keep their distance. In the morning, the sloop had weighed anchor and ridden the current back down to the mouth of the river. There it was still hovering, waiting for a favorable wind to make the run back upstream. Obviously it was going to have a considerable gauntlet of rifle fire to run from the shores as it passed and Gladwin hoped Captain Newman would not make another attempt at the passage until he had a strong wind behind him.

It was nice, however, to have something of a respite from all the firing that had been directed at the fort. It was even possible to send some of the men out on sorties. At one point, for example, a couple of Indians were seen skulking about in back of the fort and they were pursued by Captain Hopkins leading a detachment of twenty men, but the Indians escaped. Still, it gave the officers a chance to burn down a few more makeshift breastworks the Indians had thrown up from behind which to fire at the fort.

As for Pontiac, he was taking advantage of the interval himself by demanding supplies from numerous of the French residents living at a little distance from the fort—residents he had not, until now, troubled with his demands. The castigation he had received from Chiefs Kinonchamek and Plukke-motah had evidently had little effect upon him. Certainly it had not curtailed his demands made on the resident Frenchmen. Pontiac's attitude was imperious and, in fact, becoming almost tyrannical. The fault was as much that of the Frenchmen who were supporting him as it was a manifestation of his own nature. For many weeks now they had constantly praised his courage, his strength, his sagacity, his planning in the taking of the other forts, his indomitable power, and so forth. Most of these French had heard of the treaty of peace that had been signed between England and France, but few really believed it—or wanted to believe it. After all, no official word had yet been received from their own French sources; not even from Fort de Chartres on the Mississippi had any word come that there had been a settlement. As far as they were concerned, the war was still on and they intended to keep encouraging Pontiac to fight their battles for them as long as they could.

Several times in the past forged letters had been sent to the Ottawa war chief, allegedly signed by the King of France, complimenting him on his stand and exhorting him to hold firm and continue his attacks. Lately, these letters were becoming more frequent, filled with compliments and promises, telling him that if he would only continue the fighting a few weeks longer, all would be well, and that his father, the great King of France, was depending upon him. Sometimes the instigators of these letters—men such as Antoine Cuillerier and his son, Alexis, along with Mimi Chene, Pierre Labadie, Laurence Gamelin, and others—dressed their own men with whom Pontiac was not familiar in flashy French uniforms and had them palm themselves off as messengers directly from the King. And Pontiac, becoming ever more sure of himself and beginning to see himself eventually as the king of all the Indians, bought every story and every messenger at face value. The news of the fall of so many English forts to the Indians had raised his prestige to unparalleled heights among the various tribes. They began to think of him as invincible and, worse yet, he began thinking of himself in the same light.

With the growing self-confidence came a growing arrogance. And now, in the house of Meloche, he ordered that paper and pen be brought to Captain Donald Campbell and then he dictated a letter for the officer to write in English, addressing it to Major Gladwin. The Frenchman Gamelin was on hand to interpret anything Campbell might not be able to understand and to carry the completed letter to Gladwin.

Campbell, at being so ordered, shot a quick glance at Lieutenant George McDougall, winked, and sighed in English, "Well, here we go again." He got up from the bed upon which he had been sitting and took a seat at the small desk which Meloche had against one wall. Though still rather heavy, it was evident that he had lost a good bit of weight during six weeks in captivity and his clothing was loose-fitting and rumpled. Now, as Pontiac dictated, he wrote:

Major Gladwin:

I, Pontiac, herewith request and advise you to surrender the fort at Detroit immediately, on my demand, as leader of the confederacy of western tribes. Believe me, though we fight one another, I wish you to know my advice is friendly. If you surrender yourself and your garrison, I promise that you will be used well. But you must do so at once. At Michilimackinac there are 900 warriors assembled under Kinonchamek, son of Minivavana, who will return here in ten days with them. If you wait for those Indians to arrive, I will not be answerable for the consequences, as I will then not be able to control them, and as soon as they arrive they will scalp all the English in the fort. You know that all roads are closed to Detroit and there is no way you can receive any help. Your time is running out, so betake yourself of my good offer whilst you may, lest it move out of my hands and you are destroyed.

Pontiac

Immediately upon finishing the letter, he sent it to the fort in Gamelin's hand and then made preparations to visit the outlying French farms to make his demands on them. Early this morning, apparently in an effort to please the French, he had attended the Mass held across the river in Father Pothier's little chapel. What he did now, however, was hardly calculated to please the French, although it impressed a great many in one way or another.

Three chairs belonging to Meloche were securely tied at the legs just below the seat to parallel poles. In the first and third of these chairs sat two powerful-looking warriors who were bodyguards and enforcers of a sort. In the middle chair sat Pontiac himself. He now ordered Cuillerier, Meloche, Labadie and some of the other Frenchmen to furnish him with some of their workmen to act as carriers for him. Themselves growing daily more fearful of the Ottawa, they acquiesced to his demand and in a short while Pontiac and his two men were raised in their chairs to the shoulders of a score of grumbling French workers and carried from farm to farm. At each place the chief demanded their cattle, grain, meat, ammunition, or whatever they had that he could use. To appease the ruffled feelings that were rapidly developing, he passed out, as he had done before, receipts written on birchbark, each listing what he had commandeered and promising reimbursal as soon as possible, then signed with his mark—the crude sketch of an otter.

Late this afternoon when he returned to Meloche's house with several cartloads of goods to be stored there, he found that Gamelin had returned from seeing Major Gladwin and was waiting for him with a verbal message.

"I have seen the commanding officer, Major Gladwin," Gamelin began, his voice betraying his nervousness. "He sends his reply to you and these are his words: 'Tell Pontiac that he need not threaten me with Kinonchamek, for I care as little for Kinonchamek as I do for Pontiac. Tell Pontiac that I will give no answer of any kind to his questions about surrendering this fort until he sends back to me my officers, Captain Campbell and Lieutenant McDougall, whom Pontiac is keeping, contrary to the laws of even the savages. Tell Pontiac that he can save himself the trouble of sending any more messages, for I will not answer to anything until these two genltemen are returned.' That is the end of the major's reply."

That threat of Kinonchamek and nine hundred men from the north had been pure bluff, and now that Gladwin had called this bluff, Pontiac grew extremely angry. He jerked his scalping knife from his waistband and for a moment Campbell and McDougall became alarmed, thinking he meant to use it on them. Pontiac slashed the air with it, thrusting and stabbing and uttering short barking cries which caused the hackles to rise on the napes of the captives. At last he stopped and resheathed the knife. He strode up to Gamelin, who involuntarily fell back a step or two and his black eyes glittered with hatred and anger.

"Go back to the fort," he directed. "Go now. Tell Major Gladwin this: tell him that Pontiac has given him his chance and he would not take it. Tell him that it is now out of my hands. As for these two—" he pointed at Campbell and

McDougall—"tell the major that I have too great a regard for them than to send them back to the fort. If I did that, I would be obliged to boil them along with the rest of the English there, as the kettle is already on the fire!"

[June 26, 1763—Sunday, 3:45 P.M.]

No sight they had ever seen was so welcome to Ensign George Price and his seven men as the huge bulk of Fort Pitt looming before them. In wretched condition with fatigue and hunger, the eight men had been moving for eight days since leaving Fort Le Boeuf and it was obvious they could not have survived much longer. The fact that they made it to the fort without being waylaid by some of the many Indians that had been harassing the place for so long, was little short of remarkable.

They were seen coming from a distance off by one of the rampart guards who sounded the alarm. In a few minutes an armed detachment was rushing out to meet them and escort them in. Their clothing was in tatters, their flesh bruised and scored with innumerable shallow cuts and scratches from briers. Yet, without rest or change of clothing, without pausing for more than the gulping down of a great quantity of fresh water, Price went to Captain Ecuyer's quarters immediately and within five minutes more the suddenly fearful commander of Fort Pitt had learned the basic facts of what had happened to both Fort Le Boeuf and Fort Venango, and the likelihood of what had happened to Fort Presque Isle. So Chief Kitehi had not been lying after all!

Stunned by the news, Captain Ecuyer ordered that Price and his men be fed and given immediate medical attention. In less than an hour, he returned and very methodically extracted the whole story in detail from George Price. And in answer to Price's own worried query, he shook his head regretfully; no, the six men who had become separated from Price's group during that first night had not come in. The word from Price was the first real confirmation Ecuyer had gotten that the upper posts were having trouble.

"Get yourself a little rest, Mister Price," he said now. "As soon as you feel up to it, I would like you to write a letter to Colonel Bouquet advising him of everything you know about what has happened. I have to write him, too, so we can send them in the same packet later on. Hopefully, we'll be able to get them through. The colonel has to know of this."

"I'll write the letter first and rest later, Captain Ecuyer,"

Price said. "I couldn't really rest anyway, knowing this was not yet done."

Ecuyer nodded, provided the ensign with paper and quill pen and went about his own affairs. An all-out assault against Fort Pitt seemed far more likely now than it had a couple of days ago when he had talked with Chief Kitehi, and preparations had better be very thoroughly checked.

Price wasted no time in beginning his letter to Bouquet. Though his eyes were grainy and his legs were so tired that he had to keep moving them because no position he got them into was comfortable for long, still he wrote steadily and in a surprisingly legible hand.

Fort Pitt, 26th June, 1763

Sir

I arrived here this morning from Le Boeuf, which I abandoned the 18th at night.

The 3rd instant I had an express from Christie with the news of Lieut. Cuyler's defeat, etc., which I immediately forwarded to Venango and I have heard since I got in was sent to you. Another express also arrived from Christie later, I forwarded it likewise, but has never been heard of since and Capt. Ecuyer therefore desired me to give you the heads [the high points] relating to it.

About the 12th [actually, the 9th] Christie, seeing a sail standing towards Niagara, sent a batteau on board thinking the master not inclined to put in; and by a corporal, who had it from Captain Newman's mouth, learned the following particulars. viz. That on or about the 1st of May, 1,500 Indians arrived at Detroit and wanted to hold a treaty in the fort, but Major Gladwin, being told by Monsieur Baby that if they were admitted they would fall upon and destroy every man in it, ordered the garrison under arms which, the chief of the Indians seeing, asked if he was afraid.

The next day they came all together and repeated their former request of admittance and, being refused, began to fire, ending that day with the loss of 40 of their men and wounding but a few of ours.

Captain Campbell and Lieutenant McDougall were sent to enquire what was the cause of their behavior and were detained, though the Indians sent in two of their own people as hostages.

A day or two preceding these transactions they killed Sir Robert Davers, Captain Robertson, Mackay and one Fisher as they were out sounding the lake and, returning to Fisher's house, hanged his wife and took the rest of his family prisoners.

Detroit had been two weeks besieged when Captain Newman came out of the river to convey Lieutenant Cuyler in. The garrison were living upon a little provision of barley then. He was three weeks after before he saw Presque Isle, being detained by contrary winds, and was afraid all the upper posts were cut off. He was fired upon coming out of the river and Captain Campbell was sent to know if he would strike [i.e., strike colors, surrender] *and they would spare the lives of all on board, but he sent them word he was determined to fight his way and did.*

The 18th instant I was attacked and, the Indians taking possession of the lower store, fired ·my house with their arrows, so that I was obliged to retreat in the night, which I did, unseen, and brought in with me seven men—six are still in the woods, but I hope will get in safe somewhere.[114]

We arrived at Venango the 20th at one at night and found the blockhouse burned to the ground.

I am a little fatigued but in good health, as are most of those who came with me.

I hope soon to have the pleasure of seeing you and am, Sir,

> *Your most obedient and most humble servant*
> *G. Price*

Col. Bouquet

Ecuyer, too, had begun a letter to Bouquet, but had put it aside to attend to some other matters. It was not until now, at nearly four o'clock in the afternoon, when he was just on the point of getting back to it, that he was informed that two more men who were in even worse condition than Price and his men had been, had just come in. Ecuyer went to them at once and found that they were Privates Benjamin Gray and David Smart, who had escaped from Fort Presque Isle at the time that Christie capitulated. Gray was the more articulate of the two and Ecuyer listened to the man's story and then hurried back to his quarters to finish the letter. It had begun:

Fort Pitt, June 26
Sir,

This morning, Ensign Price, of the Royal Americans, with part of his garrison, arrived here, being separated from the rest in the night. The enemy attacked his post, and set it on fire, and while they watched the door of the house, he got out on the other side, and the Indians continued firing a long time afterwards, imagining that the garrison was in it, and that they were consumed with the house. He touched at Vanango, found the fort burned to the ground, and saw one of our expresses lying killed in the road.

This was as far as he had gotten with his letter writing before the interruptions, but now Ecuyer bent to the task of adding the newer information to it:

Four o'clock in the afternoon. Just now came in one of the soldiers from Presque Isle, who says Mr. Christie fought two days; that the enemy fifty times set fire to the blockhouse, but that they as often put it out; that they then undermined the house and was ready to blow it up when they offered Mr. Christie terms, who accepted them, viz., that he and his garrison were to be conducted to this place. The soldier also says he suspected they intended to put them all to death; and that on hearing a woman scream out, he supposed they were murdering her; upon which he and another soldier came immediately off, but know nothing of the rest: that the vessel from Niagara was in sight, but believes she had no provisions, as the Indians told them they had cut off Little Fort Niagara and destroyed 800 barrels of provisions: and he thinks by what he saw, Venango had capitulated . . .

[June 29, 1763—Wednesday]

In his New York headquarters, Amherst had been getting numerous reports from Colonel Henry Bouquet, of course, but equally from Major Wilkins at Niagara, from Sir William Johnson on the Mohawk, from George Croghan on the Pennsylvania frontier, and from a variety of officers at the scattered forts.

Though as yet not fully informed as to the extent of affairs in the west, he was still seething over the very fact of the Indian uprising occurring at all, not only because of the fool it had made him out to be in view of his disparagement of and underestimation of and condescension for the enemy, but because now it might have a nullifying effect on his long outstanding request to London that he be recalled from this post. For as long as possible Amherst had held off in sending the news of this uprising to his superiors, hoping that somehow the problem might be resolved.

Then had come Colonel Bouquet's letter from Philadelphia

dated the 23rd, which said that he had heard from Captain Simeon Ecuyer that while Fort Pitt was in a good state of defense from the Indians, it was nonetheless being fired upon every day and that, worse yet, a smallpox epidemic had broken out in the fort, for which victims Ecuyer had built an isolated hospital building. Further, a sergeant of militia, out cutting grass with a party right beside the fort, was killed but not scalped. Outraged at such liberties being taken against His Majesty's fort and subjects, Bouquet had decided to begin his westward march at once.

And so, the day before yesterday, Amherst had made the painful decision and wrote of the troubles in a letter to England's Secretary of State, the Earl of Egremont. In as underemphasized a manner as it was possible to state it without distortion, he told of the uprising, remarking parenthetically that he hoped this would not delay a decision giving him leave to return to England. Still unable to comprehend that it was his own policies toward the Indians which had resulted in this present uprising. Amherst had added:

It is difficult, my Lord, to account any causes that can have induced these barbarians to this perfidious attempt. They have pretended to be very dissatisfied at not getting rum, when in every formal meeting that has been held it has generally been at the request of their chiefs not to permit any. From a declaration of one of their prisoners, it appears they strike the blow to revenge the death of two of their chiefs that were killed in the action at Niagara.[115] I think it is most likely to have derived from the belt that was sent to the Miamis, which Sir William Johnson supposes to have come from the French some time ago and has lain by, and I believe the savages have really long meditated this mischief and have been waiting an opportunity.

Reports from Bouquet, who was now well on his way to the west, had been the most numerous, often with enclosures or reports that he had just received by express from the frontier. Amherst had not immediately replied to all, but instead jotted down notations of what he would say when next he wrote, and then finally referring to this when he wrote to the colonel a week ago today. Among the many things he commented upon in that letter were:

I have perused Captain Ourry's letters and entirely approve of the measures taken by him for the security of Fort Bed-

ford and the communication. The behavior of the inhabitants in so rashly throwing themselves into the power of the Indians, without the least intention or resolution to defend themselves, is indeed very unaccountable and attended with bad consequences, as it encourages the savages to repeat their attempts.

Their success in defeating Lieutenant Cuyler's party, I fear, has been a great means of spiriting up the Indians below, as they have no doubt flattered themselves with the hopes that the Detroit and the upper posts were likewise cut off: . . .

My opinion with regard to the Indians that are in our power is that they should remain as prisoners, as I am convinced they would be among the first, were they let loose, that would join the others: . . . All the troops from hence that could be collected are sent you; so that should the whole race of Indians take arms against us, I can do no more . . .

I approve of Mr. Croghan's having raised the 25 men to garrison Fort Lyttleton, which appears to have been very necessary; . . . You may acquaint Mr. Croghan that I have from time to time informed Sir William Johnson of every intelligence I have received, and that his letter to Sir William, with the enclosures, shall be forwarded to him.

The resolution of Ensign Christie, in being prepared for the defense of his post, gives me great pleasure; and I doubt not but Major Wilkins will have sent him the ammunition and provisions he required . . .

Now, settling back in his comfortable chair, Amherst read again the letter just received this evening from Henry Bouquet. He was delighted to learn that the reinforcement of three hundred and forty-seven men and officers he had sent under Major Campbell were expected soon by Bouquet and that the colonel had already formulated plans for their use. Bouquet had written:

> *New Lancaster*
> *25th June 1763* P.M.
>
> *Sir*
>
> *I had this moment the honor of your Excellency's letter of the 23rd instant with that most welcome news of the preservation of Detroit from the infernal treachery of the vilest of brutes: I regret sincerely the brave men they have so basely massacred, but hope that we shall soon take an adequate revenge on the barbarians.*
>
> *The reinforcement you have ordered this way, so consider-*

able by the additional number of officers, will fully enable me to crush the little opposition that they may dare to offer along the road, and secure that part of the country against all their future attempts, till you think proper to order us to act in conjunction with the rest of your forces to extirpate that vermin from a country they have forfeited and, with it, all claim to the rights of humanity. The route recommended by Sir J. St. Clair is good and shorter, but I doubted whether the troops not be retarded that way on account of provisions . . . the first two companies will be at Carlisle the 28th, from whence I propose to detach a party to proceed by a shorter way to Bedford and, if safe, to Ligonier, to reinforce immediately that post till I can follow up with the convoy. I shall leave no men of the 42nd Regiment—and as few as possible of the 77th—upon the communication and only then such as, by weakness, cannot easily proceed further. I have no pretention to be a judge of Indian affairs, but I should be sorry we should ever appear to be under the least obligation to the perfidious Cherokees; and as to the Catawbas, they are no more a nation. I would rather choose the liberty to kill any savage that may come in our way than to be perpetually doubtful whether they are friends or foes. I cannot finish this letter without returning my grateful thanks to your Excellency for this early communication of an event so important as the safety of Detroit and so many good men.

> *I have the honor, &ca.,*
> *Henry Bouquet*

His Excellency
  Sir Jeffrey Amherst

Amherst smiled and put the letter down. By damn, it was good to get a letter for a change that wasn't crammed with bad news. Was it possible that this whole business was just becoming blown all out of proportion and that his own early evaluation of the affair was correct, that this was just a manifestation of anger that would soon pass? Had he, perhaps, in spite of waiting as long as he thought he could, been still a trifle hasty in sending that letter to the Secretary of State? Well, it was gone, so there was no help for it. But if things continued this way, he'd soon be sending a much more encouraging letter than the last had been to the Earl of Egremont.

He raised his bulk from the comfortable chair with a soft wheezing sound and went to his desk now and set about replying to Colonel Bouquet:

. . . I received your letter of the 25th, the contents of which please me very much, your sentiments agreeing exactly with my own regarding the treatment the savages deserve from us. A proper spirit exerted now may be the happy means of preserving the lives of many of his Majesty's subjects thereafter. I need only add that I wish to hear of no prisoners, should any of the villains be met with in arms. And whoever of those who were concerned in the murder of Sir Robert Davers, Lieutenant Robertson, &ca., or were at the attack of the detachment going to the Detroit, and that may hereafter be taken, shall certainly be put to death. I have nothing new from the above since my last . . .

I have sent directions to the officers commanding at Fort Ontario [Oswego] and Fort Niagara not to permit any of the traders to pass their posts with goods; and you will please to take the like care at Fort Pitt and the communication until the savages are entirely reduced and everything again put on a proper footing, for I judge it of the utmost consequence to prevent the Indians from having it in their power to get any more goods, &ca., than have already unfortunately fallen into their hands.

J.A.

[June 30, 1763—Thursday, 10:00 A.M.]

They screamed with joy and cheered until their throats were raw and a good many of the men simply broke down and wept with relief. Such was the reaction of the garrison at Detroit when, just now, the sloop *Michigan* slid trimly through the green waters of the Detroit River and dropped her anchor with a mighty splash adjacent to the fort.

It had not been an easy passage by any means. The sides of the ship were pocked with bullet holes and her sails, just over the decks, were punctured in a number of places. Five men of the reinforcement detachment—a sergeant and four privates—had been wounded, though none seriously, and had to be assisted into the fort.

With no small show of pride, Lieutenant Abraham Cuyler met Major Henry Gladwin at the water gate to the fort and executed a snappy salute.

"Sir," he said crisply, "Lieutenant Cuyler reporting for duty as ordered by Major Wilkins, with a reinforcement of twenty-two men of the Thirtieth Regiment and twenty-eight men of the Rangers."

Gladwin, grinning rather foolishly, returned the salute and then shook the lieutenant's hand warmly. "If you live to be a hundred, Lieutenant," he said, "you'll never know what a welcome sight you were this morning."

As soon as Captain Newman came ashore and was also warmly greeted and abundantly congratulated on his handling of the *Michigan* under decidedly adverse conditions, the three men adjourned to Gladwin's office where they were joined by Captain Hopkins and Lieutenants MacDonald and Hay. It seemed as if no one could stop smiling and laughing and both parties had a great deal of news to impart.

Newman and Cuyler cheerfully stumbled over one another in their attempts to fill the Detroit commander in on everything that had occurred, without missing any points. Their levity was understandably dimmed when they told of witnessing the fall of Fort Presque Isle, and they were more than surprised that Gladwin already knew about it and that the commander of that post, Ensign Christie, was being held prisoner right now no more than a few miles from this very fort.

As for the trip up the Detroit River, it had been a frightening venture to say the least. After being forced back to the mouth of the river, they had had to wait there until a favorable wind finally came up two days ago. They had built up a fairly good speed, despite the river's strong current, and had swept past the place where they were attacked previously, without slackening speed in the least.

All along the shorelines of both Turkey Island and Grosse Isle, the Indians had dug holes in which they had hidden themselves, and the ship was under almost constant rifle fire for the better part of an hour as it progressed. Little return fire was sent at the Indians—though there had been some— simply because it wasn't worthwhile. The Indians were too well hidden to make shots from the vessel pay off, and the danger of exposing themselves to shoot became immediately apparent when, early in this gauntlet of gunfire, the five men had been wounded.

Just as they had neared the mouth of the River Rouge, the wind died and they were forced to anchor well out from shore at this point. Again they had expected attack and prepared for it, but apparently the Indians had had enough of trying to attack the vessel in canoes. Though they remained there throughout the night, all day yesterday and all through last night, no attack other than scattered rifle fire from shore had come their way. And this morning, with a fair wind blowing in their favor, they had upped anchor and made the remainder of the upstream voyage to the fort without incident, except at a point adjacent to the Huron Village.

There they had been fired on, while Gladwin and much of the garrison had watched from the ramparts, but Captain Newman had ordered several rounds of grape blasted through the village and that had ended the attack. Apparently a good many Indians had been wounded, perhaps some killed; and everyone there that could, scattered.

Even while these officers talked, the reinforcement company was getting itself established in quarters within the fort. And there were far more willing hands than required when it came to assisting in bringing to shore in batteaux the one hundred and fifty barrels of provisions and ammunition the ship had brought. Detroit might still be under siege, but it certainly was in a much better condition now than at any time since the siege began. And the boost in morale provided by the arrival of these men and goods was easily worth the weight of a barrelful of gold.

[*June 30, 1763—Thursday, 11:00* A.M.]

Only about an hour after the time that the ship was arriving at Detroit, a number of boats were arriving at their destination far to the north. On the northeasternmost shoreline of Lake Michigan, just south of the far-projecting Waugoshance Point, the flotilla of canoes carrying Lieutenant James Gorrell and his garrison from the abandoned Fort Edward Augustus at Green Bay, coasted ashore before the Ottawa village of L'Arbre Croche.

The men were edgy to the extreme and even their escorts, the Menominees, were beginning to look as if they felt they had made a serious mistake. The closer they had come to this village, the deeper they had penetrated into Ottawa country, the more gloomy they had become.

Even before they had crossed southward over the choppy waters of the Straits of Mackinac, Chief Oshkosh had confided to Gorrell that it was likely that the first thing the Ottawas would do would be to disarm the lieutenant and his men. At this Gorrell had shaken his head violently.

"No, by God! They'll have to kill us to do so! We will not give up our arms now for anyone."

He thereupon passed the word to his men to be prepared for anything, but to follow his lead. Every man was to check

494

his weapon to be sure it was well primed and the powder dry. Then they braced themselves for whatever would come next.

The reception by the Ottawas, however, showed their fears to have been in vain. They were greeted personally by Chief Mackinac and his second, Chief Okinochumake. A moment later, George Etherington and William Leslye ran down the shore and welcomed them effusively. Both men, Gorrell was relieved to see, had pistols in their belts and they were not the only ones. Most of the other survivors were similarly armed or else had rifles. It was not until then that Gorrell genuinely relaxed.

Etherington could not have been more enthusiastic in his praise for Chief Mackinac and his warriors. He assured Gorrell and Chief Oshkosh that had it not been for these L'Arbre Croche Ottawas, chances are they would have been dead long ago.

"By heaven, sir," Etherington declared, "they've been our salvation, that's what! Right now the Chippewas are still hot about it and are talking about coming to take us away or at least refusing to let us pass through the Strait on the way back to Montreal, but Chief Mackinac says he's not so worried. He intends to live up to his word to see that we're escorted there as soon as possible, but he still thinks it'd be a good idea to wait another week or two."

"Why is that?" Gorrell asked.

"Just plain old common sense, Jim. They're not afraid of the Chippewas—or at least so they say—but they can't see any point in getting a war started between 'em if they don't really have to. Okinochumake's going off to council with 'em tomorrow to see if they won't guarantee our safe passage. You know how the councils drag on. We'll be lucky if they're over in a fortnight. Anyway, things are fine here." He lowered his voice and added, "But keep your gun close at hand, just in case. You never can tell."

With great warmth, then, and with promises of extensive rewards for their service in this crisis, the officers bade adieu to Oshkosh and his men. They watched as the Menominees pushed off from shore after thanking the Ottawas for their invitation to stay, but saying that they wished to get back to their homes and their families.

When they were gone, Captain Etherington put an arm around Gorrell's shoulders and grinned. "We built a cabin that we're all staying in," he said. "Come on up there. We've got lots to talk about. Have you heard about Detroit and the other posts? Man, we're at war!"

Although there was the outward appearance of matters improving for the English in the western Great Lakes area, the same could not be said of the situation on the Pennsylvania frontier. Even those who had stubbornly upheld the belief that the massacres were being caused by a few marauding bands and did not represent the policy of the western tribes in general, now were forced to alter their opinions. There could no longer be the least doubt that a war was upon them and that matters were apt to get much worse before they got better . . . *if* they got better.

Henry Bouquet had been depressed upon his arrival at Carlisle to find that every building—houses, barns, fruit cellars, sheds, hovels—all were crowded with refugees. These were settlers and their families, driven together for protection here in Carlisle. The same thing, Bouquet learned, was happening at the various forts on the communication between here and Fort Pitt. Some of the refugees were wounded; many had buried their own relatives; others had fled for their lives while savages were still scalping their loved ones and their homes were still burning. The whole atmosphere around Carlisle was one of gloom and a deeply penetrating personal anguish. And it was little short of embarrassing to the colonel the way he was treated almost like a savior on his arrival there. It was with no little relief that today he witnessed the arrival of the reinforcement under Major Campbell and saw some of the reaction of the people transferred to them.

Everywhere—not only here at Carlisle—the news was bad. A hurried note from Ecuyer stated that he was girding himself for a major attack by the Indians, expecting it to occur hourly. A part of the Fort Pitt outer wall, weakened by erosion from the flooding runoff of spring rains, had fallen into the ditch, but by unstinting labor it had been repaired; a new line of palisades had been erected along the ramparts and the barracks were being made shot-proof in an effort to protect the women and children who were taking refuge in them. A crude fire engine of sorts had been built from a wagon belonging to one of the traders, being fitted out with a multitude of buckets for a bucket brigade and twelve barrels now filled with water had been securely fastened to its bed. Hopefully, with this machine they could effectively douse fire arrows striking at different places simultaneously before they got out of control.

Activity was no less strenuous at Forts Bedford and Ligonier. Lieutenant Blane at the former post feared that two or three of his messengers, experienced frontiersmen though they were, had already been taken by the enemy while attempting to get dispatches through. Captain Ourry sent a messy letter obviously written at various times during the day, filled with the horror of what was transpiring there:

This morning a party of the enemy attacked fifteen persons who were mowing in Mr. Croghan's field, within a mile of the garrison; and news is brought in of two of the men being killed.

Eight o'clock. Two men are brought in, alive but tomahawked and scalped more than half the head over.

Our parade just now presents a scene of bloody and savage cruelty; three men, two of which are in the bloom of life, the other an old man, lying scalped (two of them still alive) thereon. Anything feigned in the most fabulous romance cannot parallel the horrid sight now before me; the gashes these poor people bear are most terrifying ...

Ten o'clock. They are just expired—one of them, after being tomahawked and scalped, ran a little way and got on a loft in Mr. Croghan's house, where he lay till found by a party of the garrison.

The forts were being taxed far beyond their capabilities, though they still attempted to cope with everything. Scores of Indian scalping parties of anywhere from a dozen to a hundred warriors each ranged the countryside from the frontiers of Virginia and Maryland up through Pennyslvania and even somewhat into western New York. Everywhere settlements were being laid waste, the newly sprouted crops of corn and other vegetables being destroyed, people of all ages and sizes and both male and female were being butchered.

A scourge was on the land and a swirling cloud of grief enveloped the countryside and the tendrils of the mist of misery reached far and touched many. Newspapers of the East were filled with the grisly stories of massacres and the accounts of survivors and witnesses to unspeakable atrocities. Whole letters and extracts of others, written on the frontier, were lambasting the senses of the citizenry of the major coastal cities, and a growing apprehension was gripping every English person in North America.

Official dispatches—Royal proclamations from the King himself—had just arrived in New York and Boston, confirming absolutely the earlier notifications of the treaty between the French and the English, the Treaty of Paris—but what joy could be taken by the English in North America in the knowledge that the gun that had been pointed at their forehead was now a knife poised at the throat?

Probably most chagrined, shocked and unbelieving next to Jeffrey Amherst himself was Sir William Johnson. The Indian supervisor had difficulty at first putting any credence in the reports which filtered to him. Always the Senecas had been the thorn in his side, even when he had championed their cause unstintingly during the last war. From them alone he would not have been terribly surprised at an outbreak of violence, but from the others it was shattering. How could the Shawnees and Delawares have opened the throat of the frontier without his being made aware by the Mohawks or one of the other tribes of the Six Nations that they were about to do so? How could the Miamis and the Wyandot Hurons and the Kaskaskias, Cahokias, Muncees, Peorias, Kickapoos, Weas, and other tribes of the vast hinterland between Fort Pitt and the Mississippi have gone on the warpath without George Croghan not having advance intelligence of it? How could the Ottawas and Chippewas, Hurons and Mississaugis and Potawatomies have risen almost as one to demolish the English toehold in the western Great Lakes country when he himself had gone there and effected treaties with them, while at the same time carefully nurturing the fires of hatred and jealousy between them and the Senecas? How could these tribes suddenly be bonded together in common purpose, fighting shoulder to shoulder against the English?

He did not know *how* these things could be; only that they were, and the fear rose in him with palpable force that if the remaining five tribes of the Iroquois—the Mohawks, Oneidas, Onondagas, Tuscaroras and Cayugas—rose up to join those western tribes as their brothers the Senecas had already done, the bloodshed on New York's frontier would by far surpass even that of Pennsylvania's.

Day after day he counciled with them, imploring them to stand firm in their alliance with England, begging them to do all in their power to force the other tribes to cease this warfare which, in the end, could gain them nothing. And so they vowed to him that they would honor their allegiance to the English and bring the pressure of their influence to bear on the other tribes. The influence of the Iroquois, however, was not now what it once had been and the hostile tribes were listening to them little, if at all. But at least, Johnson reasoned, they weren't joining, the attackers, they weren't setting the New York frontier alive with atrocities of their own, and that was something.

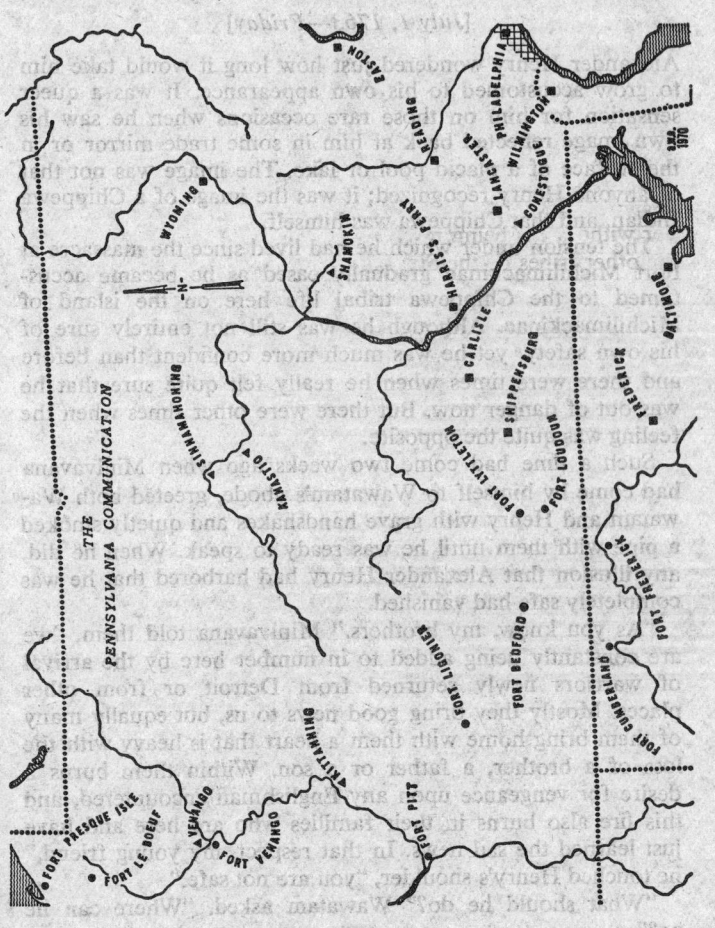

"There is no place he can go away from us here," Mink-vavand replied, "where the danger he is in is not manifold. He is safer with us here than anywhere else in this country."

they weren't *joining* the attackers; they weren't setting the New York frontier afire with atrocities of their own, and that was *something!*

But to the multitude already under the scalping knife, it was precious little consolation.

[*July 1, 1763—Friday*]

Alexander Henry wondered just how long it would take him to grow accustomed to his own appearance. It was a queer sensation for him on those rare occasions when he saw his own image reflected back at him in some trade mirror or in the surface of a placid pool or lake. The image was not that of anyone Henry recognized; it was the image of a Chippewa Indian, and that Chippewa was himself.

The tension under which he had lived since the massacre at Fort Michilimackinac gradually eased as he became accustomed to the Chippewa tribal life here on the island of Michilimackinac. Although he was still not entirely sure of his own safety, yet he was much more confident than before and there were times when he really felt quite sure that he was out of danger now. But there were other times when the feeling was quite the opposite.

Such a time had come two weeks ago when Minivavana had come by himself to Wawatam's abode, greeted both Wawatam and Henry with grave handshakes and quietly smoked a pipe with them until he was ready to speak. When he did, any illusion that Alexander Henry had harbored that he was completely safe had vanished.

"As you know, my brothers," Minivavana told them, "we are constantly being added to in number here by the arrival of warriors newly returned from Detroit or from other places. Mostly they bring good news to us, but equally many of them bring home with them a heart that is heavy with the loss of a brother, a father or a son. Within them burns a desire for vengeance upon any Englishman encountered, and this fire also burns in their families who are here and have just learned the sad news. In that respect, my young friend," he touched Henry's shoulder, "you are not safe."

"What should he do?" Wawatam asked. "Where can he go?"

"There is no place he can go away from us here," Minivavana replied, "where the danger he is in is not magnified. He is safer with us here than anywhere else in this country, yet he is not truly safe here, for the reasons I have just given. One cause of this is that he is yet too recognizable as an Englishman. He has been adopted by you, Wawatam, but he has not been adopted by the Chippewa nation, nor can he be while our people feel as strongly as they do against the English. But for the protection of his life, I recommend to you, Wawatam, that you dress him in the manner and custom of our people and color his skin so that he appears to be one of us. Then, perhaps, the people will not be so often reminded that he is an Englishman, and then, perhaps, he will be safer."

By nightfall the startling transition had been made and, when shown his own image in the trade mirror, Henry could scarcely believe it was himself who looked back. First a skinning knife, painstakingly honed to razor keenness, was used to shave off all the hair on his head except for a lock sprouting from a portion of his scalp the size of a hickory nut. Though he trusted Wawatam implicitly, young Henry could not control the trembling that went through him as Wawatam first touched the blade of the knife to his head. Wawatam discreetly pretended not to notice and, truth to tell, never had a Chippewa so gently "scalped" an Englishman before.

Then came the bath. It was Oghqua who came back from the woods with her basket filled with the bark of the white oak. She dumped all of it into a kettle of water bubbling over the fire. To this she added several handfuls of currant-like berries collected by the greatly pregnant wife of her son. When the mixture had, in her judgment, steeped enough, the kettle was removed from the fire and cold water added until the liquid was only tepid to the touch.

To Henry's intense embarrassment, the women of the household then undressed him completely and, using wads of soft moss as daubers, they rubbed the stain vigorously into his flesh. Though they managed to prevent any of it from seeping into his eyes as they stained his eyelids, a trickle of the juice ran down his face to his mouth-corner and he made the mistake of licking it. The bitterness of it was so extreme that it almost caused him to retch and it was fully two days before the awful taste left his mouth. Carefully they worked the stain into his skin everywhere, even in the most private areas of his body, and only the fact that his face was already stained prevented the deep flush on his cheeks and neck from showing. This was, Oghqua told him matter-of-factly, a permanent stain which no amount of washing would remove, and only time would wear it away. The result, when they were finished, was that his skin had become a deep coppery brown incredibly similar in coloration to that of Wawatam's own skin.

Following that, his face was painted in broad bands of red and black and yellow and he was given a shirt made of buckskin, heavy with bear grease and discolored with patches of vermilion stain. A weighty necklace of wampum was put around his throat and a cluster of it was attached to the front of his sleeveless shirt. Two wide bands of beaten silver were squeezed to fit securely around each upper arm, and three or four narrow bands of the same encircled his wrists. He was given a loincloth to cover his nakedness—which he donned with grateful alacrity—and some odd scarlet stockings called *mitasses* which reached to the knee and were greatly favored by many of the Indians and which, as Henry well knew, had become a favorite trade item over the past year. A bright red blanket was given to him, as well, which he was expected to toss over his shoulders and wear as a sort of cape when the air was chill or damp.

As a final touch, a cluster of hawk feathers were bound together at the quill end and securely fastened to the single remaining lock of his hair. With that, the metamorphosis was complete and Alexander Henry had now become, in every vestige of his appearance, a Chippewa Indian.

With his new disguise, Henry had much greater freedom and much less fear for his life. He was able to move about casually among newly arriving Indians without any of them suspecting that he was not one of themselves. He became, very quickly, a bit overconfident.

This was just now the season when Henry had expected many of his French employees to have already returned to Fort Michilimackinac with the proceeds of their eight months of wilderness trading ventures. He asked Wawatam to allow him to go back there for a visit in an endeavor to collect some of his property if possible, and Wawatam reluctantly agreed.

The journey there and back by canoe was entirely uneventful, but the effort was wholly fruitless. The men had returned, as he had expected, and they were deeply shocked when the warrior who stopped to speak with them turned out to be their employer whom they thought to be dead. Yet, though some of them professed great pleasure at seeing him well, every one of them claimed that due to the upheaval the country was experiencing, they had lost everything. In more than one case, Henry was certain it was simply an outright example of theft, but he was powerless to do anything about it. Too, he became progressively concerned that his disguise would be penetrated by the Ottawas or the Chippewas under Matchekewis who were still hovering near the fort, and so he returned to the island quickly.

He was now sure that he was destined to lead a hand-to-mouth existence with the Chippewas indefinitely and, surprisingly, he wasn't even greatly concerned about it. The very fact that he no longer had to worry about his property was something of a relief to him. After all, he reasoned, he had his life and this new existence of his could hardly have been termed uninteresting.

Several times recently councils had been held with some Ottawas who came to the island led by Chief Okinochumake. Wawatam explained to Henry that they wished to have the assurance of Chief Minivavana that when they passed through the Straits on their way toward Montreal, there would be no difficulties with the Chippewas. On this point Minivavana had thus far given no answer, though it was Wawatam's opinion that his chief would eventually agree. Queerly, though, Wawatam refused to discuss the matter further when Henry pressed him for details as to why the Ottawas might be heading for Montreal.

It was only a week or less after that when Wawatam told Henry that they were moving away from the island. A critical food shortage had developed and there was virtually no game on this island to hunt.

"We will go there," Wawatam said, pointing to the northwest, toward where the old Jesuit mission of St. Ignace had been located on the northern coast of the Straits of Mackinac. "It is Minivavana's order. There, if the English come, we will see them before they see us and they will not be able to surprise us. We are too many now to stay here. There are nearly four hundred warriors here, plus the many wives and children. Over there, at the bay which the Frenchmen called Boutchitaouy, there we will find game and berries and all we need in plenty."[116]

As Wawatam had predicted, game was in abundance in that area and stomachs that had long been on meager rations were now filled. Then, two days ago, the pregnant wife of Wawatam's son—the warrior was away fighting under Pontiac—went into labor. Immediately she was removed from the common lodge and placed in a smaller one which had been erected nearby for this occasion. It was obvious from the onset, however, that she was having grave difficulties. This, Wawatam said soberly, was extremely unusual in their tribe and he was concerned for her life and the life of his grandchild within her.

Beckoning Henry to follow him, Wawatam went out into the fields nearby and walked along watching the ground and occasionally turning over sticks or matted clumps of grasses or pieces of bark. At last, as he flipped over a plate-sized segment of dried bark, a small garter snake which had been curled beneath it attempted to escape into the heavy weeds. With an exclamation, Wawatam pounced and caught it. The little snake struck at him again and again, but he paid no attention to it. From his pouch he removed a small pewter cup and, directing Henry to hold it for him, he cut off the snake's head and held the body neck down over the cup until it had bled itself out. Then he tossed the carcass aside and together they returned to the pregnant squaw.

Gently, careful not to spill a drop, Wawatam spoon-fed the small amount of blood to her until it was all gone. Except for the winces occasioned by the continuing labor spasms, she remained expressionless during this time. When he was finished, Wawatam straightened and smiled. To Henry he nodded and said, "It is good. This is what we always do in such rare cases and I have never seen it to fail. She will now have her baby in a short while."

They left her to the ministrations of Oghqua and returned to Wawatam's lodge. Less than an hour later they heard the cry of a baby and a few moments later Oghqua entered with the news which pleased Wawatam enormously; that he was now the grandfather of a fine new boy.

"How could snake's blood have helped?" Henry asked, perplexed over this mystery.

"I do not question," Wawatam replied. "Manitou has told us that it will make a baby come when the mother fails. It is not a concern how it does so. It is enough that it happens. Tomorrow morning," he added, changing the subject with the casualness which Henry always found disconcerting in the Chippewas, "we go to St. Martin's Island in this bay and there we fish for the great long-nosed fish with fingers under his snout."

By this, Henry knew he meant the sturgeon, and he looked forward to the event. He expected that the new mother and her child would stay here, but at dawn this morning he was shocked to see her in apparent high spirits, the babe swaddled and strapped to her back on a board and contained by windings of rawhide strips—this carrier called a *papoose*[117]—as she stood knee-deep in the cold water and helped to load the canoe.

Once again Alexander Henry marveled at what amazing people the Indians were.

[*July 2, 1763—Saturday, 1:00* A.M.]

Ever since darkness had fallen about four hours ago, the three men had sat with their heads close together in the house of the Meloche brothers just north of Detroit, speaking in undertones of their plan to escape. Two of them had been in this house in the midst of Pontiac's camp for nearly eight weeks and the confinement was beginning to prey on them badly. They were Captain Donald Campbell and Lieutenant George McDougall. The third man, a newly captured trader taken on Lake Erie, Abraham Van Eps, had only been here a few days but he more than willingly fell in with the plan to escape.

"As I see it, Captain," McDougall whispered now, an hour after midnight, "in about three hours should be the best time to make our try at it. Everyone who's going to be asleep'll be dead to the world then, and those on guard will be groggy."

"I agree," Van Eps remarked. "We've got the shutter boards worked loose enough now that a good solid push'll shove the whole thing down. All we'll have to do then is jump out and run like hell for the fort."

"It's a long way," said Campbell dubiously. "You two boys don't carry as much weight around with you as I do and you're both a lot taller. You'll be taking one step for every two of mine." He shook his head, adding, "I don't know. It's a good bit better than a mile to the fort, maybe closer to two, and I'm damned sure I couldn't run that far. And if we get caught trying, it's our scalps."

"You've *got* to come, Don!" McDougall whispered fiercely. "We can't go if you don't come; there's no telling what they'd do to you if we got away and left you here. Either you come with us or we don't go."

Campbell's smile was lost in the darkness. He couldn't possibly make it and he knew it. He was too fat to run and too nearsighted to see whether a man twenty feet away was a friend or an enemy. And somehow he just couldn't picture himself tiptoeing through a camp filled with savage Indians to make his escape. Like as not, he'd step right on someone. If he went along he was sure he'd only jeopardize the entire plan. By the same token, he realized, it was manifestly unfair to him to hinder the others in their bid for escape, which a flat refusal to accompany them would do. In these weeks that they had been held captive, he had come to know Pontiac a lot better. He could understand some of the things that motivated the Ottawa—in fact, almost sympathize with him on some points—and he thought he knew what the reaction would be if the trader and the lieutenant escaped and he did not. He was pretty sure that Pontiac would be very angry and would rant and rave a bit, but he truly doubted that the war chief would cause him any greater inconvenience than perhaps putting a permanent guard with him or tying him up every night. Thinking the situation over in this way, he came to his decision easily.

"All right," he told them, "we'll do it. About four o'clock we'll make the break. George, you'll lead off. Grip Van Eps's hand and head for the secret entry that Baby and St. Martin use when they go to see the major. There's a guard there and you know the code knock. Van Eps, you keep pace and keep your hand tightly locked in George's grip, otherwise you'll wind up getting lost in the dark. I'll bring up the rear and don't worry if I fall back a ways. Remember, I'm fat and slow, but I'll be along. I know the way all right. Close and lock that entry port after you get in and keep it closed till you hear me coming. That's an order."

There was a little more discussion after that, though not much. There was really little left to say. If Meloche didn't hear them getting out and didn't raise the alarm, there was a good chance they would make it. The intervening hours now passed on the back of a snail, crawling by with excruciating slowness. Finally, when it must have been approaching the appointed hour, Campbell decided it would be foolish to wait any longer.

"Let's go," he whispered, touching the two men. Instantly they were alert and they crept to the heavily boarded window. Slowly and carefully, McDougall reached up and slid his fingers between sill and shutter, thrusting them down into the previously opened gap until they were able to curl about the bottom of the shutter. Then, holding his breath and straining, he pushed outward with controlled pressure. There was the faintest of squeaks as the shutter moved outward. He stopped, then began again. This time it moved with no sound. In another moment it was loose at bottom and sides and only barely connected yet at the top.

"Don't try to take it all the way off," Campbell warned.

"You couldn't hold it in that position if it came loose up there and if it falls we'll wake the whole camp."

"Right," McDougall whispered. Continuing to hold the shutter up from the bottom, he pushed it out until there was a gap of almost an arm's length. With his toe he touched the trader's leg and said, "Go, Van Eps! Wait outside till we get out." The trader carefully hoisted a leg over the sill, felt downward with the outside foot until it touched the ground and then drew himself out. In just a moment he stuck his head back in and whispered excitedly but in such a low voice the two officers could hardly hear him.

"Two or three Indians asleep under blankets about ten feet away. My God, we better not do it."

"Quiet," Campbell hissed. "Get hold of that shutter-bottom and maintain it till George gets out. You next," he added, nudging McDougall.

The lieutenant waited until he felt Van Eps grasp and hold the bottom of the shutter from outside and then he slipped out soundlessly in one fluid movement. Campbell quickly reached out and put his own hands under the bottom of the shutter, gripped it firmly and then whispered abruptly, "All right, Van Eps, let it go."

Without even realizing that it was Campbell who now held the shutter and not McDougall, Van Eps obeyed, and immediately Campbell pulled the shutter closed as nearly as he could. There was a momentary silence and then McDougall's urgent whisper came from directly on the other side of the shutter.

"Don!" His lips brushed the wood at the crack between shutter and frame as he spoke so softly that even Campbell could hardly make out what he said. "Don, for God's sake, push it open. *Hurry!*"

"Lieutenant," Campbell said, his voice authoritative even in his whisper, "I know I can't make it. You and Van Eps get to the fort. Now! That's an order. Dammit, *go!* I can't hold this shutter for long."

"Captain, in the name of—"

Campbell cut him off curtly, his whisper hoarse and as urgent as McDougall's had been. "Get away from here. *Now!*"

He braced himself with his knees against the wall, feeling momentarily McDougall's pull against his own. The pull stopped abruptly and after a moment he realized they had gone. He leaned his head against the shutter, wondering how long it would be before his fingers numbed beyond control and the shutter slipped out of his grasp.

"Good luck, boys," he murmured, not sure whether he had said the words aloud or had just thought them.

He was very tense at first, waiting for the shriek which would indicate they had been seen and the alarm was out. But no sound came and he began to relax a little. It was about fifteen minutes later that there was a loud, tearing squeak followed by a thud of the bottom edge of the shutter striking ground, and then the crackle of branches as the heavy shutter toppled over into a bush.

Captain Donald Campbell grinned as he straightened and then began to rub his fingers to restore the circulation. Even before they had begun to tingle with returning sensitivity, the Ottawa camp was in an uproar.

[*July 2, 1763—Sunday, 11:00* A.M.]

Father Pierre Pothier, Jesuit missionary to the Hurons, had always considered himself capable of meeting any contingency. Had it not been he who, at the very beginning of this siege against Detroit, persuaded the Hurons for a considerable while to balk Pontiac's endeavors to make them join him? Had it not been he who had stood up to Pontiac and induced him to wait until after the passage of a holy day Mass before forcing his Christian Hurons to support him? He had been courageous.

Now, as he walked swiftly toward the fort, his long black gown flapping softly against his legs, he was embarked on another matter which involved personal courage. The thought stuck him suddenly that in considering the worth of his own courage, he was giving in to the cardinal sin of pride and his step faltered. He slowed and his brow furrowed deeply as he made an effort to decide what was the best, the most selfless, the most *Christian* thing to do. Again his pace picked up. There could be no other answer than that he would have to reveal the plot to Major Gladwin.

To attract as little attention as possible, he had gone downstream from the Huron village and then crossed over to the fort side of the river in the vicinity of the Potawatomi village, hoping to attract as little attention to himself as possible. It meant a fairly good walk back to the fort, but he was accustomed to walking long distances and he maintained a steady pace. As he walked he thought again of that fantastic council held last night between Pontiac and the Frenchmen of Detroit.

Those Frenchmen, perhaps one hundred and fifty of them,

had gathered in the prescribed meeting area that Pontiac had informed them of, seating themselves on mats that had been placed for their comfort. A small fire had been lighted, Indian guards posted, and when all had assembled who were going to, the pipe were smoked in silence. Not all of them had been finished when Pontiac had risen, tossed to the ground a purple war belt he was holding, and began to address them, foregoing the usual greetings and polite remarks with which councils were generally opened and coming directly to the point:

"My brothers," he said, "how long will you French people allow this bad flesh to remain upon your lands? I have told you before and I now tell you again, that when I took up the hatchet it was for *your* good as well as ours. This year the English must all perish throughout this country!"

His voice had risen to a vicious whiplash and the Frenchmen seated before him shuffled uncomfortably beneath his stern gaze. With the tip of his tongue, Pontiac touched the points of the crescent of white stone hanging from his nostrils and then continued:

"They must perish! The Master of Life commands it; yet you, who know Him better than we, wish to oppose His will. Until now I have said nothing on this matter. I have not urged you to take part with us in the war. It would have been enough had you been content to sit quiet on your mats, looking on, while we were fighting for you. But you have not done so. No! You call yourselves our friends, and yet you assist the English with provisions and you go about as spies among our villages. *This must not continue!* Now the time has come for decision. You must be either wholly French or wholly English. If you are French, take up that war belt and lift the hatchet with us; but if you are English, then we declare war upon you!

"My brothers," he added, his voice gentling some of the dismay registering on their faces, "I know this is a hard thing. We are all alike, children of our great father, the King of France, and it is hard to fight among brethren for the sake of dogs. But there is no choice. Look upon the belt, and let us have your answer."

There was a distinctly uncomfortable silence as Pontiac stood waiting for someone to speak. It was Matthias Meloche, brother of Baptiste and François, who picked up the challenge. When he had been invited to attend this council, he more than half suspected that Pontiac was on the point of demanding active French help. Though Meloche had in his possession a message stating that the Treaty of Paris was a reality, it was still not official word and he did not want to let himself believe it; could not comprehend that Louis would really give up Canada to the English. But while he and his brothers were not averse to assisting Pontiac covertly, they had no desire to do so openly. If the treaty was an *actuality*, they were liable, in the end, to be executed. So now, instead of the treaty message, he withdrew from inside his coat a copy of the capitulation of Montreal and its dependencies, which included Detroit.

"We French here," he began slowly, "have a great love for our Indian brothers, as Chief Pontiac must by this time surely know. We also have, within our hearts, a strong desire to help the Indians in this war. But, my brothers," he now held up the document of the capitulation, "what of this? You must first untie the knot with which our great father, the King, has bound us. In this paper he tells all his Canadian children to sit quietly and obey the English until he comes, because he wishes to punish his enemies himself. We dare not disobey him, for then he would be angry with us. And you, my brothers, who speak of making war on us if we do not do as you wish, do you think you could escape his wrath if you should raise the hatchet against his French children? He would treat you as enemies, not as friends, and you would have to fight both English and French at once. Tell us, my brothers, what can you reply to this?"

With evidently the only possible answer that could have done so, Matthias Meloche had just neatly taken all the wind out of Pontiac's sails. The Ottawa war chief did not know what to say for a moment and he simply stood there frowning and apparently in deep thought. There was one thing, however, which the middle-aged Meloche had not counted upon—the heated blood of his own young Frenchmen. Suddenly a young man, Zacharias Cicotte, sprang to his feet, came to the front and scooped up the war belt with one hand.

"I have heard enough of circle talk," he shouted, waving the belt over his head. "Enough! I speak for the young men among us and for all others who love France and this I say in answer to Pontiac: my comrades and I are ready and willing to raise the hatchet for you! Those who agree with me, stand and come forward so that Pontiac will know you."

There was a gasp from the older generation as perhaps forty or more young men ranging in age from about eighteen to twenty-eight scrambled to their feet and moved to join young Cicotte, despite the shouts of "No! No!" which arose from those still seated around them. Among those joining Cicotte was Alexis Cuillerier, the son of Pontiac's closest French cohort, Antoine Cuillerier. Pierre and Jean Labadie also came forward, the sons of the elder Pierre Labadie, and with them moved Labadie's son-in-law as well, Christ Molére. Another readily recognizable face was that of Charles Dusette, who carried with him right at this moment the rifle that had belonged to Sir Robert Davers and the powder horn that had been Lieutenant Robertson's. Pierre Barth—better known as Piero—was there, a young man who worked in a little shop within the fort as a silversmith and candlestick maker. With him as well was a notorious ruffian and brawler named Jules Mayerin who, at twenty-eight, was one of the oldest who had risen to join Pontiac. There were many more, but these were representative of the young men who came forward.

The Jesuit priest, Pierre Pothier, shook his head as he continued his walk toward the fort, still hard put to believe such a council had really taken place and that young Frenchmen were planning to voluntarily raise arms against the English here. The drama of that moment last night was still a vivid picture in his mind. Pontiac had shaken the hands of each of the young men in turn, warmly welcoming them to his side, but growing angry when the greater number of older Frenchmen left the council almost as one to return to their homes and have no part of this subversiveness. The young men, some of them concerned now about what sort of reception would await them at home from their parents, elected to remain with Pontiac for the night. They discussed what their role would be under the Ottawa chief. One of the first questions asked by Pontiac was if there were more young men in or around the Detroit area upon whom he could count for help. Dusette, Barth, Mayerin and Cuillerier agreed to recruit and believed they could wind up with a total of about three hundred men willing to serve. With the help of some of these from inside the fort, perhaps, they might be able to overpower guards or in some other way get the gates open at night so that Pontiac and his warriors could attack inside the fort.

It was Piero Barth who proudly announced that he was making a set of keys which would unlock the gates of the fort and that as soon as he finished them he would turn them over to Pontiac. To the chief and his men he boasted, "The English in the fort are already half dead and a good savage cry will make them surrender!" But, he added, he would need four or five days yet to complete those keys.

In the meanwhile, some of the young men claimed they would lend active fighting assistance at once, joining with Pontiac at daybreak in the continued shooting at the fort from a distance to maintain the siege.

Considerably pleased, Pontiac ordered a great feast to be prepared and immediately a number of the village dogs were caught, butchered and roasted. It was not until nearly dawn that word finally reached Pontiac that one of his prime captives, Lieutenant George McDougall, had escaped from the house of Meloche during the night, along with the trader, Van Eps, but that Captain Campbell was still being held.

Campbell's evaluation of how Pontiac would react was amazingly accurate. The chief had been extremely angry at first and made a few dark threats, but eventually he settled for just establishing a closer guard over him at all times. Of this, Father Pothier knew little. He was aware, however, that the older and more conservative Frenchmen of the community were almost in a state of despair now—unwilling to see their sons actively support Pontiac, but equally unwilling to aid the English in any way, and certainly afraid to become informers lest some of the atrocities reserved for the English by Pontiac be visited upon themselves.

It was because of this prevailing indecision that Father Pothier had made his decision. It was quite clear to him that Major Gladwin had to be told so that steps could be taken to stop this before both French and English were spilling each other's blood here and the very flowing of it opened a new war between these powers. Since no one else had the courage to go to Gladwin, Pothier had reasoned, then he must be the one.

The fort was only a half mile ahead of him when he sensed someone behind him and spun around. There were two men—the interpreter Pierre LaButte, and another well-known drinker and brawler named Baptiste Gruereme. They caught up to the priest and blocked his passage.

"You fool!" LaButte snarled. "You're going to Gladwin to tell him about that council last night, aren't you? *Idiot!* If you go there, you are absolutely mad and you will deserve just exactly what you will get."

"And what will that be, my son?" the Jesuit asked calmly.

"Don't 'my son' me! If you haven't figured it out for yourself, I'll tell you what'll happen. Three things. First of all, Pontiac'll cross the river and he'll burn down your church.

Next, he will go to your home and he will burn that, too, and destroy all that you have. Finally, he will kill you, and the death will not be a fast one nor an easy one. You will probably beg him to kill you before he is finished. In fact, you will pray to God Himself to let you die."

Pothier felt the fear rising in his throat and tried to force it down. He tried to speak, but gave out only a hoarse little croak and then shut his mouth. His tongue was suddenly dry and there was the bitter taste of fear in his throat. With it came the equally bitter self-denunciation which remained unspoken. It had been hard enough to bear the pride he had felt in his own courage; but the knowledge that struck him now that it had been a false pride and that he was a decidedly frightened man . . . this was a blow which shattered the spirit of Pierre Pothier, Jesuit.

With shoulders slumped and eyes downcast, he turned away from the fort.

[July 3, 1763—Sunday, 3:00 P.M.]

In his New York headquarters, having yesterday heard rumors to the effect that such posts as Fort Miamis, Ouiatenon, St. Joseph and Michilimackinac had been lost, a barely containable anger had begun percolating within Lieutenant General Sir Jeffrey Amherst. Only the vague possibility—and strong hope—that the rumors were groundless prevented him from erupting violently. Nevertheless, it was only with the greatest of self-control that he had been able to write to Major Henry Gladwin in a constrained hand, declaring that:

. . . and it is my will and desire, Sir, that immediate and total vengeance be taken upon all Indians in every encounter you may have with them and that no mercy whatever be shown to these perfidious barbarians. They must be destroyed utterly as an example for any others who might hope to follow the pattern they have set. Further, I have ordered Colonel Bouquet to stop at Fort Pitt, from which place he is to direct operations. You will soon be reinforced by detachments already en route to you which are soon to rendezous at Presque Isle and then continue together to the Detroit and, should the reports I have received be true, that many of the upper posts dependent upon the Detroit have fallen, then you are ordered to march out with your men and reestablish these dependencies at once; . . .

But the vague, not-entirely-to-be-believed rumors Amherst received about the western Great Lakes were already in the process of being confirmed, as was news of an equally disastrous scope on the communication from the Pennsylvania frontier.

Yesterday, at Fort Ligonier, Lieutenant Archibald Blane had received an express that had made it through from Fort Pitt; an express bearing the news that all three posts to the north—Venango, Le Boeuf and Presque Isle—had been destroyed, with by far the greater majority of their men killed or captured. This threw Blane into such a state that when he relayed the news at once to Captain Louis Ourry at Fort Bedford, he indiscreetly mentioned that he did not know whether he should abandon his own fort at once or just wait for the Indians to appear and then immediately capitulate to avoid loss of life to his garrison.

Nor was he the only one in whose mind the thought of flight was strong. Settlers everywhere were suddenly streaming eastward, many pausing at Fort Bedford or Shippensburg, Carlisle or Lancaster, but others continuing their panicky retreat until the welcome cobblestones of Philadelphia were beneath their feet.

Only yesterday in the valley of the Juniata River, a tributary of the Susquehanna, a party of six men had been working in the fields not far from the smaller river's mouth when they had paused to eat dinner in the house of one of the settlers there. Unexpectedly the door burst open and four or five Indians fired at them, then beat down the survivors with their rifle butts. One young man escaped to spread the alarm and a party of about a dozen young men took up the trail of the Indians. This was anticipated by the Shawnee party and the settlers walked right into an ambush from which only four escaped and managed to make it to Carlisle. Understandably, their arrival increased the ever-growing alarm.

Those refugees who made it back to Philadelphia told their stories of horror and deprivation to wide-eyed audiences. The verbal pictures they painted of conditions at Carlisle and elsewhere were nightmarish. At Carlisle, for example, a great many refugees who were unable to find shelter in the town were camped at various places in adjoining fields and forest, making lean-tos of bark and branches and living mainly on what they could beg from the Carlisle residents, which was very little. Their wretchedness was almost beyond description; some were numbed by their losses which were tragic to the extreme, while others were filled with a mind-fogging fear that the same would happen to them. All felt an implacable, ever-present hatred for the Indians, but too few were so keen on vengeance that they offered their services to Bouquet or any of the various fort commanders.

Governor James Hamilton of Pennsylvania outlined to the Pennsylvania General Assembly the scope of the misery and terror and fear running rampant on the province's frontier and begged that legislative body to take measures of defense at once before the condition grew even worse. The response, however, was predictable; the pattern for it had been set during the French and Indian War which was still so very fresh in memory. The Quakers dominated the General Assembly and they adamantly refused to take any measure which might result in harm coming to the Indians. As a matter of fact, not until the screams and moans of misery became overwhelming and the threat of actual violence against them was darkly promised if they did not do *something*, did they vote to pass a measure of, as they called it, "defense for the inhabitants." What it amounted to was that they voted the wherewithal to raise a body of seven hundred militiamen, but then attached to the bill a rider which positively forbade this body to take part in any offensive operations, or even to move itself to the frontier fringe. They were limited to "protecting the farmers while they bring in their crops," although the time for harvest was still a long way off for most crops.

Virginia, unlike Pennsylvania, took immediate measures of defense and these very measures increased the problems on the Pennsylvania frontier. Not troubled by having pacifistic Quakers dominating their governmental establishment, the House of Burgesses took quick advantage of their militia law—a law which was absent in Pennsylvania—and called up a militia of a thousand experienced woodsmen and hunters to patrol their borders. There were a number of skirmishes with the Indians, who soon found that it was much safer to prey on the virtually undefended Pennsylvanians than on these tough Virginians.

And while the Indians—the Shawnees and Delawares in particular—hacked and bludgeoned and burned their way through the Pennsylvania frontier, the Senecas to the north of them began taking a more active role in their own backyards. Unable, because of the influence of Sir William Johnson, to convince their five brother tribes of the Iroquois League to raise the bloody tomahawk, they did so by themselves and now began concentrating on interrupting the supply line from

Fort Niagara to the western posts. The most ideal place to do this was on the treacherous, narrow, winding road which was the portage around the two great cataracts and the gorge below them, from Fort Little Niagara below the falls, nine miles to Fort Schlosser above, where the Niagara River again became navigable for batteaux.[118] All supplies from Montreal, New York, Albany and Oswego which were destined for Detroit and her dependencies were shipped first to Fort Niagara, where the Niagara River empties into Lake Ontario. From this point they could still be taken in batteaux upriver to Fort Little Niagara. Here the boats would have to be unloaded and everything trucked by wagon for those very difficult nine miles past the Niagara gorge, the monstrous whirlpools and the great cataracts. At Fort Schlosser—as often called the Upper Landing—the goods were then transferred to batteaux and then moved upstream around the huge Grand Island, through difficult rapids, to the mouth of Lake Erie. Here, where Buffalo Creek emptied into the lake,[119] the ships from Detroit would anchor, as it was dangerous for them to approach any closer to the shallowing waters and swiftly increasing current of the Niagara River. From this point the goods would continue by batteaux or else be transferred aboard the ships for the continuation of the supply line westward.

Far to the south, at Carlisle, Henry Bouquet quietly fumed at the delays he was experiencing. He had with him now a total of four hundred and sixty men, which included one hundred and thirty-three of the Scottish 77th Regiment, two hundred and fourteen of the proud and famous 42nd Regiment—better known as the Blackwatch Regiment—plus a party of the Rangers and a battalion from the 60th Regiment, called the Royal Americans.

Bouquet was irritated beyond expression at the apathy of the people, their unwillingness to offer any real help while at the same time demanding the utmost of protection. The news received this morning had in no way helped his bearish mood. He had been writing a series of dispatches about an hour before noon when he heard a considerable furor outside. It didn't take long to learn what occasioned it.

Captain Ourry at Fort Bedford, having received the dreadful news relayed by Blane at Fort Ligonier concerning the fall of Presque Isle, Le Boeuf and Venango, had immediately himself relayed the express to Bouquet. The rider had just come into town and, having stopped to water his horse, was immediately bombarded with questions and demands for news. With little thought to what the results would be, he excitedly told the listeners of the fall of the three forts and of the continuing attacks against Fort Pitt, Fort Ligonier and Fort Bedford. Expounding even more under the glow of being an extremely important and carefully listened-to person at the moment, he gave all the gory details he had in his possession, plus a few more that he thought up on the spur of the moment. Finally, gripping his reins to ride on to Bouquet's headquarters tent, he said loudly over his shoulder, "Yes sir, them Injens'll be here damn quick, by grab! An' they ain't no way that either Pitt or Ligonier'll stop 'em, or Bedford either!"

As if they were homing pigeons riding a tail wind, within mere minutes dozens of people had set off on foot or astride horses to spread the grim news to communities to the eastward. The stories grew with each telling and before long the reports had it that the Indians were right on their heels in force and that wholesale massacres and burnings had begun.

Bouquet himself heard the news from the rider and then read the dispatches from Fort Pitt, relayed via Forts Ligonier and Bedford. He was deeply shocked and along with the shock came an encompassing anger. The loss of Venango and Le Boeuf he might understand, small as they were, but that Presque Isle, whose defenses he himself had helped to improve not so very long ago, should have surrendered was not only unthinkable, it was unpardonable. And that Blane should have remarked to Ourry that he, too, was already contemplating abandonment or capitulation of his post, filled Bouquet with a rare and profound rage. In his immediate reply to Ourry he said:

Humanity makes me hope that Christie is dead, as his scandalous capitulation, for a post of that consequence and so impregnable to savages, deserves the most severe punishment. As for Fort Ligonier, I shivered when you hinted to me Lieutenant Blane's intentions. Death and infamy would have been the reward he would expect, instead of the honor he has thus far obtained by his prudence, courage and resolution . . . This is a most trying time, but harbor no thought of relinquishing your post. You may be sure that all expedition possible will be used for the relief of the few remaining posts.

Admonishing the express for his loose tongue and cautioning him against further demonstration of this sort of talk in public, whether true or not, Bouquet sent him back at once on the road to Fort Bedford. Then he began another letter to be carried by special courier in the fastest means possible to General Amherst in New York. He wrote:

Carlisle, 3rd July 1763

Sir

An express from Fort Pitt brings this moment the fatal account of the loss of our posts at Presque Isle, Le Boeuf and Venango. Your Excellency will see, in the enclosed letters, all the particulars I had of the unexpected disaster.

As the destruction of the important post of Presque Isle will occasion some alteration in your first plan, I beg you will favor me with your orders concerning the troops you have destined for this department.

By the enclosed return of provisions at Fort Pitt, that post does not stand so immediately in need of relief as to make us run great risks to force a convoy up, before the province can give us some assistance.

I doubt if . . . Pennsylvania can have troops raised and equipped in less than six weeks or two months, during which time they are incapable of any defense, for want of a Militia Law.

The savages must soon disperse for want of provisions and, their first impetuosity cooled, they will be more easily dealt with. I shall, however, move forward as soon as I can collect the horses and carriages I want, which the great consternation and flight of the inhabitants makes very difficult.

I have required the Governor to send them arms and ammunition and proposed to collect the people in this frontier in a few well-stockaded places inclosing mills, as a retreat for themselves, their families and provisions, to help keep possession of the country and, if the enemy should penetrate, destroy all kinds of eatables which could not be secured in their strongholds and might fall into the hands of the savages; but from the nature of this Government, I suppose nothing will be done in time.

The second company of the 42nd will be here the 5th and I expect the remains of the two regiments on the 6th and 7th.

I have secured all the provisions I could get in this country; 100 head of cattle, 200 sheep, and about 3000 pounds of fine powder from the Indian traders. I expect the flour and wagons from Lancaster by the 8th.

I received your letter of the 25th June and shall continue in the service the men so timely raised by Mr. Croghan, which the Province will, I hope, take into their pay. I am, &ca.,

H.B.

P.S. I enclose Mr. Croghan's letter to Sir William Johnson open.

His Excellency
Sir Jeffrey Amherst

[*July 3, 1763—Sunday, 9:00* P.M.]

Many individuals of the older generation of Frenchmen at Detroit were growing progressively more worried. Most of them were sure now, especially in view of the documents that had been brought to Major Gladwin aboard the *Michigan*, that a treaty of peace had indeed been drawn up and ratified between England and France and they had no wish to see their young men destroyed through their own impetuosity or through misplaced loyalty.

With quiet dignity, a group of the most influential and respected of the older French residents asked for and received a private conference with Major Gladwin. Many things were spoken of, including some of the things which had transpired at the meeting called by Pontiac the night before. General hints of what was developing were given and, even though nothing explicit was revealed, nor were the names of the French sympathizers of Pontiac, Gladwin was quick to realize the situation could have been devastating without such information.

After they had gone he called a conference of his officers and explained what he knew of the situation to them. Guards were cautioned to be extra alert and, in some cases, guard posts were doubled. The ramparts guard, which had been somewhat relaxed of late, was now trebled. A special small group of soldiers spread out within the fort to look for a set of keys allegedly already made and hidden somewhere about, to be used by someone inside during some night to let the Indians in before anyone suspected what was happening. A proclamation was issued to all French residents who might be fearful of what the Indians would do to them if they did not actively support Pontiac and they were invited, any who cared to, to take up residence within the fort proper. Those who did would be somewhat limited in their movements and would have to have legitimate reasons for leaving the fort, and get official permission to do so from Major Gladwin personally. The gates would all be doubly locked and doubly guarded and no egress of any nature permitted between the hours of sunset to sunrise.

By nightfall, nearly twoscore French families had left their homes outside the fort and taken up residence inside, and there would be more to come, apparently, on the morrow. Among those arriving with their families today were Jacques Duperon Baby and Jacques St. Martin. All of these Frenchmen who came were formed into a sort of militia which would be required to assist in the defense of the place in case of emergency. The English trader James Sterling volunteered to take command of them and see that they lived up to their newly given allegiance. Gladwin accepted his services gratefully.

The fact that so many of their countrymen were moving into the fort was a matter of frustration and anger for those Frenchmen who remained outside, and also for Pontiac. The young Frenchmen, it was true, continued to assert that they would help the chief, but now they declared they would not assist him in an all-out attack against the fort, since their friends, possibly even members of their own families, within the fort might get killed.

Adjacent to the camp of the Chippewas, in the house of Jules St. Bemand, Ensign Christopher Pauli and young John Rutherford were being held captive. It was there that another meeting of Frenchmen was held. Pauli, since being brought here after the fall of Fort Sandusky, had not once left the room he was in, although Rutherford, taken with the Robertson-Davers party, was often out for one purpose or another. This was what had happened last night.

A number of Frenchmen—among them Baptiste Campeau, Sancho Obeign, Baptiste Meloche, François Meloche, Pierre Barth, Antoine Domelte, and Louisan Denter—had come to St. Bemand's house sometime after midnight. The first that Pauli had known they were there was when he awakened to see John Rutherford being quietly led from the room by François Meloche.

As soon as the door had been closed and locked behind them, Pauli arose and crouched for an hour or more with his ear to the door, listening to the mumbled conversation of the men. From scattered words he was able to overhear in this way, added to what little he was able to extract from the frightened Rutherford when he was returned to the room,

Pauli was certain that a new plan of treachery against Detroit was ready to be put into operation in a few days.

Rutherford at first would only say that they had told him to say nothing, under pain of death, about what had gone on in the room, but little by little Pauli learned what had happened. Apparently one of those Frenchmen had gotten his hands on the papers that had been in the possession of Matthias Meloche declaring that the Treaty of Paris had been enacted. They looked quite official but since their own abilities with English writing were limited, Rutherford had been brought out to give his studied opinion about them. None of the men had been happy when he said that as nearly as he could tell they were genuine. At once a pact had been made among the Frenchmen present in the house to keep this information to themselves and continue to go ahead with their plans of aiding Pontiac in the planned surprise attack against the fort and in the construction of fire rafts to be set afire and floated downstream into the *Michigan* and *Huron* anchored beside the fort.

Shortly afterwards, Pontiac himself had arrived at the house, accompanied by an older Frenchman named Jadeau, and Pierre LaButte, the interpreter. The old man studied the documents carefully and then shook his head. Addressing himself to Pontiac, he held up three fingers close together.

"These," he said, touching the tip of each in turn, "are the kings of France and England and Spain. They have made their peace and are now close together like this and cannot be separated. By attacking the English now, Pontiac, you will be attacking the whole and you will bring down on your head the wrath of all three."

Jadeau went on with other arguments inclined to convince Pontiac that his cause was now a lost one, but abruptly LaButte jumped to his feet in a rage, snatching up the documents and tossed them into the fireplace where they quickly burned. Then he turned to face Jadeau and pointed a trembling finger at him.

"You lie!" he snarled. "Jadeau, you are no better than an Englishman yourself. Pontiac," and he turned to the chief, "do not believe what he has said. The words have been put into his mouth by the English in the fort. I have seen him there. He lies! Do not believe him. I tell you what Piero Barth told you only a short while ago—that the English in the fort are half dead now and a good savage cry will make them surrender!"

From what he could gather, Pauli sensed that Pontiac was

more inclined to listen to LaButte than to Jadeau. He heard chairs pushed back and the movement of feet and by the time the door to his room was unlocked and Rutherford shown back in, the English officer was again on his pallet feigning sleep. When they were alone again, he had risen and questioned the badly frightened Rutherford, gradually fitting together the pieces of what was shaping up.[120]

Before the light of dawn, Pauli had made his decision: he must escape to the fort and warn Major Gladwin.

[July 4, 1763—Monday, 6:00 A.M.]

Lieutenant Jehu Hay was more than pleased when he was summoned to Major Gladwin's quarters at dawn this morning and given orders to lead a sortie out of the fort. Hay, one of the oldest officers at the fort, was essentially a lazy man. It was why, after all these years of service in His Majesty's army, he was still a lieutenant. His greatest ambition was simply to take life as he found it and not aspire to great things which might cause him extra effort. Nevertheless, even for him the fact of being confined to the fort was getting on his nerves and he craved a little excitement.

"Lieutenant," Gladwin had told him, "you are familiar, are you not, with the location of Monsieur Baby's house?"

"Yes sir."

"Well, Monsieur Baby has taken up residence in the fort now with his family and it is almost certain that whatever things he left behind will be pillaged by the Indians. Unfortunately, we cannot be concerned with moving his personal items to preserve them, but he informs me that he has in storage there a fair quantity of gunpowder and lead. I want you to round up thirty men and go there to get it and bring it back here before the Indians can get their hands on it. While out, see what you can do, if it's safe enough, about destroying those breastworks the Indians built and have been firing from beyond Baby's house. You know which I mean."

And so now, at six o'clock in the morning, Lieutenant Jehu Hay was leading his party out. Expecting shots to be fired at them from a distance, they were pleased when none came and they reached Baby's house without interference of any kind. Here they located the ammunition and Hay sent a small squad of men back to the fort with it, while with the remainder he went to the Indian breastworks, constructed of old wood planking and other such materials and began tearing it down. At this point they were about four hundred yards from the fort. They completed the destruction by about half past seven and were about to return to the fort when they were met by a volley of gunfire. It seemed evident that a party of Indians had spotted them and then crept into hiding behind another small breastworks a little farther away and were now attacking.

Jehu Hay ordered the fire returned and the fight was a hot one for a little while. Then the gate of the fort opened and a reinforcement led by Captain Hopkins came out on the double, rushing up toward the flank of the attackers. Immediately the Indians broke from cover and began to flee. There were only about twenty of them and, though they were heavily painted, Hay was sure he recognized among them two or three young Frenchmen whom he knew by sight if not by name.

"After them!" he bellowed.

His party spread out in pursuit, some of the men firing as they ran. Almost immediately one of the Indians crumpled in midstride and fell, while two others screeched and clapped hands over their wounds as they continued hobbling away as rapidly as possible.

Private Frederick Dann, who had been raised on the frontier of Virginia, was the soldier who had downed the fallen Indians. All of his life he had hated the savages with a passion and now, despite Hay's order for the pursuit to cease and a return be made to the fort, he ran up to the Indian, kneeled on his back and quickly, with a well-practiced move, removed the scalp. He stood up and held it high, shaking it wildly over his head.

"Here's what's gonna happen to all you Injens!" he shouted after the retreating warriors. "An' this, too!"

A dozen times in succession he drove his knife into the body of the Indian at his feet—a warrior of about twenty— and then quickly cut off the ears and nose, punctured the eyes and kicked the head repeatedly in a vicious manner until the skull was crushed and shapeless.

From the edge of the woods came faintly the outraged screams of the Indians who had stopped and were now watching from cover. Their anger seemed to be much more vehement than any shown previously over the fall of any Indian since the siege began. As a matter of fact, it was.

The mutilated warrior now being left to the flies by Private Dann as he shook the scalp at the Indians one more time and then rejoined the troop, was named Tewalee. He was dearly beloved nephew of Wasson, chief of the Saginaw Bay Chippewas.[121]

Jules St. Bemand had just brought some breakfast to the room where John Rutherford and Christopher Pauli were being held captive when the adjoining Chippewa camp was suddenly thrown into an uproar. There were screams and woeful wailings from squaws and blood-curdling shrieks of anger from warriors. Wondering what was going on, St. Bemand allowed Rutherford and Pauli to follow him to the front door to watch.

A majority of the warriors in the camp were clustered around a small party of war-painted warriors who had just arrived. Though the prisoners could not see well what was happening, it looked as if two or three of their number were wounded. One of them, with a great quantity of blood pulsing down his back and leg, leaned against a tree and then, a moment later, sank to a sitting position.

From off to one side there was a movement and Chief Wasson, followed by a dozen of his best men, came into view. They walked directly to the center of all this activity and stood there listening as two or three warriors spoke in turn. Abruptly the wounded man sitting against the tree pitched forward onto his face and a moment later another death cry went up from the squaws.

"Back to your room," St. Bemand ordered the two Englishmen gruffly. "I'll go find out what's happening."

"Will you let us know?" Pauli asked.

"When I get back," St. Bemand agreed, nodding, then added, "if it's something you should know about."

He locked them in and was gone perhaps ten minutes when again the door was unlocked and opened. St. Bemand's face was pale. Behind him the front door of the house was open and Ensign Pauli and John Rutherford could see that by far the greater majority of warriors were following Wasson away, toward Pontiac's camp. Only a few of the men, along with a large number of squaws, were still clustered around the dead warrior.

"It is bad news," St. Bemand said, "for everybody. A small party of soldiers came out of the fort early this morning to carry in some supplies they took from Monsieur Baby's house and to tear down a place of cover that the Indians had built to fire from at the fort. Tewalee, the nephew of Wasson, who is like a son to the chief, saw them and attacked them with some of his men, but another party of soldiers came out of the fort and Tewalee's party had to flee. As they ran away, Tewalee and two others were hit by bullets. The other two came here and one has since died, but Tewalee was killed on the spot. His scalp was taken and his body mutilated. This was bad enough, but the soldier who took the scalp shook it in the air toward the other warriors and yelled something at them which they could not understand but which they took to be insults. It is a terrible insult and disgrace. Now Wasson has been told and his shame, his grief and his anger are greater than anyone has ever seen them."

St. Bemand motioned with his thumb over his shoulder in the direction Wasson and his men had been walking, but who were now passed out of sight, adding: "He has already blackened his face with soot and grease and he goes now to confront Pontiac and to take from him Captain Campbell, whom he means to kill in revenge. What he will do with you," he looked at Pauli, "when he comes back here, I do not know. He is—"

St. Bemand never completed what he was going to say. Pauli's fist shot up and collided with his jaw, snapping his head back and causing his eyes to roll up in his head as he fell backward and then hit the floor heavily and lay still. John Rutherford was aghast.

"My God," he said fearfully, "why'd you go and do a thing like that?"

"We've got to get out of here," Pauli said. "Now!"

"I don't *want* to," Rutherford objected. "We'd never make it to the fort. They'll kill us."

"You stay then," Pauli gritted harshly, "but not me. If Wasson kills the captain, then I'm next. You coming or not?"

Even as Rutherford shook his head, Pauli leaped away and raced out of the still-open front door. Knowing there was absolutely no chance of his getting away unobserved, he simply plunged through the very heart of this Chippewa camp, which lay in his path to the fort. He ran as he had never run and was into, through, and out the other side of the camp almost before the shouts of alarm were raised. Incredibly, no shots were fired at him, but a glance behind showed that six or seven warriors were already in pursuit and others joining. Pauli didn't waste much time looking around anymore.

It was close to three miles to the fort and by the end of the first, Pauli was sure he would collapse. His lungs felt on fire and his chest hurt as if a steel band was being tightened around it. He slowed a little as he glanced behind and was heartened to see that he had gained on his pursuers. His greatest worry was that he would be cut off in front, so he kept a close watch. In another quarter mile he felt better, as if he had suddenly gotten a second wind and now he was able to increase his speed a little.

As much as possible he kept to cover to avoid being seen by any Indians who might be ahead. When he was just about a mile from the fort he emerged from a cluster of trees into a little clearing where at least fifteen of Pontiac's Ottawas were squatted about a small fire, gnawing on some meat they had cooked. Their jaws dropped as he rushed past less than fifty feet away and instantly they, too, were up in pursuit.

Once again Pauli had to exert every ounce of his strength to maintain his lead and now his vision was swimming, his throat raw, his legs weakening. From far ahead of him he heard a voice shout dimly, "Sir! A white man approaching the fort, being chased!"

An instant later a few shots began being fired from the ramparts and then a barrage of gunfire came. Looking back, Pauli saw his pursuers turn and scatter for cover. Now a few shots came from them and he heard the angry buzzing of the lead balls whizzing past, saw several of them kick up spurts of earth around him, but he was not hit. Ahead, the gate was opening for him and in another few seconds he raced through it and would have fallen had he not been gripped firmly by his arms and held on his feet.

Ensign Christopher Pauli, late commander of Fort Sandusky, was once again among friends.

[*July 4, 1763—Monday, 8:30* A.M.]

There had been no amenities when Wasson came to Pontiac's camp along Parent's Creek.

The Chippewa chief, his face smeared and ugly with the combination of soot and bear grease which he had rubbed upon it, confronted the Ottawa war chief without greeting or sign of friendship. Nor did he waste words in coming to the point of his unexpected visit.

"Pontiac is a very brave chief," he said scathingly, his voice thick with rage and insult. "He is so brave that he has even stolen bread from the hands of the Frenchmen, or killed their cattle for his own meat, knowing they could make no resistance against him. Yes! He is very brave. And while he does this, Chippewas and other Indians are dying as they fight the battles which he began and does not know how to finish."

Pontiac, taken aback at the savageness of this attack upon him by one of his staunchest allies, opened his mouth to reply, but Wasson cut him off with a chopping sweep of his hand.

"Say nothing! I wish to hear no more words from the great Ottawa war chief now. He has said enough! *Now he will listen!* Pontiac is the cause of all our ills. We entered the war to fight *with* him, but instead it seems that we fight *for* him, while he is elsewhere. There have so far been many Indians wounded and killed, but not very many of these have been Ottawa. No! Most of them have been Chippewa. Our blood has soaked the ground in your fight and now, added to it, is the blood of my nephew Tewalee, who was as a son to me. His hair was taken and his body kicked and stabbed and cut to pieces. *My nephew!* Insult of the worst kind has been given to us, and now we will have our turn."

He paused briefly in this angry tirade, but now Pontiac wisely said nothing. The Ottawa was well aware that Wasson was quite capable of killing him and might yet do so. At any other time, such an act might well cause war between the Ottawa and Chippewa tribes, but such would not be the case here—not while Wasson acted in grief over his personal loss and stood here with his face blackened and his body shaking. Whatever he did now would be excused as a manifestation of that grief and neither Wasson nor his people could be held accountable for it. This was always the way. And so, saying nothing, Pontiac felt his stomach muscles tighten as he waited for whatever would come next.

"For that reason," Wasson continued at length, calmer now but his words filled with an implacable coldness, "we will take with us that with which Pontiac intended to save himself in the end. My brother, I am fond of this carrion flesh which you guard. I wish some in my turn. I will take it, and Pontiac will make no move to stop me in what I do. He knows this would not be wise."

The threat was implicit and Pontiac remained rooted, unspeaking, as Wasson turned his back on him and, still followed by a large number of his warriors, strode directly to the Meloche house. There he demanded that Captain Campbell be turned over to him instantly unless Meloche himself wished to die.

François Meloche had no such wish and with unseemly but understandable haste, he delivered the surprised Donald

Campbell into Wasson's hands. At a signal from the Chippewa chief, every shred of clothing was stripped from Campbell. Though he didn't resist, the captain's face had taken on a ghastly pallor. When he was smashed in the mouth and told to walk toward Wasson's camp, he did so wordlessly, with blood trickling from a split lip. The fat whiteness of his body as he walked, surrounded by jeering savages, would have been almost ludicrous had not the situation been so desperately grim.

Wasson's anger, which had never fully abated, was sharply rekindled when they arrived there and learned of the escape of Ensign Pauli. He ordered Campbell backed against the picket fence surrounding Jules St. Bemand's house and had the warriors spread Campbell's arms apart and bind his wrists to the top of it. Then, motioning his men back, he jerked out his tomahawk and even as the captain's eyes widened and a cry was forming on his lips, swung the weapon at him in a powerful, sweeping blow. The narrow but keenly sharpened edge of the tomahawk caught Campbell just below the rib cage and opened his stomach from one side to the other, permitting the ruptured bowels and other organs to spill forth and hang from him in a grisly mass. The captain's would-be cry emerged as a deep, agonized grunt and his knees sagged.

Now Wasson thrust the handle of the stained weapon back into his waistband and withdrew his knife. He grasped Campbell's hair in one hand and held his head up so that the officer's shocked eyes were looking into his own. Then slowly, methodically, he stuck the point of the razor-edged blade deep into the scalp and, in two movements, cut a great bleeding circle. He twined the hair around his hand and then, with the weight of his body behind it, gave a tremendous jerk. The whole scalp pulled free with a distinctly audible sucking sound.

Another moan gurgled in Campbell's throat. He was still not dead and, incredibly, he was able to straighten his legs and stand nearly erect again, practically blinded by the blood pouring into his face and eyes. His mouth was pried open and the knife thrust inside and sawed vigorously back and forth until the tongue was severed and withdrawn, impaled on the knife point.

Pushing the hanging mass of entrails out of the way, Wasson gripped the officer's gentials and severed them with a powerful slash and threw them aside. Now Campbell's knees buckled again, though his legs continued to open and close convulsively. His eyelids were severed next, followed by nose, ears and lips. Again using the tomahawk, Wasson hacked open the chest and raked the man's heart out, using his knife to cut away the blood vessels still attached to it. Even then Campbell must still have been alive, for there was a great burst of blood surpassing any amount he had yet shed.

Wasson brought the heart to his own mouth and sank his teeth into it, ripping away a great bite which he chewed and swallowed. He did it a second, then a third time, and finally tossed the remains to his men, who bit and chewed in turn as it was passed from hand to hand until it was all gone.

Satisfied at last that his vengeance for Tewalee's death and desecration had been taken, Wasson turned away, leaving the carcass to his men. They played games with it, first loosing so many arrows into it that it soon looked like some nightmarish pincushion. To save their precious arrowheads when they were finished, they merely shoved the arrows completely through by hand, exulting in the English blood that now stained them.

Both of the officer's feet were chopped off and tossed into a fire and one of his legs was hacked away at the knee. His hands, too, were cut off, allowing the body to fall to the ground now and, as it lay there, an arm was chopped off just below the shoulder. Finally the head was cut off and impaled on a pointed stake nearby, the sightless eyes now glazed and covered with grime.

The body was kicked and dragged to the river's edge and then picked up by two men and thrown far out into the current, where it sank at once. The severed arm and leg followed with smaller splashes, but the hands and feet were kept.

On the river bottom, the remains of the body bumped and slid along until, with an ironic twist of fate, the currents thrust it into the shallows directly in front of the water gate at Detroit. There it was seen from the ramparts and recovered, carried soberly into the fort and quickly buried behind the house of the commanding officer.

After an absence of fifty-three days, Donald Campbell, late commanding officer of Detroit, late first officer of Detroit, late Captain of His Majesty's Royal American Regiment, had at last returned to his fort.

[*July 6, 1763—Wednesday*]

The excitement of this venture had not worn off for Captain James Dalyell. To the contrary, it had increased to the point where now he was truly little short of insufferable. And because he was possessed of such boundless enthusiasm, he had little patience with or use for anyone who was not as indefatigable as he or who made suggestions which might delay his progress toward Detroit.

Major John Wilkins, the commander of Fort Niagara, was essentially a slow man—slow in his reactions, slow in his manner of speech, slow in his mental processes—and there was little meeting of the minds between himself and Dalyell when the eager young captain arrived with his force this morning.

No sooner had they exchanged greetings when Dalyell made his demands: he wanted all of Wilkin's remaining men of the 80th Regiment to join his detachment. Wilkins refused, saying he had no intention of giving them up. Dalyell argued that the orders he carried from General Amherst personally, *demanded* that Wilkins give them up to him. Checking these orders himself, Wilkins pointed out that Dalyell was entitled to take only so many men as the Niagara commander could justifiably spare.

Back and forth the haranguing went until finally both of the men very grudgingly compromised and Wilkins gave Dalyell forty men of the 80th, which boosted the reinforcement detachment's total strength now to two hundred and eighty men, including the twenty Rangers under Major Robert Rogers.

This matter settled, Dalyell immediately alerted his men to be prepared to set out for Detroit within the hour. The universal groan which arose from them went ignored. Dalyell was already engaged in another battle of wills with Major Wilkins. The latter told him that he ought to wait here at Fort Niagara until word came from Buffalo Creek of the arrival of the *Michigan* from Detroit, which could then return with them as an escort. Dalyell's reply was a flat refusal. The captain pointed out that the major had admitted there were more than enough batteaux at the Upper Landing—Fort Schlosser—above the falls to accommodate the forty men added to Dalyell's detachment, plus the large amount of provisions which Dalyell had demanded of him in Amherst's name; therefore, he meant to have them. Probably more to be rid of this frenetic captain than for any other reason, Wilkins gave in, though still warning darkly that he intended writing to General Amherst about Dalyell's high-handedness and near insubordination, as well as his refusal to wait for the ship as an escort.

"Major," James Dalyell remarked with pointed dryness, "the trouble with the English army today is that the majority of its officers always seem to want to wait for *something!* Detroit, sir, is under siege and there is a battle to be fought. The sooner we get at it, the sooner conditions can be returned to some degree of normalcy. I, sir, am a doer, not a waiter. Goodby, Major."

John Wilkins watched him go and shook his head with a grudging admiration of sorts. Captain James Dalyell, he suspected, was either going to quickly become the most famous general in His Majesty's Army, or else he was even more quickly going to get himself killed. And the commanding officer of Fort Niagara would not have cared to make any bets on which of the alternatives would prevail.

[July 7, 1763—Thursday]

The news of the taking of Forts Presque Isle, Le Boeuf and Venango had had a crushing effect upon Lieutenant General Sir Jeffrey Amherst. This morning had come the packet by special courier from Bouquet bearing these tidings and it had irrevocably snapped the last faltering hope nourished by the commander in chief that the uprising was relatively minor and could be quickly and simply quelled.

Apparently Major Wilkins at Niagara as yet knew nothing about the fall of these forts, as a letter Amherst had received from him yesterday had made no mention of it. Damn such faulty communications which caused important messages to travel at a snail's pace!

Jeffrey Amherst was honest enough with himself to recall bitterly how many times over the past year or more he had been warned that matters were shaping up to such an end; warned by such men as Sir William Johnson and George Croghan, by Pennsylvania's Indian agent Conrad Weiser, by many of his own officers, by traders and frontiersmen, by settlers, and by governmental representatives. A massive disgust for his own blindness in the matter settled upon him and, with it, an implacable and rather frightening hatred of all red men; a hatred further intensified by a growing fear that what he had considered as preposterous, when he considered it at all—that the Indians might thrust the English out of their country—might just come to pass.

For perhaps the first time since he had taken this command, he felt a sense of appreciation and relief in the knowledge that Sir William Johnson was still holding five of the tribes of the Six Nations Iroquois Confederacy in check. God help the English if *they* should join their western brethren in raising the hatchet! And it was clearly apparent that without Johnson constantly on hand working with them from his home on the Mohawk, such would be precisely the case. Only yesterday, along with the letter from Wilkins, Amherst had received a letter from Johnson reconfirming the fact that the Onondagas, Oneidas, Cayugas, Tuscaroras and Mohawks were still calm and peacefully inclined toward the English, and he had hopes of their continuing in this frame of mind despite the fact that the westernmost tribe of their league, the Senecas, were beginning to raise hell. He begged Amherst not to place the blame for the actions of the Senecas on the entire Iroquois League, as such was not the case at all. In fact, Johnson was far more confident of the future behavior of the five tribes around him than he was of the English inhabitants on the New York frontier. As Sir William put it:

I cannot conclude without representing to your Excellency the great panic and uneasiness into which the inhabitants of these parts are cast, which I have endeavored to remove by every method in my power, to prevent their abandoning their settlements from their apprehensions of the Indians. As they in general confide much in my residence, they are hitherto prevented from taking that hasty measure, but should I be obliged to write (which I hope will not be the case), not only my own tenants—who are upward of 120 families—but all the rest would immediately follow the example, which I am determined against doing till the last extremity, as I know it would prove of general bad consequence.

Well, Johnson was right about that. If any one person was the mainstay of that New York frontier, it was Sir William at Johnson Hall. Though many times in the past Amherst had fervently wished Johnson was not around to be such a damned irritation to him, now he thanked the Providence which kept the man here and desperately hoped for his continued safety, residency, and influence over the Iroquois.

Of course it was clear that the settlers everywhere on the frontiers wouldn't be in such turmoil if they could just get some reasonable support from their provincial governments. Jeffrey Amherst was thoroughly disgusted with the attitude of such influential powers as the Quakers, who still refused to provide provincial military support for their harassed frontier residents and who continued to mumble things about understanding the Indians and respecting their rights. *Their* rights! Good God, what about the rights of the white people they were butchering? How could they possibly, in view of the stories of such atrocities as were being published in their own Pennsylvania *Gazette*, refuse to acknowledge that help was desperately needed?

Amherst picked up from his desk a four-day-old issue of that newspaper and read again the first of a whole series of letter extracts from the frontier which were being published in every issue. The accounts were getting progressively worse. This first one, for example, was a sample of the hideous situation they sketched:

To Col. Francis Lee, or, in his absence, to the next commanding officer in Loudoun County:

I examined the express who brought this letter from Winchester to Loudown County, and he informed me that he was employed as an express from Fort Cumberland to Winchester . . . and that passing from the Fort to Winchester, he saw lying on the road a woman who had just been scalped and was then in the agonies of death, with her brains hanging over her skull; his companions made a proposal to knock her on the head to put an end to her agony, but this express, apprehending the Indians were near at hand and not thinking it safe to lose any time, they rode off and left the poor woman in the situation they found her.

Amherst slammed the paper down angrily. And the Quakers prattled on about the rights of the Indians! Even Pennsylvania Governor James Hamilton had sent him a letter, asking Amherst to intercede in person, to say *something* that would convince the Quakers to change their minds, but just this morning in writing a reply to him, Amherst had quickly quashed that absurd idea. He had written to Hamilton:

If the present situation of the poor families who have abandoned their settlements, and the danger that the whole Province is threatened with, can have no effect in opening the hearts of your Assembly to exert themselves, like men, I am sure no arguments I could urge will be regarded.

Amherst belched softly and grimaced at the bitterness of the bile which rose as a gorge in his throat. He wished he had another powder on hand to settle his stomach, which had begun rolling with the news Bouquet had imparted in the very first sentence of his letter.

Thank God that he had a man like Henry Bouquet in the field! It was a blessing to have a steady, dependable officer who would, in every respect, handle himself admirably and meet every exigency with calmness and strength, not giving way in the face of danger to either rashness or overprudence. If ever a commander in chief had a strong right arm, Bouquet was his. Major General Thomas Gage in Montreal might be the second-in-command of His Majesty's forces in North America and admittedly he was a brilliant administrator, but for sheer generalship, it was in Colonel Henry Bouquet that Amherst had the greater confidence. Now, bending to the task he could no longer procrastinate over, he wrote his reply to Bouquet:

New York, 7th July 1763

Sir:

Last night I received your letter of 29th June, and early this morning an express brought me that of the 3rd instant.

The loss of Presque Isle (which I fear is too true, although it may happen that the soldier who gave the account may prove to be a deserter) gives me great concern; but it must make no alteration in my plan. There seems to have been an absolute necessity for my sending you all the troops I could for the protection of the inhabitants, otherwise the savages would have spread their depredations all over the country. They will now retire as you advance, and I would have you follow the same directions I have already given you for your sending troops forward to Presque Isle, notwithstanding this disaster, only observing to send them in such a manner that their march may be secure and that they may be able to encounter [overcome] any body of Indians that can attack them.

I write immediately to Niagara and shall try to send troops from thence to retake possession of Presque Isle. The orders I have already sent to Major Gladwin, of which you have been acquainted, are to that purport. I shall now acquaint him of this loss and I wish I could send him immediately some more force. Should any of the corps from the West Indies come this way, I shall lose no time in forwarding them to Niagara to strengthen the force already sent; but, in the meantime, we must do the best we can with the numbers we have.

I write again to Governor Hamilton; and I trust the Prov-

ince will now enable him to raise a sufficient force to protect the back settlements, while the regulars are employed in chastizing the savages.

On your arrival at Fort Pitt you will, of course, get rid of the women and children and useless hands as fast as can be done with their safety, for the Article of Provisions is a very material one and must be attended to.

I shall forward Mr. Croghan's letter with the other papers to Sir William Johnson. I had a letter from him last night, by which I find that the Six Nations continue quiet, and Sir William is in hopes they will not be concerned with any of those tribes who are now committing hostilities against us.

Captain Ecuyer seems to act with great prudence and I approve of everything he mentions to have done. A fixed resolution should be taken by every commanding officer whose post is attacked by savages, never to trust their promises but to defend his post to the last extremity and to take every occasion he can of putting them to death while they are attempting to take every life away that they can. We have so many recent instances of their breach of faith in this particular that I am surprised any officer in his senses would enter into terms with such barbarians. I am, Sir,

> *Your most obdt. servant*
> *Jeff: Amherst*

Colonel Bouquet

Amherst blew on the paper to dry the ink and then read over what he had written. As he came to the final paragraph concerning Captain Ecuyer he paused and thought about the steps taken by that officer to preserve Fort Pitt. Like Bouquet, Amherst knew, Ecuyer was a Swiss mercenary and he found himself wishing he had a whole army of them. What soldiers they were! Things had not been easy at all for Ecuyer there at Pitt, and it was not too farfetched to believe that some other commander in that slot might have lost his head or committed errors which would have resulted in the loss of that key post, too. And the very fact that while fighting Indians outside the fort he was at the same time fighting an epidemic of smallpox inside the fort, made the holding of that place even more to his credit. Suddenly Amherst's eyes narrowed with a strange thought. He pursed his lips as he considered something and then nodded. Just the faintest trace of a smile tilted his lips as he dipped his quill pen again and added a rather startling postscript to the letter he had just completed writing to Bouquet:

P.S. Could it not be contrived to send the small pox among the disaffected tribes of Indians? We must, on this occasion, use every stratagem in our power to reduce them.

J.A.

CHAPTER IX

EACH passing day of late was bringing a new feeling of confidence to Major Henry Gladwin. The very fact that it was against all precepts of Indian warfare to maintain a prolonged siege was now evidently working strongly against Pontiac. The fact, too, that Gladwin himself was beginning to take some stronger offensive measures was also beginning to have an effect on some of the tribes.

Two days ago he had ordered the *Michigan*, carrying a detachment of soldiers under Captain Hopkins and Ensign Pauli—who was now recovered from his ordeal—to sail upstream to a point opposite Pontiac's camp and shell it with the ship's cannon. Unfortunately, the wind had been weak and the progress of the ship so slow that Pontiac had ample opportunity to move his women and children out before the actual shelling began. Still, the cannon made an utter ruin of the temporary village and killed three of Pontiac's warriors and wounded another. During the night that followed, Pontiac moved his camp three miles farther upstream from the old, putting it now five miles from the fort and on the opposite side of a dense swamp.

The fact that this one ship had been able to create so much havoc had caused much consternation among other tribes. The Hurons especially, living nearly directly across the river from the fort, were highly vulnerable to such attack; and the Potawatomies, somewhat downstream on the same side of the river as the fort, were hardly less so. It was undoubtedly for just this reason that chiefs of both these tribes had come to Gladwin yesterday under a flag of truce and reiterated what they had told the major before—that they had been forced into the war by Pontiac, who had threatened to cut them to pieces if they refused him; that they did not wish to continue it; that only some scattered bands of young men of their tribe, who were headstrong and hard to control, were still desirous of continuing the war; and that they had never really done anything except fire a few rifle shots at the fort from a distance. They also wished to consummate the previously discussed prisoner exchange, turning in all the English prisoners their nations held in trade for the release of Chief Winnemac.

Gladwin listened carefully and then, in replying, showed them that his sources of information regarding their part in this war were much better than they had realized.

"I will stand by what I told you before in regard to exchanging prisoners," the major had replied, then added with casual coldness, "but don't try to delude me with false innocence. Notwithstanding all that you promised the last time you were with me, I know that you went down the river with Pontiac and you fired against the ship as she was coming up. And I know that a few days ago you managed to steal two horses from the fort. Yet, this I will overlook, to clearly show you that I pity you for the position you are in. If you will bring in all the prisoners you or your people have, if you will promise not to do any more mischief either to the French or the English, since we are now one, if you will do these things, then I will give up Chief Winnemac to you and recommend you to the general for your good behavior. But now," his voice hardened, "hear me well: if from this point on you make the least difficulty, I will no longer listen to anything you have to say and you will have to take the consequences along with Pontiac. Is that understood?"

The chiefs hung their heads and admitted that all the major had said was true and they were guilty of what he accused them. They were sorry and now promised to do all he asked of them and they would permit none of their people to come closer to the fort any more than Campeau's Mill, which was a mile away. Where the prisoner exchange was concerned, however, they hedged a little. Many of the prisoners, they explained, had been adopted into the tribes, as was the custom, to take the places of warriors who had been lost. These people who had adopted them as sons or brothers or husbands would have to be convinced to give them up, and this would take time.

They had left, then, taking with them some wampum belts Gladwin had given them, and no less than an hour later the alarming news swept the fort that the searchers ordered out by Gladwin a week ago had finally found what they had been seeking. Buried just under the surface of the ground beside the back step of Pierre Barth's shop had been found three large keys which it was believed the silversmith had made. They had been taken to the gates and were found to be exact duplicates of the keys which fit the locks for each of them. All three opened those locks perfectly. A search was instigated at once for Barth, but the young metalworker had vanished.

More of the French residents, however, moved into the fort at once upon hearing this news, more than ever afraid of what Pontiac would do now that his latest plan for simultaneous attack from within and without the fort had been thwarted.

The garrison was in relatively good spirits now, although for a day or so after the morbid death of Captain Campbell, their morale had fallen to a new low. The full details of what had happened to Campbell had been brought to the fort by the interpreter, Pierre LaButte. The willingness with which he gave this information to the officers assembled with Gladwin, and the further information he imparted about Pontiac's present strengths and weaknesses, made Gladwin sorry that he had ever suspected LaButte was collaborating with the Ottawa war chief. It was, of course, precisely the reaction LaButte had anticipated.

Since then only two other matters had deviated from the normal events of defending the fort. The first was a court of inquiry which Gladwin ordered seated, with Captain Hopkins as president and both Lieutenant Jehu Hay of the 60th Regiment and Ensign John Perry of the Queen's Rangers as members, to inquire into the taking of Forts Sandusky, St. Joseph, Miamis and Presque Isle.

This morning a few more Frenchmen moved into the fort with their families and there also came to the water gate a crude French sailing craft about the size of a batteau. It was towing five of the long, dugout type of craft which the French called *piroques*. These were the boats of the trader Charles Maisonville, his dugouts loaded with nearly five tons of peltry and lead, the latter of which he willingly turned over to Gladwin in return for a bill of collection which the trader could present for payment when this current crisis was ended. Maisonville said that he had been on hand at Fort Ouiatenon when it was taken, but because he was a Frenchman, he had been unmolested both there and during his trip to Detroit.

Of all the duties Major Gladwin faced, that which he found least to his liking was the writing of letters. As a result, he wrote just as few as possible, but there were times when it could no longer be put off and one of those times was today. The news about Campbell's terrible death had already been written to both Amherst and Bouquet at Gladwin's request by Lieutenant James MacDonald of the 60th Regiment and dispatched eastward in the hands of a trusted Indian express. MacDonald had also detailed in his twelve-page letter to the general, all that had occurred here at Detroit since the beginning of the siege, and for that Gladwin was grateful. It would allow him to keep his own letters which he now had to write to both Amherst and Bouquet as brief as possible. It was to Amherst that he wrote first, explaining what yet needed to be explained and then concluding with:

Since the commencement of this extraordinary affair, I have been informed that many of the inhabitants of this place, seconded by some French traders from Montreal, have made the Indians believe that a French army and fleet were in the River St. Lawrence, and that another army would come from the Illinois . . . when I published the cessation of arms, they said it was a mere invention of mine, purposely calculated to keep the Indians quiet, as we were afraid of them, but that they were not such fools as to believe me; which, with a thousand other lies calculated to stir up mischief, have induced the Indians to take up arms. I daresay it will appear ere long that one half of the [French] settlement merit a gibbet and the other half ought to be decimated. Nevertheless, there are some honest men among them to whom I am infinitely obliged. I mean, Sir, Monsieur Navarre, the two Babys, and my interpreters, St. Martin and LaButte.

With this letter to Amherst quickly out of the way, Gladwin immediately wrote to Bouquet, saying:

Major Henry Gladwin to Col. Henry Bouquet
                                                  Detroit, July 8th 1763
Dear Sir,
I did myself the pleasure of writing you by the bearer hereof [a friendly Huron Indian] about two months ago—three weeks after we were attacked—but yesterday he returned without delivering my letters and reports that he lost them when he made his escape from the Delawares, who detained him some time, for which occasion—as he had nothing to show—he did not choose to go to Fort Pitt, as he might be suspected of ill designs. Be that as it may, I have trusted him

again with another packet for the general. I hope he will reach you safe.

I am sorry to acquaint you that all the outposts are cut off. For further particulars, I refer you to the enclosed papers. I should have given you a detail of our proceedings here had not Lieutenant MacDonald written fully on that subject . . . to which I refer you. But before I conclude, I can't omit this occasion of recommending to you the officers and men under my command for supporting the fatigue of this long affair with spirit and patience worthy of notice.

I have heard but once from Niagara since the commencement of this sad affair. I should be glad to know what troops I may expect and who commands.

It would also be very satisfactory to know what troops are coming your way, and what has been done by the enemy in your quarter.

The bearer has a great deal to say to the Delawares. He can let you into their designs if he chooses it.

Be kind enough to receive him well, and dismiss him as soon as possible. I should be glad if you can favor me with some late papers.

I am Dear Sir

> *Your most obedient & very humble servant*
> *Henry Gladwin*

P.S. My compliments to the Gentlemen with you.

[*July 9, 1763—Saturday, 10:00* A.M.]

For Lieutenant James MacDonald it was a melancholy day. The pall of gloom which overhung him was not even lifted much by the arrival at Detroit of Chief Teata of the Hurons who brought nine prisoners with him to surrender to Major Gladwin; prisoners he had not taken, but whom he had been keeping at Pontiac's order. Among these was a woman, a child, a trader, five privates from various forts, and Ensign John Christie, commander of the fallen Fort Presque Isle.

For practically everyone in the fort it was a bright day because of these prisoners being released. For every man here it was an augury of things to come and they were rejoicing— for every man, that is, except Lieutenant James MacDonald.

In the past week he had written long letters to General Amherst, General Gage, Colonel Bouquet and other officers about the events here at Detroit, culminating in the unfortunate death of Captain Campbell. For MacDonald it had been a terribly severe blow because Donald Campbell happened to be his dearest friend as well as his former commander. It had been hard enough to write the other letters about it, but now he had spent since sunrise of this day working on a letter to Captain Campbell's next of kin, Dr. Philip Campbell of Baltimore.

Page after page he filled with the details of what had happened at Detroit since that fateful May 9 when Pontiac had opened his war. It was as if his hand was unwilling to reach that point where he had to tell of Campbell's death, and not until sixteen pages were filled with precise handwriting could he any longer keep from telling what had happened. He had already told of how both Campbell and Lieutenant McDougall had been detained by Pontiac and what had happened through the remainder of May and during the entire month of June. Now he paused, wiped the point of his quill pen, resharpened and slit it with his penknife, then sighed and mentally berated himself for procrastinating and then bent to the unpleasant business.

. . . and on the night of the 2nd instant, Captain Campbell and Lieutenant McDougall were lodged at the house abovementioned, about a mile or so from the fort, and made a resolution to escape; but it was agreed upon between them that McDougall should set off first, which he did, and got safe into the fort. But you know, it was much more dangerous for Captain Campbell than for any other person, by reason that he could neither run nor see, and being sensible of that failing, I am sure, prevented him from attempting to escape. The 4th, a detachment was ordered to destroy some breastworks and an entrenchment the Indians had made a quarter of a mile from the fort. About twenty Indians came to attack that party, which they engaged. But they were drove off in an instant with the loss of one man killed and two wounded, which our people scalped and cut to pieces . . . Afterward the savages . . . [took] Captain Campbell, stripped him naked and directly murdered him. You cannot conceive, nor can I express, my sorrow for the loss of my dearest friend, with whom I have constantly been since we left Fort Pitt, although he is now out of the question. Being sensible of the confidence he had in me, I thought it a duty incumbent to acquaint you with his melancholy fate, which gives me pain beyond expression. My greatest comfort at present is that if charity, benevolence, innocence, and integrity is a sufficient dispensation for all mankind, that certainly

entitles him to happiness in the world to come. As I have assisted him in the transactions of his affairs since we have been together, I will pay for all the debts that he has contracted here, and charge it to Captain Barnsley, our paymaster, who will place the same to his account of arrears. I remember of his telling me of a debt of 100 pounds sterling due to Mr. Ross, Agent, since he left London. You may give Captain Barnsley or, if you choose, me, power of attorney to apply for his arrears, which, if paid, will exceed his debts, and in that case the overplus may be reimbursed to you. If he had not been too hospitable to the inhabitants of this place, he might have saved some of his subsistance, but I fancy you know he had always too much generosity to think of saving money.

I very sincerely condole with you upon this melancholy occasion, and be assured that I am, with the greatest of veracity, Sir,

> *Your most obedient and humble servant,*
> *James MacDonald*

P.S. It would be a pleasure to me to hear of your receiving this letter; therefore, pray write me and direct thus: to Lieutenant James MacDonald of the Royal American Regiment at Detroit and New York. Address to Major Gates at Mr. Darby's Tailor in Gerard Street, Soho.

[July 9, 1763—Saturday, 8:30 P.M.]

For some weeks now Pontiac had been aware that if he was ever to force a capitulation of Detroit it could only be through the total bottling up of the place. He had thought in the beginning that this was accomplished, but the fact that the *Michigan* had left the fort, gone to Niagara and returned here with a reinforcement—both times passing through gunfire on the Detroit River—convinced him that the place would never surrender so long as the English here had both the sloop and the schooner to rely upon.

He had thought of numerous ways in which these vessels might be taken or destroyed, but always wound up rejecting them because they would result in the expenditure of Indians' lives that just were not expendable. It was simply not the Indian way to deliberately allow warriors to attack into sure death except as a last desperate defensive measure. Even had he harkened to the idea of sacrificing Indian lives to achieve his aims, he would not have been able to convince the warriors of the practicality of it.

There was, however, another way the ships might be destroyed, with no loss of Indian life whatever, and it was this project upon which he had set his men—aided by a number of Frenchmen and a few captives who were forced to do the work—some weeks ago. They had been constructing a great fire raft which was just now completed and this would be the night they would float it to where it would drift on a collision course with one of the vessels, ignite it and then let it go.

This was not an idea originated by Pontiac. During the siege of Quebec in 1758 when he and his warriors had fought beside the gallant French general, the Marquis Louis de Montcalm, this same ploy had been used against the English ships in the St. Lawrence River. True, the plan had failed then, but more through the poor planning of the man who instigated the maneuver—Governor Pierre Vaudreuil—and the cowardice of the men he picked to carry it out, rather than because of the plan itself was poor.[122] No, it had been a good idea and Pontiac was sure it was even more applicable to the condition here on the Detroit River than it had been then on the St. Lawrence.

Now, in the dim light of the dusk, he surveyed the handiwork at the river's edge with a pleased eye. The raft was made of four of the batteaux captured from Lieutenant Cuyler on Lake Erie. These had been securely lashed together and then filled almost to overflowing with highly combustible birchbark, tar and faggots, along with other combustible materials. The last of the burnables were just being loaded aboard now and the canoes being readied to tow the raft to the proper position for release. The Indians were excited at the prospect. Tonight would see the culmination of a great deal of hard work on their part and they were extremely anxious for it. It was not, however, until close to midnight when the twelve canoes surrounding the raft began to nudge it into position as they drifted downstream.

The target was the sloop, *Michigan*, which was anchored farther out in the river from the fort than was the schooner *Huron*. Pontiac himself, in the leading canoe—several Frenchmen with him—directed the operation, whispering commands to the others to move the bulky raft left or right as needed until they were about a hundred and fifty yards above the *Michigan*. Then, at a dozen different places at once, the fire raft was ignited and released.

The blaze took hold well and though current was swift, before the raft had drifted half the distance to the ship it was a roaring conflagration with flames leaping twenty or thirty feet into the air. And Pontiac's calculation of the current drift had been almost perfect: the raft was drifting straight toward the bow of the *Michigan*.

Cries of alarm erupted from the watch aboard the ship at once and in the illumination from the flames Pontiac could see men running about on deck. The night was practically windless and without the wind, even if the ship weighed anchor to drift away from the fire raft, it would be floating helplessly and would eventually be torn to splinters as it ran aground on the rocks. Either way, the vessel would be destroyed and Pontiac opened his mouth and shrieked with the sheer exultation of the moment. His men, both in the canoes and ashore, echoed the cry in a wild chorus.

But as Captain Newman had foiled plots against his ship before, so now he did so again. He shouted a sharp command for the stern anchor cable to be cut and a moment later the vigorous blows of a large axe had parted the line. Already Newman was spinning the helm and the very power of the current began quickly moving the ship to one side, even though it was still bow-anchored. At Newman's order, more of the bow cable was released, allowing the vessel to move even more to port before it snubbed tightly again.

The fire shot past, enveloping the *Michigan* in its radiant heat and narrowly missing the bow cable. In a moment it was already astern and still burning fiercely as it drifted aimlessly and harmlessly on with the current. From the ship came the cheers of the crew and the detachment of soldiers kept permanently aboard her in case of attack. This was followed by a rattle of gunfire from both ship and fort toward the dark shadows of the canoes still in midriver, causing the Indians to paddle fiercely upstream to get out of range.

For the majority of the Indians it was nothing more than a disappointing failure. But to the war chief of the Ottawas, it was a turning point. He took the failure to be the gravest of omens.

All the way back to the landing place he said nothing, but as they ground ashore here, Pontiac spoke glumly to the Frenchmen with him.

"Until now," he said, "I have always told you that those in the fort were all dead men. I have been wrong. I will continue the war against them, but now I see that these dead men have come to life, and I am ruined."

545

While the Pennsylvania Assembly argued interminably about whether or not they should assist the beleaguered settlers on the frontier of this province and if so to what extent, the slaughter continued unabated in the valley of the Susquehanna and beyond. The fact that Colonel Henry Bouquet still remained poised at Carlisle to march for Fort Pitt as soon as the remainder of his provisions, wagons and some additional men arrived, was of little concern to the Shawnees and Delawares.

A permanent watch was maintained on Bouquet's army, but it was strictly surreptitious and from a considerable distance. As soon as it should begin its move westward, then runners would hasten in all directions, gathering together all the marauding parties from the Susquehanna to Fort Pitt and beyond. Somewhere in the wilderness between Fort Pitt and Fort Ligonier, they would set about positioning themselves to ambush Bouquet's army, cut it to bits and turn their attention again to the settlers and all the remaining western posts which would then be at their mercy.

In the meantime, though, the carnage being caused by these red marauders continued unabated. Though for some years the frontiersmen and settlers had lived and traded in peace with many of the Indians—and even now there were still whole communities of Indians who professed continued friendship and loyalty to the English—the hatred being fanned by these attacks was all-consuming and highly contagious among the border people.

One grizzled backwoodsman, having journeyed to Philadelphia expressly to tell the General Assembly what was happening and to learn what the Province was going to do about it, flew into a rage. Instead of hearing of steps being taken to preserve and protect his fellow Pennsylvanians, he listened incredulously to Quaker Assemblymen saying how the Indians had been mistreated, how it was a sin against God and man to consider harming them in any way, and how "In our considered judgment, the Indians have been forced to act as they have acted. We wish to live in peace with them instead of bringing war upon them. They are essentially good people."

It was more than the backwoodsman could stomach and he leaped to his feet, shook his fist with impotent fury and shouted, "By damn, sir, the only good Injen is a dead Injen!"

That did little to change the Assembly's opinions, but the

phrase stuck and within mere days it had become the most quoted comment in English North America. Everyone had it on his lips and everyone wanted to see a lot more "good Injens." The only trouble was, they were themselves afraid to the point of panic and more often ran than tried to add to the list of "good Injens."

Throughout it all, the bloodletting and rampant destruction continued. On the morning of July 10—last Sunday—a war party made up mostly of Shawnees, having assured themselves that Bouquet's force was still bogged down at Carlisle, swept up the valley of the Juniata and approached the small farm of a settler named William White. In the house with him were three men and a boy. Upon hearing a nicker from one of the Indian horses, White foolishly opened the cabin door to see who was there and was instantly killed by a bullet through his head. He fell to the ground just outside the door. A second man exposed himself in the doorway, apparently to drag White inside, and was likewise killed, but fell inside. His body was pulled out of the way and the door slammed and locked, but by the time this was done, the Indians had set the cabin afire. Another of the men and a boy tried to escape the blaze through a loft window and were both shot to death as they emerged. Deciding that these four dead represented all who had been inside and that the scalps could not be taken because of the fire, the Indians took White's horse and galloped off up the river. The last man still alive in the house used an axe to chop a hole in the roof and plunge out of it gagging and choking from the smoke. He fell to the ground and was injured, but he did get away.

Only a short while later and a mile and a half distant, the same party of Shawnees silently approached the cabin of Robert Campbell, a settler on Tuscarora Creek, which ran into the Juniata. Six men were gathered here to help Campbell with his crops and were completely surprised when the Indians abruptly burst in on them. Two of the men were killed instantly and the other four wounded, but as quickly as they had come the Shawnees withdrew when one of the wounded settlers managed to kill a warrior.

Throughout the day the party continued up Tuscarora Creek, ransacking and burning three more farms, all of which had fortunately been abandoned the day before. As they finished burning the third, they became aware that a dozen mounted Pennsylvanians had taken up their trail. They moved out quickly until coming to a good place for an ambush, where they hid themselves. A quarter hour later the twelve rode unsuspectingly into it, and when the gunsmoke cleared five were dead, one was wounded, and all that remained unhurt were in panicky flight back in the direction from whence they had come.

The wounded man was killed, all six dead were scalped, and the war party left the Tuscarora Valley, crossed the ridge into the Sherman River Valley between the Juniata and Carlisle, and continued their depredations. By the time the sun was an hour high on Monday, they had already attacked two more farms in Sherman Valley and carried in their belt pouches the fresh scalps of the settler Alexander Logan, his son John, and two other men. On the marauders went, looking for more victims—and this was only one of actually dozens of such war parties presently on the rampage.

The wonder of it all was that there were still settlers who were stupid enough or stubborn enough to remain at their cabins and cling to the hope that good fortune would be with them and they would not be attacked. Yet, for every two or three families of settlers who fled, there were one or two who remained behind, living in perpetual fear, hopeful that somehow the province would soon take action to protect them and run the Indians off.

At Lancaster, to the east of the Susquehanna, a well-educated gentleman farmer named John Hughes had been at the very moment of those recent attacks writing to Colonel Bouquet with an idea he had which might aid in putting an end to the Indian menace. After first introducing himself to the colonel, he step by step unfolded his plan:

1st: Each soldier to have a dog, which he is to lead on the march by a strap three feet long.

2nd: All the dogs to be held fast by the straps, except one or two on each flank and as many in advance, to discover the enemy in ambush.

3rd: When you are fired upon, let loose all the dogs, which will rush at the concealed Indians and force them, in self-defense, to expose themselves and fire at their assailants, with so little chance of hitting them that if 1,000 Indians fired on 300 dogs, there would be at least 200 dogs left, besides all the soldiers' fires, which must put the Indians to flight very soon.

4th: If you come to a swamp, thicket or the like, only turn loose three or four dogs extraordinary, and you are immediately convinced what you have to fear.

5th: No Indian can well conceal himself in a swamp or

thicket as a spy, for ye dogs will discover him, and may soon be learnt to destroy him, too.

6th: The leading of the dogs makes them more fierce, and keeps them from being tired in running after wild beasts or fighting one another.

7th: Keeping the leading straps short will make it much simpler for the soldier to release his dog in an instant, as might be necessary, and as he might have trouble doing if the strap were any longer. Also, it allows the soldiers to remain closer together without their dogs being able to engage one another.

8th: The greater the number of dogs, the more fierce they will be by a great deal, and the more terrible to the Indians; and if, when you get to Bedford, a few scouting parties were sent out with dogs, and one or two Indians killed and the dogs put at them to tear them to pieces, you would soon see the good effects of it; and I could almost venture my life that 500 men with 500 dogs would be much more dreadful to 2,000 Indians than an army of some thousand of brave men in the regular way.

Jⁿ Hughes

To Colonel Bouquet

P.S. Probably there is no man who ever had occasion to fight Indians in the woods who would object to a dog as an ally.

And today, Henry Bouquet, having just finished reading that letter from Hughes, found himself considerably taken by the idea. True, the use of dogs in war was not a new concept; the Spanish had used them years ago, for example, and other armies as well. But the idea of using them here against the Indians had not occurred to him and he was quick now to see the advantages which might accrue as a result. He decided that he would mention it in the letter he was preparing to write to Amherst in reply to the general's letter of July 7.

He sat at his desk and wrote swiftly about how the sheriff of Carlisle, outraged at the continuing massacres, had raised a party of men from among the refugees here at Carlisle and was at this moment out hunting Indians with them. He continued:

The list of people known to be killed increases very fast every hour. The desolation of so many families, reduced to the extremity of want and misery; the despair of those who have lost their parents, relations, and friends, with the cries of distracted women and children who fill the streets—all these form a scene painful to humanity and impossible to describe. Rage alternates with grief. Now, even those Indians who have proven their faith and loyalty to us in the past are not safe among us because of the hatred. Two such, a Mohican and a Cayuga, recently came here with their squaws and children to ask that I give them protection. For their own protection, I securely locked them up. It was with the utmost difficulty that I could prevail with the enraged multitude not to massacre them. I don't think them very safe in the jail. They ought to be removed to Philadelphia.

From what appears, the Indians are traveling from one place to another along the valley, burning the farms and destroying all the people they meet with. This day gives an account of six more being killed in the valley, so that since last Sunday morning to this day, twelve o'clock, we have a pretty authentic account of the number slain being twenty-five, and four or five wounded. Colonel Armstrong of the militia, Mr. Wilson and Mr. Alricks are now on the parade endeavoring to raise another party to go out and succor the sheriff and his party, consisting of fifty men, which marched yesterday, and hope they will be able to send off immediately twenty good men. The people here, I assure you, want nothing but a good leader and a little encouragement to make a very good defense. Nevertheless, the situation of this country is deplorable, and the infatuation of their government in taking the most dilatory and ineffectual measures for their protection, highly blameable. They have not paid the least regard to the plan I proposed to them on my arrival here, and will lose this and York Counties if the savages push their attacks . . . I have borne very patiently the ill-usage of this Province, having, still, hopes that they will do something for us; and therefore have avoided to quarrel with them. I hope that we shall be able to save that infatuated people from destruction, notwithstanding all their endeavors to defeat your vigorous measures. I meet everywhere with the same backwardness, even among the most exposed of the inhabitants, which makes everything move on heavily, and is disgusting to the last degree.

Though the party of the sheriff is out and another being formed, they are ill controlled and I fear will do little good. But it is a satisfaction to see some concern being observed by these people, since for the most part I find myself utterly abandoned by the very people I am ordered to protect.

Almost all of my men and supplies are now arrived and

we prepare ourselves for departure. The remainder is expected daily and I hope to be on the march for Bedford, Ligonier, and Fort Pitt by Monday next. I have the honor to be, Sir,

Your most obedt. & humble servant,
H. Bouquet

His Excellency
Sir Jeffrey Amherst

P.S. I will try to innoculate the bastards with some blankets that may fall in their hands, and take care not to get the disease myself. As it is a pity to expose good men against them, I wish we could make use of the Spanish method to hunt them with English dogs, supported by Rangers and some light horse, who would, I think, effectually extirpate or remove that vermin.

H.B.

[July 15, 1763—Friday]

The shock that filled the breast of every man in the detachment of Captain James Dalyell was devastating. Even for the exuberant captain himself, it was worse than merely a disquieting moment.

They had coasted up to shore in just the first light of the dawning this morning, expecting to see before them the welcome bulk of Fort Presque Isle and to be greeted by Ensign John Christie's garrision there. Instead, they found ashes and rubble and charred bones.

The two hundred and sixty men of the detachment wandered dazedly among the remains, at first too stunned to assimilate what must have happened here. Then came the fear; like a great enveloping blanket it spread over them and within moments they were teetering on the edge of panic. Their voices were high with encroaching hysteria and already some of the men were beginning to move back to the boats, apparently to flee, when there came the crash of Dalyell's rifle.

The voices and the movement stopped and every head was turned toward its course. Dalyell, disregarding the charcoal which smeared his breeches, scrambled to the top of a pile of blackened timbers so that he could be seen and heard by everyone. He faced the men with a scornful look and the sarcasm was heavy in his voice.

"What are you, soldiers or schoolchildren? Stay right where

you are. Let no man here even *think* of running away. I give you my word, I will shoot the first man who tries to do so!"

He swept out his arm to take in the ruins around him and continued, "Is this what you are afraid of? A burned fort? It shows your ignorance of matters. I had not told you this before, because I saw no reason to, but since you are afraid like little children, then I will have to explain to you as if you were children. You think the Indians attacked and destroyed this place, don't you? Well, you are wrong. Before I left New York, General Amherst told me he had sent orders for this place to be abandoned and destroyed. It was too exposed and isolated to properly protect, and so it was better that we did it ourselves than to have had the Indians do it, as they might have. Get control of yourselves! The bones you see scattered about are not the bones of men, but the bones from meat supplies which could not be kept and were discarded with other provisions which were rendered useless. The fort was then set afire by the garrison before they retreated southward to Fort Pitt. Now get back to your boats and let's get on our way to Detroit. And from now on, by God, act like men!"

He jumped down and rejoined Major Rogers and, as he did so, there was a general muttering from the men as they moved toward the boats. A decided uneasiness still prevailed among them and it was obvious to all that Dalyell's ridiculous explanations were patently false and that he had fooled no one. He had not expected them to. All he had wanted to do was nip this approaching panic in the bud, and he had done so.

"Very smooth, James," Robert Rogers remarked as they walked back toward their own boat. "You make a great liar."

Dalyell shrugged but did not smile. "Necessity," he said tersely. He motioned with his head toward the remains of the fort. "How long ago, do you think?"

Rogers shrugged in turn. "A month. Maybe less. Less, probably, since Major Wilkins didn't know about it. Now I wonder what we'll run into at Detroit?"

"We'll soon find out," Dalyell said grimly.

[*July 16, 1763—Saturday*]

The tendrils of this Indian war—already being referred to by many as Pontiac's War—were stretching ever farther.

A party of eighty Shawnees being led by their principal chief, Hokolesqua, who was better known to the English as Cornstalk, and by the great war chief of that tribe, Pucksinwah,[123] crossed the Ohio River and swept up the Great Kanawha River of western Virginia in a murderous rampage. They simultaneously struck and massacred the seven-member Frederick Lea family and the six-member Filty Yokum[124] family on Muddy Creek.

Continuing upstream to the Greenbrier River, they found assembled at the house at Archibald Glendenin a total of fifty men, women and children. Taking them by surprise, they slaughtered all the men and some of the women and children who were too weak or sick to travel. The remainder were taken into captivity, more for use as pack animals to carry the plunder than because of any merciful inclination. Two days later, their miserable prisoners still in tow, they descended on settlements in the Jackson River Valley and wiped them out completely.

Other bands, both of Shawnees and Delawares, were striking deeper into the border country of Maryland and northern Virginia, their depredations there paralleling the savagery of Hokolesqua's band.

Senecas were suddenly becoming even more active in the western New York frontier and now they were being aided for the first time by aggressive young warriors from among the Cayuga who yearned for the opportunity to strike the whites and disagreed with the ruling of their elders to maintain the neutrality they had promised William Johnson they would observe.

Abnaki Indians, along with a few of the Nipissings and Algonkins and supported strongly by the remaining small number of Caughnawagas of the central St. Lawrence River valley, were beginning to make scattered attacks on Englishmen in the Canadian country from Quebec to Montreal and in the hinterlands of New England. Only today an Abnaki had arrived at Detroit and went directly to Pontiac. Saying that he spoke for his whole nation and their allies, he informed Pontiac and the chiefs that the east was aflame and blood was ankle-deep in the streets of Montreal. Better yet, insofar as Pontiac was concerned, he asserted that a great French fleet—the one so long expected—had entered the St. Lawrence River. He claimed that the ships, bulging with troops, were heading for Quebec and Montreal to repossess both cities and the whole of Canada for the French King.

For Pontiac it was a tremendous lift. With the failure of his fire raft he had become deeply depressed. Several nights later he had attempted another try with the fire rafts, but in a different way. Expecting the *Michigan* to pull the same maneuver, he had two other rafts similar to the first fitted out and positioned. The idea was to ignite the first and let it go and then, as the ship veered to get out of the way, ignite the second, from which the vessel could not then escape. But again he was outwitted by Captain Jacob Newman.

As soon as the first raft was lighted and started on its drift, the ship's cannon were fired at the assailants. Grapeshot churned into the water around the canoes with such frightening splashes that the Indians were unnerved to the extent that they released the second raft before it could be lighted. Captain Joseph Hopkins and his detachment aboard the vessel managed to snag it as it came past and they towed it ashore to the fort with their own batteaux.

This failure, too, intensified the increasing demoralization of Pontiac, mainly because he knew only too well that for each failure, his own prestige was substantially lowered among his followers. But now, with the good news brought by the Abnaki—the veracity of which went unquestioned— Pontiac set his men to making an even bigger and better fire raft, one from which the *Michigan* could not possibly escape.

In addition, Pontiac now began preparing another large party of warriors to march against Fort Pitt, just as his party had previously gone against Forts Le Boeuf, Venango and Presque Isle so successfully. More victories like those would be required to keep his followers staunchly behind him. There was some concern in his mind, however, whether he might have difficulty in passing through the country of the Delawares, with whom relations in the past had sometimes been strained. He therefore had a large war belt prepared which he gave to a pair of energetic young warriors to carry to such of the Delaware chiefs as Pitwe-owa, Shingas, White-Eyes, Kitehi, Buckangehela, Tollema and Wingenund.

"This," Pontiac told them, "is what you will say to them in my name and in my words: 'Grandfathers the Delawares, by this belt we inform you that in a short time we intend to pass, in a very great body, through your country on our way to strike the English at the forks of the *Spay-lay-wi-theepi*, which our French brothers call *La Belle Rivière*, and which our English enemies call Ohio River. Grandfathers, you know us to be a headstrong people and we will have our way. We are determined to stop at nothing; and as we expect to be very hungry, we will seize and eat up everything that comes in our way.' "125

Lieutenant General Sir Jeffrey Amherst scratched his broad bare stomach and groaned with pleasure. In certain places his uniform was becoming too tight and it was pure luxury, after a hot day of wearing it, to shed himself of it, indulge in this personal pleasure of scratching the long-constricted flesh and then relax in a delightful bath lasting a half hour or longer. He was just reaching up to remove his heavily powdered wig when there was a sharp rapping on his door. Growling with exasperation, he quickly donned a robe, belted it about his middle and strode to the door.

"Dispatches, sir," a messenger told him. "They've just arrived from Colonel Bouquet."

Amherst held out his hand and accepted them without comment. There was a letter from Bouquet, written four days ago, plus several other reports and letters that the colonel had enclosed. Nothing seemed of an urgent nature, but Amherst looked at the messenger.

"You're returning to Carlisle?"

"No sir, I'm not, but the express who brought these is. He's having something to eat right now and then he'll be starting right back."

"Wait a minute, then," Amherst said. He moved closer to the lamp and read Bouquet's letter through. He smiled as he read the postscript. Over his shoulder he told the messenger, "Inform the express to tell Colonel Bouquet I'll be writing him at greater length very soon, but that at the moment there is nothing especially pressing to pass on. However, he can give him this note. Just a moment."

Amherst moved to the desk and swiftly wrote a few lines to the colonel:

Sir: You will do well to try to inoculate the Indians by means of blankets, as well as to try every other method that can serve to extirpate this execrable race. I should be very glad your scheme for hunting them down by dogs could take effect, but England is at too great a distance to think of that at present.

JA

He blew on the sheet, folded it, sealed it with wax into which he impressed his signet ring and then gave the paper to the messenger.

"You might have the express tell Colonel Bouquet for me," he said as the man started off, "that I am well pleased that we are of one mind in so many matters."

Major Henry Gladwin rubbed his eyes with the heels of his hands and wondered if there would ever come a time again when he did not feel so completely worn out, so completely drained of ambition. Even sleep was of little benefit anymore; somehow he always seemed to awaken feeling no less fatigued than when he had gone to sleep. He was tired of being on the alert, tired of constantly coping with the thousand and one things, large and small, which seemed to come up each day demanding his attention. For the first time in his military career, he began to consider resigning his commission. Though a military life was really just about all he had ever known, he found himself thinking increasingly of how pleasant it would be to be shed of his responsibilities here, to return to his new wife in England, to settle in the country and just live the remainder of his days peacefully and quietly.

More than once he had been tempted to write to General Amherst asking to be relieved, but there was that certain something in his character which would not permit it until this crisis was past. He was sure now that no matter how long it took, Detroit would survive Pontiac's siege. The fact remained, however, that the siege was still in effect and, since he was commander here when it began, he felt that it was his responsibility to remain so until it was ended; but he was deeply and desperately tired.

He knew that he ought to write again to both the general and Colonel Bouquet, but his dislike of writing letters, combined with his general weariness, had made him thrust aside the notion. Another time he would do so. For the moment he would relax, if possible. He lay back down on the bed and closed his eyes, but there was little rest for him. A montage of all the multitude of little things that had been occurring ran through his head.

There had been, for example, the arrival of the Potawatomies with their prisoners and the almost pathetic joy of those men on once again being among their own kind and rid of the prevailing threat of death which had overhung them since their capture. Early in the morning six days ago—on July 12—a party of those Potawatomies had arrived at the fort under Chiefs Washee and Errant, bringing along with them three soldiers. They did not stay long and they made no demands; they simply handed the captives over and left after a brief statement by Washee.

"These," he had said, "are only what we ourselves have to turn over to you, but others are being gathered from among our people where they have been adopted and they are due to be here today. We will be back with them before the sun sets."

He had lived up to his word. About four that afternoon they had come again. This time Errant and Washee and their dozen warriors had brought with them five more soldiers—four Royal Americans and one of the Queen's Rangers of Hopkins's company—along with two traders well known in Detroit and long thought to be dead. The first, Hugh Crawford, had been taken by the Miamis on the Wabash River about the time Fort Miamis was taken and he was subsequently traded to the Potawatomies. The second, Chapman Abraham, was taken at the beginning of the siege here as he reached the mouth of the Detroit River. He told how he had escaped being killed at the stake by feigning insanity and that, since then, he had been reasonably well treated.

Believing that the Potawatomies had now sincerely lived up to their promises, Gladwin had been on the point of releasing Chief Winnemac to them when Abraham spoke up.

"You say they were supposed to have given up *all* their prisoners for the return of Winnemac, Major?"

"That's right."

"Reckon then you'd best hang onto him a while more. I know damned well they got at least half a dozen more prisoners, an' perhaps some beyond that."

Gladwin's lips tightened and he rescinded the order calling for the release of Winnemac. He turned to Washee and addressed him coldly.

"You are on the right road in bringing these prisoners to me to be released, Chief Washee, but you have not come to the end of that road yet. You promised to return all the prisoners your people had in exchange for your Chief Winnemac. You have not yet done so. You still have a number of Englishmen and until they are brought here—*all of them!*—there can be no release of your chief."

Both Washee and Errant turned sullen when Jacques St. Martin interpreted the major's words. And it was at just about this time that Lieutenant George McDougall arrived on the scene, saw what was happening and immediately pointed a finger at one of the warriors amid the cluster behind their chiefs.

"Sir," he told Gladwin, "that one there—he's no Potawatomi. I saw him several times before. He's an Ottawa."

Gladwin, through St. Martin, had thereupon quickly questioned the warrior off to one side and then ordered that he be taken away to confinement. When the commanding officer faced Washee and Errant again, they looked guilty and their sullenness had evaporated.

"That man was an Ottawa," Gladwin said. "He admits that he came here for Pontiac, to see where the fort is most vulnerable, so that they might set fire to it. What do you say to this, Washee?"

The Potawatomi chief shook his head. "That is not what we believed, my brother. He joined us saying that he was part of a band of his people who had broken from Pontiac and were going home to fight no more, and that it was he upon whom the responsibility had fallen to come and tell you of this, which is why he joined us. We will take him back with us."

"You will *not* take him back with you," Gladwin remarked. "If I let him out again, the Ottawas would laugh at me, seeing how easily one of their own could enter and leave the fort of an enemy. Let me ask you this: if I sent one of my men disguised among you and you found him out, would you then turn around and release him back to me? No, you would not. You would hold him as a hostage, which is now what I will do. But this you can tell Pontiac: that I will not use this hostage as Pontiac used Captain Campbell and the rest of the English prisoners, as I have more regard for human life than this. I will guard him with the security with which I have guarded Winnemac, and when you come back with *all* the rest of your prisoners, Washee, then will I release to you both Winnemac and this Ottawa, but not before."

The Indians had gone away and within the hour after their departure Gladwin had sent the schooner *Huron*, under command of Captain Edgar Loring, off toward Niagara with some of Detroit's wounded men, along with letters written by the garrison, dispatches he himself was sending, and an urgent appeal to Major Wilkins at Fort Niagara for another reinforcement of fifty men to be sent. Loring, raising his craggy head and sniffing, testing the wind, told Gladwin that sailing conditions looked good and that if the stiff breeze continued as it was blowing, he could possibly make it to Niagara in as short as four or five days or anyway, with good tailwinds, at least within a week.

The next morning—last Wednesday—Chief Errant and a handful of his Potawatomies returned to the fort. Errant presented Gladwin with a broad belt of white wampum— peace wampum—saying that it had now been determined that there were just six English prisoners left among the Potawatomies and that they would be turned in to him very soon. In the meanwhile, he wondered if Gladwin would release the Ottawa taken the day before, into his custody, Gladwin shook his head.

"For the belt you have brought, I am glad, Chief Errant," he said, "for now I believe that you and your people are sincere and truly want peace. When you come again with the prisoners, I will have ready for you then a belt from us as a token of our fidelity and friendship. But as for the Ottawa, it must be as I have said: he will stay here in custody with Winnemac until the final six of your prisoners are released to us."

It was not long after Errant's departure that news was brought in by Jacques Duperon Baby that a large party of Ottawas under one of Pontiac's foremost chiefs, Mehemah, along with two of Pontiac's sons—Nebahkohum and Kasadah[126]—were camped on a plain about two miles to the southwest of the fort. They were all well outfitted, Baby said, and apparently readying for a long journey. Baby had heard, though he did not know how much reliance to place in it, that they were heading for the forks of *La Belle Rivière*—the Ohio River—to attack Fort Pitt. An inquiry by Gladwin in the matter confirmed what Baby had said, though the destination of the Ottawa party was still not authenticated. Nevertheless, Gladwin entrusted a message to a Christian Huron named Aaron who had faithfully carried messages for him before, warning Captain Simeon Ecuyer of the possible approach of this Ottawa force.

Three days ago, on Friday, the Frenchman Clairmont had come with news that large numbers of the young Frenchmen, who so recently had joined forces with Pontiac, were now deserting him and heading for the Illinois country, suddenly fearful that if they remained in this area much longer, they would suffer either at the hands of Pontiac or else be hung by Gladwin. Before leaving, Clairmont also commented that he had heard the rift between Ottawas and Chippewas, which had started with the death of Tewalee and resulted in the murder of Campbell, was each day growing wider and that the Chippewas might soon desert Pontiac entirely, though whether or not this would mean they would also stop fighting the English on their own was something he did not know. It was good to hear, but Gladwin found it very hard to believe.

What he did believe, however, and what worried him considerably, was the report from several good sources—St. Martin and Baby among them—that Pontiac had not yet given up the idea of a fire raft; that he had, at this moment, many men busily at work constructing one which could not fail to collide with the *Michigan*.

The raft, it was said, was being built of pine boards from two dismantled barns. It was being built over the hulls of six old batteaux. Filled with combustibles, just as the others had been filled, the six batteaux would be chained together so they would stretch broadside to the current for three hundred feet. When it was set afire at each of the batteaux and then released, such a raft could hardly be expected to miss colliding with the *Michigan*. In fact, it was reasonable to assume that, burning fiercely, they would collide with the bow of the ship and then the batteaux on either side of the collision point would be swept in an arc by the current right up against both sides of the sloop.

And try as he would, Gladwin could think of no practicable way of preventing it.

[*July 18, 1763—Monday, 8:00 A.M.*]

Far to the north of where Major Gladwin lay pondering the problems of his Detroit command, forty large canoes were in the process of being loaded.

The councils between the L'Arbre Croche Ottawas—represented by Chief Okinochumaki—and the Chippewas of Michilimackinac and the surrounding area—represented by Chief Minivavana—had finally concluded with the desired results. The Englishmen in the hands of these northern Ottawas were to be given leave to pass through the Straits of Mackinac without being molested. Lieutenant James Gorrell and his garrison from Fort Edward Augustus at Green Bay, along with Captain George Etherington and the remains of his force from Fort Michilimackinac, plus the two traders Ezekiel Solomon and Henry Bostwick, had been brought a week ago to Michilimackinac again and now they were to be escorted all the way to Montreal by sixty Ottawas. All of the English, with the exception of two privates still recovering from their wounds, were in excellent condition and all were terribly excited that the day of deliverance was in sight and that now they were leaving behind them this country in which so many of their comrades had died.

Farewells had long since been said to Chief Mackinac at L'Arbre Croche and reiterated promises given to Okinochumaki that the Ottawa escort would return heavily laden with gifts from General Gage at Montreal for the help the Ottawas had been to these English. Now, at the fort again, George Etherington had yet only to bid good-by to the Jesuit priest, Father de Jaunay, but first he was scribbling a hasty line to Major Gladwin:

> *Michilimackinac, 18 July 1763*
>
> *Dear Sir: The express which I sent off to Lieutenant Gorrell at LaBay arrived, as we are led to believe, very luckily one day before that post was to have been cut off. The savages of that post came down to the Indian village where I was prisoner, and brought with them Lieutenant Gorrell and all his garrison, and they, with Mr. Leslye, me, and the fourteen men that remain of the garrison of this place, are just embarking for Montreal under a guard of sixty savages of the Ottawa Nation.*
>
> *I have a thousand things to tell you, but I cannot trust them by this conveyance. I have heard nothing of the four men that I sent last May to St. Josephs. There are two of my men yet with the Chippewas. I have prevailed with the savages to permit all the English merchants to carry all the goods to Montreal under convoy. I have been at a very great expense here, but it was all unavoidable. I don't despair of seeing you this fall at Detroit, and am, in the meantime, Dear Sir,*
>
> > *Yours sincerely,*
> > *George Etherington*

[July 18, 1763—Monday, 9:00 A.M.]

It was with decidedly mixed emotions that the populace of Carlisle, Pennsylvania—refugees and residents alike—watched the troops under Colonel Henry Bouquet form up and begin their westward march out of town. There had been a great sense of security and comfort having the army here, even though as yet it had done nothing but wait for its final provisioning and reinforcements. Just its presence here had acted as a deterrent to any body of Indians which might have been considering attacking.

561

By the same token, it was good to see them go because the town had been for many weeks far too crowded, too filled with misery and with pain and with short tempers. Fights between soldiers and civilians had been frequent, though not severe: the civilians scornful of the soldiers for not going out to fight the Indians who were laying waste the countryside; the soldiers scornful of the civilians for not banding themselves together in strong militia groups to protect themselves and their families and possessions.

Now, with Bouquet leading the four hundred and sixty men westward, Carlisle would be quieter and more able to cope with the still-growing influx of refugees. And many who watched the soldiers go, lowered their eyes and turned away in shame because the hope was deep within them that now the Indians would concentrate their attacks on the army and leave the settlements alone.

They were apt to be correct. Less than a mile from the fort, a lithe Shawnee warrior in the uppermost branches of a tree watched with close attention the departure of Bouquet's force on the road leading toward Fort Bedford. When there could be no lingering doubt that the army was indeed on its move to the west, he lowered himself quickly to the ground, said a few words to his companion astride a horse, leaped onto the back of his own mount which the other Shawnee had been holding, and the pair kicked their steeds into a gallop toward Fort Pitt.

[*July 26, 1763—Tuesday, 8:30 A.M.*]

Although it was distinctly against his better judgment to do so, Captain Simeon Ecuyer had allowed the small party of Shawnee and Delaware chiefs to enter the fort. His basis for doing so was their approach about a half hour ago bearing on a stick raised above them the little British flag which, many months ago, he himself had given as a token of friendship.

Now, in this council room, the air had a bluish-white haze from the *kinnikinnick* that had been smoked in their pipes. Seated on the floor in a sort of semicircle before Ecuyer and his two interpreters, Simon Girty and Alexander McKee, the nine chiefs had just put their pipes aside. Six of them were Delawares, including Tollema, Turtle's Heart—Kitehi, as he called himself—Shingas, White Eyes, Buckangehela and Wingenund. The three Shawnee chiefs were Benewisica, Moluntha, and Pluk-ke-motah. It was Shingas—The Beaver—who rose to speak.

"Brother," he began, "what we are about to say to you comes from our hearts and not just from our lips. I am sorry that more of our chiefs could not come, so that you would know that we speak here for all Shawnees and all Delawares, but many of our chiefs and even more of our people need *chobeka*—what the English call medicine—for the pimple sickness which is amongst us. Many of our people who were weak have died and we are afraid that many more will die also. We do not know what this sickness is, but it makes them unable to walk and they talk without knowing what they say and their bodies are hot to the touch of a hand. We now come to you because we know you have ways of curing such sickness—because it is a white man's sickness—and we beg that you will share with us your *chobeka*, that we may stop it and have to grieve no more. We love our families, even as the white men love theirs, and though there is difficulty between us now, it is for our wives and children, who are most affected, that we ask for help from you."

The flush that had crept up Ecuyer's neck and flooded his face as Simon Girty interpreted this came from the knowledge that it was he who had given the Indians the blankets infected with smallpox. Inwardly he groaned at the thought of what beasts war could turn men into and that he himself, in the final analysis, would have to be classed with the most inhumane for the act he had committed. But the pinkening of Ecuyer's face went unnoticed by the Indians as Shingas continued:

"But brother, this is not the only reason we have come, though it is an important one to us. Brother, we wish to hold fast the chain of friendship—that ancient chain which our forefathers held with their brothers, the English. Why can we not do so? I will tell you the reason: you have let your end of the chain fall to the ground, where it has become dirty and stained and covered with rust; but ours is still fast within our hands. Why do you complain that our young men have fired at your soldiers and killed your cattle and taken your horses? You yourselves are the cause of this. You marched your armies into our country and built your forts here, although we have told you again and again that we wished you to remove from our lands. My brother, can you not understand that this is *our* land, not yours? Could you, in truth, stand by and do nothing if someone from a far-off country came to your own land and put down roots against your wishes and refused to leave when you asked them again and again to leave? No! You would have done as we have done. There is a time for talk and there is a time for talking to end and force to begin. You would not listen to our talk, so we thought you might listen to our guns and our tomahawks and our fire arrows. We did not wish to use them, but we were given no other way to have our voices heard. Could you have done less if you were in our place? No! You are the intruders here, not we! You would have struck back against intruders of your land just as we are now striking back for what is ours. We know full well that you wish us to turn and run, as many times we have done before when our lands were taken by your people, but if we continue to do this, soon there will be no land left and there will be no place left that we can run to, and what then? Somewhere there must be a place to stop and stand, *and this is that place!* This is why we have fought you and why some of your forts have been taken and some of your soldiers killed. Yet, though all of this is true, still we wish peace with you and are willing to have it if you, too, are willing."

Shingas paused and then reached under his blanket and removed a broad strand of black-and-purple wampum and held it up for the Fort Pitt commander to see. Almost simultaneously both interpreters spoke in undertones to Ecuyer. Girty said, "It's a war belt, Captain," and McKee said, "Looks like Ottawa or Chippewa design."

Ecuyer began reaching out to accept it, but Girty grabbed his arm and said quickly, "Don't take it. You ain't s'posed to. He's jist showin' you it."

As Simeon Ecuyer nodded at Girty with some embarrassment and let his hand fall back to his side, the swarthy little interpreter continued his job of interpretation as Chief Shingas looped the war belt over one arm and went on with his speech:

"My brother, two days ago we received this great belt of war wampum from the Ottawas of the Detroit. It carries the words of the Chief Pontiac who says that he intends coming through this country in a great body to attack this place and that he will not be stopped in this design and that we must move out of the way or he will eat us up, as he intends to eat you up, as he is very hungry.

"My brother," he concluded, "this is what Pontiac of the Ottawas has said and this is why we have come. If you leave this place at once and go home to your wives and children, no warrior of ours will raise his hand against you, and no harm will come of it. But, my brother, *hear well now what I will say:* if you stay, you must blame only yourselves for what will happen. Therefore, again *and for the last time* we tell you now that we desire you to remove from this place so that once again there may be peace and trade between us, you in your land and we in ours and only the good traders to come and go between us."

With this, Shingas replaced the war belt inside his blanket and then turned and took a seat on the floor between Wingenund and Buckangehela. Now it was Ecuyer's turn and when he spoke it was with an unnatural stiffness and coldness which was not reflected in Simon Girty's voice as he interpreted for the Indians.

"We, too, in this place have the smallpox, which you call the pimple sickness, and many are ill of it. We have not enough medicine for our *own* people, much less supplying our enemies with it. If your people are dying of it, then perhaps it should be a sign to you that it is not good for you to be near white people and you should move far away so that it will trouble you no more."

The fact that he had begun addressing the chiefs without any salutation, without any show of friendship or courtesy, with only a stiff, cold formality, was insult of itself, but the fact that he would say words showing so little concern for women and children who were suffering from a sickness, this was a situation which caused all of the assembled chiefs to murmur ominously. There was, of course, no way for them to know that his apparent anger was a manifestation of his own guilt. It was an anger he felt toward himself but which he directed now toward the chiefs. With hardly a pause, Ecuyer continued:

"You say that you wish trade and friendship with us, yet that is why this place was built—why *you* asked that we build it in the first place—for the purpose of supplying you with clothing and ammunition and the things we make which you need. As for leaving this place because you say the Ottawas are coming, my answer is no! We absolutely refuse to leave here. I have enough soldiers, provisions and ammunition to defend it for three years against all the Indians in the woods, and this I say now: *we will never abandon it* so long as a white man lives in America! I am not concerned by the Ottawas. I despise Ottawas! And I am very much surprised at the Delawares and Shawnees for proposing to us to leave this place and go home. This *is* our home! You have attacked us without reason or provocation. You have murdered and plundered our soldiers and traders. You have murdered settlers and their wives and children, yet you ask us to help your wives and children. You have taken our horses and killed our cattle. All this, and yet you come here now and tell us your hearts are good toward your brothers, the English? How can I have faith in you?"

Simeon Ecuyer slapped his hands to his sides, his guiltiness forgotten as he became caught up in the spell of his own righteous anger. "You come here to advise us to go away. Now it is time for you to hear my advice, and you had better heed it well. I advise you to go home to your towns and villages and take care of your sick wives and children. Moreover, I tell you that if *any* of you appear around this fort again. I will throw bombshells at you which will burst when they strike near you and blow you to bits, and I will fire cannon at you which are loaded with whole bagsful of lead balls for rifles. Therefore, take care, as I don't want to hurt you!"

He ignored the smoldering anger in their eyes as he turned to face Alexander McKee. "Tell them they can leave now. I've nothing further to say to them, except for you to say to them that they are not to come back. Sergeant!"

A noncommissioned officer appeared at the door and said briskly, "Yes, sir?"

"Have your troop escort these people out of the fort. They are not to be molested, as they came in truce, but fire is not to be withheld if they appear again."

Before the chiefs realized what he was doing, he reached up and took the little British flag they had approached the fort under and which they had wedged in a crack in the planking near the door. He broke the stick in half over his knee, ripped the flag from it and then, without another word or glance at the chiefs, stalked from the council room with the flag clutched in his fist.

[*July 26, 1763—Tuesday, Noon*]

The entire force of men under Captain James Dalyell was grim-faced as they viewed the ruins of Fort Sandusky, but this time the overpowering fear was not gripping them. They had known about the fall of Fort Sandusky before leaving on this expedition and it came as no great shock to see it. Too, there was already an aspect of age to it. In many places grasses and weeds were growing up through the blackened remains as nature reclaimed the land.

Less than three miles from this place was the Wyandot Huron village called Junundat where the heavy-jawed Chief Odinghquanooron presided. With crisp commands and precise movements, Dalyell reformed his troops and they marched there.

The place was deserted, which was no surprise to Dalyell. He had fully expected it to be and would have been surprised had it not been. After all, his flotilla of batteaux had been visible on the lake for an hour or more before reaching the mouth of Sandusky Creek. The Indians had had plenty of time to leave. But there was little doubt in the captain's mind that his actions were being closely watched.

"All right," he said in a loud voice, "check each place first to see if there's anything worthwhile inside. Then burn them. Destroy that corn crop growing there, too."

There were some implements in the lodges, crude farming tools, utensils, bowls, other items, but nothing of any real value to the detachment, so nothing was taken. Within a quarter hour the entire village was burning fiercely and the newly tasseling corn was crushed to the ground. As the flotilla pulled away from the shore near the remains of the fort. Dalyell stood looking back at the smoke rising high over the bay waters.

"That," he said aloud to no one in particular, "ought to give them the idea that we mean business."

[*July 26, 1763—Wednesday, 2:00 P.M.*]

The return of Elleopolle "Mini" Chene and Jacques Godefroy to Detroit caused a sensation. Not one word had been heard from them since they had been sent by Pontiac to Fort de Chartres in the Illinois country eleven weeks ago to ask the commandant there, Major Neyon de Villiere, to send a French army to assist in the taking of Detroit. The pair had conferred with the lately promoted officer at length and now they had returned, still with their prisoner, the trader John Welch, in tow. Immediately a major council of the principal Frenchmen of Detroit and Indian chiefs of the surrounding tribes was called.

For Pontiac, the news they brought was neither as good as he had hoped, nor as bad as he had expected. Though there were letters from the Fort de Chartres commander to both the French and the Indians, the pertinent points of what had occurred were told aloud in council by Godefroy and Chene.

"Major de Villiere was surprised and not displeased with what was taking place here," Chene announced. "He accepted from us the soldiers we brought to him as prisoners from Fort Ouiatenon and he has them still. He applauds the courage of Pontiac in taking it upon himself to pluck the fangs from the English rattlesnake and wishes it could be in his power at this moment to send the army of French soldiers which Pontiac asks for. However, this cannot be, at least not yet. The major has asked me to tell you this, which he repeats in the letters he has sent: he advises all French residents of this and other areas to take no part whatever in hostilities directed against the English. They are not required to help these English, but neither should they harm them. For their own good, they should maintain a strict neutrality. As to the Indians, as I have said, the major says that it is with great regret that he is not at this time able to send help. He cannot do so, he says, because he has heard rumors that there is now a peace between France and Great Britain. However, he has dispatched couriers to New Orleans to learn the truth and should the reports be untrue, then he will see what he can do about sending help of a significant nature, and further instructions will be given at that time to the French residents here."

Godefroy then spoke for a short while, telling more of the details of how Forts Miamis and Ouiatenon had been taken and a little more of what had been said and done at Fort de Chartres. Then the council broke up, but just as quickly another was called by Pontiac and held in the Huron village across the river from Detroit. There was a surprisingly large attendance, with only a handful of warriors watching the fort. In addition to the Potawatomies, Hurons, Mississaugis, Ottawas and Chippewas of this Detroit area on hand for the council, a body of seventy Chippewas from Michilimackimac under Chief Matchekewis had arrived, as well as a fair number of Shawnees, Delawares and Wyandot Hurons from the Ohio country.

Pontiac was at his finest. He was the only speaker and he spoke at great length of the triumphs and pitfalls of this whole war thus far. It was customary among the Indians to boast loudly and at length of past achievements and overlook entirely one's failings. Wisely, the Ottawa war chief deviated from this procedure and began his talk by telling of the Indians' failures thus far, blaming himself most of all. It had been no one's fault but his own, he told them earnestly, that Detroit was not taken by surprise, that ships had come and gone at Detroit and his Indians had been unable to stop them, that the fire rafts had failed and even the building of the great three-hundred-foot fire raft was now being abandoned. But when he had gone over every bit of the bad news, not sparing himself in the least and thus winning a rather awed respect from his listeners, then he began enumerating the Indian accomplishments in this war, emphasizing his own role in planning the attacks which had been so successful on so many fronts. Look at what had been done: of the ten English forts west of Fort Pitt and Niagara, only one—Detroit—still remained in English hands, and it was under siege and would soon be taken. Even Niagara and Pitt were being attacked, along with many of the smaller posts to the east of them. The huge military supply convoy had been taken on Lake Erie and dozens of smaller trader convoys had fallen into their hands. Had not what Pontiac promised at the great River Rouge Congress virtually come to pass? Had not he said then that their goal was to drive the English from this country, and was it not a fact that the only English who remained in it now were those in this fort at Detroit or in captivity?

On and on he talked, taking point by point every victory the Indians had won, however small or large, and exposing it to the full understanding of his audience. There could be no denying it: the Indians had gained far more than they had lost, the Indian cause was far more advanced than it had been, the whole Indian race was again acting like men, had again aquired a self-confidence and pride and self-respect that had been so long on the wane under English dominion. But above all, it had to be borne in mind that the struggle was not yet over, that there was much to be done, that there might yet be setbacks of one kind or another, that his followers must keep faith, must persevere, must uphold him and follow his wishes and commands, for was he not himself under the orders of the Master of Life to exterminate the English from this country?

His voice was strong and his manner compelling, almost hypnotic, and by the time he finished his speech he had every man present with him in every respect. As he spoke the last of his lengthy and inspired oratory, he whipped out his tomahawk, held it high and screamed out the war cry, then broke into the dance and chant of war.

They joined him—one, two, a dozen, a score, a hundred many times over! Even the faltering Potawatomies and Hurons joined him; and even the Chippewas with whom he had lately argued. Stamping, shrieking, pouncing upon imaginary enemies, driving home imaginary tomahawks and knives into imaginary bodies, scalping imaginary heads, they reaffirmed their faith in Pontiac, reaffirmed their wish to continue the war, committed themselves to the utter annihilation of the English invaders of their land!

[July 26, 1763—Tuesday, 8:30 P.M.]

The panic continued, even increased, on the frontiers of Virginia, Maryland, Pennsylvania and New York. Thus far the New York frontier had been perhaps the least affected of the four provinces, but every border-country resident there lived in a state of perpetual fear, expecting at any moment to find the massacring hordes of painted red men descending upon them. An incident at the little hamlet of Goshen gave stark evidence of the frame of mind prevailing among the residents.

Four or five men of the town decided to go hunting for partridge in the nearby hills and set out early in the morning when most of the residents were still asleep. Perhaps an hour later, when the townsfolk were mostly up and about, the hunters happened to flush some of their quarry and all of the men raised their guns and fired at nearly the same time. The crashing of the gunfire re-echoed down the hills and valley.

Instantly Goshen was in an uproar. The shots were clearly heard in town and thought to be an attacking Indian war party. Residents streamed away from the town in terror, spreading panic as they went with wild tales which grew with each telling. The rumors and the terror grew, became all-encompassing throughout that section of the country. Farmers plowing in the fields cut the traces and leaped upon the backs of the horses and galloped off, leaving behind carts or plows or whatever. Others gathered their families and valuables, abandoned their homes and fled to New England, not even pausing to rest until the mighty Hudson River was behind them. Over five hundred families abandoned their homes. Such was the state of mind in New York, where thus far attacks had been slight. In other provinces, it was even worse.

Colonel James Robertson, who had been sent by Amherst as a special envoy to the Pennsylvania General Assembly to plead for Provincial help for their own beleaguered border residents west of the Susquehanna, talked himself hoarse and got absolutely nowhere. At last he gave up and sent a disheartened message to Sir Jeffrey:

Sir:
  I found all my pleading vain, and believe even Cicero's

would have been so. I never saw any men so determined in the right as these people are in this absurdly wrong resolve.

The Pennsylvania *Gazette* offered its readers little consolation. Letter after letter was printed, extract after extract, from the terrified pens of the border inhabitants. An unsigned extract from a letter originating at Frederickstown on July 19 exemplified the existing state:

Every day, for some time past, has offered the melancholy scene of poor distressed families driven downwards through this town with their effects, who have deserted their plantations for fear of falling into the cruel hands of our savage enemies, now daily seen in the woods. And never was panic more general or forcible than that of the black inhabitants [Negro slaves], whose terrors at this time exceed what followed on the defeat of General Braddock, when the frontiers lay open to the incursions of both French and Indians.

That was not quite accurate. The fear felt at this time by the Negro slaves was not so much a fear of the Indians as it was a fear of their own masters. Immediately following Braddock's inglorious defeat on the Monongahela near Fort Duquesne—which had since become rebuilt as Fort Pitt—the blacks had rejoiced and the story had spread rapidly among them that they would be liberated by the Indians. For weeks at that time the slaves had been on the point of rioting against their masters. The situation was remembered only too clearly now, by both whites and blacks; the whites fearing such riots would become reality and that the self-liberated slaves would join the Indians against the whites, and the blacks eager enough to do just that, but fearful that at the first sign of it, there would be wholesale execution of them by their masters. It was an extremely volatile situation.

Many blacks in the past who had escaped from their slavery and fled into the wilderness had encountered Indians. In some cases they were killed, but in many instances they were, at their own request, accepted into the tribes. Often they were adopted and shared equal freedom and responsibility with the Indians they had joined. Occasionally they fought with them against the whites and sometimes they married into the tribe and had children who became, regardless of skin color, far more Indian than Negro. But this was only a segment of the far greater problem of the Indian war parties themselves.

As negligent as Pennsylvania was to its citizens on the

frontier, Maryland was not much better. Massacres were becoming daily more frequent there and the panic more general. Residents forted up together for mutual protection as best they could, but their plight was still dreadful. From his fortified home at Old Town, the hardy trader, frontiersman and former militia captain, Thomas Cresap, wrote pleadingly for aid to Governor Sharpe:

Old Town, July 15th, 1763

May it please your Excellency:

I take this opportunity in the height of confusion to acquaint you with our unhappy and most wretched situation at this time, being in hourly expectation of being massacred by our barbarous and inhuman enemy, the Indians; we having been three days successively attacked by them, viz., the 13th, 14th, and this instant . . . I have enclosed a list of the desolate men and women, and children, who have fled to my house, which is enclosed by a small stockade for safety, by which you see what a number of poor souls, destitute of every necessary of life, are here penned up, and likely to be butchered without immediate relief and assistance, and can expect none, unless from the Province to which they belong. I shall submit to your wiser judgment the best and most effectual method for such relief, and shall conclude with hoping we shall have it in time. Yours &ca.

Thomas Cresap

And in the midst of this maelstrom of fear and horror, this vast arena of death and destruction, the long, winding red line which was Colonel Henry Bouquet's army continued its progress toward Fort Pitt. The commander had tried to hire a body of frontiersmen to accompany the march, to act as flankers and scouts as the army moved, but his efforts had been in vain; the frontiersmen, by necessity, were being forced to remain to protect their own families. And though Bouquet tried to use some of his Scottish Highlander troops for this purpose, they were such poor woodsmen that almost invariably they became lost and occasioned even greater delays. As Bouquet had written to Amherst this very morning:

I cannot send a Highlander out of my sight without running the risk of losing the man, which exposes me to surprise from the skulking villains I have to deal with.

Yet, despite this, the army had moved well since leaving Carlisle. Bouquet, from the onset, was very much afraid that Fort Ligonier, the weakest link in this communication chain to Fort Pitt, would be taken. To avert this possibility, he gathered up thirty of his finest Highlanders and sent them forward at top speed to that post, ordering them to stay off the roads and travel only at night. They made it to Fort Bedford without incident but, because Captain Ourry was expecting an attack, remained there for two days. When the attack failed to materialize, they set out again, still following Bouquet's orders to march only under cover of darkness and to stay off the main road. Approaching Fort Ligonier, they heard gunfire and found the fort at that moment under attack by a party of Indians numbering about the same as themselves. Bouquet had picked his men well. With great self-control they thrust their way through the attackers and entered the fort without having a man injured, though scores of shots were fired at them. Lieutenant Archibald Blane was almost beside himself with the joy of receiving this reinforcement and with their good news that Bouquet and his whole army were not too far behind.

Nor was he. Twenty miles after leaving Carlisle, Bouquet's force had reached Shippensburg and found, as at Carlisle, a frightened and hungry multitude which actually wept with relief at his approach. They wished him to stay but he pressed on, passing little Fort Loudoun at Cove Mountain, fording streams, descending valleys, ascending hills, passing the miserable little post of Fort Lyttleton which the Pennsylvania government had refused to garrison—and where Bouquet now dropped off a few men with arms and provisions to guard the place and finally arriving intact mid-day yesterday at Fort Bedford.

"Sir," said Captain Ourry, first saluting and then shaking the colonel's hand, "if I may be permitted an understatement, you are most welcome."

Bouquet smiled and then asked what the situation was. Louis Ourry shook his head and blew out a deep breath.

"Not good, sir. The woods are full of Indians. They fire on us every day and I'm surprised you got in without some difficulty. The detachment you sent ahead passed through all right. I retained them here a couple of days, since a large party of warriors had been seen and we expected an attack. They remained two days and, considering the danger past, I sent them on. As for what lies ahead I don't know, but I suspect little good. There hasn't been a word from either Pitt or

Ligonier for a long time now and if any messengers have been sent, they've been captured or killed. The last we heard from Captain Ecuyer was that Fort Pitt was surrounded and a general attack was expected."

Bouquet had nodded gloomily. He had expected it, but it still was an added burden to carry. The thought struck him with pain that it was altogether possible he had sent his thirty best Highlanders to certain death. Since his men and animals needed a rest after this brisk march from Carlisle, Bouquet told Ourry that he and his force would be staying here for three days, and he also promised to leave behind him here as a reinforcement for Fort Bedford, poor though they might be, whatever invalids he had with him who could not well carry on farther.

This morning Bouquet had been up early, talking earnestly with the refugees gathered at the place, restoring such confidence as he could in them, and asking for volunteers from among the frontiersmen to march with him as guides and scouts. His luck here was better than it had been at Carlisle. Here all the frontiersmen had brought their families to the fort where they were under protection of the garrison and they could leave them with the reasonable assurance of their continued safety. By noon, thirty tough and experienced backwoodsmen had agreed to continue the march with Bouquet when he left here the day after tomorrow.

By nightfall, Bouquet was penning a full report of his progress and the conditions thus far to General Amherst. And now, at this same moment, one hundred miles to the west of where Bouquet now sat, Fort Pitt had just come under full-scale attack by three hundred or more Shawnees and Delawares.

At dusk this evening the Indians had begun to creep into position and, though fired upon with great briskness from the fort, they completely surrounded the place, slipping from cover to cover under the steep riverbanks of the Monongahela and Allegheny and digging holes for themselves to hide in with their knives—holes large enough to shelter their bodies from the fort's fire, yet still permit them to fire at the place with bow or gun.

Ecuyer had sounded a general alarm drum roll as the attack began in earnest only a short while ago and within moments every man not already there had reached his post and all were witnessing the awesome, terrifyingly beautiful spectacle of scores of fire arrows being launched simultaneously. They arched through the darkness like a shower of meteors, with flame and sparks trailing behind each. Most fell short of their mark, but some carried far enough to bury themselves in the pickets or in roofs and walls of structures within the fort. The clumsy fire engine so laboriously constructed became worth its value a hundred times over as blaze after blaze was doused before a real conflagration could result.

Captain Ecuyer seemed omnipresent. He was everywhere, directing gunfire and artillery, shouting encouragement, answering questions, solving problems, calling orders. A dozen times or more fire arrows lofted over the walls and thunked into the ground near his feet or into walls close to him, but except to stamp them out, he paid little attention to them. Though these fire arrows were numerous, there were only two of the vicious barbed-head war arrows which flew over the wall. One of these drove deeply into the planking of a sidewalk and was kicked and broken by a soldier. It was of little concern. The other, however, was one which demanded more attention.

A yard-long shaft fitted with a beautifully chipped head of gray flint and fletched with turkey wing feathers came over the wall in a hissing trajectory which ended as the barbed head buried itself plus an inch or so of the shaft as well in the calf muscle of Captain Ecuyer's left leg.

He called to a nearby corporal to give him a hand and, with his arm around the soldier's neck, hobbled to the hospital quarters. There he watched without a murmur as the surgeon alternately manipulated a scalpel and wiped away the blood as he gradually opened the flesh enough for the arrowhead to be gently pulled free.

Within half an hour, limping but uncomplaining, Captain Simeon Ecuyer was again the omnipresent commander directing every phase of the defense of his fort. Little wonder that Lieutenant General Sir Jeffrey Amherst longed to have an army made up of Swiss mercenaries like Colonel Bouquet and Captain Ecuyer.

[July 29, 1763—Friday]

It was 4:30 A.M. when Major Henry Gladwin came groggily erect at the urgent knocking at his door. It was still very dark and for a little while he felt dislocated and unable to do much more than stumble about confusedly while he groped for his breeches and tunic. The knocking continued insistently and the Detroit commander lurched toward the door, pausing momentarily to pick up the heavy pistol lying on his desk.

"Coming," he mumbled. "Coming." At the door he paused without opening it and, sounding a little more awake now, he demanded, "Who is it?"

"Captain Hopkins, sir," came the reply. He sounded excited.

Gladwin jammed the pistol into his waistband and opened the door. Joseph Hopkins, fully dressed and obviously keyed up about something, nodded. It was the first time he had ever forgotten to salute.

"Sir," he said, "there's something going on. Gunfire downstream, not too far off and on the other side. Sounds like the Hurons shooting at something. Sentry said he thought he heard some swivels firing, too. You don't suppose it could be Ed Loring coming back already, do you?"

Gladwin shook his head as he turned up the faintly glowing wick of his lamp on the desk. "I doubt it very much. Captain Loring's hardly had time enough to get the *Huron* to Niagara, much less bring it back here, and I can't imagine anything that would have made him turn back toward this place before he'd gotten there. Still, if it is the schooner, he's going to need some help. Joseph, get about twenty men right away and take one of the batteaux down that way a little. Also, have the drummer sound a general alarm. I'll be on the ramparts in a few minutes."

Hopkins nodded again, remembered to throw a hasty salute, and was gone on the run. Gladwin shut the door and quickly completed his dressing. He didn't have any idea what was going on, but it didn't sound good and he was worried. Even as he dressed he heard the staccato beating of the general alarm and the voices of men as they rushed to their posts. In less than ten minutes he had joined them there on the ramparts at the southwest corner of the fort overlooking the river.

The batteau carrying Captain Hopkins and his detachment had already shoved off and was still in view in the dimness of the growing morning light, but only barely. A heavy fog overhung the fort and river, limiting visibility sharply, but from diagonally across the river came the continuing sounds that had first caused the alert—a muted rattling of musketry and the occasional deeper sounds of what had to be swivels.

In a moment Hopkins's boat was swallowed up and along the ramparts eyes and ears strained for some better clue as to what was happening. Gladwin felt his eyes burning as he tried to penetrate the fog. With each passing moment the daylight grew stronger, the fog less dense. At ten minutes be-

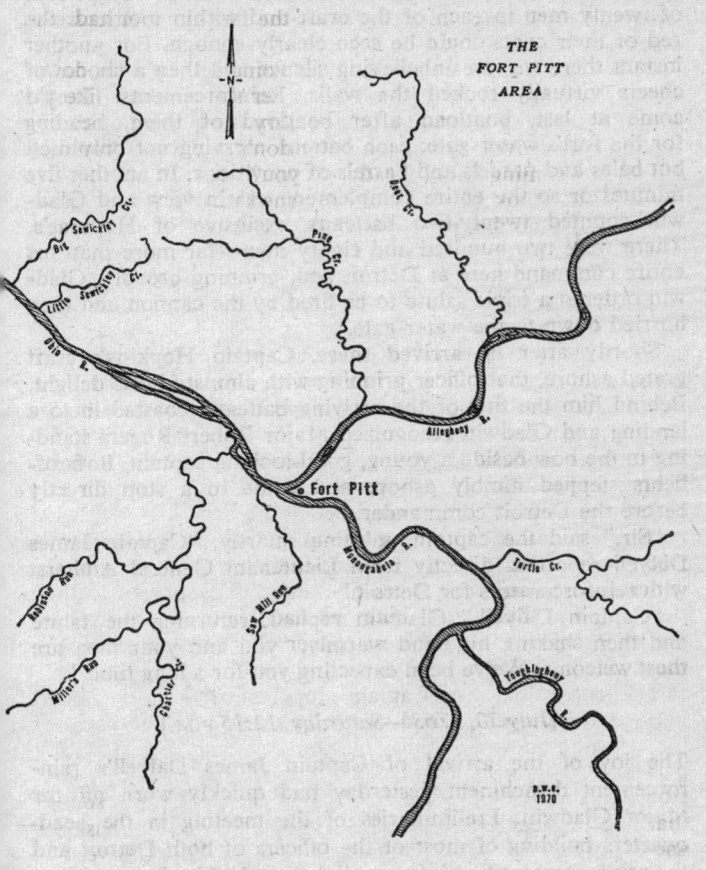

THE
FORT PITT
AREA

-N-

Big Sewickley Cr.

Little Sewickley Cr.

Ohio R.

Allegheny R.

Back Cr.

Pine Cr.

Fort Pitt

Monongahela R.

Saw Mill Run

Turtle Cr.

Youghiogheny R.

Redstone Cr.

Miller's Run

Chartiers Cr.

D.W.T.
1970

fore five o'clock he heard voices, obviously excited but the words themselves muted beyond understanding. He suspected they came from Hopkins's boat.

And then, at five o'clock exactly, a batteau hove out of the dimness at midstream, heading toward the fort. It was Hopkins. His boat was followed by another and then a second, a third, a whole string of batteaux. There were upwards of twenty men in each of the craft and within moments the red of their coats could be seen clearly enough. For another instant there was an unbelieving silence and then a chorus of cheers virtually rocked the walls. Reinforcements! They'd come at last, boatload after boatload of them, heading for the fort's water gate, each batteau carrying not only men but bales and parcels and barrels of provisions. In another five minutes or so the entire complement was in view and Gladwin counted twenty-two batteaux exclusive of Hopkins's. There were two hundred and eighty men—far more than his entire command here at Detroit and, grinning broadly, Gladwin ordered a triple salute to be fired by the cannon and then hurried down to the water gate.

Shortly after he arrived there, Captain Hopkins's craft grated ashore, that officer grinning with almost idiotic delight. Behind him the first of the arriving batteaux coasted in to a landing and Gladwin recognized Major Robert Rogers standing in the bow beside a young, good-looking captain. Both officers stepped nimbly ashore and came to a stop directly before the Detroit commander.

"Sir," said the captain, saluting smartly, "Captain James Dalyell reporting directly from Lieutenant General Amherst with reinforcements for Detroit."

"Captain Dalyell," Gladwin replied, returning the salute and then shaking his hand warmly, "you and your men are most welcome. We've been expecting you for a long time."

[July 30, 1763—Saturday, 12:15 P.M.]

The joy of the arrival of Captain James Dalyell's reinforcement detachment yesterday had quickly worn off for Major Gladwin. Preliminaries of the meeting in the headquarters building of most of the officers of both Detroit and the reinforcement had been cordial enough. The first concern, of course, immediately after the arrival, had been getting medical attention to the fourteen men of Dalyell's who had been wounded in the skirmish while coming upriver.

Rarely had a fog been as fortuitous as that one had been.

The detachment had reached the mouth of the Detroit River at nightfall and Dalyell had decided that rather than camp, it would be most to their advantage to continue the upriver progress to the fort. It had been a prudent move. Throughout the night they had rowed wearily against the current and without being detected, insofar as they could tell, by anyone on shore. At about 2 A.M. the fog had come, further cloaking their movements and muffling their sound, but causing them to hug the east shore of the river closely. In this way they had passed the Potawatomi village of the west shore undetected, but it was at the Huron village, just as light was beginning to filter through the fog, where they ran into trouble. The Indians spotted them and a general firing broke out until the flotilla was able to move out of sight in the fog with fourteen rank and file wounded.[127] They were then met in midstream by the approaching batteau under Captain Hopkins.

Quarters had been assigned to the new men at once and they gratefully turned in, having been rowing for nearly twenty-four consecutive hours. Dalyell, however, along with his second- and third-in-command—Captains Robert Gray and James Grant—and with Major Rogers on hand also, went into immediate conference with Gladwin. Dalyell delivered dispatches and copies of his orders, explaining in a rather superior manner to Gladwin that General Amherst had great confidence in his aide; so much, in fact, that he had given Dalyell a free hand to take whatever action he considered necessary upon reaching Detroit.

"Our intention, Major," he told Gladwin, "is to make Pontiac and his followers regret they ever considered attacking the English."

Gladwin replied rather stiffly, "That, too, has been our objective."

"Yes, of course," Dalyell said, nodding, then added tactlessly, "but *we* intend some strong offensive action against them."

"A good intention," Gladwin said, "provided one does not expose his men to unnecessary hazard in the process. Our garrison here is not terribly small, but it has not been large enough to permit any sort of strong offensive measure without undue risk."

"Sometimes," Dalyell pointed out blandly, "a soldier must take risks. It is, after all, his profession to do so."

Already the attitude of this young captain was grating harshly on Major Gladwin. The decided supercilious manner of the general's aide, his bluntness, his stepping in here as if he meant to command the whole show, all these were aggravating to the Detroit commander. With insinuations, even insults, becoming ever less masked in politeness, Gladwin felt his temper slipping. Realizing that Dalyell had been on his way here for some time, that it was a rigorous trip by batteau and that the young officer had had no sleep for upwards of thirty hours, Gladwin had abruptly stood up, announced that obviously Dalyell and his officers needed some rest and that discussion of what action was to be taken at Detroit now could be put off until tomorrow. Dalyell could not resist a parting shot.

"Perhaps," he said to Major Rogers as they walked out, but loudly enough for everyone in the room to hear, "it has been the timorous putting-off of things which has resulted in His Majesty's strongest western post being held under siege for so long by a band of ignorant barbarians."

As a deep flush spread on Gladwin's face, the other officers had discreetly averted their eyes from him and filed out of the room. The Detroit commander stood absolutely still until all were gone except for Captain Hopkins and then he let out a breath and chuckled without much humor.

"We have in our midst, Joseph," he commented, "an extremely ambitious young man. I can only hope that his abilities as a leader make up for his deficiency in tact. Well, he's tired and tomorrow's another day."

Whatever hopes that Henry Gladwin may have harbored, however, that Dalyell's conduct would improve with rest were unfounded. The second meeting of officers had begun just after noon today—about ten minutes ago—on practically the same footing that the first had ended, and it swiftly degenerated from that point.

Most of the talking was done by Captain Dalyell, rather than either of the two superior officers present, Majors Gladwin and Rogers. For Gladwin it was something of a ticklish situation. Dalyell was very evidently quite close to General Amherst and it was patently clear that he fully shared the general's contempt for and hatred of the Indians. It was even more apparent today than yesterday that he was extremely ambitious and abundantly self-confident. These, Gladwin knew, might well be traits which could cause him to seriously underestimate the strength and ability of the enemy. That Amherst had great faith in him was evident to Gladwin by the very fact that it was Dalyell who had been placed in command of the reinforcement rather than Rogers, who not only outranked him, but whose Indian-fighting prowess was legendary. Rogers himself seemed quite subdued, which was not at all in keeping with his character and, because of this, Gladwin became all the more convinced that Dalyell had a good deal more power than mere rank alone would indicate.

"I propose to attack Pontiac at once," Dalyell said, his very tone indicating that he expected to get no argument about it. He added, "I can see no purpose whatever in wasting any more time."

"I might remind the captain," Gladwin spoke up tightly, "that I am commanding officer of this post and the captain's orders call for him to place himself under my command."

"My orders, sir," Dalyell corrected, "both verbal and written, were to come to the aid of Detroit and to take what action I thought to be necessary for putting down this Indian trouble. I have no intention of usurping your command of this fort, but at the same time, it is *my* decision now as to what must be done to end a situation that has prevailed here for altogether much too long. It is further my considered view that the only way to put down Indian trouble is to *do* so, to strike at once, to hit with as much surprise and strength as possible directly at the stronghold of Pontiac himself."

Gladwin shook his head. "I do not agree. Nor do my interpreters here, Monsieurs St. Martin and LaButte." He dipped his head at two of the three Frenchmen in attendance. The third was Jacques Baby. The major continued: "It is their belief that the force of men Pontiac has at his disposal here— which is certainly over a thousand warriors and perhaps as many as two thousand—is simply too numerous a force to be attacked directly by us in our present numbers, even with the addition of your reinforcement. Sir, a successful attack is most unlikely, but even if successfully carried out, it could only be at the cost of many lives of our men. Until we are able to better assess the situation and strike most advantageously and with the least risk for our own force, I am of the opinion that we should wait."

The argument had no effect on Dalyell's determination to do things his own way. His reply was flat, emotionless. "Begging the major's pardon, but my orders are to proceed at my discretion. I see no point whatever in waiting. A strong blow must be struck at once. The Indians are no match for trained English forces. The longer we wait, the greater the likelihood that Pontiac will take his Indians and slip away into the woods. Sir, allow me to remind you again: I was sent here to crush him and I intend doing so. I mean to march on him tonight and take him by surprise in his camp. Are you giving me a direct order *not* to attack the Indians here? If so, sir, then I am afraid I will have to lead my detachment away, to some other post where their value and purpose will be realized. Again I ask you, sir, am I being ordered *not* to attack the Indians who surround you?"

Gladwin hesitated, then shook his head slowly. "No, Captain Dalyell, that is not my order. And I am well aware of the value of your detachment. I do, however, strongly question your judgment which I believe, at best, is hasty and ill-advised. Further, I have no intention whatever of ordering the men of my garrison here out on a mission which I deem to be hastily conceived and needlessly hazardous. If some of my men wish to volunteer to go with you, they have my permission to do so, but I will not order them to go."

He sighed, thrusting down the anger within him and forcing his voice to soften as he tried to reason with this aggressive young officer. "Captain, I wish you would reconsider. Early in the siege I might have agreed with you that direct attack was advisable. In these past three months, however, we've learned a good bit about Pontiac and his followers— how they fight and what they can do. Indians they may be, sir, but fools they are not. I don't believe you have a ghost's chance of catching Pontiac unawares. Your force—our *entire* force here—is vastly inferior in number to Pontiac's. Our only superiority arises from the protection afforded by this fort and its artillery. To try to fight him against odds and on his own grounds is apt to be disastrous."

"And I, Major," Dalyell said coldly, "am well aware of the general's thoughts and desires in this matter. He expects these Indians to be broken up and wiped out. I have been sent here for that purpose, sir, and I am not afraid to make the attempt."

The only thing, apparently, that Dalyell was concerned over was the possibility that Pontiac would flee and the greatest opportunity he had ever had for military glory would escape him. With his eyes still locked unwaveringly on Gladwin's, he added: "I regret you will not order your men to support me—as I am sure the general, too, will regret such a decision on the major's part—but that does not hinder me from going ahead as I have planned. I will gladly accept such of your men as volunteer to accompany us. We will march out of the fort under utmost silence at about three o'clock in the morning, to attack Pontiac when his defenses are weakest—just before dawn."

Gladwin sighed again and gave up. He had to admit that, despite his pessimism, there was an outside chance that such a predawn attack might result in success. No one was more weary of this siege than he, and the idea that such an attack might break the back of the uprising was appealing.

"All right, Captain Dalyell, if you believe this is what General Amherst expected you to do, then go ahead with it."

The plan of attack was thereupon gone over in considerable detail, with the three Frenchmen supplying what information they could regarding topography, location of Pontiac's camp, best line of movement, Pontiac's weaknesses and strengths and other such matters. When they were finished, Baby and St. Martin agreed to act as guides, to lead the force through the darkness to Pontiac's camp. Gladwin, not wishing to be without an interpreter, asked LaButte to remain at the fort.

The meeting broke up and as the officers left to spread the word among their men, to have them get their equipment in readiness and get some sleep before they would be assembled sometime after 2 A.M., Baby and St. Martin went to their own quarters inside the fort to get some rest, too. LaButte, however, moved through the streets of the fort to a shop bearing the sign of a silversmith. Making sure he was unobserved, he slipped inside and, at the rear, tapped a signal on a narrow door. It was opened at once by Pierre Barth and the two went into a whispered discussion.

Less than an hour later, Barth, having left the fort by mingling with a group of Frenchmen who had received permission from the commander to go to their homes to pick up some clothing and other articles, was on the way to the camp of Pontiac.

[July 30, 1763—Saturday, 8:30 P.M.]

Long before the sun had set, Pontiac and the chiefs of the various Detroit tribes and villages had already discussed and established their own plan for thwarting the planned secret attack upon them by the English. For the first time, Pontiac regretted having sent away such a sizable force of his own men to go against Fort Pitt. Nevertheless, with well over four hundred Ottawa and Chippewa warriors on hand here and the advantage on their side, they should have no real difficulty.

The Hurons under Teata were becoming progressively

583

more irksome and more difficult to deal with. Though they had been caught up again by the contagion of Pontiac's recent war speech, their fervor had quickly cooled and once more they were saying that they did not wish to attack the English.

Suppose, then, that the English attacked you?" Pontiac asked. "Would you fight then?"

Both Teata and Takee agreed they would and so Pontiac outlined a plan for them. They were to return to their village across from Detroit at once and, making a great show of it, they were to burn up a lot of their unwanted gear, load their canoes with their goods, plus their women, children and dogs, and set off downstream. The whole purpose was to give the English observers the impression that they were abandoning their town. However, as soon as they were out of sight of the fort, they were to come ashore and the warriors were to make their way back to the town unseen by a circuitous path and conceal themselves in ambush for the English. If the redcoats came across the river to destroy the town, as was possible, then the Hurons could fall upon them from one side to preserve their town, while Pontiac and his followers would hit them on the other side.

Two hours later the smoke from their camp rose and the Hurons dutifully set off downstream. The plan was followed precisely and before long the concealed Hurons had their ambush set. By the very act of doing so, they found themselves committed against the English, which was not what they had wished. But it was what Pontiac had wished, for two reasons: first, for the obvious one of getting them into a frame of mind to think of the English as enemies, which they had been disinclined to do, and secondly, to keep them away from the fort in view of what was to come. At this point he wanted nothing to interfere with the English plan. He expected the English to be curious about the supposed withdrawal of the Hurons, but he did not anticipate that they would do anything about it. Nor did they. And Pontiac was delighted because he reasoned that the English, having seen the Hurons go, would assume that his allies were leaving him in fear of the reinforcement that had arrived. It would make that reinforcement that much more eager to follow through with their plan.

Much of the afternoon had been taken up in quiet, unobtrusive preparations at Pontiac's camp. But now, with the fall of darkness at hand, hundreds of women and children left the dwellings with their belongings which could be carried and filed silently through the woods to the northwest toward a predetermined camping spot a couple of miles distant. In the meanwhile, the old men of the tribe remained in the camp here by the swamp and kept the fires going so that the appearance was one of normalcy.

As they did this, Pontiac split his force in two. Both forces were to take hidden positions in the vicinity of Parent's Creek—that little stream which entered the Detroit River a couple of miles upstream from the fort. Here, close to the mouth of the creek, a narrow wooden bridge spanned the stream and it would be an ideal location to set up an ambush. The English planned line of march was to take them over this bridge.

The larger segment of his force—some two hundred and fifty warriors—Pontiac ordered to go through the woods and get themselves in hiding between the fort and the bridge on the Chauvin farm. There were numerous trees, fences, ditches and similar cover where they could hide there, spreading themselves out on both sides of the road for a distance of nearly three-quarters of a mile.

On the other side of Parent's Creek, close to the wooden bridge, the remaining one hundred and sixty warriors were to take position on both sides of the road also; some to hide in the ridges of ground which ran parallel with the stream, others to spread themselves out around Baptiste Meloche's house, garden and orchard. Absolute silence and secrecy was to be maintained and positively no Indian was to fire or otherwise reveal his position until Pontiac himself shot first as the signal to attack, which he would do when the English had reached the middle of the bridge.

By midnight the entire Indian force was so well hidden in their ambush that, even knowing they were there, Pontiac could detect no sign of them. Crickets chirped pleasantly and the night air was sultry. The moon was behind a thin overcast, but it still shed enough subdued light through the clouds to see the road reasonably well by, yet not reveal their own presence.

All in all, it was an ideal night for an ambush.

[July 31, 1763—Sunday, 2:45 A.M.]

The tension was practically a tangible thing among the two hundred and forty-seven officers and men quietly getting themselves into readiness for the march against Pontiac's camp. There was little talk and no laughter.

Near the east gate of the fort, Captain James Dalyell stood in the darkness with a group of the officers who would take part in this foray, reviewing details of what each was expected to do. Over half of the force would be made up of men of the 55th Regiment who, along with the others, had been awakened a quarter of an hour ago. The very fact that they readied themselves quietly, without grumbling, denoted the stress they felt themselves under.

The order of march was simple and open, in the British military manner. The fact that in the past, particularly during the recent French and Indian War, English detachments or whole armies—Braddock's, for example—had been cut to ribbons when marched in such a way against Indians had made little impression upon Dalyell. It was the prescribed military manner and it would therefore be the manner followed. They would march on the road paralleling the dark river—quietly as possible, of course—cross the little bridge over Parent's Creek, go directly to Pontiac's camp from there, draw up their battle lines and attack. It was that simple.

By this time some of the officers who had shown a degree of Dalyell's enthusiasm for the affair were having second thoughts, but it was much too late for that. Lieutenant Archibald Brown of the 55th was to lead an advance guard of twenty-five men. They would be followed by the main body of the force under command of Dalyell himself and his second officer, Captain Robert Gray, also of the 55th. The rear was to be commanded by the third officer, Captain James Grant of the 80th Regiment. Lieutenant Diedrick Brehm of the 60th Regiment and Lieutenant Edward Abbott of the Royal Artillery were to pace the advancing force in two batteaux, each fitted with a swivel mounted in front. These boats were to provide covering fire, if necessary and if possible, and also to convey any dead or wounded English back to the fort, as well as to cover any retreat which might conceivably have to be made.

Major Rogers, with the main body of troops, commanded his own small force of Rangers. Among the other officers with the force were Lieutenant Abraham Cuyler of the Queen's Rangers, Lieutenant George McDougall, who was acting as adjutant, Lieutenants John Luke and Francis Nartloo of the 55th, Ensigns Robert Anderson and Garrett Fisher of the 55th and Ensign Christopher Pauli of the 60th. Both of the Frenchmen acting as guides—St. Martin and Baby—were with Lieutenant Brown's advance squad.

It was not quite 3 A.M. when the east gate of the fort opened quietly and the detachment filed out, two abreast. The scarlet coats looked maroon dark in the wan, cloud-filtered moonlight and each man carried a saber in his scabbard and musket with fixed bayonet in his hands. Though silence was desired, there was the distant rattling of sabers at each step and the measured thud of many feet.

They marched in a column of twos, passing numerous French houses fronting on the road until within a half mile or less of the bridge, at which time platoons were formed and the march continued six abreast. Not a sound or movement came from the darkness around them and this, more than anything else, worried Robert Rogers. To his Ranger sergeant he whispered. "We're in trouble. Pass the word to watch me and follow orders when it breaks. Damn me, if I don't think we're walking right into an ambuscade."

Far up in front, Lieutenant Brown led his vanguard onto the bridge and, though they stepped quietly, there was a hollow muted drumming of the feet and a faint creaking of timbers. A bit over half the bridge was behind them when Brown felt an agonizing pain as a lead ball plunged through his thigh and tumbled him. It had come from Pontiac's weapon and in that instant the silence ended. The night was rent by the explosions of scores of guns and men screaming, shouting, cursing. War shrieks split the air and a half dozen or more men dropped and lay still upon the bridge, while others fell into the water below.

With chain reaction, the firing sprang up all down the line of men, with bursts of rifle fire coming from the deeper shadows among the trees and ditches, from beside buildings and behind fences, and all of it being answered in like terms from the road. A dreadful confusion momentarily gripped the detachment until the cries of the officers could be heard above the tumult.

Brown, with the help of Baby on one side and St. Martin on the other, hopped and dragged his way back toward the main body and some of his men followed. Others plunged on across the bridge and a fair number of troops from the main body thundered across after them. The rush surprised many of the Ottawas and Chippewas hiding in the parallel ridges and a sizable portion of them broke and ran; but more than enough did not.

In the main body, Major Rogers had been ready. His eyes had flitted from one piece of cover to another as they marched and at the moment of attack his glance was on the house belonging to Jacques Campeau.

"To the house!" he bellowed, flinging himself in that direction in a low run.

The Rangers followed him and, on getting under cover there, began throwing down a covering fire for the troops and keeping them from being hit so hard on that flank.

As Lieutenant Brown had been hit, so too did Captain Dalyell take a ball through the thigh, though not as seriously and he did not fall. As he straightened from being spun around by the bullet's impact, he heard a heavy volley come from Captain Grant's rear guard and he called a private to him.

"Run back there to Captain Grant," he said. "We can't be cut off. Tell him to take possession of the houses and fences on his flanks and hold the road open for a retreat. Go!"

The man went, darting nimbly through the firing troops, hearing the buzzing of balls and the groans of more men being struck as the engagement grew general and even more fierce. He reached Grant as that officer was just ordering his rear guard to advance on the Indians that had fired on them from the flanking darkness there. He nodded as the private relayed the orders and directed his men accordingly.

All up and down the line the soldiers were fighting determinedly. The first deadly confusion caused by the ambush had passed and, with it, whatever momentary panic may have filled the men. Incredibly, though it seemed only minutes had passed, the battle had been going on for more than an hour now, yet they were holding their ground and fighting well. Dalyell, limping his way through them toward the rear to confer with Grant—having left Gray temporarily in charge of the main body—expressed his admiration for them to Jacques Baby, who was helping him. The Frenchman had become separated from St. Martin and had no idea now where his companion was. Captain Grant spotted them coming and ran up to Dalyell.

"What now, Captain?" he said.

Dalyell shook his head, his previously boundless self-assurance no longer evident. "I don't know, Jim. What do you think?"

Grant snorted. He had been opposed to the whole plan in the first place. "By God, Captain, we're going to have to either press on or fall back. We stay here and sure as hell we're going to be surrounded damned quick!"

Dalyell nodded. With each shot being fired his dream of

glory was being punctured. It was dreadfully obvious that not only were they greatly outnumbered by the enemy, they were also in a much more vulnerable position. It would be insanity to either press ahead or remain here. In the first glow of the dawn now lighting the sky through a light fog, he could see scores of men lying dead or wounded. Already many of them had been helped, carried or dragged to the two batteaux and Lieutenant Brehm's boat was just now pushing off with a full load to take them back to the fort. All up and down the line the firing continued with unabated din and the whole business had a queer, dreamlike quality to it.

Dalyell nodded again. "We'll retreat," he said. "I'm going up the line to pass the word. Hold your position here and lay down cover as we come through. Join the forward troops as they pass but, dammit, don't let them panic. A slow retreat, orderly and firing all the way."

With Jacques Baby beside him still, Dalyell limped back through the bloody detachment, pausing at each officer encountered to give him the order for a defensive retreat to begin. He noted with approval that Rogers's Rangers were still pouring out a good covering fire from the house where they had taken refuge. With frequent pauses, it took Dalyell the better part of half an hour to regain his former lead position with the main body and it was another fifteen or twenty minutes after that before those men of the vanguard who were able had fallen back to rejoin the front of the main body. On the bridge and under it there were bodies, some on the banks, some still on the planking, others in the water. And the flowing of their life's blood into the muddy little stream caused it to pinken and, in the process, lose its name. Most of the survivors, not knowing in the first place that this watercourse was named Parent's Creek, were already calling it Bloody Run among themselves. It could never have another name for them, not after what was happening here.

By now, though the sun had not yet entirely burned away the light fog, it was full daylight. The Indian force had, with approaching light, fallen back to more distant cover but there had been no slackening in their gunfire. With the survivors of the vanguard and those of the main body who had crossed the bridge now reunited with the detachment, Captain Dalyell raised his voice in a call heard well above the din.

"Retreat!" he shouted. "Orderly retreat! Fire and fall back, reload and fire again. Orderly retreat!"

It was not all that simple. Though the men kept their heads and followed these orders, a bottleneck developed. A large group of Indians had taken a strong position in the cellar excavation being dug for a new house and behind a pile of cordwood adjacent to it. From here they poured out such a concentrated fire that the main body of troops was effectively stopped in their retreat. For nearly an hour the battle raged here, with great havoc being wrought on the troops and little, if any, damage being done to their adversaries. It was clear that before the retreat could continue, they would have to be routed out with a determined charge, and Dalyell decided to lead it. He called Baby to him and asked if there was another house toward the rear which Grant might take and hold to cover the retreat, and Baby nodded.

"All right," Dalyell said, "go back there and tell him to occupy it. Show him the right one."

Baby nodded and, joining the handful of men slipping past this bottleneck, sprinted toward the rear. As he did so, Dalyell, his right trouser leg greatly stained by his own blood, called Captain Gray to him, conferred for a moment and then they split and formed the men for a charge. Dalyell may have been blinded by his own ambitions, but he was not without courage. Limping very badly, he nevertheless was a dozen feet in front of his men, saber raised, leading the charge when several bullets struck him simultaneously—one in the head and two in the chest—killing him instantly.

Captain Gray moved up to take the command and continue the charge. He was struck almost immediately by a ball which shattered his shoulder, spun him around and slammed him to the ground. Lieutenant John Luke, too, took a bullet in his side and fell. But the men coming behind them did not falter and the Indians in the excavation and behind the woodpile abruptly broke and ran.

Now the way was clear and the retreat renewed as Captain Gray, Lieutenant Luke and Lieutenant Brown were carried to the batteau of Lieutenant Abbott, which was still being loaded with wounded and dead. The body of Captain James Dalyell was not among those recovered.

Suddenly Robert Rogers and his Rangers found themselves isolated in the house, the retreat having passed them by. Gunfire was coming at them from all sides now and they were in extreme jeopardy. Without help they were sure to be lost.

"Captain!" Lieutenant George McDougall, who had been with Dalyell and Gray in the main body of troops, now rushed up to James Grant. "Captain!" he said again, "Dalyell's dead. Gray's badly wounded and on Abbott's boat. You're in command onw."

Grant nodded, not pleased. He had no time even to reply before Lieutenant Edward Blain came running up with word of Major Rogers and his men being cut off and pinned down in the Campeau house. Grant looked around, saw Lieutenant Brehm's batteaux coming upstream again for the third time from the fort and ran over to the shore, waving him in. When he was close enough, Grant called an order to him, pointing at the distant house.

"Brehm, move up as close as you can opposite that house. The Rangers are boxed in there. Lay down some cover with your swivel to give the major and his men an opportunity to get out."

He turned away, saw Ensign Christopher Pauli and ran up to him. "Mister Pauli, take twenty men back up and occupy that cellar excavation to fire cover for the Rangers while they retreat."

Pauli bobbed his head and raced off, gathering men to go with him. Grant paid no more attention to him and was already engaged in setting up several more parties of twenty men each at intervals along the road to cover the retreat. The main body of troops was now nearly halfway back to the fort.

Soon came the thumping of Brehm's bow-mounted swivel, and shortly after that Rogers and his men, bent low and running rapidly and erratically, came down the road. Pauli's fire held back any would-be Indian followers and he and his men joined the Rangers as they passed.[128] One by one they ran by the covering parties and one by one those parties joined them. It was a beautifully executed retreat, made without further loss. The gates of the fort opened to receive them as they approached and an abundance of covering fire—both rifle and cannon—now came from the fort itself under Gladwin's direction. In another fifteen minutes they were inside the walls and the gates were shut and locked behind them.

The Battle of Bloody Run was over.

From the onset it had been a lopsided affray and the battle statistics reflected that fact. Among Pontiac's entire force, seven warriors had been killed and an even dozen were wounded. The English were not so fortunate. Twenty-three men, including three who died after reaching the fort, were killed. Thirty-eight other soldiers were wounded, some of them very seriously.[129]

And Captain James Dalyell, who had yearned for fame, had found it in a way he had not envisioned. The Indians, returning to the battle scene to scalp those bodies not recovered by the English, discovered among them the body of Dalyell. Hooting savagely, they dragged it back to their camp, cut out the heart and ate it, decapitated the carcass and, after taking the scalp, impaled the young officer's head on a sharpened pole before Pontiac's lodge.

[*July 31, 1763—Sunday, 8:00 P.M.*]

Badly frightened now of Pontiac, who had become something more than they had anticipated, the anti-English Frenchmen of Detroit saw no way to decline his invitation to a great victory feast to be held just outside his camp, which was once again bustling with squaws and children.

The Indians were more than merely jubilant over their triumph and, though they had no liquor to drink, they were drunk with their achievement. Much of the afternoon had been spent in the preparation of this feast of fish and fowl and young beef and it was now, just before dusk, that the Frenchmen, having somewhat reservedly congratulated Pontiac on the victory, finally finished eating their share of the repast.

Still maintaining the elaborate deception they had been perpetrating on him—though not quite so enthusiastically of late—the Frenchmen had told Pontiac that the King of France would be greatly pleased and impressed with the accomplishment of the Indians in general and the Ottawa war chief in particular. They added that now surely all Indians would gladly fall under his leadership.

Among the guests was the dapper Pierre Descompts Labadie[130] and when the meal was concluded Pontiac walked beside him, grinning hugely, optimistic again for the future, aware that his prestige had increased enormously, immensely proud of himself.

"You liked the feast?" he asked Labadie. "The roasted birds and young beef and the fish?"

Labadie nodded and Pontiac threw back his head and laughed uproariously, the white crescent nose ornament bouncing furiously as he did so. Unable to comprehend the amusement, Labadie allowed the chief to lead him to the edge of the camp to where there was a large sack on the ground under a tree.

"Here," said Pontiac, "is the fine young beef you have eaten!"

He upended the sack and out tumbled the heads of several of the slain English soldiers. Pontiac then roared with laughter again as Pierre Descompts Labadie became an extremely sick man.

The expression on the face of Sir Jeffrey Amherst was one of murderous anger as he swiftly wrote out the orders under which he was sending another reinforcement detachment to Detroit. It had only been with the greatest of difficulty that he had induced one hundred previously discharged men to reenlist in a company to be headed by Captain Valentine Gardiner.

His extra effort to find these men had been instigated early this afternoon when an express had brought him the horrifying message from Detroit that the former commander and first officer there, Captain Donald Campbell, had been deliberately, cold-bloodedly killed during an unspeakable mutilation of his body.

Now it was nearing midnight and the company was up to strength, its captain standing by for his orders. Several pages had already been filled under Amherst's pen and at this time he concluded with the stark admonition:

You may tell your men and also the officers and rank and file of the other posts you pass, especially those of the Detroit itself, that I personally shall pay a reward of £100 to the man who shall kill the chief of the Chippewas who butchered Captain Campbell. Further, you are hereby ordered to observe that the Senecas and the Indians of the Lakes are to be treated not as a generous enemy, but as the vilest race of beings that ever infested the earth, and whose riddance from it must be esteemed a meritorious act, for the good of mankind. You will therefore take no prisoners, but put to death all that fall into your hands of the nations who have so unjustly and cruelly committed depredations.

This was the sixth day of the siege of Fort Pitt by the combined forces of the Shawnees, Delawares, the Hurons called Wyandots from the Sandusky Bay area, some Senecas, a few Cayugas, and a large body of Ottawas who had joined this group three days ago. All during this period bands of marauding warriors had arrived here until now few war parties were still out ravaging the settlements. Somewhere around five hundred Indians had gathered here to help fling their hatred at Fort Pitt. For five days and five nights they had poured an unceasing rain of gunfire upon the fort, interspersed with times when great flights of their fire arrows were lofted at the place. But the Indians were held at such a considerable distance by the fort's return gunfire that few of the fire arrows even reached the walls, much less soared over them and into the buildings inside. On the whole, the defenses of Fort Pitt were very good and the Indian attackers had made little headway in their efforts.

Now, near noon of this sixth day, a pair of Shawnees astride horses trotted into the main camp of the Indians, about two miles from the fort. Within minutes of their arrival, runners were on their way from there to fetch in the various chiefs for a council. The afternoon was still new when the council convened.

The two warriors who had come were not the first Indian messengers to arrive at this camp with news about the movement of Colonel Bouquet's army. They were, however, the bearers of news that had been anticipated for some time; news that would now divert their attention and end this fruitless siege against Fort Pitt.

The word they brought was this: Bouquet's army of less than five hundred men had rested at Fort Bedford for three days. On July 28 they struck out to the westward, guided by a band of frontiersmen. Little sniping from unexpected quarters had been possible for the Indians watching the army's move, mainly because of these sharp-eyed frontiersmen whom Bouquet had put far out in front and on either flank of the marching redcoats.

Now the army was less than a day's march from Fort Ligonier. That they would arrive there sometime in the morning was obvious, just as it was equally certain that they would not remain there long. Perhaps they would stay there the remainder of that day and overnight, but surely no more than that. The post was hardly big enough as it was to accommodate its own garrison and the refugees which were already filling it. Yes, undoubtedly the army would pause, but only briefly. Then it would hurry on to reach Fort Pitt.

Between Fort Ligonier and Fort Pitt lay a rough, hilly country full of rocky defiles and forest growth and ideal for setting up an ambush. With an Indian force just about equaling in number the size of this army, it would be a simple matter to intercept the line of march, set up an ambush, kill as many as possible in those first important moments of the attack, surround the rest and then methodically destroy them to the last man. That was precisely the plan agreed upon now. The siege was lifted and Fort Pitt was left in the midst of an uneasy, unexpected silence.

The entire body of Indians began moving through the forest, heading east.

[August 2, 1763—Tuesday]

Captain Simeon Ecuyer changed position in his desk chair and winced a little at the jagged streak of pain which shot up his leg from the arrow wound in his calf. It was ironic, to his way of thinking, that Fort Pitt should fall under siege to a horde of bloodthirsty Indians for the better part of six days and that of only seven persons injured of the entire garrison, the worst wound had been inflicted upon its commanding officer. He chuckled. It would make an interesting story to tell, years from now.

The breaking off of the siege and the withdrawing of the Indians had come as a surprise yesterday. That they were completely gone there was little doubt. The lookouts on the ramparts had used spyglasses to watch the long trains of the Indian horses, loaded with supplies, disappearing on the trails leading eastward. Yet now was no time for carelessness, and Ecuyer had issued orders that the gates were to remain locked and no one was to venture out of the fort except with his personal permission. There was always the possibility that this wholesale withdrawal was nothing more than a ruse to draw them out.

Nevertheless, Ecuyer was relieved they were gone and he felt quite confident that it was no ruse. His relief was tempered to some extent by a feeling of guilt, however, since logic dictated that the Indians must have gone eastward to cut off some reinforcement on its way here. He wished his comrades luck, whoever they might be, and wondered if it would be safe to attempt getting an express through to Bedford or Carlisle. So many of them in the past had not gotten through and he hated to risk more, yet Bouquet should be informed of these developments. He decided he would chance it once more.

Gathering together all the letters and dispatches which were to be sent, he included a report to Bouquet which he had not finished writing. Now, before putting them all together in a packet, he decided he would jot a few more paragraphs onto the report. Dipping his pen he paused a moment, tapped off the excess drop of ink and then wrote, in French as he usually did:

August 2, 1763

Sir:

The siege was lifted a little time after noon yesterday and the Indians shortly afterward were observed leaving with their baggage in the direction of Ligonier. I hope all is secure in that direction. We here came through without serious hurt. The Indians were quite a few in number and there seemed to be more at the end of the siege than at the beginning. They were all well under cover and so were we. They did us no harm; nobody killed, seven wounded, and I myself slightly. Their attack lasted five days and five nights. We are certain of having killed or wounded twenty of them, without reckoning those we could not see. I let nobody fire till he had marked his man; and not an Indian could show his nose without being pricked by a bullet, for I have some good shots here . . . Our men are doing admirably, regulars and the rest. All that they ask is to go out and fight. I am fortunate to have the honor of commanding such brave men.

I only wish the Indians had ventured an assault. They would have remembered it to the thousandth generation! . . . I forgot to tell you that they threw fire arrows to burn our works, but mostly they could not reach the buildings, nor even the rampart. Only two war arrows came into the fort, one of which had the insolence to make free with my left leg . . .

[August 5, 1763—Friday]

Colonel Henry Bouquet was reasonably sure that tomorrow morning he would be dead. He accepted the likelihood of it calmly, though not fatalistically. At the moment, like the majority of his men, he was just too fatigued for it to make much of an impact on him. The wonder of it all was that he was not already stiffening with the onslaught of rigor mortis.

Here and there in the growing darkness surrounding his tent he could hear the occasional crash of a musket, but nothing like the hellish fire there had been earlier. But what was worse, now that it had become relatively still, he could hear the agonized groaning and sobbing rising from his men and this was the sound which disturbed him most.

Well, with death so imminent, the least he could do was write one last letter to General Amherst to let him know what had happened. Possibly one of the frontiersmen who had been acting as guides and scouts could manage to slip away unseen and get the message through. He doubted it, but at least he would write and send it and perhaps, in this one case, luck would be on their side.

He grunted faintly as he straightened his back, trying to relieve the deep ache between his shoulder blades, to relax the muscles which had too long been drawn tight with tension. Then he reached into his personal effects kit and began extracting writing materials while at the same time going over in his mind how this whole hideous situation had come about and what now lay ahead.

The first problem that had faced him, other than the routine ones of assembling the men and supplies and transportation needed, had been the unexpected balkiness of George Croghan at Fort Bedford. Probably no other white man in this Pennsylvania wilderness was as familiar with these Indian tribes causing so much trouble here, or could so accurately judge their state of mind and what they would do next as this Indian agent. Bouquet had taken it for granted that Croghan would be accompanying him and the army on the march westward from Fort Bedford to Fort Ligonier and then on to Fort Pitt. Croghan, however, had absolutely refused.

"They ain't no use in the world of me going with you, Colonel," he had drawled. "Firstways, I been feelin' poorly an' I ain't much in no frame of mind for traipsing all the way out to Pitt with you. They jest ain't no need for it 'cause, secondways, I done my working 'fore this whole damned business started, though I might as well not've done it, for all the attention Gen'ral Amherst give what I reported and recommended.

"Colonel," he added, cutting off some comment Bouquet was beginning to interject, "they ain't no negotiation going on now with the tribes and they ain't apt to be, since both sides is plumb itchin' to fight a war. Why, hell, even if we got some of the Indians to hold back and help us agin the others, the gen'ral wouldn't hold still for it. He aims to get blood out of 'em all. By God, he won't even take the help of Provincials 'cause as he puts it, they ain't trained soldiers. Now what kind of figuring is that? And jest so's my not going can't be held up an' used to show I ain't doing my duties, by God, I done resigned from the Indian service! I got affairs what need tending to in London an' I aim to go there 'fore this year's out."

Nothing Bouquet could say would make Croghan change his mind, so he had coldly asked the frontiersman to put his refusal in writing. George Croghan was glad to do so and in the subsequent letter he gave to Bouquet he added:

> . . . and seven tribes in Canada have offered their services to act with the King's troops; but the General seems determined to neither accept of Indians' services, nor provincials' . . . I have resigned out of the service, and will start for England about the beginning of December. Sir Jeffrey Amherst would not give his consent; so I made my resignation in writing and give my reasons for doing so. Had I continued, I could be of no more service than I have been these eighteen months past, which was none at all, as no regard was had to any intelligence I sent, no more than to my opinion.

The upshot of the whole matter was that when the army marched out of Fort Bedford eight days ago, Croghan had not accompanied them. Bouquet's force had covered the fifty-mile distance to Fort Ligonier in good time and without incident. If anything, Indian sign seemed less prevalent than it had been around Carlisle, Shippensburg or Fort Bedford.

Lieutenant Archibald Blane had been delighted at the army's arrival on July 2. The colonel was equally pleased and relieved to find that the thirty Highlanders he had sent ahead had reached this fort safely and were now rejoined with the force. More than anything else, however, he was greatly worried about the state of Fort Pitt. It had been a month now since he had received any word at all from Captain Simeon Ecuyer and Bouquet knew that if it had been possible to get a message through, Ecuyer would have seen it was done. Blane, here at Ligonier, knew no more about what was going on at Pitt than his colonel, so it was apparent that haste was requisite for the relief of that place. Even now, though he could barely conceive of it, Fort Pitt might already have been taken.

Not quite two days of rest at Ligonier was all that Bouquet felt he could give his troops and very early yesterday morning, leaving behind all their oxen and wagons so as to make better time, they had left the little fort, Bouquet in the lead and followed by his troops and three hundred and forty packhorses laden primarily with flour, plus a small herd of cattle. All through the day the army of less than five hundred men had marched, but it was rough going and only ten or eleven miles was traversed. As camp was pitched last night, Bouquet had studied the maps he had of the terrain which lay ahead. He hadn't liked the looks of it at all. Another twenty miles ahead, more or less, was a stream called Turtle Creek. The trail ran parallel to it for a fair distance, with steep hills on both sides. It looked like an ideal place for an ambush to be set up. If the army continued traveling as it was, they would reach it about nightfall. Bouquet felt it would be much too risky to establish a camp there, yet knew that his men and animals could not continue much farther than that without rest. A few miles on this side of that Turtle Creek pass, however, was a smaller stream called Bushy Run. By moving along well, the army should be able to reach that point by early afternoon. That was good. Bouquet decided he could march them that far, allow them to stop, eat and rest there for three or four hours, and then start marching again. By moving on forced march under cover of darkness, they might be able to pass the dangerous Turtle Creek area without being attacked.

This plan resolved on, Bouquet had turned in for the night and just after dawn today the tents were struck and he had the army on the march again. It was rugged terrain to say the least—steep hills, deep ravines, dense forest and brush. The army marched at a steadily rapid pace and at one o'clock this afternoon Bouquet had gotten the cheering news from one of his frontiersmen scouts that they were now only about a mile away from Bushy Run, where he proposed resting his troops.

And then had come the shots.

With startling abruptness, the tired advance guard found itself under a hot firing coming from ambush. Immediately Bouquet ordered the two forward companies ahead to support the advance guard. They raced to the scene but instead of their approach causing the attackers to scatter, the firing became heavier.

With the first shooting, Bouquet had assumed it was just the hit-and-run attack of a small party. Now, however, it was becoming evident that this was approaching the magnitude of a major attack and so he swiftly halted the convoy, ordered the troops into battle lines and then issued the command for a general charge. With fixed bayonets the army plunged forward and, as anticipated, the enemy gave way before it. Hooting and screaming, the Indian attackers broke and ran and the troops yelled loudly, triumphantly, with their success. It was a short-lived triumph. The ruse had worked perfectly and now the Indians had drawn the whole army precisely into the midst of its major ambush.[131]

Suddenly from the rear and both flanks there came a

deafening cacophony of new war shrieks and a blistering fire erupted from the trees. The noise to the rear was especially loud and it became immediately obvious that the convoy was being very harshly assaulted. At once an order was shouted by Bouquet to fall back to protect it. The Indians tried to prevent it but, at the cost of numerous casualties, the army accomplished it. The whole field of conflict had become one of inconceivable confusion. An acrid smoke of gunpowder fogged the area and all eyes were soon red and running. The crackle of gunfire was constant and, with it, the whinnying and snorting and stamping of well over three hundred fear-crazed packhorses, the cries and screams of pain or fear or anger from the soldiers and the unnerving shrieks of the attackers.

Despite the confusion, Bouquet managed to form the army into a dense circle around the horses and pour into the surrounding woods a continuing fire very nearly as heavy as that which they were receiving, though hardly with as great effectiveness. Time and again at different places along the perimeter there would come an onslaught as the attackers bunched together and rushed the line of redcoats to break the ring, but time and again they were driven back by volleys of shots and well-directed bayonet charges.

The Indians did not press these bursting attacks. They were simply a harrying tactic, meant to force the army to wear itself out, keep it on edge, expend its ammunition and, if possible, instill panic. As soon as the redcoats had braced to meet and repulse these smaller attackers, the Indians would bound away and disappear within the thick forest, only to appear again an instant later at some other point of the encirclement to try again. They moved so swiftly, hit and fled so suddenly, that their losses were slight in the extreme. but the same could not be said for the army. A terrible toll was being taken of the soldiers and the ground was strewn with the scarlet of fallen men.

On and on through a sweltering afternoon the battle raged, with Bouquet directing operations at all quarters, meeting attack here, repulsing attackers there, encouraging his men, issuing commands, seemingly indefatigable in his efforts. There was little water and tongues became thick and swollen. Lips cracked and eyes burned and the senses were numbed with the sound and fury of the battle. Hour after hour the soldiers, who were already weary when the battle began, fought doggedly while around them their companions were struck by bullets or arrows and fell.

Not until an hour ago, at about eight o'clock, as the sun set and dusk began filtering through the woods, had the attack eased and then nearly stopped. Here and there shots were still being fired, but even they were dwindling away. Yet, not a man in this army had any illusion that the enemy had withdrawn. As soon as it became light enough again, they knew, the battle would resume.

It seemed apparent, considering the English losses during this seven-hour battle today, that by now the Indians outnumbered them slightly. Few of the men had any real hope of surviving when the battle resumed in the morning; yet Colonel Bouquet moved steadily among them, praising them for their courage and stamina, trying as best he knew to assure them that on the morrow the tide would turn and the attackers would be beaten back and scattered. The words were hollow and accepted without comment. The men were too exhausted, too shocked, too emotionally drained to do more than sit or crouch or lay where they were, too tired to even exert themselves enough to eat.

Bouquet was no less tired than anyone else, but he continued to do what could be done to improve their situation. Already in the neighborhood of sixty soldiers had been killed, along with several officers. That amounted to an eighth of the army gone. A place was prepared at Bouquet's order in the center of the camp and the dead and wounded were brought here. Flour sacks were removed from the horses and used to erect a fortification of sorts around these men. There was little medication, little treatment offered. The wounded were made as comfortable as possible and the order went out for those unhurt to see to their weapons and their ammunition and then rest as well as they could, and to sleep if possible. A guard detail was posted at close intervals on the perimeter to sound alarm if any sort of nighttime attack was launched, but it was not expected.

There was little sleeping to be enjoyed. The same thought seemed to be in every mind. The thought that only eight years ago another British army, vastly superior in numbers and arms to themselves was annihilated hardly thirty miles from this spot; an army which, like themselves, had been en route to the forks of the Ohio; an army which, like them, had been attacked by Indians; an army which, though equipped with much artillery and far outnumbering the enemy, had been utterly destroyed as a fighting force, a huge percentage of its men killed, along with its commander, General Edward

Braddock.[132] The thought of it was hardly inducive to promoting sleep or rest.

And so now, in his tent and writing by the light of a single, well-shielded candle, Henry Bouquet was penning what he was sure would be his last letter to General Amherst . . . or to anyone else.

Camp at Edge Hill, 26 miles
from Fort Pitt, 5th August 1763

Sir:

The second instant the troops and convoy arrived at Ligonier, where I could obtain no intelligence of the enemy; the expresses sent since the beginning of July having either been killed or obliged to return, all passes being occupied by the enemy. In this uncertainty, I determined to leave all the wagons with the powder and a quantity of stores and provisions at Ligonier. And on the 4th, proceeded with troops and about 340 horses loaded with flour.

I intended to have halted today at Bushy Run (a mile beyond this camp) and, after having refreshed the men and horses, to have marched in the night over Turtle Creek, a very dangerous defile of several miles commanded by high and craggy hills. But at one o'clock this afternoon, after a march of 17 miles, the savages suddenly attacked our advanced guard, which was immediately supported by the two Light Infantry companies of the 42nd Regiment, who drove the enemy from their ambuscade and pursued them a good way. The savages returned to the attack and the fire being obstinate on our front and extending along our flanks, we made a general charge with the whole line to dislodge the savages from the heights, in which attempt we succeeded, without obtaining by it any decisive advantage, for as soon as they were driven from one post they appeared on another until, by continual reinforcements, they were at last able to surround us and attack the convoy left in our rear. This obliged us to march back to protect it. The action then became general and though we were attacked on every side and the savages exerted themselves with uncommon resolution, they were constantly repulsed with loss. We, also, suffered considerably. Captain Lieutenant Graham and Lieutenant James McIntosh of the 42nd are killed, and Captain Graham wounded of the Royal American Regiment. Lieutenant Dow, who acted as ADQMG [Adjutant Quartermaster General] *is shot through the body. Of the 77th, Lieutenant Donald Campbell and Mr. Peebles, a volunteer, are wounded.*

Our loss in men, including Rangers and drivers, exceeds sixty killed or wounded.

The action has lasted from one o'clock until night and we expect to begin again at daybreak. Whatever our fate may be, I thought it necessary to give your Excellency this early information that you may, at all events, take such measures as you will think proper with the Provinces for their own safety and effectual relief of Fort Pitt; as, in the case of another engagement, I fear insurmountable difficulties in protecting and transporting our provisions, being already so much weakened by the losses of this day in men and horses, besides the additional necessity of carrying the wounded, whose situation is truly deplorable.

I cannot sufficiently acknowledge the constant assistance I have received from Major Campbell during this long action, nor express my admiration of the cool and steady behavior of the troops, who did not fire a shot without orders and drove the enemy from their posts with fixed bayonets.

> *I have the Honor to be*
> *with Great Respect*
> *Your most obedient &*
> *most Humble Servant*
> *H. Bouquet*

His Excellency
General Amherst

CHAPTER X

COLONEL HENRY BOUQUET was far more concerned than he let on to his men. Better than anyone else, he knew that the position of his army here at Edge Hill was vulnerable. The ring of men, their guns bristling with bayonets, presently encircled the wounded soldiers and those pack-horses not already killed during yesterday's battle. These soldiers might be able to hold off the attacking Indians for a while, but then what? There were no reinforcements which could be counted upon to come to this army's aid. Whatever needed to be done would have to be done by the men he had right here, or else the whole army would fall.

Most serious at the moment was the desperate need for water being suffered by all the men, especially the wounded. If he could successfully move the army just one more mile ahead to Bushy Run, then at least they would be able to satisfy their needs for water and perhaps be better able to hold off the attackers. But there was no way to move now without dangerously exposing their flanks and rear. It was a grave predicament and Bouquet had little faith that anyone in this force of his would survive to see today's sunset.

Just the first faint streaks of dawn were beginning to show in the east now and, as Bouquet expected, the Indians resumed their attack. He had hoped they would have become overconfident enough to mount an all-out assault, because in such case the army could pour a concentrated fire into their ranks and hurt them badly. Obviously the Indians knew this just as well and they did not. They had the army tightly boxed here in a rather exposed position and the advantages were all theirs. The army was not only weakened by the death or injury of many of its men from the previous day's battle, these very men surviving were also extremely weary from the long march here the day before, prior to the battle, and by the fact that there had been little if any sleep among them all through this night just ending. Therefore, knowing that the victory must eventually be theirs, the enemy fought cautiously, clinging to cover, rarely exposing themselves, making their shots at the huddled redcoats tell.

A dozen, a score, even more of the English fell as the sky became brighter and the gunfire increased from the Indians. Most of those newly fallen were wounded, but a fair percentage of them were killed and now the situation was becoming as perilous as it had yet been. Bouquet, pacing the inner circumference of his circle of men, studied the situation with a calculating eye. The army simply could not take much more of this. Already there was the growing danger of the circle caving in on itself and if that happened, if the circle was broken, the Indians would rush in and that would be the beginning of the end for them all.

Bouquet stopped and considered. Could not this very fact be used to lure the Indians into exposing themselves? The more he thought of it, the more he felt that the maneuver might at least stand a chance of succeeding. Hurriedly he conferred with Major John Campbell and several other officers, explaining what he had in mind and how the maneuver should be carried out to be most effective.

The sun was up by now and the Indians were pressing their advantage to the utmost, stepping up their already advanced firing at the encircled soldiers and howling with voices in which the knowledge of victory forthcoming was implicit. With the better visibility, the Indian fire was even more devastating. Many of the horses, hidden as well as possible behind the barricade of flour sacks that had been erected to protect them and the wounded men, were nevertheless being hit and wounded. Maddened by pain and crazed with fear, four of them here or six there or eight elsewhere would break away, screaming in their terror and gallop through the lines, dashing back and forth through the hail of bullets. The drivers, whose duty it was to keep them under control, had themselves given way to a paralyzing fear and most were now crouched under whatever cover was available, paying no mind to the horses, thinking only of protecting themselves, unhearing of any commands that were shouted at them by the officers.

At ten o'clock just when the circle appeared to be on the verge of collapse, Bouquet gave the signal for the desperate stratagem to be put into effect and at once two companies of infantrymen who had been undergoing the hottest fire turned and fell back into the center of the circle, while the line of men on either side moved and spread out toward one another in what seemed an effort to close the gap as best they could. The line of men still holding was thus not only thinned, the circle was flattened on one side and had obviously become suddenly very weak.

It was what the Indians had been waiting for and now, for the first time, they burst from their hiding places in a great body and attacked the line with fantastic energy, continuing to pour in a dreadful fire as they charged and then dropping the emptied weapons and drawing tomahawks or warclubs from their waistbands for the close-in fighting. The line of soldiers fought valiantly, holding their ground and firing until the horde was almost upon them, and then their line parting, splitting, pulling off on each side.

Into the gap the Indians charged. As they did so, the men under Major Campbell abruptly sprang to their feet, having been hidden until now by a slight depression near the break in the circle, which they had gained by moving in a small circle through the wooded hilltop here. They struck the flank of the charging Indians with every bit as much ferocity as the Indians themselves were exhibiting. Dozens of the Indians fell at the first firing and others spun about and began hobbling or dragging themselves painfully away.

Even when those two companies of charging redcoats had expended their shots, they continued their rush with bayonets extended before them. For a moment the Indians held and Bouquet sucked in his breath, fearing that his gamble had failed, but then they suddenly turned and ran. It was exactly what the colonel had anticipated, hoped for, and he was ready for it. Orders had been given for another two companies on the circle to support the men under Major Campbell when they could do so with the most favorable results. This group crouched behind every conceivable bush or tree and now, as the Indians came running back among them, pressed from behind by the bayonet charge of Campbell's men, they leaped up and poured a second withering fusillade into them, equally as destructive as Campbell's had been. The four companies joined and continued driving the now rapidly retreating Indians before them, giving them no opportunity to rally, to stop and reload or do anything more than flee for their lives. The Indian losses were heavy and those not killed or wounded scattered in a hopeless confusion before the rush of the soldiers.

At the other areas of the circle, where Indians were still pinning the English down with their fire under cover, the shooting faltered. As the circle of men suddenly leaped to their feet and came charging toward them, they broke and fled. In a remarkably short time no Indian cries were audible any longer and the only Indians visible were those that had been downed by the effects of Colonel Henry Bouquet's brilliant stratagem. About sixty of the Indians had been killed, including the Delaware chief named Kittiskung and his son, Wolf. Only one Indian was taken alive and he was stood up and shot to death immediately.

The Indians continued their flight, abandoning the attack entirely, and so almost certain defeat had, in the space of minutes, been turned into a victory for the English, but one which Bouquet knew had been bought dearly, with the lives of eight officers and one hundred and fifteen rank and file dead or wounded.

Now, expecting they would be attacked again as soon as the Indians regrouped, Bouquet ordered the flour destroyed and the remaining packhorses to be used to convey the dead and wounded. In a very short time the whole army was on the move toward Bushy Run and covered this remaining mile without further trouble. A camp was quickly made there, but even before they were settled or suitable fortifications thrown up, the Indians attacked again. It was a dispirited attack at best and when the infantry retaliated by furiously charging into them, they dispersed—but again it was at the cost of more soldiers killed and wounded.

The situation was still not good, but at least it was better now, in the afternoon, than it had been at dawn. For one thing, now they had hope; and for another, now there was the much needed water of the stream to supply their needs. A strong guard force was set up and the wounds of the injured were tended to as best as could be done under the circumstances. While this was being accomplished, Bouquet busied himself with the writing of another account to Amherst, to inform the general that they had survived thus far.

Camp at Bushy Run
6th August 1763

Sir:

I had the honor to inform your Excellency in my letter of yesterday of our first engagement with the savages.

We took post last night on the hill where our convoy halted . . . (A commodious piece of ground and just spacious enough for our purpose.) There we encircled the whole and covered our wounded with flour bags.

In the morning the savages surrounded our camp at the distance of about 500 yards and, by shouting and yelping quite round that extensive circumference, thought to have terrified us with their numbers. They attacked us early and under favor of an incessant fire made several bold attempts to penetrate our camp, and though they failed in the effort, our situation was not the less perplexing, have experienced that brisk attacks had little effect upon an enemy who always gave way when pressed and appeared again immediately. Our troops were, besides, extremely fatigued with the long march and as long action of the preceding day, and distressed to the last degree by a total want of water much more intolerable than the Indians' fire.

Tied to our convoy, we could not lose sight of it without exposing it and our wounded to fall prey to the savages who pressed upon us on every side, and to move it was impracticable, having lost many horses and most of the drivers stupefied by fear, hid themselves in the bushes or were incapable of hearing or obeying any orders.

The savages every moment growing more audacious, it was thought proper still to increase their confidence; by that means, if possible, to entice them to come close upon us or stand their ground when attacked. With this view, two companies of Light Infantry were ordered within the circle and the troops on their right and left opened their files and filled up the space, that it might seem they were intended to cover their retreat. The third Light Infantry company, and the grenadiers of the 42nd, were ordered to support the first two companies. This maneuver succeeded to our wish, for the few troops who took possession of the ground lately occupied by the two Light Infantry companies being brought in nearer to the center of the circle, the barbarians mistaking these motions for a retreat, hurried headlong on and, advancing on us with the most daring intrepidity, galled us exceedingly with their heavy fire; but at the very moment that, certain of success, they thought themselves masters of the camp, Major Campbell at the head of the first two companies sallied out from a part of the hill they could not observe, and fell upon their flank. They resolutely returned the fire, but could not stand the irresistible shock of our men who, rushing in among them, killed many of them and put the rest to flight. The orders sent to the other two companies were delivered so timely by Captain Bassett and executed with such celerity and spirit, that the routed savages who happened to run that moment before their front, received their full fire when uncovered by the trees. The four companies did not give them time to load a second time, but pursued them till they were totally dispersed. The left of the savages, which had not been attacked, were kept in awe by the remains of our troops posted on the brow of the hill for that purpose, nor durst they attempt to support or assist their right but, being witness to their defeat, followed their example and fled.

Our brave men disdained so much to touch the dead body of a vanquished enemy, that scarce a scalp was taken except by the rangers and packhorse drivers.

The woods being now cleared, and the pursuit over, the four companies took possession of the hill in our front and as soon as litters could be made for the wounded, the flour and everything destroyed which, for want of horses, could not be carried, we marched without molestation to this camp. After the severe correction we had given the savages a few hours before, it was natural to suppose we should enjoy some rest, but we had hardly fixed our camp when they fired on us again. This was very provoking! However, the Light Infantry dispersed them before they could receive orders for that purpose. I hope we shall be no more disturbed, for if we have another action, we shall hardly be able to carry our wounded.

The behavior of the troops upon this occasion speaks for itself so strongly that for me to attempt their eulogium would but detract from their merit.

> *I have the Honor to be*
> *most respectively*
> *Sir*
> *Your most obedient &*
> *most Humble Servant*
> *Henry Bouquet*

P.S. I have the honor to inclose the return of killed, wounded and missing in the two engagements.

His Excellency
General Amherst

[August 6, 1763—Saturday, 2:00 P.M.]

It was difficult to say who was the most frightened this afternoon as the party of Ottawas entered Montreal with their prisoners—the amazed populace, or the Indians themselves. Several among the Indians had been insisting for the past three our four days that, rather than place themselves in possible jeopardy among the unpredictable English, they should merely set Captain George Etherington and Lieutenant James Gorrell and their respective men of Forts Michilimackinac and Edward Augustus loose to continue the remainder of the journey themselves, while the escort hastened back toward their own country. The lure of reward, however, which had for so long been promised them, overruled the idea.

Now they had arrived in Montreal and the English captives, deeply relieved at being rescued, expressed in the strongest possible terms to General Thomas Gage just how much they owed the Ottawas and how deserving these Indians were of reward. And Gage, who understood the Indian mentality far better than did his superior, took it upon himself to load the Ottawa party down with a lavish supply of goods—even more than they thought they might get. Included in the gifts were foodstuffs, blankets, tools, vermilion, wampum beads, tomahawks, powder and lead. Gage gave this, knowing that Amherst would undoubtedly be angered by it, but feeling nonetheless that the reward was fitting and deserved.

And not far from the military headquarters, the Indian agent, Daniel Claus, was swiftly penning a letter to his supervisor, Sir William Johnson:

6 August 1703

Sir:

   Whilst I am writing this, my landlord tells me that Captain Etherington and Lieutenant Leslye passed the door coming from Michilimackinac who, I heard, with all the traders except one Tracy—who was killed by the enemy Indians—were escorted here by the Ottawas living near that place. I followed them immediately to the governor's and there learned the news of them parts . . . The officers and traders can not say enough of the good behavior of these Ottawas and General Gage is resolved to use and reward them well . . . If the Indians now here leave this place satisfied, it may be of infinite service, which I intend to represent to General Gage, and I believe you will approve of making them handsome presents as an encouragement for their good behavior, and the only means of chastizing those villainous nations who are the occasion of this unhappy event.

I am, Sir, yrs, &ca.
D. Claus

To Sir. Wm. Johnson
*   at Johnson Hall*

It had been an extraordinarily busy day for Major Henry Gladwin and now, athough he wished he could just drop into his bed and sleep the clock around, there were still many things to do. As soon as possible, the *Michigan* would be heading for Niagara again, and he must be sure that it carried along with it all the dispatches which needed to be delivered, all the reports which needed to be made.

He busied himself, therefore, in making out his reports on what had been transpiring here at Detroit, doing so with a great economy of words and lack of extraneous detail. That, he knew, could always come later and could better be presented by some of his officers—Lieutenant James MacDonald, for example—who had more of a flair for writing and who could present a great deal of detail in a more cogent manner than he.

For his part, Gladwin wrote that the schooner *Huron* under Captain Loring had returned to within sight of Detroit yesterday, dropping anchor when the wind failed and remaining in that position throughout the night without being in any manner molested. This morning it had continued to the fort, discharging its cargo of eighty barrels of provisions and a reinforcement of sixty men of the 17th Regiment and the 44th Regiment under Lieutenant John Williams. This further reinforcement now insured that Detroit would not be taken, come what may, and Gladwin was certain that the end of the uprising would not be long in coming after this. On the morrow, the sloop *Michigan* would weigh anchor for Niagara with all the dispatches and carrying along with her all the wounded men from Detroit.

Gladwin next told that the hideously mutilated remains of Captain James Dalyell had been brought to the fort by Jacques Campeau and given burial here; that young John Rutherford, who had been aboard Lieutenant Robertson's boat with Sir Robert Davers when it had been attacked and was the only English survivor of that incident, had escaped from the Indians and made his way by canoe to the sloop and then was brought safely into the fort; that since Dalyell's defeat, some two hundred and fifty Ottawas and Chippewas had been watching the fort from a safe distance each night and firing upon it regularly, though without much success; that he had sent out a detachment of fifty men under Captain Grant under cover of darkness to take post in some houses from which the Indians had been firing upon the fort, but that the Indians had not shown up, indicating that somewhere in the fort there had to be a security leak; and, finally, that at three o'clock this afternoon a Frenchman had arrived at the fort from Michilimackinac to say that Captain Etherington and his men, along with those from Fort Edward Augustus, had been escorted safely away from Montreal by the Ottawas and should be nearly reaching there by now if all went well.

On the whole, the reports were encouraging, emphasizing the fact that Detroit was now felt safe from loss—though admittedly still under siege—and could, it was believed, continue to hold its own until the war was ended. But this did little to cheer Henry Gladwin. More and more he thought of his new wife, of whom he had seen so very little after their wedding before it was time for him to come back to North America. There she sat, waiting for him in England. He yearned deeply to be with her, to doff this redcoated uniform a final time and retain no responsibility greater than that to his own family. He spoke little of this to anyone, but there was one unguarded moment when he allowed his feelings to be exposed as he wrote a brief letter to Sir William Johnson this evening. He sighed deeply as he wrote:

I am brought into a scrape, and left in it; things are expected of me that can't be performed; I wish I had quitted the service seven years ago, and that somebody else commanded here.

[August 7, 1763—Sunday]

From his desk drawer, Sir Jeffrey Amherst removed the stick of sealing wax with which he would seal the letter he had just finished writing to Henry Bouquet. It was characteristic of him, however, that before sealing and dispatching it, he would read it through again to make sure there was nothing of importance he had overlooked telling his most able field commander. He read:

New York, 7th August 1763

Sir

Last night I received your letter of the 26th July and I approve of everything you mentioned to have done for the se-

curity of the communication, and for advancing with the troops under your command, agreeable to my former orders.

The behavior of the Province of Pennsylvania upon this occasion is altogether so very unaccountable that, were the persons who are so much to blame in this affair the only ones who could be the sufferers, I must confess it would be just that they felt the effect of their supineness and timidity, which seem to spring from an obstinacy peculiar to themselves.

I have a letter from Major Campbell concerning the reduced officers of the 42nd and I herewith enclose my answer, open for your perusal. By my other letter which accompanies this, you will be fully informed of my intentions concerning the reduction of that as well as the other corps now with you.

The warrant you have received for holding Courts-Martial makes no alteration in your reporting to me as usual; the like warrants have been sent to all the commanding officers of corps.

I have letters from Major Gladwin of the 8th July. He had baffled all the attempts of the savages, even before the schooner returned with a reinforcement. But all the Upper Posts had been surprised and too many of our people suffered. Major Gladwin sent out a party who pursued the enemy for some distance and killed three (one chief.) But I fear from what he writes me, poor Captain Campbell has been butchered by the villains. Christi, with part of his garrison, was carried to the Detroit, where Pauli and Schlosser likewise were, the former having made his escape, and the latter was delivered up.

Captain Dalyell, with 26 men, had got as far as Presque Isle the 15th July, and the schooner left Niagara the second trip, with a reinforcement of 60 men, besides seamen, with Captain Loring.

I have ordered the 46th Regiment (which arrived here with the other corps from the Havana) to Niagara, and likewise the 80th from Fort William Augustus. The detachment of Royal Americans now at Niagara will advance to Presque Isle on the arrival of the 46th and I shall direct that the whole of the Royal Americans in the Upper Posts are likewise brought to Presque Isle that they may join the battalion at Pittsburgh, where I intend they shall be formed, according to the new establishment, as you will see by my other letter.

I flatter myself that we shall soon be in a condition to punish the barbarians most effectually. I need not repeat to you of my desires that the guilty, in which I include every nation *that has been concerned in this treacherous attempt, who may fall into your hands, may meet with their deserts without delay.*

I have a letter from Mr. Croghan wherein he gives it as his opinion that as soon as you arrive at Fort Pitt, the Delawares and other Indians on this side of the Lakes will remove with their families over the Lakes. My answer is that I wish there was not an Indian settlement within a thousand miles of our country; for they are only fit to live with the inhabitants of the woods, being more nearly allied with the Brute rather than the Human creation. I am, Sir,

Your most obedient Servant,
Jeff: Amherst

Colonel Bouquet

[August 11, 1763—Thursday]

At no time in his past career had such relief been felt by Captain Simeon Ecuyer at Fort Pitt as that which he had experienced yesterday at the arrival of Colonel Henry Bouquet's army here. It was the uncertainty of not knowing what the Indians were up to that had been most undermining, most frightening. Since August 1, when they had suddenly lifted the siege against Fort Pitt and disappeared into the woods to the east, not an Indian had been seen. Fearful of a ruse, however, Ecuyer had kept the fort gates locked and a constant double-strength lookout in effect.

Then, yesterday morning, the Indians had returned, moving toward the west. They moved mainly in a ragged body of about four hundred men and stayed well out of rifle range, but as they passed they howled out the scalp yell and many of them held up their grisly red trophies in triumphant display. Ecuyer had been sure they were going to resume their attack on Fort Pitt, since it seemed obvious that they had defeated whatever force it was they had attacked to the east of here. But the Indians had moved on, crossing the river and disappearing in the west.

The watch had been intensified, but not until several hours more had passed did the watch patrol suddenly shout exultantly. Hobbling on his wounded leg, Ecuyer climbed to the ramparts and saw the most beautiful sight he could imagine—the brilliant red coats of an English army approaching, its banners snapping crisply in the breeze. Many of the men were evidently injured and being transported on horses, so this was obviously the force the Indians had attacked. But they hadn't been victorious after all! They were fleeing from the advance of the army, so there was little wonder now why they hadn't reopened their attack on Fort Pitt.

The gates had been flung wide to welcome the army in and Ecuyer himself limped up to Bouquet, saluted smartly and then shook his superior's hand with an abundance of warmth. They repaired to Ecuyer's quarters and there Bouquet told him of the ambush at Edge Hill and the smaller attack at Bushy Run. Quarters were provided for the men and medical attention immediately given to those needing it. Then, under orders from Bouquet, Major John Campbell, with some of his own men and a reinforcement of rested and eager men from among Ecuyer's force—a total of four hundred soldiers—set out at once to return to Fort Ligonier to escort eastward the women and children at Fort Pitt and then to bring back from Ligonier the remainder of the convoy which had been left there. Little further trouble with the Indians was anticipated, since they had been seen to continue their westward flight, but strong precautionary steps were taken to prevent any possible ambush. Further, Bouquet pointed out that it must be assumed that the small war parties might again begin making forays against easier prey—the settlers of the western Pennsylvania wilderness.

This morning, Colonel Bouquet once again the imposing military figure after a good night's rest, along with a good dinner, breakfast, bath and change of clothing, had written a letter to General Amherst and now he gave it to Ecuyer to look at and then dispatch it to the east. The captain read with interest and approval.

Fort Pitt, 11 August 1763

Sir

We arrived here yesterday without further opposition than scattered shots along the road.

The Delawares, Shawnees, Wyandots and Mingoes[188] had closely beset and attacked this fort from the 27th July to the first instant, when they quitted it to march against us. The boldness of those savages is hardly credible; they had taken posts under the banks of both rivers close to the fort here, where, digging holes, they kept an incessant fire, and threw fire arrows. They are good marksmen and, though our people were under cover, they wounded seven. Captain Ecuyer is wounded in the leg with an arrow.

I would not do justice to that officer should I omit to inform your Excellency that, without engineer or any other ar-

tificers than a few shipwrights, he has raised a parapet of logs round the fort above the old one which, not having been finished, was too low and enfiladed.

He has traced the whole, palisaded the inside of the area, constructed a fire engine and, in short, has taken all the precautions which art and judgment could suggest for the preservation of this post [which was] open on three sides, which had suffered by the floods.

The inhabitants have acted with spirit against the enemy and in the repairs of the fort. Captain Ecuyer expressed an entire satisfaction of their conduct. The artillery and small number of regulars have done their duty with distinction. As nothing more can be done to this post for the present, I send Captain Bassett with my letters to you and an exact report of its actual condition, and to answer any questions you may be pleased to ask him concerning our march and engagements, in which he has been of great service to me. He has been so long in a bad state of health and his disorder increasing on him, that I cannot help recommending him to your Excellency's indulgence. The doctors under whose care he was for a considerable time [said] that nothing but a long course of salt waters was likely to do him any good. I have not yet received any intelligence from Presque Isle and the Detroit, and all the savages beyond this river having now openly declared war against us, it is become impossible for me to procure any intelligence from these posts; and after the heavy loss we have sustained, the troops we have left will barely be sufficient for the service of this department and escorts of provisions.

Major Campbell, with 400 men, goes back to Ligonier to bring up the remains of our convoy; all useless people go down at the same time. The lieutenant and some of the few rangers I had raised for our march have been killed. I write to Captain Ourry to pay the rest off at Bedford and transmit the account of the expense to your Excellency, which I flatter myself you will be pleased to allow.

Unless trusty Indians could be employed, it is very doubtful whether I shall receive your letters, as it is probable the enemy will keep spies upon the road to obtain intelligence of our intentions, and give themselves time to provide for the safety of their families when their own towns will be threatened. Had the Provinces assisted us, this would have been the favorable moment to have crushed the barbarians; a service we cannot effect with our forces alone, the carriage of the wounded, after every action, being a cruel incumberance upon a few troops acting in the woods at a distance from posts.

You will please to observe by the state of our provisions here, that we shall want another supply. I don't expect above twenty thousand weight of flour more from Ligonier, and no meat. I trust the Provinces will furnish the escorts.

At the request of Major Campbell, I have the honor to recommend to your Excellency, Mr. Patrick Balreaves, the eldest lieutenant with the 42nd Regiment, to succeed to the Captain Lieutenancy vacant by the death of Captain Lieutenant Graham, killed the 5th. And if you are pleased to grant that favor to that deserving officer, there will be two vacancies more for which the Major desires I would recommend Lieutenant Charles Menzies and Lieutenant John McIntosh as the two eldest lieutenants here of the second battalion, who choose to remain in full pay.

I cannot omit to mention the only volunteer still with us, Mr. Pallas, [who was] dangerously wounded. I have the honor to be with the greatest respect

Sir

> *Your most obdt. &*
> *most Hmbl Servt*
> *H.B.*

To His Exy. Sir Jeffrey Amherst

[August 17, 1763—Wednesday]

Once again Pontiac oversaw the moving of his camp. Even through the detachment that had been sent against him from Detroit had been soundly defeated, the very fact that it had been sent at all indicated a certain vulnerability of this present camp, despite the intervening swamp.

Therefore, early this morning he had issued the order: the entire camp was to be moved from this location to a new one downstream from Detroit, moving in a wide circle in the woods around Detroit and not stopping until they had reached the banks of the River Rouge, where a permanent village would be reestablished. It was more than just for the possibility of avoiding attack by a detachment sent from the fort. Too easily the fort's vessels had been coming and going. Just four days ago, for example, the two vessels called *Michigan* and *Huron* had weighed anchor and proceeded down the river with impunity to Lake Erie and by now they were well on their way to Niagara. In fact, with the rather strong west wind that had been blowing, they were likely nearing the place already. That was not good. Far too many reinforcements had come to Detroit as it was and Pontiac now meant to see to it personally that no more ships were allowed to pass up the river to Detroit. He would capture them if he could, for the provisions and arms aboard, but if he could not capture them, then they would be utterly destroyed and every man aboard them slain.

The Ottawa war chief had now accepted the inevitability that he could not take Detroit, but this did not mean that he could not cut its supply line, sever its communication, and destroy any ships or men who would come to offer assistance. And even if his forces, in the end, be themselves forced to quit this war, they would have impressed upon the English that they were not a soft people to whom anything could be done. When future Indian demands were made, such demands would be very swiftly met or there would be continued harassment of the English cause in this country.

This was a promise which Pontiac now made to himself.

[*August 27, 1763—Wednesday, 3:00 P.M.*]

The English trader, John Welch, was greatly tired of his captivity and earnestly wished he could escape. Several times he had devised plans to do so, as others had done before him, but always something had intervened to balk him. Besides, he was not a terribly brave man and considered it much wiser and healthier to undergo the inconveniences of captivity than to make an escape attempt which, if it failed, would almost certainly result in his death.

On the whole, his captivity had not been excessively uncomfortable. Because of his cooperation with Mini Chene when Fort Miamis and Fort Ouiatenon had been taken, he had been reasonably well treated. His trade goods and peltry had been taken, of course, and he doubted that he would ever get restitution for them, but at least he was alive. A fair number of the English traders, from what he heard, had not been so fortunate.

The journey with Chene and Godefroy to the Illinois country had at least been rather interesting and Welch had even seen some things which suggested that when this present trouble died away, he might extend his trading enterprises further to the west. He had hoped, of course, that Chene would leave him with the French garrison at Fort de Chartres, but such had not been the case and so he had been forced to journey back to Detroit with his captors.

That was when things had stopped being so comfortable. The Indians had not been pleased to see him, an English trader, being held captive by Chene. Pontiac, in his now more than ever imperious manner, personally demanded possession of the captive and Chene had surrendered him. Since then, Welch had been cuffed about a bit, insulted in various ways, and he had been the recipient of some rather frightening threats. All this he accepted as philosophically as possible, telling himself that all he had to do was endure and it would soon be all over.

It was to be all over for John Welch much sooner than he expected. Once again the Indians were beginning to turn on Pontiac, castigating him for leading them into this war in the first place, threatening again to desert him if some sign was not forthcoming that they were doing the right thing. Pontiac knew what they needed was to be bolstered again, to have their blood heated with hatred for the English and a new desire kindled within them to seek blood. An object was needed to instill such feeling, and John Welch would suit the purpose admirably.

The trader was not particularly afraid this afternoon when they took him from the dwelling in which he had been kept prisoner and placed him under the watchful eye of three warriors. He was not particularly afraid when he was cuffed around a little more than usual. He was not particularly afraid when a large post was sunk to an upright position in the ground of a clearing and a wide circle of kindling laid around it and numerous oak and hickory sticks placed atop the kindling. He merely thought through all these preparations that he was going to be forced to watch an execution.

As a matter of fact, John Welch did not really begin to become alarmed until now, with crushing impact, he suddenly realized that all this preparation was for himself. In succession as a rawhide loop was tied around his neck and his clothing stripped from him, his hands bound behind his back and the loose end of the neck loop attached to the post so that he could walk in a circle around the post but not get away from it, he struggled, threatened, implored, reasoned, begged and wept, but it was to no avail.

It was not until dusk that the ring of firewood ten or twelve feet from the post was lighted and the torture began. But it was not until the first light of dawn that the spark of life finally deserted the eyeless, partially dismembered, scalped, earless, blistered and blackened remains that were once the English trader named John Welch.[134]

And once again, Pontiac had whipped his followers into a frenzy to continue the letting of English blood.

[*August 27, 1763—Wednesday, 4:00 P.M.*]

"You really think there's a chance we're going to be attacked here, Lieutenant?" The sergeant of the 17th Regiment looked uneasy.

Lieutenant John Montresor grunted, his attention on the hasty fortifications still being constructed, then shook his head. "I don't know that we will be, Sergeant," he answered, "but there's a chance of it. And as long as there's a chance, I don't mean to be caught unprepared. But damn the infernal luck that put us here anyway!"

He looked out at the gray, mean-looking and heavily white-capped water which continued to pound the disabled hulk of the sloop *Michigan* and which, if the wind did not soon die down, would rip it apart. He turned his attention back to the sergeant.

"Are you ready to leave?"

"Yes, sir. Ready as I'll ever be, I guess. Don't worry, I'll make it back to Niagara all right, sir, and Major Wilkins'll have a party on the way to help right quick."

"I hope you're correct on both counts, Sergeant. Good luck."

He watched as the man turned and left, quickly passing out of sight on the lakeside trail which followed Lake Erie to the northeast. Then he centered his attention again on directing the construction of the defensive works.

John Montresor was a good engineer. Some months ago he had come under the attention of General Amherst and the commander in chief had been pleased by him. Just recently Montresor had been sent for by Amherst and handed a packet of letters destined for Major Gladwin at Detroit.

"Take these," Amherst had directed, "to Gladwin as quickly as possible. When you've delivered them, stay with him to help in the defenses until you receive further orders. You'll probably have to hold up at Niagara and wait for some transportation if none's at hand. However, urge Major Wilkins that it is my desire that all expedition be observed in getting these dispatches through to the Detroit."

As Amherst had anticipated, there was a delay at Fort Niagara. Neither of Detroit's ships were at the Buffalo Creek anchorage when Montresor arrived at Niagara on July 31 and for better than two weeks he had sat fuming at the delay. Then, on the same day—August 16—both the *Huron* and the *Michigan* had arrived, bringing with them the stunning news of the awful defeat of Dalyell's detachment and the death of that officer and others. The wounded of that battle, brought aboard the *Michigan*, were quickly transported to the fort for treatment and Major Wilkins had ordered that the sloop be immediately reprovisioned and manned with a reinforcement under Captain Edward Hope of the 17th Regiment. It was a very small reinforcement—only seventeen men—but it was the best Wilkins could do at the moment without seriously weakening Fort Niagara. The fact that numerous hostile parties of Senecas had been hovering near the Niagara Portage of late, and that just the other day a large body of Ottawas and Chippewas were reported beginning to congregate in the area, had set Wilkins on edge and caused him to enlarge the guard escorts for everything being transported over the portage.

It took ten days for the *Michigan* to be provisioned and cast away from its anchorage, heading for Detroit with Lieutenant Montresor aboard. The schooner *Huron*, under its new master, Captain Walter Horsey, would be following in a couple of days with more provisions and, if possible, more men for the aid of Detroit. But hardly had the voyage of the sloop begun and the shoreline disappeared behind them when the wind died away completely and the *Michigan* lay utterly becalmed on water as flat as ice.

To the reinforcement aboard and to Lieutenant Montresor, it was a delay, a mere inconvenience, but no more. To the skipper of the *Michigan*, however, it was something else. Captain Jacob Newman was more than just a little apprehensive. He had seen storms on many of the seas of the world, but seldom if ever did they so swiftly reach the brutal proportions with which a storm could come up on this most shallow of the Great Lakes. He desperately hoped now that this was merely a simple becalming and not the prelude to one of those vicious tempests of which Lake Erie was so notoriously capable. He hoped, too, that the *Huron* was still holding at its relatively safe anchorage. Quietly and calmly, he ordered his crew to batten down and prepare for the worst.

And the worst came.

Just after sunrise today the storm had struck. With incredible, practically unbelievable swiftness, the surface of the lake changed from glassy smoothness to a rampaging sea with waves six or seven feet in height and steadily worsening. Within minutes it became obvious that they were in extremely serious trouble, heightened by the fact that the ship was wallowing because of the weight of her cargo.

The situation became suddenly worse when the power of this thunderous sea caused a seam to split and water began gushing into the hold. As his crewmen manned the hand pumps and worked frantically, Captain Newman ordered the provisions thrown overboard and even the artillery dumped over the side. There was not even time enough to do this. With crushing violence the tornadic storm slammed the ship back toward the south shore of the lake and here she crunched wickedly against rocks, tore wide open, and settled canted to one side in twelve feet of water, still being terribly battered.

All around them the barrels and bales of provisions were washing up on shore, along with boards and timbers which were part of the *Michigan* itself. There was no hope of saving the ship; no hope of anything except possibly getting off and ashore alive. Captain Jacob Newman gave the order to abandon ship. Amazingly, no lives were lost. Newman and his crew, Captain Hope and his detachment, and Lieutenant Montresor all made the shore in safety. They were close to the mouth of a little stream called Catfish Creek,[135] about fourteen miles southwest of Buffalo Creek.

As quickly as it had come up the gale dwindled and by noon, though the surface of the water was still heavily churning, the worst was well past. It was then that Lieutenant Montresor, with the younger Captain Hope's complete acquiescence, took charge and began directing the building of a defensible position. He directed the salvageable barrels, timbers and other items to be carried to the top of a bluff seventy feet from the water and quickly had the men—both soldiers and crewmen—cutting down trees, digging entrenchments, throwing up earthworks and positioning salvaged barrels of provisions as breastworks.

Now the detachment's sergeant had been sent back afoot to Fort Niagara to ask Major Wilkins for a reinforcement until the *Michigan* could be repaired, and Lieutenant John Montresor gave up a little prayer that the man would get through. If a large party of Indians attacked here, not much could be done. The defenses would help for a little while, but without reinforcement the destruction of every man here was almost a foregone conclusion. In the meanwhile, Montresor determined to keep the men busy with constant improvements on the defenses. It just might mean the difference between life and death.

On the sixth day of this month Major Henry Gladwin had written in a very depressed manner to Sir William Johnson, saying how he wished he had left the service seven years before and that some other officer commanded here at Detroit. Nothing that had happened since then had changed his mind nor lifted the depression which so thoroughly enveloped him. The feeling that he and his garrison were just being blandly ignored in this time of greatest crisis continued to grow in the major and it became ever more of an effort to arise in the morning and face the newest batch of trouble.

Why, he wondered, had he heard nothing more from the commander in chief? Why should it be so many weeks since he had received any news at all from Amherst? Why was the garrison here at Detroit being, in essence, thrown to the wolves? This was His Majesty's most important post in the far wilderness, so why was it that the commanding general would permit it to be held under siege by a pack of Indians for what was now well over a hundred days? These were all questions for which Gladwin had no answers and his very pondering of them caused his depression to deepen.

When Lieutenant James MacDonald had shown him the letter he had written to Major Gates on August 8, Gladwin had thought MacDonald was being perhaps a bit too harsh on the French residents and Jesuit priest here at Detroit. Now, in light of what had been happening, Gladwin felt himself inclined to agree. How else to explain the fact that no matter what kind of offensive action had been attempted against the Indians, it was known of far in advance by those Indians and, in one way or another, thwarted? In his letter MacDonald had written:

I now take the liberty of giving you my opinion freely of the inhabitants in general, who are certainly the most rascally and inhumane people on earth; who make nothing of seeing an Englishman butchered in a degree too shocking to humanity and really beyond my expression; and many instances of which have happened here since May last. And whilst a priest or Jesuit remains amongst them, no peace or quietness can subsist. And until the greatest part of the present inhabitants are removed from the frontiers and the lands possessed by our own natural subjects, the priests' and Jesuits' influence will always prevail, who you well know are always sowing the seed of dissention among their own people.

Every sortie that had thus far been sent out against the Indians had come to naught—a fact which supported MacDonald's viewpoint that someone from among the trusted French in this place was feeding vital information to the enemy. Was it St. Martin? LaButte? Baby? Was it someone among the English traders? Was it, God forbid, perhaps an English soldier betraying his own people? Of the choices, the least disagreeable was that the treachery stemmed from among the French and Gladwin hoped that somehow, in some way, the traitor could be found out.[136]

During this month a number of sorties had been sent out. The first, sent out in the dead of night on August 8 with Captain Hopkins leading a detachment of sixty men, resulted in failure. Fog caused their batteaux to become separated and then daylight coming showed the Indians to be ready and waiting for them, so the attempt was aborted. Again, on August 20, Hopkins led a forty-man detachment out of the fort at 3:30 A.M. to ambush the Potawatomies on the road they used each morning to circle around the fort; but on this particular morning the Indians didn't use the road, and the detachment was itself discovered and forced to flee.

The next day a detachment was sent out four hundred yards from the fort to engage the Indians who had been firing on them from houses; but when they arrived, the houses were deserted and they were themselves fired upon. So it went, with the Indians seemingly always armed with information on the English moves before they were begun. It was highly discouraging and there was little wonder that a cloak of depression was settled upon Henry Gladwin's shoulders. His temper grew shorter with everyone and when, on August 16, he received a letter allegedly written for Chief Wasson by a Frenchman, he exploded with rage.

The letter was insulting in the extreme. Wasson—if indeed the Chippewa chief had dictated it—told Gladwin that if the English had a mind to leave the fort, they might do it peaceably at present. If they refused, however, it would be to their regret because the river would soon be stopped up and no ships could go in any direction on it except to the bottom, which was where he, Wasson, would put them. Wasson claimed that he had never yet fought against the English in the fort because if he had, the fort would have been burned long ago. There were an abnormal number of threats in the letter. Gladwin immediately replied in a terse letter to the chief:

If you have anything at all to say to me, come to the fort to say it in person under a flag of truce. I know you cannot write and therefore you may be imposed on by those who write for you. Further, this I now say to you or to any Frenchman who might write another letter such as that just received: the writer of another such letter can expect to be arrested and hanged at once!

That had effectively ended any letter writing to Gladwin by Wasson, Pontiac or any of the other chiefs for a while. Apparently none of the French were willing to test out Gladwin's resolve in the matter. But the daily skirmishing continued, the deadly, always-to-be-watched sniping which, over the past few weeks, had resulted in seven of the garrison having been wounded, two of them very seriously. Most of this shooting had come from the nearby house of Jacques Duperon Baby and so Gladwin—reluctantly, because he trusted Baby implicitly and considered him a good friend— ordered the place burned down.

And now, sending another report to Colonel Bouquet, Major Gladwin for the first time in his correspondence with his superior officer, allowed some of his inner feelings to come to the surface. He wrote:

. . . and the last I received from the general is of the 2nd July, in which I am ordered to establish the outposts immediately. At the time I received these orders I knew it was impossible to comply with any part of them: the event shows I was right. I am heartily wearied of my command, and I have just signified the same to Colonel Amherst (Sir Jeffrey's adjutant). I hope I shall be relieved soon; if not, I intend to quit the service, for I would not choose to be any longer exposed to the villainy and treachery of the settlement and Indians . . .

[August 31, 1763—Wednesday]

Almost all of the adult life of Sir William Johnson had been closely intertwined with the Indians. In many respects, especially insofar as it concerned the tribes of the Iroquois League, he knew the Indian mentality as no other white man did. He could understand and sympathize with the tribes as they sought in their own ways to follow the tack which, in the long run, would be most beneficial to the tribe as a whole.

It was because of this very thinking that he had been able to extract from five of the Six Nations their promise not to lift the war hatchet against the English in concert with the tribes of the western Great Lakes or the Ohio country. Even now, with the reluctant concurrence of General Amherst, he had six of his most trusted Mohawks en route to Detroit aboard the *Huron* out of Fort Niagara to see if they could not convince the tribes siding with Pontiac to lay aside the war club and make peace. In addition, he had sent along another Iroquois party aboard the sloop *Michigan* under his devoted Mohawk friend Oughnour—whom he called Daniel—for the same purpose and with personal messages of friendship to the western chiefs. All this was done with the approval of the Six Nations council. In fact, only with the Senecas, of the whole Iroquois League, did he continue negotiations which were singularly unsuccessful.

Now the word had come to him that these Senecas, no longer content to stir up the other tribes to mischief and themselves engage in scattered attacks on small outposts, were seriously considering the destruction of Fort Niagara. He knew he should transmit this intelligence at once to General Amherst, but hesitated in doing so. Amherst, he well knew, saw things only as black or white, and where Indians were concerned, everything was undoubtedly the deepest black. To transmit such information on to the general when he himself could scarcely give it credence might do irreparable harm. He would not put it past Amherst, upon receiving such information, to blandly declare war on the entire Iroquois League. The possibility of it was apparent in every communication he had received from the general, up to and including that which had arrived today, written by Amherst four days ago, in which, having been informed of Dalyell's defeat and death, he declared:

I shall only say that it behooves the whole race of Indians to beware (for I fear the best of them have in some measure been privy to and concerned in the late mischief) of carrying matters much farther against the English, or daring to form conspiracies; as the consequences will most certainly occasion measures to be taken that, in the end, will put a most effectual stop to their being. Indeed, their total extirpation is scarce sufficient atonement for the bloody and inhuman deeds they have committed ...

No, for a bit longer at any rate, Johnson decided, he would sit on this latest bit of bad intelligence.

[September 2, 1763—Friday]

Captain Walter Horsey, skipper of the schooner *Huron*, was a very tough seaman with a world of confidence in himself and his own abilities. And, like many another Englishman who had never before encountered belligerent Indians, he thoroughly underestimated their capabilities while at the same time overestimating his own.

Having safely ridden out the Lake Erie storm while still anchored in the protected mouth of Buffalo Creek, the *Huron* had hoisted sail for Detroit two days after the departure of the *Michigan*, confident they would find this sister ship awaiting them at Detroit when they arrived. On board the *Huron* besides her master was the first mate, Ebenezer Jacobs, plus ten soldiers and sailors who made up the protective guard and crew. The only other people aboard were six Mohawk emissaries being sent by Sir William Johnson under a subchief named Aaron, whom Johnson especially trusted, to council with the Detroit tribes. The object, apparently, was to see if they could get the tribes to reach some agreement by which the war could be ended with neither loss of pride for the Indians nor loss of position for the English.

The *Huron* was primarily a provisions ship on this trip, carrying no reinforcements for Detroit, but also having dispatches to deliver, along with the forty-seven barrels of flour and one hundred sixty barrels of pork. All had gone well on the journey up the lake, but at the mouth of the Detroit River, Captain Horsey made three related errors. First, upon entering the river about midday today, he had acquiesced to the request of the Mohawks that they be put ashore here and allowed from this point on to make their own way, visiting each village as they came to it and eventually coming to Detroit itself. Since it was their mission to visit the tribes, Walter Horsey saw no reason to deny them this permission and accordingly he put them ashore.

The second error came soon after, when he permitted two Frenchmen in a canoe loaded with fresh vegetables to come aboard to trade. While dickering over the price was going on, the Frenchmen covertly studied the ship's complement of manpower and defenses and were amazed at how weakly armed and manned the craft was. As soon as they completed their deal they shoved off again, pointed their canoe toward the mouth of the River Rouge—and Pontiac's new camp— and quickly outdistanced the schooner as its upstream progress was slowed under a diminishing breeze.

That was the third error—trying to make the run upstream in these waters without a stiff wind coming from behind, which could carry them rapidly against this current all the way to Detroit. The wind became altogether too weak to permit further headway as dusk approached, and at a point about nine miles downstream from Detroit the *Huron* was forced to anchor.

Only a short distance away, as darkness fell, Pontiac was readying a major assault party, having received word from the two French traders of the weaknesses of this vessel. Had the six Mohawks representing the Iroquois League and Sir William Johnson still been aboard, it was doubtful he would have made any attempt against the ship. His hands were full enough at the moment fighting the English; he could hardly dare to precipitate a war with as powerful a foe as the Iroquois could be. But the Mohawks were ashore and, learning this, Pontiac had them politely detained for their own safety and taken to the Huron village of Chief Teata. The assault plan was then set in motion.

Hardly more than an hour after dark, twenty-five canoes carrying a total of three hundred and forty warriors pushed out from shore and moved silently toward the anchored ship, managing to approach within one hundred yards of her before being spotted by a lookout.

"Indians!"

The cry of the lookout was harsh and filled with fear and it jerked the remaining eleven men aboard the vessel into alertness. Already a heavy gunfire was coming from the Indians and one of the light cannon aboard the ship was fired in answer. It might have created havoc had it been loaded with grape, but the single small cannonball it shot plunged harmlessly into the river and then there was no time for further artillery fire. The Indians had reached the ship and were attempting to swarm up her sides.

It was a desperate struggle. The twelve men aboard fought with every ounce of their strength and ability, tossing aside their guns when they were emptied and continuing to beat at the attackers with clubs or pierce them with spears or swords. Incredibly, for a little while they held their own. Two of the soldiers and two of the crewmen were wounded right at the beginning, though not put totally out of commission. Worse yet, another seaman had his spine severed by the slashing tomahawk of a boarding Indian and was killed, while that Indian in turn was victim of the blast of Captain Horsey's pistol full in his face.

The shrieking of the Indians made a frightful din and, though the firing of weapons on board the ship had ended and the attackers were being repelled only with club or sword, there were still numerous shots coming from the Indians. One of the big lead balls struck Captain Horsey at an angle in the temple and carried away much of the top of his head, leaving him sprawled dead on the deck.

Instantly the first mate, Ebenezer Jacobs, took command. He directed the remaining men with grim sureness and, considering the few defenders, they took a considerable toll of their attackers. Eight Indians were already dead, their bodies swirling off downstream in the dark waters. Another twenty had been wounded and of these seven were dying. Yet the attack continued and the defenders were being overwhelmed by sheer weight of numbers.

"They're taking us!" Jacobs shouted. "Blow up the magazine! By God, if we're going, we'll take these devils with us. Blow us up!"

Several of the Indians understood enough English that they now raised their own voices in shrill alarm. Quite suddenly the Indians were scrambling off the sides of the ship and back into their canoes and moving away from the big craft.[187]

Quickly countermanding his own order, Jacobs had the several cannon loaded and began throwing shot after shot at the hovering Indians. They fell back, out of range, remained a little longer and then, abruptly, fled toward shore and the battle was over.

Still not able to move without a good wind, the *Huron* remained at anchor, every gun loaded and ready, every cannon now filled with grapeshot and primed for instant firing. They were almost too prepared. Less than an hour later four batteaux loomed from upstream and Jacobs was just about to blow them out of the water when an English voice came to them.

"This is Captain Hopkins. Are you all right aboard the ship? Major Gladwin sent us down to give a hand when we heard the fight in progress."

The men aboard the *Huron* cheered and Jacobs was quick to reply: "Four wounded and two dead, including the skipper. This is Jacobs, mate, in command now. We can't move until a wind picks up. Can you stay with us?"

"We'll stay with you. Wind picks up every morning just after dawn. Don't worry, we'll get you to the fort all right. Sounded like you had quite a fight here."

"Captain," Jacobs' voice came back across the water, "we just had the goddamnedest fight you ever saw!"[138]

[September 7, 1763—Wednesday]

The depression being felt by Major Gladwin at Detroit was echoed to some degree by commanders of other posts as well. Major Wilkins at Niagara had been perpetually frightened since word first came of the outbreak of hostilities and his greatest concern was for his own safety. It would hardly have been possible for him to have done less to aid Detroit and the other posts without having turned his back on them completely. He, too, heartily wished now that he had followed a career somewhat less dangerous than as an officer in His Majesty's service.

Farther to the south, at Fort Ligonier, Lieutenant Archibald Blane was also enveloped by depression. Even though the arrival and passage of Colonel Bouquet and his army had eased the Indian attacks against his installation, the situation at Ligonier was still quite bad and the complaints in his letters to Bouquet became more numerous. He had been quick to write Bouquet a congratulatory letter on the affair at Edge Hill and Bushy Run, but in that and other letters to the colonel he penned a multitude of complaints which clearly showed his mood. He wrote:

I have now to beg that I may not be left any longer in this forlorn way, for I can assure you that fatigue I have gone through begins to get the better of me. I must therefore beg that you will appoint me, by the return of the convoy, a proper garrison . . . My present situation is fifty times worse than ever . . . I must beg leave to recommend to your particular attention the sick soldiers here. As there is neither surgeon nor medicine, it would really be charity to order them up. I must also beg leave to ask what you intend to do with the poor starving militia, who have neither shirts, shoes, nor anything else. I am sorry you can do nothing for the poor inhabitants . . . I really get tired of this post . . . I intend going home by the first opportunity, being pretty much tired of a service that's so little worth any man's time; and the more so, as I cannot but think I have been particularly unlucky in it . . .

Even the almost always lighthearted and philosophical commander of Fort Pitt, Captain Simeon Ecuyer, fell prey to the blanket of depression evidently settling over all His Majesty's troops. He had always intended making the service his lifetime career, but now he suddenly wished nothing so much as to be out of it. Having been sent by Bouquet to Fort Bedford, there to await an expected convoy and lead it back to Fort Pitt, he wrote to the colonel:

I find it extremely difficult to deal with the settlers here, who, notwithstanding their fear of the enemy, always do their best to shelter deserters from the army. I enclose, sir, a list of eighteen soldiers who have deserted within the past five days, aided, yea, even encouraged by the people of this place. I have been twenty-two years in the service, and I never in my life saw anything equal to it—a gang of mutineers, bandits, cut-throats, especially the grenadiers. I have been obliged, after all the patience imaginable, to have two of them whipped on the spot, without court-martial. One wanted to kill the sergeant and the other wanted to kill me! . . . For God's sake, let me go and raise cabbages! You can do it, if you will, and I shall thank you eternally for it. Don't refuse, I beg you. Besides, my health is not very good; and I don't know if I can go up again to Fort Pitt with this convoy.

While to a certain extent Bouquet sympathized with his subordinate commanders and even shared many of their views and moods, he had little time to devote to solving their personal problems. The vexing situation of the hostile Indians was still very much with them and there was every indication that it might grow still worse. In his own quarters at Fort Pitt this evening, he wrote to General Amherst:

Fort Pitt, 7th Sept 1763
Sir:
I had the honor to inform your Excellency in my letter of the 27th August, that I had sent to Presque Isle the Indian express, who had brought Major Gladwin's packet. He returned, after proceeding about halfway, with the intelligence enclosed.

I detain him here till I receive a letter from you, and send him daily out to be informed of the motions of the savages.

Yesterday he told me that several parties were about the fort, watching an opportunity to strike and cut off our grass guard, but as he speaks very little of their language, he could not know their numbers.

He has met this morning, over the river, two Wyandots (sent from Sandusky to inquire what was become of him), who have told him that 800 western Indians in 80 canoes were gone towards Niagara to take post at the Carrying Place and cut off all communication with the Detroit, where one of our vessels had arrived about 12 days ago, and that the Ottawas and Chippewas who were at Presque Isle were not yet come back.

If this war continues it will not be possible to keep cattle at the posts without exposing the men too much to guard them.

The Mingoes, Delawares and Shawnees are now collecting their men at the Muskingum and at the heads of the Scioto River. As it is probable that they will attempt to cut off the communication to this post, our parties must be strong to avoid a check.

> *I have the honor to be, &ca.*
> *H.B.*

His Excellency
Sir Jeffrey Amherst

[September 12, 1763—Monday]

In answer to the summons of the white man whom they trusted and respected more than any other—Sir William Johnson—today the chiefs and principal warriors of the Six Nations and other tribes gathered for council outside the imposing structure known as Johnson Hall on the Mohawk River.

Sir William, adopted brother of the Mohawks and known among the Iroquois as Warraghiyagey—The-Man-Who-Undertakes-Great-Things—stood before them and was satisfied with what he saw. That the Senecas were not here neither surprised not dismayed him. He had not expected them. But here before him were the most powerful chiefs of the Oneida and Onondaga, the Mohawk and Tuscarora and Cayuga. For over two hundred years their council fire at the village of Onondaga, heart of the Iroquois League, had burned. Compared to the Iroquois League, such loosely formed confederacies as the Mingo and that collection of tribes and villages gathered under Pontiac were as nothing.

In the months past the chiefs of the Iroquois League had

told Johnson that they meant to remain with the English, to continue to hold their end of the chain of friendship and keep it brightly polished. Now, however, it was necessary to get from them more than just an assurance that they would remain neutral. In one hand Johnson held a broad black war belt and in the other, a hatchet. He spoke fluently in the Iroquois tongue, addressing them in strong words:

"My brothers, hear me with your hearts as well as your ears. You see your white brothers, the English, attacked by angry Indians at many places. On the lakes far to the west it is the Ottawa and Chippewa, the Huron and Potawatomi and Mississaugi who wield the bloody hatchet, and at the forks of the Ohio and near there it is the Shawnees and Delawares, along with those Hurons who now call themselves Wyandots, who now wage war against the English. Closer to us here, it is our own brothers, the Senecas, along with a few of our young hot-blooded Cayuga warriors, who spread out from the valley of the Genesee to cause trouble on the frontier.

"My brothers, I call you here to tell you that we have been patient more than long enough. I wish you to know now, so that it will not cause you concern later, that in the next season an English army of redcoats must pass through your country on their way to punish the tribes in the west. They will not in any way trouble you and it is my desire that you will not in any way trouble them."

He could see from their expressions that they did not much care for this idea of an army of redcoats marching through their lands, but he went on speaking without pause:

"My brothers, you have told me before and you have repeated here that you will not raise the hatchet against your brothers, the English. This is good, but it is not enough. Now I ask you to take this belt and this hatchet and rise up against the hostile tribes who oppose your will and ours. I now deliver you a fine English tomahawk, which I desire you will give to the warriors of all your nations, with directions that they may use it against these breakers of the covenant that has existed heretofore between us; that they may use it to cut off the bad links which have caused the chain of friendship to become stained and rusted."

Johnson knew his Indians well. He expected that they would accept both belt and hatchet and that there might be some action on their part against tribes making war on the English, but he hardly expected they would vigorously pursue a war against the other tribes. His expectations were almost exactly what happened.

The reply was given by the Onondaga chief who was principal speaker for the entire league. Gravely he accepted both belt and tomahawk and promised on behalf of the League to remain faithful to the English. He promised as well to send embassies to the various tribes, encouraging them to lay aside their enmities and make peace.

"To the nearest tribe at war against you, the Delawares, who are part of them living on the Susquehanna River," he said, "we will send them this message: 'Cousins the Delawares, we have heard that many wild Indians in the West, who have tails like bears, have let fall the chain of friendship, and taken up the hatchet against our brothers, the English. We desire you to hold fast the chain, and shut your ears against their words.' This, Warraghiyagey, is what we will say to them, and we will say the same to others of more distant tribes we will see. We, for our part, will continue to hold our end of the chain and only relinquish our hold on it if your end is dropped first."

The Onondaga paused a long moment and then added to this veiled threat, one that was less subtle. "We do not like to see the redcoat army march through our country and we will watch it carefully. We will not lift a hand against it, but we will watch to see that it does not lift a hand against us. Your foot is broad and heavy. In your passing through this country, take care that you do not tread on us!"

It was a word of caution which Sir William Johnson was going to make sure Sir Jeffrey Amherst fully understood. And now, with the council ended, with gifts distributed to the Iroquois and the various bands beginning to disperse back to their own villages, Johnson returned to his own home and was greeted there by an express bearing two messages.

One of them was from his agent, Thomas DeCouagne, at Fort Niagara, and the other from Collin Andrews, who was supposedly accompanying Oughnour on the mission to Detroit, upon which Johnson had set him. Both letters were brief and not very encouraging, although Johnson was thankful he had taken the precaution of sending Indian peace emissaries aboard both the *Huron* and the *Michigan*, rather than on just one of the ships. For once, it seemed, such duplication of effort had been rewarded. With irritating brevity, as usual, DeCouagne had written:

Niagara, 8th Sept' 1763
Sir: In my last I wrote you that the sloop was lost upon Lake Erie. Since they have been on shore they have been attacked

by a few straggling Indians. We have lost three men in the breastwork and one out that was scalped. Daniel and the rest of the Indians behaved very well.

          T. DeCouagne

The letter from Collin Andrews, on the other hand, while not much longer, was at least a bit more detailed. He had written:

> *Cat Fish Creek, 9th Sept^m 1763*
> *Dear Sir: According to Daniel Oughnour's desire, I now take the freedom to write to you. The 28th ultimo we have been cast away at this place, which detained him from proceeding to Detroit, but he says he'll go forward and deliver your belts and bring you an answer from the different nations according to your directions. The 3rd Instant we had three men killed by a small party of Indians. Daniel spoke to them at a little distance from the breastwork, but they would not tell what nation they were. He says he believes they are Senecas. We expect the schooner from Detroit daily. Aaron and five Indians went in her to Detroit. Daniel gives his compliments to you and family and desires the favor of you in case you see his wife to tell her he is well. Sir, excuse my freedom in writing in such a [badly scrawled] manner, for I have had the fever and ague.*

>   *I am Sir, your*
>   *most obedient humble Servant,*
>   *Collin Andrews*

[September 14, 1763—Wednesday]

Sergeant William Stedman, astride a huge gray horse, looked back over his shoulder at the party following him along the narrow trail-like road of the Niagara Carrying Place. They were strung out in a formless grouping for fifty yards or more behind, paying no attention whatever to the cadence being tapped on the drum by the escort's thirteen-year-old drummer boy, Peter Matthews. The thirty wagoneers were now mainly afoot, having left the loaded wagons under guard at the upper landing, Fort Schlosser, to await the arrival of the schooner *Huron*. Stedman and his detachment of two dozen mounted soldiers had been ordered to escort the wagoneers back to Ford Niagara while the remainder of the escort stayed with the supplies destined for Detroit.

Those thirty wagonloads of goods, pulled by teams of oxen, had left Fort Niagara under Major Wilkins's orders at dawn yesterday. The portage was by no means an easy one but, even so, the passage to Fort Schlosser had been completed by early evening. The entire party had camped overnight together and now Sergeant Stedman was leading the wagoneeers back, protecting them with his portion of the escort party.

The roaring, ground-shaking rumble of the two great cataracts was now diminished enough behind them that the tapping from Peter Matthews's drum was clearly audible, its tinny rattle hanging in the still air over this fearsome gorge through which flowed the mighty Niagara, carrying the overflow of Lakes Superior, Michigan, Huron and Erie over the falls and into Lake Ontario for eventual discharge via the St. Lawrence River into the Atlantic.

As always, Stedman was impressed by the scene hardly more than an arm's length off the portage road to the left. The river below the falls had always been more of a fascination to him than the falls themselves. Here the earth on both sides of the river fell away in sheer rocky cliffs peppered here and there with scattered stunted trees which had somehow managed to root themselves in such less-than-ideal sites.

This spot they were presently passing was near the most awesome spectacle of all—a great dark abyss in which the waters swirled around a sharp bend in the gorge and formed a mammoth maelstrom; a whirlpool whose single black eye seemed to look with evil anticipation at all who passed above, causing in the viewer an almost hypnotic compulsion to leap from the edge of the chasm and be sucked down into the whirling, foam-flecked vortex. Devil's Hole, some people were calling it, and truly it seemed to be a fitting lair for a devil. Only a short distance upstream from the great whirlpool was where the road came closest to the edge and the cliffs, even at their lowest points, were a sheer drop of eighty to a hundred feet or more to a shoreline cluttered with immense jagged boulders which reached out of sight into the deep green waters.

Sergeant Stedman swallowed and shook his head, looking away toward the dense forest bordering the road on his right. As always, he felt that hypnotic attraction of the whirlpool reaching out to him and he was glad he was mounted rather than afoot. It was the last casual thought he was to have for some time.

With ghastly unexpectedness there came a barrage of gun-

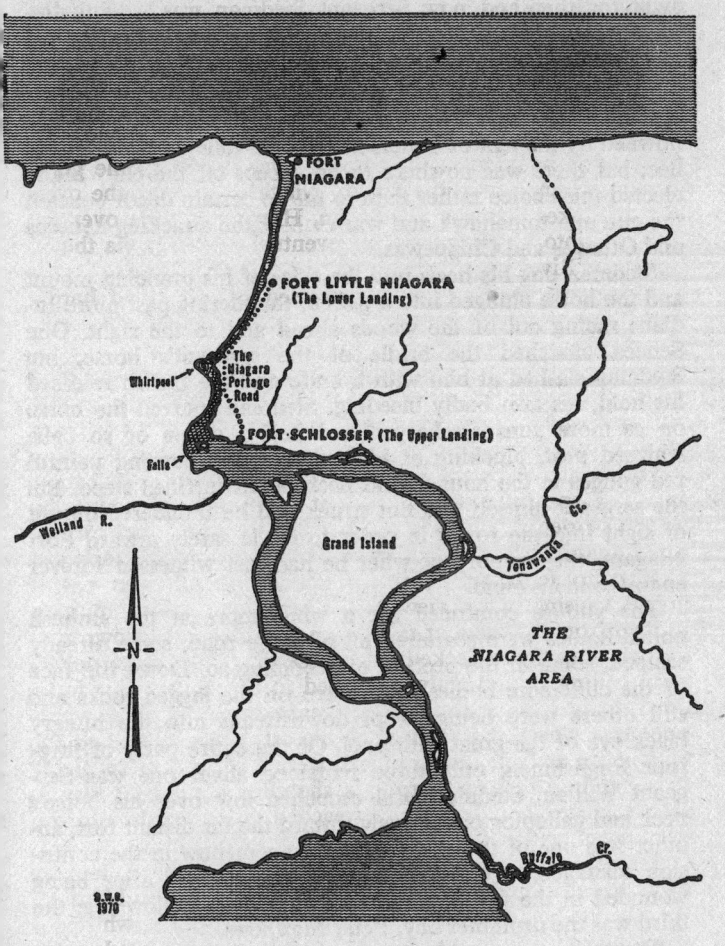

FORT NIAGARA

FORT LITTLE NIAGARA
(The Lower Landing)

Whirlpool

The
Niagara
Portage
Road

Falls

FORT SCHLOSSER (The Upper Landing)

Welland R.

N

Grand Island

Cr.

Tonawanda

THE
NIAGARA RIVER
AREA

Buffalo Cr.

B.V.S.
1970

fire from the woods and a horde of savages, perhaps as few as three hundred but maybe as many as five hundred of them, came boiling out of ambush, their fierce cries adding to the shock of their gunfire. Most of them were coming from the woods the sergeant had already passed and one swift glance over his shoulder was enough. He saw dozens, scores of the men falling to the road upon which only moments before they had been walking so casually. Soldiers were tumbling from their mounts, some of them falling over the precipice into that awful watery torrent below. Those not downed by the hail of bullets in the first volley were trying to flee, but there was nowhere to go except off the cliff. Many elected this choice rather than to fall to certain death beneath the gun and tomahawk and war club of the attacking Senecas and Ottawas and Chippewas.

Stedman dug his heels into the sides of his prancing mount and the horse plunged into a gallop, thundering past more Indians racing out of the woods ahead and to the right. One Seneca snatched the bridle of the sergeant's horse, but Stedman slashed at him with a knife and the Indian released his hold, his arm badly bleeding. Stedman spurred the horse on as more guns discharged and half a dozen or so balls whizzed past, plucking at his uniform and burning painful red gouges in the haunch and neck of his terrified steed. But the sergeant himself was not struck and he thundered on out of sight into the forest in order to circle safely toward Fort Niagara, the memory of what he had just witnessed forever engraved in his mind.

The gunfire continued for a while more at the ambush point. Bodies were scattered all over the road, some already scalped, some in the process of becoming so. Down the face of the cliff more bodies lay broken on the jagged rocks and still others were being swept downstream into the hungry black eye of the great whirlpool. Of the entire party of fifty-four Englishmen, only three remained alive: one was Sergeant William Stedman, still crouched low over his horse's neck and galloping circuitously toward the far distant fort; another was one of the wagoneers, who somehow in the confusion managed to crawl into the woods unseen after being wounded in the first fire and hide in a huge hollow log; the third was the drummer boy, Peter Matthews.

The thirteen-year-old, like the others not instantly killed in the initial gunfire, had instinctively recoiled from it and, in doing so, had toppled over the edge of the cliff. He screamed as he fell, feeling the rush of the wind and seeing the rocks and water leaping toward him and then, miraculously, his fall was checked. The projecting limb of one of those stunted cliffside trees snagged in the belt holding his drum and he bounced violently. For only a brief moment it held him before limb and belt snapped at the same time and he was falling free again, but it had been enough. The bouncing had catapulted him outward somewhat from the cliff face and now, instead of falling on the rocks, he just barely missed them and plunged into the green waters which hissed past them. A dozen feet or more from where he hit he came to the surface sputtering and coughing and his arms flailing wildly. The current swept him to the rocks and he was slammed against them, caught one, lost his hold, was slammed into another and this time managed to grip it. Slowly, using every bit of his strength, he pulled himself up and out of the water and into a crevice of the rocks and lay there gasping, unhurt and not really believing that he was still alive.

The harsh rattle of the gunfire had reverberated down the river, echoing and reechoing from the gorge walls, and it was heard a mile and a half below by two companies of soldiers of the 80th Regiment encamped at the Lower Landing—Fort Little Niagara. This was a detachment of eighty men and four lieutenants under command of Captain Benjamin Johnston. Immediately assessing the sounds correctly as an ambush of the wagoneers, Johnston ordered his men up and on the run toward the scene. He took the lead and at commanding intervals among the men were Lieutenants George Campbell, Frederick Roscoe, George Frazier, and Philip Deaton.[139]

The Indians had been well aware of this party's presence at the lower landing and anticipated it would come. Having scalped all the victims still on the road, they melted again into the trees lining the road and moved stealthily toward the Lower Landing until, with the bodies behind them on the road still in sight, they heard the panting detachment coming. They stopped and waited, well hidden behind trees and logs and rocks, no sound or movement betraying their presence.

The detachment, hoping to catch a small ambushing Indian party by surprise, themselves now plunged headlong into a second withering fire which, if anything, was far worse than that which earlier struck down the wagoneers and their escort. All five officers and about thirty-five of the men were slain in that first dreadful fusillade of shots. Half as many more were wounded. Before any could fully recover from the shock of it, the whole body of Indians was among them, war-clubs and slashing tomahawks driving through flesh and bone. It was pure carnage.

Of the eighty-five soldiers, only ten managed to escape through the woods, six of whom were wounded. They, too, circled toward Fort Niagara with their grim tidings. Soon all had become quiet at the ambush scene and thus it remained for hours.

And now, as the sun was beginning to nestle in the upper-most branches of the western trees, Major John Wilkins arrived on the scene, leading a force of virtually the entire remaining strength of the garrison. No Indian was to be seen. As far as could be determined, not one Indian life was lost. But the scene on the road was straight out of some frighten-ing nightmare. Eighty-six bodies, all of them scalped, many of them mutilated, lay strewn about like discarded dolls. A fair number had had their uniform coats taken and all of the rifles, swords, knives, and other equipment were gone. The horses that had escaped the gunfire were gone as well, either run off or taken by the attackers.

A fearful inspection down the cliff revealed more bodies on the rocks, but not enough to make up the total of thirty-five men still missing. It had to be presumed that the remainder had been swept downstream in the river, sucked deep into the eye of the whirlpool and forever lost. A young boy was now seen below, striving to climb back up to the road. A loop was made in a rope and thrown down to him and he was care-fully drawn up to safety. It was the dummer boy, Peter Mat-thews, and he confirmed the worst. There could be no doubt remaining: one hundred and twenty-seven men had been killed here.[140]

It was, for the English, the single greatest loss of life yet in this war, and it was a disaster of major importance. And now more than ever, as the bodies were hurriedly buried in a com-mon grave hastily dug and the commander quickly moved his men back toward Fort Niagara, Major John Wilkins was deeply and desperately afraid.

[September 17, 1763—Saturday]

Rarely had news from the frontier reached the commander in chief so swiftly. A light, swift canoe manned by four young privates in the peak of physical condition had been dispatched from Fort Niagara at once by Major John Wil-kins, immediately upon his return there following the Devil's

Hole Massacre. With usually all four men paddling at the same time and never more than one resting at once, they moved continually. Eastward on Lake Ontario they went, to Oswego and then upstream on the Onondaga River[141] to Lake Oneida, up Wood Creek at its eastern end, then across the Great Carrying Place to the upper Mohawk and down that stream to the Hudson and subsequently to New York. They were on the point of collapsing with exhaustion when, eighty-four hours after leaving Fort Niagara, they delivered their messages to General Sir Jeffrey Amherst; messages which struck him with the force of hammer blows.

Following the dubious "victory" of Colonel Bouquet, in which one hundred and twenty-three English soldiers had been lost as compared to sixty of the Indians, had come news of Dalyell's defeat by Pontiac, followed by word of the loss of the sloop *Michigan* on Lake Erie, which might well foretoken the ultimate loss of Detroit. This, in turn, had been followed by the report of the shipwrecked party being attacked and three of its men killed—although very likely there would have been more had it not been for the strong defensive measures taken immediately by Lieutenant Montresor. And now had come the numbing news of the incredible double ambush on the Niagara Portage, with its death toll of one hundred and twenty-seven men.

And so at last, on the one hundred forty-first day of this war, the commander in chief of His Royal Majesty's forces in North America reluctantly conceded that this was, after all, a major Indian uprising, a full-blown war.

Trembling with frustration and rage and feeling personally humiliated by it all, Amherst immediately doubled the reward for Pontiac's head and sat himself down for some serious thinking about what should be done now. For the first time he had to admit that his long-nurtured idea of reestablishing Fort Presque Isle and Fort Michilimackinac, as well as others of the upper forts, was absolutely out of the question, as both Bouquet and Gladwin had been subtly suggesting it was for many weeks now. There was only one real solution, as Amherst saw it, which was to utterly destroy the very core of the unrest. This would have to be done by sending Major Gladwin a very large and powerful reinforcement so that he could take up a strong offensive and crush Pontiac and the coalition of western tribes. At once he began starting the wheels in motion for assembling such a force to march from Niagara under Major Wilkins in October if possible.

In the meanwhile, for whatever comfort it might bring

him, he had some news for Gladwin which ought to cheer him. He sat at his desk and swiftly made an exact copy of a letter he had only this morning written to Secretary at War McEllis. Then he wrote a brief and, he hoped, inspiring note to Gladwin. The copy of the letter to the Secretary at War he appended to the note to Gladwin. It read:

New York, 17 September 1763
Sir: As there have been two Deputy Adjutants General serving here, I have taken the liberty to show a mark of my entire satisfaction of Major Gladwin's good conduct and commendable behavior, in appointing him a D. Adjt. General; but to remain with the troops at the Detroit in the same manner as has been ordered. This is no more than a name, but should it be your gracious pleasure to approve it, and honor Major Gladwin with the rank of lieutenant colonel, I am firmly of the opinion that the promotion of so deserving an officer must at any time be a benefit to his Majesty's service, and this is the sole view I have in mentioning it to you.

I have the honor to be, with the most perfect regard, Sir:
Jeff: Amherst

Right Honorable McEllis

The note to Gladwin was considerably less formal. Amherst had written:

It is always a great satisfaction to me when I can promote an officer of real merit, and should the enclosed succeed to my wishes, it will give me much pleasure, as it will be of service to you, as well as proof of the sense I have of your distinguished conduct. Success attend you![142]

[September 18, 1763—Sunday]

The fact that the small reinforcement detachment for Detroit under Captain Edward Hope was at last underway again toward that beleaguered fort was little to the credit of Major John Wilkins. The commander of Niagara had been in something of a blue funk these past weeks and the Devil's Hole Massacre had practically pitched him off the deep end. He was nervous, irritable and his actions sometimes bordered on the irrational.

As soon as the express from Montresor had arrived telling of the wreck of the *Michigan*, the fact that a breastwork was being constructed and that a reinforcement was urgently required, he had gathered a detachment of one hundred men and sent them there. When they arrived at Catfish Creek on September 2 late in the afternoon, they found that Montresor had erected quite a respectable fortification, already considerably more than just merely a breastwork.

Their arrival had been none too soon. Just before dawn the very next morning, a band of Ottawas, Chippewas and Senecas crept up to within fifty yards of the post and opened fire. A soldier who was in the woods at the time attending to a natural function was caught, killed and scalped. In the first fire, two more of Captain Hope's men were killed. Montresor, however, swiftly brought the swivel to bear on them and opened fire. Undoubtedly this, more than anything else, prevented the fortification from being taken in one great rush. The fear that the Indians reserved for the "thunder guns" was something special, and rarely if ever would they deliberately advance into artillery fire. The troops rallied well under Hope and Montresor and the battle continued in place until about ten o'clock in the morning, when the Indians suddenly withdrew.[143]

Throughout the remainder of September 3 and all during the fourth there were occasional glimpses of the enemy, but no further attack. None were seen on the morning of September 5 and a squad sent out that afternoon came back with the good news that evidently the Indians had pulled out altogether.

Now attention was brought to bear on the crushed and splintered remains of the *Michigan* being lapped by the presently gentle wave action of Lake Erie close by. It did not take very long to determine that there was no possibility of repairing her. An express was sent back to Major Wilkins at once with this news and the announcement that they would continue to hold this point at Catfish Creek and continue as well to strengthen the fortifications lest there should be another attack by the Indians.

In the ten days which followed an enormous amount of work was done, and by the evening of September 16 the works were completed. In an incredible and admirable performance, young Lieutenant John Montresor had constructed a permanent fort which was more secure a stronghold than either Fort Le Boeuf or Fort Venango had ever been.

In the meanwhile, however, the massacre had occurred on the Niagara Portage road and Wilkins was extremely upset. When the messenger from Catfish Creek arrived, the major decided it would be of great benefit to salvage everything possible from the *Michigan*, take the ship apart and raft everything back down to Fort Schlosser. Accordingly, he sent off another detachment of two hundred and forty men in twenty-three batteaux to do the job. Unfortunately his befuddlement was such that he sent them off without giving them a single tool to use in dismantling the vessel. It was, to say the least, an embarrassing situation.

Now, however, the schooner *Huron* hove into view, coming from Detroit, bearing news of the attack she had sustained and the death of her skipper and one seaman. She was used at once in aiding the dismantling party and the last of the material that was salvageable from the *Michigan* had been brought in this morning. The large reinforcements returned to Fort Niagara, the *Huron* loaded with supplies from the ox wagons at Fort Schlosser and at last, with the sun still a few degrees above the waters of western Lake Erie, the ship was on her way again. There was one difference about her now: the heavier artillery from the *Michigan* had now been mounted on the *Huron* and neither Captain Hope nor Lieutenant Montresor were very much worried about the Indians trying again to take this vessel on the Detroit River.

[*September 19, 1763—Monday*]

The little confederacy that was Pontiac's, never closely knit to begin with, was now well on its way to collapse. In past weeks numerous reports had come to the Ottawa war chief of various chiefs of other tribes going to Major Gladwin and conferring with him privately, seeking peace and safety from eventual English retaliation. Most of the rumors said that the chiefs were promising to go away, to desert Pontiac and his cause. These were stories he had heard for too long now and he had never before found them to have solid foundation. Whenever he confronted any chief said to have counciled with Gladwin, that chief promptly denied any agreement having been made between himself and the Detroit commander and reaffirmed his support of Pontiac. Even the Hurons under Teata, who had vacillated all during this siege, had sided with him when the demand was made.

But the crack which foretold the crumbling of this confederacy made its appearance ten days ago with the arrival of seventy of the St. Joseph Potawatomies under Chiefs Washee and Kioqua. Boldly, openly, almost insolently, they announced to Pontiac that they were through with this war and were going into council with the Detroit commander to make peace. Pontiac had not really believed they would do so, but for three days they came and went with regularity at the fort.

Six days ago, forty of these Potawatomies announced that they were well satisfied with what Major Gladwin had told them and that they would now do as he bade them: return to their village and remain quiet, giving no further support to Pontiac nor heed to his words. With Kioqua leading them, they set off at once for the St. Joseph area, pointedly ignoring Pontiac's entreaties, promises and threats.

The rift became even deeper this morning when the remaining thirty of these Potawatomies stood and heard Chief Washee tell Pontiac almost the same thing and then lead them all away. The Chippewas and Hurons and Pontiac's own Ottawas watched with interest, waiting for the wrath of the war chief to fall on these miscreants, but it did not happen. With sour expression but without further pleas or threats, Pontiac merely watched them go.

"I do not care that they have gone," he announced after they had passed out of hearing. "Pontiac needs not the strength of rabbits to support him. It is better that they are gone. They have listened too well to the words of the Mohawks among us, brought here by the little chief called Aaron, and they have become afraid, as rabbits become afraid when the dog barks in the distance. I do not need them! I do not *want* them! Nor do I fear the words being spoken by these Mohawks who claim that they speak for all the Iroquois League. No! Even if abandoned by my other allies here, still will my own Ottawas and I fight on to destroy the English, and soon the French army will come to help us, as we have been promised by our father, the King."

But for once the oratory of Pontiac rang hollowly in their ears and there was no rush of words as various chiefs vied to most assertively pledge their loyalty to him. And now, in his own camp on the River Rouge, had come the most unbearable blow of all. A peace chief of his tribe—Chief Manitou— who had until now supported Pontiac, arose in council and pointed a stern, unwavering finger at him.

"You have told us that all the tribes are with you, Pontiac. We have seen with our eyes that this is not true. You have told us that the French King will send you an army, but we no longer believe this to be true. You have told us that you will destroy the Englishmen and drive them from among us, but even this is not true. Where the English have been driven out, it has been by others, not by you. Here the English sit before us as they have since the beginning, safer now than when all this began. Is this how you drive the English out? Is this how you show leadership to the Ottawas? What kind of war chief is it who directs his followers so poorly that even when he is supported by over three hundred warriors, he cannot capture a little ship which cannot move and has only two times six men on it? Is this the bold, brave, unconquerable war chief we are supposed to honor and follow? Not I, Pontiac. I leave you now, and all who feel as I feel are welcome to walk beside me."

Chief Manitou gave Pontiac one last withering glare and then turned and strode out of the council longhouse. There was a shuffling as many of the seated Ottawas rose to join him and when all movement had ended and an uncomfortable silence filled the great room, more than a third of his Ottawa warriors had left him. Most of those who remained were very young men who seldom thought farther than the bloodied end of a tomahawk or scalping knife. Still, Pontiac smiled at them and there was no sign of concern in his voice as he spoke.

"I thank my brothers for showing their courage and their determination. Our fight with the English is not finished so long as their red coats can be seen in the green of our forests and on the blue of our waters. We will fight on, and we will conquer them!"

He left the council then, and though his shoulders did not sag nor his head hang nor his step falter, yet he knew within him, even if these young followers did not, that the leadership of Pontiac was coming to an end, that his prestige among his own people was dying, that his influence among other tribes was nearly gone.

Nothing in his life had ever been harder for Chief Pontiac to bear than the realization of this.

[September 27, 1763—Tuesday]

Although for quite some time he had expected it, the arrival of the news from New Orleans still came as something of a shock to Major Pierre Joseph Neyon de Villiere, commander of the French post of Fort de Chartres on the Mississippi River in the Illinois country.

The dispatches from the governor, received here six days ago, had not only borne his seal, they also carried the imperial seal of the King of France and there was no disputing their authenticity. Yet, even with the written word before him that a peace had been ratified between Britain, France and

Spain, de Villiere hesitated in his duty. In weeks past his blood had raced and his hopes soared as word filtered through the wilderness to him of the fall of post after post of the English. Perhaps even as much as Pontiac wanted it, de Villiere had yearned to send an army of French soldiers to help in this disruption of the English hold on the wild western heartland of America, which rightfully belonged to France. To him it seemed almost a betrayal of his own people that the King had put his hand to such a document.

For six days de Villiere had wrestled with himself. Suppose these messages had not arrived? Would not then the Indians have continued their war and the ultimate conquest of the English resulted? Or, if not their conquest, at least their ouster? Suppose he took it upon himself, despite these official papers, to send a body of French soldiers to uproot Detroit? What pleasure it would give him! But what then might be his own ultimate reward?

At last he reached his decision and it was a decision that somehow deep inside he had known, as a loyal officer of the King, was his only way to go, irrespective of personal feelings. There were three letters to write now, and with the decision made, he wasted no time in getting them written. The first was directed to the French inhabitants—traders, farmers, settlers, whatever—living at or near Detroit, but with similar copies to go to all French settlements or posts in this wilderness, even those living right here in the Illinois country in the shade of Fort de Chartres. Copies would be made and carried at once by couriers to the different centers of French habitation. The document was really more of a proclamation than a letter and it was to be posted immediately at each destination. It read:

27th Sept., 1763

Gentlemen:
It is well decided that the King of France, the King of England and he of Spain (undoubtedly affected with the horrors of such a long and bloody war) have at length made Peace, whereof the definite Treaty was exchanged the 4th of March last. It is by virtue of a letter with the King's Seal that the Governor, by his dispatches bearing the date the 13th of last July (and which I received the 21st instant) gives me orders to deliver up this place to the Commissaries of his Britannic Majesty empowered by his orders for the purpose, and evacuate it. I do not enter into a detail of this Cession; it is con-

formable to the articles in the Parliamentaries concerning this quarter, and which you have seen, which leaves the Inhabitants free and at liberty to retire whenever it seemeth good unto them within the possessions of the three Kings; he has then ordered me to acquaint all those who are willing to withdraw themselves hereof, and to propose to them New Orleans, the Allemants, LaPointe, Coupee, Arkansas, and Saint Gennviene, to establish themselves there with assurance of having all facility in their new settlements. If any amongst you gentlemen choose to follow this resolution, they are free to do it and may assure themselves that I will procure them every succour that will depend on me. It remains then, Gentlemen, that I exhort you agreeable to the King's intention, to put everything in practice to contribute to the peace which I demand of the Indians, being well persuaded that the English Gentlemen will take the most just means to accomplish it, in consequence whereof I have dispatched these couriers and am entirely, Gentlemen, your very humble and most obedient servant.

Neyon de Villiere

Immediately following this, the major drew up a second letter, which was actually more a set of orders for the messenger who would carry the proclamation above to Detroit. It directed:

We, Pierre Joseph Neyon de Villiere, Major, commandant of the Illinois:

Mr. De Quindre, Cadet, is ordered to set out this day with one named James la Davarette and two Indians, to go to Detroit to carry our dispatches thither.

He will be charged, moreover, with a parole from us in writing, with a flying seal, three belts and four pipes for all the Nations.

As the Ouiatenons are the first that he will find, he will cause their chiefs to be assembled together, to whom he will explain exactly our parole in assuring them of the Peace, in token whereof, he will deliver up to them one belt and one pipe.

He will do the same with the Kickapoos, Mascoutens, and Miamis, and from thence he will go to Detroit, where he will deliver our letters to the commandant.

If, contrary to our intentions, the siege of Detroit by the Indians should obstruct his entering the fort, he is to go to Pontiac, Chief of the Ottawas, where he will read over our *parole and give it up to them, enjoining them to convey it to all other nations.*

He will be on his guard in order to avoid all manner of surprises from ill conditioned Indians.

We command to him most expressly to make all dispatch. We desire, therefore, all whom it may concern, not to retard him but, on the contrary, to procure him succour and assistance.

Given at Fort Chartre, 27 Sept., 1763

It was the third letter which would be hardest for him to write and which, for this reason, he had put off until last. He sat for a long while looking at the blank sheet before him and then he dipped his pen to write the words which, he was sure, would forever after destroy any trust for the French which the Indians still harbored. It was by no means an easy thing for him to do. He wrote:

TO ALL MY CHILDREN: The Iroquois, or Six Nations, Abnakis, Shawnees, Ottawas, Chippewas, Hurons, Potawatomies, Kickapoos, Mascoutens, Miamis, Piankeshaws, Ouiatenons, Illinois, Sacs, Foxes, Menominees, Osages, Kansas, Missouris, Pawnees, and to all Red Men:

My Dear Children: as none of you can reproach me of lying, I promised you to communicate to you the news, and you to listen to my speech. Lo! Here it is, my Dear Children. Open your ears that it may penetrate even to the bottom of your hearts. The great day has come at last, wherein it has pleased the Master of Life to inspire the Great King of the French, and him of the English, to make Peace between them, sorry to see the blood of men spilled so long. It is for this reason that they have ordered all their chiefs and warriors to lay down their arms and we acquaint you of this news to engage you to bury the hatchet. Doing it, as I hope, what joy you will have in seeing the French and English smoke with the same pipe and eating out of the same spoon and finally living like brothers. You will see the road free, the lakes and rivers unstopped. Ammunition and merchandise will abound in your villages. Your women and children will be cloaked as well as you. They will go to the dances and festivals not with cumbersome and heavy clothes, but with skirts, blankets and ribbons. Forget, then, my Dear Children, all the evil talks. May the wind carry off like dust all those which have proceeded out of evil mouths. The respect and friendship which you have always had for the word of On-ontio,[144] and for mine in particular, makes me believe that you will listen to this one now: it is from a Father who loves tenderly his Children and who seeks nothing but your welfare.

The French are free, even as you. They change the land when the King orders it. He has not given yours. He has only ceded those which he had amongst you in order to avoid war for the future, and that you may always enjoy tranquility and have abundance of merchandise in your villages. I depend upon you that you will not make me lie, and that your young men will not quit their rattles or playthings to take up the hatchet and carry it amongst savage nations from whom you expect no succours and who are on the earth to embroil it. Leave off then, my Dear Children, from spilling the blood of your brothers, the English. Our hearts are now but one. You cannot at present strike the one without having the other for your enemy also. If you continue, you will have no supplies, and it is from us that you expect them. You will be always in my heart, and in those of the French, who will never abandon you.

I bid you all farewell and recommend you to respect always the French who remain amongst you. Although I expect to go off sometime after the couriers which I dispatch to you, send me your answer by them. If I do not receive it here, it will be at New Orleans, where I will consult with the great chief about the means of supplying you, thus having all the other side of the River Mississippi where the French will supply the wants to those who will be in this quarter.

I pray the Master of Life to enter into your hearts, and that He may make you know that in following the advice which I gave you to make Peace with our brothers, the English, you may never stand in need of being pitied. And finally, that the King, I, and all the French will be glad to see you live in Peace; and for the proof of what I tell you, I sign these presents with my hand and put thereto seal of my arms at Fort Chartre, 27 September, 1763.

J. Neyon de Villiere

[Seal]

[September 28, 1763—Wednesday]

As always, whenever he came face to face with the commander in chief of His Majesty's forces in North America, George Croghan felt faintly repelled by him. There was about Lieutenant General Sir Jeffrey Amherst an affected air, a detachment, a sense that whatever the man said was simply said on the basis of molding the one to whom he spoke to his own will. In short, it was damned hard for George Croghan to believe anything the general told him. It had always been the case and it was the case now. But where others tended to fawn before him, Croghan's frontier temperament would not permit him to do so. It did not do so now.

The Indian agent had not really wanted to see Amherst and had avoided the encounter as long as possible. When it became evident that there was no way he could get around doing so, he had every intention of making their meeting just as brief as possible.

For some weeks prior to this Croghan had been in Philadelphia, trying to tie up loose business ends of his own before he embarked on what he hoped would be a leave of absence from his duties to see to other business dealings in England. Whether or not Amherst would consent to his leaving at this time was the big question.

Croghan had first gone from Philadelphia to Johnson Hall some ten days ago, hoping to secure the permission he needed from Sir William and thus circumvent any necessity for confronting Amherst. Johnson was sympathetic and told Croghan he wished he could give his deputy permission to sail for England as he desired, but he felt that was out of his province and that it must be up to General Amherst as to whether or not he could be spared.

"Spared!" Croghan snorted. "Why couldn't I be spared? His High-and-Mightiness hasn't listened to one word I've said—or what you've said either, for that matter—for the past two years!"

Johnson nodded and shrugged but remained adamant about Croghan seeing Amherst. There was nothing the deputy Indian agent could do but go through with it. Johnson gave him some dispatches to deliver and Croghan had come to New York. Three days ago he was given an audience with the general and, immediately after handing Amherst the messages from Sir William, he made his request. Almost before he had finished speaking the request was denied. Amherst would not even deign to listen to his reasons for wanting to leave and dismissed Croghan in a rather peremptory way. Shortly afterward, as Amherst wrote to Bouquet, he commented:

Mr. Croghan is just now arrived here, last from Sir William Johnson's. What carried him there I know not. He has brought me dispatches from Sir William, by which I learn that the five friendly tribes of the Six Nations, at the conference he has now with them, express great firmness and steadiness in our interest; and the Canada Indians have been offered to act offensively against the Western Tribes who have committed the hostilities. This is so far good, but I shall not employ them, as all I desire is their remaining quiet, for I never will put the least trust in any of the Indian race.

Mr. Croghan has desired leave to go to England, on account of his private affairs, but I have absolutely refused to comply with his request, as I think if his presence ever was of any consequence in the department he filled, it certainly is so at the present time ...

The following day, not to be daunted, Croghan made a second request of Amherst for leave, this time in writing, stressing as best he could the many losses he had sustained because of his service in the Indian Department and saying that he never had had it in his power to properly attend to his own private affairs because of the interference by Indian duties. He delivered the letter in person and stood there trying to control his temper as Amherst, with an amused smirk on his lips, read it and then carelessly dropped it to his desk.

"This is the same thing you asked me yesterday, Mr. Croghan, and my answer is the same. Permission denied."

"Then, sir, by God," Croghan stormed, "I do what I've been talked out of doing too damned many times. I resign my office here and now!"

Before the astonished Amherst could reply, Croghan stalked out. Yesterday a note was delivered to him from Amherst which was markedly conciliatory and which requested Croghan to appear again at his office the following day. The deputy Indian agent, believing the general was relenting, had now come again to the commander's office.

Amherst smiled cordially and shook the frontiersman's hand with suspicious warmth. Croghan only nodded and, declining a proffered chair, stood watching the general warily. Amherst clasped his hands behind his back and looked for a long moment out of his window. When he spoke, it was without looking at Croghan.

"Mr. Croghan," he said, "right this moment in the Lehigh area of Pennsylvania I have reports of several outrages having been perpetrated on the settlers there."

Croghan made no reply and Amherst went on casually, "I understand the Moravian Indians are being blamed and there has been talk of destroying them."

"That's crazy talk!" the agent retorted. "The Moravian Indians are Christianized and they'd no more commit outrages on the settlers than the Quakers'd kill an Indian child! Everybody knows that."

Amherst only shrugged and went on. "I presume you have heard about the Connecticut people moving onto the Delaware Indian lands in Pennsylvania?"

Croghan frowned. "No, sir, I haven't. What people? What lands?"

"I've just been informed, sir," Amherst replied, his back still to Croghan, "that in defiance of the government of the Province of Pennsylvania and to the extreme displeasure of the Indians, a group of Connecticut settlers have taken claim to a section of the Wyoming Valley on the East Branch of the Susquehanna. They claim their right to it on the basis of a very nebulous land grant of several score years ago."

"It doesn't sound very smart at a time like this, your Excellency," Croghan commented, "but what's that got to do with me?"

"Just this, Mr. Croghan!" Amherst snapped, turning and facing the deputy Indian agent. "Your knowledge and ability with the Delawares—with all the Indians—is vitally needed now. Your resignation is absolutely not acceptable."

Croghan's eyes narrowed. "You telling me, Gen'ral, that I can't quit iffen I've a mind to?"

"Precisely, sir!"

"Then I reckon you got something yet to learn, Gen'ral, 'cause I'm quitting and they ain't no way you can stop it. And it won't do you no good to try to have me thrown in jail, neither, 'cause I won't be no more good to you there than I'd be in England."

Croghan's face had become flushed with his anger and now Amherst realized he had gone a little too far and tried another tack.

"Well, sir, there's no need to become irritated. Mr. Croghan, the reason I want you to stay is because you're so valuable to us. Why, I'd as soon consent to a whole battalion's going home right now as I would to your leaving here."

Croghan was unimpressed. "Flattery ain't going to change my mind, Gen'ral. I need to go and I damned well intend to."

Amherst shook his head in annoyance. "I'm trying to be

very patient with you, Mr. Croghan. Don't you think the Ministry would consider it very odd indeed if I gave you leave to go to England at a time like this, just when it may be that there is some hint of peace on the horizon?"

"*Peace!* Gen'ral, they ain't *no* hint of any peace yet, and they ain't going to be for a good long spell yet. Reckon I could go to England and back twice in a row 'fore any sort of peace was restored and my services needed. No sir, Gen'ral, I'm going, but I'll tell you one thing afore I do. Reckon it's high time somebody told you: it would've been one whole hell of a lot easier for you to've *prevented* this damn' needless war in the first place than it'll be for you to bring about a peace now!"

With the commander in chief spluttering angrily behind him, he stalked from the office a final time and immediately confirmed his passage for England aboard the *Britannia*, tentatively scheduled for departure from these shores about the end of the year. The interval would give him time to tie up loose ends yet remaining here.

[*October 3, 1763—Monday*]

Immediately following the rapid knocking, the door to Major Henry Gladwin's office was jerked open and a young officer—Lieutenant Diedrick Brehm—stepped a couple of paces into the room, saluted and spoke excitedly.

"Sir," he said, "good news! The *Huron* has just come into sight downriver. We haven't seen the other boats yet, but this must be the major reinforcement that was promised."

Gladwin smiled wearily and nodded. "Very good, Lieutenant Brehm. Order a cannon fired once in salute and prepare a guard at the water gate for their arrival. I'll be out shortly."

"Yes, sir!" Brehm saluted again and left, almost running.

Henry Gladwin continued smiling and then chuckled lightly. It was easy to remember when he had been an eager young lieutenant and had become easily excited. No more. Now he felt old; old and tired and very disinclined to run anywhere or get very excited about anything. Maybe that was what made a good officer. Maybe when a man no longer worked himself up to an excited pitch and when his body complained at unnecessary exertion, maybe when he took his time and allowed himself a chance to think about things thoroughly before acting, maybe that's what constituted wiseness, steadiness and reliability on an officer's part.

Thirty-five was hardly an age at which to feel old, but that was how Gladwin felt. In these past five months he felt he had aged more than in the preceding five years. He yearned so deeply again to be with his wife, Frances, that it had become almost physical anguish to think of her. When and if he saw her again, would he have changed so much that he would no longer be the man she had married? He grunted softly. Ridiculous thinking of such things as that. There were other matters to concern oneself with now. This reinforcement approaching, for example: he wondered how many men it would consist of and hoped that the rumors that had been passing about for so many days of a vast fleet of English batteaux approaching Detroit were correct. With four or five hundred men—even more, perhaps!—he could take up a strong enough offensive to end this damned siege for once and for all.

As he left his office and began moving down the street toward the southwest lookout station, he reviewed the state of matters here. It was said that Pontiac's allies were deserting him, that his siege was collapsing and could not be maintained much longer. In addition to the fact that winter was approaching again and the Indians would necessarily have to be going off to their winter hunting grounds if they were to provide for their families, there were reports that the Indians themselves were far more wary of the siege than were the soldiers they had kept bottled up here. Be that as it may, the danger was not ended; that had been made only too clear this past week.

Last Thursday, for example, after a week of quiet around the fort, Sergeant Bertram Fisher left the fort to go to the house of Jacques St. Martin with a message and on the way he was surprised by a pair of Ottawas, shot and killed. It was a sobering thing, not only because of the fact of Fisher's death, but because this same walk to St. Martin's house was one that many of the officers, Gladwin included, had taken lately.

Then, on Saturday, a Frenchman was seen putting out into the river just a little above the fort, apparently heading toward the Huron village across the river diagonally downstream. Gladwin considered it likely that the man might have been a spy, had his men hail the boat and order it back. When it refused to turn, he sent out a batteau in pursuit. They chased the craft across the river and were only thirty yards behind it when it grounded on the shore and the man leaped out and ran. At the same time another pair of Indians appeared high up on the bank, fired into the batteau and killed one of the privates.

No, despite encouraging reports—and even evidence—to the contrary, the siege was not yet lifted and the war far from ended. There were hopeful signs, of course, but Gladwin refused to let himself get overly enthusiastic about them. Chief Big Jaw of the Wyandot Hurons, for example—the one called Odinghquanooron by his own people—was one of the many chiefs who had recently come to talk with Gladwin. As the other chiefs had been, so this chief, too, seemed apprehensive of the rumors that an immense fleet of batteaux filled with reinforcements was approaching Detroit and he was anxious to sue for peace. Gladwin was skeptical, considering it no more than a matter of convenience and an attempt at self-preservation on Big Jaw's part, just as it had seemed to be with the others. Like all of them, Big Jaw feared the consequences of a major English attack; all the more so lately, since their ammunition was apparently almost exhausted and suing for peace could be the easiest method of gaining immunity from English reprisal, as well as for lulling the redcoats into a false sense of security. In this way, the reasoning seemed to dictate, they could head unmolested into their winter hunting grounds and then in the spring renew the war with a reasonable expectation of success.

This, at least, was the essence of the report brought to Gladwin by Sir William Johnson's party of Mohawks under the chief named Aaron. For some time the six Iroquois had been moving about the area, talking with the various village and tribal chiefs and gaining an insight into what the current situation was, how it had been brought about, and what might be expected in the future.

It was Aaron who reported to Gladwin that from all he could determine, it was more than a handful of Frenchmen here who were the real rascals of this whole affair; who kept the pot on the fire and well stirred. The Mohawk said as well that now there was evidence that many of the French here who had been actively supporting Pontiac were growing very afraid and that there had been occurring of late an exodus of a fair number of them toward the Mississippi, carrying with them considerable quantities of English plunder that had been given to them or that they had bought from the Indians here. True though the report might be—and Gladwin was inclined to accept it as truth, since the letter of introduction Aaron carried from Sir William Johnson recommended him highly—it was nevertheless still no time to relax.

Only yesterday Gladwin had sent out four batteaux which were armed with small cannon. Theirs was a reconnoitering mission under three lieutenants—Brehm, Abbott and Hay— as well as Ensign Robert Riggell, to go up to an island in the southern portion of Lake St. Clair to see if it was possible to bring firewood from it to the fort. They were fired on from shore by the Indians who had hidden themselves in holes dug in the bank. When the four batteaux turned to run for it, a horde of Indians launched nineteen of their own canoes and batteaux and gave pursuit. Letting them come fairly close, Lieutenant Brehm had suddenly ordered his batteau turned to face them and with the four-pounder cannon mounted in the bow, sent a point-blank charge of grapeshot into the nearest canoe, which was only forty or fifty yards distant. Of the fifteen or sixteen Indians in it, only two were capable of paddling after that and when that craft and others retreated to shore, the detachment heard the death cry raised from them. But the four batteaux had not come out of it unscathed, either. One private was killed and three others wounded.

Later in the day the Mohawk Aaron had come back to the fort to tell Gladwin that the cannon blast had killed three Chippewas and wounded seven others very badly. Worse than that, however, was that a severe spotted fever—apparently smallpox—was sweeping the nearby tribes, apparently spread inadvertently by some visiting Shawnees, whose own tribe had been suffering terribly from the disease. Already, Aaron said, many of the Chippewas, Ottawas and Potawatomies were sick with it and in the past week seven or eight Hurons had died of it. Many of the Indians were now lamenting the fact that this war prevented them from begging medical help from the fort. Gladwin told Aaron to go back and tell them that medical supplies would be provided where possible to all who ceased fighting.

Now, as he climbed to the lookout post, Major Gladwin felt a strong sense of relief that such a sizable reinforcement had at last arrived. Breathing a bit heavily, he finished his climb and looked over the ramparts and was immediately disappointed. There were no batteaux in sight at all. In fact, the only vessel visible was the *Huron*, although surely the *Michigan* could not be far behind. Perhaps it had just held back to escort the batteaux up the river.

Within the hour, however, the staggering truth was known. The ship anchored and the two officers aboard—Captain Hope and Lieutenant Montresor—reported to Gladwin. Briefly they told of the unrecoverable wreck of the *Michigan*, which was why they had not arrived at Detroit last time with the *Huron*. They told him as well of the hideous massacre at the Niagara Portage, of the fact that only one hundred and eighty-five barrels of provisions had been saved from the *Michigan*, which had now been brought aboard the *Huron* along with some other goods that had been at the Upper Landing, and, finally, that there was no massive reinforcement. Their reinforcement detachment had started out with seventeen men, but three of these had been killed by Indians after the shipwreck, so they had arrived at Detroit now with only fourteen.

Gladwin was stricken. Winter was rapidly approaching and there would not be time left for much more transportation of goods and men between Niagara and Detroit, and certainly these barrels of provisions brought on board the *Huron* were nowhere near enough for the Detroit garrison's subsistence until navigation opened again in the spring. Without substantial help immediately, Detroit could not possibly hold out for the winter.

"Alert the captain of the *Huron* that he will be setting sail for Niagara tomorrow," Gladwin ordered. "He'll have some wounded men to take back from here and I'll be sending Lieutenant MacDonald along with some dispatches to carry directly to New York for the general."

[October 7, 1763—Friday]

A great sigh of relief puffed out the flaccid cheeks of Sir Jeffrey Amherst as he read the dispatches just arrived from London. At last, after all these requests, after all these months of a situation here in America which just kept degenerating and with which he seemed unable to cope, Lieutenant General Amherst had now received His Majesty's gracious permission to return to England.

It would take four or five weeks to shift command of the North American forces over to Major General Thomas Gage, but at last now there was a real goal for him, an end in sight of all this vexation, a separation at last from having to think about or deal with or fight against a race of red barbarians. He was going home!

He sent a summons to Gage at once, ordering him to leave Montreal in command of his second and come to New York for the transfer of chief command. Few things had ever lifted Amherst's spirits as much as the thought that now he would be able to dump all these problems into Gage's lap.

He also held a hurried conference with Sir William Johnson for latest information to take with him to London on the state of Indian affairs in North America, and sent reiterating word to Major Wilkins at Fort Niagara that, despite the nearing winter, he must still mount a major reinforcement for Detroit this fall.

But while much of Amherst's concern was now lifted, the reverse was true in London. His Majesty's ministers were just now recognizing the fact that the North American Indian uprising was a full-blown war and that it really needn't have come about in the first place had affairs been properly administered. In an effort to quell it, they pushed through the Proclamation of 1763, which sternly limited the westward limit of white settlement to the crest of the Appalachian Range. It was about as useful as a declaration which would have ordered the tide to no longer rise and fall in the mouth of the Thames River.

Like it or not, westward expansion in North America had begun in earnest some time ago, and no Royal Proclamation given now could possibly stop it.

[October 17, 1763—Monday]

While the failure of the Indians to destroy Henry Bouquet's army had had something of a dampening effect on the border massacres in Pennsylvania and Virginia, it had by no means ended them. Here and there parties of Shawnees and Delawares continued with deadly frequency to descend unexpectedly on small settlements and isolated cabins, plundering, burning, killing and taking prisoners.

On September 20, two Virginia militia captains named Phillips and Moffat, along with their little army of sixty militiamen, had been lured into ambush by the Shawnees. The two captains had been killed, along with half their men, and the rest had fled eastward in panic.

The Senecas were busy, too. Ever since the Devil's Hole Massacre, they had been sniping away at Forts Niagara, Little Niagara and Schlosser, and numerous men had been killed while out gathering firewood or performing other tasks. It was not unusual for anywhere from one to six or eight men to go out and just vanish. No one needed an explanation as to what must have happened to them.

The border attacks continued worst, however, in Pennsylvania. For the first time bodies of settlers were forming themselves into illegal or only quasi-legal militia bands to rise and pursue, wherever possible, any reported Indians. No distinction was made between peaceful Indians and those on the warpath and tensions increased rather than relaxed. And since it was much easier—and considerably less dangerous!—to attack peaceful Indians, such acts were perpetrated with frequency and with total disregard to the righteously outraged cries of the Quakers in particular.

One party of drunken rangers, finding a small band of Christianized Moravian Indians—women as well as men— peacefully asleep in a barn along the Susquehanna, calmly and methodically murdered them all and then were themselves shocked and angered when several of the rangers were caught by surprise and themselves killed. It was not a time of calm thinking and, though the evidence was apparent that the rangers had been killed by a roving band of Delawares, the act was ascribed to vengeance on the part of other Moravian Indians and it was decided that it would be a fine thing indeed if *all* these proselytized red men were utterly exterminated.

There were at this time four principal communities of Indians in Pennsylvania well known for their placidity. Three of these were Moravian communities—Nain and Wequetank in the Lehigh area, and Wyalusing in the Wyoming Valley—and the other was a small community of about a score of Iroquois-speaking Conestogue Indians, who called their tiny town Conestoga. This latter band had been seated here since the very first settlement of Pennsylvania and had, in fact, taken part in the treaty drawn up with William Penn; a treaty which had been reconfirmed by every Pennsylvania governor since then. This made no difference to the self-proclaimed rangers, who viewed them as deadly enemies. Plans were already afoot to wipe out all four towns and kill every Indian inhabiting them. When the Quakers and certain responsible citizens of the frontier objected and declared that they would protect these innocents, the bordermen growled in reply that they would do so at their own risk, because they would kill anyone who stood between them and these red devils.

One of the militia groups ignoring the injunctions of the Pennsylvania General Assembly was raised by a veteran partisan of the French and Indian War, Colonel George Armstrong. Promising the destruction of every Indian village on the Susquehanna and its tributaries, he raised three hundred men, mainly residents of Cumberland and Lancaster Counties. They rendezvoused at a crossing of the Juniata River on the first of October and set out against some villages of hostile Delawares on the upper West Branch of the Susquehanna. On the sixth day of their march they arrived at the towns in the vicinity of Great Island, but found them all abandoned. Methodically they destroyed everything they saw and marched back down to Fort Augusta, arriving there on October 12, hungry, irritable, fatigued, and quarreling among themselves.

Returning to find their villages destroyed, the irate Delawares promptly descended upon Northampton County and there plundered and burned four houses and killed eleven people. Not yet satisfied, they left this area and headed northward toward a relatively new settlement of whites which was being called Wyoming[145] after the name of the stream there.

Although the Colonel Armstrong militia party was disbanded, many of the men immediately joined another which was forming at Harris's Ferry in Lancaster County to march north under Major James Clayton. Its object this time was to go against the Connecticut settlers who had refused demands of the Pennsylvanians that they leave. The idea of the mission was to drive the settlers away and destroy their corn and provisions before the Indians could sweep down on them and get these vital supplies for their own use. The band left Harris's Ferry on October 14 and late this afternoon, October 17, they arrived at Wyoming. They were two days too late and they were sickened by what they saw, as well as what they heard from the lone survivor. Twenty of the thirty-one Connecticut settlers had been taken into captivity by the Delawares and the other ten still lay on the ground here, all dead and badly mutilated. Nine of these were men, some with pitchforks sticking in their bodies, others pierced time and again with arrows and spears, a few with leather awls having been plunged into their eyes. The tenth victim was a woman who had been tortured. She had been forced to grasp red hot hinges in her hands and in many places the skin of her body had been flayed. Then, while apparently still alive, she had been scalped and roasted. The nine dead men had also been scalped.

The grim-faced Clayton party buried them hurriedly and began the march back to their own settlements, there to spread the word of the tragedy and to bring to a white heat the already flaming anger in the breasts of the border people, and to encourage the feeling that no matter whether he was a Shawnee or Delaware, a Seneca or a Mohawk, a Conestogue or a proselytized Indian, absolutely no Indian was a good Indian unless he was a dead Indian.

Despite the fact that at his back were marching his well-armed force of six hundred redcoated regulars, Major John Wilkins was very nervous. He wished he had not been ordered to lead this reinforcement detachment to Detroit. Ever since that awful massacre of the portage, his nights had been filled with bad dreams and more than once he had awakened with a fearful cry and found himself drenched with perspiration and shaking uncontrollably. Always in these nightmares he saw his own body lying there with the others, scalp gone, body mutilated, dead eyes staring accusingly at the heavens.

The orders from General Amherst that he was to lead this force to the relief of Detroit had reached Wilkins over a month ago, but it wasn't until just a few days ago that enough replacement regulars had arrived from various points to make up the requisite number of six hundred. He knew he ought to feel quite secure with so many trained soldiers under his command, but he could not shake off his worry. Worse yet, the troops sensed it in him and it had had a contagious effect upon them.

They had left Fort Niagara in this flotilla of batteaux, rowed up to the Lower Landing at Fort Little Niagara and made the portage past the site of the massacre, past the cataracts and finally to the Upper Landing, Fort Schlosser, where the batteaux were relaunched. The fear in the men as they passed the massacre place was a smothering veil over the whole force and it had diminished little even when the awful place was left behind. Now, afloat again and rowing upstream against this strong Niagara River current, they were still ripe for a disastrous panic to sweep them.

And so it did.

A mere handful of Senecas, probably no more than thirty or forty of them, opened fire on the flotilla from heavy cover on shore. Immediately thrown into confusion, the men dropped their oars and ducked for cover, making little attempt to rout the attackers. The current carried them swiftly backwards and in far less time than it had taken them since leaving there, they found themselves ashore again at Fort Schlosser. Not an Indian had been killed or even wounded, but of Major Wilkins's six-hundred-man force, two officers and six men were killed, two other officers and nine other men wounded. A small detachment was sent up the shore to drive out the Senecas, and Wilkins ordered camp to be made here "to wait for a more auspicious time for our enterprise."

Thus far, at least, the "enterprise" had not been one to inspire any great degree of confidence.

Had it not been for their complete sincerity, the position of the Quakers in regard to the Indian problem would have been positively ridiculous. Though it was galling, frustrating, and considerably more than merely irritating to many of the Pennsylvanians that the moralistic views of this religious body should dominate in the Provincial Assembly, yet there could be no denying that they not only believed what they said, they most assuredly practiced what they preached.

Human life was, to them, the most sacred thing next to God Himself. That the Indians should harass the frontiers and murder the settlers was, they agreed, a terrible thing, but it was also understandable; their lands were being taken, they were being grossly mistreated, and they were fundamentally afraid of the white man—afraid of what he would do to him with his superior weapons and superior numbers. Even the fact that they killed some whites, the Quakers pointed out, was to some degree excusable in that they were heathens and not trained to respect the value of human life, especially that of an enemy. They were not Children of God and so were ignorant of how great a wrong they did in the taking of a life. But, the Friends added darkly, that there could be Christian Englishmen—whether soldiers, settlers or whatever—who knew and understood Christian principles and yet went out deliberately to kill Indians was absolutely repugnant and sinful and must be prohibited.

They inveighed bitterly against the unlawful expeditions against the Indians which were being mounted by so-called militia groups, declaring them to be not only murderous, but seditious as well. To support their argument, they pointed out the recent case of what had occurred at the Moravian Indian town of Wequetank. On the night of October 10, a group of men whom they described as "a mob of armed border ruffians," slipped up in the woods just beyond that town with the view of destroying it and killing all its inhabitants. The Lord intervened, the Quakers declared, by sending a drenching rainstorm which soaked the men, rendered their gunpowder unusable, and drove them away. Learning of their close call, the Moravian Indians were terrified and with the help of their missionary, Bernard Grube, they had now removed to another of their towns called Nazareth. Here they waited in fear for whatever action might be taken against them. What, the Quakers wanted to know, was the Assembly going to do about it?

It was not an easy dilemma for the Pennsylvania Assembly to overcome. In fact it seemed unlikely that any sort of solution could be reached which would be acceptable to both the Quakers and their foes. But then, in a move that could only be called brilliant, a motion was made that all these so-called peaceful Indians be disarmed, taken into protective custody and moved to a part of the Province where there would be no chance of them engaging in mischief, or abetting those who did. The plan was acceptable to both factions and a ruling made to carry it out.

But that the Quakers were entirely sincere in their pacific views was unquestionable. These views were difficult enough to stand by in the comfortably secure aura of civilization in Philadelphia, but for the many Quakers living on the frontier, it was considerably more difficult. Neither threat nor actual physical violence could make them alter their stand, and the example of a Quaker named John Fincher was a case in point.

Shortly after noon today, Fincher heard a noise outside his cabin and went out to investigate. Fifty or sixty yards away he saw a band of painted Delawares on horseback. With firebrands in their hands, they were obviously intent on destroying his place. With remarkable courage and calmness, Fincher held up his right hand in the sign of peace and walked toward them smiling. He stopped at the foot of their muscular, war-painted leader.

"Welcome, brothers," he said. "May thy days be many and happy. My home and all that is in it I am prepared to share with thee. As thou may see, I am a Quaker and a friend of the Indians. I trust thou intendest no harm here."

With a movement that was almost casual, the leader of the party leaned forward to one side of his horse's neck and, laughing as he did so, buried his tomahawk to the haft in John Fincher's temple.

Pacifism, it seemed, was by no means always the easiest course.

It was over.

For Pontiac, the war at Detroit must end this day. He knew it with a great feeling of bitterness and dejection. He had failed: failed himself, failed his Ottawas, failed the Indian race in general.

Day by day during this month of miserably rainy weather he had seen it coming, had known that eventually there would come the breaking-off point, the time of the end. That time was now, this moment.

His allies had deserted him, chief by chief, village by village, tribe by tribe. Beginning October 12 many of the chiefs had gone to see Major Gladwin and sued for peace, but the major had given no answer to any of them other than that they should remain quiet and go about their hunting and he would communicate their wishes to the general. In a last strong effort to maintain his hold on his allies, Pontiac had convened, eleven days ago, another great council of the tribes here at the mouth of the River Rouge. He had expected an attendance of perhaps fifteen hundred to two thousand warriors of all tribes. Instead, a total of only sixty canoes had come bearing less than four hundred Indians, mostly Chippewas, along with a few Potawatomies and Hurons. None of the northern Chippewas or Ottawas had come, and even of his own Ottawas here, only about two-thirds attended, the rest having gone off under Chief Manitou. And so the grand council was not so grand at that.

In his best oratorical manner Pontiac had appealed to them not to desert him but to maintain the siege, for certainly Detroit could not possibly hold out against them much longer.

"My brothers," he pleaded, "hear me! Two days ago Frenchmen whom you well know in this region came to me. They told me that within only a matter of days now I can expect help from the French King, help we have so long awaited! They told me that this very moment a convoy is on the way here from the Illinois country. It is a large detachment of French soldiers under our good friend Captain de Beaujeu, who brings with him for us forty packhorses loaded with ammunition and provisions. We need only wait a few days more!"

He had held them, but just barely, and certainly not for long. They continued sporadic firing at the fort for a few

665

days more and then they began drifting away. Six days ago the last of his Huron allies vanished. Four days ago the Potawatomies disappeared. Just the day before yesterday the final contingent of Chippewas left and, with them, ten canoeloads of his own Ottawas, claiming they could no longer put off going to their winter hunting grounds.

The final crushing blow had come late last night with the arrival of the party of French and Indians from the Illinois country, led by a young cadet named DeQuindre, who first came to Pontiac with the dispatches written by Major Neyon de Villiere, read and explained them to him and then continued to the fort to deliver them to Major Gladwin and the French inhabitants.

Now, with a Frenchman beside him to take down as he dictated, Pontiac slowly formed the most difficult letter he had ever had to compose:

My Brother

The word which my Father has sent me to make peace I have accepted. All my young men have buried their hatchets. I think you will forget the bad things that have taken place for some time past. Likewise I shall forget what you may have done to me, in order to think of nothing but good. I, the Chippewas, the Hurons, we are ready to go speak with you when you ask us. Give us an answer. I am sending this resolution to you in order that you may see it. If you are as kind as I, you will make me a reply. I wish you a good day.

Pontiac

Mons. Gladwin, Major
Commandt. au Detroit

The Chippewas and Hurons were, of course, gone from him, but Pontiac thought it would make dealing with Gladwin a little easier if the major believed the other tribes still supported him. He sent the Frenchman off with the note at once, enjoining him to return the quickest possible moment with Gladwin's reply. By nightfall it was given to him, and it was even more brief than Pontiac's note had been. It said:

31st October 1763, Detroit
Pontiac of the Ottawas:

I have received your letter of this date. If I had started this war, then perhaps I would be able to grant you peace; but it was you, Pontiac, who began it, therefore you must await the pleasure of the general in this matter. I will immediately communicate to the general your peaceable inclination and your promise of good behavior, and I doubt not that if you are true to your words, all will be well. I will notify you of the General's decision as soon as I have received it. I wish you good evening.

Henry Gladwin, Major
Commander of Detroit

Pontiac nodded, his face devoid of expression. The reply neither pleased nor angered him. It was neither more nor less than he had expected, but he had no intention whatever of remaining here to await the general's pleasure, whatever that pleasure might be. Certainly it would hardly be any sort of pleasure for Pontiac and his remaining faithful people. He nodded again and dismissed the Frenchman and then called in one of his subchiefs.

"Go out among our people," he told him, "and tell them to tie up their things and prepare to go. We will leave this place tonight and we will not return. For now we will go south to the River Maumee and there we will build a new village. You may tell everyone that the war is over for the Ottawa people."

It was true—the war *was* over for the Ottawas, but not yet for the Senecas, Wyandots, Delawares and Shawnees.

667

CHAPTER XI

[*November 1, 1763—Tuesday*]

MAJOR HENRY GLADWIN made a neat packet of the letters and proclamations and some other documents received lately from Pontiac, several other chiefs, some influential Frenchmen of Detroit, and from the young French cadet named DeQuindre of Fort de Chartres. This completed, he began to write the letter to General Amherst with which these papers would be enclosed. It was a letter which he wrote with a most heartfelt sense of gratitude and relief:

Detroit, November 1, 1763

Sir:

On the 12th October, the enemy sued for peace in a very submissive manner. At that time I was so circumstanced for want of flour that I must either pass or hear them. Of the two, I chose the latter, thinking it of the utmost consequence to keep possession of the country. Nevertheless, I made them no promises. I told them the affair of peace lay wholly in your breast, but I did not doubt, when you were thoroughly convinced of their sincerity, everything would be well again; upon which hostility ceased and they dispersed to their hunting grounds. This gave me an opportunity of getting flour from the inhabitants hereabout in this country to serve from hand to mouth.

Yesterday, Monsieur DeQuindre, a volunteer, arrived with dispatches from the commandant of the Illinois, copies of which I enclose to you. The tenor of that which I enclose from Pontiac is something extraordinary. The Indians are preparing for peace. I enclose you my answer to their demands.

I believe, as things are circumstanced, it would be to the good of his Majesty's servants to accommodate matters in the

668

spring. By that time the savages will be sufficiently reduced for want of powder, and I do not imagine there will be any danger of their breaking out again, provided some examples are made of their good subjects, the French, who set them on. No advantage can be gained by prosecuting the war, owing to the difficulty of catching them. Add to this the expense of such a war which, if continued, the entire ruin of the peltry trade must follow, and the loss of a prodigious consumption of our merchandise. It will be the means of their retiring, which will reinforce other nations on the Mississippi, whom they will push against us and make them our enemies forever. Consequently, they will render it extremely difficult, if not impossible, for us to pass in that country. And, especially, the French have promised to supply them with everything they want.

They have lost between eighty and ninety of their best warriors, but if your Excellency still intends to punish them further for their barbarities, it may easily be done without any expense to the Crown, simply by permitting a free sale of rum, which will destroy them more effectually than fire and sword; but, on the contrary, if you intend to accommodate matters in the spring, which I hope you will for the above reasons, it may be necessary to send up Sir William Johnson.

I shall write your Excellency fully concerning everything in this department by Lieutenant Montresor. This letter comes by Aaron, a Mohawk, whom I shall direct to wait at Fort Pitt for your answer.

This moment I received a message from Pontiac, telling me that he will send to all the Nations concerned in the war to bury the hatchet, and he hopes your Excellency will forget what is past. If not, I believe he will retire to the Mississippi.

In a few days I shall send a duplicate of this by Andrew, a faithful Huron. He has a great deal to say with the Delawares. He will try to make matters easy that way. I shall direct him to assure them of a peace, provided they remain quiet during the winter, which may perhaps ease our frontiers of those villains and, in spring, your Excellency can do as you please with them.

No news of the troops nor of the vessel which sailed from hence the 7th of last month. If the troops do not come very soon, they will scarcely have time to return to Niagara, but I hope they will come in time enough to destroy that nest of thieves at Sandusky. When things are accommodated, if your Excellency allows an exclusive trade for a year or two to the *merchants who have suffered so much by this unhappy affair, they will be amply paid for their loss.*

I have the honor to be, with the utmost respect, Sir,

Your most obedient, humble servant,

Henry Gladwin

His Excellency
Genl. Jeffrey Amherst

[November 6, 1763—Sunday]

It was not without reason that as the pitiful procession of Moravian Indians approached Philadelphia this morning they were filled with a great fear. They had not, in fact, been without fear for many days now.

At first when the word had reached them in their villages that for their own protection the government of Pennsylvania was going to take their weapons and place them, the Moravian Indians, out of danger, they had not cared much for the idea. But the Wequetank faction, already having narrowly escaped massacre because of a providential storm, convinced them that government protection was now their only hope of survival.

With some reluctance these Christian Indians of both Wequetank and Nazareth yielded up their arms and packed their meager possessions for the journey to Philadelphia. On the morning of the day established for their departure, they all congregated in the mission church where their preacher, the Reverend Bernard Grube, gave a brief sermon and then led them all in the singing of a hymn.

By noon they were on their way, with the very elderly, the sick, the lame, the blind and the very young riding in jolting flatbed wagons, and the remainder walking before and behind them. At both Wyalusing and Bethlehem, as they passed these two towns, the Moravian Indians there joined the procession and now their number totaled one hundred and forty individuals.

It was not a pleasant journey. At every settlement, every hamlet, every town and city through which they passed, they were greeted with anger and threats and curses. Garbage was thrown at them and sometimes sticks and stones. The nearer they came to Philadelphia, the worse it became. They were paced by hecklers, jabbed at with sticks, jeered and cursed further and spat upon. Many of them prayed as they walked, asking the God whose children they now were to deliver them from this ordeal, but instead the worst still lay ahead. At

Germantown a mob of angry citizens descended upon them, screaming for their scalps and their blood and it was only through the efforts of a small body of hastily formed policemen that this mob was restrained from physically attacking them.

Now they had reached Philadelphia and the crowds before were as nothing compared to the great influx of people who surrounded them here. Hundreds upon hundreds of people milled and pushed. Most had never really seen "wild Indians" before but they had heard, as everyone had, of the frontier depredations and they now considered it their duty to aid in making everyone of these Moravian Indians into "good" Indians. Rocks were thrown and both fists and booted feet lashed out. By the time the confused and frightened Indians had been brought to the barracks assigned to their use by the governor, many were bleeding or welted and a few could no longer walk and had been placed in the wagons.

It was ten o'clock in the morning when the barracks was reached, but the haven it offered was denied them. A large squad of soldiers stood barring their way, holding rifles with fixed bayonets and, taking it upon themselves to defy the orders of the governor, refused to let the "red niggers" enter.

For five hours the refugees stood in the midst of the square before the barracks and all this while the mob abused them in a variety of ways and were prevented from killing them only by the arrival of a large group of Quakers who placed themselves between the mob and the Indians and prevented further physical damage from being inflicted upon those in the center.

And now, finally, a larger detachment of soldiers had come and was leading them away, taking them to where they could no longer be surrounded and threatened; taking them to Province Island in the Delaware River below the city. And here they were lodged in filthy, decrepit, broken-down, windowless waste buildings where half their number would have been crowded. And here, cold, hungry, tired and bewildered, many of them bleeding from minor wounds, they knelt and with folded hands and bowed heads, thanked the white man's God for their deliverance.

[*November 7, 1763—Monday*]

Wholly unaware that Pontiac had ended his war against the English, that the confederacy of tribes he had drawn together was broken apart and scattered, that Detroit was under siege no longer, and that a reinforcement was not any longer urgently required, the harried Major John Wilkins was making another effort to get his six-hundred-man detachment to the west.

With the few harassing parties of Senecas now run off and the way clear, Wilkins had once more reluctantly ordered the batteaux loaded, the soldiers aboard and the journey across Lake Erie recommenced. Without any loss greater than the shedding of a few drops of perspiration, the flotilla rowed its way from Fort Schlosser upriver on the Niagara to the mouth of Lake Erie. Here, at Buffalo Creek, they took a heading a little bit south of due west, moved across the open waters of the lake and encountered the Canadian shore sixty-five miles distant at that great, narrow, eastward-pointing peninsula known as Long Point.

The wise course to have adopted here, especially at this season, would have been to follow the shoreline closely from this point westward. Never widely acclaimed for his wisdom, however, Major Wilkins—now in great haste to get to Detroit, seeing that the journey was really underway—elected to set a course directly for Point Aux Pins, another eighty-five miles ahead of them across the open lake.

Just before the fall of night today, Point Aux Pins loomed on the horizon ahead, but so did something else. Behind it a great bank of sinister-looking black clouds was moving swiftly toward them. The men bent with extra effort to their oars, but darkness overtook them first, followed shortly afterward by a violent storm which passed almost as quickly as it had come. But in its passage, the storm had taken a grim toll.

The remains of the unmercifully battered flotilla beached themselves on the point and a quick tally was taken: fifty-two barrels of provisions were lost; all the ammunition for the entire six hundred men and for the resupplying of Detroit was lost; eighteen batteaux had sunk; two batteaux and their occupants were missing; seventy men—including three officers—had been drowned.

It was an extremely fortunate thing that Detroit was no longer under siege and was now out of danger, because if help from Major John Wilkins was required, it would still be a long time in coming. A council of the surviving officers was held and, after much discussion, it was decided that the boats remaining should be repaired and the force make its way back again to Niagara—this time hugging the shore.

If anyone wept this day at the fact that Lieutenant General Sir Jeffrey Amherst was embarking for England, leaving behind him forever the North American continent, no note was ever made of it.

He was leaving behind more than just Major General Thomas Gage as the new commander in chief: he was leaving behind a chaotic situation on the frontiers which was largely of his making; leaving behind a land whose earth was soaked with the lifeblood of hundreds, perhaps even thousands, of men, women and children—settlers, soldiers, traders, frontiersmen. Indians; leaving behind a tragedy of the first magnitude which need never have occurred at all, but for his simple lack of human understanding.

Amherst was a good soldier, and a brave one, but it was unlikely that when he reached England he would be revered as the military leader who had led His Majesty's forces to brilliant victories at the close of the French and Indian War; now as the King's officer who had wrested control and dominion of a vast wilderness empire from the French. No, things had changed. He had left England when George II was King, but since that monarch's death in October three years ago, the Crown of England rested upon a new head—that of George III—and a different ministry had come to power. It was a government intolerant of failure, and the former commander in chief of His Majesty's North American forces was returning home to a reception as the general who, with all the military resources of the British Empire at his beck, could not quash the uprising of a pack of naked savages.[146]

And in this land which he was this day to leave forever behind, perhaps no comment of the many that were made was more exemplary of the general feeling about him than that made in a single sentence written by Captain Simeon Ecuyer to Colonel Henry Bouquet:

What universal cries of joy and what bumpers of Madeira are drunk to his prompt departure!

[*December 10, 1763—Saturday*]

Major General Thomas Gage was determined that he was very quickly going to put the quietus to the Indian troubles in North America and he let no grass sprout beneath his feet before starting several important wheels turning. Unlike his predecessor, Amherst, for whom he held no brief and, in fact whom he had admired as a military leader, Gage knew the Indians well. He recognized, just as Lord Howe had recognized in the French and Indian War, that conventional battle methods were more often than not worse than useless against the Indians.[147] To fight them effectively, men accustomed to the wilderness would have to be used. Gage meant to use them.

Not a man to delude himself in any respect, Gage realized immediately that no matter what course he took, the task ahead was apt to be fraught with frustration and difficulties. That His Majesty's forces could crush the uprising, he had no doubt, but he was determined from the onset that—aside from what wilderness fighting value they might have—the onus for this job must be shared by those who would most benefit from it, the men of the various provinces. The difficulty here lay not merely in convincing the provinces to provide men—though assuredly that would be difficult—but in keeping tight military control of these men once they were obtained. Militia, whether made up of frontiersmen or clerks, could be very good fighters, but they were inclined to be an undisciplined, headstrong, vindictive and irresponsible body unless kept under tight check. Gage recognized only too well that truth in the letter written by William Smith of New York five days after Amherst's departure. As Smith put it:

Is not Mr. Amherst the happiest of men to get out of this trouble so seasonably? At last he was obliged to submit, to give the Indians so great a mark of his consideration as to confess he could not defend us, and to make a requisition of 1400 Provincials by the Spring . . . Is not Gage to be pitied? The war will be a tedious one, nor can it be glorious, even though attended with success. Instead of decisive battles, woodland skirmishes; instead of colors and cannon, our trophies will be stinking scalps. Heaven preserve you, my friend, from a war conducted by a spirit of murder rather than of brave and generous offense . . .

Gage's first moves, therefore, were swiftly and decisively made. On his first day in his new command he confirmed Amherst's recommendation of November 15 calling for the provinces of Virginia, Maryland, Pennsylvania, New York and New Jersey to draft men for militia service in ratio to the population of each province. There were complaints about it, but these were met and overcome without undue difficulty. The greatest complaint, especially from Pennsylvania and Virginia, as well as their strongest demand, was that since the people of New England would share in the benefits of crushing the Indian uprising, then it behooved them to share equally in furnishing militiamen. It was a reasonable request and Gage saw to it at once.

While yet it was not known precisely how many militiamen he would get, Gage was hoping for a force of at least six thousand men. Three thousand of these he planned to put under command of Colonel Henry Bouquet, with which that officer could lead an expedition next spring from Fort Pitt into the Ohio country against the Shawnees and Delawares. The other three thousand would be prepared for a simultaneous expedition to the western Great Lakes country under command of Colonel John Bradstreet, this force to rendezvous at Fort Niagara. Bouquet was to be responsible directly to Gage. Bradstreet was to be responsible to—and concert his actions with—Colonel Bouquet. It was, of course, Bouquet who had thoroughly outlined such a two-pronged attack to General Amherst shortly after the battle at Edge Hill and Bushy Run. It was an excellent plan, which Amherst had strongly recommended that Gage give his approval to, and Gage had done so. Now Gage wrote to Bouquet:

The nature and service you have been upon this campaign must, I am certain, have greatly harassed and fatigued the troops, and the difficulties in getting up your convoys extremely great. I hope, however, you have been able to get up the last convoy, which I am pleased to find will leave your fort well supplied. I am sorry the two Provinces of Pennsylvania and Maryland have been so backward in affording you that assistance which is so much in their interest to do. It is, as you observe, next to impossible to march in the woods with Regulars alone, without being every moment subject to a surprise from which a body of good woodsmen would effectually secure you.

In respect to the expedition you propose . . . if it should be too late to be attempted this year, it must be refused till Spring. And as soon as you shall have finished the operations possible to be effected his year, put your fort in a proper state of defense and secured your communication, I shall be very glad to see you at New York, to concert with you the operations for the ensuing Spring . . .

I am with great regard, Sir,

Your most obedient servant,
Thos. Gage

[December 31, 1763—Saturday]

The incredibly eventful year of 1763 drew to a close with a bitter, howling blizzard ripping its way down from the north across the Michigan and Ohio country wilderness—now coming to be called the Northwest Territory—and whining through the forests and hills and river valleys of Pennsylvania. At Detroit numerous buildings lost their roofs to the screeching wind and eight inches of new snow was dumped atop that already on the ground.

Great snowdrifts piled up against the walls of Detroit and Fort Niagara and Fort Pitt, and just as the Pennsylvania settlers huddled about the fireplaces in their tiny log cabins, so too the Indians squatted blanket-covered and fur-wrapped around their lodge fires in wegiwas, tepees, quonsets, cabins and longhouses in their villages across the wilderness from the Green Bay and Sault Sainte Marie areas to the valleys of the Mohawk and the Genesee, the Susquehanna and Allegheny, the Scioto and Ohio rivers. Theirs was more than just an effort to keep warm, because in nearly every village, especially among the Shawnees and Delawares, the ravages of smallpox were still taking their toll; and among the victims who died was, ironically enough perhaps the greatest champion of the English among the Delawares, Shingas—he whom the English often called Chief Beaver.[148]

Movement was virtually at a standstill in the wilderness and an uneasy, weather-dictated cessation of hostilities filled the land. That the maraudings would begin again, that there would be strife and woe and unimaginable sufferings yet to come, was a depressing knowledge in the minds of everyone, but for now there was a chance to breathe a little more freely, to relax the tiring vigilance, to reflect a bit on what had happened in this incredible year and what was yet to come in 1764.

The siege of Detroit was ended and the war in that theater supposedly over, yet the events of the past two months there had indicated that this might not really be the case at all. Soldiers who left forts by themselves or in small groups were somehow never seen again and words of war and hatred still ose in the air over lodge fires. Rumor had it that Pontiac, though he had relocated his village on the banks of the Maumee River, had stopped en route at Sandusky and had encouraged the Wyandots under Chief Odinghquanooron to continue the war with him in the spring. It was also said that Pontiac was preparing to go to the Illinois country, there to rouse the bloodlust among the tribes of the Illinois Confederacy—the Peorias, Muncees, Piankeshaws and Cahokias, the Kaskaskias, Kickapoos and Kankankees, the Weas and Mascoutens. With Pontiac and egging him on were still such renegade Frenchmen as Baptiste Campeau, Alexis Cuillerier, Pierre Barth, John Maiet, Jacques St. Vincent and others, all of them men who had fled the Detroit area immediately upon hearing that Major Gladwin had ordered a roundup of suspected French agitators and had already arrested Mini Chene and Jacques Godefroy. No, the possibility of a renewed siege against Detroit in the spring was not to be laughed off. No treaty had yet been made, no end of the war confirmed. It was with distinct dread in the hearts of many that they viewed the coming of spring.

At Detroit, many things had happened since the ending of the siege. The critical shortage of food had almost immediately been alleviated by the French residents who now—either through no longer harboring fear of reprisal from Pontiac, or to ingratiate themselves to the English whose dominion here was no longer in doubt—sold Major Gladwin great stores of wheat and meat. Within four days following the lifting of the siege, the bins of Detroit were bulging with 8,000 pounds of wheat and by November 10 there was an additional 9,000 pounds of flour and 23,000 pounds of meat in storage. It was more than enough to maintain a garrison of two hundred and fifty men all winter long. This was a fortunate thing, for anticipated supplies never had arrived from Niagara. Instead had come two friendly Hurons to Gladwin, one of them carrying a message concealed in the false bottom of his powder horn, which told of the disaster suffered on the lake by Major Wilkins's detachment and the return of that force to Fort Niagara. It was a bitter pill indeed for Gladwin, not so much because of the lost supplies, since they were no longer so desperately needed here, but because he had eagerly anticipated being relieved of his command, and now this meant he would have to stay on at least until spring when navigation opened again. With a cold implacability he had grown to detest Detroit more than any other place he knew.

With the need no longer acute for so large a garrison here, the commander of Detroit took advantage of a last stretch of warm weather and ordered a detachment of two hundred and forty men back to Fort Niagara and eventually the east. Under command of Major Robert Rogers and with Captain Joseph Hopkins and Lieutenant John Montresor along, they left in a flotilla of nineteen batteaux on November 20, carrying along with them numerous dispatches for General Gage, Colonel Bouquet, Sir William Johnson and other officials, as well as a great volume of personal letters from the garrison to their families and friends. Following the north shore of Lake Erie, with favorable winds all the way, they reached Niagara after an uneventful trip of only seven days. Major Wilkins begged Rogers to stay on at the fort, but the former commander of the Rangers refused, declaring he had messages to deliver to General Gage in New York. And so he did, but he took a long while getting there, detouring to New England on the way to spend a lengthy and delightful respite with Betsey, his beloved wife. Montresor, however, continued directly to New York, delivering his messages to General Gage on December 18.

Far to the north of Detroit, wearied of the responsibility of holding Fort Michilimackinac for the return of the English, who could now come with probable safety to reclaim it anytime, Charles Michel de Langlade turned command of the fort over to Frenchman Pierre Parent, packed all he owned, and with his wife and children moved across Lake Michigan to Green Bay, determined to remain there in peace with the world until his life should end.[149]

At Fort Niagara, the difficulties with Indians had not ended. Little bands of Senecas still harassed the place and preyed upon individual soldiers or small detachments of them which were sent out. On November 5, for example, a wood-cutting party of men was sent out at the lower landing and was promptly captured within sight of Fort Little Niagara. Even as the soldiers still inside the fortifications watched fearfully, they saw eight of the captives deliberately and cold-bloodedly killed one after another. The head of their corporal was cut off and impaled on a post. All eight were scalped. The remaining two captives were taken away with the Indians. And the nightmares of frightened Major John Wilkins increased.

To the south, on the Mohawk River, Sir William Johnson—aided by George Croghan who had not yet departed this land—continued to hold council with the Iroquois.

Knowing that none of the five tribes of this confederacy who were still loyal to the English would even consider attacking the sixth—the Senecas—Johnson conspicuously appealed to the Caughnawagas of near Montreal to raise the hatchet against that western-most tribe of the Iroquois, knowing even as he made the appeal that they would refuse, but that it might concern the Senecas enough to cause them to come to council here. As usual, he had foreseen their reaction correctly. They came, surly and uncommunicative. This bothered Johnson not at all. In front of the other five tribes he told the Senecas of the great armies being prepared to march in the spring, warning them to leave the redcoats alone. He wound up by castigating them in an example of Iroquoian oratory so blistering that they were unable to reply and slunk off to consider the fact that perhaps they had been making a grievous error and that it was time to mend their ways.

Both Johnson and Croghan made written reports to the Lords of the Board of Trade in London—Croghan in an attempt to estimate the loss to England thus far in this uprising, and Johnson in reply to a request from them to clearly outline what lands were in question which the Iroquois League and various tribes were fighting to retain or recover, as well as why the Indians had uprisen against the English in the first place.

Croghan, as always, was blunt to the extreme in his communiqué:

> *The Indians can, with great ease, enter our colonies and cut off our frontier settlements and thereby lay waste a large tract of country, which, indeed, they have effected in the space of four months in Virginia, Maryland, Pennsylvania, and the Jerseys, on whose frontiers they have killed and captivated not less than two thousand of His Majesty's subjects, and drove some thousands to beggary and the greatest distress, besides burning to the ground nine forts or blockhouses in the country, and killing a number of His Majesty's troops and traders. All this with a loss to themselves of only about eighty killed in actual fighting of this war.*

William Johnson was considerably more detailed in his response, writing in answer to the first question:

Johnson Hall, November 18, 1763

My Lords:
In obedience to your Lordships' commands of the 5th Au-

gust last, I am now to lay before you the claims of the Nations mentioned in the State of the Confederacies. The Six Nations have, in the last century (when known as the Five Nations), subdued the Shawnees, Delawares, Miamis, and western Indians so far as Lakes Michigan and Superior, received them into an alliance, allowed them possession of the lands they occupied, and have ever since been in peace with the greatest part of them; and such was the prowess of the Five Nations Confederacy that, had they been properly supported by us, they would have long since put a period to the Colony of Canada, which alone they were near effecting in the year 1688. Since that time they have admitted [in 1710] the Tuscaroras from the southward, beyond Oneida, and they have ever since formed a part of that Confederacy, making it then the Six Nations.

As original proprietors, this Confederacy claim the country of their residence: south of Lake Ontario to the great Ridge of the Blue Mountains, with all the western part of the Province of New York towards Hudson River, west of the Catskill, thence to Lake Champlain, and from Regioghne (a rock at the east side of said lake) to Oswegatchie (or La Gallette) on the River St. Lawrence, (having long since ceded their claim north of said line in favor of the Canada Indians as hunting ground), thence up the River St. Lawrence, and along the south side of Lake Ontario to Niagara.

In right of conquest, they claim all the country (comprehending the Ohio) along the great Ridge of Blue Mountains at the back of Virginia, thence to the head of Kentucky River, and down the same to the Ohio above the Rifts, thence northerly to the south end of Lake Michigan, then along the eastern shore of said lake to Michilimackinac, thence easterly across the north end of Lake Huron to the great Ottawa River (including the Chippewa or Mississaugi country), and down the said river to the Island of Montreal. However, these more distant claims, being possessed by many powerful Nations, the inhabitants have long begun to render themselves independent, by the assistance of the French and the great decrease of the Six Nations; but their claim to the Ohio and thence to the Lakes is not in the least disputed by the Shawnees, Delawares, etc., who never transacted any sales of land or other matters without their consent, and who sent deputies to the grand council at Onondaga on all important occasions.

The second question asked by the Lords of the Board of

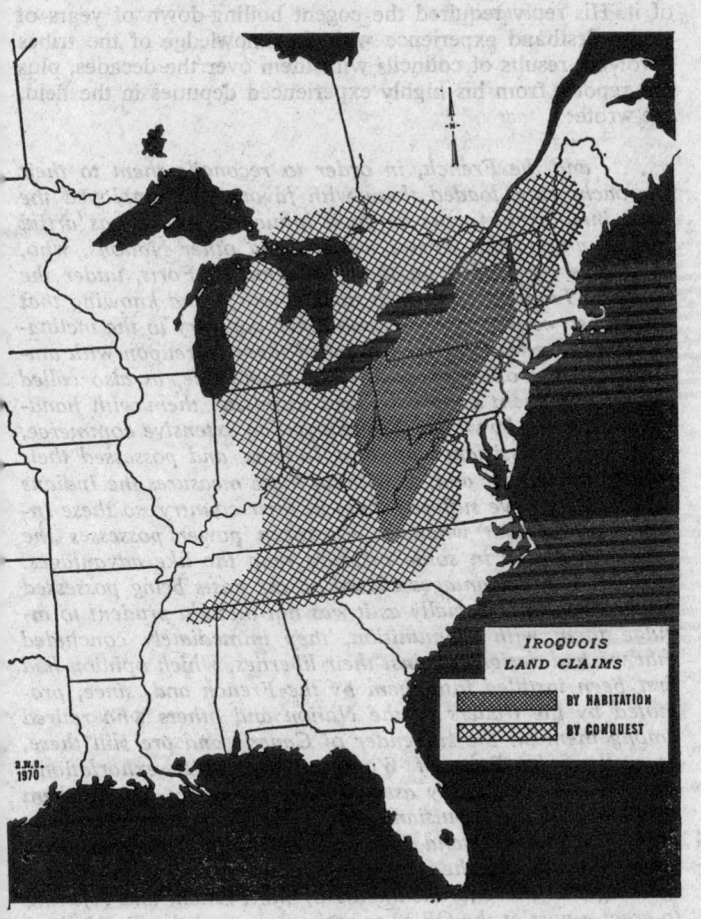

IROQUOIS
LAND CLAIMS

BY HABITATION

BY CONQUEST

Trade—why the Indians had declared war on the English to begin with—was no easy matter to answer. Probably no other white man in America could have done so admirable a job of it. His reply required the cogent boiling-down of years of study, firsthand experience with the knowledge of the tribes involved, results of councils with them over the decades, plus the reports from his highly experienced deputies in the field. He wrote:

. . . and the French, in order to reconcile them to their encroachments, loaded them with favors, and employed the most intelligent Agents of good influence, as well as artful Jesuits, among the several western and other Nations, who, by degrees, prevailed on them to admit of Forts, under the name of Trading Houses, in their country; and knowing that these posts could never be maintained contrary to the inclinations of these Indians, they supplied them thereupon with ammunition and other necessaries in abundance, as also called them to frequent congresses and dismissed them with handsome presents, by which they enjoyed an extensive commerce, obtained the assistance of these Indians, and possessed their frontiers in safety; and, as without these measures the Indians would never have suffered them in their country, so these Indians expect that whatever European power possesses the same, they shall in some measure reap the like advantages. Now as these advantages ceased on the posts being possessed by the English, especially as it was not thought prudent to indulge them with ammunition, they immediately concluded that we had designs against their liberties, which opinion had first been instilled into them by the French and, since, promoted by the traders of the Nation and others who retired among them on the surrender of Canada and are still there, as well as by Belts of Wampum and other exhortations, which I am confidently assured have been sent among them from the Illinois, Louisiana, and even Canada for that purpose. The Shawnees and Delawares about the Ohio, who were never warmly attached to us since our neglects to defend them against the encroachments of the French, and refusing to erect a post at the Ohio, or assist them and the Six Nations with men or ammunition when they requested both of us, as well as being irritated at the loss of several of their people being killed upon the communication of Fort Pitt in the years of 1759 and 1761, were easily induced to join with the western Nations; and the Senecas, dissatisfied at many of our posts in their country, jealous of our designs, and displeased

at our neglect and contempt of them, soon followed their example.

These, My Lords, are the causes the Indians themselves assign and which certainly caused the rupture between us, the consequence of which, in my opinion, will be that the Indians (who do not regard the distance) will be supplied with necessaries by the Wabash and several rivers which empty into the Mississippi, which it is by no means in our power to prevent, and in return the French will draw the valuable furs down that river to the advantage of their Colony and the destruction of our trade; this will always induce the French to foment differences between us and the Indians; and the prospects many of them entertain, that they may hereafter become possessed of Canada, will incline them still more to cultivate a good understanding with the Indians which, if ever attempted by the French would, I am very apprehensive, be attended with a general defection of them from our interest unless we are at great pains and expense to regain their friendship, and thereby satisfy them that we have no designs to their prejudice . . .

The grand matter of concern to all the Six Nations (Mohawks excepted) is our occupying a chain of small posts on the communication through their country to Lake Ontario . . . ; in order to obtain permission for erecting these posts, these Indians were promised that they should be demolished at the end of the war.[150] General [William] Shirley also made them a little promise for the posts he erected; and as about these posts are their fishing and hunting places—where they complain they are often obstructed by the troops and insulted—they request they may not be kept up, the war with the French now being over.

In 1760, Sir Jeffrey Amherst sent a speech to the Indians in writing (which was to be communicated to the Nations about Fort Pitt, etc., by General Monckton, then commanding there) signifying his intentions to satisfy and content all Indians for the ground occupied by the posts, as also for any land about them which might be found necessary for the use of the garrisons; but the same has not been performed, neither are the Indians in the several countries at all pleased at our occupying them, which they look upon as the first steps to enslave them and invade their properties.

And I beg leave to represent to your Lordships that one very material advantage resulting from a continuance of good treatment and some favors to the Indians will be the security and toleration thereby given to the troops for cultivating lands about the garrisons, which the reduction of their rations renders absolutely necessary . . .

Page after page the letter continued, extremely recriminatory—and justifiably so—of the English treatment of the Indians under Amherst's policies since the close of the French and Indian War. Brutal the Indians might be, and horrible in the atrocities perpetrated upon the English, but they had come not unexpectedly, but rather as a last resort by Indians whose land this was, whose words were not listened to, whose demands were not met, whose people were deprived and insulted by the English and who had no other way of communicating their displeasure left to them other than the necessity of direct and violent warfare.

George Croghan had stayed with Sir William for a number of days, engaging in lengthy discussions with him and getting his advice on what to do when he reached London. Sir William listened sympathetically to Croghan's personal business problems and admitted he might possibly be of some help. He prepared and gave to Croghan two letters of introduction—one to Lord Halifax, Secretary of State in charge of American Affairs, the other to former Massachusetts governor Thomas Pownall, who was considered an expert on land matters regarding the Colonies. Johnson felt that the patronage of these two powerful men might go far in Croghan's goal to eventually acquire restitution for his heavy trade losses and also to help him relocate in New York Province the 200,000 acres of Pennsylvania territory granted to him by the Iroquois in 1749 and which Pennsylvania had balked him from claiming on the grounds that the title was not legal. Such relocation of this Indian grant by the Crown would, Johnson knew, not only confirm the legality of the grant, but it would also enable his deputy to settle much closer to Johnson Hall. It was a thought which pleased Johnson, for he and George Croghan had much in common.

Finally, on the eve of Croghan's departure back to New York, Johnson gave him the letter he had written to the Lords of Trade with instructions for him to deliver it in person and to do all in his power while there to convince the Court that the Indian Department in North America should be autonomous—completely freed of any military or provincial control—in order to be most effective.

And just two days ago, with Croghan aboard in the company of such individuals as Colonel George Armstrong of Cumberland County, and Lieutenant James MacDonald, fresh from Detroit, the *Britannia* cleared the Delaware Capes and pointed her prow toward England.

From Armstrong, who not very long ago had led the abortive raid against the Delaware villages on the upper Susquehanna, Croghan learned greater details of an event that had set all of Pennsylvania on its ear lately and which was still not cleared up: the attack of a band of vigilante-type bordermen from the Paxton area near Harris's Ferry against the Conestogue Indians.

Croghan knew the Conestogues very well and had often visited them in their tiny town of Conestoga, about six miles from Lancaster. He knew also that at last count there had been only twenty-two of these Iroquois-speaking Indians left, of what had once been a sizable tribe. Further, he knew them to be harmless and likable, and that anybody should even consider attacking them was shocking to him. It would be comparable to attacking your pet hound dog because there was a wolf reported in the woods nearby. With mounting anger, Croghan listened to George Armstrong's story.

On December 11, it seemed, one of the Conestogues, a gangly, sad-faced individual known only as Bill Soc, had somehow broken the pipe end of his tomahawk[151] and took a walk to Lancaster to have it fixed. He took it to the shop of a Mennonite gunsmith named Abraham Newcomer, a narrow-minded bigot who had always referred to the Conestogues—or any other Indians, for that matter—as "red niggers." Newcomer refused to mend it and ordered Soc away. Angry, Soc had shaken the broken tomahawk at Newcomer and said words to the effect that, "If you won't fix it, then I'll have it mended somewhere else to your sorrow!"

Incensed at such impudence from this "red nigger," Newcomer spread the story about Lancaster, enlarging it at each telling until his very life, according to him, had been in jeopardy. Most of the people who were familiar with Newcomer and his ways just laughed the story off, telling the gunsmith he was lucky to have gotten off that easy, but the story spread and the next day—December 12—it reached Paxton and the ears of one Matthew Smith.

Smith, immediately setting himself up in his own mind as an extra-legal sheriff, prosecutor, judge, jury and executioner, decided that it was up to him and others who thought as he did to arrest, try, judge, find guilty and execute not only Bill Soc, but *all* the Conestogues. He rounded up five armed companions and they thundered off toward Conestoga. Arriving at the vicinity after dark, Smith left his horse with his companions and set off to reconnoiter ahead on his own. After a little while he came back to his companions and told them he had seen a large war party too big for them to attack and that they should all go back and raise a powerful body of men for the job ahead.

Returning to Paxton, Smith got the strong support of an educated but hot-headed neighbor, Lazarus Stewart. Together they raised a body of fifty-seven tough bordermen and set out at once, arriving at Conestoga before daylight on December 14. Seeing firelight in the Indians' cabins, they separated into several smaller groups and, having surrounded the town, advanced on all sides. Within the seven little cabins were twenty of the total population of twenty-two Conestogues—seven men, five women, and eight children—all of them sound asleep.

With terrifying cries, Stewart and Smith and their men burst in upon them. In the great confusion that ensued, twelve of the Indians managed to flee in the darkness, but the other eight were killed and scalped. The Paxton Boys, as the gang called itself, did not pursue the escapees, satisfied with triumphantly heading back toward Paxton in the first light of morning with their grisly trophies. They set the seven cabins afire before leaving.

On the road during their return they met a Lancaster resident, Thomas Wright. Seeing the bloody scalps they were carrying, Wright reined up and asked what had happened and they told him. Wright was so horrified that he was speechless and Stewart sneered at him.

"No reason to be upset, friend. We've only followed the Lord's word in respect to what should be done with heathens, as given to us in the Holy Bible."

"The Bible?" Wright responded, frowning. "Where?"

"Deuteronomy, sir. Chapter seven, verse twelve. I quote for you: *'And when the Lord thy God shall deliver them before thee, thou shalt smite them and utterly destroy them; thou shalt make no convenant with them; nor show mercy unto them.'* That's what it says, friend, and that's what we did."

They left then, continuing the ride to Paxton and a short while later they stopped along the way at the house of another resident, Robert Barber, for some refreshments. It had, after all, been a rather strenuous night and morning. Though here they did not confess what they had done, they talked and joked around the subject enough that Barber guessed the truth. As soon as they had ridden on, Barber gathered his neighbors and they went to Conestoga, where they found the cabins still burning, some with corpses in them, and the remaining fourteen Conestogues—including the two missing ones, who had returned at dawn—gathered fearfully together, moaning and crying in grief. Barber and his friends helped the Indians bury those dead who were outside the cabins and then escorted these survivors into Lancaster where, for their own protection and amid great excitement of the residents, they were lodged in Sheriff John Hay's strong stone jailhouse. An express was dispatched at once to Philadelphia to inform the governor what had occurred.

"The matter didn't die there, though," Armstrong went on to Croghan. "Two days later, on the sixteenth, the governor issued a proclamation denouncing the massacre and offering a reward for information leading to the arrest and conviction of the so-called Paxton Boys. Didn't bother them in the least. They knew damned well there wasn't anybody going to turn them in for killing Indians. Fact is, it made them mad, so they planned another attack for the second night after Christmas."

Armstrong went on to tell how Stewart and Smith sent out men to learn where the other Conestogues had gone and quickly found out they were lodged in the jail. One of the survivors was Bill Soc, who had escaped from the massacre in the cabins. In discussing it, one of Stewart's men announced that it was Bill Soc who, some time back, had killed a relative of his somewhere around Carlisle. No one thought to question who the relative of this man was, when it had happened and who had identified Bill Soc as the perpetrator of the crime, if crime there was. Frankly, no one cared. The comment merely added flame to the fire and they decided they'd just meander down to the Lancaster County Jail on December 27th and put Bill Soc in their own custody, take him to Carlisle to be identified as the killer and then hang him.

Accordingly, on the morning of the 27th, they left Paxton, numbering now about a hundred men. Before they left the Reverend John Elder had tried in vain to make them change their minds, but they refused to listen. A mile or so out of town the preacher, astride his own fine steed, overtook them and stopped the horse broadside across the narrow road, blocking their path. He told them that as God-fearing men, they just could not do such a thing.

"Preacher," drawled Matthew Smith, "you shouldn't ought'a do nothin' like this." He kneed his horse forward, stopped when directly facing the Reverend Mister Elder, raised his rifle and aimed it at the head of the minister's horse. "Now," he continued calmly, "I reckon you'll move your animal aside or in about two shakes he's gonna be stone dead."

Elder's courage deserted him then and he moved his horse out of their way and watched sorrowfully as they went on. By nearly three in the afternoon, the mob was on the edge of Lancaster. Rousing their horses into a gallop, they thundered into the town. They stopped their horses in the yard of the innkeeper named Slough and then ran across the street to the jail. Felix Donnelly, the keeper, saw them coming and locked the door, but they smashed it in, ran to the cells and began killing the Indians, who offered no resistance.

Sheriff John Hay, with the Lancaster County coroner at his heels, now rushed in from outside and flourished his pistol, demanding that the carnage cease. Threatening to kill the two county officials next if they dared to interfere, the Paxton Boys kept slashing with their tomahawks until the floor was a sea of red and every Indian dead.

The last of the Conestogue Indians were gone, their tribe forever extinguished.

Satisfied with their work, the Paxton Boys left the jail as hurriedly as they had entered it, leaped onto their horses and rode off, shouting something to the effect of going on to Philadelphia to wipe out similarly the Moravian Indians lodged on Province Island.

"That's how it stands now," Armstrong concluded. "You saw the turmoil in Philadelphia today. They're bordering on panic there. They've heard that armed mobs are already on their march to the city and nobody knows what's going to happen next."

"What about the Moravian Indians?" Croghan asked concernedly.

Armstrong shook his head. "Hard to say what'll be done with 'em. They sent boats out this morning to take them off the island and started them downriver, but then somebody sent a messenger and recalled 'em, so there they are, still on Province Island, scared to death. Rumors are going around that the governor's going to ship 'em to some other province where they'll be safe."

George Croghan shook his head and looked toward the west across the heaving gray surface of the Atlantic. The shoreline had long since dropped out of sight and he sighed.

"Poor devils," he muttered. "They's times when it don't take no great effort to see why the Indians hate us so much."

And strangely, now that he was finally on the way to England, Croghan found himself wishing he could be back in Philadelphia to help these red men in whatever way he could.[152]

[February 8, 1764—Wednesday]

Rarely had tempers run so high or the population of an American colony been so divided as had been the case during the past two months in Pennsylvania. There was little room for those who wished to carefully evaluate both sides of the situation and take a sensible conservative stand on matters. The lines were sharply drawn: a man was either an Indian lover or an Indian hater; a Presbyterian or a Quaker; a dweller of the massacre-torn borders or a dweller of the secure easternmost cities, especially Philadelphia; a too-placid Assemblyman who wanted peace at any cost, or a hot-tempered and hate-blinded frontiersman who wanted blood at any risk. The Pandora's box that had been opened with the massacre of the Conestogues had let loose an aura of hatred, fear, suspicion, anger, consternation and bloodlust which settled on the shoulders of every resident of the province.

With most Philadelphians expecting momentarily to see rifle-and-tomahawk-wielding frontiersmen surging into town bent on killing the Moravian Indians and anyone who stood in their way, a proposal was hastily laid before the Pennsylvania General Assembly in the first session of the year that these Indians be removed from Province Island and taken to England. Almost as soon as it was proposed, the plan was rejected as being costly and inexpedient, but on January 2, it was decided to send them to New York Province where, supposedly, they would be safe under the protection of Sir William Johnson. The only thing wrong with the plan was that no one thought to ask either Johnson or the governor of New York if this plan was acceptable to them.

January 4 was not more than a few minutes old when the proselytized Indians were loaded into boats and the journey begun into and through the city. Despite the hour and the darkness, word of the exodus got out. Mobs quickly formed after the boats discharged their fearful passengers and it was only with the greatest of difficulty that the Indians were led off in the direction of Trenton without a riot.

Upon reaching Trenton, they were transferred into the

hands of a commissary official named Thomas Apty, who had them escorted to the town of Amboy where three small vessels lay waiting to carry them to New York. However, on January 9 just before sailing time, an express thundered up bearing a letter from the lieutenant governor of New York, Cadwallader Colden, who had gotten wind of the plans and who now forbade bringing these Indians into New York, that province having enough Indian problems already.

Not sure what should be done now, Apty gave lodging to the Indians at Amboy until January 15 when Governor Franklin of New Jersey, sharing Colden's view, said they could not remain in his province either. Dejected, and existing in a state of almost perpetual fright, the Moravian Indians were marched back to Philadelphia, arriving there on January 24. On their heels came the report that three hundred frontiersmen, mustered under Lazarus Stewart and Matthew Smith, were on their way to take them, no matter what. Again the city bordered on a panic and even the peaceful Quakers took up rifles and joined the armed citizenry on the streets, determined that, God help them, they would shed the blood of these bordermen before they would let them murder those innocent Indians. During the forty-eight hours of February 4 and 5, Philadelphia was virtually under a state of martial law. Barricades were thrown up across the streets and artillery positioned to mow down the frontiersmen when they approached. Several alarms were raised during this interval, but the frontiersmen had prudently stopped outside the city.

In a frantic effort to settle this matter quickly, Benjamin Franklin and three other citizens of substance were named by the governor to go and negotiate with the frontiersmen and, if possible, convince them to depart peaceably.

By now these bordermen were themselves quite concerned with the way this whole matter had snowballed out of control and they snatched at this opportunity to settle it. They agreed—threatening possibly even to leave the province—but before doing so they wrote a declaration and a paper which they termed a "remonstrance" for Ben Franklin to deliver to both the governor and Assembly. Filled with their grievances and outrage, the documents penned by Lazarus Stewart were very lengthy, but their essence was implicit in one particular passage which stated:

To protect and maintain these Indians at the public expense, while our suffering brethren on the frontiers are almost destitute of the necessaries of life and neglected by the public, is sufficient to make us mad with rage and tempt us to do what nothing but the most violent necessity can vindicate.

Furious as well with the government's order that Stewart and Smith and others of the Paxton Boys be arrested and that they be tried in Philadelphia rather than in Lancaster County, Stewart could not resist adding a more personal clause to the declaration:

Did we not brave the summer's heat and the winter's cold and the savage tomahawk, while the inhabitants of Philadelphia, Philadelphia County, Bucks, and Chester "ate, drank, and were merry"? If a white man kill an Indian, it is a murder far exceeding any crime on record; he must not be tried in the county where he lives or where the offense was committed, but in Philadelphia, that he may be tried, convicted, sentenced and hung without delay. If an Indian kill a white man, it was the act of an ignorant heathen, perhaps in liquor; alas, poor innocent! He is sent to the friendly Indians, that he may be made a Christian. What I have done was done for the security of hundreds of settlers on the frontiers. The blood of a thousand of my fellow creatures called for vengeance. As a Ranger, I sought the post of danger, and now you ask my life. Let me be tried where prejudice has not prejudged my case. Let my brave Rangers, who have stemmed the blast nobly and never flinched, let them have an equitable trial; they were my friends in the hour of danger—to desert them now were cowardice! What remains is to leave our cause with our God and our guns.[153]

No, at the moment there was no room for any would-be middle-of-the-roaders in Pennsylvania. Those who even suggested calmness and reason and common sense were publicly reviled and verbally castigated, sometimes even threatened by extremists of one viewpoint or the other. That it would undoubtedly remain this way for some time was evidenced by the spate of partisan verse which began being published in Philadelphia and continued for some time, giving the Presbyterians and the Quakers a bloodless outlet for tearing at each other's throats. A partisan of the Quaker faction launched this broadside at the bordermen, who were mainly Scots and Irishmen:

O'Hara mounted on his steed
(Descendant of that self-same ass
That bore his grandsire, Hudibras,)
And from that same exalted station,
Produced a great inspired oration.
For he was cunning as a fox,
Had read o'er Calvin and Dan Nox;
A man of most profound discerning,
Well versed in Presbyterian learning.
So, after hemming thrice to clear
His throat, and banish thoughts of fear,
And of the mob obtaining silence,
He thus went on—"Dear Sirs, a while since,
Ye know as how the Indian rabble,
With practices unwarrantable,
Did come upon our quiet borders
And there commit most desperate murders;
Did tomahawk, butcher, wound and cripple,
With cruel rage, the Lord's own people;
Did a war most implacable wage
With God's own chosen heritage;
Did from our brethren take their lives,
And kill our children, kine, and wives.
Now, Sirs, I ween it is but right,
That we upon these Canaanites
Without delay, should vengeance take,
Both for our own, and our King's sake;
Should totally destroy the heathen
And never, till we've killed 'em, leave 'em;
Destroy them quite from out the land!
And for it, men, we've God's command..."
He paused, as orators are used,
And from his pocket quick produced
A friendly vase, well stored and filled
With good old whiskey, twice distilled;
Then, having refreshed his inward man,
Went on with his harangue again:
"Is it not a pretty story
That we, who are the land's chief glory,
Who're in the number of God's elected,
Should slighted thus be, and neglected?
That we, who're the only Gospel Church,
Should thus be left here in the lurch
While our most antiChristian foes,

Whose trade is war and hardy blows,
(At least while some of the same color
With those who've caused us all this dolor,)
In matchcoats warm and blankets dressed,
Are by the Quakers much caressed
And live in peace by good warm fires
And have the extent of their desires?
Shall we put by such treatment base?
By Nox, we won't"—and broke his vase.
"Seeing, then, we've such good cause to hate 'em,
What I intend's to extirpate 'em;
To suffer them no more to thrive
And leave no root nor branch alive!"
But here he paused, and, on reflecting,
He hemmed and hawed while thoughts collecting
Deciding now 't'would safer be
To strike defenseless enemy.
So, to his listeners he appealed
And quickly had the bargain sealed
A savage wild could fight or flee,
But not Moravians, so, quoth he:
"But would we madly leave our wives
And children and expose our lives
In search of those who infest our borders
And perpetrate such cruel murders?
It is most likely, by King Harry,
That we should in the end miscarry!
I deem, therefore, the wisest course is
That those who have 'em, mount their horses,
And those who've none should march on foot,
With all the quickness that will suit
To where those heathen, nothing fearful
(That we will on their front and rear fall,)
Enjoy sweet opium in their cots
And dwell securely in their huts;
And as they've nothing to defend 'em,
We'll quickly to their own place send 'em!"[154]

Hardly to be outdone by this bitter sarcasm—which was too uncomfortably close to the truth—penned by their pacifistic adversaries, partisans of the Paxton Boys were not long in having their own reply published:

"Go on, good Christians, never spare
To give your Indians clothes to wear;

Send 'em beef and pork and bread,
Guns and powder, flints and lead,
To shoot your neighbors through the head.
Devoutly, then make affirmation
You're Friends to George and British Nation!
Encourage ev'ry friendly savage
To murder, burn, destroy and ravage!
Fathers and mothers here maintain
(Whose sons add numbers to the slain
Of Scotch and Irish) let them kill
As many thousands as they will!
Thus you may lord it o'er the land
And have the whole and sole command ...

Yes, throughout the Province of Pennsylvania it was quite apparent that the Quaker harbored no abiding love for the border people. On the other hand, of course, the hatred of the border people for the Indian only slightly outweighed that which he harbored for the Quaker.

[February 11, 1764—Saturday]

For Colonel Henry Bouquet it was a pleasure to be at Fort Bedford again, not particularly because he cared a great deal for the place, which he did not, but because it was one step closer on his return to New York for the war conferences with General Gage on the forthcoming spring campaign against the Northwest Territory Indians.

It had been very quiet around Fort Pitt for many weeks now, although scattered outrages were still being committed in small settlements and on isolated families. Fort Pitt, however, seemed quite secure and was being quite competently operated by its new commanding officer, Captain William Grant of the 42nd Regiment. Captain Simeon Ecuyer, having been granted the discharge that he desired, had been quick to leave the frontier post behind him and, so far as Bouquet knew, was by now getting ready to grow cabbages, as he had half-facetiously expressed a wish to do. After his departure, Fort Pitt had somehow seemed a lonelier place to Bouquet, who always had enjoyed Ecuyer's quick wit and intelligence and who had considered him a better than average subordinate commander.

From all over the frontier, in fact, especially where His Majesty's posts were concerned, the news was much better. It had been a great satisfaction to learn of Pontiac's withdrawal from Detroit, but it was no time to relax one's guard. As Major Gladwin had cautiously pointed out in his last letter, the war was not yet over and there was absolutely no guarantee that Detroit—and Fort Pitt, too, for that matter—would not again be put under siege come warmer weather. Apparently the biggest force at work to keep the Indians quiet at the moment was nature itself, in the form of a particularly severe winter and the smallpox epidemic, both of which were playing havoc with the weakened and ill-provisioned tribes.

Pleased though he was at the alleviation to some degree of hostilities, Bouquet found it difficult to be quite as callous of the human condition of the Indians as some others of His Majesty's officers were. It was evident that there were more than just a few who took considerable delight in their wretched condition. Lieutenant Diedrick Brehm, still at Detroit, had written on January 4 that:

. . . the Indians (those nations who were obliged to take up arms against us by the Ottawas and Chippewas) are coming from time to time, begging Major Gladwin to intercede by the general for to procure peace for them, representing the starving condition they are in for want of ammunition and clothing, but they obtain very little.

Our garrison is in perfect health and we are well provided with provisions, etc. . .

Obviously a good part of the slackening of hostilities was due to the very elemental necessity of the warriors to provide for their families. With no ammunition available to them, it took strenuous daily effort for fresh meat to be taken with bow or snare. Small wonder that so many of the village chiefs were anxious for a definitive treaty to be made so that trade could return to some degree of normalcy. As Lieutenant George McDougall, also still at Detroit, put it in his letter to Bouquet of January 8:

Since my last letter to you by Aaron the Indian, we have had nothing new here; the savages are all gone to their hunting and seem earnest of making peace. Enclosed is a return of the Royal Americans that are here. The savages of Saginaw have brought in three of the Royal Americans and beg earnestly for pardon . . .

Now, in the yellow glow of the large glass-fronted pewter lantern on the desk, Bouquet was himself writing to his commander:

Fort Bedford 11th Feby 1764

Sir

I have the honor to acknowledge your Excellency's letters of 22nd of December and 26th January.

Your dispatches for Major Gladwin were forwarded immediately by two Indian expresses.

Your orders dated at Headquarters the 5th of last month have been transmitted to the different posts in this Department.

If the zeal of these troops was susceptible of aggrandizement, it would have been effected by so great a condescension of his Majesty's most gracious approbation of their services.

I left Fort Pitt on the 21st January, after having finished the temporary repairs that appeared necessary for the defense of that post, agreeably to your orders of the 18th November. And as the last supply I had received had fallen short of my expectation, I have improved the opportunity of the communication being clear of Indians to form another convoy and tomorrow I shall have here 500 horses to carry flour to Fort Pitt, which will give us some ease in the spring. As soon as they are dispatched, I shall proceed without delay to New York to receive your further commands. No motive but my desire of forwarding the service, to which I have devoted all my time, could have detained me so long in this wilderness where, for want of assistance, I have been obliged to take upon me every branch.

I am sorry for the distressed situation of the three companies relieved from Niagara, though it is no more than might be expected from the hard service that battalion has been employed in for six years, scattered among the savages and in the remotest part of our new frontiers. I shall put them in order as soon as possible.

I see with the greatest satisfaction that you have determined to punish the Delawares and Shawnees. The Senecas, the better protected, do not deserve a milder treatment and I wish they might be compelled to incorporate and mix with the other Five Nations and lose their odious name, as, after

*their unparalleled treachery, a sincere reconciliation can
never be placed on either side.*

I am, with deep esteem, Sir,

*Your most obedient and
most humble Servant,
H.B.*

*His Excellency in New York
Genl. Thomas Gage*

[*March 19, 1764—Monday*]

Chief Pontiac of the Ottawas was down, but he was most certainly not yet out. In fact, if he could gather the support he needed—and he was quite sure he could—then sometime this summer, or perhaps autumn at the latest, he would deliver a hammer blow to the English which would make the events of last year look like child's play.

There was no denying it, he had lost face badly in his own country and he could expect no help whatever from the tribes in that quarter; at least not until he could return with a force strong enough to deliver the English such a severely crippling blow that the tribes would, in awe and fear, have to fall again under his command. It was to the task of gathering this force that he now devoted all his energies and he was confident of ultimate success. The tribes of the Illinois country, as well as the Osages and Kansas, the Missouris and the Mandans and Dakotahs to the west of the Mississippi River, all these still accorded to Pontiac an extremely high measure of prestige. Of them all, the Dakotahs might be hard to convince, since they favored the English, but Pontiac thought he might get their power behind him when he explained how they had deluded themselves and pointed out how the English had gobbled up lands to the east and would soon come west and take Dakotah lands.

He really did not think it was possible that any of the tribes, Dakotahs included, could fail to fall in with him when he explained to them how the English destroyed the forests and fields, killed the game, laid waste wherever they went, spread sickness and hurt and, most of all, drove the Indians from their own land and took it as theirs. The English were all the same—give them one tree and they took the forest, given them one foot of ground and they took acres. Give them acres and they took the country.

Yes, there was good reason to believe these tribes would

join his fight and, when they did, there would be many others who would still fall in behind. Nor were the French to be overlooked. As Alexis Cuillerier—along with other young Frenchmen who were constantly in his camp now—still kept telling him, the treaty papers, the orders from Neyon de Villiere, the story that the French King had given the English King his holdings here, all these were lies that had been fabricated by the English to discourage Pontiac's followers; and look, they insisted, at how well it had worked!

His greatest strength at the moment, Pontiac knew, lay in the hard core of seventy or more warriors who had stayed with him and who had moved here to the Maumee River with him. To them he was little short of a god and his slightest wish was their absolute command. Many of these he would use as emissaries to distant tribes, to take them the word of Pontiac's greatness and his struggle to regain for the red man—not just the Ottawas, but *every* red man!—what was rightfully his. In another few days, Pontiac himself would set out for Fort de Chartres to confront Major Pierre Joseph Neyon de Villiere. Even if that officer would not give him troops, Pontiac could not conceive that he would deny him all he required of ammunition and provisions. Certainly the English were as detestable to that French officer as they were to Pontiac.

The disintegration of his forces at Detroit and his subsequent loss of prestige there had caused a transformation in Pontiac. Where not too infrequently before he had laughed and joked among his warriors and was gentle to his women and children, now he was hard, unsmiling, cold. The air of the tyrant, which he had exhibited to the French inhabitants at Detroit, he was now exhibiting here, as if by doing this he felt within himself a restoration of power. It amused him especially to make outrageous demands of his young French followers and force them to obey. Each time they did so, it put them more completely than ever under his control, as well as increasing his prestige in the minds of any Indians who heard of it.

Only last week he had sent eight of his fiercest and most devoted warriors upstream to the village of the Miami chief, Cold Foot, as a small test of his own power. Cold Foot was not principal chief of all the Miamis; that was Michikiniqua—he whom the English called Little Turtle—who lived with his people at present on the upper reaches of the Miami River at the sprawling Indian Lake which gave the river its genesis.

Thus far Michikiniqua had kept himself relatively aloof from the war. Because of the remoteness of his location, where there was little contact with either French or English, this had not been difficult for him to do. Yet, it was said that he leaned toward the English still. He was a strong chief and a factor with whom Pontiac would eventually have to contend, but he hoped to change the Miami's mind. Perhaps he could not convince him to give friendship to the French, but surely he could sway him to throwing the power of his Miami Nation behind Pontiac in a struggle that was for the benefit of Indians against whites. And the first place to test this out would be with Chief Cold Foot on the Maumee.

Michikiniqua had been greatly displeased, so Pontiac had learned, at the knowledge that Cold Foot had helped the Detroit Frenchmen who came to him; that he had helped considerably in the downfall of Fort Miamis. For this Cold Foot had been severely reprimanded by Michikiniqua and warned that he must not again allow himself to be so used. Now Pontiac was testing the strength of that order.

The eight warriors he had dispatched to Cold Foot's village had been sent because Pontiac had heard that two Englishmen—a soldier and a trader—were still being held captive there, but that plans were afoot to take them to Detroit and give them up to Major Gladwin as a measure of good faith. Pontiac's eight warriors had been given explicit instructions: they were to force Chief Cold Foot to kill these prisoners, using whatever coercion was necessary to do so.

This very morning the eight had returned and their report was good. The prisoners had been there and, as expected, Cold Foot had objected to executing them at first. But through a judicious application of intimidation, the Miami village chief had been forced to change his mind. Pontiac was pleased to learn that the soldier had been tied to the stake and burned to death and the trader, who had been a friend of the Miamis for many years, had mercifully been shot through the head. Already word of this was streaking through the tribes of the Indiana and Illinois countries and there the power of Pontiac was increasing proportionately.

Pontiac had been sitting beside the outside fire with his head bent in thought, oblivious to the camp activities occurring around him. Suddenly now he sniffed, frowned and looked up. His frown deepened to a heavy scowl. There she was again, that filthy, disgusting little English captive. She was thin and weak and cried almost constantly now with the cold and her sickness and Pontiac was angered anew that she had been brought along.

This was little Betty Fisher, now seven years old. Her family had been the first to suffer at Detroit. On the very day that Pontiac had declared his war, his men had gone from the gate of the fort to Isle au Cochon—Belle Isle—where retired Sergeant James Fisher lived with his wife and four children. One of these four had been little Betty. No words could describe the terror she had undergone when she had been snatched and held and made to watch while her father was tomahawked to death; while her infant brother, John, had been held by the ankles and swung around and his head crushed as it slammed viciously against the cabin wall; while her mother was held as a rawhide loop was tied around her neck and she was hanged from a tree as the Ottawas laughed and joked while she kicked and struggled as she strangled.

Betty had been taken prisoner, along with her year-old sister Marie and three-year-old sister Mildred. Milly had been taken by the Chippewas to Saginaw Bay and apparently was still there, but Marie had not been so fortunate. She had contracted smallpox from her captors and died last October.

Ever since the capture, Betty had been kept by the Ottawas. When the siege had ended and Pontiac had his village moved here along the Maumee River, she had been brought along. She had fared poorly, however, especially since contracting dysentery a week or so ago.

Because of the malady, even though she tried desperately not to do so, she soiled her ragged clothes frequently. With nothing else to wear but what she had on her back, it meant that she had to go down to the river bank, break away the ice, wash the vile feces off her clothing and herself and then come back to the fire to try to get warm and dry.

Just a short while ago she had voided on her clothing again and now, naked, blue with cold and trembling convulsively after having rinsed them, she approached the fire and was holding her garment toward it to dry. The warmth of the blaze made it steam slightly and, since she had not been entirely successful in washing the feces away, a highly distasteful odor began emanating from them. It was this that Pontiac had smelled.

With an angry exclamation he leaped to his feet and in one stride he had snatched her up to throw her off to one side. He frightened her so severely that her already weakened sphincter muscle failed and the loose bowels gave way. The diarrhea spurted from her and sprayed all over Pontiac's leggings and moccasins. His face suffused with rage and there was an instant silence in the camp as all eyes were suddenly on this little drama. Still holding her aloft, but well away from him now, Pontiac walked to the riverbank and pitched her out into the open water beyond the margin of ice along the shore.

Her scream was cut short by the splash and in an instant she had surfaced, standing mid-chest-deep, suffering from the frigid water swirling around her, yet afraid to come to shore. Pontiac turned away and his smoldering gaze fell on Alexis Cuillerier. He pointed at the young Frenchman.

"Mushett," he ordered, using the name he had dubbed him with, "go drown her."

Cuillerier, abruptly paling, remained rooted where he stood.

Pontiac's eyes narrowed and he dropped the pointing hand to his waistband where it rested on his tomahawk. When he spoke the second time, his voice was absolutely flat, wholly implacable.

"Mushett, you boasted to me of your great courage. I will see now whether you are a man or not. *Go drown her!*"

Walking as if he were in a trance, Alexis Cuillerier stepped past Pontiac and waded through the margin of ice he broke. With her teeth chattering uncontrollably, Betty Fisher watched him come. At the last moment she tried to get away but the Frenchman seized her by the hair and pulled her back and then, as she struggled frenziedly, thrust her head beneath the surface of the Maumee.

For fully two minutes after she stopped moving he held her thus and then he pulled her limp body up into his arms and carried her ashore. He moved past Pontiac without looking at him and walked out into the woods a short distance where he laid her on the ground and began digging a hole in the frozen earth with his tomahawk.

After a few minutes one of his companions, John Maiet, approached with a shovel and together they buried the little body.

[*March 20, 1764—Tuesday*]

No blow inflicted on the Delawares by the English, regardless of how destructive, could have been so damaging or produced more of a demoralizing effect than that which was brought down on them by the Iroquois.

The very fact that Indian now fought Indian was disheartening to all the tribes, just as the adopted Mohawk who had set it up—Warraghiyagey, alias Sir William Johnson—had known it would be. It had taken a great many councils and feasts and war dances, beginning late in December, but little by little Johnson had convinced the Iroquois that it was not enough that they had not joined the other tribes in making war against the English. If they wished to continue as recipients of English largesse, then they must themselves raise the hatchet against the foes of England and let their position be known.

The break in their aloofness toward the idea had come on January 25 at Johnson Hall when at last, after much exhortation by Johnson, they picked up the feather-decorated, red-painted war hatchet and broke into the traditional war dance with its chilling chants and howls and stampings. The din became all the more bombastic as Johnson brought out cider and rum and promised that he would pay fifty dollars each for two trophies. These trophies were, specifically, not just the scalps but the whole heads of two Delaware chiefs who were leading many of the border attacks, which were once again on the increase in Pennsylvania. Both of these chiefs lived in the village of Kanastio, built initially by the Delawares high up the Susquehanna, but now a polyglot village of Mingoes —Shawnees, Delawares, Senecas, Wyandots, Cayugas and a scattering of other tribes. The names of the chiefs in question were Petacowacone and Onuperaquedra, known respectively to the English as Chief Long Coat and Chief Squashcutter.

The war dance lasted for four days and then, on January 29, led by George Croghan's half-breed associate, Andrew Montour, two hundred warriors set out, generally following the Pennsylvania-New York border westward. Another one hundred, led by the Mohawk chief named Steyawa, headed directly west, first to order the Senecas not to interfere and then to move south along the border to the Northwest Territory to destroy Delawares and their villages.

The second group did not kill many Delawares, but they did destroy three large towns, a dozen or more small villages and camps of the Delawares, and at least one hundred and thirty permanent Delaware cabins. One of the principal towns destroyed was Kanastio, but neither of the chiefs with rewards on their heads was taken.

Montour's band, on the other hand, paused in their march by a little Delaware village on the main branch of the Susquehanna. While they rested the Delaware chief known as

Captain Bull—son of the famed self-proclaimed prophet, Teedyscung—came out of the woods with seven of his warriors and, unsuspecting, joined the party. Montour made a signal and after an extremely brief resistance, all eight Delawares were bound hand and foot. Montour and about half his party then followed Bull's trail to his camp and there they very neatly and with just a little effort captured twenty-two more Delawares, including eleven warriors, eight squaws and three children.

Brought directly back to Johnson Hall, the prisoners were ordered by Sir William to be taken to Albany. From there they would be shipped to New York and incarcerated for the duration. Bull, angry but not intimidated, shot an angry look at Johnson.

"I have with my own hands, Warraghiyagey," he boasted, "killed twenty-six English since last spring. I will kill more."

Johnson merely shook his head disgustedly and waved them off. He had other things to attend to. Since the Iroquois war parties had gone out he had, with the full sanction of General Gage, sent out two dozen or more Indian runners in various directions with an important message and powerful wampum belts. These runners were to stop at every village and tell the chief there that a great congress would be held by Warraghiyagey in July at Fort Niagara. All tribes, friendly, neutral or enemy, were asked to be on hand as this would be the last opportunity to discuss peace and sign a strong and binding treaty with the English. Two great armies were being formed to march to the west—one under Colonel Bouquet and the other under Colonel Bradstreet. So strong would these armies be that no band of Indians, no village or tribe, not even any confederacy of tribes could stand before them. All who did not make peace in July would be crushed.

It was Sir William's close Mohawk friend, Peter,[155] whom the Indian supervisor named to make the canoe journey first to Detroit and then to Sandusky with the message of the forthcoming congress, with its offer of peace or promise of destruction. Peter had made the journey swiftly, arriving at Detroit four days ago. The day after his arrival he addressed the combined Huron factions in a large assembly, telling them:

"You know of your brother, Warraghiyagey, and of the strength of his arm and of the love that the Iroquois hold in their hearts for him. For more years than I am old, he has been the eyes and ears and tongue of our people among the English. His promises made are always kept. He promises you peace if you come to Niagara four moons from now. He promises you destruction if you do not. Why does he do this? My children I will tell you: he has looked on every side of him and he has found himself struck from all parts. He is so covered with blood that he can scarce see, and he knows not for what reason this should be. He said first that he deserves pity from you; but then, when thinking on this, he changed and said no, why should he want pity from you when it is in his power to destroy you and all others who do him ill? He said he could see that it was the Hurons who needed pity and that, notwithstanding your ingratitude to him, he would give it to you if you will accept it. What is your answer?"

Both Teata and Takee spoke for their own bands and their replies were essentially identical: "We see that the eyes of our brother Warraghiyagey are shut with blood because of the strokes they have received from all sides. We dip our hands in the clear water and wash the blood away so that he can see we have no more war in our hearts. We will hand up our war hatchet far up in the air where only the Master of Life can reach it. We will come to Niagara and we will come for the purpose of peace, which we have long desired."

But the reception that Peter received today at Sandusky was considerably different. In spite of the fact that Chief Odinghquanoonron had only recently been in Detroit professing his friendship to Gladwin—and asking for supplies in the same breath—now he scowled as he heard the Mohawk's message.

"Go back," he said stiffly, "to your white-skinned Mohawk who is called Warraghiyagey and tell him this: tell him that the chief of the Wyandots, who are no longer a part of the Hurons, needs no pity from Englishmen. It may be as he has said, that the English have as many men as there are leaves upon the trees, but tell him to remember that those leaves fall, as will the English. We look upon one Wyandot warrior as being worth a thousand of them. They are the leaves, but we are the tree. We do not fall! In numbers we are but mice in comparison to the English, this we know, but our kick can be as strong as theirs and much better directed. Tell your white Mohawk that I am sorry to hear that the English are coming here in an army, because by that I take it to mean that they wish to leave their bones here, and this much I promise you: *they will!*"

Not even the confirmation that he had recently received from England via General Gage that his promotion to lieutenant colonel was approved could raise the spirits of Henry Gladwin. Long before this he had resolved that the instant he should be relieved from his post here at Detroit—which each day he grew to detest more—he would end his military career. This promotion, which was a very high rank in the regular army for a man only thirty-six years old, did not alter his feelings in the matter.

Lieutenant Colonel Henry Gladwin was very tired and depressed, extremely discouraged and quite thoroughly frustrated. Not having been relieved at the end of the siege, he had hoped that somehow during the winter a relief might perhaps get through for him or, failing that, certainly one would come in the spring. In neither case had this happened and now the Indian situation here, so relatively placid all winter long, was beginning to degenerate again. If something didn't happen soon to alter matters, Detroit would be right back in the position it had been in last summer.

A time or two over these past months Gladwin had tried to analyze matters, to see if he could determine what the bones of contention were between the Indians and the English and what might be done to alleviate the tensions. Such alleviation was hopeless, though; even the shallowest of thought showed that. The facts were simple: the Indians were hungry and they were cold and they were sick. Here, in the midst of this land they called their own was a fort they did not want to have there, filled with people they disliked, and these people were annoyingly well provided with food and ammunition and everything else the Indians so badly needed but were denied. It was not a situation calculated to instill friendly feelings. Worse yet was the fact that even with General Amherst now gone, there was no change of policy yet and there would apparently be none until a new treaty had been made with *all* the tribes; and that would not be until July at the very earliest, when Sir William Johnson held his grand congress at Niagara. Even then, though there was hope for it, there was no guarantee whatever that trading regulations would ease. The letter just received from General Gage was dated March 23 in New York and there had been a temporary sense of great relief from Gladwin as he read what Gage had written:

You will be informed, I accepted of the proposals of peace which the Detroit Indians had made to you and am now to desire, if you find the savages amicably disposed and sincerely inclined to conclude peace with us in earnest, that you would give them notice in a proper manner to repair to Niagara by the end of June, at which time Sir William Johnson will be there to meet him. You will best know what is proper to do on such occasion; shall therefore add that it may be necessary to acquaint them that the representatives that they send to this business need not be apprehensive of receiving any insults from the troops which they will probably meet in their way, as, when we find they are sincere in their overtures, the troops will have orders not to molest them; and they should likewise have notice to collect all the prisoners and deserters which they may have amongst them, who should all be delivered up to us on this occasion. If you think of any proposals proper for Sir William Johnson to make on this occasion of peace, you will write to Sir William on that head.

Well, he'd informed the Indians and there was considerable excitement shown, but no great deal of change in the way they'd been acting. The letter from Gage could have done a lot more good had it come two months ago. Now it was a little late.

At first, following the siege, Gladwin had welcomed all the chiefs who came to pay their respects and profess friendship. He knew they expected gifts, but he had none to give them; most especially, he had no ammunition to give them. In most cases they had come in a friendly way, often bringing along English prisoners, both traders and soldiers, to turn in at the fort. When, for this show of good faith on their parts, they received nothing in return but some half-hearted promises that things would get better, their anger upon leaving was understandable. Even the fact that Gladwin returned his hostage, Chief Winnemac, to the Potawatomies did not appreciably alter their mood.

The commander of Detroit had kept track of those Indians who had visited the fort since the beginning of the year and they made a rather impressive role.

First had come the massively-mandibled chief of the Wyandots, Odinghquanooron—Big Jaw—and, with him, Chief Teata of the Hurons across the river. Chief Takee, too, had come several days afterward. All three had gone away scowling and with apparently dark thoughts.

Some of the Potawatomies, now free of the fear that reprisal would be taken on Chief Winnemac, fired in anger on the fort again and one of Gladwin's privates had been wounded. When Chiefs Ninivois and Washee of that tribe came allegedly to apologize, Gladwin had been informed that they intended mischief and refused to let them enter. The same occurred when the great Chippewa chiefs Minivavana and Matchekewis came to visit from the Michilimackinac area.

Wabbicomigot of the Mississaugis near Toronto also came, expressing his desire for peace and expecting gifts. Gladwin expressed appreciation at the peaceful desires but told him what he had told the others, and Chief Wabbicomigot had gone away displeased.

Again had come word that two Ottawa chiefs, Mintiwaby and Manitou were coming, allegedly in friendship but with the plan of assassinating Gladwin, so when they arrived at the fort they were turned away. Shortly after they had gone, and much too late for Gladwin to use the information to at least partially mollify the many irritated chiefs, the Mohawk messenger named Aaron showed up with dispatches from Gage telling about the forthcoming treaty congress. He confirmed that there was a general uneasiness among all the Indians who had ceased fighting and it would not take much to get them on the warpath again. The Delawares and Shawnees, he reported, were still raising great havoc on the Pennsylvania frontier. The only encouraging note was the forthcoming congress at Niagara, at which perhaps a binding peace treaty might be concluded. In the event that it would not be, both Bouquet and Bradstreet were going to lead armies against those tribes who had refused, and crush them. One final bit of good news imparted almost as an afterthought by Aaron was the fact that all winter long work had progressed at the east end of Lake Erie on three new English ships, two of which were now finished and a third very nearly so. These were the schooners *Boston* and *Victory* and the sloop *Charlotte*.

But the news Gladwin had been hoping for—word of when he might expect relief from this post—had been absent and the Detroit commander groaned. In just the past few weeks matters here had begun degenerating at a more alarming pace. If he was not able to be relieved before another outbreak occurred, God only knew how much longer he might be stuck here.

On March 12, early in the morning, there was an alarm

when it was discovered that a firebrand had been placed against the door of the powder magazine. It had not been detected and had scorched the door, but fortunately it had burned itself out before the door could ignite. Gladwin trembled at the thought of what would have happened had it burned its way through. It also brought into sharp focus again the unnerving realization that somewhere in this fort there was a Frenchman who still wished to see the English brought to their knees and was willing to take desperate chances to help make it happen.

Shortly after that, one of Monsieur Moran's cows came in from the woods bawling and grunting in pain, with ten arrows sticking out of her, and she had to be butchered. A number of other cattle, some belonging to the fort, disappeared in the woods and it was evident they had been killed and eaten by the Indians, and most likely the Potawatomies.

Three weeks ago, on March 23, Chief Osa of the Sacs had come from the Green Bay region to visit Gladwin and was admitted to the fort. He reported that though he wished nothing but peace, the birds of war were singing in the woods. Not only he, but Chief Oshkosh of the Menominees and Chief Taychee of the Winnebagoes had received war belts recently from the Chippewas, which they had refused. And on his way here he had stopped at St. Joseph and found that the Potawatomies there and the Miamis to the south of them had just received war belts from the Delawares and Shawnees.

About a week later, when a band of thirteen war-painted Indians had been seen skulking in the woods beyond Detroit, Gladwin sent out a detachment of twenty men under Lieutenant George McDougall, who routed them with gunfire, but it could not be determined whether any had been hit or not.

And today a soldier escaped into the fort who had been one of a detachment of four sent to Fort St. Joseph from Fort Michilimackinac just prior to the outbreak. They had been captured en route and the other three had long since been killed, but this soldier had been taken to the Chippewa village at Saginaw Bay and held there ever since. He reported that on the day of his escape, eight days ago, he had seen the Chippewas under Wasson paint themselves, do a war dance and then murder a little English girl captive, cut her up, boil her and eat her. Her name, he said, was Mildred Fisher.

Now, in the privacy of his own quarters, Lieutenant Colonel Henry Gladwin felt like weeping at the sheer frustration of his situation here. With his elbows on the desk before him, he buried his face in his hands.

"Will I never . . . never . . . *never*," he muttered, "get away from this damnable post?"

Alexander Henry did not know whether to laugh or cry, but he did know that he was teetering on the edge of hysteria and he closed his eyes to try to get a grip on himself. How incredibly, incredibly ironic it was that now he has come full circle—that after the passage of just short of a year, here he was again, crouched in a dim attic listening for a conversation to begin below him as a Chippewa chief, seeking his blood, demanded of a Frenchman that he be turned over to them.

As he waited, Henry slipped deeper into a sort of retrospect, seeing again in his mind's eye a swift montage of pictures of what had occurred this past year. It was all so unbelievable, like some idiotic nightmare from which there was no awakening.

Last summer, after the Chippewa band had left Michilimackinac Island and gone to the Bay of Boutichouy for hunting, the insults suffered by Henry had not ceased, even though now he was, in appearance, as much a Chippewa as anyone in Wawatam's family. Fearful still that his adopted friend and brother and son would eventually be slain, Wawatam had suggested they leave early for the winter hunting grounds, where they would be by themselves, with only the seventeen members of Wawatam's family group. Henry was only too happy to agree.

And so they had gone, stopping first at Michilimackinac where supplies were procured on credit from a French trader there, and then proceeding west on the Straits of Mackinac to Waugoshance Point and down the east shore of Lake Michigan to L'Arbre Croche. For two days—August 25 and 26—they had visited there with Chiefs Mackinac and Okinochumaki and learned how the survivors of the fort and the garrison from Green Bay, under Captain George Etherington and Lieutenant James Gorrell, had only the week before been escorted away toward Montreal. How strongly Henry wished that he had been on hand to accompany them, but by then it was too late.

Soon they left L'Arbre Croche and continued south along the Lake Michigan shoreline toward the family winter hunting ground. Along the way they took a surprising number of fowl and beaver and finally, having passed Little Traverse

Bay and Grand Traverse Bay, having continued always southward along the shoreline, they had come to the mouth of the River au Sable.[156] Here the legs of one of the family's dogs were tied together, a prayer offered up to the Great Spirit asking for blessing on a good winter's hunt, and then the dog pitched overboard into the river mouth as a sacrifice. The ritual drowning having been attended to, the canoes were drawn up on shore and cached very carefully and the whole party moved inland some fifteen miles and made their first hunting camp.

Apparently the blessing had been bestowed, because the hunting was good. Though ammunition was very scarce and they relied mainly on bow, deadfall and snare, along with some iron traps, by December 20 when it was decided to move to another campsite, they had already taken over a hundred pelts each of beaver and raccoon, plus numerous otter, mink, marten, fox, wolves and muskrat, and the tiny weasel which, having shed its brown summer coat and now clad in a pelt of purest white with black-tipped tail, had magically become the valuable ermine. They also had, by now, a considerable quantity of venison, most of which they had flayed and dried. All of this material was carefully bundled and then stored atop a high scaffolding to keep it safe from wolves and other animals, and then camp had again been moved inland. For three days more they moved, until Wawatam killed a huge stag, and then camp was made again.

The next day Henry had gone out hunting by himself and promptly became lost. Momentarily he panicked and it had nearly cost him his life. Finally, when exhaustion had overcome him, he began using his head and trying to figure out what to do. He found a huge lake he could only barely see across[157] and, knowing he had not seen it before, he set a course southwest through the bitterly cold, snow-filled wilderness. Not until December 28 did he run across a trail and, following it, eventually made his way back to Wawatam's camp. The entire family was in mourning, thinking him dead, and so they held a feast of rejoicing at his providential return.

On January 8 Henry discovered a huge black bear in a tree which was six feet in diameter at the base. He led the family to the scene and, working in shifts and using only tomahawks, they managed to cut the tree down in two days. The Indians just stood there as the angry bear came boiling out of the shattered branches and it was Henry who threw his rifle to his shoulder and used one of their precious ammunition charges to kill the animal. It was well over five hundred pounds. Now another strange ritual followed, in which all the members of the family prayed for forgiveness and asked the Great Spirit not to blame them, because it was the Englishman among them who had killed the bear. It had amused Henry, but it bothered him, too. He had been living as a Chippewa Indian for all these months and yet he still could not comprehend their ways. The bear was cleaned and rendered down to oil and meat and fur, and then the hunting continued.

Late in February Wawatam had announced that the winter's hunt was over and it was time to return to the canoes, make sugar, then head back for Michilimackinac. The proceeds of the hunt—over four thousand pounds of furs, oil, and dried meat—were divided into packs and each person carried a share on his back and dragged another on a pair of poles pulled behind, carrying and pulling this load a total of seventy miles to where the canoes were cached. Near the lake shore, in a dense woods of sugar maples, they tapped trees and, catching the sap in vessels of birchbark and then boiling it in kettles, they made a remarkable supply of coarse sugar. Usually this was a festive occasion, but this time the pleasure was marred when one of Wawatam's little granddaughters accidentally toppled into one of the boiling kettles and was scalded. For two days prayers were said almost continually as she was treated with bear oil, but eventually she died.

A large grave was dug and carefully lined with fresh birchbark, upon which her body was placed. In the grave with her was placed a hatchet, a pair of snowshoes, a small kettle filled with venison, several pairs of moccasins, her own beads, a canoe paddle, and a load-carrying belt. All these items, Wawatam explained, were things she would need during her journey through the land of devils to the land of happiness. The body and goods were covered with more birchbark, then with logs laid side by side and then with more bark over these so that no dirt would fall upon the corpse. Then the hole was filled with the sandy soil amid the wrenching wailings of the mother and the more subdued lamentations of the rest of Wawatam's family.

On April 2 the journey north was begun in the canoes and now all the Chippewas in this party became very nervous and Henry discovered that they were fearful of meeting reprisal from the English for the Fort Michilimackinac massacre. He assured them that he would permit no harm to come to them, just as they had not let harm come to him. At Grand Traverse

Bay they met another family band on its way back from winter hunting and they, too, were extremely fearful of what lay ahead.

For two days they stayed at L'Arbre Croche, visiting the Ottawas there, and then pushed on again, arriving at Fort Michilimackinac on April 26. Henry was deeply disappointed. No English had returned and the only traders on hand were two Frenchmen. It was with them that Wawatam bargained for the furs, meat and oil they had. The proceeds were divided and Alexander Henry's share had come to one hundred beaver pelts, sixty raccoon pelts and six otter pelts. For these he was alloted the equivalent of $160 by the traders and he thereupon bought his own supplies.

Many Chippewas were coming back from hunting—as they would continue to do until about mid-June—and on May 5 a large band of them arrived under the huge Chief Matchekewis, who was still seething over the rebuff he had received from the commander of Detroit. Recognizing Alexander Henry despite his Indian garb and appearance, he let it be known that he proposed to take Henry, kill him, cook him and eat him. Once again the young English trader's life was in jeopardy.

During the night Wawatam and his family spirited Henry across the Straits to Point Saint Ignace and here they camped. Worried that they would be followed, Henry begged Wawatam to escort him to the Sault Sainte Marie, where he had learned his old friend Jean Baptiste Cadotte was still living and engaging in trade with the Indians. Wawatam agreed and they prepared to go, but on the morning of their departure Wawatam's wife balked. Oghqua said she was very sick and that she had had bad dreams during the night and one of these was that if they went to the Sault, all of them would be killed. Dreams were powerful medicine among the Chippewas and now there was a dilemma, with Henry in jeopardy if he stayed here and the family apparently in jeopardy if they went.

The problem was solved for them on the morning of May 11 when Henry spied a sail coming across the Straits from the direction of Fort Michilimackinac. As it turned out, the craft was a huge canoe in which were a number of Frenchmen in Cadotte's employ. With them was none other than the Chippewa woman Henry knew so well, Madame Cadotte. They were en route back to the Sault and she agreed at once that Henry could accompany them.

So the time had come at last for Henry to leave Wawatam's family, and it was an emotion-filled experience. For his own use, Henry packed two shirts, an extra pair of leggings and a blanket. He returned to Wawatam the beaten silver armbands and wristlets and also gave him everything else that he possessed. Then he gravely shook hands with each member of the big family, reserving his farewell for Wawatam until last. They lit a pipe and smoked it together in silence. Several times Henry tried to say the words that were struggling to leave him, but he could not. At last he merely embraced Wawatam and the tears coursed silently down his cheeks. Wawatam was not so tongue-tied.

"My son," he said gently, "this may be the last time you and I shall smoke out of the same pipe. I am sorry to part with you, for now you are a part of us and your leaving will make an emptiness. You know the love I have for you and the dangers I and my family have faced to save you from your enemies. This is the measure of my love and I can say nothing more than that I am happy that my efforts to help you have not been in vain. With pain in my heart I say one final word to you who are my son, my brother, and my friend. Good-by."

Within a quarter hour the boat was pulling away. On the shore stood the whole family behind Wawatam, who, with his face upturned, prayed aloud to the Great Spirit that good fortune should ride with Henry. The young trader watched the family group until he could hear Wawatam's voice no longer.

The next morning, after they had turned north around the Pointe de Détour, they suddenly found themselves being overtaken by twenty canoe-loads of Chippewa Indians and Henry's heart sank. They greeted Cadotte's wife with great respect, and his French workers in a friendly enough manner, saying they were on their way to the Mississaugi River on the north shore of Lake Huron; but suddenly one of them looked more closely at Henry, who was dressed now as a Frenchman, and gave an exclamation. He said aloud to his companions that that one—pointing at Henry—looked very much like an Englishman. The others agreed and the leader, first in the Chippewa tongue and then in broken English, accused Henry of being an Englishman. Henry, pretending an inability to understand, shrugged and mumbled something in French. Taking her cue from this, Madame Cadotte came to the rescue. Speaking in the Chippewa she said:

"He is French, not English. He is a Canadian who has just come up for the first time from Montreal and he is to help my husband in his business."

The Indians accepted this, but they still looked suspiciously at Henry and he was sure that at least one of them actually recognized him as the English trader of Fort Michilimackinac a year ago. The journey was continued, however, and the next morning they reached the Sault Sainte Marie. A village of about a hundred Chippewas, including several chiefs and thirty or more warriors, was adjacent to the good house where Jean Baptiste Cadotte now lived. Cadotte was at first deeply shocked and then greatly pleased at seeing Henry again, having several times heard that he had been killed.

Immediately the Frenchman put Henry's fears about the Indians in the adjoining village aside. These, he said, were his good and trusted friends who had no hatred for the English and who, at Cadotte's encouragement, had declined the invitation last year of Minivavana to raise the hatchet and help take Fort Michilimackinac. No, Cadotte assured him again, they would do him no harm.

For five days Henry had felt secure, but now the terror had come back again as strongly as ever. Only half an hour ago a young warrior from the adjoining village came rushing to Cadotte's house to say that a party of Chippewas from Michilimackinac had just arrived here, that they were this moment at the village inquiring into the whereabouts of Alexander Henry—calling him by his English name—and the youth was sure they meant to make trouble. His chief had sent him here to warn Henry to conceal himself at once.

So here he was, in the garret of Cadotte's house and below he could hear the door open and the voice of his French host greeting the visitors. A greater thrill of fear shot through Henry as he recognized the deep baritone voice of Chief Matchekewis.[158]

"Matchekewis," Cadotte said when the greetings were finished, "I am told that you come here seeking to harm my good friend, the English trader named Alexander Henry."

There was a pause and Henry held his breath, straining to hear. The voice of Matchekewis, however, carried clearly to him when that chief spoke.

"My brother," he said to Cadotte, "I was told that he had come here and that was one of the reasons I came, intending to kill him. I had not known that he was your friend and under your protection and so if it is displeasing to you, I will trouble him no more."

"It is indeed very displeasing to me," Cadotte replied, "and I am grateful for your consideration of my feelings in this matter. Now, you say that he was *one* of the reasons you came here. What other reason may have brought you?"

"I wish to have the chiefs of the village assembled that they may hear what I have to say," Matchekewis replied. ·

Answering that he would see to it, Cadotte sent word for the village chiefs to come and they did so, along with a sizable number of their warriors, all armed. They took their places and the speech of Matchekewis began. It was the intention of the Chippewas under Minivavana and Matchekewis, he told them, to leave very soon for Detroit, which they intended to take as Fort Michilimackinac had been taken last year. Pontiac had failed, but they would not. He had come here to see if his brother Chippewas would join them in this endeavor. The voice of the chief who answered below was unfamiliar to Henry, but he felt a huge relief at the reply again now. Further, we have learned that you came here exoverheard.

"Brother," the chief said, "more than once in this war we have told you that we wish no part in it. We tell you that pecting to take from among us the English trader from Michilimackinac, who has sought sanctuary in the home of our brother Cadotte. This we say now in addition: this man is under the immediate protection of all the chiefs you see before you and they will consider it an insult against themselves if he is harmed. Go back where you came from, Matchekewis, as none of the young men in our village will be foolish enough to join you."

There was no way of knowing what Matchekewis might have replied to that, for just at this moment a warrior hurried in with the report that a canoe had just arrived from Niagara. This caused quite a stir and the chief who had replied to Matchekewis now directed that the warrior go back to these strangers and request that they come to council here with whatever news they brought.

As soon as he had gone, Cadotte came to the garret and led Henry back downstairs, reassuring him that he had nothing at all to fear now. Henry very nervously took a seat, aware that Matchekewis was eyeing him darkly. He was convinced, despite the reassurances of Cadotte and the words of the chief, that Matchekewis still meant to kill him as soon as an opportunity presented itself.

In another moment the messenger arrived back at the house, bringing with him the delegation from Niagara. They were Mohawks. Holding a large belt of wampum, their leader introduced himself, but it was an involved name which Henry could not understand. The Mohawk went on:

"My friends and brothers, I am come here with this belt from our great father, Sir William Johnson, who is also our brother Warraghiyagey. He desired me to come to you as his ambassador and to tell you that he is making a great feast and council fire at Fort Niagara. His kettles are all ready and his fires have been lighted. He invites you to take part in this feast, along with your friends, the Six Nations,[159] who have all made peace with the English. He advises you to seize this opportunity of doing the same, as you cannot otherwise keep from being destroyed; for the English are already preparing to march with a great army and this army will be joined by many different nations of Indians. What this means is that before the fall of the leaves, they will be again at Michilimackinac and here. And harken to this—when they come, the Six Nations will be with them."

The talks continued and eventually Matchekewis and his warriors left without making any promises to attend. The chiefs of the Sault Sainte Marie village, however, consulted briefly among themselves and then addressed the Mohawk:

"We accept the offer to attend this feast and to make peace with the English and the Six Nations. We have not taken part in this war, yet we will come to reaffirm our peacefulness, and on this you have our word. We will at once prepare a party of our men to attend. Go now, in peace, and may your further journey be safe and to your desires."

Abruptly the hopes of Alexander Henry flared to brilliant life. At last there was a chance for him to get back among the English. He immediately asked for permission to accompany the party and the chief smiled and nodded.

"When we go, Englishman, you will go with us."

And Alexander Henry nearly wept with joy.

[June 15, 1764—Friday]

Pontiac's great trouble was that he flatly refused to accept the inevitable. Though the proof was overwhelming, he still refused to believe that the French would not eventually support him militarily in a continuing war against the English. He even managed to convince a great many of the Illinois country tribes and those farther down the Mississippi of the same thing and he was greatly pleased by the fierceness with which some of them had attached themselves to his goals and leadership.

716

When, just as he was embarking from the Maumee to come to the Illinois country, he heard that a large force of English regulars would soon be coming up the Mississippi to take over command of Fort de Chartres, he immediately sent runners to some of the tribes of the lower Mississippi. His messengers asked the Tunicas and Ofogoulas, the Avoyelles and the Choctaws to ambush any such detachment that might start upriver.

Pontiac himself reached Fort de Chartres on April 15. On the way he was stopped at numerous villages of the Illinois confederacy and his reception had been extremely good. While as yet he had asked no commitment of them, he suggested that they stand ready and they promised they would. Then had come some exciting news.

Major Edward Loftus, leading a detachment of four hundred regulars from Pensacola in the Florida country, had stopped at New Orleans to pay his respects to the French governor, d'Abbadie, and inform him of his orders to go at once to take Fort de Chartres out of French hands in accordance with the provisions of the Treaty of Paris and occupy it with his men for His Britannic Majesty. D'Abbadie had wished him well and Loftus had set off upstream. They were following the west bank of the river some two hundred and forty miles above New Orleans at a place called Roche à Davion when there came the crack of a rifle and a private standing in the lead boat fell dead. At once there was a whole volley of shooting from the bushes and trees rimming the bank.

Loftus made a bad blunder then. Instead of ordering his boats into the middle of the river, he directed them to head for the opposite shore. They did so and as they neared it, another strong volley met them from under cover there, dropping upwards of a score or more of his men, dead or wounded.

Doing now as he should have done in the first place, Loftus ordered the boats out into midriver and they held their place there against the current for a while. But scattered shots kept coming at them and, though now they were having little effect, he decided that the mission was too hazardous and ordered his flotilla to turn about and drift back down to New Orleans. And what pleased Pontiac more than anything else, because it tended to prove his claim that no English force was any match for even a considerably smaller Indian force, was the fact that this detachment of four hundred regulars had been turned back by less than two score Indians.

His prestige among the Illinois tribes having risen even higher with this news, Pontiac proceeded to Fort de Chartres and was given an immediate audience with Major Pierre Joseph Neyon de Villiere. There he went into a very long speech which was heavily peppered with lies, half-truths, threats, pleas and exhortations.

Among the many things that he told the major was that his army of warriors was still fighting at Detroit; that he had had several conferences with Englishmen, whom he did not name, and that universally they spoke with great contempt for the French King and also for de Villiere; that the English also claimed to have the French in their pocket and that they could brush them away like mosquitoes if they chose; that they considered all Indians to be no more than a lump of earth which they could break in their hands and scatter to the wind as dust; that he was still waiting for the help that was supposed to come from the French army.

Astounded, de Villiere asked him if he had not received the word he had sent to Detroit last fall in the hands of the cadet, DeQuindre. Pontiac admitted that he had received the belts and messages and pipes, but that he didn't believe them. Even now, when de Villiere himself said that they were indeed true, Pontiac refused to accept it. Almost as if he had not heard the French commander, he began reiterating demands, requests, boasts and threats. He asked de Villiere to carry a message from him to the French King, letting him know of the Indians' devotion to him, asking that he take pity on the Indians and send them provisions and ammunition and troops; asking that both Major de Villiere and Captain Belêtre, the former Detroit commander, be given command of such troops; begging that the King not abandon his Indian children here. He added a request to de Villiere that he ask Governor d'Abbadie in New Orleans—which Pontiac referred to as "the warm town"—that he send provisions and ammunition to support the Indians while they waited to hear from the King.

Growing exasperated, Major de Villiere again explained that England and France were now at peace and that there could be no French troops or support. Pontiac merely continued his exhortation. If de Villiere had come to Detroit when first asked, the Ottawa chief told him, ". . . we would have made you the greatest man in the world!" He went on to say that in refusing to attack Detroit and the English everywhere, de Villiere was going against the command of the Master of Life, who had ordered it; that the Indians would not finish their war against the English while one red man remained alive.

Major de Villiere interrupted to tell Pontiac in a firm, measured tone that he simply had to make peace with the English, that there was no other way for him and his people if they wished to avoid annihilation.

Pontiac sneered at this, saying that he would never make peace with them, that he hated them, and that if the French made peace with them, such a peace would not last for forty moons. He now pulled from his waistband a dark war belt, tossed it onto the floor and asked the major to pick it up, to show that he would continue to support Pontiac.

"Pontiac!" de Villiere exploded, the anger spilling from him at last, "Can you not understand? Can you not hear? *Listen to me!* The French and the English are at peace and there will be no more war between them. If you attack the English, it will be as if you are attacking us. You will be destroyed!" Savagely he kicked the war belt across the room. "Take that away and stop this foolishness of stirring up the tribes. If you persist, you will bring bloodshed next to the Illinois country."

Pontiac looked at him in a speculative way for a moment and then, amazingly, he smiled and picked up the war belt, stuffing it back into his waistband. He looked levelly at de Villiere and his words were filled with subtle threat which the French officer found disturbing.

"Be easy, my father. I will not spill blood upon your lands here." The chief smiled more broadly and added, "What I spill will be on the water of this river, which the current will carry away."

Then, taking up the rum and presents de Villiere had laid out for him on his arrival, Pontiac left at once. He went directly to the Illinois villages again, demanded and got a major council and exhorted them to war. He gave them the war belt de Villiere had refused and the rum de Villiere had given him, and they accepted both. From village to village, tribe to tribe he moved, asking and getting the promise of support to stop the English.

And at Fort de Chartres, under orders of Governor d'Abbadie, early this morning—June 15—Major Pierre Joseph Neyon de Villiere turned over command of the fort to Captain Louis St. Ange de Bellerive and left for New Orleans with all but forty men of his garrison.

St. Ange, who had long been in command of the tiny post called Port St. Vincent—but better known among the inhabi-

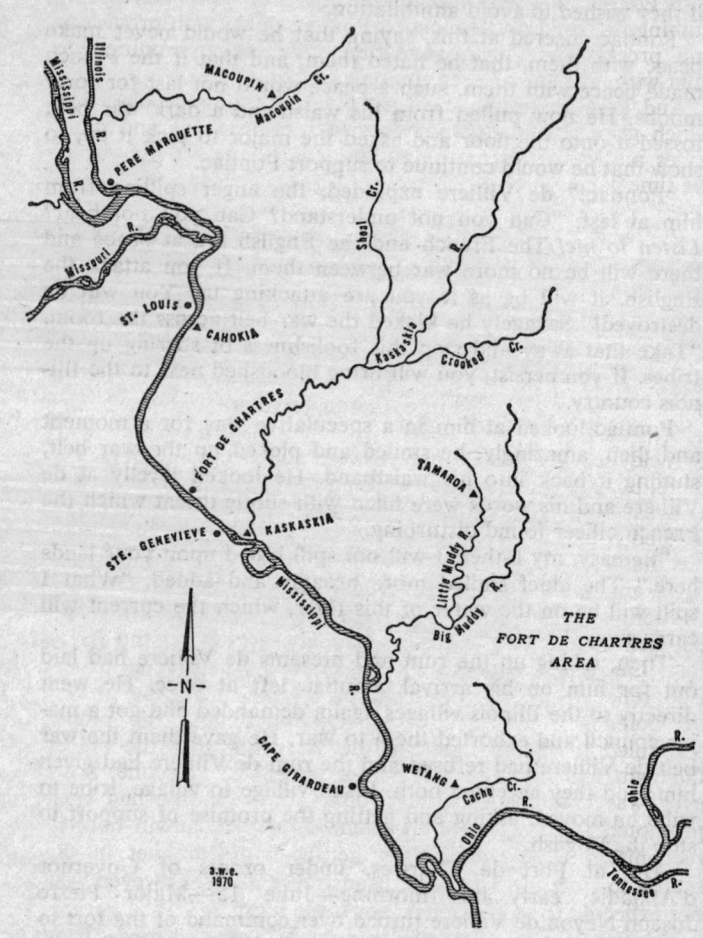

THE
FORT DE CHARTRES
AREA

j.w.e.
1970

ants as Vincennes—on the Wabash River, was visited during the afternoon of this very day by Pontiac. Once more the Ottawa chief went through almost the same routine as he had with Major de Villiere.

No lover of the English, St. Ange listened and sympathized with Pontiac, but told him regretfully that there was simply nothing he could do. He loaded Pontiac down with provisions and presents and even gave him sufficient ammunition to hunt with, and then he sent him away.

And Pontiac, not in the least diverted from the obsession which gripped him, set out to visit more villages and more tribes and convince more Indians yet to support him when the time came.

[June 22, 1764—Friday]

The situation in the western Great Lakes area was a strange one. The whole country was abuzz with talk of the forthcoming Indian congress to be held at Fort Niagara by Sir William Johnson. There was also considerable concern over the armies being formed under Bradstreet and Bouquet, which were poised to arrow deeply into Indian territory and crush any tribe that had not made peace.

Incidents of a hostile nature were still occurring here and there, but rather more covertly than openly and nowhere with as great frequency as previously. That the Indians here still loathed the English was clearly evident, but it was also obvious that they were starting to believe that if they did not wish to be annihilated, they had better make peace.

Along with the word of the forthcoming congress and the planned expeditions, the news had filtered among the tribes that Lieutenant Colonel Henry Gladwin had been promised relief from his command of Detroit upon the arrival of Colonel Bradstreet's army. Oddly enough, the officer scheduled to relieve him had the same name as the officer Gladwin had first relieved here—Campbell. This one, however, was Lieutenant Colonel John Campbell, who had been promoted from major at the same time as Gladwin had, in recognition of his exemplary action with Bouquet in the march to Fort Pitt last year. Bradstreet's army, however, was not expected to reach Detroit for some time.

Nevertheless, the Detroit area tribes *were* worried. They knew Gladwin well by now, knew how he would react under various circumstances and how they would be treated. John Campbell, however, was at this point an unknown factor and it frightened them some. Even the French here were bothered by the news and more of the Detroit inhabitants quietly packed up and slipped off to the Illinois country.

On April 29 the two Huron chiefs, Takee and Teata, came very submissively to Gladwin with some of their men, asking for a council. The commander complied. It was quite brief and it clearly revealed the state of mind these Indians were in now. Teata spoke first, his expression grave, his manner earnest.

"My brother," he said, "we beg you may take pity upon us and hear us, that the words we now say may be as a carpet for your successor to walk upon.

"Brother, we beg you to have pity upon us and be assured of our good intentions, as we have most faithfully repented of all the ill we have done. We do most sincerely promise never to be guilty of any bad thing in the future, having thrown ourselves into the hands of God. If any evil happens to us, it must be from Him, as you may be persuaded. Let the earth turn how it will, we shall never be advised to do a bad thing again."

He paused and then took a large white wampum belt from where it was draped over his arm and handed it to the interpreter, Jacques St. Martin, who in turn gave it to Gladwin as Teata concluded:

"This, brother, we beg you will inform the general at the first opportunity."

Lieutenant Colonel Henry Gladwin smiled benignly and promised that he would relay the good words of Chief Teata to General Gage.

Takee was far more nervous than Teata had been. His facial expression changed rapidly as he stood before the officer and for a short while he could not seem to find the words he wanted. At last he spoke:

"Brother, ever since the English have had possession of this place we have been used very gently, agreeable to the promise you made us when you first came here, for which reason we hope our brother will grant us the small favor we are going to ask.

"Brother, as wood and bark have become very scarce at the place where our village is now, we hope you will give us leave to make a new village up a small creek near the bottom of the settlement, where everything will be more convenient."

Without hesitation Gladwin granted the request, surprised that Takee should have felt that he needed the Detroit commander's permission for such a move. Takee nodded and continued:

"Brother, when first you came here you told us that you had conquered our French father and sent him over the great water far to the east, and all that then belonged to him was yours, but that we should be allowed to keep our possessions and be allowed to have our Jesuit priest, Father Pothier. Now that you have said we may change our village place, we hope you will not prevent him going with us, for he wishes to and we are in need of him."

He too, as Teata had done, presented a string of wampum and Gladwin again gave his permission readily. Within minutes the Indians had gone.

The same sort of concern was evident among the other tribes. Although both the Potawatomies and Chippewas had bands which continued to act in a hostile manner, the majority stepped lightly and took pains not to offend the English of Detroit in any way. One band of forty Chippewas under Chief Wasson, coming to do some mischief around Detroit, quietly turned back and did nothing when they heard the news of the Niagara congress and the army, and way up at Michilimackinac there was another noteworthy happening. Nearly two hundred and fifty Sacs, Menominees, Winnebagoes and Foxes from the west side of Lake Michigan came through the Straits of Mackinac en route on their regular annual visit to Montreal. But at Michilimackinac they heard of the grand congress being called by Johnson at Niagara and immediately they pointed their flotilla of canoes in that direction.

From all over the wilderness—on foot, on horseback or in canoes—there was a great general movement of tribal delegates toward the head of Lake Ontario, the site of Fort Niagara. One of the canoes plying its way down the eastern shore of Lake Huron contained sixteen Indians and a white man. The Indians were Chippewas from the Sault Sainte Marie and the white man was Alexander Henry, hardly able to believe that at last he was really heading back to his own people and that the threat of death which had overhung him for more than a year was soon to be lifted.

They had left the Sault on June 10, but the trip had not been lacking in hazards for Henry. Shortly after passing the mouth of the Mississaugi River they put ashore for rest at Point aux Grondines. Here, as he was gathering some firewood, Henry encountered a large timber rattlesnake and was on the point of killing it when interrupted by the Chippewas.

Motioning him back, they surrounded it, all of them addressing it as their grandfather and paying it the utmost respect, yet while keeping a discreet distance from it. They lit their pipes and for thirty minutes or more blew puffs of smoke toward the coiled snake. The reptile was at first irritated and rattled menacingly, but after a short while it seemed to relax and almost to take enjoyment from the attention being received. The Chippewas told Henry this was the manifestation of a very special spirit and they prayed to it that it would open the heart of Sir William Johnson toward them when they arrived at Niagara.

The next morning the journey was continued under good weather conditions and finally, since it was such a calm day, they decided they would head directly for a fair-sized island just barely visible on the horizon across the open water, some five or six miles distant. Though rarely did the canoes venture into such unprotected water, by doing so now instead of following the shoreline, they could save themselves about thirty miles of paddling.[160]

Hardly more than a quarter of the way across, however, the wind began picking up. The water rippled, became choppy and then was suddenly a very heavy sea, and numerous times they were nearly swamped. The Indians were terrified and frequently called on the rattlesnake to come to their help, calling that spirit by the name of *Manitou-kinibic*. One of the chiefs took a small dog which was aboard, tied its forelegs together and threw it overboard, beseeching *Manitou-kinibic* to satisfy its hunger with the carcass of the dog rather than themselves.

When this had no immediate effect, another chief did the same thing with another dog and also tossed some tobacco overboard as an offering. Still the storm did not abate and now angry looks were being cast at Henry. The chief sitting near him pointed a finger at him and shouted above the noise of wind and water:

"You have brought this upon us! You were going to kill the *Manitou-kinibic* until we stopped you and this is what he has brought upon us for the insult you gave him, and because we have harbored you. If we drown, it will be for your fault alone. Perhaps we should tie your hands and throw you into the water as we did the dogs. Perhaps that way the anger would be smoothed away from *Manitou-kinibic*."

For a few frightening moments Henry was sure they were going to do just this to him. Then, more suddenly than it had arisen, the wind providentially died down and they continued

724

in safety. But the incident made Henry realize that he was yet far from being safe.

On June 17—five days ago—they had reached the foot of this great bay of Lake Huron[161] at Beausoleil Island. Here they entered the stream which led up to Lac aux Claies.[162] On June 19 they crossed the twenty-two-mile-wide lake, left their canoes on the south shore and moved overland until they reached the headwaters of a stream which the Indians called the Taranta River, after the name of a small tribe once said to have lived here, and they followed it to its mouth on Lake Ontario.[163] Here, stripping wide sheaths of bark from elm trees, they made several small canoes and began following the shore of Lake Ontario west and south toward Niagara.

Last night they had made camp just four miles short of their goal, the Indians becoming a little afraid of what lay ahead and unwilling to go farther in the darkness. But early in the morning today, being again assured by Henry of a friendly welcome, they had continued. And just an hour ago the mouth of the mighty Niagara River appeared before them and, on the point of land on the far side of it, Fort Niagara.

Tears filled Henry's eyes as he saw the fort, saw the red coats of a great multitude of soldiers, saw at last the only real haven he had seen in so very long a time. His Chippewa escort expressing a wish to camp on the opposite side of the river mouth from the fort, Henry bade them farewell for now, manned a paddle and went across alone.

And now, standing in the very shadow of the fort, he stared at the scene before him. Several thousand soldiers, many in the uniform of the regulars, many more in the nondescript dress of the militia, were camped all about the fort; and beyond them, everywhere he looked, were the thin columns of blue-white smoke rising from not just dozens or scores of Indian campfires, but actually hundreds of them.

Within the hour, Alexander Henry, Englishman, was explaining in detail to Sir William Johnson and Colonel John Bradstreet how Fort Michilimackinac had fallen and what had happened since then.

[June 30, 1764—Saturday]

As usual when a major campaign was in prospect, matters were bogging down badly. And, also as usual, still at his headquarters in Philadelphia, Colonel Henry Bouquet was becoming ever more frustrated at the delays. The war plan agreed upon had called for the absolute and unconditional submission of the tribes, but in order to bring this about an enormous amount of material and a great number of men had to be collected. Already the prime period for beginning the onslaught into the Northwest Territory was past.

Bouquet considered Thomas Gage to be far more competent a commander for a job such as this one of quelling the Indian uprising than Amherst had been. For one thing, Gage did not make the inexcusable blunder that so plagued Amherst here; he did not underestimate the enemy. The Indians were, the new commander admitted, a strong and worthy adversary. They would demand greater effort and resolution on the part of His Majesty's troops to put them down. They might be bestial in many ways and their customs greatly different from the English, but it would be a grave error to underestimate their fighting ability or the mentality of the chiefs who led them. Of Pontiac in particular—as it would have been inconceivable for Amherst to have admitted—Gage commented:

"There is reason to judge of Pontiac not only as a savage possessed of the most refined cunning and treachery natural to the Indians, but as a person of extraordinary abilities."

Despite a new and better commander in chief, however, the campaign preparations had gone on at a snail's pace. Bouquet had hoped to be able to take his army downstream on the Ohio in a great multitude of batteaux. The journey in such manner would have been more swiftly and less fatiguingly done than by land, and in relatively good time they could sweep up the Muskingum River of the Ohio country to the Delaware villages on its headwaters and then, after crushing them to submission, float back down to the Ohio, continue downstream to the Scioto River and then move up that stream to do the same against the Shawnees.

But by now the time of high water was already past and such passage, especially on the Muskingum and Scioto, would be extremely difficult. Now, if and when everything was assembled that was needed, the only means of getting to those villages would be by marching overland from Fort Pitt through the wilderness. Remembering the awful ambush he had undergone last summer, it was without any great degree of eagerness that Bouquet considered tramping through country so well known to the Indians and so poorly known by himself and the army.

Even the fact that Pennsylvania had finally taken some action to defend itself and also join the general offensive effort failed to raise his spirits very high. It was a tragic thing when it took an invasion of frontiersmen against the principal city of a province to frighten the legislative body to its senses. After the Paxton Boys had created their stir, the Quakers in the Assembly seemed to realize it was time to put into abeyance their age-old quarrels with the governor and the Pennsylvania proprietors and the Presbyterians; time to ease off on their morally sound but too abundantly idealistic scruples about bringing war to the Indians. The Assembly voted to raise three hundred men to guard the borders and an additional thousand to join Bouquet's army for the campaign. They even went so far as to promise Bouquet that they were going to send to England for a hundred bloodhounds to be used in the hunting down of Indian scalping parties.[164] But perhaps the most amazing thing of all was when Governor Penn issued a proclamation offering high bounties for Indian scalps. Copies of the document were posted on trees and sides of buildings throughout the entire province and almost overnight Indian hunting became a decidedly profitable business for those who didn't mind the occupational hazards involved. The proclamation stated:

I do hereby declare and promise, that there shall be paid out of the moneys lately granted for His Majesty's use, to all and every person and persons not in the pay of this Province, the following several and respective premiums and bounties for the prisoners and scalps of the enemy Indians that shall be taken or killed within the bounds of this Province, as limited by the Royal Charter, or in pursuit from within said bounds; that is to say, for every male Indian enemy above ten years old, who shall be taken prisoner and delivered at any fort garrisoned by the troops in the pay of this Province, or at any of the county towns, to the keeper of the common jails there, the sum of one hundred and fifty Spanish dollars, or pieces of eight. For every female Indian enemy taken prisoner and brought in as aforesaid, and for every male Indian enemy of ten years old or under taken prisoner and delivered as aforesaid, the sum of one hundred and thirty pieces of eight. For the scalp of every male Indian enemy above the age of ten years, produced as evidence of their being killed, the sum of one hundred and thirty-four pieces of eight. And for the scalp of every female Indian enemy above the age of ten years, produced as evidence of their being killed, the sum of fifty pieces of eight.

But despite this tardy and rather over-reactive move by Pennsylvania and the fact that already some of the provincial troops were on their way to Fort Pitt to await his coming, Henry Bouquet was depressed. His entire adult life had been devoted to a military career, but it seemed to him that now he was at a dead end, that he had come as far as it was possible for him to come. What possible advantage could there be for him to continue leading troops and risking his life in the wilderness frontier when, as a Swiss mercenary, it was obvious that he had advanced in rank as far as he could go in the British army? The melancholy grew on him daily until, on a gloomy, rainy day just ten days ago, he had written a brief note to General Gage at headquarters in New York:

Sir:

I flatter myself that you will do me the favor to have me relieved from this command, the burden and fatigues of which I begin to feel my strength very unequal to.

Now had come Gage's reply, telling Bouquet what a fine soldier he was, what a great strategist, what a superb officer and leader of men; that no other officer in North America had the experience in fighting the Delawares and Shawnees that he possessed, nor so well understood what needed to be done. He sympathized with Bouquet to the extreme and piled him high with plaudits and expressions of greatest confidence, but no matter how many times Bouquet read the letter, the answer was always the same: no, the request was denied—Colonel Bouquet would not be relieved of his command and resignation would not be acceptable.

And so, with the resolution and lack of complaint that had been a characteristic of him throughout his military life, Colonel Henry Bouquet turned his eyes to the west and prepared to invade the savage wilderness that was called the Middle Ground by some, the Ohio country by others, and, by a great many, the Northwest Territory.

[August 6, 1764—Monday]

Fort Niagara held many memories for Sir William Johnson. Here it was that he had won part of the aura of greatness which still attended him, by taking command of the army brought here after its commander was killed accidentally, and in a maneuver worthy of the highest accolades for generalship destroying a French force attacking from the west while at the same time bringing the French garrison within the fort to its knees. Yet, even during that important period here in 1759, during the French and Indian War, there had not been so many people on hand as there were at this moment.

Not only did the fort's garrison and Colonel Bradstreet's army total to the impressive figure of over three thousand men, but also assembled here were well over two thousand Indians representing twenty-two different tribes. Everywhere one looked there were campfires and gatherings and the wonder of it all was that there were no volatile incidents. But the officers, for the military, and the various chiefs, for their tribes, kept a tight check on their men and maintained a strictly adhered-to policy of neutrality on these grounds, with sober warnings made of severe punishment to be meted out to whatever man—white or Indian—caused disturbance.

Here were the Ottawas and Chippewas, the Hurons and Mississaugi and Potawatomies and the representatives of seven or eight other western Great Lakes tribes. Here were the Six Nations and the Abnakis, the Algonkins and Caughnawagas and Nipissings and representatives of other tribes to the south and east and north. Here were the Miamis and Kaskaskias, the Kickapoos and Cahokias and representatives of other far western tribes.

But here were *not* the Delawares or the Shawnees or the Senecas. The former two tribes had sent a runner bearing a terse little message to Sir William Johnson. It was, in fact, not only a terse message, it was insolent in the extreme, saying:

Although we have no fear of the English and regard them as old women and hold them in great contempt, yet we feel pity for them and if another invitation should come to us, accompanied by presents, begging us to come, we will then do so and perhaps treat for peace with you.

William Johnson merely shook his head and would not even deign to send these Shawnees and Delawares a reply. But it was another matter indeed when a runner arrived with a message from the Senecas. Discarding the preliminary treaty they had already made with Sir William and breaking their promise to appear at the Niagara Congress to complete and ratify that treaty, their message was a distinct slap in the face to Johnson, a strong insult to their Mohawk brother, Warraghiyagey. It said:

We prefer to go our own way. We find the company of our brother Shawnees and Delawares much more to our liking. We will not come.

Johnson was so furious he trembled and for the briefest of moments he seemed on the verge of striking down the smirking Seneca warrior who had delivered the message. But then he caught himself and, in a voice frightening in its threat, he gave the warrior a message to carry back to the valley of the Genesee.

"Go back to your chiefs," he said, "and tell them that these are my words: tell them that it is not my wish but rather my *command* that they come to Niagara instantly! Tell them that if they do not arrive here within four days—*only four!*—that I will bank my council fires here and I will gather behind me the three thousand soldiers you see waiting here for my command, and I will march to the Genesee. And tell them that if I do this, it will be too late for them, because the anger will blind my eyes against seeing them kneel to beg mercy from me and my ears will be deaf to their pleas and I will destroy every town and every house, *and I will destroy every Seneca!* Four days, that is all. Tell them."

At dusk of the third day the Senecas arrived and very meekly turned over to Sir William a total of fourteen prisoners, along with several army deserters and a number of runaway Negro slaves they had been harboring. Quite satisfied, Johnson now opened the Niagara Congress, with the first councils beginning on July 11.

It was a much different type of congress than any of the Indians had expected or were accustomed to. In past congresses there had always been one grand council, with all the tribes spread out on the ground in a dense semicircle before the speaker. Not so this time. A point of policy had been agreed upon long in advance by Johnson and Gage: positively no *general* council with the Indians was to be held. Instead, separate and private treaties were to be made with each individual tribe. The reason for this was shrewdly contrived: in this way there would be no assurance for any one tribe that it was getting as much as any other tribe. They would ask one another, of course, what the details of the other's treaty were, but more than likely the answer given would not be believed. This would immediately create and promote intertribal jealousies and rivalry which might never end, promote much distrust among the tribes for each other, and very likely act as a barrier against possible future alliances or a union against the common enemy, the whites. It was, in conception and effect, a brilliantly strategic negotiative maneuver which had precisely the expected results.

As treaty after treaty was consummated, intertribal resentment grew more and more heated and there was even some fear that there would be an eruption of violence between the tribes before the congress ended. That did not occur, but the wedges which had been driven by Johnson were firmly lodged and were splitting old alliances and new friendships. Suddenly many of the old and nearly forgotten animosities between various tribes flared to new life.

The English, as had become customary, gave far less than they received. As so often promised in the past, they agreed that settlement on Indian lands would be prohibited and that good relations with the tribes would be maintained. The Indians were promised full pardon for all past misdeeds of the war or before, and given assurance that immediately the trade would be reopened to all the tribes involved in making their peace with the English here. Further, that they would be given, for a price, all of whatever they needed, including even alcohol and ammunition. In exchange, the Indians were to faithfully give up any designs against the subjects of soldiers of His Britannic Majesty, give up all prisoners and deserters and runaway slaves amongst them, give their own promises to maintain a friendly alliance with the English, give their word to do their utmost to promote peace and preserve His Majesty's interests in America and, finally, to give the English the right to certain specific parcels of land that the individual tribes claimed.

Johnson had been particularly hard with the Senecas, verbally castigating them for their actions in defying the rulings of the Iroquois League and for their impudence in sending that insulting message to him before the congress convened. And, still holding the club of three thousand soldiers over their heads, he virtually forced them to cede to the English all claim to a four-mile-wide strip of land on either side of the Niagara River, from Lake Erie to Lake Ontario.

As each treaty was signed, William Johnson loaded the delegates with bountiful gifts such as they had not seen since the war or before, and they went away pleased with themselves, pleased with the English, and often at odds with practically every other tribe. Regardless of what vantage point it was viewed from, this had to be ranked as one of the most important and triumphant treaty sessions for Great Britain that had ever been concluded to this time.

For Sir William himself, it was a victorious time in more ways than one. Not only was a definite and permanent peace established with all the heretofore troublesome tribes—with the exception only of the Shawnees, Delawares and Wyandots—there was at this very moment a document being written in London by the Lords of Trade under direction of the Crown that gave the Indian Department in North America precisely what it had yearned for—autonomy; an independence from, and in some cases authority over, the English military command of the continent.

Sir William Johnson and the South Carolinian, John Stuart,[165] as the supervisors respectively of the Northern and Southern Indian Departments, would be responsible directly to the Crown. They would have the right to serve as *ex officiis* members on the provincial councils of all colonies within their jurisdiction. This meant, in Johnson's case, that he now had the right to sit in on the councils of Virginia, Maryland, Pennsylvania, New Jersey, New York, Connecticut, Massachusetts, New Hampshire, Nova Scotia and Quebec. In addition, to quash such interference with the Indian Department as the Quakers and other bodies had heretofore been guilty of, it was ordered that the Indian Superintendents *alone* would have the authority to call Indian congresses, to deal with the Indians politically and in matters of trade, and to be the final word in whether there should be war or peace with them. The traders would have to procure licenses through both the military commander and the authorities of the provinces from which they operated, but the moment they entered the territory of the Indians, they were under the sole and complete jurisdiction of the Indian Superintendent. No Indian land was to be sold by anyone except at a general council convened by the Indian Superintendent and, for their own protection, authorized tribal representatives were to attend such councils and approve all surveys.

As yet, however, the new edict was not known here on the American continent and the military commander in chief was still the supreme power. And, acting under his direction, Colonel John Bradstreet prepared to drive straight westward from Niagara and Colonel Henry Bouquet prepared to do the same from Fort Pitt. The Niagara Congress had been a powerful treaty-making affair, but there was one thing yet which needed attention.

The Shawnees and Delawares were still at war with the English.

If ever any officer in the services of His Royal Majesty, George III, was candidate for enshrinement in the Halls of Megalomania, it was Colonel John Bradstreet. Though plagued with a recurring incompetency, he was incapable of conceiving that there was anything he could not do, if given the chance. How many times since that thrilling day of August 27, 1758, had he relived his greatest triumph? How many times had he congratulated himself on his strategy, his incredible brilliance, his military genius? Was he not the officer who, in the midst of defeat after defeat for the English at the hands of the French and Indians, led the force which surprised and utterly destroyed the French Fort Frontenac at the foot of Lake Ontario, which was the principal communication between Montreal and the posts of the western Great Lakes? Had he not accomplished this feat without the loss of a man? Had not the fact that he had been responsible for this destruction of Fort Frontenac hastened the end of the war?

As with most megalomaniacs in reviewing their past accomplishments, there were facts which were conveniently shunted aside. Bradstreet's victory at Fort Frontenac, if victory it could be called since there was no fighting involved, was the supernova of his career to this point, but its importance was largely in his own mind. The little post, commanded at that time by none other than Pierre Joseph Neyon de Villiere, who was then a captain, had been garrisoned by one hundred and ten men. In the dead of night Bradstreet's force of three thousand soldiers and forty Mohawk warriors had surrounded it. In the morning when he announced his presence and Neyon de Villiere quite sensibly capitulated immediately, the French garrison and its commander were set free to make their way back to Montreal, the fort and its goods had been burned, along with the supply ships in its little harbor, and Bradstreet's army hotfooted it back to Albany.[166]

Since that time, John Bradstreet had become an absolute bore to his superiors and a fatuous tyrant to his subordinates. He had also, in his own mind, become the foremost military figure in His Majesty's service, if not in the entire world. For the ensuing five years since then he had been waiting for a chance to once again show what he could do; to prove to the world that he was a man of destiny. And now, with a force of twelve hundred soldiers and three hundred Indians, he was moving westward from Niagara, determined to let nothing stand in his way to that glorious destiny.

His orders had been quite clear: to move first to the site of Presque Isle and then, following the southern shore to Lake Erie westward, to crush any opposition offered by Indians—specifically Shawnees and Delawares—and then to batter into submissiveness any Wyandots or Ottawas of a hostile nature still in the Sandusky area and force them to deliver up to him every English captive they had. If the situation warranted it, he was to move southward from there to the headwaters of the Scioto River and follow that stream down to a union with Bouquet—who would be ascending it with his force—and between them to wipe out all Shawnee and Delaware resistance remaining. If, however, such uniting of forces was not deemed necessary or practicable, he was to go on from Sandusky to Detroit, relieve Lieutenant Colonel Henry Gladwin by putting Lieutenant Colonel John Campbell in command of the fort, use discretion on whether or not to attack any Indians in the Detroit area, but not to hesitate in attacking any Shawnees or Delawares encountered, and, finally, he was to send a detachment to reoccupy Fort Michilimackinac.

The possibilities that all this presaged brought a glitter to Bradstreet's eye. He had a number of ideas of his own about things he was going to do very soon, above and beyond what his orders called for. And some of his orders he had no intention whatever of obeying, simply because to obey them would take out of his grasp the very destiny he knew awaited him. One such order, for example, was Gage's directive that if any Indians were encountered who wished to sue for peace, they were to be immediately sent on to Sir William Johnson. Neither Bradstreet nor Bouquet was empowered to make treaties or grant peace. Which, Bradstreet reasoned, was ridiculous; how could a man possibly become known as the officer who crushed the hostiles and brought peace to the west if, when peace delegates from the tribes came to him, he simply relayed them on to someone else? Who then would reap the glory? No, sir! In his own boastfully spoken words, he was a man "seeking great honor" and *that*, by God, was no way to get it!

On August 8, two days following the close of the Niagara Congress, Bradstreet's army embarked from Fort Schlosser above the falls in a great fleet of batteaux. For some reason explainable only to himself, when they reached the long peninsula of Presque Isle stretching out into the lake, instead of going around it in the water which was customary, he ordered that a portage be made of the cumbersome boats and supplies. The distance was not great and apparently he thought he was saving time. As a matter of fact though, at the cost of considerable effort and fatigue to the men and much damage to the boats as they were dragged and bumped along, the portage wound up taking about three times as long as the much simpler journey by water around it would have done.

But Bradstreet, giddy already with mental images of a fantastic new triumph shaping up for his crown of glory, thought little of it, And his first crack at such triumph appeared to present itself right here at Presque Isle. With a storm in the offing, the army took refuge on the shore to camp for the night, and it was during this night of August 12 that a small party of ten Delawares and Shawnees was discovered skulking about the camp. Surrounded unexpectedly, they surrendered and were brought before Bradstreet who, incredibly, over the objections of his officers, concluded that these ten were peace emissaries from their tribes. The Indians quickly latched onto this golden opportunity to get out of a ticklish situation. Rummaging about in their pouches, they managed to find one very little string of wampum which they held before Bradstreet's eyes and announced that they were, indeed, ambassadors who had come on behalf of their nations to beg peace.

Bradstreet's officers were quick to point out to the colonel that this was ridiculous and that the ten warriors were obviously spies. The army's Indian allies, mostly Iroquois, agreed and were strong for putting the ten to death at once.

Completely ignoring all this unsolicited advice, Colonel John Bradstreet, to the immense shock and complete incredulity of his entire force, did not ask the Shawnees and Delawares what chiefs had appointed them to this mission or even if any of them were chiefs themselves; nor did he pay any attention to the fact that their wampum was no more than any party of Indians might be carrying; nor would he believe the reports received that the Pennsylvania frontier was still alive with parties of marauding Indians just like these.

Savoring every second of this moment, which he was positive would forever be revered in times to come, Colonel John Bradstreet granted a full pardon to the entire Shawnee and Delaware tribes, provided that they would meet him again at Sandusky to deliver up their prisoners there. And then, to the further consternation of his officers and men, he gave his solemn promise to the little party of warriors that he would not advance down the Scioto to destroy their villages. In conclusion he signed, for them to take with them, a preliminary treaty of peace in the name of George III.

Nervously grasping the document and not even asking for presents—which probably more than anything else should have alerted Bradstreet that they were not what they claimed to be—the ten Indians hastened away and were quickly swallowed up in the darkness. And Bradstreet, a great glow of pride virtually bursting in him—and wholly ignoring the dark glances and mutterings of his Indian allies and the protests of his officers—retired to his tent to add a final damning exclamation mark to his utter cupidity of this day.

He quickly wrote and dispatched letters to General Gage in New York and Colonel Bouquet, who was already on the march himself through the hills of western Pennsylvania. In both he outlined the details of the treaty he had made and pointedly extolled his own consummate skill in bringing about this peace which Sir William Johnson had not been able to do. And in the letter to Bouquet, although that officer was his superior in this operation, he had the inconceivable brashness to write:

. . . and since I have reduced the Delawares and Shawnees to submission without your aid, you may withdraw your troops, as there is no longer any need of your advancing farther.

Little wonder that now, as the batteaux were launched and reloaded, that such mundane matters as a mere unnecessary portage, badly leaking boats and exhausted men failed to penetrate the aura of self-glory he emanated. There were other things to think about. Ahead lay the rest of Lake Erie and, toward the far end of it, Sandusky. Perhaps more glory awaited him there and, if not there, might it not be a good idea to act with a little initiative of his own? What about the *far* western country? What about such tribes as the Weas and Muncees, the Piankeshaws, Sacs and Foxes, and what about the whole Illinois Confederacy? What fantastic glory and honor might not attend the officer who single-handedly pushed the advantage he had made and brought peace all the way to the Mississippi River?

It was assuredly food for thought.

As had become glaringly apparent to a good many people by now, Chief Pontiac of the Ottawas did not discourage easily. When an idea became fixed in his mind, it was a measure of his character that he held to it against the most formidable of obstacles. But even he, as he now approached his Maumee River village again after his long stay in the Illinois country, had been forced to reluctantly admit that his great plans to balk the English, to drive them from these lands, had failed. One by one his hopes had been shattered and he was both angry and discouraged.

All the war fervor he had been able to inspire in the Illinois tribes was evaporating. Their desire for English blood had been sired in brains fogged by rum; there had been second thoughts with the return of sobriety and the principal tribes of the Illinois Confederacy—the Cahokia, Peoria and Kaskaskia—had abruptly backed off. The rejection was not absolute, but it might as well have been. They were willing to fight under Pontiac only if Pontiac's own people would be leading the field and other tribes than their own joined in support; but, they warned ominously, they had no intention of being used by Pontiac to accomplish the Ottawa war chief's own aims. What it amounted to was this: if the English came to their country and it was then deemed by the Illinois Confederacy that their presence was a bad thing, *then* would they raise their tomahawks in war.

Continued appeals by Pontiac to Captain Louis St. Ange at Fort de Chartres were equally unavailing. The commanding officer remained most sympathetic to Pontiac but, other than providing the chief with moral support, he had nothing to give. Even the moral support had dwindled of late and he had begun advising the Ottawa to return and make his peace with the English. St. Ange himself was anticipating the time when, as called for by the Treaty of Paris, the English would come and relieve him of Fort de Chartres and let him be rid of the uneasiness of the Indians of the surrounding area.

So now Pontiac was approaching his own village again, determined despite his gnawing discouragement to do as his Illinois allies requested: get his own people firmly behind him and renew the war. He did not expect it to be very easy, but he had no doubt that in the end he could do it. At least he had no doubt until this moment. But now, reentering the

Maumee River village he could see something was wrong. It did not take long to discover what it was.

Not one of the four elder Ottawa chiefs he had left behind here remained. They had come with him to this place still believing in Pontiac's design, still helping through their age and respected positions in the tribe to hold the younger men together with the firm conviction of driving the English out. But that had been before the arrival of Chief Manitou.

A month or so after Pontiac had gone to the Illinois country, Manitou had come to this village and, just as he had at Detroit, inveighed against Pontiac and undermined what he had established. In long deliberations with the elder chiefs, he convinced them of the futility of the course they were taking and of the fact that the last opportunity for snatching the proffered peace from the English was diminishing and soon it would be too late; then there would be nothing left for them but destruction.

When Manitou left the Maumee River village, only two weeks ago, the body of Pontiac's warriors whom he had converted and who accompanied him back to Detroit was not large, perhaps no more than twelve or fifteen men. But among them were all four chiefs and now, at last, Pontiac was alone. The warriors left to him were all young men, many not yet into their twentieth summer, and all were motivated to fight still more not because of any marked degree of idealism, but simply for the excitement of waging war and taking scalps. Even the handful of young Frenchmen who had been here, Alexis Cuillerier among them, had slunk away into the forest and disappeared.

Now Pontiac must depend entirely upon himself.

CHAPTER XII

COLONEL JOHN BRADSTREET wore a half-smile on his ruggedly handsome military face as the wooded shoreline of the Detroit River moved past on both sides. Soon they would be at Detroit where, he had little doubt, more laurels were waiting to be plucked. Obviously, from comments made at the Niagara Congress, there were still many bands of Indians in this area who, despite the actions of their brothers, had not made peace at Niagara. It was upon these that he would concentrate and, just as he had brought peace to the entire Ohio country and the far west, so now he would bring peace here.

His smile broadened some as he thought of the events of this campaign till now. He could visualize the stories already appearing about him in the eastern newspapers and he could virtually hear his own name on the lips of everyone as the word was passed of his grand accomplishments. Soon, perhaps, he would be getting dispatches from General Gage and he very nearly squirmed with anticipation of the praise they would contain. Perhaps—certainly it was not an impossibility!—he would return from this campaign to find he was advanced in rank to brigadier. After that, who knew what? Eventually there would be need for another military commander in chief in America; why not John Bradstreet?

There had been times, as his army continued westward along the south shore of Lake Erie after having left the Presque Isle area, that it had been impractical in the extreme for the Indian detachment traveling with them to continue afoot on shore as they had been, At such times they were wedged into the already crowded and leaking batteaux. It was quite uncomfortable. They could have kept pace on shore had Bradstreet slowed his pace a little, but this he adamantly refused to do. When, at one rest stop, several officers came to him with a number of the chiefs in tow, he heard them out impatiently.

"Sir," one of the young officers asked hesitantly, "how are these Indians to get along, when the boats are too crowded and yet they can't keep pace on shore?"

"By God," Bradstreet snorted, waving them off with a disparaging motion of his hand, "let them swim and be damned, or let them stay and be damned!"

The fact that a number of the chiefs understood English well enough to follow perfectly what he had said concerned him not in the least. Whether or not they continued with his force made little difference to him.

Arriving at Sandusky, where his orders called for him to attack and destroy any Ottawas, Wyandots or Shawnees who appeared hostilely inclined, Bradstreet was met by a deputation of warriors who said they had been sent by their chiefs to beg that no attack be made against them, that they wished peace, and that if Bradstreet would continue to Detroit, they would meet him there in fifteen days and conclude a peace with him there. Again ignoring the advice of his officers that this was no more than a ploy to keep the army from destroying their villages, Bradstreet again entered into a preliminary treaty. He was not at all disturbed by the fact that the Shawnees and Delawares, with whom he had treated at Presque Isle, had not shown up here to surrender their prisoners as promised. After all, the army had traveled fast and he was certain they had merely been delayed, that they would soon be here to see to that matter. Since Bradstreet himself would undoubtedly soon be back here too, there was no problem.

At the mouth of the Maumee River, the army paused again. Bradstreet had given much thought to the idea of ascending that river and moving westward into the Illinois country, but it was such a flagrant breach of his orders that he decided against it. He did, however, dispatch Captain Thomas Morris with an escort of Indians to go up the Maumee and down the Wabash, to make peace with each tribe he came to until he reached the Illinois country. Morris was selected because he could speak French, which Bradstreet assumed would be an advantage when the young, round-faced officer presented himself at Fort de Chartres to take over command of the place. He also gave Morris, as bodyguard, a Frenchman who was being returned to Gladwin at Detroit from Niagara. He had authority to hang the man but now told him that he would spare his life if he would go with

Morris, interpret between the captain and the Indians, and take good care of the officer. Quite naturally, the Frenchman, expecting to be hung upon reaching Detroit, jumped at the chance. When Morris asked his name, he identified himself as Jacques Godefroy.[167]

That sending Captain Morris and his party out on such a mission was an extremely rash move of highly doubtful benefit, not in accordance with his orders, and subject to the sacrificing of this officer's life, did not seem to concern Colonel Bradstreet in the least. In the morning, having seen Morris's party off, the flotilla set out again for Detroit.

Now, as the Detroit River shoreline slid past, Bradstreet began writing a letter to General Gage. A private in the boat obligingly bent over to allow his back to be used as a sort of makeshift desk, steadying the inkpot with one hand and himself with the other. The colonel wrote proudly of what had occurred at both Sandusky and the mouth of the Maumee River, and then added:

. . . and I will hold an Indian council at Detroit and intend to demand that Pontiac be given up, to be sent down the country and maintained at his Majesty's expense the remainder of his days.

The booming of a cannon and a great cheering smote Bradstreet's ears now and he looked up, then quickly put away his writing materials. Billows of white smoke puffed far in the distance from the walls of Detroit, followed moments later by more throaty boomings of the cannon as an excited welcome was given the approaching army. The ramparts were lined with soldiers cheering wildly and waving their hats.

It was precisely the sort of welcome Bradstreet expected and he was highly gratified. This, he reasoned, was only a sampling of what awaited him when he returned to New York.

[August 27, 1764—Monday]

Rarely in his life had Colonel Henry Bouquet ever completely lost his temper. An extraordinarily levelheaded individual, he generally considered uncontrolled outbursts of anger as rather juvenile manifestations which accomplished little. When something came up which irritated him, it was characteristic of him either to do whatever was in his power to set matters right again or, if this was not possible, to accept the situation as philosophically as could be and look ahead from there. It was an admirable disposition which had gone far in contributing to his notable success as a leader of men. But there were exceedingly rare instances when an all-consuming rage gripped him. This day was one such time.

For the first two hours after receiving the impertinent, astonishing, and utterly unbelievable message from Colonel Bradstreet written from Presque Isle, he had been enveloped by a rage more blinding than any he had ever before experienced. Had Bradstreet been before him, he believed he could have gladly, and with malice aforethought, strangled the man with his bare hands. The nincompoop! The blindly ambitious unmitigated ass! Were not matters on this frontier bad enough as it was without being hampered by the actions of an absolute idiot?

Little had gone as Bouquet might have wished since he had left Philadelphia at the time that the Niagara Congress was being held by Sir William Johnson. The force he had hoped to have available to take with him had been nowhere near the strength he had anticipated, and on his arrival at Carlisle on August 5 he had with him considerably fewer of the new provincial troops than were necessary, and his regulars were mainly the veterans of his battle at Bushy Run and Edge Hill a year ago.

Within five days after arrival at Carlisle, some two hundred of his provincials had deserted—some because they were afraid, others because they wanted to hunt Indians on their own and claim the high bounties being offered for scalps and prisoners, which they could not claim if they were in the pay of the province for such purpose. As a result, Bouquet had been forced to send an express to Colonel Andrew Lewis, commanding the Virginia Militia, and request two hundred of his men as volunteers to take the place of the deserters.

Supplies had not been available as they should have been and much of the gunpowder had been so damaged by persistent rains that it was worthless. The season was already extremely advanced to attempt still carrying out the Ohio expedition before winter closed in. Everything was chaotic and to this was added the continuing peril of red marauders all around them. The arrival of the army under Bouquet had done little to discourage the Indian war parties roaming this frontier. Five days ago, for example, insolently and within almost a stone's throw, six of Bouquet's men had been captured and killed. Throughout the whole countryside cabins were still being attacked and burned, their inhabitants butchered or led away as captives into the Ohio country.

Determining to carry on as best he could with what he had, Bouquet had led the army farther westward and it was today, at the tiny, disintegrating post of Fort Loudoun, that the express from Bradstreet had reached him. Not until three hours after he received it was he able to calm himself down enough to write in a still-trembling hand to General Gage:

Fort Loudoun, 27th August 1764

Sir:

I received this moment advice from Colonel Bradstreet which it is impossible for me to comprehend and which threatens our entire enterprise. He has treated with some Indians at Presque Isle the 12th instant and the terms he gives them are such as to fill me with astonishment . . . Had Colonel Bradstreet been as well informed as I am of the horrid perfidies of the Delawares and Shawnees, whose parties as late as the 22nd instant killed six men, he could never have compromised the honor of the nation by such disgraceful conditions; and that at a time when two armies, after long struggles, are in full motion to penetrate into the heart of the enemy's country! Permit me likewise humbly to represent to your Excellency that I have not deserved the affront laid upon me by this treaty of peace, concluded by a younger officer—in the department where you have done me the honor to appoint me to command—without referring the deputies of the savages to me at Fort Pitt, but telling them that he shall send and prevent my proceeding against them! I can therefore take no notice of his peace, but shall proceed forthwith to the Ohio, where I shall wait till I receive your orders . . .

Completing that letter, he immediately wrote another, similar to it, to Governor William Penn in Philadelphia, stating the affair briefly:

Sir:

I have the honor to transmit to you a letter from Colonel Bradstreet, who acquaints me that he has granted peace to all the Indians living between Lake Erie and the Ohio; but as no satisfaction is insisted on, I hope the general will not confirm it, and that I shall not be a witness to a transaction which would fix an indelible stain upon the Nation.

I therefore take no noice of that pretended peace, and

proceed forthwith on the expedition, fully determined to treat as enemies any Delawares or Shawnees I shall find in my way, till I receive contrary orders from the General . . .

Not trusting himself to write more, Bouquet signed and sealed the two letters and sent them off to Gage and Penn at once by express. Then, with his hands clasped tightly behind his back, he paced to and fro within his headquarters tent, trying to compose himself enough to sit down and write to Colonel Bradstreet. But in the end he gave it up, deciding that in his present frame of mind he would be unable to refrain from verbally crucifying John Bradstreet, as he would be more than pleased to do physically if that officer were here. In four or five days, he decided, when this all-encompassing wrath within him cooled, then he would write to the officer whom he now thought of as "that buffoon on Lake Erie."

[August 31, 1764—Friday]

Behind him still, in the distance, Lieutenant Colonel Henry Gladwin could see the crowds of Indians and soldiers lining the banks of the Detroit River and the ramparts of the fort. Three cannon in succession belched smoke and flame and their rumbling roar swept past the schooner *Victory* and reverberated down the river. At last—at long, long last!—he had been relieved of the command of Detroit and he knew beyond any shadow of doubt that he was looking at the fort for the last time in his life.

It was hard for Gladwin to remember any time over the past fifteen months that he had not felt perpetually weary, nor any time over the past nine or ten months when his thoughts and desires had not been more in England than here. And now there was a need, as well as a desire, for him to go home. Among the letters and dispatches brought to Detroit recently had been one for Gladwin from England bearing the sad news that his father had died and that Gladwin had been appointed executor of the estate. His presence was therefore required to attend to urgent matters.

He had made his decision and he meant to stick to it. Already he had requested and received permission to retire with his rank from His Majesty's service, and he wished with all his heart that the deck beneath his feet at this moment was, instead, that of the ship which would soon be carrying him to London and home. He was tired of everything: tired of war, of sieges, of Indians, of negotiations, of Frenchmen, of military life. Existence at Detroit these months past had become a monumental tedium which nearly drove him out of his mind.

What was in store for Detroit now, he had no way of knowing, but he was thankful that he would not be there to witness it. The extreme joy of welcoming Bradstreet and his army had quickly paled and in just this very short time he had come to dislike that officer intensely. As everyone else had been, he was shocked to learn what Bradstreet had done since leaving Fort Niagara. And the actions of the man since he arrived at Detroit were hardly conducive to inspiring trust and confidence.

One of the very first things Bradstreet had done upon arrival was to summon all the neighboring tribes to a council. The Chippewas were represented by Wasson, the only chief present who had taken an active part against Detroit during the siege. On hand to represent the Ottawas were Chief Atawang and Chief Manitou. Instead of the principal chief of the Miamis, Little Turtle—who called himself Michikiniqua—it was Chief Naranea who was on hand, and instead of Ninivois or Washee for the Potawatomies, the tribe was represented by Kioqua and Nanequoba.

Again in defiance of his orders, John Bradstreet now consummated still another treaty of peace, this time with all the Detroit area Indians who had not treated at Niagara. In the process of doing so, he clearly gave evidence of his total ignorance of Indian protocol, courtesy, custom, honor and pride. He tried to make a grand impression; and impression he made, though there was grave doubt as to how grand it was. He boasted of his prowess, of how he had brought the fierce Delawares and Shawnees into submission, of how he was the engineer of peace for this whole country. When, at one point, it seemed to him that the listeners were paying more respect and attention to the Indian speakers than to him, he leaped to his feet and snatched a belt of war wampum that had been sent to Detroit by Pontiac and was being circulated among the tribes here. Before the incredulous eyes of all the Indians, Bradstreet proceeded to chop the belt to bits with a tomahawk—such an extreme breach of Indian parliamentary procedure that it was almost beyond belief to them that it had actually happened. Had they not witnessed it, they could not have believed it. He then demanded that the Indians present declare themselves to be "subjects of King George III," but there was no term for this in the Indian languages. The interpreters, already considerably upset themselves, improvised by telling the assembled Indians that they must now refer to the English King as "Father" rather than as "Brother."[168]

When the council was terminating, the Indians, as straight-faced as possible, bestowed upon Colonel John Bradstreet an Indian name, calling him with seeming respect, *Peshikthi Matchsquathi*. He took it to be a great honor and carefully memorized the two alien words, while the interpreters, nearly bursting from containing their laughter, did not dare to tell him that it meant "The Timid Deer."

It was wholly without reluctance that Henry Gladwin had turned over the reins of command to his successor, Lieutenant Colonel John Campbell of the 17th Regiment. He wished him the best of luck with fervent sincerity and had immediately set about packing his things to go.

Some other matters of interest occurred before he left, however. The first was that on August 26, Bradstreet had organized a detachment of three hundred soldiers under Captain William Howard to head north and take possession again of Fort Michilimackinac. Among those nonmilitary people accompanying this detachment was a young trader who had joined Bradstreet at Niagara, intent on recouping his losses in the Michilimackinac area—a trader named Alexander Henry. Bradstreet also, by promising a payment of fifty cents per day per man—which he had absolutely no intention of ever paying—was able to raise two companies of fifty Frenchmen each from among the Detroit inhabitants to escort the detachment to that place.[169]

Another thing Bradstreet did was to send the former commander of Fort Sandusky, Ensign Christopher Pauli, back with a small detachment to where the fort had been, there to establish a new post and to meet the Shawnees and Delawares who were due to arrive with their prisoners to be liberated.

Finally, at nine o'clock yesterday morning, John Bradstreet had assembled all the inhabitants of Detroit over fourteen years of age and made them renew their oaths of allegiance to the King of England.

Now, as the schooner coasted around a bend in the river and he could no longer see Detroit, Lieutenant Colonel Henry Gladwin turned away from the rail and went to his cabin. There, propped against a lamp, was a little note written by the captain of the ship in a precise and flowing hand:

It is a great pleasure having you aboard. I have the honor to inform you that upon reaching the harbor at the lower end of Lake Erie, this vessel, the Victory, *is to be rechristened and will thereafter be officially known as the* Gladwin.

[September 2, 1764—Sunday]

The fury of Major General Thomas Gage at his New York headquarters was hardly less than had been Henry Bouquet's. The commander in chief had just received both the letter from Bouquet and the letter, report, and preliminary treaty copy from Bradstreet. That one of his two principal field commanders should so blatantly thwart his orders and act in the manner Bradstreet had acted was unthinkable. Yet, here was the evidence of it, in his own boastfully written words.

Unlike Bouquet, Gage had no hesitancy about writing to Bradstreet. His pen flew across the page in line after line of bitter denunciation and chastisement. For nearly an hour he wrote, filling page after page, and then finally he concluded with a stinging reprimand:

They have negotiated with you on Lake Erie, and cut our throats upon the frontiers. With your letters of peace I received others giving accounts of murders, and these acts continue to this time. Had you only consulted Colonel Bouquet before you agreed upon anything with them (a deference he was certainly entitled to, instead of an order to stop his march), you would have been acquainted with the treachery of those people, and not have suffered yourself to be thus deceived, and you would have saved both Colonel Bouquet and myself from the dilemma you have brought us into. You concluded a peace with people who were daily murdering us. Your instructions called for you to offer *peace to such tribes as should make their submission. To* offer *peace, I think can never be construed a power to* conclude *and dictate the articles of peace, and you certainly know that no such power could with propriety be lodged in any person but in Sir William Johnson, his Majesty's sole agent and Superintendent for Indian Affairs. I again repeat that I annul and disavow the peace you have made!*

[September 17, 1764—Monday]

The Captain Thomas Morris who staggered into Detroit this day was a far cry from the neatly dressed, enthusiastic young officer who had been dispatched westward toward the Illinois country at the mouth of the Maumee by Colonel Bradstreet. His eyes were sunken and haunted with fear and malnutrition, he was dressed in tattered remnants, he had obviously been badly mistreated and he was on the point of collapse from exhaustion. He asked for Colonel Bradstreet, but it was Lieutenant Colonel John Campbell who saw him.

"My God, man," the new Detroit commander exclaimed, "what happened to you?"

Morris shook his head and waved the question aside, saying instead, "Where is Colonel Bradstreet, sir?"

"Back at Sandusky by now," Campbell replied. He added grimly: "Apparently things were not as he thought they'd be. The Delewares and Shawnees came to Sandusky all right, but evidently they took Ensign Pauli and his detachment prisoner and have gone again."

Morris groaned. "He's been duped! Every step of the way. There is no peace with the Shawnees and Delawares."

Little by little Campbell got the story out of him. After leaving Bradstreet on his mission, Morris continued up the Maumee River until, on August 20, he had come to Pontiac's village. There he found himself immediately treated very badly by the Indians and was in constant danger of his life. He was saved by Jacques Godefroy, who had hidden him in a cornfield all night. Then Pontiac had arrived, and had treated Morris reasonably well. They had conversed in French and Pontiac had boasted of a great alliance growing under him, claiming that he had forty-seven tribes and one hundred and eighty villages at his command, with more joining him daily. Surprisingly, he restrained his men from harming Morris further and allowed him to continue his journey upstream. Perhaps he had known what was awaiting the officer there. Only a few days before Morris arrived at the deserted Fort Miamis, the Miami Indians there under Chief Cold Foot were visited by a band of Shawnees and Delawares who were carrying a war belt toward the Illinois country. The Miamis were asked to kill or turn back any English who came this way.

When Morris had arrived, he was immediately seized, all his goods taken, his clothing stripped from him and there he was bound to a stake to be tortured and burned. Only through the efforts of a young Miami chief named Pacanne, son of the principal chief of the whole tribe, Michikiniqua, had he been spared. A council was held on September 9 and when it was concluded, Captain Morris was given the choice of either returning to Detroit or being killed. The decision had not been difficult for him to make. The next morning he had set out overland for Detroit and it had taken a week of steady, extremely difficult traveling for him to get here to warn Bradstreet, and now he was dismayed to find the colonel was gone.

Refusing to accept any care for himself until he had gotten word to Bradstreet, he sent that officer the journal which he had kept of his travels since leaving the colonel, and enclosed with it a covering letter in which he wrote:

. . . thus, Sir, have the villains nipped our fairest hopes in the bud. I tremble for you at Sandusky; though I was greatly pleased to find you have one of the vessels with you, and the artillery. I wish the chiefs were assembled on board the vessel and she had a hole in her bottom. Treachery should be paid with treachery; and it is more than ordinary pleasure to deceive those who would deceive us . . .[170]

[October 12, 1764—Friday]

"You sail when, Henry?" Thomas Gage asked.

"Within two hours, General," replied Lieutenant Colonel Gladwin.

Gage shook his head. "Lord knows, you deserve it, but I'm damned sorry to see you go, sir. A general whose field officers are incompetent is severely crippled, but when he has officers of the caliber of yourself and Colonel Bouquet, he is well-nigh invincible. You will be sorely missed here."

He shook Gladwin's hand and then handed him a folded piece of paper that was on his desk. "This may interest you. Take it along and read it when you get on board. Good-by, Henry, and good luck."

Gladwin, impressive in his immaculate uniform, snapped to attention and saluted his general. "Good-by to you, too, sir," he said. "And especially good luck. God bless you, sir."

He turned and left, tucking the paper into his pocket as he did so. Returning to his quarters he gathered up his things and boarded the ship. Not until the shore had dropped out of sight in the sea behind them and he had retired to his cabin did he recall the paper Gage had given him and he took it out of his pocket. It was a copy of a letter from Gage to the Secretary of War, which said:

Major Gladwin, having come here from Detroit and his affairs long ago requiring his presence in England, I have given him leave to go home before the 80th Regiment, to which he belongs, is reduced. The services this gentleman has performed will alone be sufficient to recommend him to your protection. I would only presume to hope that his merit will procure him the same rank that every other officer has hitherto obtained who has served in the station of Deputy Adjutant General.[171]

[October 17, 1764—Wednesday]

From the very beginning of this campaign, Colonel Henry Bouquet had resolved to take no nonsense whatever from the Indians. He had no intention of making any sort of hasty council with them just for the sake of establishing a makeshift peace. If and when a peace would be asked of him by the Indians, as he was sure it would be on this expedition, it would be entirely on his terms and *only* after there was no vestige of doubt left in the minds of any of the chiefs of both Shawnee and Delaware tribes that he could—and, if necessary, *would*—crush them to oblivion.

The action of Bradstreet at Presque Isle had stripped from him all good humor and the orders which he issued thereafter to his men were neither questioned nor disobeyed. His manner was stern and in every soldier's mind—regular or militia—was implanted the knowledge that, during this campaign, at least, the word of Henry Bouquet was absolute law and the final authority. In short, he was not a man to be trifled with in any respect.

Also, he was through with waiting.

Disregarding the weakness his force had sustained through desertion, and disgusted with waiting any longer for the party of Iroquois which were supposed to have been sent by Sir William to join him, he put his men on the move and did not allow the pace to flag. Between Fort Bedford and Fort Ligonier, and again between Fort Ligonier and Fort Pitt, several of his men were picked off on the flanks and in the rear by tiny parties of Indians, but other than ordering the men to keep alert, he paid little attention to such parties.

On September 15 they passed the site of his bloody battle fourteen months before, and two days later they arrived at Fort Pitt. Here Bouquet found that only the day before his arrival, a large party of Shawnees and Delawares had appeared on the other side of the river and set up camp, then sent a deputation of three men across to the fort, saying they wished to make peace. Suspecting them to be spies rather than peace emissaries, Captain Grant had ordered that they be held as hostages and immediately the camp on the other side of the river was broken up and the remaining Indians fled westward.

Bouquet, pleased at Grant's action, questioned the three captives himself and agreed that they were hardly qualified to act in the name of their tribes. He determined to send one of them back to the tribes with a message and, through the fort's young but able interpreter, Simon Girty, he addressed the Indian.

"Are you Shawnee or Delaware?"

"Shawnee, and you will never conquer my people."

When Girty interpreted, Bouquet stared coldly at the native and said, "Tell him to speak no more, only to listen and listen well. If he speaks again, I'll have him executed and send one of the others back with the message for his people."

Girty rattled off a string of guttural sentences and the Shawnee lost some of his composure and clamped his lips tightly together. Girty grunted, then grinned at the officer.

"He'll listen now, Colonel."

"Will he be able to repeat what I tell him?"

Girty nodded. "Not only the gen'rul idee of what you say, Colonel, but he'll be able to quote you word for word. They got a knack for that."

"All right, here it is," Bouquet said. He faced the Indian and began speaking strongly and emphatically. "I have received an account from Colonel Bradstreet that your nations had begged for peace, which he consented to grant, on the assurance that you had recalled all your warriors from our frontiers. In consequence of this, I would not have proceeded against your towns if I had not learned that in open violation of these promises, you have since murdered many of our people.

"I was therefore determined to attack you as a people whose word could not be relied on. However, I will one final time put it in your power to save yourselves and your families from total destruction. This can only be done by your giving us satisfaction for the hostilities you have committed against us. First, you are to leave the path open and safe for my messengers from here to Detroit. I am today sending two men with dispatches to Colonel Bradstreet, who commands on the lakes. You will send two of your own people along with them and bring them back safe with an answer. If these two receive any injury, either in coming or going, or if the letters are taken from them, I will immediately put to death the two Indians now in my custody here, and I will show no further mercy for the future to any of the people of the Shawnee or Delaware Nations who may fall into my hands. I allow you ten days to have my letters delivered at the Detroit, and ten days to bring me back an answer."

The strong, unrelenting nature of Bouquet's speech had a profound effect on the Shawnee. Girty whispered to Bouquet that he'd never seen a Shawnee so shaken before. Not commenting, Bouquet ordered the warrior released and then instructed Grant on what to do, since he had no intention of staying here himself for twenty days waiting for the return of messengers. The word, he knew, would be passed swiftly through the forest. They would know now with what sort of man they had to deal.

Before moving the expedition out, Bouquet, who had finally been able to write a markedly restrained letter to Bradstreet, had the satisfaction of having Gage's letter of chastisement to Bradstreet sent to him first, to read, then seal and relay to the colonel on Lake Erie. In the letter of that packet which was directed to Bouquet by Gage, the condemnation of Bradstreet continued. In fact, Gage had concluded by saying:

. . . and if they find Colonel Bradstreet is to be thus amused, they will deceive him till it is too late to act and then insult him and begin their horrid murders. There is nothing will prevent this but the fear of chastisement from you, and I think myself happy that you are in a condition to march against them.

But though it was personally satisfying for Bouquet to read such words from his commander, there was little inclination on his part to gloat. He issued final marching orders on September 28 and they were very strict. Under penalty of death, no man was to fire his gun, whether at Indians or for any other reason, except at the colonel's own command. This order was not to be questioned, only obeyed. On October 1, the sheep and cattle were moved across the Allegheny in preparation for the march and the next day the expedition into the wildnerness began. Fifteen hundred men crossed the river and began following their commander into a land where never before had an army marched.

On October 6 they camped thirty-two miles from Fort Pitt.[172] Here they encountered their first fresh Indian sign—the tracks of fifteen Indians and the skull of a child impaled on a stake. If it was meant as a warning, it had no effect on Bouquet. He kicked it down and in the morning the march was resumed.

On October 12 they reached a little stream called Sandy Creek,[173] a tributary of the Tuscarawas River, which was itself one of the two principal branches of the Muskingum. Now they began encountering small Delaware villages, but all were deserted. Continuing down Sandy Creek, they camped at a point on the north bank of the little stream, exactly eighty-three miles distant from Fort Pitt.[174] While his men prepared for the night's rest, Bouquet dictated an order. At 7 A.M. the next day, it was read aloud to the troops, who listened attentively:

BY ORDER OF THE COLONEL: This army has already penetrated to the heart of the enemy's country. These perfidious savages have already and severally experienced the valor of Britons, which must have struck them with terror, as they now shun encountering the same gallant troops that formerly put them to flight, and this instance of so distant a progress of his Majesty's successful arms in this part of the vast continent of North America has hitherto met with no serious opposition. Nor have the barbarians, who brutally destroyed the defenseless inhabitants of the back settlements of our colonies, dared to appear in the face of this small but well composed army in a hostile manner.

The troops will this day proceed to Tuscarawas, a settlement now abandoned but formerly inhabited by a numerous tribe of the enemy Indians.

From the pacific disposition of several savage Nations to the northward, who applied for and have had peace granted to them by Sir William Johnson, and from appearances lately in this quarter, it is probable that a deputation from the Shawnee and Delaware Nations will sue for peace. Colonel Bouquet desires every person in this army may be acquainted it is his orders that, to avoid unnecessary bloodshed, the troops are generously to forbear treating the savages hostilly till their intentions are fully known. And should they meanly and servily attempt to recover the countenance and favor of any person whatsoever it is positively forbidden to hold any kind of friendly intercourse with them, by speaking, shaking hands or otherwise. But, on the contrary, to look on them with utmost disdain and with that stern and manly indignation justly felt for their many barbarities to our friends and fellow subjects. They will continue to be regarded as enemies till they submit to the terms that will be offered them and till they have in some measure expiated the horrid crimes they have been guilty of, by a strict compliance with those terms. Ample satisfaction will be demanded and insisted on for all possible reparation of wrongs and such satisfaction as will be adequate to the spirit now exerted by an injured people, and equally consistent with the honor and dignity of the British Empire. Should the savages have the audacity to dispute the access of this army to Tuscarawas, the conduct and bravery of the officers and men will soon retaliate their cruelties on their guilty heads in a manner more becoming their resentments, although repugnant to their humanity.

It was while the reading of the order was going on that the messengers Bouquet had sent off to Detroit caught up to the army. They had not made it. The men related that they had been held by the Delawares and not permitted to go to Lake Erie. They had not, however, been in any way mistreated, nor had their letters been taken from them. They had been asked to tell Bouquet that within a few days the principal chiefs would arrive to hold council with him.

Having no intention of waiting on their favor, Bouquet again put his army on the march and followed the main Indian trail to the site of Tuscarawas.[175] Here the branch they were following emptied into the much larger Tuscarawas River many miles upstream from where the Tuscarawas and Walhonding Rivers joined to form the Muskingum River. Here there was a fording place and here a number of Indian trails branched off, leading to Detroit, Cuyahoga and the Shawnee towns on the Scioto. Bouquet ordered camp made and a strong palisade erected to protect stores and baggage.

In the morning the march began again downstream on the river. And finally there was Indian contact.

A deputation of Delaware, Shawnee and Seneca chiefs appeared in the twilight, unarmed, and came directly to Bouquet, paced by a guard of soldiers. Without preamble they told Bouquet that their warriors were massed in great numbers just eight miles away. They asked Bouquet to name the time and place for a council and Bouquet agreed. After a short discussion the chiefs turned and left in the direction from which they had appeared. As soon as they were gone,

Bouquet set his men to constructing a sort of arbor beneath which the council could be held.[176]

And now it was the morning of October 17 and the time for the first council had arrived. Bouquet, knowing the Indians would be impressed by the greatest possible show of strength, suitably situated his troops; and the sight of fifteen hundred men bristling with weapons, their fixed bayonets glittering in the morning sun, was indeed an impressive sight. Here were the Royal Americans in uniforms that were a splash of scarlet across the meadow, and there were the tartans of the Highlander regulars. Here were the moccasined and leather-shirted frontiersmen, and there the quaintly garbed provincials. Abruptly there was a brief roll of the drums and an expectant hush fell over the assemblage as a group of seventy or eighty Indians approached, being led by the principal chiefs of the three tribes gathered here—Custaloga, chief of the Delawares, and better known to the English as White Eyes, beside whom walked Turtle's Heart,[177] chief orator of that tribe, in whose hand was a bulging leather pouch containing wampum belts; Hokolesqua, principal chief of the Shawnees, well known as Chief Cornstalk, beside whom strode his war chief, Pucksinwah; and Kyashuta, chief of the band of Senecas who had broken from the rest of their tribe when it had agreed to meet Johnson's demand and attend the Niagara Congress.

With amazing calmness and dignity, looking neither to left nor right at the ranked soldiers who stared murderously at them, they walked to the huge arbor that had been constructed, where Bouquet and his officers sat waiting and, behind them, several secretaries poised to take down on paper all that was spoken.

At a motion from Custaloga the greatest part of the following warriors stopped and sat on the ground. This was about a dozen yards from the arbor. The chiefs, however, along with half a dozen others, did not stop and sit until they were well under the arbor.

No words were spoken by anyone as the calumets were packed with *kinnikinnick* and the ceremony of smoking began. In turn, from each of the chiefs, Bouquet and the officers accepted and puffed a time or two on the pipes and handed them back. At last, when all smoking was finished and the calumets laid aside, it was Kitehi who rose and began to speak, offering wampum belts at the appropriate pauses.

"Brother," he began, "I speak in behalf of the three nations

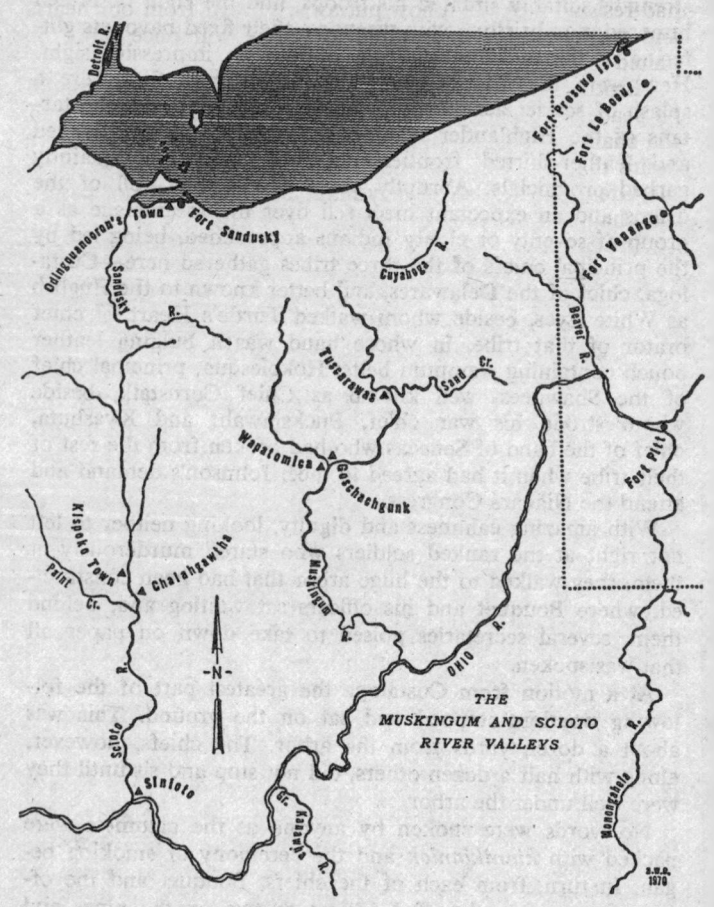

THE
MUSKINGUM AND SCIOTO
RIVER VALLEYS

Detroit R.

Fort Presque Isle

Fort Le Bœuf

Fort Sandusky

Fort Venango

Odinequanoran's Town

Cuyahoga R.

Sandusky R.

Tuscarawas R.

Sand Cr.

Beaver R.

Fort Pitt

Wapatomica

Goschachgunk

Kispoko Town

Chalahgawtha

Paint Cr.

Muskingum R.

OHIO R.

Kanawha R.

Scioto R.

Sinioto

Monongahela R.

—N—

B.W.R.
1970

whose chiefs are here present. With this belt I open your ears and your hearts, that you may listen to my words.

"Brother, this war was neither your fault nor ours. It was the work of the nations who live to the westward, and of our wild young men who would have turned and killed us if we had resisted them. We now put away all evil from our hearts and we hope that your mind and ours will once more be united together for the common good.

"Brother, it is the will of the Great Spirit that there should be peace between us. We, on our side, now take fast hold of the chain of friendship; but, as we cannot hold it alone, we desire that you will take hold also, and we must look up to the Great Spirit, that he may make us strong and not permit this chain to fall from our hands.

"Brother, these words come from our hearts and not only from our lips. You desire that we should deliver up your flesh and blood who are now captive among us; and to show you that we are sincere, we now return to you as many of them as we have at present been able to bring."

He made a circular motion with his hand above his head and immediately the horde of warriors gathered in the distance opened and a party detached itself and walked forward. Within five minutes, eighteen English prisoners had been turned over to Bouquet's officers.

Kitehi nodded when this was finished and added, "You shall receive the rest as soon as we have time to collect them."

Having completed the principal address, Kitehi now took his place with the others. One by one then, chief after chief of tribe and village arose and came forward to speak, each of them saying in one way or another virtually what Kitehi had said, and each of them, before returning to his place, presenting Bouquet with a bundle of smooth cedar sticks bound together with rawhide. Each of these sticks represented one prisoner and each bundle was the number of prisoners the individual chief pledged himself to give up.

Since it was not proper, in the procedures of formal council, for Bouquet to give his reply on the same day, the council now broke up, to be resumed tomorrow morning. As the officers moved away, Chaplain John Thomas of the 60th Regiment moved up beside Colonel Bouquet.

"It looks," he murmured to the commander, "as if they're serious about ending the war and giving up their prisoners, doesn't it?"

"Nowhere near serious enough," Bouquet replied shortly.

"They'll be surprised at what I have to say to them tomorrow, I'll wager."

Colonel John Bradstreet looked with mild disgust at the wet and shivering men crouched naked around the fires here at the mouth of the river, trying to get their clothing dry before the journey resumed. The delay irked him but he supposed he had to at least give them this respite anyway. He ignored entirely the murderous looks which were being directed his way. What the rank and file thought of him bothered him not at all. In fact, he didn't even care what his subordinate officers thought of him. He was lost in new thoughts of what glory would come to him when his great plan for the elimination of all the Indians was made public.

He'd been working on this plan ever since leaving Sandusky to head east and now, even though most of his notes had become wet and many of them were illegible, still he had the plan fixed well enough in his own mind that he could quickly write it out again. As a matter of fact, this might be the ideal time to do it, while these idiot soldiers of his continued to wring themselves out around the fires.

He strode to the tent and got out fresh, dry writing material and then carefully separated the soggy sheets. The words written on them had little to do with the campaign behind him. In the manner of most megalomaniacs, since it was a distasteful episode pointing to his own ineptitude, he simply refused to think about it. The glory lay ahead, not in what was behind.

It was just as well that he didn't dwell on those events that had occurred since leaving Detroit. To dwell on them would have been to admit his own incompetence, and this was something he would not, *could not*, do. Having left Detroit upon hearing that the English detachment at Sandusky had been taken prisoner, Bradstreet led his army back to Sandusky Bay. It was immediately apparent that the area was deserted. Absolutely refusing to believe that the Indians could have hoodwinked him and had no intention of coming back, Bradstreet waited. At last, after three or four days, a little group of warriors hesitantly approached, though with no chiefs among them. They said they were emissaries from their tribe and that if the colonel would keep waiting and refrain from attacking their villages, they would begin bringing their prisoners in by the next week.

It was vindication for Bradstreet and his face became wreathed with a great smile as he agreed—against the advice of practically every other officer in his army. They waited . . . and waited. The colonel was still positive that there must be some mistake in the report of Ensign Pauli's detachment having been taken captive and reasoned that they had probably returned to Detroit by now and the whole thing was no more than a rumor.

But then had come the double blow that had sent him mentally reeling. Letters from both General Gage and Colonal Bouquet came—letters which severely raked him over the coals, made him out to be a fool and reprimanded him in a way he had never in his whole military career been reprimanded before. The harsh words of Gage in particular almost made him physically ill. And not content in reprimanding him, Gage now had given him an order to immediately lead his army south through the Ohio wilderness to launch an attack against the Shawnees living along the Scioto River.

Even while he staggered under the enormity of all this, the second blow had come. A messenger arrived from Detroit, bearing with him the journal of Captain Morris's abortive trip up the Maumee River, along with that officer's accompanying letter—undeniable proof that he, Bradstreet, had been duped by the Indians; that he, a skilled military commander had been outthought, outmaneuvered, entirely outwitted and made a complete ass of by a pack of ignorant savages!

His wrath made him inchoate and only after a long while did some degree of normalcy return to him. His officers, who had stood back, now came to him, wondering aloud if they should get their men ready for the move southward into the enemy territory. All he did was rebuke them severely for bothering him. Day after day they continued to perch at Sandusky and, to the consternation and incredulity of his officers and men, it became clear that he was still determined to wait here for the Indians to honor their promises to him! His temper became such that it was a decided risk for anyone even to address him. His actions were at best capricious and the harshness with which he treated his troops increased and, with it, the discontent of the whole army. Most inexplicable to them was his continued tenderness of thought toward the Indians of these woods while at the same time never missing any opportunity to curse his own Iroquois allies, which enraged them no little.

Finally, on October 14, he dispatched one of the French volunteers with him, Louis Hertel, along with a small party of his discontent Indians, to Colonel Bouquet with a message; a message which declared that because of the advanced season, he was no longer able to remain in the Indian country and would soon be returning east.

Two days later, after having sent out a party of five Iroquois to hunt for some venison, which he had a taste for, and two of his New Jersey privates to catch some fish for his table, he abruptly decided that he had had enough of this country. He charged out of his tent bellowing orders for the men to load the boats and the army to be ready to embark for Niagara within the hour. The camp became a beehive of activity as gear was gathered and the loading of the batteaux began. Then several concerned officers came to him in a little group and one of them self-consciously cleared his throat.

"Sir," he said, "what about the men who are out? The Indians you sent out deer hunting? And the Jersey men?"

"What about them?" Bradstreet growled.

"They're not back yet, sir."

"Then that's their problem. We'll go without them."

The officers were shocked. "But Colonel," their speaker protested, "those men were sent out on your orders. Can't we at least leave one of the batteaux here for an hour or two for them? It could catch up to us easily enough."

"No!" Bradstreet roared. "They can stay here and be damned! Not one boat will stay here to wait one minute for them. We're ready to leave now and so, by damn, we're leaving!"

And so they did.

Several of the more high-ranking officers hesitantly asked the colonel why they were going east, when the general's orders specifically had been for them to move south and attack the Shawnees to support Bouquet. At first Bradstreet refused to discuss it, but at last he mumbled such excuses as the season growing too late, provisions failing, the way there being too difficult a passage, and no good maps to guide them. When the officers declared that they were willing to try anyway, he silenced them and would not discuss it further.

On October 21 they had reached the vicinity of the mouth of the Cuyahoga River.[178] Great black clouds were piling up over the lake and it looked as if a good storm was in prospect. Although a thousand boats could have found relatively safe harbor just a short way upriver and weathered nearly any storm, Bradstreet ignored all suggestions in this respect and ordered camp to be made on an exposed beach. Within mere hours one of those fierce Lake Erie tempests was full upon them. Great waves formed and rolled ashore and the beached boats were beaten and capsized and smashed to pieces. For three days the storms raged on and when at last it was over and they took stock of the damage, it was found that most of the ammunition, provisions, arms, baggage and six cannon were lost and the remaining boats, all of them in very bad shape, were no longer enough to carry everyone.

Bradstreet solved this problem by ordering all his Indians and one hundred and fifty of his provincials to make their way to Niagara as best they could on shore. With that, he set out with his remaining force in the boats that were left. And on November 4, seventeen days after having left Sandusky, they arrived at Niagara.[179]

By this time, having for many days already been working on his grand plan for the extermination of the Indians, Bradstreet was in no mood to rest, though his men needed it badly. What he wanted to do was get back east so he could expand and promote his ideas. He discharged the few Indians with him in a few curt words, the next morning had his men get aboard the remaining batteaux and a couple of schooners from the fort and set off for New York via Oswego, the Mohawk River, and Albany.

This afternoon they had reached Oswego but, as luck would have it, another storm caught them before they landed. One of the schooners loaded with troops foundered and a number of men were drowned. It was only with the greatest of exertion that the others were saved.

And so now, while his troops wrung themselves dry before roaring fires and muttered imprecations against a commander whom many of them could have joyfully slain without qualm or conscience, Colonel John Bradstreet busied himself with dashing off on fresh paper his ideas on annihilating the Indians. The strange thing was, however, that the Indians he inveighed most against were the staunch allies of the English, the Iroquois, while those for whom he recommended the most tender treatment were the Indians of the upper Great Lakes. He knew he'd still have a bit of revising to do on it, but now he read over the first brief outline he had made:

Of all the savages upon the continent, the most knowing, the most intriguing, the less useful and the greatest villains are those most conversant with the Europeans and deserve attention of the government most by way of correction, and these are the Six Nations, the Shawnees and Delawares. They are all well acquainted with the defenseless state of the in-

habitants who live on the frontiers and think they will ever have it in their power to distress and plunder them. And they never cease raising the jealousy of the Upper Nations against us, by propagating amongst them stories such as to make them believe the English have nothing so much at heart as the extirpation of all savages. The apparent design of the Six Nations is to keep us at war with all savages but themselves, that they may be employed as mediators between us and them—at continuation of the expense to the public, which is too often and too heavily felt, and the sweets of which these Six Nations will never forget nor lose sight of if they can possibly avoid it. That of the Shawnees and Delawares is to live on killing, captivating and plundering the people inhabiting the frontiers, long experience having shown them that they grow richer and live better thereby than by hunting wild beasts.

This campaign has fully opened the eyes of the Upper Nations of Indians. They are now sensible that they are made use of as dupes and tools of those detestable and diabolical Six Nations, Shawnees and Delawares, and it would require but little address and expense (the posts and trade properly fixed) to engage the Upper Nations to cut them from the face of the earth (and they deserve it) or to keep the Six Nations in such subjection as would put an end to our being any longer a kind of tributary to them. And their real interests call upon the Upper Nations to destroy or drive out the Shawnees and Delawares out of the country they now possess, to hunt in. This they know and would soon put either into execution if assured his Majesty would not suffer any other savages to live there. Happy it will be when savages can be punished by savages, the good effects of which the French can tell. That we can punish them is beyond doubt, whenever wisdom, secrecy, dispatch and good troops in numbers proportionate to the service are employed.

He intended to write more—much more—but this would do for a start, and John Bradstreet was pleased with it. Already he could see himself being hailed as the master planner, the brilliant strategist who, with stroke of pen, wiped out the great deterrent to expansion and scourge of the English, which had for so many years plagued them.

Yes, indeed, laurels were ahead for Colonel John Bradstreet.[180]

Colonel Henry Bouquet was back!

Fort Pitt virtually split its seams with excitement as the weary army led by Bouquet hove into view on the west side of the Allegheny, moved to the river's edge and began the crossing. The riverbank of the fort side became mobbed with cheering people—soldiers, settlers, frontiersmen, shopkeepers, traders, people of every description and state—and the air was filled with the din of their voices. Soldiers lined the ramparts shoulder to shoulder, raising their rifles time after time to fire into the sky, while for more than an hour the heavy artillery rumbled and roared and belched great bursts of fire and smoke.

Bouquet was back and the Indian War was ended and there was peace!

Never in its turbulent history had Fort Pitt been so wild with excitement. Never had the huts and cabins and houses of adjacent Pittsburgh seen so much laughter and backslapping and delight. Never had so many happy reunions been effected. And the story of how it had all come about was on everyone's lips.

After the initial council session Bouquet had held with the Indians there had been a delay. The council scheduled for the next day had been postponed because of a driving rainstorm which had come up at dawn and lasted most of the day; but on October 19 the council had resumed. Colonel Henry Bouquet had not been wrong in his comment that the Indians might be surprised at what he had to say. Obviously they had expected him to be all smiles and generosity and eager to settle things quickly and be off. Such was not at all the case.

With such interpreters as Simon Girty, his brothers James and George, Matthew Elliott and Alexander McKee reiterating in the Delaware, Seneca and Shawnee Indian tongues every phrase as he finished uttering it, Bouquet had launched into them with a tongue-lashing such as none of them had ever before received. Even in his opening statement it was obvious that this was going to be a tough speech, for he began to talk without any of the usual courteous addresses such as "My children," or "Brothers," or the like. He simply stood before them and when every ear was attuned to what he would say, he began:

"Sachems, war chiefs and warriors. The excuses you have offered are weak and have no weight with me. Your conduct has been beyond defense or apology. You could not have acted, as you pretend you have done, because of fear of the western nations, for had you stood faithful to us, you knew that we would have protected you against their anger. And as for your own young men threatening you, this I cannot accept, for it was your duty to punish them if they went amiss."

Already the eyes of his listeners were widening as the interpreters caught up to him in this first lengthy pause, and many of the Indians looked startled. It was not at all what they had expected to hear. As soon as the interpreters stopped, Bouquet went on in a loud voice.

"You have drawn down our just resentment by your violence and perfidy. Last summer, in cold blood and in a time of profound peace, you robbed and murdered the traders who had come among you at your own express desire that they do so. You attacked Fort Pitt, which was built at the forks of the Ohio not only with your consent, but at your request. You have destroyed our outposts and garrisons wherever treachery could place them in your power."

Again he paused to let the interpreters catch up, and then flung a hand out to point at the ranks of soldiers standing on both sides. "You assailed our troops—the same who now stand before you—in the woods at Bushy Run, and when we had routed you and driven you off, you sent your scalping parties to the frontier and murdered many hundreds more of our people.

"Last July," he continued after another pause, "when the other nations came to treat for peace at Niagara, you not only refused to attend, but you sent an insolent message instead, in which you expressed a pretended contempt for the English, calling them old women. At the same time you told the surrounding nations that you would never lay down the hatchet.

"Afterwards, when Colonel Bradstreet came up Lake Erie with his army, you sent him a deputation of your men and concluded a treaty of peace with him, but your engagements were no sooner made than broken. And from that day to this, you have scalped and butchered us without ceasing!"

Bouquet stopped and looked sharply at each of the principal chiefs and then at the horde of at least a thousand warriors standing silently several hundred yards beyond the ranked soldiers. The colonel shook his head. "Nay," he said, "I am informed that when you heard this army was penetrating the woods, you mustered your warriors to attack us and the only reason you did not do so was because you discovered how greatly we outnumbered you with the men of this army and that to the north under Colonel Bradstreet, which could join with us swiftly to destroy you all.

"This," he added, "is not the only instance of your bad faith, for since the beginning of the last war you have made repeated treaties with us and promised to give up your prisoners, but you have never kept these engagements, nor any others."

Bouquet slammed his fist into his palm with a loud smack and cried out, "We shall endure this no longer! I am now come among you to *force* you to make atonement for the injuries you have done us. I have brought with me the relatives of those you have murdered, and they are eager for vengeance! Nothing restrains them from taking it but my assurance that this army shall not leave your country until you have given ample satisfaction.

"Your allies, the Ottawas, Chippewas and Hurons have begged for peace; the Six Nations have leagued themselves with us; the Great Lakes and the rivers around you are all in our possession; your friends, the French, are in subjection to us and can do nothing more to aid you. You are all in our power and, if we choose, we can exterminate you from the earth!"

He let the interpreters catch up and when he continued, his outrage had abated some and his voice had become gentler, though by no means friendly. "Yes, you are in our power, but the English are a merciful and generous people. We are averse to shedding blood, even that of our greatest enemies. If it were possible that you could convince us that you sincerely repent your past perfidy, and that we could depend on your good behavior for the future, you might yet hope for mercy and peace. Therefore, if I find that you faithfully execute the conditions which I shall prescribe, I will not treat you with the severity you deserve.

"I give you twelve days from today to deliver into my hands all the English prisoners in your possession, *without exception!* All of them—men, women, children, whether or not you have adopted them into your tribes, whether or not they have married among your people, whether or not they have sired or borne children with you or among you, whether or not they wish to stay among you—*all of them* who are living among you under any denomination or pretense whatsoever!

"Further, you are to furnish these prisoners with clothing, with provisions, and with horses to carry them to Fort Pitt. When you have fully and faithfully complied with these conditions, then and only then will you know on what terms you may obtain the peace you sue for."

If ever a group of men had been whipped by words and awed by threats, it was this body of Shawnees, Delawares and Senecas now before Bouquet. Never had any white commander dared to bring his army so far into their territory; never had any white man ever before spoken so harshly to them; never had any other commander refused to bargain until such far-reaching conditions were met. They were chagrined and they were more than a little frightened.

On the next day their replies had been lifeless, even insipid, with none of the flamboyance of oratory which so often before had issued from them. And though they approached the matter in a roundabout way, attempting in every way possible to preserve face and dignity, their reply boiled down to this: they would return to their different villages at once and return with their prisoners—all of them—in the prescribed manner and in the prescribed time.

Lest they think he had been too easily mollified, Bouquet gave them one final word. "I will not wait here," he told them, "but you will know where I am. I will move my army into the very center of your nation, beginning at once, so that if your promises are not met, mine will be more swiftly fulfilled! And that you will make no attempt at deception, I will keep with me as hostage your principal chiefs who spoke here, who will be well treated and returned to your people safely—but not until every prisoner has been surrendered."

A coincidence occurred then, but it had the appearance of a plan to emphasize his strength and ability to carry out his threats. Under Captain William McClellan, a tardy corps of Maryland volunteers which had arrived late at Fort Pitt, had found Bouquet gone and had followed his path, chose this moment to arrive. The same thought was instantly in every Indian mind: how many other smaller forces like this were still coming? Enough were already here to cripple them, perhaps enough to annihilate them. Looking fearfully over their shoulders, the Indians departed at once.

As he promised, Bouquet moved his army downstream at once, down to near the head of the Muskingum River. This was not only the heart of the Delaware nation, it was equally the traditional meeting place of both the Shawnees and Delawares for their intertribal councils. It was a beautiful site, where the Walhonding River flowing in from the west and north joined the Tuscarawas River flowing in from the east and north. Their merging formed the great Muskingum River which flowed south and east, eventually to empty into the Ohio River.

On the east side of the Muskingum here was the sprawling Delaware principal town of Goschachgunk, and on the west side of the river directly across from Goschachgunk[181] was the somewhat smaller Shawnee town of Wapatomica. Bouquet knew that from this point, should it become necessary for the army to march against them, it was only a matter of about ninety miles southwest to the principal Shawnee villages on the Scioto River.[182]

Even though he was holding the principal chiefs as hostage, Bouquet took no chances on a sudden massive surprise attack against him. He ordered the immediate erection of a substantial fortification, as well as makeshift barracks for the prisoners to be released and the construction of another council arbor. Awed as much by their commander as the Indians had been, the soldiers worked hard and they worked fast. Hundreds of trees were felled and very quickly a surprisingly good defensive works was erected, along with the rude but functional structures to be used as hospitals, storehouses, cabins and dormitories for liberated prisoners, plus the necessary council arbor. A score or more of sturdy married women, mainly wives of frontiersmen and border settlers brought along for just this purpose, prepared themselves to take charge of any women and children prisoners to be delivered up.

And the prisoners came.

In singles or small groups, by the tens or by the scores, they were led to this place by the returning Indian parties and turned over to Bouquet's army. Day by day these parties came, meekly and submissively handing over all their prisoners, including even those who had no desire to return, who wept and screamed and fought against such liberation—those who had become adopted into the tribes, had become part of them, had been brought up through childhood in them, had married in them, had children in them. There were as many tears of anguish shed as there were tears of joyful reunion. In some cases the released prisoners had to be physically restrained from running away to rejoin their adopted people.

During the midst of this activity the Frenchman carrying the message from Colonel Bradstreet, Louis Hertel, arrived. The dispatch he carried informed Bouquet that the northern campaign was being given up and that Bradstreet was going home. Hertel confirmed that no prisoners had been given up to him by the Wyandots or the Shawnees or the Delawares and, in fact, Ensign Christopher Pauli and his small detachment, sent to rebuild Fort Sandusky, had been taken captive. The colonel's shoulders slumped at the news.

Now, in addition to his own difficult job here, Bouquet had to send a detachment to the Wyandot country near Sandusky Bay—along with an escort of Shawnees and Delawares willingly given by his hostage principal chiefs who guaranteed success of the mission—to demand the return of Pauli and his men, along with the other prisoners which Bradstreet should have liberated.

Nor was the fact lost on Bouquet that once again Bradstreet had, by failing to follow his orders, narrowly missed placing Bouquet's force in jeopardy. Had this message from Bradstreet come only a few days before this and fallen into Indian hands here, it could have greatly encouraged the red men to consider Bouquet not quite so strong as he let on, perhaps resulting in attack rather than in full submission and deliverance of prisoners. But, thankfully, the time for that was past. He had cowed them—using the threat of Bradstreet's force as an extra club—as they had never before been cowed, and the liberation of prisoners continued.

Throughout it all, Bouquet maintained his stern attitude, permitting no fraternizing with the Indians by his men and reminding the tribes that until conditions were fully met, he must continue to treat them as enemies. He knew only too well that any softening on his part, any show of leniency or friendliness by him or his men, might yet be interpreted as weakness or indecision or timidity. The cardinal rule was clear in his mind: only when he had proved to them clearly and beyond any doubt that he could subdue them at any time by force, only then could he indulge the luxury of treating them with the kindness and natural clemency toward which he was naturally inclined.

By early November so many prisoners had been returned that it was becoming difficult to care for them and so, on November 9, Bouquet had given orders for a detachment under Captain Abraham Buford[183] to lead this first contingent of one hundred and ten liberated prisoners back to Fort Pitt.

Still more prisoners were brought in—including Ensign Pauli and his men and the captives of the Wyandots—and day after day their numbers mounted and the scenes of misery or joy that accompanied them were wrenching to every heart there, Indian or English. And when at last the conditions had been met and the council reconvened, Colonel

Henry Bouquet released the hostages he had been holding and the speeches began anew.

"Brother," said Kitehi, extending a broad belt of white wampum, "with this belt I dispel the black cloud that has so long hung over our heads, in order that the sunshine of peace may once more descend to warm and gladden us. I wipe the tears from your eyes and condole with you on the loss of your brothers who have perished in this war. I gather their bones together and cover them deep in the earth, that the sight of them may no longer bring sorrow to your heart, and I scatter leaves over the spot so that it may depart forever from your memory."

When Simon Girty had interpreted the guttural intonations to English, Kitehi continued:

"The path of peace which once ran between your dwellings and ours has lately become choked with weeks and thorns, so that no one could pass that way. So long has it been overgrown that both of us have almost forgotten that such a path had ever been. I now clear away all such obstructions and make a broad, smooth road so that you and I may freely visit each other, as our fathers used to do. I light a great council fire, whose smoke shall rise to the skies in view of all nations, while you and I sit together in friendship again and smoke the calumet of peace before the blaze."

Kitehi's speech was only the first of many along the same line and a multitude of belts were given, along with speeches of peace. For one of the few times in a long career of dealing with Indians, Bouquet felt the wonderful conviction within him that they spoke with absolute sincerity. It took several days for all the chiefs to speak but then, at last, it was Bouquet's turn. He replied:

"My children, by your compliance with the conditions which I imposed upon you, I have been satisfied completely of your sincerity in wishing peace between us, and I now receive you once more as brothers. The English King, however, has commissioned me not to make treaties for him, but rather to fight for him. Although now I offer you peace, it is not in my power to settle the precise terms and conditions of it, by which both of us must be bound. For this I refer you to Sir William Johnson, who you know is His Majesty's agent and Superintendent for Indian Affairs. It is he who will settle with you the articles of peace and determine everything in relation to opening trade among you again. Two things yet, however, I must insist on. First, you are to give hostages freely, as security that you will keep faith and will send, at once, authorized deputations of your chiefs to Sir William Johnson. Second, these chiefs must be fully empowered to act for you and speak for you, to treat for peace in behalf of your entire nations, in a manner which will be binding upon all of you. Finally, you must, without the slightest deviation, bind yourself to adhere completely to everything that these chiefs shall agree upon in your behalf."

Such a demand was not unexpected and it was agreed to with alacrity. Even before Bouquet himself left the area, the delegation of chiefs with two hundred or more unpainted warriors in tow was on its way for the treaty talks with Johnson at Fort Stanwix on the upper Mohawk River. And as Bouquet prepared to give his own army the command to return to Fort Pitt, he was visited by Hokolesqua—Cornstalk—principal chief of the Shawnee tribe.

"When you came among us," Hokolesqua said, "you came with hatchet raised to strike us. We now take it from your hand and throw it to the Great Spirit, that he may do with it what shall seem good in his sight. We hope that you, who are brave warriors, will take hold of the chain of friendship which we now extend to you. We, who are also brave warriors, will take hold as you do and, in pity for our women and our children and our old people, we will think no more of war."

And so now it was all over and today, with his weary but exultant army behind him, with two hundred more liberated prisoners among them, Colonel Henry Bouquet recrossed the Allegheny and was once again at Fort Pitt.

[December 13, 1764—Thursday]

For many years past, nothing had given Major General Thomas Gage so much pleasure as writing the letter he was just now finishing to Lord Halifax. Step by step he had gone over the brilliance of the campaign just concluded by Bouquet, from the gathering of the troops and their departure from Fort Pitt to his dealings with the tribes that had caused so much woe, the subsequent submission of the Indians and liberation of their prisoners and the ultimate, victorious return to Fort Pitt again, where the army had been disbanded.

Now, in conclusion, he dipped his pen again and wrote the words which brought him such utmost satisfaction:

I must flatter myself that the country is restored to its former tranquility and that a general and, it is hoped, lasting peace is concluded with all the Indian Nations who have taken up arms against his Majesty.

I remain,
etc.
Thomas Gage

EPILOGUE

[*September 2, 1765—Monday*]

HENRY BOUQUET lay quietly in the dimness of his quarters in the fort at Pensacola on Escambia Bay, not far from the broad blue waters of the Gulf of Mexico. He hadn't especially cared for the assignment that had taken him to this Florida Territory, far from the crispness of the more temperate climate which he liked so well. But it was here that he had been ordered to come and, a dedicated servant always of His Royal Majesty first, his own desires had been thrust aside.

When the Indian War had ended, it had been fully his intention to retire from his career. After all, he had performed his job and received the honors and praise that went with a campaign beautifully executed, but there was no further advancement available to him in the service. As a Swiss mercenary, he had reached the uppermost rank of colonel and—no matter what his value in leadership and strategy—this was a plateau beyond which advancement was traditionally denied.

He had made no secret of his desire to quit the service. In fact, on the turn of the year immediately after the war ended, he had begun his preparations for booking passage to England. After that, who knew what?

The people were sorry. To them he was a man of heroic proportions, a true champion, and they revered him as they had revered few military commanders before him. Just a month and a half after the end of the war the Pennsylvania General Assembly, in an unprecedented move, devoted an entire day to honor him. No one could remember a time when the always turbulent Assembly had ever voted unanimously on any matter, but on this day they had:

IN ASSEMBLY, January 15, 1765
  To the Honorable Henry Bouquet, Esq., Commander in

chief of his Majesty's Forces in the Southern Department of America:

The address of the Representatives of the Freemen of the Province of Pennsylvania, in General Assembly met:

Sir:

The Representatives of the Freemen of the Province of Pennsylvania, in General Assembly met, being informed that you intend shortly to embark for England, and moved with a due sense of the important services you have rendered to His Majesty, his Northern Colonies in general, and to this Province in particular, during our late wars with the French and barbarous Indians; in the remarkable victory over the savage enemy united to oppose you, near Bushy Run, in August 1763, when on your march for the relief of Pittsburgh, owing, under God, to your intrepidity and superior skill in command, together with the bravery of your officers and little army; as also in your late march to the country of the savage nations, with the troops under your direction, thereby striking terror through the numerous Indian tribes around you, laying a foundation for a lasting as well as honorable peace, and rescuing from savage captivity upwards of two hundred of our Christian brethren, prisoners among them.[184] These eminent services, and your constant attention to the civil rights of his Majesty's subjects in this Province demand, Sir, the grateful tribute of thanks from all good men; and therefore we, the Representatives of the Freemen of Pennsylvania, unanimously for ourselves, and in behalf of all the people of this Province, do return you our most sincere and hearty thanks for these your great services, wishing you a safe and pleasant voyage to England, with a kind and gracious reception from his Majesty.

Signed, by Order of the House,
JOSEPH FOX, Speaker

Moved by this measure and deeply appreciative of it, Bouquet nonetheless continued to prepare for his journey. But then had happened the unbelievable. On the seventeenth day of the following April he was taken completely by surprise when he received a letter from Major General Thomas Gage, happily informing him that it had been the pleasure of His Majesty to promote Colonel Henry Bouquet to the rank of brigadier general.

Dazed, *General* Bouquet sat and penned a reply, saying:

I had, today, the honor of your Excellency's letter of the 15th instant. The unexpected honor which his Majesty has condescended to confer upon me fills my heart with the utmost gratitude. Permit me, Sir, to express my sincere acknowledgements of my great obligation to you . . . The flattering prospect of preferment, open to the other foreign officers by the removal of that dreadful barrier, gives me the highest satisfaction, being convinced that his Majesty has no subjects more devoted to his service.

From all over America came letters from his many friends and fellow officers, and the one he received from Captain George Etherington, former commander of Fort Michilimackinac, was representative:

Lancaster, Pa., 19 April, 1765

Sir:
Though I almost despair of this reaching you before you sail for Europe, yet I cannot deny myself the pleasure of giving you joy on your promotion, and can with truth tell you that it gives great joy to all the gentlemen of the battalion, for two reasons: first, on your account; and, secondly, on our own, as by that means we may hope for the pleasure of continuing under your command.
You can hardly imagine how this place rings with the news of your promotion, for the townsmen and boors [German farmers] *stop us in the streets to ask if it is true that the King has made Colonel Bouquet a general; so you see, the old proverb wrong for once, which says he that prospers is envied; for sure I am that all the people here are more pleased with the news of your promotion than they would be if the government would take off the stamp duty . . .*

Geo. Etherington

Brigadier General Henry Bouquet

It had changed the entire picture, of course. Gone was his resolve to leave the service, gone his plans to return to England, gone the deep melancholy that had so long filled him and, most happily, gone the sense of military stultification he had so long borne. How could he leave such men, such fine officers, who wished to serve beneath him? He could not.

And so he had remained in His Majesty's service and by midsummer had been assigned here to Florida in a climate alien to him and unappreciated by him.

Ironic in the extreme it was that, though he had survived the bullets of the formidable French army and equally the tomahawks and warclubs of fierce Indian adversaries, now it was a tiny mosquito which brought him down, inflicting him with yellow fever so that today, this moment, he lay in his chambers, his forty-six-year-old body burning with a temperature which would not stop climbing. He was out of his head with delirium, trying to croak out a whisper for water but unable to speak, his breath coming faster and faster until suddenly there was a wheezing sound and then a deafening silence.

Brigadier General Henry Bouquet was dead.

[April 20, 1769—Thursday]

Pontiac was forty-nine years old now, but he looked considerably older. Premature wrinkles creased his brow and lined the skin of his neck, but they were not unattractive. His aspect was still one of command and the wrinkles added an interesting touch of age and dignity.

Month following tedious month after the war had ended he had visited the tribes of the Mississippi Valley, constantly exhorting them to rise beneath him and keep the English out; but though his oratory always stirred them, it was never quite enough. Sometimes he pleaded with them, often he tried to bribe them, frequently he threatened them, but then he himself had finally given in and made his peace with the English at last. He had gone to Oswego in June of 1766 to meet with Sir William Johnson and there he had signed a treaty with the English. But though he signed it, this was more a matter of self-preservation than anything else and he still harbored within him a deep, implacable hatred of the English. And, even though a bit more surreptitiously, he still continued to seek support for another uprising. But on the way home from signing that treaty, traveling with a party of the Illinois Confederacy who had also signed, he had gotten into a severe argument with one of the chiefs. It had degenerated to an actual fight and Pontiac had wound up stabbing him quite badly. The chief did not die, but he was never quite well again afterwards and perhaps that was the reason the Illinois tribes never quite let themselves be led into a new war by the

775

Ottawa; and quite possibly that was equally the event which was culminating in another event this very day.

As Pontiac had warned they would, the English had come to this Illinois country. They now occupied Fort de Chartres and Vincennes and all the forts that had been taken from them during Pontiac's uprising, plus the addition of others that had been built since then. Yes, the English had come and now the whole continent from the eastern sea to the grandmother of rivers was theirs, and still they continued to reach out, always grasping for more.

Now they were trickling down the valley of the Ohio, entering the sacred Can-tuc-kee hunting lands of the Shawnees, defying the treaties which prohibited their doing so. He told the Illinois Indians about this, trying to explain that this was what would soon be happening to their country, that it would become overrun by settlers and then what would happen? Settlers and Indians were incompatible, they could not possibly live close to one another in peace and there could therefore be only one conclusion: the Indians would be ousted from their lands, the forests would be cut, the waters despoiled, the game slaughtered. If then the Illinois Indians objected, it would be too late and they would still be ousted or, if they refused to leave, only their bones would remain in the land.

But the Illinois Confederacy would not listen.

In recent months, Pontiac had taken to wearing the impressive full-dress French officer's uniform which General Louis de Montcalm had personally presented to him just before his death at the battle of Quebec. It was Pontiac's hope that his wearing of it would impress the Illinois chiefs and make them more inclined, as so many of their young warriors were already inclined, to take to heart the words he spoke to them and to rise up under the strength of his arm. There was still time, yes! Still time to thrust the English back to the eastern mountains, perhaps even drive them into the sea and then reclaim this whole broad land which belonged to the Indians first.

Now another council was scheduled and, his determination dented but undaunted, he was going to try again to make them see the urgency of his plea and the deadly peril that the English posed for them—for *all* Indian tribes.

It was about ten o'clock this morning when, in Cahokia, having some time to spare before the council began, he entered the English trading post of Baynton, Wharton and Morgan in the center of town. With him was a smiling, friendly young Peoria warrior who seemed entranced by the once-mighty war chief of the Ottawas and to whom he had attached himself some time ago.

Together they looked at some of the merchandise in the store, but bought nothing. When it was time to go, the Peoria warrior stepped aside deferentially to let the Ottawa chief pass. As the elder Indian went out, the warrior followed him, at the same time jerking from his belt the war club he carried there.

Pontiac was just stepping into the street when the young Indian behind him swung the club in a mighty arc and struck Pontiac a blow which caved in the entire back of his head. Even as the war chief was falling, the Peoria jerked a knife from his belt and leaped upon him, driving the blade deep into Pontiac's heart.

Pontiac, war chief of the Ottawas, was dead.[185]

The time for the Illinois Indians to rise was not yet. It might come in time, but the English settlers were far away to the east and thus the bite of their plow was not felt in these prairies, the ring of their axe unknown in these woods. Perhaps another day at another time, another chief would rise whose strength was great and whose vision was clear and who could once again lead the Indians to rise and stand to fight for this land in which their council fires burned and beneath which lay the bones of their fathers and the fathers of many generations before. But not now. Not yet. The time for it had passed.

Pontiac was dead.

AMPLIFICATION NOTES

THESE notes have been placed at the rear of the book in order not to detract from the narrative flow, as so often occurs with footnotes. Though the reader may enjoy doing so, it is not *necessary* that he refer to this note section each time a supernumeral is given in the text. These are merely amplification notes and they are primarily intended for added interest; the narrative is not dependent upon them.

As much as possible, these amplification notes have been held to a minimum. In many cases they merely transpose the eighteenth-century locales of *The Conquerors* to modern-day landmarks, thus enabling the reader to acquire a better mental image of where the activity in question is occurring. However, there is also a certain amount of information included which, while it may not be directly germane to the narrative itself, is of such pertinence and interest tangentially that it should not be altogether omitted.

In the previous two volumes of this historical series—*The Frontiersmen* and *Wilderness Empire*—the amplification notes were numbered consecutively chapter by chapter, beginning with number one at the start of each new chapter. To avoid the confusion possible in such a system and to facilitate the reader's being able to quickly find the note he is seeking, the amplification notes in *The Conquerors* have been consecutively numbered from beginning to end of the narrative.

PROLOGUE

1. The tribal designations of Chippewa and Ojibwa are synonymous. Anthropologists now class the Ojibwa stock as having been divided into four great tribes: Chippewa, Ottawa, Mississaugi, Potawatomi. Generally speaking, however, an Indian referred to as an Ojibwa is a Chippewa. It should be further noted, however, that the Chippewa was composed of numerous small bands and had no real claim to any sort of formalized tribal government. The

aims or actions of one band did not necessarily reflect that of another, or of the tribe in general. To a lesser degree, as will be seen, this was also true of the Ottawa, Potawatomi and Mississaugi.

2. The island is today called Mackinac Island, just northeast of the Straits of Mackinac separating Lower Michigan from Upper Michigan.

3. The story of this incredible moose hunt first appeared in Nicholas Perrot's own account of his journey through this territory in 1670–71. He published his journal under the title *Memoir on the Manners, Customs, and Religion of the Savages of North America,* and parts of it were subsequently quoted in *The Indian Tribes of the Upper Mississippi Valley and Region of the Great Lakes,* edited by Emma H. Blair, I, 31, 272.

CHAPTER I

4. The Six Nations, also known as the Iroquois League and the Iroquois Confederacy, was made up of six tribes: Mohawk, Oneida, Onondaga, Cayuga, Seneca, and Tuscarora. Of these, the Senecas had long favored the French and only gradually was William Johnson winning them over. The Mohawks, who were geographically closest to the English, leaned strongly toward them. The other four tribes maintained a somewhat vacillating neutrality. All were supposedly bound, however, by the rulings of their central government. League councils were held annually (or more often if events required) and each of the Six Nations had delegates to the councils which were held at Onondaga, located at the south end of present Onondaga Lake in New York on the site of present Syracuse.

5. The Mingo Confederation simply evolved without benefit of formalized agreement between participating tribes. It had neither principal chief nor central government and was held together merely through a common goal to harass the frontier and destroy the English. Tribes participating included the Shawnee, Delaware, Cayuga, Seneca, and a few occasionally from the Nipissing, Caughnawaga, and Algonkin tribes.

6. Pennsylvania had never succeeded in regulating its Indian trade, despite a law and proclamations which sought to license traders and penalize abuses. In 1758 the provincial Assembly passed a stronger Indian trade act, naming commissioners to supervise the trade, banning the sale of liquor to the Indians, and creating a monopoly for the province of all trade west of the mountains. Three stores were set up by the commissioners: at Fort Augustus, at Fort Allen, and at Pittsburgh. Goods were sold to the Indians at established rates, and the furs and hides taken in exchange were auctioned in Philadelphia. From the very beginning, however, the Indian trade commissioners ran into difficulties. The sum of £4,000 which they were permitted to borrow to finance their stores was too small. Even when it was increased to £10,000, the capital proved inadequate. Croghan completely disregarded Pennsylvania's law, taking it upon himself not only to license Indian traders but to set prices. It mattered not to him that the commissioners had set their own prices; he called on their agent to adopt his schedule, which gave the Indians better trading values. Entirely opposed to a government monopoly and a bitter enemy of

the store, Croghan claimed Stanwix had given him the right to open the trade to all. Actually, the inability of the commissioners to send enough goods to Pittsburgh doomed their expectation of engrossing the Indian trade. *George Croghan: Wilderness Diplomat,* by Nicholas Wainwright, 162–163.

7. This tribe was originally called the Lenni Lenape by themselves, but soon after English Colonization began, the river on which they lived was named the Delaware River after Lord Delaware, second governor of Virginia. Before long the Indians residing there had become known (and still are) as Delawares.

8. He was often referred to as King Beaver, Chief Beaver or just The Beaver. However, the "King" designation was of English origin and actually meant "Chief" and was therefore not part of the name.

9. In this siege, Colonel John Prideaux was accidentally killed by his own artillery and Sir William Johnson took over command, won the battle and forced the capitulation of Fort Niagara, effectively severing the French communication with their forts of the western Great Lakes. For complete details of this incident, as well as the fall of Quebec and other occurrences leading to the conclusion of the French and Indian War in America, see the author's *Wilderness Empire,* 577–608.

10. Although the French called their installation at Venango Fort Machault, it is more familiarly referred to as Fort Venango, which name was officially adopted when the place was rebuilt by the English.

11. Quite frequently in historical accounts, the vessel *Michigan* is referred to as the *Gladwin.* This is an error. The *Gladwin* was a schooner which was originally christened the *Victory* and which was not built until the winter of 1763–64.

12. Gladwin's name is frequently spelled Gladwyn or Glandwin in historical writings and even in some of the original documents of the period. Even in the military "Report of General Braddock's Defeat on the Monongahela," in which he took part, his name is spelled Glandwin. The correct spelling is Gladwin.

13. Gladwin was promoted from second lieutenant, Irish Half-pay, to lieutenant of the 48th Regiment of Foot in 1753. In December, 1757, he was promoted to the rank of captain.

14. This was the same Robert Rogers of New Hampshire who formed and led the famous Ranger Company which provided the English such useful service under extremely hazardous conditions all through the French and Indian War, particularly in spying missions in the French-occupied area of Lake Champlain. See *Wilderness Empire* for expansion of these exploits.

15. The Canadian capitulation, a long and detailed document, was dictated by Amherst and signed by the Marquis de Vaudreuil.

16. Michilimackinac is pronounced Mish-ill-lah-mack-in-naw. Ouiatenon is pronounced Wy-ah-tee-non.

17. Originally, the Royal Americans were the 62nd Regiment. They became the 60th in the reorganization of 1758, but many of the officers continued to bear the designation of the 62nd. The Royal Americans were not originally riflemen, despite many claims to the contrary. (See *The Orderly Book of Colonel Henry Bouquet's Expedition,* page 54, number 4.)

18. A thin, hard mattress made of a sack constructed of strong fab-

ric, such as canvas, generally stuffed with straw and used as a pallet to sleep upon.

19. The village was located near the site of present Geneseo, Livingston County, New York. The river is still called the Genesee River, which empties into Lake Ontario at Rochester, N.Y.

20. Iroquois League councils were held at Onondaga (site of present Syracuse, N.Y.) not because the Onondagas were the most powerful tribe of the confederacy, which they were not, but because the site was centrally located to the entire League.

21. There are a variety of spellings of the names of these two chiefs. The one, for example, has been listed as Teantoriance, Teantoniance, Teantorianee, and Tahaiadoris; the other as Gayachiouton, Kiashuta, Kayathshutha and Kyashuga. However, the most commonly used spellings are Kyashuta and Teantoriance.

22. Often incorrectly spelled Belestre, Beletree or Belletry.

23. George II had died October 25 and was succeeded by George III, a fact not yet known on the American frontier.

24. Fort Miamis, at the confluence of the St. Joseph and St. Marys rivers, where the Maumee River is formed, is the site of present Fort Wayne, Indiana. Fort Ouiatenon, on the Wabash River, was near the site of present Lafayette, Indiana.

25. In the original letter, Campbell made a mistake in the date, saying they arrived at Detroit on the nineteenth instead of the twenty-ninth. He also dated this letter November 2 instead of December 2. Both errors have been corrected in this text.

26. The Wyandots were a branch of the Huron tribe who had separated from the segment of their nation at Detroit and moved to the Sandusky Bay area. See also the details in Amplification Note Number 30.

27. Lieutenant Brewer arrived with the cattle for Detroit on November 30.

28. Monsieur Nevarre, a respected French inhabitant of Detroit, was helpful in many ways to the English and, for a time, acted as a sort of liaison between the English and French here.

29. As a further basis for his anti-English stance, Cuillerier was related, through Captain Belêtre, to Alphonse Tonti who, in 1701, had helped Antoine de la Mothe-Cadillac to found this very post. Tonti had been one of the post's earliest commandants.

30. Wyandot (which is often spelled Guyandot) was the Huron terminology for "People-who-live-on-an-island-or-peninsula." The Wyandots were so named because the village was located on the Sandusky Bay peninsula. In accuracy, therefore, only those Huron Indians who had settled at Sandusky Bay under the two chiefs named Orontony and Odinghquanooron could properly be called Wyandots. Later, through misuse, the name became associated with all the Hurons who migrated to and settled in the Ohio country. Although the Wyandots had virtually the stature of a tribe on their own, they were nonetheless Hurons.

31. Fort de Chartres was originally built by the French in 1720 and rebuilt in 1753. It was one of the strongest of the French forts in America, having four stone bastions. At this time it was the center and citadel of a curiously isolated forest settlement located on the east bank of the Mississippi River, downstream from present St. Louis, about halfway between the mouths of the Missouri and Ohio Rivers. It was on the site of present Prairie du Rocher, in Randolph County, Illinois.

32. David Duncan was eventually slain by Chief Logan in the events leading up to Lord Dunmore's War of 1774. For details see *The Frontiersmen*, 15–89.

33. In his narrative, Alexander Henry erroneously calls this individual M. LeDuc.

34. La Chine—meaning China—was so named when the French explorer La Salle fitted out his expeditions at this place in his efforts to discover a northwest passage to China. Because of the extremely shallow rapids just above Montreal, loaded canoes could not fight the upstream current. The boats were therefore sent empty upstream to La Chine, nine miles distant, to which point, as was customary, merchandise and equipment were transported in wagons.

35. A livre, at the time of the conquest of Canada, was equivalent to one Canadian shilling or about 25¢ American. The middlemen therefore were paid a wage of about $37.50 and the end men $75, which was quite a substantial amount for the time.

36. The birth, lifetime career, and death of Sir William Johnson are chronicled in detail in the author's *Wilderness Empire*.

37. Johnson, who in the later years of his life suffered the ravages of syphilis, was allegedly the father of at least several hundred children, especially among the Iroquois Indians.

38. Among the tribes recorded as being on hand were the Huron, Ottawa, Sac, Fox, Potawatomi, Chippewa, Miami, Delaware, Kaskaskia, Peoria, Muncee, Mohawk, Oneida, Seneca, Mississaugi, Kickapoo, Mohican, Abnaki, Wea, Nipissing, Menominee, Piankeshaw, Eel River Miami, Winnebago, Shawnee, Cayuga, Onondaga.

39. By this he meant not a confederacy of tribes, but the confederation of the four separate bands which made up the Ottawa tribe—the Nassauaketons, the Sinagoes, the Kiskagons, and the Sables.

CHAPTER II

40. Also called the Grand River, La Grande Rivière, Ottaway, Outaouais, and Utawas.

41. Present Georgian Bay.

42. Minivavana's name is occasionally spelled Menewehna or Menewhena. To the French he was frequently called Le Grand Saulteur, which is how he was referred to by Jonathan Carver in 1767.

43. Different tribes had different ways of preparing *kinnikinnick*, although in almost all cases the ingredients included willow leaves, dried sumac, dried and shredded or pulverized dogwood bark and actual tobacco. In some cases marijuana was used in place of or in addition to willow leaves. The aroma of burning *kinnikinnick* was distinctly pungent but not displeasing, though it was said to be harsh to the tongue of the smoker.

44. The term "covering the bodies" was a common metaphor in Indian usage and signified the making of restitution by means of a payment to the relatives which they felt satisfactory for the injury done them and which was acceptable in lieu of physical vengeance. It was, however, elective on the part of the relative whether or not he wanted the body covered. In many cases vengeance was preferred.

45. Milo Milton Quaife, in his edition of *Alexander Henry's Travels*

and Adventures in the Years 1760–1776, states in a footnote on page 47 that L'Arbre Croche was located at the site of present Harbor Springs, Michigan, on the north shore of Little Traverse Bay. This is approximately thirty-two miles south by southwest of where Fort Michilimackinac stood. Yet, Alexander Henry consistently says they had to go west to get to L'Arbre Croche (though there were trails going both south and southwest from the fort) and that it was a one-day journey. Harbor Springs, no less than forty water miles (and one land portage) away from the fort, was at least a two-day journey. Quaife also calls Waugoshance by the name of Fox Point, yet present maps still identify this peninsula as being Waugoshance Point. L'Arbre Croche could not have been far from this point. Howard Peckham in *Pontiac and the Indian Uprising* states that L'Arbre Croche is the present Cross Village, Michigan. Indeed, historical markers in that area claim the same. While this is more apt to be correct than Quaife's assertion, yet there is still a distinct likelihood that L'Arbre Croche was at neither of these locations but, instead, within two miles of Waugoshance Point. Henry definitely states (Quaife, pp. 95–96) that the Ottawa village of L'Arbre Croche lay "about 20 miles to the westward of Michilimackinac on the opposite side of the tongue of land on which the fort is built." Henry also describes (p. 96) Waugoshance as being "distant 18 miles from Michilimackinac," and therefore within two miles of L'Arbre Croche. It is the author's firm conviction that L'Arbre Croche was located by the mouth of the little stream which empties Neil Lake into Lake Michigan, the mouth of this stream being only about two miles south of Waugoshance Point.

46. The spelling of Lieutenant Leslye's name has been given in a number of different ways in various accounts. Henry, in his journal, spelled it both Lesslie and Lesslye. Most often, even in official military records, it has been spelled Leslie. However, in a letter the lieutenant wrote (which the author has inspected) to the French inhabitants of Fort Michilimackinac on September 30, 1761, he signs his own name as Leslye, so obviously this must be correct.

47. This body of water was originally named Lac Sainte Claire, using the feminine gender, but already by 1761 it was being spelled in the masculine gender as Lac Saint Clair. To avoid confusion, the modern spelling, Lake St. Clair, has been used.

48. Sand Point and Point Lookout on opposite shores of Saginaw Bay still retain the same names today. The two islands, then unnamed, subsequently became the present Charity Island and Little Charity Island.

49. Present Green Bay on the eastern shore of Wisconsin was known to the French as Bay des Puants—Stinking Bay—because of the large number of dead fish, mainly alewives, which each spring drifted ashore and for weeks caused an almost insufferable smell.

50. The Ottawa tribe, however, was in some respects like the Chippewa. It had little real central government and the term "principal chief" did not give its holder the absolute power of his whole tribe as the same title did among the Shawnees or some other tribes. In the same way, the title of "war chief," while tribally important, was not as much so as with other tribes. In most respects the Ottawas of Michilimackinac and Detroit acted entirely inde-

pendently of one another and often, as will be seen, at cross purposes to each other.

51. For greater details of this incident in particular and the Quebec battle in general, see *Wilderness Empire*, 590–604.

52. Fort Pitt was located on the point of land where the Monongahela and Allegheny Rivers converged to form the Ohio River, on the site of present Pittsburgh, Pennsylvania. Fort Niagara was located at the mouth of the Niagara River, on the east bank of that river and overlooking Lake Ontario, about one mile north of present Youngstown, Niagara County, N.Y. Fort Presque Isle was located within the city limits of present Erie, Erie County, Pennsylvania. Fort le Boeuf, fifteen miles south of Fort Presque Isle, was located on the site of present Waterford, Erie County, Pennsylvania. Fort Venango was located at the mouth of French Creek where it empties into the Allegheny River on the site of present Franklin, Venango County, Pensylvania.

53. Fort Miamis was located on the site of present downtown Fort Wayne, Allen County, Indiana, on the southeast bank of the Maumee River immediately below the confluence of the St. Joseph and St. Marys Rivers.

54. Fort Ouiatenon was located on the bank of the Wabash River just downstream from Lafayette, Tippecanoe County, Indiana.

55. Fort Edward Augustus (Fort La Baye) was located at the southern end of Green Bay at the mouth of the Fox River on the site of present Green Bay, Brown County, Wisconsin.

56. Fort St. Joseph was located on the east bank of the St. Joseph River about one mile upstream (south) of present downtown Niles, Berrien County, Michigan.

57. This is precisely what occurred. The mortally ill young man, Robert Davers, preceded his father in death and never inherited his father's title; hence, there never was, legally, a Sir Robert Davers. The actual identity of the imposter, however, has never been ascertained.

58. Thomas Hutchins was commissioned an ensign in the 2nd Pennsylvania Regiment on November 1, 1756, and lieutenant on December 18, 1757. He served through 1758–59 as a supply officer under General John Forbes. In 1766 he accompanied Captain Harry Gordon on a trip down the Ohio and Mississippi. He was promoted to captain lieutenant on August 7, 1771 and to captain in 1776. He resigned his commission in 1777 rather than oppose his country and went to England where he published his *Topographical Description of Virginia, Pennsylvania, Maryland and North Carolina*. Imprisoned for six weeks in London on suspicion of holding correspondence with Ben Franklin in France, upon his release he fled to France, then to Charleston, South Carolina, where he joined the American army under Captain Greene. He left the army September 3, 1783 and immediately thereafter became a United States Geographer and, later on, Geographer General of the United States. He was involved in a fraudulent sale of Ohio Valley land in Paris, France (for details of which see *The Frontiersmen*, 320, 331–332), and finally died at the age of 59 in 1789 at Pittsburgh and was buried there in the Trinity churchyard.

59. Many of the maps executed by Thomas Hutchins of the frontier areas of Pennsylvania, Virginia, the Carolinas, Maryland, Ohio and the Great Lakes were so skillfully rendered that even in this

present day, with all our modern mapmaking and both ground and aerial surveying equipment, his maps of vast areas have been found to be accurate within fractions of inches. In fact, many of his maps are far more accurate than the maps currently in use for these locales. To Hutchins goes the credit for having devised the rectangular system of surveying the western lands, known to the world now as the American Land System.

60. The surname of Elleopolle "Mini" Chene is very often misspelled because it was pronounced "chain." Therefore, it was often spelled Chain. Quite frequently, too, it was spelled Chesne. The correct spelling, however, seems to be Chene.

61. For more complete details on what the Walking Purchase consisted of and the problems which followed, culminating in the chastisement of the Delawares by the Iroquois, see *Wilderness Empire*, 26–30.

62. Johnson was often referred to by his militia rank of General, although at this time the title was more honorary than actual.

63. For greater details of Bouquet's service under General John Forbes, see *Wilderness Empire*, 525–526, 530–531, 552–553, 555.

CHAPTER III

64. Black rainfalls such as this, though not common, have been recorded numerous times in history, as have red rains which gave the apearance of blood. Both black rains and red rains are normally accompanied by a most unpleasant sulphurous odor. Science is still largely mystified by such phenomena.

65. Isle aux Pêches, meaning Fish Island, has been corrupted to present Peach Island.

66. Isle au Cochon—Hog Island—is now Belle Isle.

67. Present Southfield Road in the Lincoln Park and Ecorse areas of Detroit bisects the area where the council was held.

68. Presently known as Mud Island.

69. Although there were a number of vagrant hints that the Detroit French were threatened by Indians during the summer of 1746, as Pontiac claims in his speech, there has never come to light any clear account of what this trouble might have been or how it was settled. There is mention of the fact that in 1747 Chief Mackinac was suspected by the Detroit commander to be conspiring with the Huron chief, Orontony (whom he called Nicholas), to attack the French at Detroit. In *Pontiac and the Indian Uprising*, Dr. Howard Peckham in a footnote commentary (p. 35) tells of letters written from Michilimackinac in the summer of 1747 which mention that the new commandant, on arriving there, "has found that post very quiet; the Ottawas are beginning to be sorry for what occurred last year." It seems evident that some sort of friction had developed between Mackinac's Ottawas and the French, and that Pontiac somehow managed to settle things through personal intervention, which is what that chief refers to in his speech at the Ecorse River council.

70. The Rivière à la Tranch is the present Thames River of Ontario, which empties into Lake St. Clair.

71. What was then called the Huron River is the present St. Clair River, carrying the overflow of Lake Huron into Lake St. Clair and thence down the Detroit River to Lake Erie.

72. This attack occurred on the west shore of the present St. Clair

River somewhere between present Algonac and Roberts Landing, St. Clair County, Michigan.

73. James Sterling did, eventually, marry Angelique Cuillerier dit Beaubien, but it was apparently an unhappy marriage and one that Sterling entered into primarily in the belief that because Angelique had been close to Sir William Johnson, he might get favors or advantages in the Indian trade from Johnson. He even asked for some of these favors in letters to Johnson, but the favors were never granted.

74. A great deal of confusion and dispute exists in regard to the identity of Major Gladwin's informant. Various accounts give various identities to the individual who brought the word to Gladwin the evening before the planned attack. Francis Parkman suggests that Gladwin was informed by Thomas Gouin and the Indian woman named Catherine. Some say a beautiful young Indian maiden, alleged to be Gladwin's mistress, exposed the plot to him. Others say it was an old squaw. Gladwin himself never revealed in writing the identity. He did, however, tell the Indians when questioned about it by them, that it was one of themselves who told him, although this was quite likely a subterfuge to divert suspicion from the real informant. Even to Amherst, Gladwin only remarked that "I was luckily informed the night before . . ." Years later, the Indian interpreter at Detroit, Henry Connor, declared that the informant was a young Indian girl named Catherine who was in love with Gladwin, but he gives no authentication for his statement. He adds that long afterward the same squaw was killed when she stumbled while drunk and fell into a huge kettle of boiling maple syrup. Parkman visited Detroit in 1845 and at that time Francis Baby, son of Jacques Duperon Baby, said he knew nothing of any squaw named Catherine. He said that he had always been told that Gladwin had been warned by the fort's two interpreters, St. Martin and LaButte, and that LaButte learned of it first from his daughter who had overheard the plan being discussed by the Indians. In 1824, Gabriel St. Aubin, Jr., declared that it was his mother who had warned Gladwin personally after she had seen the Indians cutting their guns down. In that same years, Charles Gouin, son of Thomas Gouin, said that his father learned of the plot from the Indians and sent another Frenchman, Jacques Chovin, to warn Captain Donald Campbell. Another story has it that an adopted white youth among the Chippewas, William Tucker, who had been captured on the Virginia frontier, was informed of the plan by his Indian sister and he thereupon informed Gladwin. Ten years after the siege, the then commander of Detroit, Major Henry Basset, wrote to Major General Haldimand recommending to him the trader James Sterling and naming him as the informant of Gladwin. Yet, these are all identifications made many years after the incident in question and subject to doubt. The only identity made in writing *at the time of the siege* was by Ensign George Price, commander of Fort Le Boeuf. On June 26, 1763, he wrote to Colonel Henry Bouquet as follows: ". . . but Major Gladwin, being told by Monsieur Baby that if they were admitted, they would fall upon and destroy every man in it, ordered the garrison under arms . . ." Since Jacques Baby was one of the most respected and influential Frenchmen of Detroit and a good friend of Gladwin's in addition, the author believes him to be the person most likely responsible for inform-

ing Major Gladwin of the plot on the night before the attack was to occur. More probable yet is the conclusion reached by Dr. Peckham who states (p. 121): "The multiplicity of claims suggests what is highly probable: namely, that more than one person brought the dread news into the fort."

75. It seems likely that Major Gladwin said this in an effort to create disunity and distrust among the Indians themselves.

76. Some accounts claim that Catherine died of the blows received by Pontiac; others that she was thereafter a cripple; still others that she was ostracized, became alcoholic, tumbled into a kettle of boiling maple syrup while drunk many years later, and was scalded to death.

CHAPTER IV

77. Turkey Island is now known as Fighting Island.

78. This incident and how Pontiac came to be given his name is discussed in *Wilderness Empire*, 11–15.

79. Cuyler's name is often erroneously spelled Keiler or Kyler.

80. Peckham (pp. 156, 175) says there were 10 boats. Lieutenant Jehu Hay's *Diary of the Siege of Detroit* (pp. 17, 17n29, 18, 18n29) and Norman Wood's *Lives of Famous Indian Chiefs* (pp. 155–156) say 18 boats. Peckham is ordinarily the most accurate but, considering the number of men and large amount of supplies involved, 18 boats seems to be the more realistic figure.

81. Fort Schlosser, also known as the Upper Landing, was located within the limits of present Niagara Falls, N.Y., at the foot of Portage Road. The fort was named after John Joseph Schlosser, who was commissioned a lieutenant on December 27, 1755, and was one of the first officers in the Royal American Regiment. Promoted for bravery to the rank of captain July 20, 1756, he succeeded to the command of the company of Baron Munster and on July 8, 1758, was wounded at Ticonderoga. It was he who, in 1759, rebuilt the French fort just above the Falls and it was named in his honor. Though the relationship is not entirely clear, it is believed that Ensign Francis Schlosser, commander of Fort St. Joseph, was the son of Captain John Joseph Schlosser.

82. In *Diary of the Siege of Detroit* (p. 89) it is noted that a trader named Prentice was released by the Hurons to Major Gladwin on April 27, 1764, who had been captive of the Sandusky Wyandots since May, 1763. Apparently Prentice was taken while en route to Fort Sandusky from Fort Pitt shortly after the former was destroyed. It was unlikely that he was at Fort Sandusky when it was taken, as all accounts agree that the only survivor was Ensign Pauli. Also, in his own account of the frontier massacres at this time, the Moravian missionary Loskiel relates (as quoted in Parkman's *The Conspiracy of Pontiac*, p. 9) that "In the villages of the Hurons or Wyandots, probably meaning those of Sandusky, the traders were so numerous that the Indians were afraid to attack them openly and had recourse to the following stratagem: they told their unsuspecting victims that the surrounding tribes had risen in arms, and were soon coming that way, bent on killing every Englishman they could find. The Wyandots averred they would gladly protect their friends, the white men; but that it would be impossible to do so unless the latter would consent, for the sake of appearances, to become their prisoners. In this case,

they said, the hostile Indians would refrain from injuring them, and they should be set at liberty as soon as the danger was past. The traders fell into the snare. They gave up their arms and, the better to carry out the deception, even consented to being bound; but no sooner was this accomplished, than their treacherous counsellors murdered them all in cold blood." No other account gives this version and it is unlikely to have occurred at Sandusky without Ensign Pauli having been aware of it. What is far more likely is that it is an embroidered account of the affair between the English traders and the Delaware Indians at the village of Tuscarawas, as recorded further along in this volume.

CHAPTER V

83. Again we find Pontiac discussing a matter with the French about which he and they are apparently quite familiar but of which incredibly little is recorded. This is obviously related to the incident he mentioned at the Ecorse River Council (see Note 69), but precisely how is unclear. A close study of all available documents relating to the French regime in Michigan in the period 1745–48 reveals only one small soiled scrap of paper in the Francis Parkman Papers collection which attests to the veracity of Pontiac's claims. Parkman, when conducting his own research, visited with the descendants of Lt. George McDougall at St. Clair, Michigan. Among the old papers in that family's possession relating to Pontiac's war and events prior to it was this intriguing glimpse of what Pontiac was evidently referring to: "Five miles below the mouth of Wolf River is the Great Death Ground. This took its name from the circumstance, that some years before the Old French War, a great battle was fought between the French troops, assisted by the Menominees and Ottawas on one side, and the Sac and Fox Indians on the other. The Sacs and Foxes were nearly all cut off; and this proved the cause of their eventual expulsion from that country." Pontiac, in his speech to the French here at Detroit, indicates that the leader of the anti-French Indians at that time was named Mackinac, but this is another matter for confusion, since Mackinac was an Ottawa and the Ottawas, as inferred in Pontiac's speech and confirmed in the above written record, were allied to the French and helped drive off the intruders; unless, of course, the Ottawa tribe was split at this time. It was possible that the chief here named as Mackinac was a chief of either the Fox or Sac and not the Ottawa chief with whom we are familiar. By the same token, if indeed it was Mackinac of the Ottawas, then perhaps this is why, during the uprising by Pontiac, Mackinac not only would not wage war against the English, but helped, as will be seen, in the rescue of many of the Englishmen who would surely otherwise have been butchered. Perhaps at some future time further documents will be uncovered which will shed some new light on this mystery.

84. None of these notes are known to exist now. Lieutenant Jehu Hay in his *Diary* states that the totem was a raccoon, but all other accounts refer to it as an otter.

85. Apparently this camp was located somewhere in the vicinity of present Leesville, Crawford County, Ohio, about nine miles east of the present city of Bucyrus.

86. Kispoko Town, under Chief Pucksinwah, was located on the west

bank of the Scioto River in Pickaway County not far below the site of present Circleville, Ohio. It was named after the Kispokotha sept of the Shawnee tribe. Chalahgawtha, somewhat farther south on that river, just above the mouth of Paint Creek, was named after the Chalahgawtha sept of the Shawnees and was at this time the center of the Shawnee tribal government. Chalahgawtha has since been corrupted in the English to Chillicothe and several present cities have this name, including Chillicothe, Ohio, located near where the original Chalahgawtha was situated.

87. Wilkins received his commission of major in the Royal Americans on June 9, 1762, having previously been a captain in Lord George Howe's 55th Regiment since December 30, 1755. After the reduction of 1763 he retired on half pay, but was on active duty again as of August 15, 1764. He was in Lancaster with the Royal Americans in 1765 and he commanded Fort (de) Chartres in 1768. His name disappeared from the army lists after 1776.

88. There are several dubious accounts which claim that Campbell boarded the vessel to speak with Newman, but such assertion appears in error.

89. The reader should take care not to confuse this St. Joseph River of southwestern Michigan with the St. Joseph River of northeastern Indiana, which is one of the two main sources of the Maumee River. The former St. Joseph River empties into Lake Michigan at Benton Harbor-St. Joseph, Michigan.

90. Though his name is almost as frequently spelled Welsh as it is Welch, the existing evidence indicates Welch to be the correct spelling.

91. Hambach (often spelled Hambough) and Winston were hidden in Chevalie's attic, remaining there for four days and nights before being discovered by the Potawatomies. At that time Hambach was taken prisoner to Fort de Chartres and Winston was held hostage at St. Joseph.

92. Later, at Detroit, in apparent fear of repercussions to come, Godefroy paid Barns for the buckles, saying that he had always intended to do so.

93. At the junction of Sandy Creek and Tuscarawas River on the site of present Bolivar, Tuscarawas County, Ohio.

94. Lake Erie is still regarded as the most treacherous of the Great Lakes because of its penchant for erupting into such violence in so swift a time. Thousands of boats have been lost throughout our history in these waters as a result of extremely sudden storms. Even modern meteorologics have not solved the problem of giving ample warning. At the very time the author wrote this, winds of tornadic force struck Lake Erie unexpectedly during the Fourth of July weekend (1969); over one hundred boats were smashed, capsized or sunk, and the death toll was very high.

95. At the site of present West Newton, Pennsylvania.

96. This island still retains the name of Pelee and is part of the Province of Ontario, Canada.

97. Present Kelley's Island, several miles off Marblehead on the Sandusky peninsula, Ottawa County, Ohio.

98. Mr. Lorrain, whose first name has not been recorded, was a respected French resident of the little village which sprang up adjacent to Fort Ouiatenon. Like many of the Frenchmen at Detroit, he chose to take oath of allegiance to England rather

than lose his home and holdings. It was on his behest that Lieutenant Jenkins was permitted to write the letter to Gladwin informing him of the fall of Fort Ouiatenon, and it was Lorrain who carried the letter to Detroit and delivered it to Major Gladwin.

CHAPTER VI

99. Site of present Cheboygan, Cheboygan County, Michigan.
100. Though referred to on several occcasions, this Englishman was never identified other than as Samuels. There are, however, a few inconclusive hints that this man may have been a business associate of Ezekiel Solomon from Boston who had come to Michilimackinac via Montreal and the northern trade route via the Ottawa River, Lake Nipissing, Georgian Bay and Lake Huron.
101. Site of present Bedford, Bedford County, Pennsylvania.
102. Ourry was commissioned a lieutenant on January 14, 1756, in the 62nd Regiment, promoted to captain-lieutenant of the 60th Regiment on August 29, 1759, and to captain on December 12, 1760. He commanded Fort Bedford during 1762–63 and is reported to have died in Ireland in 1779.
103. Site of present Ligonier, Westmoreland County, Pennsylvania.
104. Though Presque Isle was a reasonably strong fortification, both Le Boeuf and Venango were weak in construction and in manpower and almost certain to fall if atacked.
105. Although quite frequently the name is spelled Dalzel, the correct spelling is Dalyell.
106. Major John Campbell was no relation of Captain Donald Campbell of Detroit, though they knew one another.
107. Grand River enters Lake Erie from present Ontario about twenty-five miles west of Buffalo, New York.
108. Quite frequently it was referred to as "the" Detroit, which was a carryover from when the fort was first built by Cadillac in 1701. Then called Fort Pontchartrain, it was located on the strait—or in French, the *détroit*—connecting Lake St. Clair with Lake Erie. The fort became more commonly called "the Detroit" than Fort Pontchartrain, and the English renamed it Fort Detroit when they took possession. However, many people—General Amherst included—continued to refer to the fort and the area around it as "the Detroit."
109. Now the capital city of Pennsylvania—Harrisburg.

CHAPTER VII

110. Oshkosh was the father of the Indian of the same name who later became chief and was a friend of the whites. In honor of this friendship, the two towns at the head of Wisconsin's Fox River, where it emerges from Lake Winnebago—Saukeer on the north side, and Algoma on the south side—merged and incorporated themselves in 1840 to become Oshkosh, Wisconsin.
111. Kinonchamek neglects to mention the four soldiers and the trader, Samuels, who were butchered after the taking of Fort Michilimackinac, with one of them cut up, cooked and eaten. There is some indication, however, that this act was perpetrated without either the knowledge or approval of Minivavana and that the guilty chief was punished for doing as he did, or at least suffered the stern disapproval of the other chiefs of the tribe.

790

112. Isle au Deinde or Turkey Island, now called Fighting Island, is presently a part of the Province of Ontario.

CHAPTER VIII

113. For greater details on why Rogers established his Ranger force and how he trained them, see *Wilderness Empire*.
114. Four of the missing six did eventually make it to Fort Pitt, but two were never heard of again and evidently died of exposure in the woods or were killed by Indians.
115. Amherst here refers to the battle and siege of 1759 when Johnson took Fort Niagara (see note 9).
116. The Bay of Boutchitaouy is presently St. Martin's Bay.
117. The term "papoose" signified just the vehicle for carry the baby, and not the infant itself; although in present usage, papoose has become almost synonymous with "Indian baby."
118. Fort Little Niagara—the Lower Landing—was located at the site of present Lewiston. New York.
119. Site of present Buffalo, Erie County, New York.
120. A very peculiar aspect of the meeting of these Frenchmen was brought out later when, on the evening of December 24, 1763, Jadeau (whose name is occasionally given as Jadoc) made a complete declaration of it to Major Gladwin and Captain James Grant and it was put into the form of a deposition and signed by both of the officers and the Frenchman. The peculiarity was that Jadeau declared that while the meeting was going on and further discussion being made on the planned surprise taking of the fort, that LaButte, claiming that he was speaking for Antoine Cuillerier, requested of Pontiac that when the fort was taken, the life of Captain Joseph Hopkins be spared as, according to Cuillerier, "he is one of us." Pontiac allegedly replied that he would spare Hopkins if he knew him, meaning if he recognized him during the furor of the attack. The intimation is certainly that Hopkins was acting in the role of a spy for the French here, but if such was the case, it has never been proved. That there was a spy for the French in Detroit became obvious, but existing evidence points to LaButte rather than to Hopkins. At no place in the records is it indicated that Hopkins was ever questioned about this allegation, as certainly he must have been, and the loyalty of that officer makes the allegation very doubtful. It is likely that either Jadeau dreamed this up to make trouble for Hopkins, or that LaButte and Cuillerier were lying.
121. Although it is not authenticated, there is some evidence to indicate that Tewalee's father, the brother of Wasson, was killed by a bear when Tewalee was an infant, whereupon Wasson allegedly raised his orphaned nephew as his own son, of which he had none.

CHAPTER IX

122. For details on Vaudreuil's fire rafts used during the siege of Quebec, see *Wilderness Empire*, pp. 590–604.
123. Pucksinwah was also chief of the warrior sept of the Shawnees, the Kispokothas. At this time his eldest child was a son named Chiksika. He also had a young daughter named Tecumapese. In five years from this time, his wife Methotase would give birth to a second son, who would be destined for greatness. This son would be named Tecumseh. For details of this and a full account

of the death of Pucksinwah and the rise of Tecumseh to become one of the greatest Indian leaders in American History, see the author's *The Frontiersmen.*

124. Yokum's name has variously been spelled also as Yolkum, Yocum and Yoakum. Yokum seems to be correct.

125. Common Indian metaphor. To destroy an enemy is to eat him up.

126. Pontiac's other two sons were Atussa and Shegenaba, but it is doubtful that all four sons were out of his number one wife, Kantuk-keghun.

127. Parkman states (*The Conspiracy of Pontiac,* I, 306–307) that Dalyell had fifteen men killed in this action, but he is in error.

128. This ended for Major Robert Rogers the last Indian fight of his career.

129. As is not uncommon in frontier battle statistics, there are numerous tallies at variance with one another regarding the number of dead and wounded in this Battle of Bloody Run. Parkman (*The Conspiracy,* I, 316–317) says there were 59 killed and wounded. This same figure is given in Lt. James MacDonald's letter to Major Gates of Aug. 8, 1763 (original in Sterling Letter Book, Clements Library, Ann Arbor). However, in the letter of James Sterling to William McAdams, Aug. 7, 1763, he states there were about "50 men killed and wounded." Wood, (in *Lives,* 158–161) gives the final total of killed and wounded as 110. Peckham (*Pontiac,* 204–208, 233) says there were 23 dead and 31 wounded, for a total of 54. However, it would seem that the most accurate accounting was that given by Lt. Jehu Hay (*Diary,* 54, 61) who tallies by unit and gives the following breakdown:

> 55TH REGIMENT—Killed, Dalyell, 1 sergeant, 16 men
> Wounded, Gray, Luke, Brown, drummer, and 22 men.
> 60TH REGIMENT—Killed, 1 private
> Wounded, 7 privates
> 80TH REGIMENT—Killed, 2
> Wounded, 3
> QUEEN'S RANGERS—Killed, 2
> Wounded, 1
> 1 trader's servant wounded
>
> TOTAL WOUNDED, 38
> TOTAL KILLED, 23

Total killed and wounded in battle, 61

130. Pierre Descompts Labadie's first name is often given as Peter, the English form of his French name.

131. This was at Edge Hill, 26 miles east of present downtown Pittsburgh, Pennsylvania.

132. Full details of Braddock's Defeat may be found in *Wilderness Empire,* 289–299.

CHAPTER X

133. Bouquet was evidently referring to the Mingo faction as a tribe, rather than as the loose confederacy which it was; a common mistake then and since (see Note 5).

134. This was a representative example of the true "burning at the

stake" of a captive. It was not at all the purpose of such an execution to immediately burn the victim and end his life. To the contrary, the object was to torture him unbearably, yet keep him alive as long as posible. For full details on precisely what occurs at a "burning at the stake," read the account of the death of Colonel William Crawford in the author's *The Frontiersmen*, 253–264.

135. Catfish Creek is now known as Eighteen Mile Creek.

136. Not until many years had passed had enough evidence—circumstantial and actual—accumulated to indicate that Pierre LaButte was the traitor in the English midst. However, he escaped any form of punishment for his actions during the siege of Detroit.

137. Whether First Mate Ebenezer Jacobs actually meant to blow up the ship or not is not known, but it is assumed he would have, as he was known to be extremely obstinate as well as courageous. His obstinacy, however, was his ultimate undoing. Three years following the attack, while still master of the *Huron*, he adamantly refused to take on more ballast when urged to do so. When a severe storm suddenly struck, Jacobs and his entire crew were lost, along with the ship.

138. Deeply impressed with the heroism of these few men in the defense of their vessel against such an incredible number of attackers, Sir Jeffrey Amherst ordered a medal to be struck and presented to each of the surviving men and to the family of Captain Horsey and the crewman who was killed. Major Gladwin, too, was so proud of the men that out of his own pocket he gave $100 to be divided among the ten survivors as a reward for their gallantry.

139. Lt. Philip Deaton's surname is sometimes recorded as Dayton, but apparently this is an error.

140. There is considerable confusion about the exact number of men who lost their lives in this double ambush, which became known as the Devil's Hole Massacre. In his letter to Bouquet on Oct. 3, 1763 (Bouquet Papers, Old Series, A.4, p. 241), Major Wilkins states that 81 of the military were lost: 1 captain, 4 lieutenants, 6 sergeants, 70 rank and file. Parkman (*The Conspiracy*, II, 76–79) states that 70 men's bodies were recovered and a good many more lost over the cliff. Peckham (*Pontiac*, 224–225) sets the toll at 72 dead among the military alone: 67 soldiers and 5 officers. However, a careful scrutiny of correspondence (i.e., *Amherst to Egremont*, Oct. 13, 1763, in Sir Jeffrey Amherst Papers, Clements Library, Ann Arbor, Mich.; several anonymous letters from officers at Fort Niagara, written Sept. 16–17, in Sir Jeffrey Amherst Papers, War Office, 34, Public Records Office, London; appendix to Seaver's *A Narrative of the Life of Mrs. Mary Jemison;* letter extracts published in newspapers at the time, especially in the Pennsylvania *Gazette* No. 1815; and miscellaneous reports in the Sir William Johnson Papers) indicate that the total dead of both military and wagoneers, reached 112; and that of the thirteen survivors, seven were wounded.

141. The Onondaga River of that time is the present Oswego River, emptying into Lake Ontario at Oswego, N.Y.

142. The promotion was immediately approved and Gladwin held the permanent rank of lieutenant colonel until his promotion to colonel in 1777.

143. There is no actual proof that these Indians were of the same

large party which subsequently engaged in the Devil's Hole Massacre, but in the light of all available evidence, there is good likelihood of it.

144. Onontio was the Indian term of respect and endearment for the French governor of Canada.

145. Near present Wilkes-Barre, Luzerne County, Pennsylvania.

CHAPTER XI

146. Though he was still a powerful military figure in England, Amherst had lost a great deal of face with the powers that were due to his poor showing against the Indians. For over two years after returning home, Amherst more or less marked time, only gradually winning back to himself the favor of the Crown. In 1776 he was created a peer and two years later he was promoted to the rank of full general. In 1780 he helped to suppress the Gordon Riots. Except for a short interval in 1782–83 he was commander in chief of British Military Forces. In 1795 he retired from the Horse Guard. In 1796 he was made Field Marshal. On August 31, 1797, he died at "Montreal," his residence in Kent.

147. See *Wilderness Empire*, 486–489, 491, 501–505, 509–510.

148. There were at this time at least three Delaware chiefs known by the name of Beaver or The Beaver, but Shingas was the eldest and most powerful in influence. The Delaware names of the other two chiefs called Beaver are not known, but it was definitely Shingas who succumbed to smallpox at this time.

149. He did so, dying there in 1800.

150. Complete details of this arrangement in *Wilderness Empire*.

151. The most common tomahawk—and the most favored—was one of English manufacture which had a good steel head that was, on one side, a narrow blade some five inches long and, on the other a small, bottom-drilled pipe bowl. Through a handle which had properly been drilled for its entire length, the Indian could smoke his tomahawk as well as put it to more energetic use. Generally, these pipe tomahawks used in Indian trade came equipped with a handle already drilled and installed, but the wood was soft and too easily broken and almost always the Indians replaced them at once with hickory or ash handles which they themselves laboriously carved and drilled.

152. Croghan's ship was subsequently struck by a three-day storm (January 25–28, 1764) and wrecked on the coast of France. Barely able to save his life, he eventually made his way to the Seine near Le Havre and there he and some of the other castaways hired a small sloop to take them to England. He remained there until mid-October 1764, at which time he returned to America and, at the persuasion of General Gage and Sir William Johnson, resumed his Indian Department duties.

153. It was amazing how many people ascribed to Stewart's reasoning. An Indian was an Indian, period. As it turned out, the affair gradually died away and none of the Paxton Boys were ever tried for their part in the extermination of the last twenty-two Conestogue Indians.

154. A slight degree of modernization for the sake of clarity has been performed on this verse by the author.

155. No Indian name is known for the Mohawk whom Johnson called Peter. There is the good likelihood that Peter was one of his great

multitude of illegitimate children out of Indian—especially Iroquois—women.

156. Present Big Sable River, north of Ludington, Michigan.

157. Apparently this was Lake Mitchell at present Cadillac, Wexford County, Michigan.

158. Cadotte's wife was evidently in some way related to Matchekewis, but exactly in what way has never been ascertained. Matchekewis, also often referred to as Mutchikiwish, was, of course, the chief who shared the leadership with Minivavana in the massacre at Fort Michilimackinac. In 1866 in Chicago, a chief named Alexander Robinson told the historian Lyman Draper that when the English eventually reoccupied Fort Michilimackinac, Matchekewis and two or three older chiefs who helped in the attack were arrested and taken to Quebec where they were imprisoned for some time. The English authorities at length released him and the others, presented him with a medal, a flag and some other presents and sent him home, where his prestige had grown even more. He led his Chippewas against the forces of General Anthony Wayne in the Battle of Fallen Timbers in 1794 and was one of the chiefs who signed Wayne's Greenville Treaty the following year. He was described as being a large, tall chief, who weighed over 200 pounds. A man of great distinction among his people, he died in 1806 at about the age of 70.

159. Although he calls the Chippewas the "friends of the Six Nations," this is only a pattern of speechmaking. Actually, the Iroquois and the Chippewa were ancient and inveterate enemies, and the Chippewa feared the Iroquois League immensely.

160. This meant they would go straight southeast from Point Grodine to about Byng Inlet, rather than hugging the shore to that point.

161. Georgian Bay.

162. Present Lake Simcoe in Ontario, Canada.

163. This is the present Humble River, at the mouth of which is the city of Toronto, Ontario, Canada.

164. Concerning this, Bouquet wrote to his commander on June 7, 1764: "They have agreed at my recommendation to send to Great Britain for 50 couples of bloodhounds to be employed with Rangers on horseback against Indian scalping parties, which will, I hope, deter more effectually from that sort of war than our troops can possibly do."

165. John Stuart, a Scot, was close to 50 years old when he came to South Carolina in 1748 and established a firm friendship with the Cherokees. In 1762 he was appointed Superintendent of the Southern Indian Department and was a capable man in this position, but he was never able to acquire the power and prestige held by Sir William. When these two men clashed over who should have jurisdiction in the Illinois Country, Johnson won handily.

166. For greater details of this incident, see *Wilderness Empire*, 514, 523–525.

CHAPTER XII

167. Godefroy had been sent to Niagara to be tried for his part in the fall of Fort Miamis. At this time Bradstreet was returning him, still a prisoner, to Detroit for possible execution there. That he had no authority to either release or pardon this prisoner did not seem to occur to Bradstreet.

168. When told of this occurrence, Sir William Johnson literally trembled at what the consequences might have been in Detroit at that moment if someone had explained to them the meaning of what they had signed. Johnson wrote (Sir William Johnson Papers, XI, 395–396): "The very idea of subjection would fill them with horror, nor would they ever consider themselves in that light, whilst they have any men or an open country to retire to. They have no ties amongst themselves but inclination. Suppose that it's explained to them that they shall be governed by the laws, liable to the punishments for high treason, murder, robbery, and the pains and penalties on actions for property or debt. Then see how it will be relished, and whether they will agree to it!"

169. In 1775, Governor Hamilton of Detroit wrote to General Guy Carleton: "I have been informed by a person of character here that Col. Bradstreet had promised to pay the Canadians who went with Howard half a dollar per day, which was never given to them, tho they had neglected their harvest and returned half naked. Such a precedent must be of the worst consequence and I mention the fact to your Excellency as it has left a deep impression upon those who were sufferers from such a dishonourable breach of word and credit." From Reuben Gold Thwaites and Lucy P. Kellogg, *Revolution on the Upper Ohio* (Madison, 1908), pp. 133–134.

170. The journal sent by Morris to Bradstreet is currently in the collection of the State Papers Office in London, along with a record of an examination of Morris's Indian and Canadian attendants, made in the presence of Bradstreet at Sandusky. Later, Morris rewrote his journal and added many more details. After the war, when he returned to England, he lost all his properties through poor speculations and then attempted to get himself awarded a government pension on the basis of the service he performed on his embassy to the Illinois. It was with this goal in mind that he rewrote the journal, but he failed to find anyone to lay it before the King and so he had it published in extremely limited edition, together with several of his own poems and his translation of the Fourth and Fourteenth satires of Juvenal. The book was published in London in 1791 under the title *Miscellanies in Prose and Verse*.

171. The 80th Regiment was disbanded December 5, 1764. Gladwin remained in service for a while yet and, before he retired, was promoted to colonel in 1777. He never returned to America and he achieved the rank of major general on the retired list, receiving half pay for the remainder of his years. He settled down to the life of a country gentleman at Stubbing, Derbyshire, after having been presented to the Court. Following a long illness, he died at his home at the age of 62 on June 22, 1791. His wife, Frances, died October 16, 1817, at the age of 74.

172. Camp was made at the extreme northeast corner of present Ohio Township, Beaver County, Pennnsylvania.

173. This was present Sandy Creek, which was first encountered by the army in the area of Minerva, Carroll County, Ohio.

174. This camp was one mile north of Magnolia, Stark County, Ohio, in the southeast corner of Sandy Township.

175. This town was called Tuscarawas and also King Beaver's Town, after Shingas, who had been chief here. At his death of smallpox early in the past winter, the town had been abandoned.

176. His council site was five miles from present Coshocton, on the west bank of the Tuscarawas.

177. Turtle's Heart was Chief Kitehi, but all through the counciling he was referred to only by the English name for him.

178. Site of present Cleveland, Ohio.

179. There were many deaths among the provincials who were put afoot and of those who survived to reach Fort Niagara after many arduous days of wilderness travel, all were suffering from cold, hunger, exposure, and severe fatique. They had had to swim icy creeks and rivers, and slog through great swamps and tangled undergrowth.

180. Incredible as it may seem, John Bradstreet, far from having his career wrecked by his inconceivable actions on this campaign, ultimately was promoted to the rank of brigadier general, though his subsequent career was singularly undistinguished. He did manage to get his "grand plan"' published, completing the writing of it in Albany on December 7, 1764. It was published ten days later under the grandiose title of: *A Brief State of Our Interior Situation with the Savages, the Disadvantages Occasioned by the Indian Traders Following them to their Hunting Country, Castles and Villages: The Benefit to all His Majesty's Subjects by Confining the Trade to Particular Posts and the Danger of Fixing these Posts nearby the Colonys of New York and Quebec than St. Mary's* [meaning the Sault Ste. Marie,] *Michilimackinac, La Baye, & Detroit, etc., etc.* Fortunately, no great heed was ever paid to this pretentious publication.

181. Goschachgunk was eventually corrupted to Coshocton, the name of the city now on that site.

182. Those villages along the Scioto River from present Circleville, Ohio, to the mouth of the river where it enters the Ohio River at present Portsmouth, Ohio.

183. Captain Buford became Major of the 14th Virginia in 1776. He served in the Carolinas as a lieutenant colonel under Lincoln. When his whole corps surrendered at Waxhaws on May 29, 1780, Buford and the rest of his force were brutally massacred by the notorious Colonel Tarleton.

EPILOGUE

184. Actually, there were over three hundred prisoners liberated, but of these, only two hundred were Pennsylvanians.

185. There have been many theories advanced for why Pontiac was assassinated—and even some argument concerning by whom, as English traders were suspected of being behind it—but no absolute proof for any of them. Probably the most likely reason is that it was an act of vengeance by a member of the family of the Illinois chief he stabbed and crippled in the summer of 1766.

LIST OF INDIAN CHARACTERS

IN the following identification key, the Indian characters in *The Conquerors* are listed by tribe or subtribe, with the meaning of the tribal name given, if known. For easier reference, the tribes and subtribes are listed alphabetically, as are the names of individuals under each tribal heading. Included where it may be of help or interest are other names the individual was known by, his tribal rank and, in some cases, family relationships. In cases where the Indian name may be difficult to pronounce, a phonetic pronunciation is given.

THE CAHOKIA TRIBE

(The meaning of the name of this tribe is unknown.)

TAMEROIS [TAM-ur-roy]. A tribal chief.

THE CAYUGA TRIBE

(Significance of name unknown. Member of Iroquois League.)

LOGAN. English name for Tal-gah-yee-tah.

SHIKELLIMUS [Sheh-KELL-ee-muss]. Principal chief of tribe; father of Tal-gah-yee-tah.

TAL-GAH-YEE-TAH. Chief of Cayuga splinter group in Mingo Confederation; called Logan by the English; son of Shikellimus.

THE CHIPPEWA TRIBE

(The name of this tribe means "People-Who-Roast-Until-Puckered," referring to the tribal practice of heating newly made moccasins over a fire to cause the seams to pucker. This tribe also known as the Ojibwa tribe.)

KINONCHAMEK [Kin-nun-CHAM-eck]. A subchief of the tribe; son of the principal chief, Minivavana.

KOLOPESH [KO-low-pesh]. A tribal chief; also called Le Grand Sable by the French.

LE GRAND SABLE. French name for Kolopesh.

LE GRAND SAULTEUR. French name for Minivavana.

MATCHEKEWIS [Match-ee-COO-iss]. A tribal chief and village chief; tribal war chief.

MINIVAVANA [Min-ah-vah-VAN-ah]. Principal chief of tribe; also called Le Grand Saulteur by the French; father of Kinonchamek.

MUSINIGON [Muss-SIN-uh-gahn]. A village chief.

MUVARRON [Moo-VAIR-on]. A village chief.

OGHQUA [OAK-kwa]. Wife of Wawatam.

OWL. A warrior. Indian name unrecorded.

PERWASH [PURR-wash]. A village chief.

SANPEAR [SAN-pair]. A village chief.

TEWALEE [Tee-WAH-lee]. A subchief; nephew of Wasson.

WASSON [WAH-sahn]. A tribal chief; second war chief; uncle of Tewalee.

WAWATAM [Wuh-WHAT-um]. A village chief; husband of Oghqua.

WENNIWAY [WEN-uh-way]. A tribal chief.

THE CONESTOGUE TRIBE

(Significance of the tribal name is unknown.)

BILL SOC. Villager; Indian name unknown.

THE DAKOTAH TRIBE

(In the Santee or eastern dialects, their name signifies "allies." They are a branch of the Sioux, which is an abbreviation of Nadouessioux, the name applied to them by the Chippewa, as transmitted through the French, signifying "adders" and, by derivation, "enemies.")

SAHAGI [Sak-HA-ghee]. A tribal chief.

THE DELAWARE TRIBE

(The name of this tribe derives from the stream on which they lived, the Delaware River. which in turn derived from Lord Delaware, early Virginia governor. The tribe referred to itself as the Lenni Lenape, which means "True Men.")

BEAVER (or Chief Beaver, or King Beaver). A tribal chief; name given to Shingas by the English.

BUCKANGEHELA [Buck-ANG-uh-HEE-luh]. A tribal chief and village chief.

CAPTAIN BULL. Son of Teedyscung; village chief; Indian name unknown.

CUSTALOGA [Cuss-tuh-LOW-guh]. A principal chief; village chief;

also called White Eyes by the English; chief of a Delaware sept.

EAGLE CLAW. Warrior. Indian name unknown.

KITEHI [KIT-tuh-hee]. A tribal chief and council orator, also called Turtle's Heart by the English.

KITTISKUNG [KIT-eh-skung]. A subchief; father of Wolf.

LONG COAT. English name for Petacowacone.

ONUPERAQUEDRA [Oh-NOOP-er-ah- KWAY-druh]. A tribal chief; also called Squashcutter by the English.

PETACOWACONE [PET-uh-cow-uh-KO-nee]. A tribal chief; also called Long Coat by the English.

PITWE-OWA [PIT-twee-OH-wah]. A war chief; also called The Wolf by the English.

SHINGAS [SHIN-gess]. A tribal chief and village chief; also called Beaver, Chief Beaver or King Beaver by the English.

SQUASHCUTTER. English name for Onuperaquedra.

TEEDYSKUNG [TEE-dee-skung]. A self-proclaimed prophet without tribal standing; father of Captain Bull.

TOLLEMA [Toe-LEE-muh]. A tribal chief.

TURTLE'S HEART. English name for Kitehi.

WHITE EYES. English name for Custaloga.

WINGENUND [WIN-guh-nund]. A tribal chief and village chief.

WOLF. A warrior; son of Kittiskung; Indian name unknown.

WOLF, THE. English name for Pitwe-owa.

THE EEL RIVER MIAMI TRIBE

(A subtribe of the Miami. For significance of name, see Miami Tribe).

SHE-NOCK-IN-WAK. A tribal chief.

THE HURON TRIBE

(The name of this tribe signifies "rough," derived from the French *hure*.)

AARON. A warrior. Indian name unknown.

ANAISA [An-NAY-sah]. An elder tribal chief.

ANDREW. A warrior; Indian name unknown.

TAKEE [TAH-kee]. A principal chief and village chief.

TEATA [Tee-AH-tuh]. A principal chief and village chief, in some measure proselytized by Jesuits.

THOMAS. A warrior; Indian name unknown.

THE KASKASKIA TRIBE

(Significance of tribal name is unknown.)

CHACORETONY [Chuh-CORE-uh-toe-nee]. A tribal chief.

THE MENOMINEE TRIBE

(Tribal name means "The Wild Rice People." The French name for the tribe was *Folle Avoine*.)

OSHKOSH. Principal chief of tribe; village chief.

THE MIAMI TRIBE

(The name of this tribe signifies "People of the Pigeons," referring to the great flocks of passenger pigeons which nested near their villages.)

COLD FOOT. A village chief; Indian name not known.

LITTLE TURTLE. English name for Michikiniqua.

MICHIKINIQUA [Mish-ee-KIN-ee-kwah]. Principal chief of tribe; also called Little Turtle by the English.

NARANEA [Nair-uh-NEE-uh]. A village chief.

OUISKE-LOTHA NEBI [WHIS-key-lo-tha NEE-bee]. Maiden; name means "Water Bird"; also called Whiskey by the English.

PACANNE [Puh-CAN]. A subchief; son of Michikiniqua; name means "a long nut" (as in pecan).

UNEMAKEMI [Unuh-MAK-uh-me]. A village chief.

WHISKEY. English name for Ouiske-lotha Nebi.

THE MISSISSAUGI TRIBE

(Actually began as a subtribe of the Chippewa but by this time with autonomy increased enough for independence, although often referred to as Mississaugi Chippewa. Name of tribe thought to mean "Snake People" because they considered snakes to be deities.)

MINDOGHQUAY [Min-doak-KWAY]. A tribal chief.

SEKAHOS [See-KAH-hoz]. A principal chief and war chief.

WABBICOMIGOT [Wob-bee-KOM-ee-got]. Also known as Wabacumaga; a tribal chief and village chief.

THE MOHAWK TRIBE

(Significance of tribal name uncertain, but probably meaning "Wolf People," referring to their ferocity. Member of the Iroquois League.)

AARON. A warrior; Indian name unknown.

DANIEL. A warrior; English name for Oughnour.

OUGHNOUR [OOH-nor]. A warrior; also called by the English, Daniel or Daniel Oughnour.

PETER. A warrior; Indian name unknown.

SCARROYADDY [Scare-oh-YAD-ee]. A subchief.

STEYAWA [Stay-YAH-wah]. A subchief; also called Abraham by the English.

THE ONEIDA TRIBE

(Significance of tribal name unknown. Member of Iroquois League.)

TORACH [Toe-RAHsh]. A tribal chief.

THE ONONDAGA TRIBE

(Significance of tribal name unknown. Member of Iroquois League).

CANASSATEGO [CAN-nuh-sah-TEE-go]. A tribal chief and village chief; one of the principal orators for the Iroquois League.

ROZINOGHYATA [RAHZ-in-oh-ghee-YAH-tah]. Principal chief of tribe; a village chief.

THE OTTAWA TRIBE

(The name of the tribe means "The People Who Trade." Sometimes called the Tawas.)

ATAWANG [AT-uh-wang]. A village chief.

BRETON [Bree-TAHN]. A village chief.

CHAUVIN [Shah-VEEN]. A village chief; father of Chavinon.

CHAVINON [SHAV-uh-non]. A village chief; uncle of Golletah.

GOLLETAH [GO-leh-TAH]. A subchief; nephew of Chavinon.

GRETON [GREE-ton]. A village chief.

KANTUK-KEGHUN [Kan-TUCK KEEG-un]. Number one wife of Pontiac.

KASAHDAH [Kuh-SAH-duh]. Warrior; a son of Pontiac.

MACATEPILESIS [Muh-CATTUH-pah-LEE-sis]. A village chief.

MACKINAC [MACK-in-naw]. Principal chief; village chief; also called Le Tourtue by the French and The Turtle by the English.

MANITOU [Man-ih-TOO]. A tribal chief.

MEHEMAH [Muh-HEE-mah]. A tribal chief.

MESSEAGHAGE [Meh-SEE-uh-gage]. A tribal chief.

MINTIWABY [Min-tuh-WOB-bee]. A village chief; secondary war chief.

MUKEETA [Moo-KEE-tah]. A village chief.

NEBAHKOHUM [Neb-uh-KO-hum]. Warrior; a son of Pontiac.

NEEWISH [NEE-oo-ish]. A subchief.

OKINOCHUMAKE [OH-kin-oh-chu-MOCK-ee]. A tribal chief; second principal chief of tribe.

OTUSSA [Oh-TOOSE-ah]. Warrior; a son of Pontiac.

OULAMY [OO-lum-mee]. A subchief.

PINAASEE [Pin-nah-AH-see]. A subchief.

PONTIAC. War chief of tribe; village chief; founder of western Great Lakes tribal confederacy; father of Kasahda, Nebakohum, Otussa, and Shegenaba; husband of Kantuk-keghun.

SHEGENABA [Sheg-uh-NOB-uh]. Subchief; son of Pontiac.

TOURTUE, LE. French name for Mackinac.

TURTLE, THE. English name for Mackinac.

WAUBINEMA [Waw-bin-EE-muh]. A village chief.

THE PEORIA TRIBE

(Significance of tribal name unknown. Member of Illinois Confederacy.)

BLACK DOG. English name for Makatachinga.

MAKATACHINGA [Mack-uh-tuh-CHING-guh]. A principal chief; village chief; also called Black Dog by the English.

THE POTAWATOMI TRIBE

(The name of the tribe means "People of the Place of Fire" and thus they are sometimes known as the "Fire People" or the "Fire Nation.")

ERRANT [AIR-ant]. A tribal chief.

KIOQUA [Kee-OH-kwa]. A village chief.

NANEQUOBA [Nay-nee-KWO-bah]. A subchief.

NINIVOIS [NIN-uh-voy]. A tribal chief; a village chief.

NONTENEE [NON-ten-nee]. A village chief.

WASHEE [WAH-shee]. War chief; tribal chief; village chief.

WINNEMAC [WIN-nuh-mack]. A tribal chief.

THE SAC TRIBE

(The name of this tribe, which is also often spelled Sauk, comes from Osakiwug, meaning "People of the Outlet" or "People of the Yellow Earth.")

OSA [OH-sah]. A principal chief.

THE SENECA TRIBE

(Significance of tribal name unknown. Member of Iroquois League.)

GROTA YOUNGA [GROW-tuh YUNG-guh]. Tribal chief.

HALF KING. English name for Monakaduto.

HANGING BELT. Tribal chief. Indian name unknown.

KAENDAE [CANE-die]. Tribal chief.

KENEGHTAUGH [Ken-NEG-taw]. Village chief.

KYASHUTA [Ky-ah-SHOO-tuh]. War chief; tribal chief.

MONAKADUTO [Mah-nah-kah-DOO-toe]. Village chief; also called Half King by the English.

TEANTORIANCE [Tee-an-TORE-ree-ants]. Tribal chief.

THE SHAWNEE TRIBE

(The name of this tribe means "People of the South.")

BENEWISICA [Ben-ee-WIS-sick-kuh]. A subchief.

BLACK SNAKE. English name for She-me-ne-to.

CORNSTALK. English name for Hokolesqua.

HOKOLESQUA [Ho-ko-LESS-kwah]. Principal chief; chief of Chalah-

gawtha sept of tribe; village chief.

KI-KUSGOW-LOWA [KEE-KUSS-go-LOW-wah]. Tribal chief; chief of Thawegila sept of tribe; village chief.

MOLUNTHA [Mo-LUN-tha]. Tribal chief; chief of Maykujay sept of tribe; village chief.

PLUK-KE-MOTAH [Pluck-kee-MO-tah]. Tribal chief; third war chief called Pluggy by English.

PUCKSINWAH [Puck-SIN-wah]; tribal chief; chief of Kispoko-tha sept; war chief of tribe; village chief; father of Tecumseh.

SHE-ME-NE-TO. Second war chief of tribe; village chief.

THE WEA TRIBE

(A subtribe of the Miami; significance of name unknown.)

WA-PA-MAN-QUA. Principal chief; village chief; also called White Loon by English.

WHITE LOON. English name for Wa-pa-man-qua.

THE WINNEBAGO TRIBE

(Tribal name signifies "People of the Filthy Water." Also called the Puants by the French and Stinkards by the English.)

TAYCHEE [TAY-chee]. A principal chief.

THE WYANDOT TRIBE

(A subtribe of the Huron; "Wyandot" [or "Guyandot"] meaning "People of the Island [or Peninsula].")

BABI. French name for Odinghquanooron.

BIG JAW. English name for Odinghquanooron.

GOOSE. English name for Ska-ki.

ODINGHQUANOOROON [OH-ding-KWA-new-ron]. A principal chief; a village chief; a war chief; also called Babi by the French and Big Jaw by the English.

ORONTONY [Oh-RAHN-tuh-nee].

A principal chief; a village chief; also known as Nicholas by the French.

SKA-KI [SKAH-kee]. Subchief.

PRINCIPAL SOURCES

AN enormous number of original documents of the period
covered in *The Conquerors* have been ferreted out and
studied in depth for use in the preparation of this third volume of *The Winning of America* series. Included has been
such material as many hundreds of manuscript letters, diaries,
logbooks, depositions, journals, council reports, personal narratives, newspaper accoounts, military records, notes, mem-
oranda and maps sifted through from private collections, public records offices, university libraries, private libraries, attics,
trunks, storage boxes and elsewhere. The information contained in such original sources makes up the research foundation for this volume; information that not infrequently opens
new doors, sheds new light, alters or supplements generally
accepted history.

Such papers are only one part of the research for such a
volume as this. Important, too, are the histories written for
the period, whether such histories were contemporary to that
time, or were written in the century following, or are contemporary to our time. As principal sources of research I have
leaned heavily upon three major collections: that portion of
the Michigan Pioneer and Historical Society Collection
housed in the Clements Library at Ann Arbor, Michigan; the
Lyman Draper Manuscript Collection in the Wisconsin Archives at Madison; and the Sir William Johnson Papers in the
collection of the New York State Library at Albany. Much
valuable material was obtained from that excellent history by
Dr. Howard H. Peckham, *Pontiac and the Indian Uprising*,
and I must acknowledge with sincere gratitude the important
assistance received both personally and in correspondence
from Dr. Peckham and his colleague, Dr. William Ewing, of
the Clements Library. Francis Parkman's two-volume work
The Conspiracy of Pontiac has proven of considerable worth,

as has the well-researched work by Nicholas Wainwright, *George Croghan: Wilderness Diplomat*. Another fertile field of research has been the vast number of unpublished theses and dissertations on this period and subject which are on file in college and university libraries throughout the nation. Many of these efforts contain heretofore unpublished material of great benefit.

Because of the extensive nature of the research that has gone into *The Conquerors*, it becomes impractical to attempt to list each source individually; therefore, only the major authenticative sources for each chapter are provided in the following bibliography. Exceptions are those sources of a minor nature which would not normally be individually listed but which substantiate some deviation from presently accepted historical fact.

PROLOGUE AND CHAPTER I

Blair, Emma H., ed. *The Indian Tribes of the Upper Mississippi Valley and the Region of the Great Lakes* (Cleveland, 1911), I, 31–272.

Butterfield, Consul Willshire, *History of the Girtys* (Cincinnati, 1890), 16.

Cuneo, John R., *Robert Rogers of the Rangers* (New York, 1959), 129–139.

Documents Relative to the Colonial History of the State of New York (hereafter cited as *Documents Relative*), edited by E. B. O'Callaghan (Albany, 1849–51), II, 783.

Drimmer, Frederick, *Scalps and Tomahawks* (New York, 1957), 75.

Flexner, James Thomas, *Mohawk Baronet: Sir William Johnson of New York* (New York, 1959), 125–126, 218–219, 239–244.

Hatcher, Harlan, *The Great Lakes* (New York, 1944), 139–146, 154–155.

Hay, Lieutenant Jehu, *Diary of the Siege of Detroit in the War with Pontiac*, edited by Franklin B. Hough (Albany, 1860), 6n16, 54n53.

Henry, Alexander, *Travels and Adventures in Canada between the Years 1760 and 1766* (New York, 1809), 3–4, 17, 74, 177.

Henry Bouquet Papers (on microfilm in Historical Society of Pennsylvania Collection), series 21652, 235; 21655, 49, 75–76.

Kenny, James, *Diary*, 1759 (in Historical Society of Pennsylvania Collection), entries for May 21, June 28, July 10, July 14.

Kinietz, W. Vernon, *The Indians of the Western Great Lakes, 1615–1760* (Ann Arbor, 1940), 317–329.

Michigan Pioneeer and Historical Society Collections (hereafter cited as *Michigan Pioneer*) (Lansing, 1892, 1897), IX, 41, 43–48, 68, 76–79, 86–88; XXVII, 606–608, 612, 612n, 613, 628, 672.

Minutes of a Council held by Deputies of the Six Nations with the Wyandots, Ottawas, Ojibwas, and Potawatomies, at the Wyandot Town near Detroit, July 3, 1761 (in *Sir William Johnson Papers*, III, 515).

North American Indians, The, edited by Roger C. Owen, James J. F.

Deetz and Anthony D. Fisher (New York, 1967), 196–199, 202–204, 576–580.

Orderly Book of Colonel Henry Bouquet's Expedition Against the Ohio Indians, 1764, The, edited by Edward G. Williams (privately printed; Pittsburgh: Mayer Press, 1960), 54, no. 4. The original manuscript is in the William L. Clements Library, Ann Arbor, Michigan.

Parkman, Francis, *The Conspiracy of Pontiac and the Indian War after the Conquest of Canada* (Boston, 1894), I, 175n, 176–177, 177n, 180n 1–2, 181n, 213–216.

————, *Montcalm and Wolfe* (Boston, 1894), I, 222–227; II, 147–149, 157–160, 361–374.

Peckham, Howard H., *Pontiac and the Indian Uprising* (Princeton, 1947), 45–47, 53, 56–59, 62–70, 74–81, 88, 91–92, 96, 105–106, 122, 128–137, 148, 193.

Pennsylvania Archives, 1st series, 5 vols. (Philadelphia, 1852–1853), III, 675.

Pennsylvania Colonial Records, 10 vols. (Philadelphia, 1851–1852), VII, 284–286, 320, 382–390.

Pennsylvania *Gazette,* 1759, July 26 and August 16.

Pennsylvania Magazine of History and Biography, LXXI (1947), 313–314, 316–317, 319n27, 327.

Pitt, William, *Correspondence . . . with Colonial Governors and Military and Naval Commissioners in America,* 2 vols. (New York, 1906), II, 192, 265–267.

Sir William Johnson Papers (under various editors for the University of the State of New York), 12 vols. (Albany, 1921–1957), III, 515.

Stanwix to Pitt, Nov. 20, 1759 (manuscript letter in William Clements Library collection).

Sterling, James, *James Sterling's Letterbook* (bound set of manuscript letters in Clements Library collection, page-numbered in author's collection), 2, 5–8, 48, 67, 69.

Wainwright, Nicholas B., *George Croghan: Wildernesss Diplomat* (Chapel Hill, 1959), 165–168, 170–175, 179–184.

Wood, Norman B., *Lives of Famous Indian Chiefs* (Aurora, 1906), 123–126.

CHAPTER II

Army Lists, 1771–1772, Library of Congress.

Cuneo, John R., *Robert Rogers,* 195.

Documents Relative, II, 900.

Fenwick, Charles G., *International Law* (London-New York, 1924), 83, 223.

CHAPTER III

Andrews, Matthew Page, *Virginia: The Old Dominion* (New York, 1937), 236.

Cotterill, R. S., *The Southern Indians: The Story of the Civilized Tribes before Removal* (Norman, 1954), 31–32, 32n.

Drimmer, Frederick, *Scalps and Tomahawks,* 74–75.

Flexner, James Thomas, *Mohawk Baronet,* 251–255.

Hay, Lieutenant Jehu, *Diary,* vi–ix, xviii, 1, 1n1, 2, 2n4, 3, 3n5–6, 9n4, 9n20, 16–17, 19, 86.

Henry, Alexander, *Travels and Adventures*, 33, 52, 62–68, 70–72, 120–121.

Henry Bouquet Papers, series 21634, 162; 21649 part I, 5, 9, 23, 62, 79, 89, 97, 108; 21655, 182.

Howe, Henry, *Historical Collections of Ohio* (Cincinnati, 1888), I, 310, 471.

Lanman, James H., *History of Michigan* (New York, 1839), 106.

MacDonald (James) to Dr. Campbell, ms. lettter in Henry E. Huntington Library Collection, San Morino, Calif.

Michigan Pioneer, VIII, 341, 358–359 (Depositions of Meloche, Parent, and Peltier); IX, 202, 209, 212–214; XXIII, 615–619, 633–634, 641, 647–650, 654–657, 661, 665–666, 669.

Mississippi Valley Historical Review, XXI (1934), 147–162, "The Identity of Major Gladwin's Informant," by Helen Humphrey.

New York *Gazette*, Letter of anonymous soldier, Aug. 4, 1763.

Parkman, Francis, *The Conspiracy*, I, 178n, 186–187, 189, 189n, 193, 196–199, 200–209, 211, 218–220, 220n, 224–225, 229–231, 234, 234n; II, 2, 271, 329–331.

———, *Montcalm and Wolfe*, II, 407

Parkman Papers, 1565–1768, 100 vols., especially vols. 22–27d on Pontiac's war.

Peckham, Howard H., *Pontiac*, 34, 93–107, 112–137, 145, 147, 154, 158, 163, 174–175, 193.

Rogers, Robert, *Journals* (Hough, ed.), 126.

Sir William Johnson Papers, X, 460–465, 467, 471, 475, 648, 689.

Sterling, James, *Letterbook*, 48–50, 70–73.

Wainwright, Nicholas B., *George Croghan*, 185, 192–196.

Wood, Norman B., *Lives of Famous Indian Chiefs*, 131–136, 142–144, 147.

CHAPTER IV

Carver, Jonathan, *Travels through the Interior Parts of North America* . . . (London, 1778), 92.

Drimmer, Frederick, *Scalps and Tomahawks*, 75.

Hatcher, Harlan H., *The Great Lakes*, 150–151.

Hay, Lieutenant Jehu, *Diary*, 3, 3n9, 4–5, 5n12, 6–10, 10n21, 11, 15, 15n27, 86, 89.

Henry Bouquet Papers, series 21635, 162.

Michigan Pioneer, IX, 188, 201–203, 213–216; XXIII, 619–623, 628, 632, 635–636, 640–645; XXVII, 644–645.

Parkman, Francis, *The Conspiracy*, I, 212, 227n, 228n, 230–231, 233–234, 234n, 235–244, 254, 254n, 255, 261–265, 271, 278–278n, 279, 279n; II, 9.

Parkman Papers, XXII, 293.

Peckham, Howard H., *Pontiac*, 127, 135, 135n, 140–149, 154–156, 175, 199.

Pennsylvania *Gazette*, Numbers 1807 and 1808.

Pennsylvania Magazine of History and Biography, LXI (1947), 436.

Sir Jeffrey Amherst Papers, Public Record Office, London, War Office 34, microfilm copy in University of Michigan General Library; 7 volumes of originals in Clements Library, II, 28–34, 140.

Sir William Johnson Papers, X, 648, 689.

Wainwright, Nicholas B., *George Croghan*, 196.

Wood, Norman, *Lives of Famous Indian Chiefs*, 128–131, 144–147, 155.

Flexner, James Thomas, *Mohawk Baronet*, 236–239, 246–247, 250–251.
Hatcher, Harlan H., *The Great Lakes*, 147–150.
Hay, Lieutenant Jehu, *Diary*, xiii–xiv, xviii, 86, 109, 109n71.
Henry, Alexander, *Travels and Adventures*, 17, 46–52, 52n1, 58–63, 70, 70n, 71, 73–74, 89–90.
Henry Bouquet Papers, series 21634, 57–58; 21647, 161–162, 210; 21648, 1; 21655, 181.
Historical Register of Officers of the Continental Army, n.d., Library of Congress.
Michigan Historical Magazine. X (1926), "Hutchins' Report to Croghan," 372–373.
Michigan Pioneer, IX, 117, 122; XIX (1891), 116, 168; XXIII, 608–609, 614, 614n, 647–648, 669, 673–674, 678.
McCoy, Raymond, *The Massacre of Old Fort Mackinac* (Bay City, 1939), 102.
Parkman, Francis, *The Conspiracy of Pontiac*, I, 186–187, 193, 196–199, 361n1.
———, *La Salle and the Discovery of the Great West* (Cambridge, Mass., 1869), 139n1.
Peckham, Howard H., *Pontiac*, 76, 81, 92–97, 102–107, 163, 234.
Pennsylvania Archives, 5th series, I, 90, 98–99, 184.
Quattrochi, Anna M., *Biography of Thomas Hutchins* (unpublished dissertation submitted for Ph.D.), in Carnegie Library Collection, Pittsburgh.
Sir William Johnson Papers, III, 269–275, 277, 331, 354, 506–507, 513–516, 520, 559, 570, 582, 601, 643, 665, 759–791, 799–818, 822–827, 837–851, 908–909, 954; IV, 82, 444; VI, 19; VII, 154; X, 20, 211, 222, 232, 269–270, 291, 319, 340–342, 475, 537, 553–554, 556–557, 665, 878.
Sterling, James, *Letterbook*, 14, 23, 30–34, 37, 67–71.
Wainwright, Nicholas B., *George Croghan*, 176, 180–185, 187, 189, 192, 194–195.

CHAPTER V

Drimmer, Frederick, *Scalps and Tomahawks*, 76, 85.
Hatcher, Harlan H., *The Great Lakes*, 151, 154–155.
Hay, Lieutenant Jehu, Diary, 9, 9n19, 9n20, 10–11, 11n22, 12–13, 13n25, 14–17, 17n29, 18, 18n30, 19–20, 20n31, 20n32, 20n33, 22–26, 29–36, 36n45, 37, 44.
Henry, Alexander, *Travels and Adventures*, 72–77, 106.
Parkman, Francis, *The Conspiracy*, I, 233, 238, 240, 244, 246–249, 249n, 250–263, 266n, 267–269, 269n, 270, 273–274 274n 277, 277n, 278, 278n, 279, 287, 299, 304n, 333, 359; II, 5–8.
Peckham, Howard H., *Pontiac*, 145–146, 149–151, 158–159, 163–164, 166–167, 171–172.
Pennsylvania *Gazette*, Number 1798 (Letter of Ecuyer to Bouquet, May 31, 1763).
Sterling, James, *Letterbook*, 52–54.
Wainwright, Nicholas B., *George Croghan*, 186–187, 196.
Wood, Norman, *Lives of Famous Indian Chiefs*, 137, 154–156.

CHAPTER VI

Cuneo, John R., *Robert Rogers*, 161–162.
Drimmer, Frederick, *Scalps and Tomahawks*, 80–86.
Hatcher, Harlan H., *The Great Lakes*, 151–154.

Hay, Lieutenant Jehu, *Diary*, 17, 17n29, 18, 20–24, 30, 30n40, 31, 31n41, 32, 32n41.

Henry, Alexander, *Travels and Adventures*, 80–86, 92–108, 124, 155.

Henry Bouquet Papers, series 21634, 180, 182, 184–185; 21649 Part I, 137.

McCoy, Raymond, *The Massacre*, 112, 118–119, 130–132, 142–145.

Michigan Pioneer, IX, 90–91, 188–189, 201–202, 212–219; XXIII, 631–633, 666–667.

Parkman, Francis, *The Conspiracy*, I, 266, 266n, 267, 267n, 275–276, 279–280, 282, 334, 353, 367; II, 11, 32–37, 46, 336–337, 364.

Peckham, Howard H., *Pontiac*, 163–165, 167–168, 171–176, 180–184, 186–187.

Schoolcraft, Henry R., *Algic Researches* (New York, 1839), II, 159.

Sir Jeffrey Amherst Papers, WO-34, XXII, 22; XL, 73.

Sir William Johnson Papers, IV, 138–139; VII, 211–216.

Sterling, James, *Letterbook*, 46, 54–58, 68.

Wisconsin Historical Society Collections, II, 197, "The Recollections of August Grignon."

Wainwright, Nicholas B., *George Croghan*, 198–199.

Wood, Norman, *Lives of Famous Indian Chiefs*, 136–137.

CHAPTER VII

Documents Relative, VII, 582; IX, 1055.

Drimmer, Frederick, *Scalps and Tomahawks*, 86–87.

Hatcher, Harlan H., *The Great Lakes*, 155.

Hay, Lieutenant Jehu, *Diary*, 8n18, 20n33, 24–30, 33–34, 36, 36n45, 37, 50, 50n49, 50n50, 52, 84–85.

Henry, Alexander, *Travels and Adventures*, 108–112.

Henry Bouquet Papers, series 21634, 184; 21649 Part I, 143–144, 160, 218; 21653, 179.

McCoy, Raymond, *The Massacre*, 142–143.

Michigan Pioneer, IX, 191–195, 198, 201–203, 209–210, 217–219; XXIII, 624–625, 633–634, 637–639, 651, 658, 668–669.

Mississippi Valley Historical Review, XI (1924), 400.

Parkman, Francis, *The Conspiracy*, I, 240–241, 241n, 242, 242n, 272–274, 274n, 275, 275n, 276, 279, 281–284, 284n, 285, 285n, 286, 286n, 287–290, 305n, 321, 364–365; II, 11–13, 15–16, 16n, 16n2, 17–21, 35, 44–47, 58, 332–333.

Parkman Papers, XXII, 293–300, Gladwin letter report to Amherst, July 8, 1763; Evidence of Benjamin Gray, soldier, in the 1st Battalion of the 60th Regiment, before a Court of Inquiry held at Ft. Pitt, 12 Sept., 1763; Evidence of David Smart, soldier of the 60th Regiment, before a Court of Inquiry held at Ft. Pitt, 24 Dec., 1763, to take Evidence Relative to the loss of Presque Isle, which did not Appear when this Court last Sat; Vol. 27, 441.

Peckham, Howard H., *Pontiac*, 160, 165, 167–170, 174–176, 184–189, 214–215.

Pennsylvania *Gazette*, July 21, 1763, and Number 1802.

Pennsylvania *Journal*, July 7, 1763.

Sir Jeffrey Amherst Papers, WO-34, 49, 73.

Sir William Johnson Papers X, 648, 689, 727–728.

Sterling, James, *Letterbook*, 46–47, 54, 58–59, 159.

Swanton, John R., *Indian Tribes in North America* (Washington, 1953), 254, 256–259, 280–284.

Wainwright, Nicholas B., *George Croghan*, 198–199.
Wood, Norman, *Lives of Famous Indian Chiefs*, 156, 157.

CHAPTER VIII

Cuneo, John R., *Robert Rogers*, 162.
Drimmer, Frederick, *Scalps and Tomahawks*, 87–88.
Flexner, James Thomas, *Mohawk Baronet*, 260.
Hay, Lieutenant Jehu, *Diary*, 5n12, 9n19, 10n21, 34–36, 36n45, 37–40, 40n47, 41, 47.
Henry, Alexander, *Travels and Adventures*, 106, 113–115.
Henry Bouquet Papers, series A, IV, 232, and original series 21634, n243.
Michigan Pioneer, IX, 128, 195–204, 206–207, 209, 211, 218–219; XXIII, 625–626, 636, 639–640.
Mississippi Valley Historical Review, XI (1924), 400.
Parkman, Francis, *The Conspiracy*, I, 211, 260, 289–291, 295, 295n, 296–300, 305–309, 366; II, 11, 16, 16n2, 17, 17n, 20, 20n, 21 21n2 22, 28–31, 35–38, 38n2, 39–45, 47, 49–52, 52n1, 52n2, 74, 86n, 95–97, 159, 203n3, 204, 204n, 225, 262, 333–335.
Parkman Papers, XXII, 302–309, Testimony of Ensign George Price, Corporals Jacob Fisher & John Nash, & Privates John Dogood, John Nigley, John Dortinger, & Uriah Trunk, survivors of Ft. Le Boeuf.
Peckham, Howard H., *Pontiac*, 155, 168, 170–172, 176–178, 180–181, 189–195, 201, 210–211, 218–226.
Pennnsylvania *Gazette*, Number 1802.
Sir Jeffrey Amherst Papers, WO-34, LIV, 171.
Sir William Johnson Papers, VII, 260.
Sterling, James, *Letterbook*, 46–47, 55, 59.
Wainwright, Nicholas B., *George Croghan*, 198–199, 201.
Wood, Norman, *Lives of Famous Indian Chiefs*, 158–159.

CHAPTER IX

Cuneo, John R., *Robert Rogers*, 162–166, 190.
Gentleman's Magazine, XXXIII, 486.
Hay, Lieutenant Jehu, *Diary*, 7n15, 20n32, 36n45, 41–49, 52–56, 56n55, 60n58, 61n58.
Howe, Henry, *Historical Collections of Ohio*, I, 472.
McCoy, Raymond, *The Massacre*, 144.
Michigan Pioneer, IX, 219–220, 223–224; XXIII, 625–627, 633, 636, 639, 646–647, 660, 678.
Parkman, Francis, *The Conspiracy*, I, 246n, 247n, 295n, 305–308, 308n, 309–317, 336–337, 359; II, 22–27, 38–40, 40n, 41, 41n, 42, 52, 52n2 52n3 53n, 54, 54n, 55–56, 56n2, 57–58, 58n1, 58n3, 59, 64, 64n, 75, 86–87, 91n, 96, 159–160, 204, 204n, 333–334, 338–339.
Parkman Papers, XXII, 413–414.
Peckham, Howard H., *Pontiac*, 165–166, 170, 196–209, 211–217, 233.
Pennsylvania *Gazette*, Numbers 1807 and 1811.
Sterling, James, *Letterbook*, 39–41, 48–56, 59–65, 68.
Wainwright, Nicholas B., *George Croghan*, 179–200.
Wood, Norman, *Lives of Famous Indian Chiefs*, 158–161.

CHAPTER X

"A Relation of the Gallent [sic] Defense made by the Crew of the Schooner on Lake Erie, when Attacked by a Large Body of Indians," as published by order of Sir Jeffrey Amherst in the New York newspapers.

Andrews, Matthew Page, *Virginia*, 236.

Bouquet Papers, Old Ser., A.4, 241.

Carver, Jonathan, *Travels*, 164.

Cotterill, R. S., *The Southern Indians*, 32.

Documents Relative, VII, 552.

Drimmer, Frederick, *Scalps and Tomahawks*, 372.

Flexner, James Thomas, *Mohawk Baronet*, 257–261.

Hatcher, Harlan H., *The Great Lakes*, 156.

Hay, Lieutenant Jehu, *Diary*, 2n, 9n20, 30, 31n41, 32n41, 56–58, 60n56, 60n57, 60n58, 61n58, 62–68, 71–75, 75n65, 76–79, 80n67, 81n67.

Henry Bouquet Papers, series 21634, 243n1, 257, 277; 21653, 219, 232.

Howe, Henry, *Historical Collections of Ohio*, I, 471.

Lanman, James H., *History of Michigan*, 108.

McCoy, Raymond, *The Massacre*, 144.

Michigan Pioneer, VIII, 361.

Parkman, Francis, *The Conspiracy*, I, 278n, 279n, 317n, 318–320, 320n, 321n, 366–367; II, 20, 27n, 39n, 64–70, 70n, 71n, 72–73, 79–80, 97–98, 100–103, 103n, 104, 106–108, 113–115, 116n, 128n, 130–132, 159–161, 339–341.

Parkman Papers, XXII, 413–414.

Peckham, Howard H., *Pontiac*, 105–111, 165–166, 178–179, 208–210, 212–213, 218–219, 222–225, 227–231, 235–238, 241–242.

Pennsylvania *Gazette*, Number 1816.

Royal Society of Canada Transactions, Section II, Series III, XXII (May, 1928), 1–31, "Life of John Montresor," by J. C. Webster.

Seaver, James E., *A Narrative of The Life of Mrs. Mary Jemison* (Canandaigua, N.Y., 1824).

Sir Jeffrey Amherst Papers, PRO-WO-34, XLI, 227; XLIX, 695; WO-34/38, foll. 264, 265; WO-34/39, foll. 413–414; Vol. VII (Ms. Letters, Clements Library).

Sir William Johnson Papers, X, 825–827, 858–859.

Sterling, James, *Letterbook*, 41–43, 59, 63–66.

Wainwright, Nicholas B., *George Croghan*, 201–202.

Wisconsin State Historical Society First Annual Report, 61.

Wood, Norman, *Lives of Famous Indian Chiefs*, 161–163.

CHAPTER XI AND EPILOGUE

Butterfield, Consul Willshire, *History of the Girtys*, 19, 19n.

Cuneo, John R., *Robert Rogers*, 169.

Documents Relative, VII, 650.

Drimmer, Frederick, *Scalps and Tomahawks*, 88–104.

Flexner, James Thomas, *Mohawk Baronet*, 261–262, 264–268, 273.

Hatcher, Harlan, H., *The Great Lakes*, 156–157.

Hay, Lieutenant Jehu, *Diary*, 2n, 80–81, 81n67, 84–89, 91–94, 97–103, 270.

Hazard's Pennsylvania Register, IX, 114; XII, 10–12.

Henry, Alexander, *Travels and Adventures*, 80–81, 123–151, 166–180.

Henry Bouquet Papers, series 21634, 216–218.

Historical Account of the Late Disturbances, anonymous pamphlet, n.d., in City Library, Philadelphia.

Howe, Henry, *Historical Collections of Ohio*, I, 471.

Illinois Historical Collections (Springfield), XI, 1.

McCoy, Raymond, *The Massacre*, 169.

Michigan Pioneer, VII, 352–360; IX, 243–250, 255; XXIII, 609–610, 630, 643, 664–666, 671–672, 675–677, 680.

Parkman, Francis, *The Conspiracy,* I, 255–256; II, 96, 103, 105, 108–109, 109n, 112–114, 116n, 117n, 120–125, 125n, 126, 126n, 127–128, 128n, 134n, 139–148, 148n, 149–150, 156–157, 160, 161n, 162–164, 164n, 165–178, 180–181, 181n, 186–199, 199n2, 200, 200n, 201, 201n, 204–205, 205n, 206–207, 207n, 208n, 208n2, 209–220, 220n, 221–235, 235n, 236, 236n, 237n, 238n, 240–248, 259–263, 263n, 266, 266n, 267–268, 268n, 269–277, 315–316, 318–320, 342–359, 360–361.

Parkman Papers, XXII, 441.

Peckham, Howard H., *Pontiac,* 134, 219, 238–258, 260–261, 263–268, 301.

Pennsylvania Archives, 1st series, IV, 532.

Pennsylvania General Assembly Records, V, 284–285, 313.

Pennsylvania Colonial Records, IX, 212, 228, 256.

Pennsylvania *Gazette,* Number 1833.

Pennsylvania Historical Society Collection, 390, Deposition of Lazarus Stewart; Deposition of Felix Donnelly.

Sir William Johnson Papers, VII, D-674; XI, 395–396.

Sterling, James, *Letterbook,* 67–68.

Thwaites, Reuben Gold, and Lucy P. Kellogg, *Revolution on the Upper Ohio* (Madison, 1908), 133–134.

Wainwright, Nicholas B., *George Croghan,* 202–203, 210–213.

Wisconsin Historical Society Collection, VII, 189–200.

Wood, Norman, *Lives of Famous Indian Chiefs,* 163–166.

INDEX

agara Congress, 723
Saginaw Bay, 88, 195, 226, 246, 524, 695; map of area, 89; Chippewas of, 280, 386, 402, 440–443
Sahagi, Dakotah chief, 419, 421, 422
St. Ange de Bellerive, Captain Louis, 719, 737
St. Aubin, Gabriel, 205
St. Aubin, Madame, 206
St. Bemand, Jules, 520–522, 524–525, 528
St. Clair, Sir John, 465, 491
St. Clair River, 198, 331; map of, 202. *See also* Lake St. Clair
St. Joseph, 708. *See also* Fort St. Joseph
St. Joseph River, empties into Lake Michigan, 102, 302, 645
St. Joseph River, empties into Maumee, 102, 165, 300
St. Lawrence River, 16, 19, 22, 30, 56, 73, 107, 114, 141, 540, 544, 553, 636; valley, 165
St. Louis, Gerrieu, 258, 259–260, 261, 270
St. Martin, Jacques, 213, 221, 230–231, 270, 271–272, 281, 331, 343, 440, 466, 468, 506, 558, 560, 581, 624, 655, 722; and Gladwin, 296–297, 401, 481; moves family inside the fort, 520; Gladwin commends to Amherst, 540; guides Dalyell's force to Pontiac's camp, 583, 586, 588
St. Vincent, Jacques, 677
Samuels, English drifter, 352, 354, 358, 375, 377, 390, 394
Sandusky Bay, 26, 49, 65, 111, 248, 272, 328, 386, 676, 734, 735, 748; English traders at, 45–46; Indian councils at, 45–48, 52, 61, 196; site of new fort, 62, 63, 67, 84, 104, 112; Johnson's emissary (Peter) arrives at, 704; Bradstreet arrives at, 740. *See also* Fort Sandusky
Sandusky Hurons, *see* Wyandots
Sanpear, Chippewa chief, 248
Sault Sainte Marie, 2, 62, 84, 101, 124, 126, 135, 136, 336, 344, 676, 712–714, 716, 723. *See also* Fort Sault Sainte Marie
Scarroyaddy of the Mohawks, 127
Schlosser, Ensign Francis, 104, 136, 302–308, 401–403, 613; exchanged for Indian prisoner, 439–440, 461
Scioto River, 26, 286, 287, 288, 676, 726, 734, 736, 754, 759, 767; map of, 756
Scottish Highlanders, 572, 573, 574, 598
Sekahos, Mississaugi chief, 140, 293, 321, 333, 386, 468–469; and attack on Fort Presque Isle, 415
Senecas, 21, 29, 141, 150, 383, 532, 633, 662, 682, 702; seek revenge against English, 30–31, 45–47, 49–52, 67; and Johnson, 30, 55, 498, 515; and the Ottawas, 51, 70; in siege of Quebec 95; at Easton council, 127; and Pontiac, 159, 167, 172; at Fort Pitt, 163, 593; in attack on Fort Venango, 413,

414, 416; take prisoners at Fort Presque Isle, 439; attack Fort Le Boeuf, 444–449, 456; interrupt supply line to western posts, 515–516; on western New York frontier, 553; near Niagara Portage, 621; and Johnson's peace negotiations with Iroquois Confederacy, 626, 632, 678–679; and Fort Niagara, 626, 643, 659; attack wagoneers at Niagara, 637; and Niagara Congress, 729–731; and Bouquet's march west, 754–755; Bouquet councils with, 755–757, 763–770, 465
17th Regiment, 382, 611, 619, 621
77th Regiment, 382, 491, 516; Amherst orders to Philadelphia, 411, 465–466
Sharpe, Governor, 572
Shaw, Sergeant Patrick, 186, 208, 211, 330, 334
Shawnees, 7, 9, 26, 30, 43, 83, 131, 150, 167, 182, 287, 364, 498, 568, 683, 702; at Sandusky council, 45, 46, 48; and settlers, 113, 119; at Easton council, 127–130 *passim;* at Pontiac's secret councils, 140, 143, 149, 158, 172; and Pontiac, 196, 254, 386, 451; at Fort Pitt, 317–318, 386, 574, 593, 615, 750–752; and Croghan, 381; in attack on Fort Venango, 413–415; take prisoners at Fort Presque Isle, 439; at Parent's Creek council, 452, 453, 469; attack Fort Ligonier, 470–471; attacks on Pennsylvania settlers, 514, 515, 546–551, 659, 707; attacks in western Virginia, 552–553; council with Ecuyer, 562–566; smallpox among, 563, 657, 676; gather at Muskingum and Scioto Rivers, 632; Villiere's letter to, 649–650; in 1763 blizzard, 676; and Six Nations 680; and Bouquet's march west, 726, 750–757; and Niagara Congress, 729, 731; Bradstreet and Bouquet set out to quell, 734, 735; and Bradstreet, 735, 740, 743, 761–762; take Ensign Pauli to Sandusky, 748; Bouquet councils with, 755–757, 763–770
She-me-ne-to (Black Snake), Shawnee village chief, 140
She-nock-in-wak, Chief, 141
Shikellimus, Cayuga chief, 127
Shingas (The Beaver), Delaware chief, 12–14, 127, 554; at Pontiac's secret council, 140; and the trader Calhoun, 315, 323, 325, 326–327, 338; councils with Ecuyer at Fort Pitt, 562–563; death of, 676
Shippensburg, Pennsylvania, 431, 434, 436, 514; Bouquet's forces reach, 573, 598
Shippin, Edward, 389–390
Shirley, General William, 683
Sioux Indians, 84, 172, 349, 421
Six Nations, 8, 30–31, 111, 388, 478, 498, 535, 680, 716; composition of, 29; and revenge against

NARRATIVES OF AMERICA
a sweeping four volume series by
ALLAN W. ECKERT

This noted author has created four epic novels, each drawn from actual history, which together span the early days of our country. You will follow heroic men and women as they fight to wrest the land from the Indians, the French and the English.

The Frontiersmen (Book I, #13944-4 $3.50)
The true saga of the conquest of the Northwest Territory. Driven from their homeland, the Indians valiantly fought a losing battle against the white invaders—staunch men and women who loved the land as much as the Indians.

Wilderness Empire (Book II, #13993-2 $3.50)
In 1755, the Iroquois were on the warpath. Whipped to a frenzy by the French, they cut a swath of desolation on a rampage that terrified white settlers from New York to the Virginias. Yet, in the end, the Iroquois would pay the highest price for their destruction.

The Conquerors (Book III, #13384-5 $3.95)
English soldiers and traders trekked across the wilderness to man former French outposts. But they were unprepared for the wrath of the Indians who had united behind the war chief Pontiac.

The Wilderness War (Book IV)
Spanning 1763 to 1780, this stirring volume will be on sale in Spring 1982.

Read NARRATIVES OF AMERICA, available wherever Bantam paperbacks are sold or order directly from Bantam Books by including $1.00 for postage and handling and sending a check to Bantam Books, Dept. EK, 414 East Golf Road, Des Plaines, Illinois 60016. Allow 4-6 weeks for delivery. This offer expires 3/82.

LOOKING IN

Books that explore Eastern and Western spirituality and examine man's concepts of God and the universe.

☐	13269	THE GOSPEL ACCORDING TO PEANUTS Robert L. Short	$1.75
☐	20084	"WITH GOD ALL THINGS ARE POSSIBLE" Life Study Fellowship	$2.95
☐	14216	THE GREATEST SALESMAN IN THE WORLD Og Mandino	$2.25
☐	14784	MYTHS TO LIVE BY Joseph Campbell	$3.50
☐	14385	THE BIBLE AS HISTORY: A CONFIRMATION OF THE BOOK OF BOOKS Werner Keller	$3.50
☐	14928	THE PASSOVER PLOT Dr. Hugh J. Schonfield	$2.95
☐	12853	THE GIFT OF INNER HEALING R. C. Stapleton	$1.95
☐	14932	I CHING: NEW INTERPRETATION FOR MODERN TIMES Sam Reitler	$3.50
☐	13515	HOW TO MEDITATE Le Shan	$2.50
☐	14782	JOURNEY OF AWAKENING Ram Dass	$3.50
☐	13593	WHATEVER BECAME OF SIN? Dr. Karl Menninger	$2.50